RENAISSANCE
HUMANISM

Volume 2

RENAISSANCE HUMANISM &

FOUNDATIONS, FORMS, AND LEGACY &

VOLUME 2 · HUMANISM BEYOND ITALY &

Edited by Albert Rabil, Jr.

UNIVERSITY OF PENNSYLVANIA PRESS
PHILADELPHIA 1988

Library of Congress Cataloging-in-Publication Data

Renaissance Humanism.
  Bibliography: p.
  Includes index.
  Contents: v. 1. Humanism in Italy—v. 2. Humanism
beyond Italy—v. 3. Humanism and the disciplines.
  1. Humanism. 2. Renaissance—Italy. I. Rabil, Albert.
B778.R43 1988   001.1'094   87-13928
ISBN 0-8122-8066-0 (set)
ISBN 0-8122-8063-6 (v. 1)
ISBN 0-8122-8064-4 (v. 2)
ISBN 0-8122-8065-2 (v. 3)

To

MARISTELLA LORCH

Catalyst Among Scholars
Whose Initial Idea Has Developed into These Volumes

CONTENTS

VOLUME 2 ❧ HUMANISM BEYOND ITALY

PART III · HUMANISM BEYOND ITALY

VOLUME 3❧HUMANISM AND THE DISCIPLINES

PART IV • HUMANISM AND THE DISCIPLINES

PART V • THE LEGACY OF HUMANISM

PREFACE

The study of Renaissance humanism became a recognized scholarly enterprise after the publication of Georg Voigt's *The Revival of Classical Antiquity or the First Century of Humanism* (1859) and, more significantly, of Jacob Burckhardt's *The Civilization of the Renaissance in Italy* (1860). Both writers maintained that the Italian Renaissance gave rise to a new personality type, one who had a thirst for fame and adopted a naturalistic attitude toward the world. Burckhardt called this new person a "spiritual individual," which meant, variously, a self-centered person, one who embodied a new kind of moral autonomy or emancipation from traditional religious standards and political authorities, or one always seeking to give full expression to his personality. Accordingly, for a long period the great debate was over the nature and cultural significance of the new kind of consciousness embodied by the humanists. Wilhelm Dilthey, Giovanni Gentile, and Ernst Cassirer, writing during the earlier decades of the twentieth century, regarded humanism as a new philosophy of human values, the chief among which were those values of individualism, secularism, and moral autonomy which had been identified by Burckhardt. The implication of this view was that humanism was hostile to Christianity and, indeed, initiated the development of modern paganism. This view was challenged in 1952 by Giuseppe Toffanin, who argued that far from being pagan and heterodox, Renaissance humanism was the champion of the authentic Latin-Catholic tradition against late medieval Aristotelian science.

These parameters of interpretation have largely been supplanted by the work of Paul Oskar Kristeller during the past generation. On the basis of the most comprehensive study of its sources ever undertaken, Kristeller has effectively established the claim that humanism is part of a rhetorical tradition that has been a continuous aspect of western civilization since classical antiquity. Moreover, humanism has specific roots in the medieval culture from which it arose, notably in the theory and practice of letter and speech writing, the study of classical poetry, prose, and grammar in the cathedral schools of France, and the study of Greek. That the humanists belong to a rhetorical tradition is now generally accepted, though different constructions are placed on what this means. Kristeller has gone on to argue that a study of the humanists' works leads one away from the conclusion that they were professional philosophers. They have no consistent philosophical position and are not concerned with philosophy in the traditional sense. Their preoccupations were those of the rhetorical tradition from which they emerged: grammar, poetry, history, rhetoric, and moral philosophy. Kristeller's formulations constitute the most widely accepted paradigm of humanist studies today. Most of the essays in these volumes reflect adherence to it in one way or another. This paradigm has had a profound impact on the earlier debates about the nature of humanism. The idea that humanism is either a radical departure from the past or a radical defense of traditional values has given way to more mediate studies, which have attempted to reveal the specific relations of the humanists to institutions and their specific ideas on particular issues. This more nuanced discussion of their relationships and ideas is reflected in many of the essays collected here.

Among Kristeller's generation of scholars, his definition of humanism has been challenged by the leading Italian scholar in the field, Eugenio Garin, who regards Renaissance philosophy (for example, Platonism and Aristotelianism) as integral to humanism and treats the philosophers as part of the humanist tradition. While widely respected, Garin's views have not found general acceptance; the writings of the humanists in their various forms and locations bear out to most interpreters the general applicability of Kristeller's paradigm, as the great majority of the essays in these volumes make clear.

Garin has exercised more influence in incorporating the notion of "civic humanism"—first formulated by Hans Baron to designate a specific historical situation in early Quattrocento Florence—into a broader view of humanism and Renaissance thought. He began with the questions: What inspired the humanists to turn from medieval rhetoric to the classical tradition? What motivated their commitment to the disciplines in which they were most interested? Both Garin and Baron believe that humanism as a cultural movement cannot be understood apart from the social and political conditions under which it arose. Their exploration of these conditions, especially in medieval and Renaissance Florence, has led to the recognition of a greater variety within the humanist movement than was previously suspected. Civic humanism, which is explored in these volumes, does not, however, replace Kristeller's paradigm, inasmuch as it applies only to a small group of humanists largely in one location and for a limited period. But it is an important contribution to our understanding of humanism itself and, equally important, to its legacy.

*   *   *

The initial idea for these volumes grew from a course on "Renaissance Humanism" taught at Barnard College/Columbia University by Professor Maristella Lorch and me in the spring of 1979, one of several courses developed through an institutional grant from the National Endowment for the Humanities. We used funds made available through that grant to invite a number of distinguished scholars in Renaissance humanist studies to participate in the course. Professor Lorch suggested the idea of a textbook based on the course, and her initial idea has developed, through several permutations, into the present collection.

We believe we have produced something unique and uniquely valuable for students of the Renaissance at all levels. During the past generation our knowledge of Renaissance humanism in its particular manifestations has grown so vast and at such a rate that the kinds of syntheses mentioned earlier by scholars of a past generation would be much more difficult today, especially if humanism is conceived as a Europe-wide movement interacting with other major movements and institutions. What we have done here is to bring specialists together to accomplish what no one scholar working alone could have achieved.

Each writer, a close student of the field about which he or she writes, was instructed to synthesize the state of the field on the assigned topic. In some cases this task involved a study of what other scholars have discovered, in others an attempt to create a synthesis that has not existed or been perceived before. In a number of cases the articles here represent condensations of book-length studies, which are themselves the major statements of the topics in those areas, for example, the articles by Marianna D. Birnbaum, John F. D'Amico on Rome, Margaret L. King on Venice, Claude V. Palisca, Mario Santoro, Retha M. Warnicke, and Ronald G. Witt. With five exceptions, the forty-one essays published here were written explicitly for these volumes. The five exceptions are Kristeller's essay on humanism and moral philosophy, King's on women and humanism in Italy, and the essays by Deno J. Geanakoplos, Anthony Grafton, and David B. Ruderman. Three of these (King, Geanakoplos, Ruderman) are not readily available; one has been expanded (Ruderman), and in all five the notes have been updated. In very large part, then, this is an originally conceived and executed collaborative scholarly project.

Each essay is addressed to a wide audience. Undergraduates studying in this field for the first time will find here the closest approximation to a textbook that is available in the field. The various essays will introduce a student to any topic that might be addressed in a course on humanism and to the various contemporary interpretations of humanism. The volumes should be of equal or greater value to advanced students, including college and university teachers, whether scholars in the field or not, who want to introduce themselves and their students to Renaissance humanism. We have tried to ensure that all essays are clear, and to this end all quotations have been translated into English. At the same time, all studies relevant to a topic have been included in each essay, regardless of the language in which they were written; many of these are repeated in several essays, and all, both books and articles, have been included in the bibliography located at the end of Volume 3.

A word should be said about the title of these volumes and the scope they promise. The "foundations" and "forms" of humanism are treated in comprehensive fashion. In the "foundations" section, classical, patristic, and medieval backgrounds to humanism are dealt with, and Petrarch, the "father" of humanism, is treated in relation to his ties to all three backgrounds. The forms of humanism have been divided into two frames of reference, geographical (Volumes 1 and 2) and disciplinary (Volume 3). The geographical is further divided into Italian (Volume 1) and European outside Italy (Volume 2). These proceed in chronological fashion, the essays on Italian humanism focusing primarily on the Quattrocento and those on humanism in other countries including the fifteenth century but also extending into and often proceeding to the end of the sixteenth. The disciplinary frame of reference cuts across geographical regions, and each essay proceeds in chronological order, sometimes up to 1700.

The section on the "legacy" of humanism is confined to one essay by Kristeller, a general overview. Actually, the legacy of humanism may be said to involve in part its impact on art, law, music, science, and theology, topics addressed in the final sections of the disciplinary treatment of humanism. It also involves, of course, the impact of humanism on the development of classical scholarship and of the disciplines central to the *studia humanitatis,* all of which are treated in the section on disciplines and institutions. The legacy has thus been more broadly confronted than the one essay in the "legacy" section implies. At the same time, the focus has been placed deliberately on humanism itself, tracing its development as long as it is discernible as a movement in European culture. To trace the impact of humanism after it merged into the broader currents of European culture is a very large task, perhaps as large as the task undertaken here. All readers should therefore be aware that although the legacy of humanism is addressed in various ways in these volumes, the topic itself is not systematically analyzed to the same extent as the foundations and forms of humanism.

*   *   *

Editing these volumes has been at times a trying, but at times also, and ultimately, a rewarding experience. I would like to thank the National Endowment for the Humanities, which provided not only the institutional grant through which this project was initiated but also a personal research fellowship during 1981 and 1982, which enabled me to complete an initial draft of several essays I have contributed, to edit essays in hand, and to enlist many new contributors.

I would like to thank two secretaries at the State University College at Old Westbury: Marion Pensabene, who typed about half of the essays in their final form, and Rosemary Smith, who entered the bibliography in its various phases into a computer; and a colleague, Professor Michael Taves, for help in generating the index on a computer. In addition, I would like to thank the College at Old Westbury for extensive support with respect to the copying and mailing costs involved in bringing the manuscript to its completed form. Most especially, I owe a deep debt of gratitude to Selby Hickey, the college's academic vice-president, through whose efforts the college has contributed toward underwriting the costs of producing these volumes. An underwriting grant has also been received from the Center for International Scholarly Exchange at Barnard College/Columbia University, whose help is here gratefully acknowledged. In addition, several individuals have contributed significantly toward underwriting the costs of publication, and to all of them I extend a deepfelt thanks.

My greatest debt of gratitude is to Paul Oskar Kristeller. These volumes themselves are in an important way a tribute to his scholarship. But in a more personal sense, I am grateful for his constant counsel through letters and (more frequently) telephone conversations. In addition to helping frame the general outline of these volumes, he assisted in the solicitation of contributors—especially during the early stages of the project—and he has read a number of the essays. His graciousness to younger scholars working in the field has become legendary in his own time; this project is certainly a wonderful instance of it.

The volumes are dedicated to Maristella Lorch, the initiator of the original course and the instigator of the idea that has now become this anthology. As the concept of the project matured, we have tried it out together in subsequent incarnations of our initial course on humanism. Without her patient and enduring goodwill and her genius for bringing people together this project would never have been begun, let alone completed.

ALBERT RABIL, JR.

RENAISSANCE HUMANISM

Volume 2

PART III

HUMANISM BEYOND ITALY

17 ❧ HUMANISM IN ENGLAND
Richard J. Schoeck

THE CLASSICAL HERITAGE OF EUROPE, THOUGH NOT ALWAYS CON-
tinuous in all parts of the Continent, is immensely broad and deep;
and here and there it was—in the mind of an Augustine, a
Bede, or a Dante—brought to a fresh synthesis and endowed with a new
immediacy. A study of humanism (which is the ideal of classical education, learning, and imitation) must consequently consider the whole even
while examining one of its phases separately, recognizing that medieval
humanism grew out of the classical *studia humanitatis* and that the roots
of Renaissance humanism lie deep in the fabric of medieval thought and
letters.[1] From the time of the early church fathers and continuing through
the Middle Ages, Britain possessed a tradition of learning that produced
many scholars of great distinction, men like Aldhelm, Bede, and John of
Salisbury.[2] Although the patristic and medieval approaches to learning
were different from that of Petrarch (1304–1374), who brought a revival
of learning to Italy which in more modern times has taken on the name
of humanism,[3] those traditions also shared much common ground in
their study of classical texts, and certain of the patristic and medieval
traditions must be seen as continuing into the Renaissance period. For
example, the thorny question of the relation between pagan learning and
Christian piety haunted some of the church fathers and their successors.
Tertullian had asked: What has Athens to do with Jerusalem? And the
great Anglo-Saxon scholar Alcuin, in a letter of 797, addressed the question of what should be read at a corporate priestly meal, asking: "What
[has] Ingeld to do with Christ?"—a questioning echoed by St. Bernard
of Clairvaux in the early twelfth century, by Petrarch in the fourteenth,
and by Erasmus in the sixteenth. Renaissance humanism was not secular,
and consequently this tension between faith and reason, piety and learning, or Christianity and classical culture continued to occupy Erasmus,
More, and their successors.[4]

Despite many shared concerns and values, however, the pace of humanist development and the rooting and growth of traditions of learning
were different in England and on the Continent, and it was to be some
time before a Renaissance England emerged in which the influence of
Petrarch would be clearly visible, not only through his poetry (which so
strongly influenced, in differing ways, the poetry of Wyatt, Spenser,

Sidney, Donne, and Shakespeare),[5] but even more deeply through his moral essays and letters (which exercised an even wider influence for generations), and the new love of Cicero and eloquence.[6] Nonetheless, even during the early Quattrocento, when Petrarch's ideas were taking root in Italy, important connections were being established between Italy and England. I would like to begin with these links (at the cost of ignoring continuing cultural connections with France and the Burgundian Netherlands) in order to continue the story of humanism's development in England. First, then, there will be an examination of the so-called Oxford Reformers who were so strongly influenced by their Italian studies, then a concentration on John Colet, Erasmus in England, Thomas More, and others. Later developments will be more briefly sketched. The primary concern of this essay is with humanism in England during the reigns of Henry VII and Henry VIII.

*   *   *

During the fifteenth century there was a growing number of Italian (as well as other European) humanists who came to England, as Roberto Weiss and Paul O. Kristeller have informed us; and what was of perhaps even greater and more lasting influence was the growing number of Englishmen who went to Italy to study under great master-teachers of humanism like Guarino of Verona and Demetrius Chalcondyles, and to establish personal relations with other humanists of their own generation.

Under the patronage of Humphrey, Duke of Gloucester (1391–1447), important classical manuscripts were copied in Italy to be sent back to England, and Tito Livio Frulovisi, an Italian schoolmaster, lived in England as early as 1437, writing a Latin life of Henry V, the duke's brother, and seven Latin plays in a style somewhat influenced by classical models. Duke Humphrey made significant bequests of manuscripts to Oxford. There were other Italian humanists who came to England,[7] and in the reign of Henry VII several Italian clerics were rewarded with English bishoprics for service as Latin orators and letter writers; Pietro Carmeliano was appointed Latin secretary, and a French scholar from Toulouse, Bernard André, tutored the king's son and lectured on classics at Oxford.[8]

By 1500, then, one can speak with some firmness of a heritage of Italian humanism: there were, especially at Oxford (owing in part to Duke Humphrey's patronage), individual scholars trained in the new humanistic techniques of reading, teaching, and writing; there was a growing interest and competence in Greek (although it was not yet part of the university curriculum at either Oxford or Cambridge); and there was a growing number of Greek and Latin classical manuscripts, often specially copied for English friends and patrons.

Unfortunately, nearly all of the English who went to Italy for studies were churchmen—unfortunately, because in general they had been sent to such Italian universities as Bologna and Padua to study law, with the consequence that upon their return to England these humanistically inspired scholars (humanism being nearly always something they studied in addition to the prescribed courses for law degrees) were put into administrative or diplomatic appointments and assignments.[9] Many of these fifteenth-century Englishmen left little in the way of publications to show for their humanist interests; but a scholar communicates (as Harbison has justly observed) "through his teaching, his conversation, and his correspondence just as truly as through his printed works."[10]

But, to repeat, there was enough by 1500 to speak of a heritage of Italian humanism in England. One of the aspects that must be stressed is the pattern of master-student and other personal relationships—with Chalcondyles and Thomas Linacre, for example, or (to cite a different kind of relationship) with Marsilio Ficino and Colet—and we have come to appreciate the unique importance of a very small band of scholars who provided the essential keys both to the story of humanism in Tudor England and to Thomas More's remarkable development as a humanist. To say this and to focus on one small group is neither to deny the importance of such individuals as William Sellyng and John Free nor to deny the importance of the group of humanists at the court of Henry VII.[11] Yet in the light of present knowledge about Tudor humanism, three stand out, and they were friends who interacted upon one another and who were recognized as a group.

These three were William Grocyn (ca. 1446–1519), Thomas Linacre (1460–1524), and John Colet (1466–1519), and the greatest of them, by all testimony, was Colet. All three had studied Latin and Greek, as well as medicine and law, in Italy, and they had returned to and were teaching at Oxford together while More was an undergraduate. This small band of scholars is still called the Oxford Reformers, even though both Colet and More spent the latter part of their lives in London and the term has been challenged.[12]

*   *   *

In Weiss's writings we may read the story of the studies in Italy pursued during the fifteenth century by Linacre, Grocyn, Colet, and others; we know something of how deeply their teaching and thought were shaped by Italian humanism. With John Colet we are on somewhat firmer ground; although a new intellectual biography is urgently needed, in the ironic words of J. B. Trapp "it should not take longer to do than a life-time."[13] Recent scholarship has gone into Colet's studies and made available Colet's marginalia on the printed text of the letters of Ficino (the only printed book, it would seem, in Colet's library). In addition, two letters from Ficino to Colet are extant, and one from Colet to Ficino. Based on an analysis of these documents, Colet's most recent editor has written about their similarities and differences:

> The volume [annotated by Colet] tends to emphasize the differences between the two men rather than their similarities, contrasting Colet's moral zeal with Ficino's intellectual enthusiasm, Colet's search for order and pattern with Ficino's search for mystery and sophistication, Colet's Augustinian ethics with Ficino's Platonic metaphysics.[14]

This much is sound enough, and one may even go a step farther in seeing a distinction between a practical and a theoretical mind. It may well be that these differences were strongly influenced by social differences; but one cannot follow Jayne in his assertion that "the speculative life was all very well for a man like Ficino, protected by a benevolent patronage and subsidized for the purpose," for Colet's great family wealth gave him a "benevolent patronage" as well.[15] There is more to the story than a simple black-and-white contrast of a Florentine aristocratic milieu with that of a bourgeois London cleric—even if it were true.

Although what Colet "published" in his own lifetime was not bulky, there can be no doubting the quality of Colet's mind and character, or his impact on key men in his own age, notably Erasmus and More.

Colet gave a series of lectures on the New Testament in the autumn of 1496 in Oxford. As has been remarked by others, he was not yet a doctor of divinity and was barely thirty, yet all of the Oxford scholarly world seems to have turned out to hear him. What he had to say was nothing less than a revolution in biblical study and scholarship, and the technique had been learned from Lorenzo Valla, that stormy petrel who opened new paths for Quattrocento humanism.[16] Put in simplest terms, Colet stripped away the apparatus of scholastic biblical study—the "luxuriant growth of dialectical and dogmatic glosses": the commentaries, summas, notes, summations of commentaries, and disputed questions—and went straight to the original text itself. It is worth visualizing the typical text of the late medieval Bible, the text not only of the manuscripts but also of the early printed Bibles, such as that of Nicholas of Lyra.[17] There the text was not simply surrounded by, it was all but overwhelmed by notes and commentaries: the apparatus visually as well as intellectually dominated the text.

Colet lectured on 1 Corinthians and Romans, and Harbison catches the essential technique and well-nigh revolutionary thrust of Colet's lecturing:

> How exciting—and perhaps unsettling—it must have been to many in his crowded audience when young Colet got up and began to talk about Paul, the person who wrote the epistles—about the Christians in Corinth to whom he was writing—about the moral and political situation in Rome—about what Paul was trying to say to these two groups of early Christians, particularly his moral advice—about his tact, his firmness, and his vision of Christ. The hardest effort in all scholarship is to rise from grasp of the minute and disconnected to grasp of the whole. Colet made it clear from the start in both series of lectures that he was concerned about the whole of what St. Paul had to say in the whole Epistle. "Everything Paul said must be cautiously examined before any opinion is offered about his meaning." "We have tried so far as possible," he concluded his lectures on *Romans*, "with the aid of God's grace, to express Paul's true meaning. How we have succeeded, we hardly know. But we have had the best will to do it." [18]

Colet's genius—and we cannot doubt that he was a man of genius, in his tremendous saneness and his ability to balance or fuse oppositions and even contradictions—lay in his lecturing to such audiences as the 1496 Oxford one or to an audience fifteen years later of the convocation of English clergy, to whom he preached on reform; in his conversing with students and friends; and in his letter writing. The far-flung world of Renaissance humanism, which was dominated to be sure by Erasmus, More, and a few others, but which was filled with so many other humanists that it has been called the republic of letters (*respublica litterarum*), was bound together, it now seems to us, by correspondence: for the epistle was, along with the dialogue, the favorite form of communication for the humanists.[19] There were other lectures by Colet, and beyond Harbison there is the recent scholarship of Trapp, which offers deeper penetration into the mind and work of this remarkable person.[20]

Colet was also a man of vision in education. He was able to devote much of the fortune inherited from his father, who had twice been lord mayor of London, to the endowment of St. Paul's School in the heart of London, which served as a model for many grammar schools later established or reformed, as well as a focal point for humanism in the city.

Colet chose as master William Lily (ca. 1468–1523)—godson of Grocyn and grandfather of the John Lyly who wrote *Euphues* (with its humanist flourishes) in the Elizabethan period, thereby marking off the several stages of humanism and humanist developments in Tudor England within one family. Erasmus was involved in framing the constitution of St. Paul's, with its detailed provisions for instituting humanism into the grammar-school curriculum, and he collaborated with Lily and Colet in the preparation of a new Latin grammar for its pupils; this influential grammar (known as Lily's Grammar) was not only the model for all English grammars in the next three centuries, it has aptly been called "the most influential of all English textbooks."[21]

*   *   *

Erasmus was of course a Dutch humanist and very much the product of a northern humanism that was in many ways different from the Florentine humanism of Giovanni Pico della Mirandola and Ficino, although Erasmus knew Italian humanism well and had lived for some years in Italy. But Erasmus had made a number of trips to England, he had several close English friends, he enjoyed English patronage, and his period of teaching in Cambridge was of great significance both to Erasmus himself and to the development of Tudor humanism, as well as to scriptural scholarship in England. It is well, therefore, to consider Erasmus in this survey of humanism in Renaissance England.

Erasmus's first trip to England was in 1499, but like the 1505 trip it was short. In 1509–1510 Erasmus stayed for some months at the house of Thomas More, and that trip is associated with the writing of Erasmus's celebrated *Moriae encomium,* with its pun on the name of his host. On that trip Erasmus lectured on Jerome at Cambridge, early in 1510, and he may well have stayed with John Fisher. Well before he came to Cambridge for his extended stay from 1511 to 1514, then, Erasmus had made a number of personal contacts and several lasting friendships: with More, of course, but also with Fisher, president of Queen's College and chancellor of the university in 1505. Erasmus then taught at Cambridge from the late summer of 1511 to 1514, lecturing first on the Greek language and a little later on theology. Finally, in July 1514, having lectured on his beloved Jerome and having revised Jerome's letters—as well as working on the New Testament, a revision of the *Adages,* Seneca, several school texts, *De copia* and *De conscribendis epistolis,* and the revision of Lily's Grammar—Erasmus left Cambridge, not to return.[22]

The 1499 visit was clearly a memorable event for Erasmus, and for others. In the autumn of that year, when about thirty-three years of age, Erasmus spent two months in Oxford, where he would have stayed in St.

Mary's, the college of the order of Augustinian canons to which he himself belonged. At Oxford Erasmus met Colet and attended some of his remarkable lectures on the letters of St. Paul, so strongly influenced by the humanist concept of text and context and so different from the scholastic lecturing through glosses that had already irritated Erasmus in his early theological studies in Paris. But if Colet influenced Erasmus on the study of the Bible, so too did Erasmus influence Colet on the need for further study of Greek.

After returning to London from Oxford in December 1499, Erasmus wrote to express his enthusiasm, in a celebrated encomiastic passage:

> [I find here, he wrote his former student, Mountjoy,] such a quantity of intellectual refinement and scholarship, not of the usual pedantic and trivial kind either, but profound and learned and truly classical, in both Latin and Greek, that I have little longing left for Italy, except for the sake of visiting it. When I listen to Colet it seems to me that I am listening to Plato himself. Who could fail to be astonished at the universal scope of Grocyn's accomplishments? Could anything be more clever or profound or sophisticated than Linacre's mind? Did Nature ever create anything kinder, sweeter, or more harmonious than the character of Thomas More? But why need I rehearse the list further? It is marvellous to see what an extensive and rich crop of ancient learning is springing up here in England.[23]

This paragraph, and this letter which so favorably compares English humanism with Italian, tell us much about the state of humanism in England in the year 1499; they also tell us much about Erasmus himself, and they explain why Erasmus returned for at least three trips of increasing duration. Behind him, Erasmus left a legacy of humanism among fellows and students: Thomas Lupset, Richard Sampson, John Watson, Richard Croke, and many others who read his writings.

A few words must be said about translations of Erasmus's writings into English during the sixteenth century. The earliest extant editions of English translations of Erasmus, Devereux has firmly established, were three—all published by Thomas Berthelet between 12 October 1524 and 12 March 1525—and significantly, while two were works of piety, the third, Berthelet's own rendering of proverbs from Erasmus's *Opuscula aliquot,* "was a humanist compilation of classical wisdom."[24] Other translations or renderings of Erasmus came steadily from English presses as well as from continental printings of the original Latin, and one must signal Sir Thomas Chaloner's excellent translation of the *Moriae encomium* in 1549 with its important preface on the work and on the matter of translation. In Devereux's summary: "The English translators of the Renaissance used his writings because they admired him and knew that his name would lend weight to what they had to say. [There were also, to be sure, many instances in which Erasmus's writings were used, but not his name.[25]] They selected works carefully and they manipulated or ignored their contexts, but they never succeeded in making him one of their own. The first translation, in 1522, challenged the authority of the old priest, and the last in the seventeenth century challenged the authority of the new presbyter."[26]

In studying the thought and letters of Tudor England one cannot ignore the presence of Erasmus and the centrality of Erasmian humanism, and it would be difficult to overstate the importance of that influence.[27]

*   *   *

Thomas More, we might be inclined to say, was lucky to have arrived in Oxford just at the time that Linacre, Grocyn, and Colet were teaching there: men and women of the Middle Ages and Renaissance, however, would have been more likely to have spoken of fortune's agency or of providence in such a timing. Yet one might think of what More might have done had he been given four years at Oxford instead of only two, because his father, a common lawyer, thought that he was wasting too much time on classical studies and that it was high time to get to the serious business of the law. In the early Tudor period few lawyers combined humanistic studies with legal studies, and it was to be a very long time before a Tudor merchant would dream of allowing, much less supporting, his son in humanistic studies.

However, we still lack some of the vital evidence needed to write definitively of the development of More's thought in general and of his humanism in particular. For one thing, we still do not know what was in More's library (as we know what was in Pico's, for example); Thomas Cromwell's seizure of More's books and papers when he was arrested and sent to the Tower and the apparent destruction of his library must be counted a great loss to English Renaissance scholarship. For another thing, against the two-year gap between the death of Pico in 1494 and the edition of his *Opera* (Bologna, 1496) by his nephew Gianfrancesco, more than twenty years elapsed between More's death in 1535 and the publication of his English *Works* in 1557 (which by no means included all of his writings); for numerous reasons, work on his literary remains was too long delayed, much was lost, and his legal writings, like his lectures on Augustine's *City of God*, have yet to see print and are probably now lost forever.[28]

I have already pointed to Colet as a key bridge between the humanism flourishing in Florence at the end of the Quattrocento and the rapidly developing classical scholarship in Oxford and London. For Colet it was clearly Ficino who was the energizing force in this transmission, this *traditio;* for More it was Pico. If Colet's role in the movement of ideas and ideals was as vital as I have been urging, then full weight must be given to Colet's influence upon More, along with that of Pico and of the Charterhouse in London, where More himself lived the monastic rule while he was studying law from about 1500 to about 1504. Like Colet in his range of interests, More was able to balance the conflicting claims of father, legal studies, classical studies (especially the study of Greek), and the spiritual life at the Charterhouse.[29] Yet a comparison of More and Pico will highlight some crucial differences between them. For Pico there were the extraordinary interests in the Jewish kabbalah, in Arabic and other languages, and in Hebrew philosophy and theology. In More there is virtually no interest in magic or in oriental languages and religions. These differences are important in themselves; and the further discovery that there seem to have been for these young men two different concepts of the nature of truth—Pico's concept ranging very widely outside the established canon and leading to a belief in there being some truth in all monotheistic religions; and More's working within the established traditions and canons of Christianity and respecting authority to a fault, becoming in later years more and more dogmatic, even by comparison with his friend Erasmus—then something further becomes apparent about the different thrusts of their kinds of humanism. For, quite significantly, the earliest of More's finished works was his Life of Pico, published in 1509 or 1510 (though very likely written toward the end of More's years in the Charterhouse, that is, around 1504),[30] and this work can tell us much with respect to More's deepest thinking at that time about humanism and about his sense of vocation: was he to be a priest, or would he be a married man living in the world? And, whichever way he took, what was the role of humanism to be for him?[31]

It has been shown that More's revisions in his translation of Gianfrancesco Pico's biography of his uncle were extensive; that there had in fact been more cutting than adding. M. P. Gilmore stresses that More, while emphasizing Pico's spiritual life,

> omitted numerous passages describing Pico's intellectual background and his philosophical work. In his account of the prepa-

ration of the *Conclusiones,* for example, More, omitting the
references to Origen, Hilary, and natural magic, summarizes the
preparation of Pico's theses . . . [dealing with Pico's philosophical
learning and debts to particular authors]. Of all the names listed by
Gianfrancesco, only that of St. Thomas, who receives particular
praise, is retained in More's version. The effect of the changes introduced by More is . . . to emphasize Pico's spiritual life and commitment to orthodox Christianity and to simplify and generalize
the description of his intellectual interests.[32]

Young Thomas More was about twenty-six when he made his translation of the *Life of Pico,* and the act of translating seems to have coin-
cided with his decision not to remain in the Charterhouse and to live
instead a secular life. It is not unreasonable to infer that More consciously or unconsciously took Pico as a model for the lay intellectual
living in the world, yet able to pursue both an intellectual life and a life
rich in spirituality—the *vita mixta,* as opposed to the singlemindedness
of either the *vita contemplativa* or the *vita activa.* For More, therefore,
humanism was a complex matter, and very much a part of his decision
not to remain in the Charterhouse and become a monk. And in 1499 two
of his models had been a part of his life: John Colet and Erasmus.

Earlier I gave Erasmus's testimony about More in the year 1499,
when he was about twenty-two, and have commented on the extent to
which Erasmus and Colet evidently deeply influenced each other; clearly
Colet gave a vital focus to Erasmus's program of studies, so that the Bible
and the church fathers occupied the bulk of Erasmus's scholarly activities
for the next thirty-six years. It is even more evident that More and Erasmus became the closest of friends, and soon they collaborated in studying
and translating Greek, particularly Lucian, whose ironic satire gave each
of them a place to stand, a mode of relating their own personas to the
world in which each found much to criticize, yet without surrendering to
cynicism or despair.[33] If it is an overstatement to assert that Erasmus and
More restored irony to Europe, it is not too much to say that the kind of
irony that both Erasmus and More mastered enabled them to control
multiple points of view, to generate (in Huizinga's terms) a rich sense of
homo ludens, and not least to take a giant step forward in fusing classical
learning and Christian piety.

In discussing Erasmus, I quoted from his letter of 1499 which asked
whether Nature had ever created "anything kinder, sweeter, or more harmonious than the character of Thomas More?" That letter is more than
a summation of the achievement of Tudor humanism by the end of the
fifteenth century: it gives a further indication of the interrelationships of

this band of humanists into which young Thomas More had at the age of twenty-one or twenty-two been accepted as a peer among men a generation older. Yet while the More extolled in the 1499 letter was so clearly a man of rare promise, unfortunately little remains of his youthful writings: only a few letters, some verses, and some translations remain (in addition to the translation of the *Life of Pico*, there are translations of epigrams from Greek into Latin). His lectures on Augustine's *City of God* (ca. 1504), which were much praised, have been lost, and so apparently have his early legal writings (such as his readings at Lincoln's Inn a few years after his lectures on Augustine). We must turn to a somewhat older More to perceive the growing complexity of the man's mind and to two texts that project his concept of humanism. Those two texts are the *Utopia* of 1516 and his letter to Oxford University of 1518. Each is a masterpiece of its kind, but obviously it is the *Utopia* that has become one of the enduring classics of our heritage. Yet I want to reverse chronology and take up the letter to Oxford first, because it is a defense of humanism, and it will display more directly than the prismatic *Utopia* the rhetorical quality of and the ironic play in More's mind. Together they offer the dialectic defense of humanism and its creative power.

*   *   *

The Thomas More of 1518, the date of his letter to the University of Oxford, was a man of about forty who had nearly reached the pinnacle of success within the practice of the common law: he had twice been selected reader of his inn of court (the double readership being the last state before moving upward to become serjeant, and then judge); he had been the top legal officer of London, the undersheriff; and he had distinguished himself as attorney and counselor, as arbitrator of wills and estates, and as a member of a number of royal commissions. In his own characterization of his busy life (in the letter to Pieter Gillis, another busy humanist-lawyer who was town clerk of Antwerp, prefixed to the *Utopia*), he gives a brief self-portrait:

> Yet even to carry through this trifling task [the writing out of the *Utopia*], my other tasks left me practically no leisure at all. I am constantly engaged in legal business, either pleading or hearing, either giving an award as arbiter or deciding a case as judge. I pay a visit of courtesy to one man and go on business to another. I devote almost the whole day in public to other men's affairs and the remainder to my own. I leave to myself, that is to learning, nothing at all.[34]

Therefore, when in 1518 Henry VIII wanted someone in England, someone at his court, to answer the attack on humanism that was gaining strength at Oxford, who better than Thomas More? It is quite remarkable that More was twice called upon by superior authority to defend the two things he most cherished: in 1518 by his king to defend humanism, and in 1529 by his bishop to defend official Catholicism; in 1518 he defended humanism in humanist Latin, and in 1529 he defended his church in English.

The letter to Oxford University, as we are informed within the letter itself, was directed by the king in reply to attacks on humanism being made from the pulpit within Oxford. The letter follows the conventional five-part structure of formal letters prescribed in the manuals and letter books, but not always followed by the most skilled writers.[35] In this letter More is almost at pains to call attention to the conventional parts of the letter, and the *salutatio* is carefully precise, with a full listing of the officials of the university. The second conventional part of the epistle was the *captatio,* in which the writer was supposed to work to gain goodwill, usually in combination with the address and tone of the *salutatio.* Perhaps the most elaborate *captatio benevolentiae* (seizing of goodwill) in all of More's letters is to be found in this letter: "I have been wondering, gentlemen, whether I might be permitted to communicate to scholars of your distinction certain conclusions to which I have recently come."

After this "communicating" More moves to the giving of advice, but only after the delicately turned wit of his *exordium:*

I have been wondering, gentleman, whether I might be permitted to communicate to scholars of your distinction certain conclusions to which I have recently come. Yet I have hesitated in approaching so brilliant a group, not so much on the ground of my style as on that of seeming to give an exhibition of pride and arrogance. Who am I, the possessor of little prudence and less practice, a scholar of mediocre proportions, to arrogate to myself the right to advise you in anything? And how can I dare to offer advice in the field of letters, especially when any one of you is fitted by his wisdom and erudition to give advice in that field to thousands?

At first sight, Venerable Fathers, I was therefore deterred by your unique wisdom, but, on second thought, I was encouraged, for it occurred to me that only ignorant and arrogant fools would disdain to give a man a hearing, and that the wiser and more learned you were, the less likely you would be to think of yourselves or to scorn the advice of others. I was further emboldened by the thought that no one was ever harmed by just judges, such as you are above all, simply on the ground that he offered advice without thinking of the consequences. On the contrary, loyal and affectionate advice, even if imprudent, has always deserved praise and thanks.

Finally, when I consider that, with God's help, I ought to offer you whatever slight learning I have acquired, since it was at your University that my education began. . . .

The *narratio* follows directly—the stating of the issue—and it almost casually tells of the formation of a society named after the Trojans, which ridiculed the study of Greek. More soon focuses on a single individual whose intemperance makes the matter more than a triviality and who has created a situation that more than anything in recent years requires serious attention in order to maintain the honor of the university:

> However, since I have been here in Abingdon in attendance at the court of His Victorious Majesty [Henry VIII], I have found that the silliness is developing into a form of insanity. For one of the Trojans, a scholar in his own estimation, a wit of the first order in that of his friends, though slightly deranged in that of anyone observing his actions, has chosen during Lent to babble in a sermon [the favorite vehicle for attacks on humanism] against not only Greek but Roman literature, and finally against all polite learning, liberally berating all the liberal arts [*sed valde liberaliter adversus omnes liberales artes blaterasse*].

More quickly moves from this account of the matter, the usual ambience of the *narratio*, into his refutation of the Trojan's attack: "Now as to the question of humanistic education being secular. No one has ever claimed that a man needed Greek and Latin, or indeed any education, in order to be saved." And he rises to eloquence in pursuing a logic used earlier in Salutati's defense of humanism:

> But really, I cannot admit that theology, that august queen of heaven, can be thus confined [i.e., to English]. Does she not dwell and abide in Holy Scripture? Does she not pursue her pilgrim way through the cells of the holy Fathers: Augustine and Jerome; Ambrose and Cyprian; Chrysostom, Gregory, Basil, and their like? . . .
> To whom is it *not* obvious that to the Greeks we owe all our precision in the liberal arts generally and in theology particularly; for the Greeks either made the great discoveries themselves or passed them on as part of their heritage. Take philosophy, for

example. If you leave out Cicero and Seneca, the Romans wrote their philosophy in Greek or translated it from Greek.

I need hardly mention that the New Testament is in Greek, or that the best New Testament scholars were Greeks and wrote in Greek.

Having presented with eloquence the traditional humanistic arguments that secular learning trains the soul in virtue, and that it is the proper handmaid for the study of theology and Scripture (which, indeed, without humanistic enrichment would degenerate, as in fact it has done, into the invention of petty and meretricious questions of late fifteenth-century philosophy against which More and Erasmus so arduously campaigned, as Petrarch, Coluccio Salutati, and Valla had done earlier against their scholastic contemporaries), More then moves to his *petitio*. He is not simply giving good advice, he is exhorting the masters of Oxford to do their duty. Without overtly holding out the king's favor as a carrot, or his displeasure as a club, the *petitio* flows smoothly into a *conclusio* that hints such a warning:

> I have no doubt that you yourselves will easily in your wisdom find a way to end this dispute and quiet these stupid factions: that you will see to it not only that all the liberal arts may be free from derision and contempt but that they shall be held in dignity and honor. . . . May God preserve your glorious seat of learning unharmed; and may He grant that it flourish continually in virtue and in all the liberal arts.

Thus in the letter to Oxford More brought to full development in Tudor England the tradition, begun by Petrarch and followed by his successors, of defending humanism in the epistolary form. While revealing More's mastery of the genre, the letter also reveals his mastery of a persuasive, subtle, and witty prose style in Latin. (It is noteworthy that the attacks against humanism came from Oxford, not Cambridge; for Erasmus had been at Cambridge, and his influence was very strong in 1518—although both universities maintained the scholastic curriculum in the university as a whole.)

I have discussed the letter to Oxford before discussing *Utopia*—despite the fact that the letter was written in 1518, whereas *Utopia* was published in 1516—for two reasons beyond what was briefly indicated above. First, I wanted to show that humanism, though it was highly regarded by some, was under attack by others, especially within the universities, where scholasticism was still (and in many places would continue for another century to be) the dominant element or mode of the curriculum,[36] and where some individuals felt threatened—perhaps it is not too unfair to suppose because they themselves lacked both Greek and the intensive study of the classics which were the hallmarks of humanism. Second, I wanted to show More's great skill in marshaling a complex argument and in controlling his tone, especially his irony, in a complex and learned Latin before I engaged in an analysis and discussion of *Utopia*.

*   *   *

There are countries of the mind, and Utopia is one of the most famous.[37] It is a favorite of tourists on the accelerated tours of Renaissance literature, history, and political theory conducted in the university, and still more it is a place to which many have returned in later life. That none, I think, want to stay there to live is not the point of it all.

Recall that More was a contemporary not only of Erasmus but also of Luther and Machiavelli, to name only the more famous. In nearly all of the seminal figures of this generation there is a complex sense of urgency, and—turning to look at England itself, as book 1 of *Utopia* compels us to do—we are led to see that there was an economic and social crisis of great seriousness. Far more than just the problem of sheep grazing and enclosure was involved, though like the problem of executing thieves, it serves to focus on the greater problems of war, disease, decadence, the breakdown of institutions, and the inefficacy of the law. From all sides voices had been raised for a century to reform the church, and humanists had spoken out with passion and learning. Just before the publication of *Utopia*, the Fifth Lateran Council had begun in 1512 with a moving appeal by Egidio of Viterbo for a massive reform of the visible institution of the church together with a genuine *renovatio* (or renewal) of the spiritual life of individuals. But the Fifth Lateran Council was nearing its end as More wrote, and in April 1517 it concluded, with great historical irony, its final session with the solemn pronouncement that reform was now assured—only a few months before a then-obscure Augustinian monk was to nail ninety-five theses concerning the need for reform on a church door in Germany. More too was concerned with reform, as was his friend Erasmus and many of their friends; *Utopia* was his unique contribution toward reform. It was a humanist's effort.

Published in 1516 (but begun at least a year earlier, and with roots in his mind and imagination years earlier still), the *Utopia* was addressed to an international audience. First printed in the Low Countries, next in Paris, and then in Basel, it was set within a framework of supporting letters from humanists of European reputation, adding Guillaume Budé in the Paris edition and Erasmus in the Basel. More wanted his little book read by learned men everywhere in Europe as well as in England, and it was therefore in Latin, which was international and the language of scholars of all nations and all fields of interest. It was, moreover, in a Latin that was up-to-date, mature, sensitive to nuances of tone and emphasis, capable of great clarity and precision, and alive to the potential enrichment by allusiveness and evocation—that is, to intertextualities— as English in general was not capable of being at the time, at least not in prose. To illustrate this point, one may take the concept of pleasure as a theme in the book and analyze the techniques by which More enlarges our thinking about pleasure, bringing into play other words for pleasure (*voluptas*, *laetitia*, and so on), thereby suggesting other meanings and other points of view that come from such a technique (which was being practiced in the Latin poetry of the age).[38]

The pursuit of pleasure is central to the Utopian philosophy, and their social system is developed to enable the individual to pursue individual pleasure, but only to that point at which it conflicts with larger interests, whether society's claims or God's. In the manifold conceptualizing of pleasure and in the multiple words employed for it and its related meanings, a crucially important and illuminating example of the richly allusive texture of More's Latin is revealed. For he begins with the basic term *voluptas* for pleasure; then he uses a Ciceronian term with a connotation of bodily gratification, embracing (as Surtz has noted) "everything pleasant, from the scratching of an itch to a self-approving conscience and eternal beatitude." More extends the range of this connotation of pleasure by synonyms of joy (*laetitia*) and gladness (*gaudium*), both of which have both classical and patristic overtones. He continues to enlarge the concept of pleasure by further synonyms: convenience, comfort, delight, enjoyment (*delectatio*, *suavitas*, *iucunditas*), and the like. By making the performance of good and virtuous deeds the source of the greatest pleasure, More has cunningly reconciled not only Stoic philosophy (then beginning its ascendancy in the Renaissance) but Christianity as well with what was potential in Epicurean philosophy at its best, just as Erasmus in his *Praise of Folly* had Christianized Epicurus by making Christ the supreme exemplar of the Epicurean.[39] In both More and Erasmus it is the play of reason and irony in this richly allusive mode that has generated such extension of conventional meanings.

Throughout the text of the *Utopia* and even in the marginal glosses that were added after the first edition, there is this kind of textual richness, this interplay that we now call intertextuality, which few translations manage to suggest, much less to succeed in rendering.[40] The fullest appreciation of this kind of prose would require the learning and the stylistic sensitivity of a Valla or a Poliziano, but many of his humanistic friends—especially Erasmus and Budé—caught more than just flashes of it, for both entered into the game of Utopia. Thus Thomas More was recognized and praised as a consummate Latin stylist.

From its heightened use of Latin we awake to and respond to other humanistic aspects of this work, both literary and nonliterary techniques. There is above all the form, which includes the mode, the spirit, and the discovering and enabling technique of dialogue—More's *Utopia* is a many-leveled multistructured dialogue. There is a full dialogue in book 1 among More, Gillis, and Hythloday, together with the dialogues within that enfolding dialogue that take us from Bruges in the Low Countries back to England twenty years earlier, successfully capturing the complexity of the contemporary world problem by means of this complex form. Then there is the narrative of Hythloday in book 2 within the larger dialogic structure, all of which in turn operates within the narrative frame of an account that Thomas More purports to be giving. As if all of this were not prismatic enough—and I use not simply the word in the sense of brilliant or varicolored, but for the metaphor as well of a prism, deliberately, for it suggests clarification by refraction (and by extension, of magnification), producing a field of vision and a clarity of sight that only such instruments can produce—the *libellus*, the golden little book, is itself set within a humanistic dialogue that the surrounding letters (the *parerga*) develop. And finally, all of the dialogue is carefully left open-ended when, on the closing pages, the character named More says: "I cannot say what features of this marvellous commonwealth I would hope to see adopted. . . ."

But we have not begun to exhaust the possibilities of the dialogue, for there is a sense of non-Europe (Utopia) entering into dialogue with Europe, of the present with the past, of the non-Christian with the Christian world. Nor have we begun to exhaust the possibilities of the concept of form, what Rosalie Colie has so aptly called *The Resources of Kind* (1973). The very idea of form in written expression—the concept, the emphasis, the organizing and shaping—is literary, and it becomes a predominantly literary concern. It is therefore important for a humanist who always works through a literary text and returns to it; it was this exploratory and shaping experience, surely, with which More was involved in the year after his return to England—not simply a writing down or copying out of what might have been projected earlier with Pieter Gillis. The map of Utopia and the Utopian verses, which were such essential features of the work from its first publication, are useful to the reader, to be sure; but to the critic they mark the incorporation of the visual with the primarily verbal and literary. In speaking of the dialogue as form, then, one must make the effort to understand the humanist imagination at work: conceiving the idea of the Utopian commonweal and then incarnating it within a dialogue. The isolated formal notion of dialogue does not exist by itself, off in some speculative vacuum. Form *is* only *in* a poem, or a dialogue: it is that work's mode of existence.[41] So *Utopia* is one of a number of dialogues from the fifteenth and sixteenth centuries that exemplify the dialogue form; but it is a unique work, and it is a dialogic masterpiece, a masterwork of humanism.

"Is the success of *Utopia* due to dialogue?" Surtz has asked (xxvi). For, after all, he writes, "dialogue is symbolic of open-mindedness, humility, and inquiry. Somehow or other More succeeds in involving readers in the dialogue" of *Utopia*. And the work ends with challenges to the reader: it is, again, an open-ended work, a dialogue with an indeterminate close. Further, on the island of Utopia itself, it has been observed, dialogue is never lacking: the Utopians seem to converse endlessly about everything, and their very religion is a dialogue with God. And through Hythloday, dialogue between the Utopians and sixteenth-century Europeans has begun. Yes, much of the success of Utopia and of the *Utopia* is due to dialogue, and to the quality and structure of that dialogue.

Its language, Latin; its form, the dialogue: these elements are vital, and not to be missed by the modern reader, as they assuredly were not missed by Renaissance readers. A third technique "calling for humanistic admiration" (in Surtz's phrase) was More's wise choice of a central point of view, as admirable a tactical decision as any made by Henry James. First, this choice arises from a fictional concern for verisimilitude: book I persuades us of certain qualities in Hythloday—he is sincere, learned, and experienced; a man of feeling as well as intelligence; and he asks the right questions—so that we may accept the picture he gives us so clearly in book 2 as a reasonable picture of a most reasonable society, and by focusing so much on the account by Hythloday More gains sharpness and achieves directness. But Hythloday—though his last name suggests in Greek a "teller of idle tales," his first name Raphael means "healing of God"—was no ordinary sailor. He was more than competent in Latin and most learned in Greek; he was, in short, on the side of the humanists' angels. He had sailed not like a Palinurus (who was the pilot of Aeneas, but slept at the helm and was drowned) or a modern traveling salesman, but like a Ulysses or rather a Plato: devoted to philosophy and letters, he had been able to observe shrewdly and reflect wisely. Anyone, we are told, can travel and bring back tall tales: "Scyllas and greedy Calaenos and folk-devouring Laestrygones [figures from the *Aeneid* and the *Odyssey*] and similar monsters are common enough, but well and wisely trained citizens are not everywhere to be found." The reference here is to the travelers' wonders that were frequent enough in the late Middle Ages and the *Voiage* of Sir John Mandeville, to name one, was a popular book in More's time. By means of such contrasts it is made clear that Hythloday was a man to listen to. And so Hythloday has the opportunity to speak for himself in presenting the Utopian achievement throughout book 2, and the character More adds his expression of opinion only at the very end of the book.

"Unity is attained" (again to quote Surtz) "through keeping Hythloday at the center of the stage. On the question of the best state he meets all challengers and triumphs in his way, at least by leaving the field undefeated. Hence the strong sense of conflict shared with the readers. Hythloday doughtily battles the lawyer on capital punishment and enclosure, the royal councillors on foreign and domestic policies, the historical Thomas More himself on the traditional arguments against communism, and Pieter Gillis in his defense of European superiority. All these points, of course, are side issues of the main conflict: the nature of the state." The title, "The Best State of a Commonwealth," echoes the traditional inquiry of humanists, and scholars have only recently begun to realize how much the fifteenth-century humanists who followed in the footsteps of Dante and Petrarch had discussed and written on the best kind of state, and the nature of the true commonweal.[42]

Having stood against all comers in book 1—but without vanquishing them as in a scholastic disputation, rather by having with them worked to the strength of his position—Hythloday has the field to himself in book 2: he has earned the right to describe Utopia as fully as possible. Indeed, he was asked to do so at the end of book 1. Throughout book 2 he shows his awareness of his listeners, for again and again, as Surtz has noted (xviii), the description of Utopia "contains answers and arguments against the implied queries or objections of his auditors." Above all, Hythloday colors the second book by what he is and by what he believes. "The courtiers, councilors, and kings with whom he would have to associate [were he to enter royal service] are enemies to what he holds dearest: reason and truth, freedom and open-mindedness, justice and peace. All his sympathies are therefore with the poor, the oppressed, the workers, the propertyless. Because of his philosophic principles as well as his experiences in Utopia and elsewhere, he indignantly rejects the course of accommodation proposed by More, impatiently refutes halfway measures, and takes an uncompromising stand for the elimination of money and property." Thus Surtz, writing eloquently on Hythloday (xx); and, may we add, in an age fascinated by rhetoric and conceiving of eloquence at its best as the final virtue of the educated man, sixteenth-century humanists would surely have admired Hythloday for his right kind and use of eloquence. The necessity for Hythloday's stand is reasonably put, but he goes further to argue from the authority of what he has seen work in Utopia. Surtz then continues: "He announces and testifies to what he has heard, what he has seen with his own eyes, what he has looked upon and his hands have handled: 'you should have been with me in Utopia and personally seen their manners and customs as I did.' After his detailed description, he rises to the stature of a prophet, who thunders against injustice and greed and pride and who climaxes his harangue with a joyful apocalyptic vision of holy Utopia. Almost as if blinded and weakened by the revelation, he is meekly taken by the hand and led indoors by More at the close of the work" (xxi).

Numbers of More's contemporaries—Erasmus in 1511, Richard Pace in 1517, Beatus Rhenanus in 1518—stressed More's love of jesting, and there are numerous examples of it in the later lives of More by William Roper and Nicholas Harpsfield. More carried his jesting to the scaffold, as is well known. It is impossible to exhaust the verbal play in the names and their relationships in *Utopia,* or the larger ironies that work from such smaller details as an intended discrepancy between the marginal gloss and the main text, up to fuller reaches of dramatic irony. In More's *Utopia* as in Erasmus's *Praise of Folly* there is ample grounding for J. A. F. Thomson's assertion that More and Erasmus restored the full play and reach of irony to western letters (though that statement requires some qualification, as already suggested). There is therefore a further aspect of *Utopia* that is of prime importance both to English literature and to European humanism: in so many ways, *Utopia* stands at the full flood of More's long and deep relationship with Erasmus. Their friendship may well have continued for some years beyond 1516, but the fruitful period of collaboration appears to have been over by the year 1520.[43] For now it must be observed that a great deal of the Tudor literature, both in English and in Latin, imaginative literature as well as polemic, that followed More's *Utopia* was indebted to the concept of dialogue as a genre and inspired by its spirit.[44]

More's *Utopia,* then, is a deeply humanistic work, and as its author himself best exemplified the humanistic tradition in early Tudor England, so the work itself is the masterpiece of that tradition, subsuming all elements of that complex tradition and, like a Calder mobile or a Buckminster Fuller building, putting all these elements into play with one another. The total structure is much more than a mere addition of its parts, and the vision is greater still.[45] There is so much of More and of his *Utopia* that I have not touched upon—the symbolism of sheep, gallows, dining, and all, and the richness of metaphors, for example—but I have attempted to develop a view of the *Utopia* as a humanistic whole. As with More himself, the marvel is in the completeness of the work, in the many-sidedness that does not break down into unrelated parts.

His influence was humanistic as well as religious. More enjoyed both on the Continent and in England a reputation as one of the foremost Latinists of the century: for epigrams, translations of Lucian, and epistles. Later controversialists looked back on More's writings as models; Sidney obviously reflected on the meaning of *Utopia*, and Shakespeare mirrored his thought in the May Day speech in *The Book of Sir Thomas More*; and Jean Bodin, in order to reject it, took seriously More's *Utopia* in his own work on historical method, the *Methodus* of 1566. Perhaps most of all, if least tangible, More's contribution to the dialogue form was inestimable.

*   *   *

The question of patronage, as McConica remarks in his pioneering volume *English Humanists and Reformation Politics*, which has provided illumination and guidelines for future studies, "itself requires further exploration." While the More circle was of course of central importance in the Henrician period,[46] there were others as well: the royal courts, the circles of Henry VIII's queens, of Lady Margaret Beaufort, of some prelates, and some others. In all of them there was a common Erasmian element, as James McConica summarizes:

> So the Erasmian gospel, undogmatic yet definite and discoverable, provides the continuous thread, turned and twisted in the course of controversy, yet always retaining its essential identity as the link between the "fellow-work" of the Oxford Reformers and the peculiar climate of the Elizabethan settlement.[47]

Patronage was a major force in the growth and redirection of humanism in Tudor England, and there was a pronounced shift from the patronage of the late medieval church—manifested through the Lancastrian and early Tudor bishops, who were primarily interested in supporting the education or work of future theologians, canonists, administrators, and parish priests—to that of a small number of individual Tudor prelates who more strongly and directly supported humanism, such as Bishops Richard Fox and John Fisher, or clergy such as John Colet, and then still later in the Tudor period influential laity.

St. John's College, Cambridge, demands attention, for it was created by John Fisher and Lady Margaret Beaufort and was the academic home of Sir John Cheke, Roger Ascham, Sir Anthony Cooke, Sir William Cecil, and Thomas Smith—all notable humanists or patrons of humanism, all (as McConica has observed) "contemporaries at St. John's, and all were to influence the world of Elizabethan England."[48] Outstanding as a humanistically oriented college, it was not unique, and one could add Richard Fox's Corpus Christi College, Oxford, as an example of such a college at the other university.[49] I have already mentioned Colet's St. Paul's School as an example of the institution of humanistic programs in whole or in part in the schools; and this school produced scholars like Thomas Lupset, Sir Anthony Denny (a future privy councillor and patron of humanism), the antiquarian scholar John Leland, and (later in the Elizabethan period) the schoolmaster and humanist William Camden.[50]

There are a number of women significant in the story of humanism in Tudor England, not only as active scholars themselves (as Retha M. Warnicke details in the essay following this one), but also as patrons. Lady Margaret Beaufort, dowager countess of Richmond, was (in the summary statement of McConica) "the principal bridge between the humanism of the Yorkist court and that of the new age."[51] Not only was she vitally important for her endowments at Cambridge, where she worked with and through Fisher, she was also the patroness of William Caxton and of certain religious houses connected with humanistic circles: the Carthusian house of Shene, the Brigittine house of Syon, and the Observant Franciscan convent at Greenwich.[52] Among the scholars of humanistic orientation who were connected with these three houses so strongly supported by Lady Margaret was the productive Richard Whitford.[53]

While the full story of humanism in Renaissance England cannot be identified with patterns of patronage, nonetheless even the work of Erasmus required the continuing assistance of patrons, and the need for patrons became if anything even stronger in the seventeenth century, as the careers of John Donne and Ben Jonson confirm. There are other aspects that call attention to the complexity of learning and letters in the Renaissance. One of them is that the patronage of the writing and illumination of manuscripts continued for some time—well more than a century—after the introduction of printing into Britain. Certainly the introduction of printing had a great impact on the study of humanism and the production of texts: English scholars were far more dependent on European presses for the printing of classical scholarship than was the case in other kinds of literature; but that field of inquiry has been relatively little studied. The significance of the countless dedications that paid homage to the individuals and institutions that "made this work possible" has of course begun with the labors of Franklin B. Williams and others; but further studies will help to clarify the trends and patterns of patronage of Tudor humanism.

*   *   *

In England the 1530s were turbulent years, and the 1540s still troubled ones. There was—in the terms Douglas Bush used to challenge R. W. Chambers's thesis of the arrest of humanism under Henry VIII[54]—a continuity of humanism in the years after More's execution in 1535 and through to the end of Henry's reign. During these years Cheke was teaching Greek at Cambridge, and Ascham rejoiced at that golden age (as he looked backward from later years[55]), as did Walter Haddon and, later, John Lyly in comparing Oxford to Athens. Further, there were numerous new foundations of grammar schools and colleges during the entire reign of Henry, and toward the end of his reign there was the provision for regius chairs in Greek and Hebrew. At best, in the wise words of Bush,

> the purpose of Tudor humanism was education. The broad aim was training in virtue and good letters, the special aim was preparing young men for public life. It was these Tudor humanists who established what was to remain the ruling motive of English classical study down to the days of the "Jowett mind."[56]

But there were differences, however much there was continuity. One must recognize the impact of the Reformation and Counter-Reformation on humanists and the nature of their studies; and there must be an account of the politicizing of humanism by Cromwell, if not by Henry himself.

Cromwellian recruiting reached even into the humanistic school-household of Reginald Pole in Padua. For Pole maintained a large household and a humanist school of studies there; his own studies in England and in Padua had in large part been subsidized from 1521 to 1536 by Henry VIII, his royal cousin. Among Pole's household were such humanists as Richard Morison, Thomas Starkey, and Thomas Lupset. These three, along with Sir Thomas Elyot, will serve to represent the various directions of humanism, and two of them have direct links with Thomas More.

Sir Thomas Elyot (ca. 1490–1546) was something of a friend of More—though in a well-known letter to Cromwell he denied too much closeness after More's refusal to take the Oath and his imprisonment[57]— and his wife was associated with More's school. Like More he was trained as a lawyer, though his training was both in the common law (at the Middle Temple) and in the civil law; and he was even more a popularizer of humanism than More. His works include a series of some eleven translations or adaptations written under the influence of Erasmus: *The Doctrine of Princes . . . translated out of Greke into Englishe* [from Isocrates] (1534), a Latin–English dictionary (1538) that was widely used, *The Image of Government* (another translation from the Greek), and several Platonic dialogues. But he is primarily celebrated for his *Boke Called the Governour* (published 1531), which drew in part from Baldassare Castiglione's *Book of the Courtier* and in part from Erasmus's *Institutio principis christiani*, as well as from Plato, Cicero, and other humanistic sources.[58] It is, in simplest terms, a humanist's guide to those who have been or are hoping to be appointed by the king to some responsible office as "governours of a publike weale." However much the *Governour* draws from noble works in the tradition of humanism, it is essentially utilitarian in its aim. And although it accepts the status quo and defends Tudor society and its ruling class, as Caspari observes, "he makes very high demands of that class."[59] One must recognize the depth of Elyot's conviction that true justice had to lie at the heart of that system and had to be the good that governors would know through humanistic studies and administer through the wisdom gained from those studies.

Less known than Elyot but an even more remarkable figure in embracing so much of the development of Tudor humanism, through its several phases from the end of the fifteenth century through the first third of the sixteenth century, was the much-admired Thomas Lupset. Lupset (ca. 1495–1530) was one of the first to study under Lily at St. Paul's, where he resided with Dean Colet; at Cambridge he aided Erasmus in work on the New Testament, and in Paris he helped in the publication of Linacre's Latin translation of Galen and in the preparation of the second edition of More's *Utopia*. He was thus a significant bridge between the generation of the Oxford Reformers and some of the younger humanists. One of the first professors of the humanities at Oxford, he lived for a while with Pole in Padua. His influence reaches into the humanism of the Elizabethan period, for among his students was Nicholas Udall, the scholarly playwright and schoolteacher, as well as Edmund Withypoll, later friend of Gabriel Harvey. In addition to More and Erasmus, Lupset was the friend of Budé, Nicolas Bérauld, and Germain de Brie (Brixius) in France, of Johann Botzheim in Switzerland, of Juan Luis Vives in Spain and the Low Countries, and of Janus Lascaris, originally from Greece. As J. A. Gee remarks: "Intimate with the small group of English humanists, he was also intimate with many of the greatest scholars of the continent."[60] The friendship with Budé is especially significant as one of the prime avenues for the influence of French humanistic scholarship to come to England.

It remains to comment briefly on Richard Morison, Thomas Starkey, and the two Heywood brothers. Richard Morison (ca. 1510–1553), the author of two tracts against the Pilgrimage of Grace, was born about 1510 and studied in the new humanistic foundation established by and named after Cardinal Wolsey, soon transformed into Christ Church.[61] A member of Thomas Winter's household in Paris, where apparently he had leisure to study, he was connected with Pole's group in Padua until 1536; he returned to England to join Cromwell's staff and immediately set about writing for the royal propaganda campaign; and in the words of his most recent editor, "the young humanist who, poverty-stricken, had left Italy at the end of May for exciting prospects in England close to the center of power, was by the end of October on the way to realizing the rewards for talent in the service of the state."[62] He was amply rewarded by Henry and by Edward, and he died in 1556, leaving a family and a large fortune. Thomas Starkey (1495/1499–1538) studied Greek at Oxford, where he took the B.A. in 1516 and the M.A. in 1520; he too was with Pole in Padua, and in 1534 he became chaplain to the countess of Salisbury, Pole's mother, and early in 1535 the king's chaplain. Starkey's *Dialogue Between Reginald Pole and Thomas Lupset* (begun 1533, finished 1535, but not published until 1871) is a remarkable dialogue in the English tradition of humanistic dialogues, and it is centrally concerned with the adoption of Roman law in Britain,[63] marking the common concern of Elyot and others with law and education.[64] The Heywoods—Ellis (ca. 1530–1578) and Jasper (1534–1598)—were sons of John Heywood, poet and playwright, who married a niece of Thomas More, and one of whose daughters was the mother of John Donne.[65] They mark yet another hinge, for both were educated at Oxford, where Ellis studied Roman law; both entered the Society of Jesus and ended their lives in exile on the Continent, with Ellis especially contributing to the educational work of the Jesuits at Louvain, Cologne, and Munich. Ellis served for some time as secretary to Pole, to whom he dedicated his dialogue on More, *Il Moro*, in 1556. Morison and Starkey thus exemplify one group of Tudor humanists who entered the royal service; a generation younger, Ellis and Jasper Heywood are examples of Tudor humanists who remained Roman Catholic and contributed to the recusant traditions of learning.

✻   ✻   ✻

Several characteristics of humanism in England before about 1550 must be mentioned. There was a gradual shift from clerical to lay humanism, through there is no point at which a dividing line can be sharply drawn, and the continuing status of clerical humanists carries into the seventeenth century. There was continuity, but with the needs of Cromwell and Henry VIII—largely over the divorce question and the break with Rome—humanists were drawn into the administrative web in a new way; and the demands of the Reformation and Counter-Reformation inevitably drew away energies that might have gone more directly into humanistic scholarship.

The main lines of Bush's thesis that the purpose of Tudor humanism was education, and the broad aim training for a virtuous life, do not appear to have been challenged. Public life was very much an end in view for many of the young humanists to whom attention has been called—from Elyot to Morison and Starkey.

The question of how international Tudor humanism was has not been fully examined as yet. It is clear that the generation of the Oxford Reformers depended on their firsthand contact with Italian humanists and that Italian humanism was for several decades thereafter the model and source for much humanistic study; Thomas More was unusual, if not unique, in this respect among his generation of English humanists. The Paduan household of Pole signals the expectation of the middle generation of English humanists that an extended period of study abroad was necessary in the fields of law—the break with Rome produced profound effects for the study of canon law, and consequently of civil law[66]—as well as in the core concerns of humanism. It would seem to have been largely the political and religious effects of the break with Rome that generated in Ascham his profound distrust of things Italian and his deeply felt remark that "Inglese italianato è un diavolo incarnato."[67] Anti-Italian prejudice was to remain with Englishmen for a long time, though neither Sidney nor Milton felt his education complete without a visit to Italy. Connections of Tudor humanists with other countries remain to be studied more carefully: Lupset is perhaps remarkable for the extent of his friendship with European scholars, but others like Richard Croke and Leonard Coxe not only traveled among German universities but taught there as well.

One may remark that preparation for public life as the ruling motive of English classical study was good for the commonwealth, and so it has been for England down through the centuries from Cheke, Smith, Milton, and others down to those fine examples offered by Bush: Gilbert Murray, Sir Alfred Zimmern, and Sir Ronald Storrs. But there has been a price, which is that Ascham, for one, like so many of his humanistic colleagues, did not contribute scholarly editions of the classics in anything like the measure that Elie Vinet and J. J. Scaliger did on the Continent; nor did Ascham's generation leave the rich heritage of Latin commentaries on classical authors that their contemporaries did. This omission mattered for the history of classical scholarship, and I think it also contributed to a growing isolationism in English scholarship.

Yet the heritage of early Tudor humanism remains, and we are its beneficiaries not only through the original works, both in Latin and in

English, of the Mores, Elyots, and Aschams, but also through their products as teachers: the Spensers, Sidneys, and Shakespeares, who were schooled in the humanistically oriented curricula of the Shrewsbury and Merchant Taylors' Schools as well as in the grammar schools of England, like that in Stratford. Looking forward to the work of Jonson and Rubens in the seventeenth century, one may conclude with the now-classic formulation of D. J. Gordon:

> Both artists had learned the great lesson of Renaissance humanist scholarship: that the ancient world existed as an entity, a separate, distanced, autonomous cultural domain—not merely a compendium from which fragments could be taken over and transmogrified, with no sense of context, of historical and cultural distance. This attitude toward the past was, in the period, relatively new. . . . The classical world, that most prized of ancient cultures, had to be got right because it was real and recoverable.[68]

NOTES

1. On Anglo-Latin writers generally, see M. L. W. Laistner, *Thought and Letters in Western Europe, A.D. 500–900* (Ithaca, NY, 2d ed., 1957); J. D. A. Ogilvy, *Books Known to Anglo-Latin Writers from Aldhelm to Alcuin* (Cambridge, MA, 1936). For a broad survey, see R. R. Bolgar, *The Classical Heritage and Its Beneficiaries* (Cambridge, 1954), and *Classical Influences on European Culture, A.D. 500–1500*, ed. R. R. Bolgar (Cambridge, 1971). In addition to the older work of J. E. Sandys, *A History of Classical Scholarship*, 3 vols. (Cambridge, 3d ed., 1921), see also R. Pfeiffer, *History of Classical Scholarship from 1300 to 1850* (Oxford, 1976). The standard work for early humanism in England is that of R. Weiss, *Humanism in England During the Fifteenth Century* (Oxford, 2d ed., 1957). The splendid work of the Warburg Institute (London) in exploring and assaying the survival of the classical tradition continues under the present director, J. B. Trapp. For a recent approach to these vital questions of the heritage of Renaissance humanism, see W. Ullman, *Medieval Foundations of Renaissance Humanism* (Ithaca, NY, 1977); but I have expressed my reservations about the book and its methodology in a review in *Classical Journal* (1979). On the thorny question of defining Renaissance humanism, see below, note 3. The recent bibliography by C. Kallendorf has many lacunas but is still useful: *Latin Influences on English Literature from the Middle Ages to the Eighteenth Century: An Annotated Bibliography of Scholarship, 1949–1979* (New York, 1982).

2. See especially Laistner, *Thought and Letters*, and Bolgar, *Classical Heritage*. From a European and modern perspective the tribute of Wilamowitz-Moellendorff is eloquent: "What was incomparably more important was that Irishmen and Anglo-Saxons brought their learning and their books

over with them and founded new monasteries, some on territory which they had first to win for Christianity themselves, such as Luxueil in the Vosges, Bobbio on the Trebbia, St. Gallen, Reichenau and Fulda" (*History of Classical Scholarship*, ed. H. Lloyd-Jones [London, 1982], 16). It must not be forgotten that the monasteries founded in Britain also continued the transmission of the classical heritage up to the Reformation. Thomas More, for one, studied in a Carthusian monastery, as did other humanists in other monasteries; and the role of the monastic orders in the history of humanism has yet to be studied fully. I have discussed the concept of *translatio studii* from Paris to England in an essay to appear in the Erasmus number of *Classical and Modern Literature* (1987).

3. "Tudor humanism" would artificially limit consideration to the period from 1485 to 1603; "Renaissance England" is a somewhat looser, more flexible, and (as I take it) chronologically broader concept, used here to cover from about 1450 to about 1650—but the scope of this essay is only the humanism in England in the first of these centuries. The concept of humanism here employed follows in general that of P. O. Kristeller: "Thus Renaissance humanism was not as such a philosophical tendency or system, but rather a cultural and educational program which emphasized and developed an important but limited area of studies" (*Renaissance Thought: The Classic, Scholastic, and Humanist Strains* [New York, 1961], 10). This area of studies stressed grammar, rhetoric, history, poetry, and moral philosophy. Some modifications have been made in later essays by Kristeller; but this definition provides a clear-cut, core signification that seems to have great validity for Florentine humanism especially, and I prefer it to the looser definition of Joachimsen as "an intellectual movement, primarily literary and philological, which was rooted in the love and desire for the rebirth of classical antiquity" (on which see Chapter 21, "Humanism in Germany," in this volume). Joachimsen, it seems to me, is both too general and also in his stress on "rebirth" susceptible to misreading, especially for humanism in England.

4. Especially valuable for his probing of this conflict is E. H. Harbison, *The Christian Scholar in the Age of the Reformation* (New York, 1956), with its studies of Erasmus, Luther, Calvin, Pico, and Colet.

5. For a splendid overview of the Petrarchan tradition in European poetry, see L. Forster, *The Icy Fire: Five Studies in European Petrarchism* (Cambridge, 1969). The intertextualities of Petrarchism are considered in the same author's *Dichten in fremden Sprachen* (Munich, 1974); and on intertextuality, see R. J. Schoeck, *Intertextuality and Renaissance Texts* (Bamberg, 1984).

6. Roger Ascham's love of Cicero in *The Scholemaster* marks the high tide of Ciceronianism as both a sense of style and a force in the teaching of the humanities. See T. Zielinski, *Cicero im Wandel der Jahrhunderte* (Leipzig, 3d ed., 1912); and A. C. Clark, "Ciceronianism," in *English Literature and the Classics* (Oxford, 1912).

7. See Weiss, *Humanism in England*, Kristeller, *Renaissance Thought: The Classic, Scholastic, and Humanist Strains*, and idem, "The European Dif-

fusion of Italian Humanism," in *Renaissance Thought II: Papers on Humanism and the Arts* (New York, 1965), as well as R. Weiss, *The Spread of Italian Humanism* (London, 1964).

8. See W. Nelson, "The Scholars of Henry VII," in *John Skelton* (New York, 1939), 4–39.

9. For a general picture, see Weiss, *Humanism in England*, amplified and, in a few instances, corrected by more recent studies. A general view of the importance of law is provided in R. J. Schoeck, "Canon Law in England on the Eve of the Reformation," *Medieval Studies* 25 (1963): 125–47.

10. Harbison, *Christian Scholar*, 64. But the old charge that John Colet "wrote no works" has been disproved by J. B. Trapp, who has demonstrated that "Colet seems to have had a rich man's preference for manuscripts over printed books, joined with a reluctance to publish," though he did commission a "sort of uniform, authorized edition [of his writings] in a single copy." See "John Colet: His Manuscripts, and the Pseudo-Dionysius," in *Classical Influences on European Culture, A.D. 1500–1700,* ed. R. R. Bolgar (Cambridge, 1976), 216.

11. See Weiss, *Humanism in England;* and Nelson, "Scholars of Henry VII."

12. It seems that the phrase "the Oxford Reformers" was coined by F. Seebohm in his classic volume entitled *The Oxford Reformers of 1498* (London, 1867), where it was focused on this small group at a limited period of history; later, however, the full title was generally shortened to *The Oxford Reformers* (as in the Everyman edition, which also reduced Seebohm's often qualifying or expanding footnotes). As a term applied to that small group of Grocyn, Linacre, Colet, and More, the descriptive term has merit, provided that we do not limit all humanistic activity in England at the end of the fifteenth century to that group, or indeed to Oxford, or extend that group beyond Seebohm's limits. It is now too late to protest the term "New Learning" as well, for it has been given currency by Elliott-Binns, T. Brooke, and others. Yet it should be noted that A. C. Chester has written in protest, pointing out that in the sixteenth century all of the early usages referred not to humanism but to the currents of theological thought coming from Germany—i.e., Lutheranism. See "The New Learning: A Semantic Note," *Studies in the Renaissance* 2 (1955): 139–47. On Linacre, see now *Essays on the Life and Work of Thomas Linacre, c. 1460–1524,* ed. F. Maddison, M. Pelling, and C. Webster (Oxford, 1977), which illuminate so many aspects of Linacre's life, his Latin grammars, his connections with Italy, and his role in founding the College of Physicians.

13. Trapp, "John Colet: His Manuscripts," 221. On Colet, see E. F. Rice, Jr., "John Colet and the Annihilation of the Natural," *Harvard Theological Review* 45 (1952): 141–63; and P. A. Duhamel, "The Oxford Lectures of John Colet: An Essay in Defining the English Renaissance," *Journal of the History of Ideas* 14 (1953): 493–510. I have not yet seen the edition of Colet's lectures edited by B. O'Kelly.

14. S. Jayne, *John Colet and Marsilio Ficino* (Oxford, 1963), 77–78.

15. *Ibid.,* 78. For an introduction to the study of such questions in Tudor

England, see F. Caspari, *Humanism and the Social Order in Tudor England* (Chicago, 1954); see also the review by R. J. Schoeck in *Catholic Historical Review* 41 (1955): 206–7.

16. For a brief but excellent introduction to Valla's thought and achievement, see P. O. Kristeller, *Eight Philosophers of the Italian Renaissance* (Stanford, 1964), chap. 2; see also Chapter 13, "Lorenzo Valla," in the first of these volumes, and sources cited there.

17. The best introduction to the field of medieval Bible study is that of B. Smalley, *The Study of the Bible in the Middle Ages* (Oxford, 2d ed., 1952); but see also *The Cambridge History of the Bible*, especially its chapter on Erasmus in relation to the medieval biblical tradition by L. Bouyer (ed. G. W. H. Lampe [Cambridge, 1969], 2:492 ff.); and the valuable volume on *Erasmus' Paraphrases of Romans and Galatians*, ed. R. D. Sider, vol. 42 of *Collected Works of Erasmus* (Toronto, 1984).

18. Harbison, *Christian Scholar*, 59–60.

19. This paragraph treats summarily what I have discussed more fully elsewhere. On the concept of the *respublica litterarum*, see my introduction to the special number on Sir Thomas Browne, *English Language Notes* 19.4 (1982), 199–213. On the importance of the epistle, see idem, *The Achievement of Thomas More* (Victoria, BC, 1976), 25–38; and, much more fully, in *Der Brief im Zeitalter der Renaissance*, ed. F. J. Worstbrock (Weinheim, 1983). On the humanist concepts of the text, see R. J. Schoeck, "The Humanistic Concept of the Text: Text, Context and Tradition," *Proceedings of the Patristic, Medieval, and Renaissance Conference 1982* (Villanova, PA, 1985), 13–31.

20. See especially Trapp, "John Colet: His Manuscripts."

21. Thus T. Brooke, *A Literary History of England*, ed. A. C. Baugh (New York, 1948), 328. Brooke notes that the editions of the Lily Grammar "make up nearly 140 entries in the Short-Title Catalogue." See further, V. J. Flynn, "The Grammatical Writings of William Lily," *Papers of the Bibliographical Society of America* 37 (1943): 85–113; his edition of *A Shorte Introduction of Grammar by William Lily* (London, 1945); and C. G. Allen, "The Sources of Lily's Latin Grammar," *Library* 5th ser. 9 (1954): 85–100.

22. The preceding paragraph has drawn largely from H. C. Porter's introduction to *Erasmus and Cambridge*, ed. H. C. Porter, trans. D. F. S. Thomson (Toronto, 1963).

23. Letter to Robert Fisher (from London, 5 December 1499), trans. by R. A. B. Mynors in *Correspondence of Erasmus* (Toronto, 1974), 1:235–36.

24. E. J. Devereux, *Renaissance English Translations of Erasmus: A Bibliography to 1700* (Toronto, 1983), 6, 18. See further J. K. McConica, *English Humanists and Reformation Politics Under Henry VIII and Edward VI* (Oxford, 1965); and C. R. Thompson, "Erasmus and Tudor England," in *Actes du congrès Erasme* (Amsterdam and London, 1971), 29–68.

25. Thus Hugh Latimer in sermons before Edward VI was almost certainly alluding to or recalling proverbs in the *Adagia*, but he did not mention Eras-

mus by name (see *Selected Sermons of Hugh Latimer*, ed. A. G. Chester [Charlottesville, VA, 1968], 72, 76). In *The Tudor Books of Private Devotion* (Madison, WI, 1951), H. C. White makes a strong case for the unacknowledged but extensive and continuing use of Erasmus in much of this important literature of private prayer.

26. Devereux, *Renaissance English Translations*, 18.

27. See H. C. Porter's introduction to *Erasmus and Cambridge*, 3ff.; and McConica, *English Humanists and Reformation Politics*. Thompson provides an excellent survey of Erasmian influence in "Erasmus and Tudor England."

28. The lectures on Augustine and the legal readings are two concerns among More's lost writings; his humanistic writings—possible marginalia on humanist texts, notes, letters, and the like—are another.

29. See Schoeck, *Achievement of Thomas More*, especially chap. 6; and brief reflections in idem, "On the Spiritual Life of St. Thomas More," *Thought* 52 (1977): 324–27, which provides a brief bibliography.

30. See Schoeck, *Achievement of Thomas More*, chap. 3.

31. Implicit in my comments is the view that More worked out his own fusion or conflation of several modes that, except for the example of Pico, had generally been perceived as distinct and mutually exclusive.

32. M. P. Gilmore, "More's Translation of Gianfranceso Pico's Biography," in *L'Opere e il Pensiero di Giovanni Pico della Mirandola nella Storia dell-'Umanesimo* (Florence, 1965), 1:301–4; and R. J. Schoeck, "Thomas More and the Italian Heritage of Early Tudor Humanism," in *Arts libéraux et philosophie au Moyen Âge* (Montreal and Paris, 1969), 1191–97. More's translation was probably dedicated to a nun, which doubtless explains some of his revisions. But there still remains his selection of that biography for translation and his act of modifying his original, as well as his act of dedication. In a searching review of the study by E. F. Rice, Jr., *The Renaissance Idea of Wisdom* (Cambridge, MA, 1958), H. Baron has discussed the controversy over the *vita contemplativa* and the *vita activa* in terms that throw much light on More's eventual decision: see "Secularization of Wisdom and Political Humanism in the Renaissance," *Journal of the History of Ideas* 21 (1960):131–50.

33. R. Marius has recently questioned the depth and durability of the More–Erasmus friendship in his biography *Thomas More* (New York, 1984). I do not accept his interpretation and have offered my reasons in a paper delivered at the Thomas More Conference, Columbia University, November 1985 and published in *Moreana* (1987).

34. I have quoted from the edition of *Utopia* by E. Surtz, S.J. (New Haven, 1964), 3. Further quotations from *Utopia* and from Surtz's introduction will be indicated by page references in the text.

35. See my discussion of More and the epistle in *Achievement of Thomas More*, chap. 2. The five parts are *salutatio*, *captatio*, *narratio*, *petitio*, and *conclusio*. For the text of the letter, I follow *St. Thomas More: Selected Letters*, ed. E. F. Rogers (New Haven, 2d ed. 1967), 94–103.

36. On the continuity of the scholastic curriculum in England, see W. T.

Costello, *The Scholastic Curriculum in Early Seventeenth-Century Cambridge* (Cambridge, MA, 1958). One should note that in another "defense of humanism" letter, More's "Letter to a Monk," the principles of textual criticism are carefully set forth, together with the humanistic concept of how to read a book. The second section of the letter is printed in *Selected Letters*, 114–44 and the complete text in *The Correspondence of Sir Thomas More*, ed. E. F. Rogers (Princeton, 1947), 165–206.

37. See the chapter on *Utopia* in Schoeck, *Achievement of Thomas More*, for further documentation and selective bibliography.

38. See E. Surtz, S.J., *The Praise of Pleasure: Philosophy, Education, and Communism in More's Utopia* (Cambridge, MA, 1957), chap. 2. In the introduction to the paperback edition of *Utopia* (1964), Surtz aptly observes that "humanists would also have appreciated the Latin style of *Utopia*. More is far from being a narrow Ciceronian; instead, he shows the flexibility and breadth demonstrated by Erasmus in *De duplici copia verborum ac rerum* (1512). In fact, just as More was composing the *Utopia*, Erasmus praised the improvement in style of his Latin letters" (xxiii).

39. See M. A. Screech, *Ecstasy and the Praise of Folly* (London, 1980).

40. On intertextuality, see Schoeck, *Intertextuality and Renaissance Texts*.

41. For further discussion of work and text, see *Intertextuality*, chap. 2.

42. In addition to the survey of medieval models in L. K. Born's introduction to his translation of Erasmus, *The Education of a Christian Prince* (New York, 1936), E. Surtz has surveyed sources, parallels, and influences upon More in part 2 of his introduction to *Utopia*, where the reader will find discussion of writers like Filippo Beroaldo (1453–1505), whose *De optimo statu* was widely current. This field has been explored thoroughly by H. Baron in *Humanistic and Political Literature in Florence and Venice at the Beginning of the Quattrocento* (Cambridge, MA, 1955) and *The Crisis of the Early Italian Renaissance*, 2 vols. in 1 (Princeton, rev. ed. 1966), though his general theory of civic humanism has not gone unchallenged. See, for example, Chapter 7 in these volumes, "The Significance of 'Civic Humanism' in the Interpretation of the Italian Renaissance." See also L. C. Warren, *Humanistic Doctrines of the Prince from Petrarch to Sir Thomas Elyot: A Study of the Principal Analogues and Sources of "The Boke Named the Governour"* (Chicago, 1939).

43. On this point, see note 33, above.

44. I would go further than R. L. Deakins's recent study, *The Tudor Dialogue* (Cambridge, MA, 1980), which is based on the later (1561) *De dialogo* of Carlo Sigonio.

45. Cf. Surtz's perceptive statement: "Above all, *Utopia* contains hardly a detail for which the scholar cannot find a source or an analogue in classical, patristic, medieval, or humanistic works. Some of the pleasure to be experienced in reading *Utopia* arises precisely from the recognition of familiar and common features. Yet the novelty of More's masterpiece is universally acknowledged. The small fragments of colored stone and glass are placed together to form a picture of incomparable design. In a word, the originality

of the *Utopia* lies less in the details than in the ensemble or the whole" (xiii).

46. See R. J. Schoeck, "The School of More," in *New Catholic Encyclopedia,* 17 vols. (Washington, D.C., 1967) 9:1142.

47. McConica, *English Humanists and Reformation Politics,* 208.

48. Ibid.

49. Richard Fox (or Foxe, ca. 1448–1528) had been chancellor of Cambridge University in 1500 and master of Pembroke College, Cambridge, from 1507 to 1519, and he not only founded Corpus Christi College, Oxford, in 1515 for the education of secular clergy, but also built and endowed schools at Taunton and Grantham and was benefactor of Magdalen College, Oxford, and Pembroke College, Cambridge, as well as other foundations. See the preface and biographical essay in *Letters of Richard Fox, 1486–1527,* ed. P. S. Allen and H. M. Allen (Oxford, 1929). The purpose of Fox's college at Oxford—with which the names of John Clement, Thomas Lupset, Gentian Hervet, Nicholas Kratzer, and Juan Luis Vives are associated, though they were never fellows—was humanistic, and "how readily he had adopted the new ideas may be seen by comparing the medieval books at Auckland with those of the classical revival which he gathered for Corpus" (ibid., xiv). For the Elizabethan period there is the survey of M. Curtis, *Oxford and Cambridge in Transition, 1558–1642* (Oxford, 1959); and in the first volume of *The University in Society,* ed. L. Stone (Princeton, 1975), there are two relevant essays: G. F. Lytle, Jr., "Patronage Patterns and Oxford Colleges, c. 1300–1530," 111–49; and J. K. McConica, "Scholars and Commoners in Renaissance Oxford," 151–81.

50. On John Leland, see T. S. Dorsch, "Two English Antiquaries: John Leland and John Stow," *Essays and Studies* n.s. 12 (1959): 18–35; and J. Hutton, "John Leland's *Laudatio pacis,*" *Studies in Philology* 58 (1961): 616–26. On William Camden, see M. Powicke, "William Camden," *Essays and Studies* n.s. 1 (1948): 67–84. On Camden's *Britannia,* S. Piggott, "William Camden and the *Britannia,*" *Proceedings of the British Academy* 37 (1951): 199–217; and F. J. Levy, "The Making of Camden's *Britannia,*" *Bibliothèque d'humanisme et Renaissance* 26 (1964): 70–97. On Lupset, see J. A. Gee, *The Life and Works of Thomas Lupset* (New Haven, 1928).

51. McConica, *English Humanists and Reformation Politics,* 55.

52. Ibid., 56.

53. Ibid.

54. D. Bush, *The Renaissance and English Humanism* (Toronto, 1939).

55. See Roger Ascham, preface to *The Scholemaster,* ed. R. J. Schoeck (Toronto, 1966).

56. Bush, *Renaissance and English Humanism,* 78.

57. On Elyot, see S. E. Lehmberg, *Sir Thomas Elyot: Tudor Humanist* (Austin, TX, 1960); and J. M. Major, *Sir Thomas Elyot and Renaissance Humanism* (Lincoln, NE, 1964). In his famous letter to Cromwell (ca. 1537), Elyot described his relation to More as "but *usque ad aras* . . . consydering that I was never so moche addict unto him as I was unto truthe and fidelity

towards my soveraigne lord." R. S. Sylvester, in availing himself of the 1552 *Dictionary,* has clearly shown that Elyot, in doing "all the pleasure that a man can for his frend, sauing his conscience," was "simply informing Cromwell that he had indeed been friends with More, but that their intimacy had ceased when the latter refused to swear the Oath to the Supremacy." R. S. Sylvester, "Revision of S. E. Lehmberg, *Sir Thomas Elyot, Tudor Humanist* (Austin, 1960)," *Renaissance News* 14 (1961): 178–81, at 180. On the important question of the sources for Elyot's *Boke Named the Governour,* see Warren, *Humanistic Doctrines of the Prince.*

58. See Caspari, *Humanism and the Social Order,* 84 ff.

59. Ibid., 102.

60. Gee, *Life and Works of Thomas Lupset,* xii.

61. D. S. Berkowitz, *Humanist Scholarship and Public Order* (Washington, DC, 1984), 19.

62. Ibid., 32.

63. See *A Dialogue Between Reginald Pole and Thomas Lupset by Thomas Starkey,* ed. K. M. Burton (London, 1948).

64. See Caspari, *Humanism and the Social Order,* for a full discussion of the social themes of the Tudor humanists, as well as A. B. Ferguson, *Clio Unbound* (Durham, NC, 1979), esp. chaps. 8–9.

65. See R. J. Schoeck on the Heywood family in *New Catholic Encyclopedia,* 17 vols. (1967), 6:1094–95.

66. The larger question of law and humanism is dealt with in Chapter 34, "Humanism and Jurisprudence," in these volumes. But for England, see Schoeck, "Canon Law in England."

67. *The Scholemaster,* ed. L. V. Ryan (Ithaca, NY, 1967), 66, and in the edition by Schoeck, 65. On Ascham's continental travels and connections, see Ryan, *Roger Ascham* (Stanford, 1963), especially on his intellectual association with Johannes Sturm. The Italian phrase in the text means: "An Englishman who has been italianated is like the devil incarnate."

68. D. J. Gordon, *The Renaissance Imagination,* ed. S. Orgel (Berkeley, 1975), 23. I have enlarged upon this perception in "'Lighting a Candle to the Place': On the Dimensions and Implications of *Imitatio* in the Renaissance," *Italian Culture* 4 (1985): 123–43, and in lectures on European humanism from Dante to T. S. Eliot delivered at the University of Dallas, October–November 1985, to be published in another form.

18 &~WOMEN AND HUMANISM IN ENGLAND
Retha M. Warnicke

C HRISTIAN HUMANISM GREATLY INFLUENCED THE EDUCATION OF
the Tudor aristocracy. Its apostles in England, John Colet, Thomas
Linacre, Thomas More, and others, including their visiting Dutch
friend Erasmus, promoted the study of classical languages and literature
in the belief that the ancient Greeks and Romans had developed an ethical
system that was compatible with Christian ideals. Calling for young men
to be trained as governors of society rather than as clerks, the humanists
anticipated that their students would be able to use their knowledge of
the classics to cure diverse social ills, ranging from political corruption
to religious superstition. This utilitarian education, which emphasized
rhetoric rather than the logic of medieval scholarship, was to begin in the
nursery where children were to be taught a few Latin words. For more
advanced training, some humanists, including Colet who endowed St.
Paul's as a prototype, advocated sending young men to schools. Subsequently grammar schools, following his guidelines, were founded, and
by the end of the century, many of the male aristocracy, and even some
members of other classes, were attending them.[1]

While increasing numbers of young men entered these institutions,
their female counterparts continued to acquire an essentially vernacular
education in the home. Ineligible for secondary education at grammar
schools, only a few women, indeed in the entire century only about sixty
of them, are known to have received humanist training, a number that
can be put into perspective by comparing it to the 153 boys admitted to
St. Paul's in its opening year early in the reign of Henry VIII. Though
relatively few in number, because of their social prominence these educated women have captured the imagination of scholars. The extant, albeit meager, evidence of their accomplishments lies at the heart of the
modern assumption that virtually all aristocratic women in Tudor England had access to classical learning and that, in fact, it was a golden age
for women. The numbers obviously do not support this assertion.

Despite their belief that women were less capable intellectually than
men, some Christian humanists, especially Thomas More, did advocate
that they be trained in classical languages and literature. To understand
More's educational program and the reasons it failed to gain support in
England, his household school must be studied and its influence on

decisions about women's education must be analyzed. The impact of his ideas will be traced through four generations of women humanists: the pre-Reformation, the Reformation, the mid-Elizabethan, and the Jacobean. Special attention will be given to the influence of the Reformation and the Counter-Reformation on his educational ideals.

References to these women as humanists may seem extraordinary since they rarely wrote original treatises or functioned as public leaders. In fact, because they sought to perform the special role that male humanists deemed proper for women with their education, the word "humanist" defines them more correctly than any other term. They were indisputably instructed by standards and for purposes different from those of their female contemporaries. The language training of women was and traditionally had been limited to learning to read English, although a few wealthy and noble women had also learned to write English and to speak a little French. Unlike the humanists, these women had not been expected to supervise the advanced education of their children or to share in intellectual conversations with their husbands. Their primary responsibilities, which continued to fall upon the more learned women, were the significant ones of feeding, clothing, and caring for the well-being of the members of their household. The contention of this essay is that for humanism, as for many other historical phenomena, definitions must be extended or enlarged in order to encompass women participants.

*   *   *

The first generation of women humanists was composed mainly of the students of More's household school. In it he had his three daughters, one son, and at least one other youth taught Latin, Greek, rhetoric, philosophy, theology, logic, mathematics, and astronomy.[2] Because he used double translations, a method that involved translating a work into English and then retranslating it into its original tongue, English composition played a central role in the curriculum. Although his students may also have studied French, a popular language at court, no evidence of that training has survived. In a 1518 letter to William Gonell, a tutor of his children, and in other writings, More explained why he offered this instruction to women. He believed, he said, that a woman should be well educated in order to be a guide in her children's education and an erudite conversationalist for her husband, who would gladly desert male companionship for her company. One of More's goals was to change family relationships. He and other humanists hoped to use their educational system to create closer spiritual and intellectual ties between husband and wife and between parents and children. As part of this program, they encouraged the family to oversee religious functions, such as family prayers, and challenged priestly influence over wives in the private confessional.

Two of the women in his household demonstrated great ability as classical scholars. His eldest daughter Margaret, the wife of William Roper, translated from Latin into English a work of Erasmus, which was printed under the title of *A Devout Treatise upon the Pater Noster,* despite her father's written assertion that her scholarship needed no other readership than the members of her own immediate family. In its introduction, the editor, Richard Hyrde, noted that her felicitous marriage was without equal because she and her husband delighted in each other's learning.

The daughter of Margaret Roper's nurse, who was also named Margaret, demonstrated similar academic excellence. Especially fluent in Greek, she became known for her aptitude in mathematics and medicine, interests that she later shared with her husband, John Clement, a court physician.

Outside More's household, the only other woman humanist of this generation was a member of the royal family. Margaret Roper and her sisters had already begun their study of Greek and Latin when Mary, the daughter of Henry VIII and his first wife, Catherine of Aragon, was born. This queen and Katherine Parr, Henry's sixth wife, have traditionally been credited with providing the advanced education of Mary and his other offspring. Although they did promote classical study, the influence of Henry's wives was not the determining factor in his support for the academic ideals of Christian humanism. Along with his brother Arthur, a former pupil of Thomas Linacre, Henry himself had been given a rigorous education at a time when the European royalty was moving generally toward providing classical scholarship to their offspring. The king possessed a copy of Erasmus's *Institutio principis Christiani,* a handbook for the education of royalty that was first published in 1516, the year of Mary's birth, whose title, princess of Wales, proclaimed her premier position in the succession. Henry appointed Linacre as her tutor and also encouraged Juan Luis Vives to assist her studies. Moreover, the king personally consulted with More and others about the advanced education of his illegitimate child, Henry, Duke of Richmond, and provided a splendid education for his daughter Elizabeth during the years in which she lacked a stepmother concerned about her welfare.

Henry's consort, Catherine of Aragon, had a similar interest in their daughter Mary's education. A Latin scholar, the queen personally corrected some of her Latin letters. She also joined the king in attempting to persuade Vives, who had written *De ratione studii puerilis,* a special study plan for the princess, to become the child's tutor.

Vives is best known as the author of *De institutione foeminae Christianae,* a publication in 1523 that was dedicated to the queen and that was later printed (probably in 1529) in an English version by Richard Hyrde. Although in this work, which became the leading theoretical manual on women's education in sixteenth-century Europe, Vives promoted classical instruction for women, his program of study for them was not as rigorous as More's. Missing from his curriculum were many of the difficult subjects, such as astronomy and mathematics, that were offered to Margaret Roper and Margaret Gigs.

Partly because Mary confined her literary interests almost exclusively to works of piety and to the Scriptures, her intellectual and cultural interests have been treated perfunctorily. That her sister, Elizabeth, loved music, for instance, is well known, but that Mary was similarly accomplished in music has seldom been mentioned. Although she did not view her linguistic abilities as a topic for boasting, as did Elizabeth, who prided herself on her mastery of languages, Mary may well have surpassed her half-sister as a Latin scholar. She read More's *Utopia* and the works of Erasmus in their original tongue and translated a prayer of St. Thomas Aquinas that was printed in the primer of 1545. Her stepmother, Katherine Parr, also asked her to translate one of Erasmus's paraphrases of the New Testament as part of a project for making them available in English.

Mary knew French, had some knowlege of Greek, and could understand Castilian and Italian. While she was probably not fluent in Greek because of its difficulty, she may have lacked motivation to excel in Italian. Sir Thomas Wyatt, who introduced Petrarch's love sonnets to England, along with other court humanists who were experimenting with Italian literary forms, was associated with Anne Boleyn and her Howard relatives. Irrevocably alienated from that circle and its celebration of the chivalric tradition, Mary, an apostle of Christian humanism, viewed classical languages as the ones most capable of serious literary expression and looked to education as a means by which family members could be drawn closer together spiritually.

*   *   *

In the next generation, which has been greatly celebrated in historical writings, at least three forces besides Christian humanism influenced decisions about education. First, there was the poetry of the court humanists, like Wyatt, the interpreter of the Petrarchan convention in English. Along with others, such as Henry Howard, earl of Surrey, Wyatt emphasized vernacular expression, thereby helping to make Italian fashionable. While these courtiers have not usually been associated with any new trend in education, at least one—Surrey, whose daughters qualify here as humanists—supported advanced language training for women.

Along with Christian and court humanism, two other movements, Erasmianism and Protestanism, were influential in this generation. Although Erasmus had fostered a study of ancient literature, he had also encouraged a more pietistic, spiritual experience than that of the contemporary Roman church. Some of his followers, especially Katherine Parr, differed with him about the value of reading a wide variety of profane authors. These Erasmians, as they have been identified by James McConica, promoted the study of early Christian or biblical writers, doubting the need for reading the pagans. The work of Erasmus that they most admired was his New Testament paraphrases.[3]

Denying that individuals could be transformed into moral creatures, some of the Protestants, patronized by Edward VI's uncle and aunt the duke and duchess of Somerset, believed that the chief purpose of education was to aid in the understanding of divine ordinances. Since the aim of their instruction was to foster the obedience, the honor, and the glorification of God, church reform assumed more importance than any other social problem. Adopting the theories of Christian humanism on family relations, these Protestants emphasized the need for reading the Bible and early Christian works. Primarily because English versions of these volumes were not always readily available, the reformers sometimes permitted women to study classical languages. These women were expected to function as deputies to their husbands, who, like domestic bishops, were to head "spiritualized" households, wielding religious authority over their families.[4]

Since all of these forces cannot be fully treated in an essay of this size and scope, the reason for including a few statements here is to present background material that will provide a perspective for the available information about female scholarship in this period. In fact, all of these forces had an impact, in varying degrees, on the education of Henry's younger daughter, the most celebrated of the learned women of the second generation.

Because Elizabeth's childhood is usually associated with Katherine Parr, an inquiry must be made into her stepmother's role at court. Although biographers have claimed that when she became queen consort, Katherine was already both a classicist and a Protestant, the evidence suggests otherwise. As C. Fenno Hoffman has pointed out, because most of her handwriting and all of her printed works are in English, she probably did not receive classical training as a child. A study of the books she wrote has also led James McConica to identify her as an Erasmian.[5]

She almost certainly did not exercise great control over the selection of her stepchildren's classical instructors, as has often been claimed. The eminent scholar Sir John Cheke, who became the prince's Greek tutor, had long enjoyed the king's patronage, and Anthony Cooke, a Protestant, did not join Edward's household until after his succession as king. Furthermore, far from choosing Elizabeth's instructors, Katherine acquiesced in the appointment of Roger Ascham in 1548 only after her stepdaughter had persistently requested him as her schoolmaster.[6]

Despite her objection to Ascham, Katherine did have a positive influence on Elizabeth's instruction. In 1544 the princess rendered into English a French treatise by Margaret of Navarre, which was then in Katherine's possession. Elizabeth's translation, along with her rendition of the fourteenth Psalm, was later published by John Bale under the title of *A Godly Medytacyon of the Christen Sowle*. In 1545 she rendered into Latin, French, and Italian the queen's English prayers, which had been printed under the title of *The Prayers Styring the Mynd unto Heavenlye Medytacions*.

Even while Katherine was emphasizing the religious education of her stepchildren, they continued to read profane literature. Although Elizabeth, for example, had commenced her studies after More's execution, she was still trained according to some of his ideals because she studied with Ascham, among others, who claimed More as his intellectual antecedent. As Ascham was both her instructor and the author of *The Scholemaster*, published posthumously in 1570, his work has rightly been recognized as an excellent representation of humanism. Because he valued profane works, however, his curriculum differed from that of many reformers.

While Elizabeth was learning to appreciate classical wisdom, she was also developing an enthusiasm for the ideals of the vernacular literature that circulated at her father's court. In their celebration of an unobtainable love, Wyatt, Surrey, and other poets had helped to popularize the Italian culture by blending the chivalrous tradition with the Petrarchan love sonnet. Doubtless the foreign vernacular that Elizabeth most esteemed was Italian, a language in which she was instructed as a child and in which her earliest extant letter, dated 1544, was written. Her continuing efforts in that language as well as in French were so successful that by 1550 when she was seventeen she could speak both of them fluently.

This generation has been celebrated not only because Elizabeth was a member but also because the daughters of four politically ambitious noble families, the dukes of Somerset and Suffolk and the earls of Surrey and Arundel, were too. Remarkably, the daughter of each of these families with the greatest contemporary reputation for her classical abilities was named Jane. The four girls were all the namesakes of Jane Seymour, Henry VIII's third consort and the mother of his only legitimate son, Edward. Undoubtedly, these noble families offered humanist education to their daughters in the hope of preparing them for marriage to the young prince.

Jane Grey, the best known of the four Janes, was born to Frances Brandon, a niece of Henry VIII, and her husband, Henry Grey, earl of Dorset, later the duke of Suffolk. Jane studied Latin, Greek, Hebrew, Italian, and French and corresponded in Latin with Heinrich Bullinger, Martin Bucer, and other Protestant divines. Her devotion to Protestantism and her family's alliance with the reformers are reflected in the decision to have her learn Hebrew, a language rarely studied by the women of this generation. Surely, the interest that these divines had in Jane's education arose because of her position in the English succession.

The Grey family also hoped she would marry Edward, who was born the same year as she. With the intention of furthering this royal alliance, her parents placed her in the custody of Thomas, Lord Seymour, Edward's younger maternal uncle. This and other conspiracies touching the throne led to the execution of Seymour in 1549 and to that of Jane and her father in 1554. All that survives of her erudition are her letters and prayers, some of which were published by John Foxe in 1563.[7]

Edward's lord protector was Somerset, who chose to provide classical instruction for three of his daughters. Claiming that he used his position at court to pursue important marriage alliances, his political enemies later charged that not only had he hoped to wed his well-educated child Jane to the young king, but that he had also planned to wed Jane Grey, the royal claimant, to his heir, the earl of Hertford. Except that the Seymour girls had a superb command of Latin and also studied Greek and French, little information has survived about their education. Since the Protestant Thomas Becon, who dedicated *The Governance of Virtue* to Jane Seymour, approved of their instruction, they may have read only Christian works. When in 1550 the hundred Latin distichs they had written to commemorate the death of Margaret of Navarre were published, they became the first Tudor women to have an original Latin work printed in their lifetime.

Besides Somerset and Suffolk, two other noblemen, Surrey (the heir of the third duke of Norfolk) and Arundel, were the fathers of learned daughters. Although some members of these families later became Catholic recusants, their primary goal in early Tudor England was the survival and social enhancement of their lineage through intermarriage with the royal family. Surrey's three girls and two boys by his wife Frances de Vere, daughter of the fifteenth earl of Oxford, were given Greek, Latin,

French, and Italian instruction. In 1544 Surrey's father appointed Hadrianus Junius, a Dutch scholar, as their tutor. Apparently Jane, who was born the same year as Prince Edward, benefited most from Junius's instruction, as the next oldest child, Thomas, the future fourth duke, remained an indifferent scholar. After their father's execution for treason in 1547, their aunt the dowager duchess of Richmond, who gained custody of them, appointed John Foxe as their tutor. Foxe was so impressed by Jane's skill that he compared her scholarship favorably to that of the learned men of her day.[8]

The fourth duke of Norfolk, Jane Howard's elder brother, married Mary Fitzalan, the younger daughter of the earl of Arundel, who had provided his children with a humanist education. Although four manuscripts by Mary with Greek and Latin pieces are still extant, her elder sister Jane, the wife of John, sixth Lord Lumley, has generally been recognized as the more brilliant of the two women. Jane, the first person known to have rendered into English a work by a Greek dramatist, Euripides's *Iphigenia at Aulis,* deserves credit for a pioneering effort that one modern scholar has suggested was "extraordinary and rare for one of her years and period."[9] As all of her extant manuscripts, like those of her sister, are translations of ancient works, her father, who acquired books for his library only in his native English and in classical languages, apparently chose not to have his two daughters tutored in French or Italian.

Outside the nobility and the continuing tradition in the More circle, only two other households, both Protestant and associated with the Edwardian government, are known to have offered humanist training to their daughters. One was that of John Hooper, bishop of Gloucester, who had a daughter named Rachel about whom almost nothing is known except that she did learn Latin. The other was that of Anthony Cooke, one of King Edward's tutors.

Cooke chose to have his five daughters instructed in Greek, Latin, and Hebrew, as well as in Italian and French. Although the eldest, Mildred, did not have any of her manuscripts published, her contemporaries were well aware of her expertise in Greek. In 1545 when she wed William Cecil, later Lord Burghley, she entered into a marriage that approached the ideal predicted by the Christian humanists. She read ancient authors with her husband and educated at least her elder daughter as a classicist.

The most published author of the family was Anne Cooke, the wife of Nicholas Bacon. Anne's translation of the Italian sermons of Bernardino Ochino and her version of *Apologia pro Ecclesiae Anglicanae,* a Latin work by John Jewel, bishop of Salisbury, were both printed. C. S.

Lewis has remarked about the Latin work: "If quality without bulk were enough Lady Bacon might be put forward as the best of all sixteenth-century translators."[10] This is extraordinary praise for a woman living in a century replete with famous scholars.

Of the three remaining Cooke sisters, only one other, Lady Elizabeth Russell, had a work published in her lifetime. In 1605, when she was well over seventy, her translation of a Latin book by John Poynet was printed under the title, *A Way of Reconciliation of a Good and Learned Man.*

Finally, in this generation can be found descendants of More's students. His daughter Margaret had offered a humanist education to her three daughters, one of whom, Mary, taught by John Morwen, became a celebrated scholar. During her marriages, first to Stephen Clarke and then to James Basset, she continued to study the classics as her grandfather had advocated. Before Mary's succession as queen, Lady Basset had bound together in a volume for the princess her translations from Greek into Latin of the first book and into English of the first five books of Eusebius's *Ecclesiastical History.* After Mary's succession, when William Rastell felt free to print the *English Works* of More, he included Lady Basset's version of the second part of her grandfather's treatise, *History of the Passion.* Rastell noted that the excellence of her translation led many to protest that it had deserved separate publication. She was the only woman whose work appeared in print during Mary's reign.[11]

The other outstanding member of More's circle had been Margaret Clement, who tutored her five daughters in Latin and Greek. While three of them, including the one named Helen, did marry, two decided to join convents on the Continent. Some interesting information has survived about the eldest daughter Margaret, her mother's namesake. In 1569, despite her English ancestry, she was elected prioress of St. Ursula's, a Flemish Augustinian convent at Louvain. When, after several decades of successful leadership, she was forced to resign because of blindness, Mother Clement decided to join six of her compatriots at Louvain in establishing St. Monica's, the second convent founded for Englishwomen in exile after the Reformation.[12]

In this generation, with some differences in emphasis, the few parents who offered their daughters instruction in ancient literature did so for the reasons advocated by the Christian humanists: to train them as suitable companions for their husbands and as godly mothers for their children. Among the Catholics, of course, a few daughters still had the option to join convents. The four noble families surely offered their girls classical training because this education was fashionable at court and because it might make their daughters attractive as potential consorts to Edward, the heir to the throne. It is interesting to note that it was largely the male relatives of these learned women who appointed their instructors and who made the major decisions affecting their advanced academic training. Although both Margaret Roper and Margaret Clement fulfilled More's educational goals by directing their daughters' classical instruction, there is no reason to believe that any of the other mothers performed those supervisory roles. The duchess of Richmond was the sole woman outside the More circle with an unquestionably positive role in offering this education to her female relatives.

*   *   *

In the third generation, classical instruction for women became less fashionable. An important reason for this change was that this kind of education was not encouraged at Elizabeth's court. Unmarried and childless, she did not establish a royal nursery with an educational standard to which aristocratic families could aspire. Her lack of children also meant that the English nobility could not generally hope to wed their offspring to royalty.

Probably no woman classicist among the Protestants of this generation had exceptional ability. Arbella Stuart, because she was a cousin to the king of Scotland and had, therefore, a claim to the English throne, received Latin instruction. Reputed to be a scholar, she did not reach the academic heights of Margaret Roper, of the Cooke sisters, or even of the queen. The only other identifiable Protestant classicist of this generation was Anne, Lady Oxford, but this young woman, whose education was probably directed by her mother, Mildred Cooke Cecil, Lady Burghley, was not a great scholar either.

That only two reformed female classicists can definitely be counted in this generation may have been a result of the Protestant emphasis on the reading of religious material in the vernacular. In Elizabeth's reign most of the Christian works, including the Bible, were made available in English. Furthermore, a person knowledgeable in Latin was sometimes suspected of being a papist or a witch. As a consequence, family instruction in Latin greatly diminished with most boys waiting until they reached grammar school for classical education. The household, where young women were instructed, turned almost exclusively to vernacular training.

Among Catholics there were no great scholars in this generation either. The descendants of More's circle through the female line were represented only by Margaret Clement's granddaughter, Magdalen Pridieux, who was taught Greek and Latin by her mother, Helen Clement.

There were only two other Catholic households with women classicists. The author Elizabeth Grymeston left some Latin and Greek translations in her work, *Miscelanea, Meditations, Memoratives,* published posthumously in 1604. And Mary Wiseman, the first prioress of St. Monica's, translated several works from Latin to English for the sisters to read. In all, Catholic and Protestant, there may have been only five or six English households with classically trained daughters.

This dearth may seem surprising because of the praise Elizabeth's court has won for its many accomplished linguists. In *The Description of England,* published in 1577 and greatly enlarged in 1587, William Harrison helped to create this myth by boasting that the men and women at court had a "sound knowledge" of Greek and Latin and were no less skilled in Spanish, Italian, and French. For reasons of his own he greatly overestimated the linguistic abilities of both sexes. Not only did most lack a "sound knowledge" of Greek, very few were fluent in Spanish or Italian. Furthermore, a closer look at Harrison's remark about the language abilities of women will be revealing. In his paragraph on courtly women, Harrison said:

> I could in like sort set down the ways . . . our antient ladies of the court do shun and avoid idleness . . . some in continual reading either of the Holy Scriptures or histories . . . and divers . . . in translating of other men's into our English and Latin tongue, whilst the youngest sort in the meantime apply their lutes, citerns, prick song and all kinds of music.[13]

Apparently, when contemporaries, such as Harrison, boasted about female classicists they were referring to the older women, the members of the second generation, Elizabeth and the Cooke sisters, for example, all of whom were well into their forties and fifties. One of the younger women at court was Mary, Countess of Pembroke, who because of her English "imitations" of the Psalms is usually reputed to be a classicist. Though well educated, Lady Pembroke almost certainly had only vernacular training, the Psalms having been taken from the French psalter of Theodore de Béze. When modern scholars have compared her versifications to similar efforts of her brother, Philip Sidney, hers have been judged of greater merit.[14] Harrison's *Description* is valuable because it highlights some of the differences between the generations of the queen and of Lady Pembroke and also because it indicates that classical studies remained a respected pastime at court, even if limited to the older generation.

* * *

This activity was ridiculed at the court of James I, whose style as monarch was different from that of his predecessors. His hostility to classical education for women became apparent to the English almost immediately after his succession in 1603, for he had his own daughter Elizabeth, the namesake of the last Tudor monarch, trained only in vernacular tongues. Indeed, the story was soon circulating that when he was introduced to a lady who could speak Greek and Latin, James retorted, "But can she spin?"

Consequently, the learned women of the Jacobean generation, with one exception, were not members of the fashionable set. Protestant hostility to women's classical instruction also did not weaken greatly during the Elizabethan period. Reformed scholars continued to fear that learned girls either would say magical incantations in Latin or would be tempted to read the tales of Vergil and Ovid. The concern was also expressed that they might become too proud to adopt a submissive demeanor toward their husbands.

Despite these reservations, at least seven reformed women of the fourth generation did receive advanced training, perhaps because the Protestant faith had become more secure in its struggle against Catholicism. Unfortunately, the evidence for the skills of reformed women depends primarily on contemporary references rather than on extant scholarship. Samuel Clarke, an aged Puritan minister, for example, gave information about two women classicists. In praising the ability of one, he boasted that the academic accomplishments in which she "so much exceeded her Sex" had not caused her to be "puffed up" with pride. He recalled that she had been an ideal wife: "she would always lower her Saile to him her Lord and Head" who remained a "perfect Stranger and wholly unacquainted with all of those inconveniences, which some have fancied to necessarily accompany a learned wife."[15]

One of the other learned women of this generation repeated his refrain. Elizabeth Jocelin, a bishop's granddaughter and trained in Latin, wrote a treatise, *The Mothers Legacie to Her Unborne Childe*, in which she discussed the education of her unborn child. If a boy, he should go to school, but if a girl, she should be taught housewifery, reading, writing, and good works at home. Denying that her daughter needed advanced academic training, Jocelin confessed that there were already too many women with more learning than wisdom. As though she had made this negative comment because it was expected of her, Jocelin then stated: "But where learning and wisdom meet in a vertuous disposed woman, she is the fittest closet for all goodness. Shee is like a well-ballanced ship that may beare all her saile." Deciding to leave the educational decisions to her husband, Jocelin then pleaded with him to take care that a female child learn humility, for pride, she admitted, was a particularly onerous vice in a female.

Even though Elizabeth, Lady Falkland—probably the only fashionable woman to learn Latin in this generation—converted to Catholicism, she is counted Protestant here simply because she acquired her education before the conversion, a spiritual move that caused her outraged husband to reject her as his wife. Although her family had offered her only vernacular instruction, she had chosen to teach herself an assortment of tongues, including Latin. Like other aspiring dramatists, she had realized the need to study Seneca and had understood the value of reading his works in their original versions. She is noteworthy as the author of *Marian,* the first original play to be published by a woman in English.

The ideas of the Counter-Reformation had an important influence on Catholic education in Elizabethan England. Because learning to pray in Latin was as important to members of this faith as praying in the vernacular was to members of the reformed religions, elementary Latin instruction began early in many Catholic households, often supervised by mothers who, in the absence of priests, assumed unprecedented control over their family's religious devotions. Even though a knowledge of this language facilitated their meditations, only a few Catholic families, perhaps only eight, had women with this training. Two of the most outstanding were Mary Ward and Elizabeth Jane Weston.

The impact, which was hardly felt in England, of Mary Ward's educational ideas cannot easily be assessed. In exile because of her faith, she founded the Institute of the Blessed Virgin Mary, an order that sponsored day schools for girls. Referring to them as Latin schools, Ward, in a letter of 1627, congratulated her Munich director on the quality of her students' Latin theses. She also commented: "All such as are capable invite them to it, no talent is to be so much regarded in them as the Latin tongue."[16]

Elizabeth Jane Weston was probably the most erudite of the classical scholars of this generation. A few years after her birth in London in 1582, her family fled to Bohemia, probably because of their strong commitment to Roman Catholicism. After her father's death, when she was in desperate financial straits, she dedicated some Latin poems to a number of Bohemian patrons. In 1602 some of them were published at Frankfurt under the title of *Poemata.* Four years later another volume, *Parthnicon,* was printed at Prague. She wrote with a careful meter and exceptional diction in the Ciceronian style, and her work has been compared favorably to that of Thomas More.[17] Besides Latin, English, and German, she also knew Greek, Italian, and Czech.

❖ ❖ ❖

Throughout this century the contributions of the More circle to women's education can be discerned. At least one of the female descendants of More's student Margaret Clement, through the female line, can be found in each of the succeeding three generations. Her great-grandchildren, Mary and Helen Copley, the only daughters of Magdalen Pridieux Copley, took their copy of Vergil with them when they left home to join St. Monica's.

While only a few Tudor women were classicists, at least for them the new developments had opened pathways to higher education. This fourth generation, ignored in modern works because its membership was not of the socially prominent circles, was perhaps the most brilliant of the four. Its women not only wrote original Latin pieces rather than translations but also founded secondary schools for girls on the Continent. A scrutiny of the education and personal characteristics of these women indicates the failure of the humanists to popularize their program of study for women. By the Jacobean period Protestants generally viewed classical education as an impediment to the husband's control of the "spiritualized" household. In contrast, many of the Catholic women who were also Latin scholars remained unmarried, unable to use their education to effect closer family relations, as the Christian humanists had hoped. And finally, even More's circle failed in this generation: the two daughters of Magdalen Pridieux Copley joined St. Monica's, thereby bringing to an end the More tradition of mother to daughter classical training.

NOTES

1. For more detailed discussion, see R. M. Warnicke, *Women of the English Renaissance and Reformation* (Westport, CT, 1983). The following list of works is far from complete but will be helpful to those who are interested in further reading. Some of the manuscripts of the learned women mentioned in this essay have been printed in two modern volumes: *The Female Spectator: English Women Writers Before 1800*, ed. M. Mahl and H. Koon (Bloomington, IN, 1977); and *The Paradise of Women: Writings by Englishwomen of the Renaissance*, ed. B. Travitsky (Westport, CT, 1981). For references to religion and the family, see R. H. Bainton, *Women of the Reformation in France and England* (Boston, 1975); J. K. Yost, "The Value of Married Life for the Social Order in the Early English Renaissance," *Societas* 6 (1976): 25–39; S. J. R. Hood, "The Impact of Protestanism on the Renaissance Ideal of Women in Tudor England" (Ph.D. diss., University of Nebraska, 1977); L. Fitz, "What Says the Married Woman? Marriage Theory and Feminism in the English Renaissance," *Mosaic* 13 (1980): 1–22; M. Cioni, "Women and Law in Elizabethan England with Particular Reference to the Court of Chancery," in *Tudor Rule and Revolution: Essays*

for G. R. Elton from His American Friends, ed. D. Guth and J. McKenna (New York, 1982); C. Levin, "Advice on Women's Behavior in Three Tudor Homilies," *International Journal of Women's Studies* 6 (1983): 176–85; and n. 4, below. For works on women and literature see K. Rogers, *The Troublesome Helpmate: A History of Misogyny in Literature* (Seattle, 1966); B. S. Travitsky, "The New Mother of the English Renaissance: Her Writings on Motherhood," in *The Lost Tradition: Mothers and Daughters in Literature*, ed. C. Davidson and E. M. Broner (New York, 1980), 33–43; L. Jardine, *Still Harping on Daughters: Women and Drama in the Age of Shakespeare* (Totowa, NJ, 1983); L. Woodbridge, *Women and the English Renaissance: Literature and the Nature of Womanhood, 1540–1620* (Urbana, IL, 1984); and M. Hannay, ed., *Silent but for the Word: Tudor Women as Patrons, Translators, and Writers of Religious Works* (Kent, OH, 1985). Only the most recent works on women's education are listed here: P. Hogrefe, *Tudor Women: Commoners and Queens* (Ames, IA, 1975); P. Stock, *Better than Rubies: A History of Women's Education* (New York, 1978); N. McMullen, "The Education of English Gentlewomen, 1540–1640," *History of Education* 6 (1977): 87–101; G. Kaufman, "Juan Luis Vives on the Education of Women," *Signs* 3.4 (1978), 891–96; L. Yates, "The Uses of Women to a Sixteenth Century Bestseller," *Historical Studies* 18 (1979): 422–34; J. K. Sowards, "Erasmus and the Education of Women," *Sixteenth Century Journal* 13 (1982): 77–90; C. Jordan, "Feminism and the Humanists: The Case of Sir Thomas Elyot's *Defence of Good Women*," *Renaissance Quarterly* 36 (1983): 181–201; M. Friedman, "The Influence of Humanism on the Education of Girls and Boys in Tudor England," *History of Education* 25 (1985): 57–70.

2. E. E. Reynolds, *Margaret Roper, Eldest Daughter of St. Thomas More* (London, 1960), 15–26.

3. J. K. McConica, *English Humanists and Reformation Politics Under Henry VIII and Edward VI* (Oxford, 1965), 208–81.

4. M. Todd, "Humanists, Puritans, and the Spiritualized Household," *Church History* 49 (1980): 18–34. For books on the family, see especially L. Stone, *The Family, Sex, and Marriage in England, 1500–1800* (New York, 1977); S. E. Ozment, *When Fathers Ruled: Family Life in Reformation Europe* (Cambridge, MA, 1983); and R. A. Houlbrooke, *The English Family, 1450–1700* (New York, 1984).

5. C. F. Hoffman, Jr., "Catherine Parr as a Woman of Letters," *Huntington Library Quarterly* 23 (1960): 349–67; McConica, *English Humanists and Reformation Politics*, 215–51.

6. L. V. Ryan, *Roger Ascham* (Stanford, 1963), 102–3.

7. John Foxe, *The Acts and Monuments of John Foxe*, ed. G. Townsend, 8 vols. (New York, repr., 1965), 6:384 and 415–25.

8. Ibid., 1:24

9. D. H. Greene, "Lady Lumley and Greek Tragedy," *Classical Journal* 36 (1941): 537–47.

10. C. S. Lewis, *English Literature in the Sixteenth Century, Excluding Drama*

(Oxford, 1954), 307; see also S. Harvey, "The Cooke Sisters: A Study of Tudor Gentlewomen" (Ph.D. diss., Indiana University, 1981).

11. Mary Basset, *St. Thomas More's History of the Passion*, ed. P. H. Hallett (London, 1944), introduction.

12. Dom A. Hamilton, *The Chronicle of the English Augustinian Canonesses Regular of the Lateran at St. Monica's in Louvain*, 2 vols. (London, 1904), vol. 1.

13. William Harrison, *The Description of England*, ed. G. Edelen (Ithaca, NY, 1968), 228–29.

14. G. F. Waller, "The Text and Manuscript Variants of the Countess of Pembroke's Psalms," *Review of English Studies* n.s. 26 (1975): 1–18.

15. Samuel Clarke, *The Lives of Sundry Eminent People in This Later Age*, 2 vols. (London, 1683), 1:197–202.

16. M. C. E. Chambers, *The Life of Mary Ward*, 2 vols. (London, 1882), 2: 237.

17. Thomas Fuller, *The History of the Worthies of England*, ed. P. A. Nuttall, 3 vols. (New York, repr. 1965), 3:217.

19 HUMANISM IN SPAIN
Ottavio Di Camillo

W HEN ONE EXAMINES RENAISSANCE HUMANISM IN SPAIN, ITAL-
ian humanism readily comes to mind because it has long been
recognized that this historical phenomenon originated in Italy
toward the middle of the fourteenth century and from there spread to the
rest of Europe within a period of a century and a half. Documentary
evidence from various sources confirms an early diffusion of this movement to Spain and reveals, at the same time, the existence of certain
favorable conditions that made the reception of Italian humanism possible and even necessary.

The acceptance of ideas and the emulation of intellectual trends
elaborated by Italian humanists in response to the growing demands of
their urban society indicates that there were in Spain, despite the vast
differences between the two cultural traditions, needs and interests of a
similar nature arising from the pressures of a changing society. This
search for solutions and new directions seems to have been well under
way by the second quarter of the fifteenth century. It was at this time that
the number of works by classical authors and Italian humanists reaching
various parts of the Iberian peninsula began to show a marked increase,
especially in Castile where such texts were avidly sought by a small group
of patrons and scholars.[1] With a deeper and broader understanding of
the ancient world and its literature, acquired chiefly through readings of
classical authors whose books were either bought or commissioned in
Italy, some Spanish men of letters became increasingly aware of the restoration of learning and ideas taking place in many Italian cities. Following the example of Italian humanists and learning from their advances in
the study of eloquence and of classical letters and thought, Spanish scholars in turn arrived at a historical consciousness of their own cultural
revival and at a conviction of living in a new era, totally different from
the past.

* * *

Unfortunately, historians and literary critics in general have not paid
much attention to this movement in Spain, helping to perpetuate thereby
an early Romantic notion that humanism was an imported movement,
alien to the spirit of the nation and thus of little or no consequence

to the development of Spanish culture.[2] Because of this prevailing attitude, the few studies on humanism that have appeared from time to time over the past hundred years have not had any impact, other than to attract the brief attention of a few specialists in the field.[3]

The reason humanism has been largely disregarded can ultimately be explained by the historiographical trends and methodological assumptions that have prevailed in Spanish studies since the early decades of this century. With Menéndez Pidal's emphasis on the Middle Ages and Dámaso Alonso's reappraisal of the Baroque period, all attention has shifted to centuries that fall outside the chronological limits of humanism. Two other dominant trends, one initiated by Marcel Bataillon's investigations into Erasmian spirituality, the other by Américo Castro's preoccupation with the problem of the *conversos,* have also overshadowed humanism and contributed to reducing it to a problem of minor importance.

The present view of Renaissance humanism in fifteenth- and sixteenth-century Spain is the outgrowth of ideas formulated by Menéndez Pelayo at the turn of the century. As a reaction to Protestant historians of northern Europe who identified the true Renaissance with the Reformation while rejecting the Italian Renaissance for its paganism, Menéndez Pelayo claimed that it was in sixteenth-century Spain that the real Renaissance took place. The explanation he gave and reiterated in many of his writings was that only Spanish humanists had been able to "christianize" the Italian revival of arts and letters, while northern humanists, in rejecting the achievements of Italian humanism, had only replaced it with heresy and thus with "barbarism." In denying the existence of a northern European Renaissance on the basis that Protestant thinkers, because of their race and cultural tradition, could not understand Italian humanism and the lessons it had to offer, Menéndez Pelayo was even critical of Erasmus. Despite his biased interpretation of Erasmus, we should credit Menéndez Pelayo with perceiving the development of spirituality as only one aspect of Spanish humanism, a distinction that has been blurred by recent critics and historians, who seem to confuse spirituality and humanism. As the concept of a Christian Renaissance, whether Catholic or Protestant, gained acceptance among European historians, Erasmus came to be seen as its most articulate representative. The new interest in this northern humanist prompted Bonilla y San Martín to undertake in 1907 a detailed history of Erasmus's influence in Spain.[4] In 1937, Marcel Bataillon published his monumental study *Erasme et l'Espagne* and showed how extensive Erasmian views and ideas had been in the Spanish Golden Age. Although his objective was to illustrate primarily the impact of Erasmus on the spiritual life of Spain, he also touched on other aspects of Spanish culture without which Erasmian influence could not be properly understood.

Bataillon's revision of the Catholic interpretation of the Spanish Renaissance has been carried even further by Américo Castro's investigation of the contributions made by *conversos* to the spiritual and intellectual life of the Spanish Renaissance. The present generation of scholars who take Bataillon and Castro as their point of departure have devoted themselves to searching for new facts and to adding new findings to those of their masters. By restricting their research to spiritual manifestations or to the peculiar modes of thinking of the *conversos* in literature, they have overlooked the significance of humanism and its effect on all branches of learning.

If sixteenth-century humanism has not been properly investigated, its early phase during the previous century has remained virtually unknown. The reason for this disregard may again be found in Menéndez Pelayo, who, in *Poetas de la corte de Don Juan II,*[5] described the fifteenth century as "el pórtico de nuestro Renacimiento." Basing his judgment on aesthetic grounds, he did not see in the literature of this period the purity of style that is to be found in the writings of sixteenth-century humanists. He did point out some Italian influences and classical strains in the literary compositions of this century, but they were not sufficiently polished or stylistically refined to be considered the product of humanism. His idea of the fifteenth century as a preparatory stage for the cultural explosion of the next century has been widely accepted and has gained added popularity through the influential study of Maria Rosa Lida de Malkiel, *Juan de Mena, poeta del prerrenacimiento español.*[6]

Only in very recent years has there been a noticeable interest in this area of study. And although of late some outmoded assumptions have been abandoned, we still find under a modified garb some of the old misconceptions and simplifications that have always surrounded the concept of Spanish humanism. At the root of these misunderstandings invariably lies a conception of Italian humanism as both uniform and unchanging, erroneously used as a criterion for defining Spanish humanism. What is not taken into account is a recognition that the movement in Italy manifested itself in a variety of ways, different features being emphasized in different places, and that the early Quattrocento humanism of Salutati and Bruni is not the same as that of Angelo Poliziano, Ermolao Barbaro the Younger, or Giovanni Pontano at the end of the century. Further adding to the confusion is a poor understanding of the reception of Italian humanism in Spain, due largely to the fact that only a fraction of the existing documentary material has thus far been studied. As a result, while some scholars have been inclined to find hasty similarities between the two humanisms or between the representative figures of both countries, others, few in number and of a more skeptical bent, have tended to exclude from the movement those Spanish authors who do not exhibit obvious affinities with Italian humanists.

Although at present it is impossible to give satisfactory answers to the many questions this complex movement raises, progress is being made in delineating some of its features. There still remains, however, a pressing need to explore further the unique characteristics of Spanish Renaissance humanism and to clarify its origins and early development. A growing interest in fifteenth-century Spanish history is providing useful information regarding economic changes, social relationships, political strife, religious thought, and other developments crucial to an understanding of humanism in its historical context. Even more important is the invaluable data that is coming to light from a number of recent studies dealing with little-known authors, their works, and where relevant, their contacts with Italian humanists.[7] Related to these inquiries is what seems to be a trend toward editing texts and documents that are not readily accessible. One of the surprising revelations of these endeavors is the massive number of works by Quattrocento Italian humanists that were acquired or specifically sponsored by Spaniards in Italy.[8] Most of these manuscripts now extant in Spanish libraries and in provincial and cathedral archives, some of them rare or unique, entered Spain in the fifteenth century. Although scholars have always been vaguely aware of their existence and some have been identified and described, the significance of such a wealth of Italian humanist literature in Spain has eluded all those who have dealt with this movement, with the exception of the indefatigable Paul Oskar Kristeller who, in an essay written in the early 1960s, urged a thorough exploration of these holdings, at the same time reminding investigators of Italian and Spanish humanism of their relevance to the history of European humanism.[9]

Another remarkable facet of fifteenth-century Spanish humanism that has not been clearly perceived in the past and which only now is coming into focus as a result of the reevaluation of old and new evidence, is the unusually large number of classical works that were translated into the vernacular at this time. This phenomenon seems to be peculiar to Spain; it is not found in any other European country, at least not to the same extent. What is most distinctive about these works is that they were translated into Spanish and, at times, even into Italian, at the request of Spanish patrons.[10] In addition to this body of vernacular renderings, including several Greek texts that had first been translated into Latin by Italian humanists, there are also some translations of contemporary Italian humanist writings. Most notable and most telling of the prestige they enjoyed is a translation and adaptation to a Spanish setting of Bartolomeo Facio's *De vitae felicitate,* which Juan de Lucena tried to pass off as his own work.[11] The need for translations must have been so keenly felt that even the Spanish humanists writing in Latin at the time translated some of their own works into the vernacular.[12]

This vernacular component, which remains a constant of Spanish humanism, cannot be explained away as a continuation of a medieval current or as a practice that is extraneous or even antithetical to the humanist movement. The truth is that this sudden surge of vernacular translations had no precedent in Spanish culture and was clearly motivated and inspired by humanism. Consequently, it would be unwise to disregard or underestimate such a widespread practice in the cultural life of fifteenth-century Spain. Without taking into account this intellectual activity, the people it involved and served, the function it played in society at large, and ultimately the force it exerted in shaping the movement and its evolution, it would be difficult indeed to arrive at a fair assessment of Spanish Renaissance humanism.

✳ ✳ ✳

Stirrings of humanism as an intellectual and literary movement are already discernible in the cultural life of Spain by the second decade of the fifteenth century. A cursory look at the writings of this period will reveal a new interest on the part of many authors in ancient literature and thought, usually expressed in a cumbersome latinized style and diction. The recurrent use of the classics by poets, historians, and moralists of this time denotes, in fact, a radical departure from traditional literature, in which ancient figures and authors were utilized sparingly and for entirely different purposes.

Examples of this new orientation in writing and thinking coincide with a significant rearrangement taking place in the curriculum of the schools, mainly in the trivium, a subdivision of the liberal arts, which comprised the three arts of verbal discourse: grammar, logic or dialectics, and rhetoric. The importance of logic, to which the scholastics had assigned and were still assigning a special role by placing it among the philosophical disciplines, was slowly being eroded by a renewed appreciation of rhetoric, the art that, together with grammar, the same scholastics had relegated to a subordinate role as a discipline of primary education.

Although there is hardly any information regarding the curriculum of schools in Christian Spain before the fifteenth century, it is safe to assume that education there was similar to the instruction generally given elsewhere in Europe. We know for a fact that at the University of

Salamanca, which was modeled after Bologna, the most prestigious discipline was jurisprudence. It occupied the most prominent place in the curriculum, followed by medicine. Theology, curiously enough, was not introduced at the university until the fifteenth century,[13] at the same time that humanism was encroaching on the trivium and modifying it. The absence of a faculty of theology meant that in Spain scholastic logic did not have the same preeminence it had in the universities of northern Europe, thus facilitating to some degree the ascent of rhetoric. It is, in fact, at Salamanca that the first change in the trivium is documented. The chair of rhetoric, which had been in the statutes of the school since its foundation in 1254, was first occupied in 1403 by an Italian, as his name, Bartolomeo Sancii de Firmo, would imply.[14] Since no further information is provided beyond the date of the appointment, we can only speculate on the text he may have used in his course. It is quite possible that he availed himself of some commentaries on Cicero's *De inventione* and the pseudo-Ciceronian *Rhetorica ad Herennium*, which were the texts customarily used at the University of Bologna from the beginning of the fourteenth century.[15]

For a new course to be given at Salamanca at this time, there must have been mounting pressure from law students who were most likely aware, through their compatriots returning from Bologna, that such a course was normally taught at that Italian university. The fact that before this time the chair of rhetoric had remained vacant suggests that some other subject had taken its place. This substitute was, in all likelihood, the *ars dictaminis*, an indispensable tool of lawyers, which supplied rules and models for the composition of letters, legal documents, and other records of everyday affairs. It is evident that by the beginning of the fifteenth century the medieval *dictamen* was being slowly abandoned as university students and graduates felt the need to enhance the efficacy of their written and oral communication. In their search for ways to improve the style of their writing and the delivery of their speeches, they found a satisfactory answer in the rhetorical texts of ancient Romans. With rhetoric restored to its original value, the trivium itself underwent a transformation and amplification. In the new scheme, dialectics was excluded while moral philosophy was added; poetry and history, which formerly were part of grammar, were isolated as independent pursuits. Fifteenth-century intellectual life in Spain reflects the gradual process by which the trivium evolved toward the *studia humanitatis*, which ultimately was to comprise grammar, rhetoric, history, poetry, and moral philosophy.[16]

This reorganization of the liberal arts, on which humanist education was based, did not appear all at once in Spain. It was, rather, a slow process by which each discipline gradually gained acceptance, beginning with rhetoric very early on, as we have seen, and ending with the reform of grammar during the last decades of the century. Subsequent to the renewed interest in rhetoric, there developed a new emphasis on moral philosophy. This attitude is clearly reflected in the reception of such Italian Trecento authors as Dante, Petrarch, and Boccaccio, who were equally esteemed by Spaniards as orators, philosophers (moralists), and poets. Somewhat later, with the revival of classical antiquity and the diffusion of early Italian humanist writings, the link between rhetoric and ethics was further strengthened as eloquence became a primary objective in the minds of many scholars. Following Cicero's precept of the ideal orator as the person who combines eloquence with wisdom, that is to say, rhetoric with moral philosophy, ethics became essential to the formation of the humanist.

The new perception of rhetoric and ethics soon extended to history, a discipline that made ample use of both ethical and rhetorical notions and shared with literature the narrative discourse. As the works of ancient historians came to be more closely studied, and most major humanists tried their hands at writing about contemporary events, the place of history, until then merged with grammar, also underwent a reappraisal, resulting in a fundamental change in its meaning, function, and manner of composition.[17] The creation of the posts of historian and secretary of Latin letters at the royal court by the middle of the fifteenth century illustrates the advances being made by humanist studies.[18]

The gradual acceptance of a more classical concept of rhetoric and eloquence did meet with some opposition. Of the lay and religious groups that felt a great deal of mistrust for the new learning, scholastic theologians exerted the greatest influence. Their rigorous adherence to more traditional doctrines and their reliance on logic and dialectics as the most suitable studies for verifying truths and for conveying ideas without appealing to passion checked the spread of humanism to some extent. Suspicious of literature in general, they viewed the revival of pagan authors as a threat to Christian beliefs and morality. Their fears had a considerable effect on the humanistic conception of poetry, to the point that the views on poetry expressed by Petrarch, Coluccio Salutati, and above all Boccaccio, remained unknown in fifteenth-century Spain. In fact, if we are to judge from the extant manuscripts, Boccaccio's polemical theories on poetry seem to have been intentionally left out of the various Spanish translations of *De genealogia deorum*, a work that had a relatively wide circulation. Every existing manuscript, in fact, omits the last two books, in which Boccaccio dealt with the nature and function of poetry.[19]

It is perhaps for this reason that only in the second half of the fifteenth century do we observe a gradual affirmation of poetry, which eventually was to be incorporated into the school curriculum. In 1465, almost sixty years after the chair of rhetoric was occupied for the first time, a chair of poetry was finally created at the University of Salamanca.[20] Shortly thereafter, grammar—the first discipline of the trivium and the only one that had remained unmodified—was made the primary target of reform by the new generation of humanists that had been formed in the second half of the century, of whom the best known is Antonio de Nebrija.

Some scholars have argued that Spanish humanism began in the 1480s, due exclusively to the efforts of Nebrija and to the intellectual climate being fostered by the Catholic kings.[21] This claim, however, is no longer tenable, though it is still very much cherished in manuals of literary history. It originated with Nebrija himself and was later popularized by Romantic historians, always prone to exalt the isolated genius who alone can change the cultural orientation of an entire society. A closer look at the intellectual activities of many Spaniards throughout the fifteenth century will cast serious doubts on Nebrija's role as the first Renaissance humanist. When seen more objectively and in the proper historical perspective, he appears to be rather the last representative, though without doubt the best, of fifteenth-century Castilian humanism.

*   *   *

With regard to the specific factors or to the historical conditions that favored the emergence of humanism in Spain, very little is known for, as I have already noted, it is an area of inquiry that has not attracted any critical attention. On the basis of the scanty evidence available, it is only possible to speculate about a combination of long-term changes in the economic, social, and political life of the country over the previous centuries that had gradually modified Spanish society to the extent that, by the beginning of the fifteenth century, support was to emerge for the earliest efforts at a revival of learning and ideas.

Agriculture, for example, chiefly based on cereal products, and which in the past had barely met the needs of the rural population, was producing by the fifteenth century new crops for luxury consumption and for export. The growth of commercial activities and the ensuing expansion of urban centers opened up Castile to international maritime trade with the Mediterranean world as well as with northern Europe through its Atlantic ports. There is no doubt that the development of the cities and of the commercial routes, the main channels of communication at the time, were essential to the development and the diffusion of Renaissance humanism not only in Spain but throughout Europe.

A more remote factor, but an equally decisive one, was the introduction of Roman law toward the end of the twelfth century, an event that eventually had far-reaching repercussions on the educational, social, and political institutions. Juridical studies in large measure did, in fact, contribute to a secularization of culture and to the increase, however modest, of literacy. It is no mere coincidence that the first known literary authors of Spain all seem to have had a juridical background. The preeminence of law graduates in the formation of Spanish culture is not altogether surprising. In the *Partidas* of Alfonso X the Wise, compiled in the second half of the thirteenth century, professors of law at the University of Salamanca enjoyed particular privileges that were not granted to teachers of other disciplines.[22] Because of their social distinction, members of the legal profession were the first to develop an awareness of belonging to an intellectual group, namely the *letrados*, with a special function in society.[23] Later, the title came to designate any university graduate with a specific preparation recognized by the society of the time as being suitable for political or administrative positions. In Spain, it was precisely the *letrados* who were the medieval precursors of fifteenth-century humanists.

As to the immediate historical circumstances surrounding the early manifestations of humanism, I should point out certain developments that, together with cultural changes that were occurring, prepared the ground for the movement to assume its unique characteristics. The most important series of events was Spain's participation in the councils to end the schisms. First at the Council of Constance (1414–17) and later at the Councils of Basel and Ferrara–Florence (1431–39), Castilian scholars, ambassadors, diplomats, and secretaries came in contact with the most distinguished European minds of the day. Journeys to the councils and travels for diplomatic missions were to affect their outlook and widen their understanding of other peoples and customs. Between debates and shifting alliances a great deal of cultural information was exchanged and, as can be seen by their correspondence, they developed lasting friendships.[24]

In the years preceding the councils, Spaniards had become increasingly familiar with the papal curia at Avignon and with the controversies regarding the end of the schism and the return of the popes to Rome. The turbulent pontificate of Benedict XIII (Pedro de Luna) first at Avignon and later in Spain, the country to which he transferred the papal library, was, at least for many of his compatriots, beneficial in a number of ways. The new pope bestowed favors and privileges on the universities of his nation, redressing the inequitable policy of his predecessors, who had generally favored French schools and universities.[25] In so doing, Benedict XIII was also establishing new bonds of mutual interests between himself and his policies and representatives of Spanish academic centers, who stood to gain by continuing to support his decision not to renounce the papacy. A fundamental change he helped to institute was to assign vacant bishoprics to a number of *letrados*. Whereas the higher ranks of ecclesiastical offices were usually reserved for candidates from the nobility, Benedict XIII began to recruit from among university graduates whose origins were not necessarily aristocratic. For example, the good fortune of the Santa Marías of Burgos, a Jewish family that converted to Christianity, is tied to this pope. Three members of this outstanding family, the father and two sons, were elected bishops.

Naturally bishops who themselves came from the universities would turn to the academic world when staffing their administrations, selecting the most promising and competent students. Moreover, in journeying to Rome to obtain new benefices and to expedite pending matters, these prelates would take along the most accomplished men of letters in their entourage. Often these subordinates were sent alone as agents and procurators to represent or to further the interests of their masters. Whatever the purpose of their missions, once in Rome these learned men eventually became acquainted, through their dealings, with the curia's functionaries, most of whom either had a humanist training or shared the ideas and aspirations of the humanists. Whether Spaniards spent only a few years or stayed behind, having obtained important posts in the curia, it is certain that their success provided an incentive to others who may have been hesitant to undertake such a costly and often dangerous journey to the papal city.[26]

It was in these early decades of the fifteenth century, with the return of the popes to Rome, that the number of Spaniards traveling to Italy increased considerably. Although the majority went to the papal curia to solicit favors and positions, there were others who went on diplomatic missions and for commercial reasons, visiting princely courts and cities of the Italian peninsula. Of particular relevance to this discussion is the growing number of students going to Italy. Until this time most university students who chose to complete their education abroad had gone to Paris for theological studies or to Toulouse or Montpellier for civil and canon law. The few who had opted for Italian schools attended mainly the University of Bologna. The presence of Spanish students and masters became conspicuous after Cardinal Gil de Albornoz founded the Spanish College (College of San Clemente) in 1367. The shift from French to Italian centers of learning began to be noticeable during the pontificate of Martin (1417–31) and continued under later popes.

Because most of these students belonged to the clergy or to religious orders and were usually pursuing juridical studies, they were not only attracted by the type and quality of education but were also drawn there because fewer regulations were imposed and fewer restrictions placed on degree candidates. According to Beltrán de Heredia, who has contributed more than any other scholar to our knowledge of Spanish universities, many students attended the Roman *studium* or the one in Siena because in these schools a clergyman could easily obtain a degree in law unhindered by the various rules of incompatibility.[27] But besides being able to circumvent theological studies, a requirement that the secular clergy had traditionally tried to evade, it is quite possible that there was also among Spanish students some degree of prestige attached to attending schools in a country that was becoming increasingly known for its intellectual activity.

If on the one hand these contacts led Spanish scholars and noblemen to venerate early Quattrocento Italian humanists for their works and for their translations of classical texts, on the other, it was precisely from these cultural interactions that Spanish thinkers became aware of the distinct characteristics of their own national culture. Because of their monarchic institution, for example, they felt more affinity with Italian humanists in the service of kings and princes than with those of republican Florence or even Venice. Instances of this process of selection and preference, dictated by the political, social, and intellectual conditions prevailing in Spain at this time, explain many of the traits that were to characterize the development of Spanish humanism.

A most distinctive feature, and one that was central to humanist thought, was the manner in which Spanish humanists interpreted the revival of antiquity. Whereas Italian humanists considered themselves the direct descendants of Roman civilization and felt an intellectual and emotional attachment to the world of classical Rome, Spanish humanists, though they acknowledged and respected Roman antiquity, tended to look to Spain's historical past, especially to classical authors and historical figures of Iberian origin.[28] Although they felt an intellectual admiration for Roman, Greek, and patristic writings, they still felt closer politically to the Visigothic period. The fascination for this period resided in the notion that the entire Iberian peninsula had been united under one monarch and one religion, an ideal of considerable significance in the drive for political centralization around which all of Castilian society, especially the humanists, rallied. It is surprising to note that

it was precisely when some Italian humanists were calling the Goths barbarians and blaming the destruction of Roman civilization on their in-
vasions, that Spanish thinkers were reviving the idea of the Visigothic
origin of Spain, to the point of trying to establish a direct line of descent
from the Gothic to the contemporary kings. Even though the myth of the
Visigothic origin of Spain was shaped by the political reality of the Re-
conquest (the long-drawn-out process of retaking Arab lands) and served
many propagandistic purposes, it did condition, nevertheless, the view of
Spanish humanists toward the preceding centuries. Unlike the Italian humanists who considered those centuries a period of darkness, the Spaniards found in them the origin of their state. In explaining the positive,
but detached, attitude of Spanish humanists toward the Middle Ages and
classical Rome, one should not overlook the fact that a number of intellectuals of the time were *conversos* (Jews recently converted to Christianity) who, like Alonso de Cartagena, were also aware of Hebrew
antiquity.

   Another trait common to Spanish humanists and one that, in my
judgment, is directly related to their interpretation of classical antiquity,
is their understanding of rhetoric and its application to vernacular compositions. The pursuit of eloquence in Spain did not lead to a flourishing
literature in Latin, as was the case in Italy, but it did contribute to the
improvement of Castilian literature. The preferred use of vernacular over
Latin has often provided grounds for certain historians and literary critics to deny, without further inquiry, the presence of any serious humanistic activity in fifteenth-century Spain. While this claim can be easily
disproved by the fact that there is also a considerable body of Latin writings, it should not be forgotten that by the end of the fifteenth century
the humanists themselves took notice of the preponderant use of the vernacular in speaking and writing. This pervasive tendency became, in fact,
a much-debated issue in the sixteenth century.[29]

*   *   *

The introduction of rhetoric at Salamanca in 1403, as I have already
observed, did have an impact on the generation of students then attending the university. The practical application of this rhetorical training can
be seen in the ensuing years as young graduates, in their quest for remu-
nerative positions, strove to elevate their style in accordance with the
newly acquired principles of composition.[30] Concerned with a more elegant form of expression, they soon discovered in classical literature,
above all in Cicero's writings and rhetorical theories, a new notion of
eloquence. But what definitely marked a turning point in the rhetorical
tradition of Spain was the vernacular translation of two classical rhetor-

ical texts during the third decade of the fifteenth century. In effect, Cartagena's translation of Cicero's *De inventione*, begun in 1422 and completed a few years later, and Enrique de Villena's translation of the pseudo-Ciceronian *Rhetorica ad Herennium*, done in 1427, represent the earliest manifestations of Spanish humanism.[31]

Cartagena's translation was begun at the request of Don Duarte, eldest son of the Portuguese king, while he was on a diplomatic mission to Portugal. It seems that in the course of the negotiations over the possession of the Canary Islands, the delegates were forced to resort to ancient historical, geographical, and cartographic documentation as they searched for a peaceful settlement. In these sessions, discussion often arose over their generally inadequate knowledge of classical languages, particularly Greek, and the need for reliable vernacular translations. This subject inevitably invited comments from participants who had been in Italy about the familiarity of Italian scholars with Greek and Latin and the exemplary use they made of their knowledge by translating Greek texts into Latin.

Motivated by these conversations and taking advantage of whatever time he had at his disposal, Cartagena undertook the translation into Spanish of Cicero's *De officiis* and *De senectute* at the request of the Castilian royal secretary, Juan Alfonso de Zamora, a member of the same peace mission.[32] In this period, which seems to be one of intense intellectual activity, Cartagena composed the *Memoriale virtutum*, his first extensive work. It is a treatise written for the education of the prince Don Duarte in which he utilizes numerous precepts derived from Aristotle's *Nicomachean Ethics, Politics, Economics,* and *Rhetoric.*[33] Soon after, Cartagena was asked to translate another Ciceronian text, *De inventione*, by the Portuguese prince who, having learned some of Aristotle's views on rhetoric from the *Memoriale*, wanted to know what Cicero had to say on the subject. As Cartagena explains in the prologue, this new undertaking could not be completed until a few years later, due to his return to Castile and to other pressing professional matters.[34]

Why Cartagena would have been asked to translate a Latin work into Castilian for a prince whose native language was Portuguese and who evidently understood Latin, as Cartagena's first treatise dedicated to him seems to show, is still unclear.[35] Although all explanations would necessarily be conjectural at this time, it is not unreasonable to deduce from this unusual case that Castilian had a linguistic, if not a cultural, hegemony in the Iberian peninsula and that Cartagena's reputation as a knowledgeable Latin scholar was widely recognized by his contemporaries. This supposition is further supported by the fact that he was asked by his king, Juan II, to translate the major works of Seneca into Castilian.

Another important question that still remains unanswered for lack of evidence concerns the ownership of the Latin texts used by Cartagena in his translations and in the *Memoriale*. To ascertain whether these books were in the library of the king of Portugal, in the collection of some other magnate or learned man, or belonged to Cartagena himself would certainly be of value in understanding the manner and extent to which these much sought-after works circulated. I am inclined to believe that the classical texts Cartagena was handling at the Portuguese court were his personal books, since it was not unusual for scholars to carry their favorite works with them for reading and studying in moments of leisure.

Regarding the *Rhetorica ad Herennium,* the classical text translated by Enrique de Villena at approximately the same time that Cartagena completed *De inventione,* there is little to be said, for no copy has yet been found. A possible explanation for the loss of this translation and others prepared concurrently and with the same objective in mind, since they dealt with grammar, *ars dictaminis,* and *ars arengandi,*[36] is that they were rendered obsolete very early on by the advances of humanism in the fifteenth century. If we are to judge by another work of Villena, also dealing with literary composition, this hypothesis seems plausible. His *Arte de trovar,* a kind of *ars poetriae,* has survived in a fragmentary form only because a sixteenth-century humanist, Alvar Gómez de Castro, who collected early Castilian writings out of an antiquarian interest, transcribed numerous passages of historical and linguistic importance.[37]

Villena's lost translations dealing with rules of written and oral composition were all undertaken between 1427 and 1428. During this period he also rendered into Spanish Vergil's *Aeneid* for the king of Navarre and Dante's *Divine Comedy* for the marquis of Santillana, Iñigo López de Mendoza.[38] It is obvious that Villena did not aim at an accurate and polished version of the texts, for he managed to complete in a little over a year two major works and some minor ones. His purpose seems to have been rather to facilitate an understanding of the works for readers who had little or no knowledge of Latin and who lacked a good grasp of Italian. If the only extant copy of the *Divine Comedy* in Spanish, found transcribed in the margins of a fourteenth-century Italian codex that belonged to the marquis of Santillana,[39] is Villena's version, the intent was most certainly to clarify the meaning of obscure words and of difficult passages. Similarly, in his translation of the *Aeneid*—which happens to be the first ever made of the entire work in a modern language—he illuminates the text with numerous commentaries drawing on his vast and eclectic erudition.

The fact that before the 1420s there were no classical translations from Latin to speak of,[40] and that within a short period of time, in Portugal and Catalonia, two geographically distant locations in the Iberian peninsula, there was a sudden manifestation of interest in classical rhetoric and literature, confirms the radical transformation that was taking place in the cultural orientation of Spain. This trend, however, does not mean that the revival of classical antiquity had filtered down to people with no formal education. The circumstances surrounding the scholarly activities of Cartagena and Villena seem to show that the cultural renovation first found expression in the royal courts and chancelleries of the Iberian states. These places were, after all, where jurists, secretaries, chroniclers, and other *letrados*, together with the more learned members of the nobility, were exposed to a variety of views and ideas through personal contacts with visiting dignitaries, many of whom were scholars in their own right. Here too they became acquainted with a new type of eloquence and a different writing style as they handled diplomatic correspondence and propagandistic tracts.

The appeal of these trends, which combined scholarly and literary concerns with official business, was without doubt a factor in creating a demand for functionaries with skills appropriate to the increasingly sophisticated ways of conducting state policy. It is very likely that those who requested Cartagena's and Villena's translations of classical rhetorical texts were lawyers and notaries trained in the *dictamen* who felt the need to keep up with the latest advances in letter writing. The constraints of the traditional *ars dictaminis* and *ars arengandi* did not permit the expression of subtle policy shifts or allow for any digressions or spontaneity that might be effective means of moving or persuading. Classical authors, by contrast, had not been bound by the *dictamen's* compositional procedures, and their literary and rhetorical texts were therefore viewed as appropriate models and instruments for attaining similarly eloquent results.

To be sure, when a merely rudimentary knowledge of the techniques of Latin prose and poetry or an indiscriminate imitation of Latin syntax and diction was applied to the Spanish vernacular the result was inevitably a clumsy style and a discordant effect, as is frequently the case with Villena.[41] Although he translated the *Rhetorica ad Herennium,* he never really abandoned the *dictamen,* and in striving to imitate classical oratory he forced the syntactical patterns of Latin phraseology onto vernacular sentence structure. A sounder understanding of rhetorical theories and of the Latin language is evident in Cartagena's Latin and Spanish works, with the result that his style is striking for its clarity and eloquence.

The significance and novelty of Cartagena's translation of *De inventione* lie not so much in making available a Ciceronian text that had been

known for some time to medieval scholars as in the fact that he clarifies
the proper meaning and function of rhetoric, which had eluded many of
his contemporaries.[42] In the prologue he warns that by merely reading a
rhetorical text, either in Latin or in the vernacular, one does not necessarily acquire an eloquent style. Rhetoric, an offshoot of moral philosophy and one of the liberal arts, is a discipline that requires a great deal
of study. Without specifically mentioning the *ars dictaminis*, which even
learned men like Villena confused with rhetoric, he points out the differences between the two. Rhetoric, he states, does not consist of special
rules for writing and speaking well, nor can it be reduced to the mere
arrangement of words within the sentence. Although any eloquent discourse is based on well-ordered language, the latter is only a means to
an end. The primary objective of rhetoric is to persuade or to stir people's
emotions and feelings.

In order to dissipate much of the misunderstanding concerning the
notion of classical rhetoric, Cartagena recognized the need to explain the
purpose rhetoric served for the Greeks and the Romans. Among the ancients rhetoric was cultivated mainly by the jurists, who pleaded their
cases by delivering elegant and forceful orations. In contrast, modern
lawyers (*abogados*), in their litigations, supported their arguments by
citing innumerable laws and by adducing hairsplitting distinctions.[43]
Cartagena, who was himself a jurist, was aware that judiciary speech-
making had fallen into disuse since Roman times and that the rein-
troduction of Roman law in the Middle Ages had not brought a
concomitant revival of ancient oratory. He also perceived that the practice of rhetoric in his own day was different from what it had been in
ancient times. It was now being applied not only by enlightened jurists
but by members of other professions as well as in personal letters, literary compositions, moral and political treatises, and public speeches. Recognizing that there were no formulas or fixed rules for achieving
eloquence and that it was attained only through the study of classical
rhetorical theories and other writings on the subject and through practice, he urged the reader to heed the general principles of classical orators
and to make use of their examples in accordance with his own abilities
and for whatever endeavor he might deem appropriate.[44]

With regard to the practice of translation, Cartagena shared the
view of early Quattrocento Italian humanists. In his brief remarks on the
subject, he states that since every language has its own peculiar manner
of communicating, any literal translation of a text from one language to
another will necessarily result in a loss of clarity and eloquence. Following the principles set forth by St. Jerome, he favors a translation *ad sen-
sum*. The first task of a translator-interpreter is to be faithful to the

author's intention by striving to reproduce his thoughts as accurately as possible. He allows, however, for a considerable amount of freedom when it comes to conveying in the translation the meaning of the text. For this reason the words of the original can be abridged, paraphrased, or changed as required by the language into which they are translated in order to convey as best one can the style of the author. This flexibility is not permissible, however, with the Scripture; since one is dealing with the word of God, only an exact word-by-word translation is appropriate.[45]

*   *   *

This sketchy summary of Cartagena's views on rhetoric and translation is meant to clarify somewhat a poorly understood chapter of Italian and Spanish humanism, namely, the polemic over Leonardo Bruni's translation of Aristotle's *Nicomachean Ethics*. The *controversia Alfonsiana*, as Bruni was to call it in a letter to Pier Candido Decembrio,[46] was initiated by Cartagena and was to involve most of the better-known humanists of the day, such as Decembrio, Poggio Bracciolini, Francesco Filelfo, Lorenzo Valla, Cardinal Bessarion, Panormita (Antonio Beccadelli), and several others of the next generation.[47] Although some scholars have dealt with a few of the issues that were raised in the polemic, and new data have been added to whatever scanty information was available to those who first called attention to it, a satisfactory assessment of this international controversy is yet to be given. The main reason is that the scholars who have analyzed it knew very little about one of the contenders, that is, Cartagena. This shortcoming has led to a great deal of conjecture as to the intention and purpose of Cartagena's criticism and has seriously impaired a just evaluation of Bruni's replies.

To some scholars the polemic is another debate between scholasticism and humanism or between Renaissance philology and medieval dialectics, while to others it is an attempt at reconciling Aristotelianism with Christianity or an argument over rhetoric and philosophy. In all of these interpretations Cartagena invariably is described as a scholastic theologian opposed to humanistic rhetoric, a champion of medieval culture in the face of an advancing Renaissance, or simply another "barbarian" unable to grasp the new ideals of humanism. Historically, however, these assumptions cannot be substantiated, for they are belied by his accomplishments and by the numerous works that have come down to us. Cartagena was by training a jurist in both civil and canon law, and he refers to himself as such and never as a theologian or anything else. Besides, at the time that he was a student at Salamanca there was not yet a faculty of theology at the university.[48] Although he was rewarded with a series of high ecclesiastical positions, culminating his career by succeeding his father as bishop of Burgos, he distinguished himself more as an effective diplomat than as a spiritual leader.[49] He was, in a sense, a moralist well-versed in classical and biblical studies and, without doubt, the only Spanish intellectual of his generation who was acutely aware of the cultural trends of the time both at home and abroad.[50]

Years before the dispute, Cartagena had been a sincere admirer of Bruni's works, especially of his translations of Greek texts.[51] We do not know why he decided to write a treatise of considerable length divulging his objections to Bruni's translation of the *Nicomachean Ethics*. However, since the controversy lasted from 1436 to 1439, precisely the years in which he was the Castilian representative at the Council of Basel, it is most likely that the polemic started in the heated political atmosphere of the council. Whatever the nationalistic or personal reasons that may have prompted Cartagena's criticism of Bruni's translation, Bruni could not dismiss Cartagena's objections as easily as he had those of previous critics.[52] While the central question is Bruni's interpretation of Aristotle, Cartagena's criticism touches upon a number of minor issues such as the danger of a subjective re-creation of ancient texts, the limitations and responsibilities of the translators, the nature and value of classical versus vernacular languages, the purity of classical Latin, the constant changes and evolution of language and their borrowings, the attainment of eloquence, and the role of philosophy.

Cartagena's attitude toward classical antiquity was different from that of Bruni. The Spaniard approached ancient authors in a more detached fashion and from a more objective point of view. In his opinion, the translator's primary concern in works of a philosophical nature should be with the actual text, for the written word is the only sure ground on which to base an accurate rendering of the author's thought. Trying to guess what the author may have felt in his heart, a most futile attempt when one considers his historical remoteness, seemed to Cartagena a most unreasonable approach to the translation of an ancient philosophical work.[53]

Despite his admitted ignorance of Greek, Cartagena still considered himself qualified to judge Bruni's translation on the basis that "reason" (*ratio*), being common to all people, could be expressed in any language. Since the philosopher did not achieve reason on account of his authority, but authority on account of his reason, it followed that whenever Bruni's translation did not make sense, that is to say, did not conform to reason, there he had departed from the original Aristotelian text.[54] Cartagena's criteria for reason were based on his knowledge of ancient ethical schools, on the older translation of the *Nicomachean Ethics*, which Bruni had so disdainfully scorned, and on the writings of classical Roman authors, chiefly Cicero and Seneca, who had also dealt with ethics and the nature of virtue, though in a less scientific manner. Cartagena's reliance on the older translation derived from his belief that it was not the work of a medieval scholastic, because it was historically impossible for a Dominican friar to have executed it, as Bruni claimed. His reasoning was that passages of the *Nicomachean Ethics* were included in the *Partidas*, a code of laws written in Castilian and assembled in the thirteenth century at approximately the time that the Dominican order was founded. He contended that it would have been difficult for the Latin translation to have reached Spain and to have been translated into the vernacular in time to be inserted in the *Partidas*. For this reason he tended to believe that the older translation had been made by Boethius and, being therefore more ancient, would also have been closer to the Aristotelian text.[55]

In defending the previous translator, he questioned whether the older rendering of the *Ethics* was so obscure as to be totally useless. This contention had been Bruni's primary consideration in wanting to undertake a more readable translation and one that was, above all, closer to the eloquence of the original text. Cartagena concurred with Bruni that philosophical writings ought to be clear and precise. But he argued further that, since philosophical terms are open to many interpretations, any textual ambiguity should be accompanied by explanatory notes. Concerning Bruni's objection that the older version contained a number of Greek words, Cartagena reminded him that many Greek terms had been assimilated into vernacular languages and that Latin, on the knowledge of which the Florentine prided himself, had borrowed numerous words from the Greek. He asks why the earlier translator's use of Greek terms should be considerd inappropriate, especially in those instances in which the meaning could not otherwise be expressed with equal brevity and clarity. In fact, according to Cartagena, the Latin equivalents that Bruni had substituted for these "barbaric" words were unsuitable for conveying the meaning intended by Aristotle.[56]

It is, in fact, on the basis of his subtle understanding of the Latin terms used by Bruni that Cartagena could hold his ground and even elicit his opponent's admiration. Against Bruni's assertion that in translations into Latin one should always follow the language customarily used by the best authors of Roman antiquity, chiefly Cicero, Cartagena emphasized that Cicero's diction was inappropriate for rendering Aristotle's discussion of moral concepts. Judging from Cicero's writings, Cartagena speculated, the Roman orator either had not chosen to inquire scientifically into the nature of ethics or had never read Aristotle on the subject.[57] Proficiency in a language and an excellent knowledge of a discipline, in this case Greek and rhetoric, respectively, do not ensure a person's mastery in another area of study, namely philosophy. The thrust of Cartagena's criticism actually called into question Bruni's understanding of Aristotelian ethics. To this end he pointed out a number of words that Bruni had substituted for those of the medieval translation, indicating their unsuitability for the rightful interpretation of Aristotelian concepts. His aim, however, was not to deny the value of eloquence, as some scholars have claimed, but to warn his contemporaries against the misuse of this art. Far from condemning the union of rhetoric and philosophy, he actually reaffirms it and makes them both the domain of the true man of wisdom.[58]

In his rebuttal of Cartagena's objections, Bruni seized on his opponent's unfamiliarity with Greek.[59] By elaborating at length on this most vulnerable point, he tried to discredit Cartagena's criticism. Bruni asked, and with good reason, how a person with no knowledge of Greek could be in a position to determine the appropriateness of Latin equivalents when he did not even know the meaning of the Greek words. The Latin of his translation, he maintained, was based on the usage of the most renowned and trustworthy authors of Roman antiquity, whose purity of language was irreproachable. In the first reply, Bruni also included a discussion of his choice of *summum bonum* as a proper translation for the Greek *tagaton*, a point not raised by the Spaniard. It was in effect an answer previously made to Ugo Benzi of Siena, who contended that the Ciceronian *summum bonum* was not as accurate as the scholastic *bonum per se*. What Cartagena's views on this question were is a matter of conjecture, since his rejoinder to Bruni's reply has been lost. All we know is that Cartagena had only mentioned in passing that the *summum bonum* was better rendered with a simple *bonum*.[60]

This dissension over the interpretation of certain Aristotelian concepts, in which neither Bruni nor Cartagena was entirely correct or entirely wrong is, to my mind, the first manifestation of a conflict between two currents within the humanist movement, which was to continue until the end of the century, becoming even more pronounced during the last decades of the Quattrocento. That Cartagena's disagreement with Bruni was not another battle between a medieval and a humanist outlook can be gathered by the correspondence of their mutual friends, namely, Pizolpasso, Decembrio, and Poggio.[61] Decembrio, who at first came to the defense of Bruni, became soon afterward the Spaniard's most cherished friend, as can be seen by what has survived of their correspondence. It was Decembrio who, on his own initiative, collected all the writings on the polemic in six books, a compilation that unfortunately has never been located or identified.[62] A sincere appreciation for Cartagena's erudition and humanist interests was again shown when Decembrio began to translate Plato's *Republic*. Besides sending the learned bishop the first book, asking him to make any corrections and modifications he saw fit, he also promised to dedicate the sixth book to Cartagena.[63]

A similar respect for the Spaniard is expressed by Poggio Bracciolini who, from the very beginning of the *controversia Alfonsiana*, praised Cartagena's civility and erudition. In a letter to Bruni, Poggio informed him of Decembrio's unsolicited defense of his translation. While he condemned the Milanese humanist's unwarranted acrimony toward Cartagena, he praised the moderate tone in which the Spaniard had presented his case. Of the letters that Cartagena wrote to Poggio, none has been found thus far. Judging by a reply from Poggio in which there are indications that Cartagena had commented at length on one of Poggio's works, most likely *De infelicitate principum*, one can be sure that the missing correspondence of Cartagena, if ever located, would tell us a great deal about his thoughts on ethics during the years immediately after the polemic.[64]

The letters of these Italian humanists indicate that the controversy arose between two learned men with dissimilar backgrounds and temperaments who, while they shared the same goals, tried to achieve them through different approaches. Interestingly, a careful reading of Bruni's second letter shows that his attitude had changed considerably from what it had been at the time of the first reply, when he knew little about Alonso de Cartagena. Whereas in the first rejoinder he had made a vehement denunciation of his critic's lack of familiarity with the Greek language, in his second reply his tone is surprisingly conciliatory. A few years later, in a letter to Cartagena, Bruni reminisces about the polemic in the friendliest of terms and asks Cartagena, with a profusion of praise for his learning and critical judgment, to let him know his opinion of the *Isagogicon moralis disciplinae*, a work he had just sent to Juan II of Castile.[65]

*   *   *

Among the men of letters who lived during the first half of the fifteenth century, the marquis of Santillana, Iñigo López de Mendoza, deserves mention, for he is the best representative of a peculiar mode of humanism that I would call "vernacular humanism." Although the use of the term "vernacular" to qualify humanism may seem contradictory in that it is generally understood that the primary concern of early humanists was the recovery of ancient literature and thought and the restoration of classical Latin, the word, nevertheless, appropriately describes an unusual but consequential form of humanism in Castile. Paradoxically, Santillana and other proponents of this type of humanism, who relied on the study of classical and humanist texts in translation and on the use of Castilian for their written compositions, were the ones who tried to imitate most closely what they perceived to be the objectives of Italian humanists, not particularly concerned that the latter held the vernacular in low esteem.

In Santillana's life and writings, one finds many of the cultural aspirations of early fifteenth-century humanists. If his intellectual curiosity, coupled with an openness to new ideas, made him receptive to the works of classical authors and of contemporary Italian humanists, his reverence for books led him to assemble a fine selection of their writings. His library, which contained what was certainly the most outstanding collection of humanist texts in Spain at that time, can also be counted among the best of its kind in Europe.[66] However, the fact that he had only a rudimentary knowledge of Latin, and thus lacked an essential tool of the humanist scholar, greatly diminished the scope and depth of his intellectual activities. Possessing neither the learning nor the critical ability necessary for a sound understanding of classical literature, his approach to ancient authors and to Italian humanist culture was based more on aesthetic than on academic grounds. Unable to grasp the full meaning of classical literature and ancient thought, he could never attain an adequate historical comprehension of antiquity.[67] In short, that vision of man and the world upon which the intellectual and philosophical convictions of the humanists rested remained always vague in Santillana's mind.

Because of these limitations some modern scholars have been reluctant to consider Santillana a humanist. But this assessment does not take into account a point that is central to all his cultural activities as an author and bibliophile, namely, that his undertakings were inspired by humanist readings and can only be explained within a humanist context. The inadequacies he may have had as a scholar are interesting in themselves and should be made the object of serious analysis, for he provides a case study of the way less educated persons, far removed from the centers of humanist learning in Italy, interpreted and assimilated Italian humanism.

Despite Santillana's shortcomings, his taste and inclinations are no longer oriented toward the Middle Ages as a source of writing and learning.[68] Even if his break with the immediate past is more for stylistic than for scholarly reasons, it is a choice that implies a denial of the prevailing culture of his day and an endorsement of classical antiquity as a model for the intellectual activities of his time. Although his interpretation of the new humanist movement did not go beyond rhetorical innovations and a fascination for ancient history, he contributed immensely to the spread of the revival of ancient literature and popularized to a certain degree the works of Dante, Petrarch, and Boccaccio, as well as those of some contemporary Italian humanists.

Santillana's efforts to replace traditional culture with what he perceived to be a new learning was confirmed and even overestimated by his friends and collaborators. In the eulogies that were written on the occasion of his death in 1458, amidst the usual praises for his virtues and literary accomplishments, he was credited with having changed the traditional culture of Castile by introducing to his country the study of letters. To Gómez Manrique, another poet and nobleman, Santillana was indeed "the first in our time who combined science [liberal studies] with chivalry, and armor with the toga."[69] In so doing, Manrique adds, the illustrious marquis eradicated from Spain the long-held idea that the active and contemplative lives were incompatible. Even though the *topos* of arms versus letters employed by Gómez Manrique to illustrate Santillana's achievements is medieval in origin—for it arose from the literary debates fictionalizing real conflicts between jurists and knights[70]—the Latinized expression he uses, "congregó la loriga con la toga," has an unmistakably humanist flavor. To be sure, Santillana was not the first nobleman who had cultivated literary studies. Beginning with Alfonso the Wise in the thirteenth century there had been an uninterrupted line of kings, princes, and magnates such as Don Juan Manuel, Pero López de Ayala, Enrique de Villena, Pérez de Guzmán, Gómez Manrique himself, and many more who, while carrying on their practical activities, found time for writing and studying.

That Santillana was regarded as responsible for altering the course of Castilian intellectual life was reiterated by his secretary, Diego de Burgos, who holds the distinction of being the first humanist to articulate an awareness of a Spanish cultural Renaissance. He attributed this rebirth to the activities of his patron who, he maintained, had dispelled the darkness that had prevailed in Spain since the fall of the Roman Empire. By emulating in his writings the famous authors of Greece and Rome and by acquiring from abroad books in different disciplines that could not be found in his country, Santillana had saved Spain from blind ignorance. According to Diego de Burgos, these works, which Santillana and his associates brought to the attention of other learned men, were instrumental in ushering in the revival of learning they were at present enjoying.[71]

Diego de Burgos's exaggerations with respect to his patron do not invalidate the fact that by the middle of the fifteenth century there were a number of people in Castile, at least in Santillana's entourage, who sensed that they were living in a new age and who characterized the preceding centuries as a period in which arts and sciences had declined. It was precisely this situation, Diego de Burgos contended, that prompted Santillana to restore Spain, a land that had given birth to Seneca, Lucan, Quintilian, and other renowned ancient figures, to its past glory. Although it would have been impossible for the marquis to have taken the initiative he did were it not for the Italian humanists, his accomplishments, Diego de Burgos affirmed, were even greater. Drawing an analogy from ancient literature, he wrote that just as Cicero had learned eloquence from the Greeks and had soon surpassed them in this art, so Santillana had outdone all the Italian orators who had been his models.[72]

Similar praises for Santillana's achievements are expressed by Pero Díaz de Toledo, the marquis's spiritual adviser, who lauded him for having fostered the transcription and translation of many classical texts, thus preventing ancient wisdom from being lost forever. A humanist in his own right, Pero Díaz had been asked by Santillana to translate into Spanish several works, including Plato's *Phaedo*. In a treatise he wrote commemorating his patron's death, there is a passage in which he seems to be describing the humanist atmosphere that Santillana had created around himself and the motivations behind the group's literary and philosophical pursuits. Scholars, he affirms, endure many personal hardships when they search out, procure, and restore classical works. They do so only because the written word can bring ancient and modern men together. The bond established through the act of reading permits the reader and the author to engage in a dialogue and to talk to each other not only from distant places but across the centuries.[73]

The novelty in Diego de Burgos's and Pero Díaz de Toledo's assertions crediting Santillana with the restoration of eloquence and the arts has not been noticed by scholars who have dealt with the culture and literature of this period. More attention has been paid instead to sporadic occurrences of the *topos* of arms versus letters or to occasional remarks found in fifteenth-century writings voicing opposition to learning and study. These comments have been construed as evidence of a pervasive antihumanist bias, which they presume to have been a constant in Spain during this period. Yet signs of anti-intellectualism can be found anywhere in Europe at that time, and the argument that in Spain it constituted a strong current hostile to the development of humanism is not very convincing. At the same time, the exaggerated praises for Santillana, inspired as they were by official patronage, should not be taken as evidence of a sweeping humanism permeating all aspects of Castilian cultural life. Well-defined articulations concerning the revival of letters such as those made by Santillana's secretary and his spiritual adviser are uncommon around the middle of the fifteenth century. But this dearth is to be expected if one considers that humanism was an elitist movement and, at least in Spain, still in an incipient stage.

The claim made by those surrounding Santillana that through a conscious effort he had brought about a revival of learning, though important for the history of humanism, cannot be taken literally. Evidently the practice of ascribing such a complex phenomenon to an illustrious scholar or to a special event was not unique to Spain, for it is also found among contemporary Italian humanists. In the *Rerum suo tempore gestarum commentarius*, Bruni considered Manuel Chrysolaras's arrival in Florence, where he had been brought to teach Greek, as the turning point in the restoration of classical antiquity.[74] Likewise, in the treatise *Della vita civile*, the Florentine Matteo Palmieri attributed to his fellow citizen, Bruni, the recent revival of letters. Although a copy of Palmieri's work appears in Santillana's library,[75] it is unlikely that Diego de Burgos or Pero Díaz de Toledo borrowed their explanation of the Spanish Renaissance from this particular source.

Despite these similarities, the assessment of the cultural revival given by Spanish humanists was quite different from that offered by the Italians. In Italy the revival was identified with the flourishing of Greek and Latin studies in the early years of the Quattrocento. The contributions of all men of letters prior to this time were excluded. This exclusion applied even to Petrarch who, in their minds, had come close to but had not attained an elegant and polished Latin style. In Spain, as we have seen, the beginning was set at a somewhat later date, coinciding with Santillana's intellectual activities. Although the revival of learning was made contingent on the introduction of classical works, read either in the original or in translation, the study of Latin and Greek did not seem to be a factor. If humanists in both countries believed in an intermediate period of darkness separating the present from classical civilization, in Spain there was no feeling of antagonism toward medieval culture. Judging from Diego de Burgos's account, the study of the classics did not replace any rival teaching. It came to fill, rather, a cultural vacuum that had been created by centuries of intellectual neglect and stagnation. His metaphors, "blind ignorance" and "illumination of true wisdom" ("ciega ignorancia" and "lunbre de caridad verdadera"), though applied to a secular interpretation of history, still have religious overtones.[76] It is, perhaps, this spiritual connotation in his concept of a cultural rebirth that prevented him from perceiving the historical causes behind the humanist movement.

The failure to discern what was behind the radical transformation of the "old coarse tradition" into something new was not due entirely to Diego de Burgos's belief in divine intervention as the determining factor ruling the course of human history. His inability to grasp the forces at work may well be attributed to his inadequate preparation. This shortcoming, a prevalent trait among the vernacular humanists of the first generation, explains their general but uncritical awareness of what was occurring. This limitation screened out, as it were, most of the complexities of the cultural revival, thus reducing the movement to a purely literary and aesthetic renovation.

In view of the preceding remarks, it can be argued that these vernacular humanists were not humanists at all, especially if they are measured against their Italian counterparts who used the purest Latin, translated from the Greek, and engaged in philological scholarship. But even though these specific activities were inaccessible to them due to their poor schooling, their presence in the intellectual life of fifteenth-century Spain and the crucial role they played in the development of their national literature make it impossible to disregard them altogether.

One has to recognize that in Spain, unlike any other country in Europe, humanism in its earliest stage was favorably received and promoted by two different groups: the *letrados* or university graduates invariably associated with the church, and a number of less formally educated poets, historians, and moralists, mostly members of the nobility, whom today we would classify as "amateurs." Though united by the same enthusiasm for the classics and by a similar dissatisfaction with traditional culture, they differed in some fundamental ways. Besides the obvious distinctions deriving in part from their respective social origins, educational backgrounds, and professional positions, their general outlook and their views on particular issues were different. But what really distinguished the two groups was the fact that the *letrados,* who had a deeper understanding of the cultural renovation, were able to assimilate the lessons of antiquity and utilize them in matters relating to their educational, social, and religious concerns. And even though they represented the ecclesiastical tradition—since they were usually affiliated with the church—they were more socially oriented than the laic, aristocratic authors who were chiefly interested in literature and history and who dealt with moral problems in the abstract. The best illustration of this attitude can be found in the contrasting views each group held with regard to rhetoric. Alonso de Cartagena understood rhetoric to be the art of persuasion and thus an effective instrument of communication, for he considered social discourse as the essential bond that united citizens of different ranks and varying functions within an organized community. To vernacular humanists such as Santillana, Juan de Mena, and other poets, rhetoric was the art of verbal embellishment, a means of adorning one's literary compositions.

Of these two groups that shaped fifteenth-century Spanish humanism, the vernacular humanists are far better known to students of Spanish culture for the conspicuous place they occupy in the history of literature. The *letrados'* contributions to humanism, by contrast, have remained largely unknown because their works, many of them in Latin, cannot easily be categorized under our modern concept of literary genres. Yet it was this group that most closely adhered to the new humanistic culture by engaging in those scholarly pursuits characteristic of humanists in fifteenth-century Europe.

The tendency until now has been to consider early Spanish humanists, whether from the ranks of the *letrados* or from the nobility, as a homogeneous group having the same aims, ideas, and intellectual outlook.[77] This supposition, based on what meager information has been available until now about their lives and works, has served to hinder further investigations into the possible ideological or factional dissensions that might have existed among them. Knowing how prevalent and how bitter were the personal enmities and rivalries among humanists elsewhere in Europe, one might reasonably assume that this infighting occurred in Spain as well. An exploration of these private and professional contentions would undoubtedly reveal the diversity of views and positions held by individual humanists. But along with this discord there were also examples of friendship and collaboration. Hence there is a need for an in-depth analysis that would determine the type and extent of the intellectual exchanges that took place among particular humanists and collectively between the two groups. Such an examination would certainly shed some light on the mutual dependence that existed between the *letrados*, who did the translations, and the vernacular humanists, who had the resources to buy books. It would explain also how one mode of humanism conditioned the other and would ultimately clarify each group's impact on the formation of Spanish humanism.

Whatever their similarities and differences, the question still remains as to why some university graduates and a few members of the nobility embraced the same intellectual movement. A factor that cannot be discounted in their joint acceptance of the revival of classical antiquity was the desire to rise above the internecine strife and the ensuing anarchy that plagued all sectors of Castilian society. By espousing an elitist movement such as the revival of learning, they were assigning to themselves a new intellectual and moral position within their respective classes. Those members of the nobility who were more responsive to cross-cultural currents and cognizant of the duties and responsibilities their status entailed sought in erudition a way to elevate themselves above their peers. Because of their learning and university training, the *letrados* aspired to "honor," that is to say, public recognition and social advancement, as recompense for the role they played in the cultural and administrative organization of the state.[78]

The principle of "honor," meaning recognition of virtue and a prerequisite for attaining royal rewards—which had always been the premise on which the nobility justified its wealth, privileges, and power—underwent during the fifteenth century a radical change in meaning. As the authors of numerous social and moral treatises of the time repeatedly emphasized, honor was not to be bestowed on account of a person's lineage or wealth but for one's personal qualities and virtuous actions.[79] Humanists from whatever social background derived virtues from the active and contemplative lives and agreed as well in identifying the attainment of virtues with true nobility. In theory, at least, the true noble was the person who knew and practiced all moral, practical, and above all intellectual virtues. The model of the virtuous person was no longer exclusively the man of action but the new man who combined action with erudition.

Paradoxically, the vernacular humanists, with their aristocratic background, were more responsible than the *letrados* for expanding the reading public. By soliciting the translation of classical and humanist works into the vernacular, they were, in fact, placing the new learning in the hands of people who had previously been excluded from literate circles. This new readership, admittedly exiguous in the beginning, with the advent of the printing press and in time was to become the "consumer" of the literature of the Spanish Golden Age.

Since vernacular humanists played such a crucial role in the development of Spanish culture, it seems appropriate to mention in passing Nuño de Guzmán who, after Santillana, more than anyone else embodies the qualities of this particular type of humanist. Among all the biographies that Vespasiano da Bisticci wrote in his *Vite di uomini illustri,* the life of Nuño de Guzmán is without doubt the most intriguing and the one most resembling literary fiction.[80] There is little information about this Spanish nobleman who traveled extensively through most of the known world of the time, for not much has been added to what we have learned from the Florentine bookseller.[81] Vespasiano first met Nuño de Guzmán when the latter arrived in Florence in 1439 to witness the union of the eastern and western churches. Considering that in those days Florence was teeming with famous humanists from both the Christian and the Byzantine worlds and that all scholars of note visited Vespasiano's bookshop, the fact that he was so profoundly impressed by an undistinguished young Spaniard tells us something about the personality of Nuño de Guzmán. What in all likelihood caught the Florentine's atten-

tion was that, unlike other humanists who searched out and studied ancient works in order to learn about past civilizations and political
institutions, this modern-day Ulysses sought to expand his knowledge by
direct observation of the way people lived. He had been traveling, in fact,
for eight years before arriving in Florence. In his wanderings he had visited many cities and lands ("quasi tutte le terre abitabili"), gathering so
much information about other people's religions, customs, and forms of
government as to enable him to write, if he ever wanted to, a fascinating
account of his experiences.

Selecting those events of Nuño de Guzmán's life that would best
characterize his intrinsic qualities, Vespasiano tells of the Spaniard's filial
love and anguish at having displeased his father by his long and unauthorized absence. Moved by the young man's grief, Vespasiano recommends that he discuss the matter with a distinguished Florentine,
Giannozzo Manetti, who writes for the repentant son an apology in the
form of a letter asking his father's pardon. The *Apologia Nunnii*, written
in the first person, is a skillful humanist composition, meant more to
impress Luis de Guzmán than to appease his anger.[82] Manetti's *Apologia*
had its desired effect. Nuño's father, according to Vespasiano, had someone who knew Latin read it to him several times, and each time it was
read, we are told, the father could not hold back his tears "per la degnità
della materia." Not only did Luis de Guzmán forgive his son, but he even
sent him a large sum of money in order for Nuño to solicit certain favors
from the papal curia, then residing in Florence because of the council.
But, Vespasiano relates, Nuño was by nature so generous and trusting
that he was soon swindled out of the money by some deceiving Florentines.[83] The friendship between Nuño de Guzmán and Manetti that began under these circumstances was to last for many years. Within months
Manetti wrote two other works for his new friend: *De illustribus longaevis*, dedicated to Luis de Guzmán, and the *Laudatio Dominae Agnetis
Numantinae*, in honor of Nuño de Guzmán's mother, Inés de Torres, a
remarkable woman who cared a great deal about her son's education and
even sponsored his travels with her own money.[84] In addition, Manetti
dedicated the *Vita Socratis et Senecae* to Nuño, who had by then returned
to Spain.[85]

Although he had visited many countries and had resided in various
courts, it was only in Florence that Nuño de Guzmán became friends
with many humanists, and with Manetti and Bruni in particular. While
his stay in Florence could not have been more than a year, and I suspect
that the total amount of time he spent in Italy could not have been very
long, he managed to acquire an excellent knowledge of Italian, for Vespasiano claims that he could read it better than a Tuscan. What also set

him apart from other foreigners with whom Vespasiano da Bisticci came in contact was the fact that he had "infiniti volumi" of classical works translated into Italian, forming thereby a considerable library ("degnissima libraria"), which unfortunately became dispersed after his death. Among the translations he commissioned, Vespasiano mentions Cicero's *Tusculanae* and *De oratore*, Quintilian's *Declamationes* and Macrobius's *Saturnalia*. With the exception of *De oratore* and the *Saturnalia*, which have yet to be found, the others, and a few more not mentioned by Vespasiano, have been identified. They are Aristotle's *Nicomachean Ethics* in Bruni's translation, Bruni's *Vita di Marco Tullio Cicerone* from the Latin original *Cicero novus*, Decembrio's Italian translation of Seneca's satire *Apocolocynthosis Claudii*, known as *Ludus de morte Claudii*, as well as Plutarch's *Life* of Alexander, which Decembrio added to Quintus Curtius Rufus's *Istoria d'Alexandro Magno* to fill in certain gaps in the text.[86]

In view of the many translations of classical texts into Italian that Nuño de Guzmán solicited, we would expect that he himself, like so many of his compatriots, would have translated some of these Italian versions into Spanish. But evidently such is not the case. No proof has come to light that he ever translated or had someone else translate any of the works he had commissioned, even for the three compositions that Manetti wrote explicitly for his family, though it is almost certain that none of them knew Latin. The only translation we can be sure he was responsible for is that of Manetti's *Orazione a Gismondo Pandolfo de' Malatesti*, which Nuño executed for the marquis of Santillana.[87] As for Seneca's *De ira*, he simply revised a previous transcription made by his mother's chaplain. More important, but also more problematic, is a Spanish translation of a compendium of Aristotle's *Nicomachean Ethics*, tentatively ascribed to Nuño, though a case can be made for attributing it to Alfonso de Paléncia.[88]

The reconstructed inventory of Nuño's books gives an insight into the reading habits of a vernacular humanist. The peculiarity of his commissioning only Italian translations remains unexplained. Did he intend to translate them into Spanish at some future time or did he consider Italian to be a prestigious idiom similar, perhaps, to classical languages? Whatever the case, the underlying impression is that Nuño, like so many other vernacular humanists, did not have a good grasp of Latin. As a fifteenth-century Spanish treatise on Italian phonology clearly states, one does not have to be an expert in Latin to be a very good man of letters (*literatisimo*).[89]

*   *   *

By the second half of the fifteenth century, humanism in Spain was well established along the lines described above. The first generation of scholars, represented by Cartagena, Santillana, and Mena, who had first introduced and fostered the rebirth of letters and ideas, had virtually disappeared by the year 1460. A new group of young men, some with direct ties to the major figures of the older generation, continued the trends initiated by their mentors. What they had in common was that they all had lived, studied, and worked in Italy. Their relations with Italian and Greek humanists were often personal and direct, and they even participated actively in the controversies that arose among Italian humanists.

A most peculiar case is that of Fernando de Córdoba, a child prodigy with an unusual memory, who had contacts with many humanists at the court of Alfonso V in Naples and at the papal curia.[90] Known to his contemporaries for some supposed intellectual feats in his youth and for the attacks that in later years he directed against some highly regarded humanists, his fame clearly outweighed his merits. Judging from his extant works, he seems to have been a good scholastic theologian with some humanist pretensions but devoid of any real fervor for serious speculation or philological investigation. His ability to retain information as well as his mastery of mnemonic techniques may not have been sufficient to secure a good position at the Aragonese court in Naples. Hence his decision to go to Paris and challenge university doctors to a series of theological debates, thinking that his extraordinary powers of recall and the excellence of his scholastic formation would gain for him the recognition that had eluded him in the humanist court of Naples. Detained by the university after he failed to appear twice for the debate he had requested, he was finally set free, for the university could not force him to keep his word.

It is somewhat puzzling that, in view of his lively intelligence and his exposure to humanist culture, Fernando did not adopt some of its values and aspirations. Of his many treatises, the one that is most akin to a humanist work is *De laudibus Platonis*, written as a reply to George of Trebizond's critical attack on Plato and dedicated to Cardinal Bessarion, whose position Fernando de Córdoba supported. Fernando's contribution to the famous polemic regarding the superiority of Plato over Aristotle is indeed disappointing. His treatise is simply a compilation of pronouncements about Plato taken from pagan and Christian sources and arranged in forty-five *veritates*, which supposedly were to prove the superiority of this philosopher. These *veritates* not only do not address themselves to the basic issues of the controversy between George of Trebizond and Bessarion, but I doubt very much that they could have lent much support to the cardinal's cause.[91] Nevertheless, Fernando's work must have carried considerable weight if, years later, as Kristeller points out, Andreas, George of Trebizond's son, tried to defend his father from the Spaniard's attacks.

From the writings of Italian humanists it seems that, despite his shortcomings, Fernando de Córdoba had gained acceptance in the learned circles of the time. We know that Valla wrote a letter of presentation to Alfonso V when Fernando, as a young man, first arrived in Italy. But while Valla praises at length the Spaniard's incredible memory and debating skills, he qualifies his laudatory remarks by pointing out that his Latin was seriously deficient and that this problem could only be remedied by extensive classical studies under the guidance of a good teacher.[92]

It seems that Valla and Fernando did not remain on good terms for very long. In the controversy between Valla and Poggio Bracciolini a few years later, Fernando's name keeps reappearing in their vitriolic exchanges. Poggio relies on Fernando, who by then was teaching theology at the Roman *studium*, when trying to discredit Valla on theological matters. References to Fernando in Poggio's *Invectivae* 2, 4, and 5 are made, in fact, to prove Valla's heretical tendencies with regard to the problems of the Trinity, predestination, and free will, the relation between philosophy and theology, and the reevaluation of Epicureanism.[93] How Poggio became acquainted with the Spaniard's views is, at present, a matter of conjecture. While he could have heard of Valla's heterodoxies directly from Fernando or indirectly from mutual friends at the curia, the reference Poggio makes in the *Invectiva* 2 suggests that Fernando might have written an attack on Valla.[94]

Concurrent with the polemic between Poggio and Valla was a less sensational controversy, which had originated earlier in the court of Alfonso V. The main contenders in this secondary but equally bitter quarrel were Bartolomeo Facio and Valla. The merging of these two controversies and the repercussions they had in humanist circles in the years that followed constitute the historical context in which some Spaniards residing in Rome lent their support to one side or the other.

If Fernando de Córdoba became involved in the theological implications of the polemic against Valla, a younger Spaniard, Juan de Lucena, who arrived in Italy only a year or two after Valla's death in 1457, caught the literary and ethical dimensions of the famous controversies. Instead of participating directly in the dispute, Lucena chose to translate into Spanish and rework Facio's *De vitae felicitate*, a treatise in dialogue form intended to refute Valla's *De vero bono*. Lucena's *De vita beata*, composed in Rome around 1463, is in a way a continuation of the debate over Valla's Epicurean solution to the problem of man's ultimate good or happiness, but fashioned for a different audience.

In adapting Facio's work, Lucena changes the setting to recognizable Castilian surroundings. To this end he introduces Spanish interlocutors and additional passages and even makes significant structural and stylistic modifications in order to give the work a distinctive literary character of its own. Although he replaces the Italian humanists appearing in the work with Spanish participants, historically speaking the latter's views only vaguely resemble those of their Italian counterparts. In reality the positions they sustain do not even reflect their own actual thinking. But it should be emphasized that Lucena, who knew the world of Spanish and Italian humanism, found it not only normal but appropriate to place Alonso de Cartagena, the marquis of Santillana, and Juan de Mena in the same category as Guarino of Verona, Panormita, and Giovanni Lamola. As he explained in the prologue, the reason he "resuscitated these Petrarchs" ("resuscité estos Petrarcas") who had been dead for some time was to lend more authority to his treatise by using their names.[95]

What is difficult to understand about Lucena is why he would appropriate another man's work, pass it off as his own, and dedicate it to his king without the slightest reference to the rightful author. A possible excuse might have been Facio's recent death, but a more likely explanation would be that all the additions to and modifications of the text would, in Lucena's mind, invalidate the idea of plagiarism—just as Facio had extensively reworked Antonio da Barga's *Libellus de dignitate et excellentia humanae vitae* in his *De vitae felicitate* without any acknowledgment.[96]

Be that as it may, Lucena's adoption of Facio's views unequivocally places him in that faction which considered Valla's *De vero bono* a defense of Epicurean doctrines, a reprehensible body of ideas in the minds of many Spaniards of this time. Charges and countercharges were being made under the term "Epicurean," as social and political transgressions began to be confused with ominous religious beliefs and disbeliefs.[97] That he identified with a non-Epicurean group whose orthodoxy was above reproach may have been motivated by his being possibly a converso and thus always wary of being associated with any school of thought that could conceivably be judged heretical.[98]

This glimpse into Lucena's motivations may help to clarify why he deemed Facio's ideas worthy of being translated into Spanish. Similarly, it provides a clue about certain interpolations he made in reworking the treatise. Behind seemingly disinterested observations are references to topics of the day or allusions to scandalous rumors that his contemporaries would readily understand but which escape us most of the time. On occasion he lets biases of a more personal nature surface, as in the biting attack on the archbishop of Toledo, Alfonso Carrillo, who was accused, falsely it seems, of being a squanderer and a believer in alchemy. It is difficult to ascertain why he singled out this particular figure from all the other prelates of the time who were just as greedy, superstitious, and given to political intrigue. Other than the possibility of some private disagreement, a plausible explanation is that Lucena was trying to please some powerful figures. His bold accusations and the risks he faced in making them publicly implies that Lucena was securely protected by very potent people, such as King Enrique IV himself, to whom the work is dedicated, and other magnates who supported the royalist cause.

Seen against this background, Lucena's characterization of Alfonso Carrillo was indeed an indictment that could not pass unnoticed in Spanish learned circles. As far as we know, Carrillo never answered Lucena's charges. But a work dedicated to Carrillo by Alfonso Ortiz, a little-known humanist who, if studied, might turn out to be a very important figure, seems to have been written as a rebuttal to Lucena's accusations. In Ortiz's *Liber dialogorum*, the archbishop of Toledo holds the distinction of being the only contemporary participant and the only interlocutor who engages in a debate with Zeno, Plato, Cicero, and Boethius on the meaning of happiness.[99] The treatise, a series of dialogues, argues from a perspective more akin to Valla's line of reasoning a wider range of issues than those discussed in Lucena's *De vita beata*.

There is little doubt that Ortiz was inspired by Valla's *De vero bono*. The main thrust of the argument is to prove, through Archbishop Carrillo, that Christian morality does not have to be ascetic or pessimistic. Pleasure, instead of being an impediment to virtue, actually enhances it. Since everyone seeks pleasure, it follows that all actions of the perfect man are necessarily filled with pleasure, for pleasure is connatural with happiness.

Unfortunately, both the *Liber dialogorum* and its author have received little attention. All the information we have about Ortiz's life and works is provided by Giovanni Maria Bertini in a sketchy study published many years ago. Lately, Bertini has resumed his investigations and has published Ortiz's treatise on education.[100] Despite these meritorious efforts there remains much to be done. A study of the six hundred volumes ("seiscientos cuerpos de libros") that he bequeathed to the University of Salamanca and of his several known works would be the first step toward an assessment of his contribution to Spanish humanism.

Alfonso Ortiz is not the only forgotten humanist who lived during the second half of the fifteenth century. An unidentified Al. Hispan. is another, the only Spanish humanist I know who wrote Latin verse, as we learn from his unfinished poem, "Sigismundiane ad Pium II Pontificem Maximum," consisting of 292 hexameters, a denigrating attack on Sig-

ismondo Pandolfo Malatesta. Other minor humanists have been con-
signed to oblivion, most of whom were the translators of classical and
humanist texts—with whom I shall not deal for reasons of space. When
a more comprehensive account of fifteenth-century Spanish humanism is
finally written, the labor of the translators will constitute a most important chapter.[101]

*   *   *

The gradual affirmation of Spanish humanism around the middle of the
fifteenth century became, in the last decades of that century, a widespread
movement that affected many aspects of Castilian cultural life. Two humanists who best exemplify the idea of continuity, for their link to the
earlier generation of humanists, but who also represent the radical transformation taking place toward the end of the century, are Alfonso de
Palencia and Antonio de Nebrija. Palencia was, in fact, the humanist who
dedicated his life, intellectually and politically, to promoting the cause
and the final ascension of the Catholic kings, while Nebrija was the one
who provided a new educational foundation for the state.

Palencia was the only Spanish humanist of the fifteenth century
whose major works were inspired by civic concerns. He attracted some
attention in the late 1800s but was subsequently ignored, for reasons too
extensive to go into here, until very recently. As we gather from his writings, he spent a few years while in his teens in Alonso de Cartagena's
household, where he was introduced to classical studies. At an undeter-
mined age, perhaps in his early twenties, he went to Italy. While in the
service of Cardinal Bessarion he studied with George of Trebizond, either
privately or at the *studium*.[102] It is curious that although Palencia was
associated with these Byzantine scholars for some years, I have never
encountered any references to his possible knowledge of Greek.

The humanist education he received in Italy was certainly a factor
in his being appointed royal chronicler and secretary of Latin letters to
Enrique IV, a post left vacant by the death of Juan de Mena. Within a
short time, however, he became a severe critic of the king and embraced
the cause of the king's younger brother, Alfonso, and after the latter's
death of Alfonso's sister Isabella and her future husband Ferdinand, later
known as the Catholic kings. His active and at times crucial participation
in these events is recorded in his four *Decades,* written in Latin, ironically
enough, in order to make them accessible to present and future generations.[103] Following the examples of Sallust and, above all, Tacitus, he was
guided by a sense of responsibility to examine critically and to record the
events of the day. In his zeal he did not spare kings, magnates, or
church dignitaries. He even subjected the actions of those on whom he

directly depended to close scrutiny, passed harsh judgment on their behavior, and often denounced their proclivities for baseness and in-
decency.

The same political and civic motives underlie his two allegorical
works: the *Batalla campal de los perros y los lobos* and *De perfectione
triumphi militaris*, better known as the *Tratado de la perfección del
triunfo militar*. The *Batalla campal*, originally written in Latin but now
lost, was meant, as Palencia explains, as a "tuning" exercise prior to his
beginning to write the history of Castile.[104] Clearly inspired by the *Batrachomyomachia* (*Battle of the Frogs and the Mice*, a Greek work of unknown date), he tells of the antagonism between the wolves and the dogs,
their pitched battle, and the defeat of both factions, visited equally by
death and destruction. This allegory is a synthetic fictionalization of a
world drawn from critical observations of people and events with which
Palencia was very familiar. For this reason the protagonists, in the garb
of animals, as well as the actions and deeds he relates, do not correspond
to particular persons and events of the time. All attempts at establishing
exact parallels with contemporary figures and situations have been un-
convincing.[105] This failure, however, does not prove that the work is
merely a writing exercise devoid of any political or social meaning. The
fact that behind the plot and the characters one constantly perceives cor-
respondences to real people and historical circumstances is indicative
that the work was intended as a social and political document. Although
the message is encoded in a fable, it did not conceal for those contemporaries who were most alert Palencia's critical understanding of current
events.

In the other allegorical work, *Tratado de la perfección del triunfo
militar*, which he himself translated into Spanish, Palencia pays tribute
to the humanist centers of Italy. The protagonist, Exercise, who symbolizes all the attributes of the leader as a perfect warrior, goes in search of
Triumph, who never visits Spain. An old lady, Experience, recommends
that he first find her daughter, Discretion, who is now living in Italy. He
finds Discretion in Tuscany and with her letter of recommendation he
sets out to find Gloridoneo, who is fighting in southern Italy (Gloridoneo
is presumably Alfonso V, the Magnanimous). Exercise joins Gloridoneo
in battle, and after he emerges triumphant he is unanimously acclaimed
and rewarded by being granted sole use of the name Exercise. The plot
is a pretext for dealing at length with various issues: outspoken criticism
of the nobility, the importance of the burghers, the type and quality of
education, the hygienic system, and social organization. Palencia reserves
his greatest admiration for thriving commercial centers such as Barcelona and, above all, Florence. But it is Florence of all cities that alone can

be called excellent, for it is a city with a thousand Catos. Echoing the observation of Aeneas Silvius Piccolomini about Salutati, Palencia reaffirms how by enlightened government the leaders of Florence often defeated tyrants without having to bear arms. Palencia's enthusiastic description of the type of education found in Discretion's house coincides, in many respects, with the account of Florentine scholarly and intellectual life around 1463 contained in a letter to Palencia by Donato Acciaiuoli, who was writing for Vespasiano da Bisticci.[106]

Without going into all of Palencia's works, one should mention at least his translations into Spanish of Josephus's *Judaic Wars* and Plutarch's *Lives,* as well as his studies in lexicography, namely, the *Opus synonimorum* and the *Universal vocabulario* in Latin and Spanish. Of humanist interest is a short treatise on the ancient names of Spain's topography in Roman times. With regard to his contribution to the spread of humanism, he can be credited with having introduced George of Trebizond to Spanish humanists. George of Trebizond's works, however, only gained a certain degree of popularity after Palencia's death—with the generation that was active in the early sixteenth century.[107] The translations he made of his own works deserve special attention, for they constitute a unique case in which the influence of Latin on the development of vernacular prose can be studied. His Spanish translations of works initially conceived and written in Latin can actually be considered variants of the original. For this reason they are rare examples of how the author-translator, in transferring the literary qualities of the original Latin to the vernacular, patterns the Spanish text after the classical model in the most natural fashion and without much interpretive interference.

Palencia's achievements in lexicography, philology, and historiography were surpassed by Antonio de Nebrija, who because of the quality of his scholarly production and his philological maturity is without doubt the most influential humanist of the last decades of the fifteenth and the beginning of the sixteenth centuries. At the same time that he brings to fruition all the ideals and aspirations of the fifteenth-century intellectual awakening, his effort to introduce the new learning in the official teaching of the university points to the beginning of a new period. In fact, with the exception of a brief interlude in Seville at the service of Bishop Fonseca, who had also protected Palencia, he spent the rest of his life at the universities of Salamanca and Alcalá.[108] Although he assigned to himself a revolutionary role, his success in integrating humanist methods and ideas into traditional university teaching was due in part to the fact that over the years the universities had been gradually assimilating the new humanist trends and in part also to Nebrija's willingness to compromise with the old establishment. For this reason, in Nebrija's academic writings all of his commentaries are made on ancient Christian authors such as Sedulius and Prudentius, or Persius who, though a pagan, was very popular with the church fathers for his *anima naturaliter christiana*.[109]

Nebrija, like Palencia, aspired to the post of royal historian, which he finally obtained after competing with other able humanists. But his *Rerum gestorum decades duae* are simply a Latin version of Fernando del Pulgar's chronicles, with a few substantial interpolations. His concerns were directed more to the formal aspect of writing history than to its content. He stressed, besides the accuracy of language and the style in which the accounts should be written, a certain personal involvement in reporting the events, and he even claimed that a foreigner could not correctly interpret the history of another nation.[110] His main contributions, however, did not lie in historical writings but in his arriving at a new concept of history that underlay all his scholarly activities. For Nebrija the restoration of a culture identical to that of classical times was impossible, but his own age, being a new and distinct epoch, could still be measured against the accomplishments of ancient civilizations from which it emerged. Although Nebrija set the premise for the *querelle* of ancients and moderns, it was a younger contemporary of his, Cristóbal de Villalón, who initiated in Spain—and perhaps in Europe—the debate that was to continue for the next three hundred years.[111]

In view of this conception of history, one can understand why Latin for Nebrija did not have a mere aesthetic appeal. It was, above all, the basic instrument for learning all other disciplines, because it was this language on which all religious, political, and juridical institutions of the present were based. For this reason he set out to reform, amidst much opposition, the teaching of Latin at the University of Salamanca. His *Introductiones latinae*, written in 1481, became the standard book for every university and secondary-school student learning Latin. While it retained the verse form in order to facilitate the beginner's memorization of rules and precepts, its aim was to impart a type of Latin that was closer to the classical model. The new grammar, which did away with all medieval manuals, was used well into the sixteenth century, for it enjoyed a virtual monopoly. Initially well received, it soon became the object of criticism and protest from younger humanists, who continuously rebelled against a grammar that they felt had outlived its usefulness.[112] Nebrija's concern for educational reform was multifaceted, as we see in his *De liberis educandi*. In this treatise he deals with many pedagogical issues and methods of teaching, some of which he had encountered at Bologna, where he had studied for almost ten years.[113] Nebrija's scholarly activities, such as his studies on the pronunciation of Greek and his contribution to the *Biblia políglota complutense*, challenged many traditional assumptions.[114] And while he was truly innovative in linguistic studies and in history, he showed little interest in the other disciplines of the *studia humanitatis*. Contrary to Italian humanists, he identified the "barbarians" of the university only with teachers of grammar, jurists, and anyone else who did not have a good grasp of Latin, but he never applied this epithet to theologians and teachers of dialectics.

In conformity with the vernacular component inherent in Spanish humanism since its inception, Nebrija applied his philological expertise to vernacular Spanish. In 1492, after completing a Latin–Spanish dictionary, he wrote the *Arte de la gramática castellana*, long before any other European humanist wrote a grammar of his own vernacular language. Without going into the merits of this pioneer work, I should emphasize that in Nebrija's mind the Castilian language had acquired sufficient importance to be placed alongside classical languages. As he made clear in the introduction, the value of this grammar was inextricably tied to the political and cultural interests of the newly formed Spanish nation. Implicit in the idea of the maturity of the Spanish language is the concomitant growth of the nation's power. By comparing the evolution of a nation and of its language to the organic development of the human being, he was affirming that politics and culture are inseparable, for they grow and die together.[115] This natural law, which explains the rise and the fatal decline of past empires and civilizations, was for Spain the harbinger of good news. Having observed from the course of history that great empires had been gradually moving from east to west, Nebrija was certain that it was his country's turn to rule over many people. For this reason he prepared a grammar that would serve the new civilization the Spanish empire would produce.

Unbeknownst to Nebrija when he was making these predictions in 1492, the new generation of humanists formed during the reign of the Catholic kings would find themselves the representatives of a national culture that was indissolubly bound to the greatest empire ever known, extending from the Old World to the New. The new breed of humanists was in general less nationalistic and had an outlook that was decidedly more international. The largely Flemish court of Charles of Habsburg, who ascended the throne in 1516, brought with it views and ideas associated with the Dutch humanist Erasmus. His philological studies and reformist endeavors were enthusiastically received by a minority of scholars placed in positions of political and religious power. The appeal of Erasmus's thinking among Spaniards was certainly widespread and lasting, but his influence in Spain was not as total as most modern critics and historians, who make sixteenth-century Spanish culture revolve around this learned humanist, would have us believe.[116]

Before the first occurrence of the word *humanista* was to be recorded in 1552, the impact of humanism, as it manifested itself in Spain, had been felt in all aspects of the cultural life.[117] The voices of humanists could be heard on all sides of the many controversies of the time: from the debate on the treatment of Indians in the New World to historical, political, and even religious issues.[118] There were staunch defenders of Erasmus as well as strong opponents. Some followed Aristotle and others Plato, while still others tried to reconcile the two. There were Ciceronians and anti-Ciceronians, those who upheld the superiority of Latin and those who pointed to the excellence of the vernacular. By the end of the sixteenth century, while the role of the humanist had remained unchanged, the term *humanista* had become so popular that treatises had to be written to distinguish the real from the false *humanista*.[119]

NOTES

1. When speaking of Spain, as in the title, I mean exclusively those regions of the Iberian peninsula that comprised the kingdom of Castile. For the development of Renaissance humanism in Aragon and Catalonia, see J. Rubió i Balaguer, *La cultura catalana del Renaixement a la Decadéncia* (Barcelona, 1964); and idem, "Humanisme i Renaixement," *VIII Congreso de historia de la Corona de Aragón V*, 3.2 (Valencia, 1973), 9–36.

2. This view was popularized in Spain during the early decades of the nineteenth century by F. Bouterwek, *Historia de la literatura española*, trans. J. Gómez de la Cortina and N. Hugalde de Mollineda (Madrid, 1829); S. de Sismondi, *Historia de la literatura española*, trans. L. de Figueroa and J. Amador de los Ríos (Seville, 1841); and G. Ticknor, *Historia de la literatura castellana*, trans. P. de Gayangos and E. de Vedia, 4 vols. (Madrid, 1851–56).

3. The concept of humanism made its appearance relatively late in European historiographic thought. It was first discussed by Karl Hagen and Georg Voigt around 1850 and at a somewhat later date in Spain by M. Menéndez Pelayo (1875). In the thirty years that followed, Menéndez Pelayo, Fabié, Morel-Fatio, and Bonilla San Martín uncovered and published some fifteenth-century texts related to this movement, despite the fact that they did not seem to have a clear idea of what humanism was. In 1905, Mario Schiff's *La bibliothèque du marquis de Santillane* (Paris) brought attention to the uniqueness of Iñigo López de Mendoza's private collection, one of the rarest examples in all Europe of an early Quattrocento humanist library. However, with the early death of Mario Schiff and the gradual disappearance of the small group of critics and historians mentioned above, interest in fifteenth-century letters and ideas began to decline. In the period between the wars the only monograph to provide some new information on this

subject was an extended review of Schiff's book, published by A. Farinelli in his *Spagna e Italia*, 2 vols. (Turin, 1929). When A. Soria published *Los humanistas de la corte de Alfonso el Magnánimo (según los epistolarios)* (Granada, 1956), his book passed virtually unnoticed, despite a valuable introduction based on the interpretations of humanism current at that time. Twenty years later, in the colloquium on Spanish humanism organized at Tours in 1976, only a few papers dealt with humanism proper. The papers of the colloquium were later published in *L'humanisme dans les lettres espagnoles*, ed. A. Redondo (Paris, 1979). O. Di Camillo, *El humanismo castellano del siglo XV* (Valencia, 1976), which is a revised and expanded version of my doctoral dissertation (1972), focuses on the emergence and development of Castilian humanism. H. Nader, in *The Mendoza Family in the Spanish Renaissance, 1350–1550* (New Brunswick, NJ, 1979), oddly enough pays hardly any attention to humanists or humanist works of the period. She argues that the Renaissance in Castile came about as a result of the lucky pairing of two powerful noble families, the Ayalas and the Mendozas, in the second half of the fourteenth century, and that it continued uninterruptedly for the next two hundred years, or as long as the family tradition lasted. The Renaissance and this family tradition, which were exclusively and inextricably bound together, flourished for about a century, but began to decline in the following years until both were destroyed by the rising culture of the *letrados*. Her contention that a historical phenomenon of such magnitude and complexity as the Renaissance can be made to depend on the alleged tradition of a single family is highly questionable. But inaccuracies and undocumented assertions make her study unreliable anyway.

4. A. Bonilla y San Martín, "Erasmo en España," *Revue hispanique* 17 (1907): 379–548.

5. M. Menéndez Pelayo, *Poetas de la corte de Don Juan II* (Madrid, 1943).

6. M. R. Lida de Malkiel, *Juan de Mena, poeta del prerenacimiento español* (Mexico, 1950).

7. For the latest investigations on various aspects of fifteenth-century Spain, see the special issue of *Anuario de estudios medievales* 7 (1970–71): *La investigación de la historia hispánica del siglo XV: problemas y cuestiones*. See also the comprehensive and up-to-date study of A. MacKay, *Spain in the Middle Ages: From Frontier to Empire, 1000–1500* (New York, 1977), chaps. 6–9. See, as well, *Historia de España*, ed. M. Tuñón de Lara, vol. 4, *Feudalismo y consolidación de los pueblos hispánicos (siglos XI–XV)*; vol. 5, *La frustración de un imperio (1476–1714)* (Madrid, 1982). For recent studies on fifteenth-century authors not always specifically related to humanism, see R. H. Trame, *Rodrigo Sánchez de Arévalo, 1404–1470: Spanish Diplomat and Champion of the Papacy* (Washington, DC, 1958); J. M. Laboa, *Rodrigo Sánchez de Arévalo, Alcaide de Sant'Angelo* (Madrid, 1973); D. Cabanelas, *Juan de Segovia y el problema islámico* (Madrid, 1952); J. González, *El maestro Juan de Segovia y su biblioteca* (Madrid, 1954); K. Kohut, *Las teorías literarias en España y Portugal durante*

los siglos XV y XVI (Madrid, 1973); idem, "Der Beitrag der Theologie zum Literaturbegriff in der Zeit Juans II. von Kastilien," *Romanische Forschungen* 89 (1977): 183–226; idem, "El humanismo castellano del siglo XV. Replanteamiento de la problemática," *Actas del séptimo congreso de la Asociación de Hispanistas,* ed. G. Bellini, 2 vols. (Rome, 1982), 2:639–47; S. González-Quevedo Alonso, ed., *"Oracional" de Alonso de Cartagena* (Valencia and Chapel Hill, 1983); idem, "Alonso de Cartagena, una expresion de su tiempo," *Crítica hispánica* 1 (1982): 1–20; E. F. Jacob, *Essays in Later Medieval History* (Manchester, 1968), chap. 6; C. Vasoli, "Il *De pace fidei* di Niccolò da Cusa," in *Studi sulla cultura del Rinascimento* (Manduria, 1968), 122–79; V. Beltrán de Heredia, *Cartulario de la Universidad de Salamanca,* 3 vols. (Salamanca, 1970), vol. 1; *Pedro Martínez de Osma: Homenaje en el V centenario de su muerte* (Soria, 1980); C. Romero de Lecea, *Antecedentes de la imprenta y circunstancias que favorecieron su introducción en España* (Madrid, 1972); R. Lida de Malkiel, *La tradición clásica en España* (Barcelona, 1975). On Villena, see P. M. Cátedra, "Enrique de Villena y algunos humanistas," *Academia literaria Renacentista* 3 (1983): 187–203; R. G. Keightley, "Alfonso de Madrigal and the *Chronici Canones," Journal of Medieval and Renaissance Studies* 7 (1977): 225–48. On Giacomo Publicio, a Spanish humanist who changed his name to an Italianate form and who taught in many cities of central Europe, see A. Seppilli, "In margine al catalogo dei codici petrarcheschi per la Germania occidentale," in *Il Petrarca ad Arquà,* ed. G. Billanovich and G. Frasso (Padua, 1975), 293–314; idem, "Note biografiche sui petrarchisti Giacomo Publicio e Guiniforte Barzizza e sull'umanista valenziano Giovanni Serra," in *Petrarca 1304–1374. Beiträge zu Werk und Wirkung,* ed. F. Schalk (Frankfurt, 1975), 270–86.

8. Although most of these works can be found in various catalogs and inventories of public and private libraries and archives, there are still others that appear from time to time. See, for example, P. O. Kristeller, "The Humanist Bartolomeo Facio and His Unknown Correspondence," in *From the Renaissance to the Counter-Reformation: Essays in Honor of Garrett Mattingly,* ed. C. H. Carter (New York, 1965), 55–74. A general catalog with accurate descriptions of the extant Italian humanist works in Spain is being prepared by P. O. Kristeller.

9. P. O. Kristeller, "The European Diffusion of Italian Humanism," *Italica* 39 (1962): 1–20, reprinted in *Renaissance Thought II: Papers on Humanism and the Arts* (New York, 1965), 69–88.

10. See Schiff, *Bibliothèque du marquis de Santillane,* 449–59. See also J. N. H. Lawrance, "Nuño de Guzmán and Early Spanish Humanism: Some Reconsiderations," *Medium aevum* 51 (1982): 55–85.

11. Juan de Lucena's work has been edited by A. Paz y Mélia, *Opúsculos literarios* (Madrid, 1892), 105–208; by G. M. Bertini, *Testi spagnoli del secolo XV* (Turin, 1950), 97–182; and by A. M. Arancón, *Antologia de humanistas españoles* (Madrid, 1980), 171–239. While Bertini's text is the most accurate, it is not the critical edition that Juan de Lucena's work deserves.

12. We know for certain that Alfonso de Cartagena and Alfonso de Palencia translated into Spanish some of their works written in Latin.

13. M. Andrés, "Las facultades de teología españolas hasta 1575: Cátedras diversas," *Anthologica annua* (1972): 123–78.

14. C. M. Ajo y Sainz de Zuñiga, *Historia de las universidades hispánicas*, 2 vols. (Madrid, 1957), 1:220.

15. P. O. Kristeller, *Renaissance Thought and Its Sources*, ed. M. Mooney (New York, 1979), 238ff.

16. Ibid., 244; see also other writings by the same author. See, as well, Di Camillo, *El humanismo castellano*, 39–40, note.

17. R. B. Tate, *Ensayos sobre la historiografía peninsular del siglo XV*, trans. J. Díaz (Madrid, 1970), 280–96. This book, the best on the subject to date, is the translation of a collection of essays written in English that appeared in various journals. See also R. B. Tate, "Alfonso de Palencia y los preceptos de la historiografía," *Academia literaria renacentista* 3 (1983): 37–64.

18. J. L. Bermejo Cabrero, "Orígenes del oficio de cronista real," *Hispania* 145 (1980): 395–409; idem, "Los primeros secretarios de los reyes," *Anuario de historia del derecho español* 49 (1979): 187–286.

19. Di Camillo, *El humanismo castellano*, 90ff.

20. The first professor of poetry was Nicolao Antonio, followed in 1473 by another Italian, Pomponio of Mantua, perhaps a nickname for his licentious life, fashioned after Pomponio Leto's bad reputation in Spain. See F. G. Olmedo, *Nebrija en Salamanca* (Madrid, 1944), 41–42; Beltrán de Heredia, *Cartulario*, 2:50.

21. J. A. Maravall, *Antiguos y modernos* (Madrid, 1966), chap. 5, and reiterated in "La diversificación de modelos del Renacimiento: Renacimiento francés y Renacimiento español," *Cuadernos hispano-americanos* 390 (1980): 551–614; and in "El prerenacimiento del siglo XV," *Academia literaria renacentista* 3 (1983): 17–36. See also F. Rico, *Nebrija frente a los bárbaros* (Salamanca, 1978).

22. V. Beltrán de Heredia, *Bulario de la Universidad de Salamanca*, 3 vols. (Salamanca, 1966), 1:130ff.

23. J. A. Maravall, "Los *hombres de saber* o letrados y la formación de su conciencia estamental," *Revista de estudios políticos* 70 (1953), reprinted in *Estudios de historia del pensamiento español* (Madrid, 1967), 345–80; S. de Moxó, "La elevación de los *letrados* en la sociedad estamental del siglo XIV," in *XII semana de estudios medievales* (Pamplona, 1976), 183–215.

24. There are no studies on the intellectual activities of the Spanish representatives at the Council of Constance and on their possible contacts with foreign humanists. Although our knowledge of those who attended the Councils of Basel and Ferrara–Florence is somewhat better, it is far from being extensive. For the sketchy introduction to the participants of the councils, see Beltrán de Heredia, *Cartulario*, 1:250–85, 314–409; M. Avilés, "La teología española en el siglo XV," in *Historia de la teología española* (Madrid, 1983), 1:495–577. As an example of the type of friendship that developed between two participants, Francesco Pizolpasso and Juan de Cervantes, see

T. Foffano, "La costruzione di Castiglione Olona in un opuscolo inedito di Francesco Pizolpasso," *Italia medioevale e umanistica* 3 (1960): 153–87.

25. Beltrán de Heredia, *Bulario*, 1:63ff.

26. Examples of Spaniards who were promoted to high posts are Rodrigo Sánchez de Arévalo, Juan de Torquemada, Juan de Carvajal, and Fernando de Córdoba, among many others.

27. Beltrán de Heredia, *Bulario*, 1:130.

28. That the Spanish origin of Seneca was a major factor in contributing to his revival in the otherwise Aristotelian fifteenth century can be seen in K. A. Bluher, *Seneca in Spanien. Untersuchungen zur Geschichte der Seneca-Rezeption in Spanien vom 13. bis 17. Jahrhundert* (Munich, 1969), Spanish trans. revised and expanded, *Séneca en España*, trans. J. Conde (Madrid, 1983). On Aristotle's influence, see A. R. D. Pagden, "The Diffusion of Aristotle's Moral Philosophy in Spain, ca. 1400–ca. 1600," *Traditio* 31 (1975): 287–313; and J. Soudek, "Leonardo Bruni and His Public," *Studies in Medieval and Renaissance History* 5 (1968): 49–136.

29. The preferred use of the vernacular among Spanish students, professors, and even scholars, taken as a disparaging trait of Spaniards in general, has its origin in the university ambience at the end of the fifteenth century. It probably started with the malicious criticism of Italian humanists who were then teaching or living in Spain and who had a low opinion of Spanish universities. The use of Latin or vernacular became an ideological issue in the following century. See L. Giles Fernandez, "El humanismo español del siglo XVI," *Estudios clásicos* 51 (1966): 211–97; idem, *Panorama social del humanismo español (1500–1800)* (Madrid, 1981), 3–116, 231–95.

30. Although no study has been made that would analyze the language and style of this generation, there is evidence that these young graduates do differ in their way of expressing themselves from that of earlier generations. For the noticeable change in composing poetry, the only area that has received some attention, see R. Lapesa, *La obra literaria del marqués de Santillana* (Madrid, 1957), 32ff.

31. Only the first book of *De inventione* translated by Cartagena has survived. It has been edited by R. Mascagna, *La rethórica de M. Tullio Cicerón* (Naples, 1969). Of Villena's translation there are no extant manuscripts.

32. L. Serrano, *Los conversos Don Pablo de Santa María y Don Alfonso de Cartagena* (Madrid, 1942), 246ff.; A. M. Salazar, "El impacto humanístico de las misiones diplomáticas de Alonso de Cartagena en la Corte de Portugal entre medioevo y renacimiento (1421–31)," in *Medieval Studies Presented to Rita Hamilton*, ed. A. Deyermond (London, 1976), 215–26.

33. Biblioteca del cabildo de la Catedral de Burgo de Osma, MS 117 (also on microfilm in the Archivo Histórico Nacional, 130).

34. Alonso de Cartagena, "Prólogo en la translación," *La rethórica*, 27–29.

35. A logical hypothesis is that Cartagena had foremost in his mind the Castilian reader who, like Juan Alfonso de Zamora, would greatly benefit from this timely translation.

36. That these minor works dealt with these *artes* can be gathered by Villena's glosses on his translation of the *Divine Comedy*, as quoted by D. C. Carr in his introduction to Don Enrique de Villena, *Tratado de la consolación* (Madrid, 1976), xlix, note.

37. Don Enrique de Villena, *Arte de Trovar*, ed. F. J. Sánchez Cantón (Madrid, 1923).

38. Don Enrique de Villena, *La traducción de la Divina Comedia atribuida a D. Enrique de Aragón: Estudio y edición del "Inferno,"* ed. J. A. Pascual Rodríguez (Salamanca, 1974); idem, *La primera versión castellana de la "Eneida" de Virgilio*, ed. and trans. R. Santiago Lacuesta (Madrid, 1979).

39. Schiff, *La bibliothèque*, 275–303.

40. The only translations of note are those of Pero López de Ayala: Boccaccio's *De casibus*, left unfinished and completed much later by Alonso de Cartagena; and Livy's *Decades* translated from the French version of Pierre Berçuire.

41. A good example would be his translation of the *Aeneid*. See *La primera versión*.

42. See his "Introduccion" to *La rethórica*, 29–34.

43. Ibid., 34.

44. Ibid., 33.

45. Ibid., 31. See A. de Petris, "Le teorie umanistiche del tradurre e l'*Apologeticus* di Giannozzo Manetti," *Bibliothèque d'humanisme et Renaissance* 37 (1975): 15–32.

46. The letter is quoted by R. Sabbadini, *Storia e critica di alcuni testi latini* (Padua, 2d ed. 1971), 235; and in V. Zaccaria, "Pier Candido Decembrio e Leonardo Bruni," *Studi medievali* 3d ser. 2 (1967): 508.

47. For studies that have dealt with one aspect or another of the polemic, see G. Gentile, *Storia della filosofia italiana fino a Lorenzo Valla* (Florence, 2d ed. 1962), 308–23; A. Birkenmaier, "Der Streit des Alonso von Cartagena mit Leonardo Bruni Aretino," in *Vermischte Untersuchungen zur Geschichte der mittelalterlichen Philosophie* (Muenster, 1922), 129–210, in which he edits Cartagena's critical tract and Bruni's responses, together with a letter of Poggio and one of Bruni; G. Saitta, *Il pensiero italiano nell'umanesimo e nel rinascimento*, 3 vols. (Florence, 2d ed., 1961), 1:172ff.; E. Franceschini, "Leonardo Bruni e il 'vetus interpres' dell'*Etica a Nicomaco*," in *Medioevo e Rinascimento: Studi in onore di Bruno Nardi*, 2 vols. (Florence, 1955), 1:299–319; F. Gaeta, *Lorenzo Valla: Filologia e storia nell'umanesimo italiano* (Naples, 1955); R. Fubini, "Tra umanesimo e concili: Note aggiunte a una publicazione recente su Francesco Pizolpasso (1370–1443)," *Studi medievali* 3d ser. 1 (1966): 322–70; V. Zaccaria, "Pier Candido Decembrio traduttore della "Republica" di Platone," *Italia medioevale e umanistica* 2 (1959): 179–206; J. E. Seigel, *Rhetoric and Philosophy in Renaissance Humanism* (Princeton, 1968), 121–33; Di Camillo, *El humanismo castellano*, 203–26.

48. "Don Alfonso always called himself Doctor of Law from the University of

Salamanca" (Serrano, *Los conversos*, 122). For a different view, see Kohut, "Der Beitrag der Theologie."

49. See M. Penna, *Prosistas castellanos del siglo XV* (Madrid, 1959), xxxvii–lxx; Serrano, *Los conversos*, 119–83.

50. Di Camillo, *El humanismo castellano*, chap. 5.

51. He repeats this admiration at the beginning of his critical tract, in "Der Streit des Alonso," 163.

52. See Seigel, *Rhetoric and Philosophy*, 121ff.

53. In Birkenmaier, "Der Streit des Alonso," 173.

54. Ibid., 166.

55. Ibid., 167.

56. Ibid., 169ff., 180ff.

57. Ibid., 179ff.

58. Ibid., 175.

59. Bruni's rebuttal is written in the form of a letter which he sent to Francesco Pizolpasso. See ibid., 202.

60. Ibid., 180ff.

61. The letters exchanged among these scholars are discussed and documented in Fubini, "Tra umanesimo e concili"; Zaccaria, "Pier Candido Decembrio e Leonardo Bruni," 506–14; and Birkenmaier, "Der Streit des Alonso."

62. V. Zaccaria, "Sulle opere di Pier Candido Decembrio," *Rinascimento* 7 (1956): 58–60. The work was dedicated to Humphrey, Duke of Gloucester.

63. The letter is reproduced in V. Zaccaria, "Pier Candido Decembrio traduttore," 204.

64. The letter from Poggio to Bruni is reproduced by Birkenmaier, "Der Streit des Alonso," 193; Poggio's other letter to Cartagena is found in Soria, *Los humanistas*, 223–24 (3.11.9, pp. 66–67 in Tonelli's edition of Poggio's works).

65. The letter is reproduced by Birkenmaier, "Der Streit des Alonso," 209–10; and in Soria, *Los humanistas*, 120–21 (from Mehus, 9.4, pp. 155–60).

66. Schiff, *La bibliothèque*. For a revised assessment of this library's holdings, see M. Penna, *Exposición de la biblioteca de los Mendoza del Infantado* (Madrid, 1958). Of all known fifteenth-century private libraries, there is no doubt that the one assembled by the marquis of Santillana contains the greatest number of classical and humanist texts. The only other library of similar importance for humanism is that of the cathedral of Burgo de Osma, whose holdings have not been studied with regard to their acquisition and provenance. For a comparison with other libraries, see the reconstruction of the library founded by Pedro Fernández de Velasco, Count of Haro, in A. Paz y Mélia, "Biblioteca fundada por el conde de Haro," *Revista de archivos bibliotecas y museos* 1 (1897): 18–24, 60–66, 156–63, 225–62; 4 (1900): 335–45, 661–67; 6 (1902): 198–208, 372–82; 7 (1902): 51–55; N. López Martínez, "La biblioteca de D. Luis de Acuña en 1496," *Hispania* 78 (1960): 81–110; M. C. Quintanilla Raso and M. A. Ladero Quesada, "Biblioteca de la alta nobleza castellana en el siglo XV," in *Livre et lecture en Espagne et en France sous l'ancien régime* (Paris,

1981), 47–59, with bibliographical references to other studies on libraries; I. Beceiro, "La biblioteca del conde de Benavente a mediados del siglo XV y su relación con las mentaliades y usos nobiliarios de la época," *En la España Medieval: III. Estudios en memoria del Profesor D. Salvador de Moxó,* ed. M. A. Ladero Quesada, 2 vols. (Madrid, 1982), 1. 135–45.

67. In the letter to his son, Pero González de Mendoza, asking him to translate into Spanish Decembrio's version of the *Iliad,* he is interested in the Trojan war as the most ancient and largest military conflict that ever took place. See *Obras de Don Iñigo López de Mendoza,* ed. J. Amador de los Riós (Madrid, 1852), 481–82. A similar ambiguity is shown in his concept of knighthood and ancient soldiers when he asks Alonso de Cartagena to clarify certain ideas he had read in Bruni's *De militia;* see the letter to Cartagena and the response to Santillana in Penna, *Prosistas castellanos,* 235–45.

68. See his *Prohemio e carta quel marqués de Santillana enbio al condestable de Portugal con las obras suyas,* in *Marqués de Santillana: Prose and Verse,* ed. and trans. T. B. Trend (London, 1940), 3–18.

69. For Gómez Manrique's eulogy for Santillana, see *Obras de Don Iñigo López de Mendoza,* clii ff.

70. Arms versus letters and other variations of this *topos* have been taken by many critics as a constant in Spanish social life. Based on the proposition that the knightly class shunned learning and any type of professional or compensatory work, this assumption has been made to explain various features of Spanish culture. It originated with A. Castro in *El pensamiento de Cervantes* (Madrid, 1925), and since then it has been widely accepted in spite of occasional objections. Yet Diego de Valera, a fifteenth-century author widely read at home and abroad, states that the Spanish nobility, contrary to that of other nations, feels no shame in undertaking commercial activities or in using offices inappropriate to its rank (see his *Espejo de verdadera nobleza,* in Penna, *Prosistas castellanos,* 107). The issue of arms versus letters has even been made a major factor in historians' understanding of Castilian humanism: see P. E. Russell, "Arms Versus Letters: Towards a Definition of Spanish Fifteenth-Century Humanism," in *Aspects of the Renaissance: A Symposium,* ed. A. R. Lewis (Austin, TX, 1967), 47–58; now translated and expanded in his *Temas de la "Celestina" y otros estudios* (Barcelona, 1978), 207–39. But since references to this *topos* do not necessarily imply a conflict between arms and letters, it seems that the issue is not so much one of arms versus letters but rather of arms and letters, as a historian of law has aptly perceived: "Nor should we forget that the idea of an equilibrium of *arma et leges,* to which Justinian referred in the proems to the *Institutes* and the *Code,* was transformed by Renaissance artists into the related ideal of *arma et litterae* and was reflected by emblematic art as well as by literary disputes, e.g., between *militia* and *jurisprudentia* or *Ars* and *Mars*" (E. Kantorowicz, "The Sovereignty of the Artist," in *Selected Studies* [Locust Valley, NY, 1965], 352–65). The case in Spain was precisely one of equilibrium, with a nobility becoming more involved in learning and studies, and the jurists, the *letrados,* assuming for the first time the role of

defenders of society, a role that had been until then the prerogative of the warrior class. These *letrados*, in fact, are called by Cartagena "knights of the unharmed knighthood" (*caballeros de la caballería desarmada*), "Respuesta del muy noble y sabio obispo de Burgos al marqués de Santillana," in Penna, *Prosistas castellanos*, 239.

71. Diego de Burgos, *Triunfo del marqués*, in Schiff, *La bibliothèque*, 461.

72. Ibid., 462.

73. Pero Díaz de Toledo, *Diálogo e razonamiento en la muerte del marqués de Santillana*, in *Opúsculos literarios*, 249.

74. Leonardo Bruni, *Rerum suo tempore gestarum commentarius*, in *Rerum Italicarum Scriptores*, 19.3, ed. C. di Pietro (Bologna, 1926), 431, quoted in W. K. Ferguson, *The Renaissance in Historical Thought* (Cambridge, MA, 1948), 22.

75. Schiff, *La bibliothèque*, 356.

76. Ibid., 461.

77. This tendency seems to prevail even in studies that deal with sixteenth-century humanists whose intellectual, ideological, and literary concerns are significantly distinct.

78. For a more detailed analysis of the semantic change in this word throughout the fifteenth century, see Di Camillo, *El humanismo castellano*, 176–93.

79. See, among others, Alonso de Cartagena, *Discurso sobre la preheminencia*, in Penna, *Prosistas castellanos*, 207; also Diego de Valera, *Espejo de verdadera nobleza*, ibid., 101, a work translated into French at the end of the fifteenth century.

80. Vespasiano da Bisticci, *Le vite*, ed. A. Greco, 2 vols. (Florence, 1970–74), 1:435–41.

81. In his recent study, "Nuño de Guzmán and Early Spanish Humanism," Lawrance has somewhat clarified the matrimonial relationship of Nuño de Guzmán's parents, but much more remains to be done to explain the many discrepancies in Nuño's life and travels as they are related by Vespasiano and by Manetti in the *Apologia* and in the prologue to *De illustribus longaevis*, such as the time he spent in Florence and in Italy sufficient to learn Italian, the real intention behind the three works written by Manetti, and the real possibility that one of his trips to Florence may have been fictionalized.

82. The *Apologia Nunnii* is in the Vatican Library, Pal. Lat. 1601, fols. 94–134v. In my study, *El humanismo castellano*, 127, note, I mistook the *Laudatio Dominae Agnetis* for the *Apologia Nunnii*. The error was due to various factors, primarily the impossibility of my seeing the actual manuscript.

83. Vespasiano da Bisticci, *Le vite*, 1:438. The enigmatic words used by Vespasiano may refer to legitimizing his parents' marriage, but, according to Vespasiano, whatever dispensation Nuño may have been looking for, he certainly did not obtain it.

84. Ibid., 436. The *Laudatio Dominae Agnetis* is in the Vatican Library, Pal. Lat. 1606. For additional information concerning Nuño de Guzmán's

mother, see M. A. Ladero Quesada, "Aristocratie et régime seigneurial dans l'Andalousie du XVe siècle," *Annales: Économies, Sociétés, Civilisations* 6 (1983): 1362.

85. Giannozzo Manetti, *Vitae Socratis et Senecae*, ed. A. de Petris (Florence, 1979).

86. A significant contribution on Decembrio's translation has been made by A. Bravo García, "Sobre las traducciones de Plutarco y de Quinto Curcio Rufo hechas por Pier Candido Decembrio y su fortuna en España," *Cuadernos de filología clásica* 12 (1977): 143–85.

87. *La oracion de miçer Ganoço Manety*, in Schiff, *La bibliothèque*, 364–65.

88. P. E. Russell and A. R. D. Pagden, "Nueva luz sobre una versión española cuatrocentista de la *Etica a Nicomaco:* Bodleian Library MS Span. D.1," in *Homenaje a Guillermo Guastavino* (Madrid, 1974), 125–46. There is a strong reason for attributing the work to Nuño de Guzmán, since the translator mentions that he is relying on an Italian translation made at his request. In fact, an Italian version of Bruni's *Ethics*, commissioned by Nuño de Guzmán, does exist, and is now at the Yale University Library, MS 151. Nevertheless, a claim can be made for Palencia, for he also was in Seville in 1467 and was better prepared than anyone else to translate without the aid of a rough draft. In explaining the procedure of his work, the translator tells us that he relied on a Catalan version and on an Italian translation. What merits consideration is that Palencia knew Italian well, for he had studied and lived in Italy longer than Nuño. Moreover, he did translate an Italian devotional work, whereas we know for certain that Nuño translated only an oration. While there is no connection between Nuño and Catalonia, we know that Palencia had traveled extensively in that region and had strong sympathies for the Aragonese kings. But a reason that carries even more weight is the interest that Palencia showed in the ongoing controversies about the translations of Aristotle into Latin. In a letter written from Rome and dated 1465 (now in the Biblioteca Nacional, Madrid, MS 7446, fols. 2642–2672), he asks his old teacher George of Trebizond for his opinion about which translation then available was closer to the Greek text. Trebizond's answer is in the Biblioteca Riccardiana, MS 907, fols. 107r–109v. According to Russell and Pagden, the translator's style is typical of a humanist, and Palencia would fit this description much better than Nuño de Guzmán, who probably had a passable or poor knowledge of Latin. Finally, since some manuscripts attribute the translation to Alonso de Cartagena, it is more probable that Palencia may have been confused with Cartagena, since he had the same first name. Such a confusion in attributing a work to a better-known author who bears the same first name as a less familiar writer has also happened in the case of *La poliscena*, a humanist comedy attributed to Leonardo Bruni, when it was actually by Leonardo della Serrata: see C. Nonni, "Contributi allo studio della commedia umanistica 'La Poliscena,'" *Arcadia: Accademia letteraria italiana* 6 (1975–76):393–451.

89. See E. J. Webber, "A Spanish Linguistic Treatise of the Fifteenth Century," *Romance Philology* 16 (1962): 32–40.

90. A. Bonilla y San Martín, *Fernando de Córdoba (1425?–1486?) y los orígenes del Renacimiento filosófico en España: Episodio de la historia de la lógica* (Madrid, 1911).

91. Di Camillo, *El humanismo castellano*, 234ff.

92. Bonilla y San Martín, *Fernando de Córdoba*, 55.

93. For a discussion of the controversy between Valla and Poggio, see S. Camporeale, *L. Valla, Umanesimo e teologia* (Florence, 1972), 311–403, esp. 339.

94. Ibid., 336.

95. Juan de Lucena, *De vita beata*, in *Testi spagnoli del secolo XV*, 98.

96. See C. Trinkaus, *In Our Image and Likeness: Humanity and Divinity in Italian Humanist Thought*, 2 vols. (Chicago, 1970), 1:200–29; and Bartolomeo Facio, *Invectiva in Laurentium Vallam*, ed. E. I. Rao (Naples, 1978).

97. On the accusation of being a "Sadducee," a term equivalent to "Epicurean," see Di Camillo, *El humanismo castellano*, 249–50; for the same use of the word, see also Valla, *De vero bono*, as quoted in M. Fois, *Il pensiero cristiano di Lorenzo Valla nel cuadro storico-culturale del suo ambiente* (Rome, 1969), 143, note. The trend of associating social and political revolt with religious transgressions was first begun by Alonso de Cartagena in his *Defensorium unitatis christianae*, ed. P. M. Alonso (Madrid, 1943). After a lengthy analysis, his conclusion was that the person who caused civil unrest was not only preventing his fellow citizens from achieving their ultimate goal—which for a Christian is his spiritual salvation—but was also going against the *corpus mysticum* of a Christian society. How these ideas contributed to the establishment of the Inquisition in Spain has not been studied. On the Inquisition, see E. Benito Ruano, *Los orígenes del problema converso* (Barcelona, 1976); H. Kamen, *La inquisición española*, trans. E. Obregón (Madrid, 1965); and B. Bennassar, et al., *Inquisición española: Poder político y control social*, trans. J. Alfaya (Barcelona, 1981).

98. In *De vita beata*, 132–35, Lucena intentionally interpolates a passage that identifies Cartagena as a converso in order to show the pride and unequivocal Christian beliefs of the newly converted.

99. Alfonso Ortiz, *Liber dialogorum*, was first described by G. M. Bertini in "Un diálogo humanístico sobre la educación del principe Don Juan," in *Fernando el Católico y la cultura de su tiempo* (Zaragoza, 1961), 37–62. The only extant copy is in the Library of the Cathedral of Burgo de Osma, MS 40.

100. Alfonso Ortiz, *Diálogo sobre la educación del principe Don Juan, hijo de los reyes católicos*, trans. G. M. Bertini (Madrid, 1983). With this edition one more humanist educational treatise has been added to the few written in Spain during the fifteenth century. See A. Keniston, "A Fifteenth-Century Treatise on Education by Bishop Rodericus Zamorensis," *Bulletin hispanique* 32 (1930): 193–217, who edits Rodrigo Sánchez de Arévalo's *De arte, disciplina et modo alendi et erudiendi filios, pueros et juvenes;* idem, "Notes on the *De liberis educandis* of Antonio de Nebrija," *Homenaje a*

R. Menéndez Pidal, 3 vols. (Madrid, 1925), 3:126–41; J. López de Toro, "El primer tratado de pedagogía en España (1453)," *Boletín de la Universidad de Granada* 5 (1933): 259–75; 6 (1934): 153–71; 7 (1935): 195–218, compares Arévalo's treatise with Antonio de Nebrija's *De liberis educandis*. See Alonso de Cartagena, *Un tratado de Alonso de Cartagena sobre la educación y los estudios literarios*, ed. J. N. H. Lawrance (Barcelona, 1979), a letter most probably written by Cartagena setting forth general guidelines for the education of a large sector of the nobility uninterested in the *studia humanitatis*.

101. A translation from Latin of the first three decades has been published as *Cronica de Enriqúe IV* in *Biblioteca de autores españoles*, 3 vols. (Madrid, 1973–75), 1:155. There is an urgent need to study the numerous translations of classical and humanist texts and to inquire into the scholarly activities of people like Martín de Ávila, Vasco Ramirez de Guzmán, and Juan de Segura, the translators of Bruni, Bessarion, and other humanist authors. See now P. E. Russell, *Traducciones y traductores en la península ibérica* (Bellaterra, 1985).

102. For Palencia's association with Alonso de Cartagena, see *Cronica de Enrique IV, 1:13;* and the letter to George of Trebizond, Riccardiana MS 907, fol. 107. From a letter of Vespasiano da Bisticci to Palencia we also learn that he was in Florence during the papacy of Nicholas V. The letter has been published by A. Mundó, "Una lletra d'Alfons de Palencia a Vespasiá da Bisticci," in *Studi di bibliografia e di storia in onore di Tammaro de Marinis* (Verona, 1964), 3:271–81. Mundó also reproduces Palencia's answer, which he discovered in the Library of Montserrat, MS 882. Vespasiano da Bisticci's letter is also published by G. M. Cagni, *Vespasiano da Bisticci e il suo epistolario* (Rome, 1969), 150–53.

103. No edition of their Latin original has yet been published. The only edition in Latin is the *Quarta decas*, which, until recently, was considered lost: Alfonso de Palencia, *Quarta decas hispaniensium gestarum ex annalibus suorum dierum*, ed. J. López de Toro (Madrid, 1970); Spanish trans., idem (Madrid, 1973).

104. Alfonso de Palencia, *Batalla campal de los lobos y perros*, in *Dos tratados de Alfonso de Palencia*, ed. M. M. Fabié (Madrid, 1876).

105. This work has attracted some attention in the past few years. See M. Pardo, "Le 'Batalla campal de los perros contra los lobos' d'Alfonso de Palencia," in *Mélanges offerts à Pierre Le Gentil* (Paris, 1973), 587–603; R. B. Tate, "Political Allegory in Fifteenth-Century Spain: A Study of the *Batalla campal de los perros contra los lobos* by Alfonso de Palencia (1423–92)," *Journal of Hispanic Philology* 1 (1977): 169–86.

106. This passage (in Cagni, *Vespasiano da Bisticci*) has been commented on by E. Garin, *Medioevo e Rinascimento* (Bari, 1966), 236ff.

107. Many of George of Trebizond's works circulated in manuscripts, such as Madrid, Biblioteca Nacional, MS 7446, which contains, among his philosophical treatise, the letter that Palencia wrote to him inquiring about the translation of Aristotle. His *Rhetoric* was printed in Alcala in 1511 as *Opus*

absolutissimum rhetoricum, cited by A. Bonilla y San Martín, "Un antiaristotélico del Renacimiento: Hernando Alonso de Herrera y su *Breve disputa de ocho levada contra Aristótil y sus secuaces,*" *Revue hispanique* 50 (1920): 61–196, at 65. See also J. López de Toro, "Jorge de Trebisonda traducido por Alonso Ortiz de Castro," in *Studi in onore di Riccardo Filangieri* 3 vols. (Naples, 1959), 2:129–31.

108. See F. G. Olmedo, *Nebrija (1441–1522) debelador de la barbarie, comentador eclesiástico, pedagogo-poeta* (Madrid, 1942); idem, *Nebrija en Salamanca.*

109. See E. Asensio in his introductory study to *Paraenesis ad litteras: Juan Maldonado y el humanismo español en tiempos de Carlo V* (Madrid, 1980), in collaboration with J. Alcina Rovira, who prepared the text of the *Paraenesis.*

110. See Olmedo, *Nebrija (1441–1522),* 172ff.

111. Cristóbal de Villalón, *Ingeniosa comparación entre lo antiguo y lo presente* (Madrid, 1898). See also A. Giannini, "Il libro X dei *Pensieri diversi di A.* Tassoni e *La ingeniosa comparación de lo antiguo y lo presente,*" *Revue hispanique* 41 (1917): 635–72. Of Villalón's works, there is an edition of *El scholastico,* ed. R. J. N. Kerr (Madrid, 1967), a very important but generally ignored treatise on education.

112. Nebrija's linguistic and philological innovations have received varying evaluations. See the introduction of A. Quilis to his edition of the *Gramática de la lengua castellana* (Madrid, 1980), esp. 62–77; Rico, *Nebrija frente a los bárbaros;* idem, "Un prólogo al Renacimiento español: La dedicatoria de Nebrija a las *Introduciones latinas* (1488)," in *Seis lecciones sobre la España de los siglos de Oro, Homenaje a M. Bataillon,* ed. P. M. Piñero Ramírez and R. Reyes Cano (Seville, 1981), 61–85; L. Gil, "Nebrija y el menester del gramático," *Academia literaria renacentista* 3 (1983): 53–64; idem, "El humanismo español del siglo XVI," *Estudios clásicos* 51 (1966): 211–97; J. Closa Farrés, "Notas sobre la difusión medieval hispana del *Arte menor* de Elio Donato," *Anuario de filología* 2 (1976): 37–67; idem, "La difusión hispana de la *Ars menor* de E. Donato en los siglos XVI y XVII," *Anuario de filología* 3 (1977): 47–80; E. Ridruejo, "Notas romances en gramáticas latino-españolas del siglo XV," *Revista de filología española* 59 (1977): 47–80; C. Codoñer, "Las *Introductiones latinae* de Nebrija: Tradición e innovación," *Academia literaria renacentista* 3 (1983): 105–22.

113. See above, note 97.

114. M. Bataillon, *Erasmo y España,* trans. A Alatorre (Mexico, 1950).

115. Nebrija, *Gramática de la lengua castellana,* 97ff.

116. The only serious revision was advanced by E. Asensio, "El erasmismo y las corrientes espirituales afines, conversos, franciscanos, italianizantes," *Revista de filología española* 36 (1952): 31–99. His lead, however, has not been followed, and today "Erasmismo" in Spain is often confused with humanism and other Renaissance trends.

117. See J. L. Abellán, *Historia crítica del pensamiento español,* 4 vols. (Madrid,

1979–85), vols. 1 and 2. From a sixteenth-century perspective, see Alfonso García de Matamoros, *Apologia pro adserenda hispanorum eruditione*, ed. J. López de Toro (Madrid, 1943).

118. Studies on aspects of humanism during this period are far too numerous to list here. The most important is certainly Bataillon, *Erasmo y España*; idem, *Erasmo y el erasmismo*, trans. C. Pujol (Barcelona, 1977); idem, *Estudios sobre Bartolomé de las Casas*, trans. J. Coderch and J. A. Martínez Schrem (Barcelona, 1976); J. A. Maravall, *Estado moderno y mentalidad social*, 2 vols. (Madrid, 1972); idem, *Carlo V y el pensamiento político del Renacimiento* (Madrid, 1960); L. Giles Fernández, *Panorama social del humanismo español (1500–1800)* (Madrid, 1981); J. López Rueda, *Helenistas españoles del siglo XVI* (Madrid, 1973); A. Gerbi, *La natura delle nuove indie* (Milan, 1975); J. Pérez Villanueva, ed., *La Inquisición española: Nueva visión, nuevos horizontes* (Madrid, 1980); J. C. Nieto, *Juan de Valdés and the Origins of the Spanish and Italian Reformation* (Geneva, 1970); B. Rekers, *Benito Arias Montano* (Leiden, 1972); C. G. Noreña, *Juan Luis Vives* (The Hague, 1970); idem, *Studies in Spanish Renaissance Thought* (The Hague, 1975); K. A. Kottman, *Law and Apocalypse: The Moral Thought of Luis de Leon (1527–1591)* (The Hague, 1972); A. Redondo, *Antonio de Guevara et l'Espagne de son temps* (Geneva, 1976); A. Rallo Asunción, *Antonio de Guevara en su contexto renacentista* (Madrid, 1979); M. Fernández Álvarez, *La sociedad española del Renacimiento* (Salamanca, 1970); E. Spivakovsky, *Son of the Alhambra: Diego Hurtado de Mendoza, 1504–1575* (Austin, TX, 1970); a translation and study of F. Sánchez de la Brozas ("El Brocense"), *Minerva o de la propriedad de la lengua latina*, trans. F. Riveras Cárdenas (Madrid, 1976); R. Kagan, *Students and Society in Early Modern Spain* (Baltimore and London, 1974); J. M. López Piñero, *Ciencia y técnica en la sociedad española de los siglos XVI y XVII* (Barcelona, 1979); W. Bahner, *La lingüística española del Siglo de Oro*, trans. J. Munárriz Peralta (Madrid, 1966); C. Vasoli, "Aspetti dei rapporti culturali tra Italia e Spagna nell'età del Rinascimento," *Annuario dell'Istituto storico italiano per l'età moderna e contemporanea* 29–30 (1977–78): 459–81, reprinted in *La cultura delle corti* (Bologna, 1980), 13–37; J. Varela, *Modos de educación en la España de la Cotrarreforma* (Madrid, 1983). On theories of history, see J. H. Franklin, *Jean Bodin and the Sixteenth-Century Revolution in the Methodology of Law and History* (New York, 1963), chap. 7, on Melchior Cano; G. Cotroneo, *I trattatisti dell'"Ars historica"* (Naples, 1971), dedicates a chapter to Fox Morcillo and another to Melchior Cano. For a revision of the Complutensian Polyglot, see J. H. Bentley, *Humanists and Holy Writ: New Testament Scholarship in the Renaissance* (Princeton, 1983), chap. 3.

119. Juan Lorenzo Palmireno, *Vocabulario del humanista* (Valencia, 1569). See the recent study on this humanist by A. Gallegos Barnes, *Juan Lorenzo Palmireno (1524–1579)* (Zaragoza, 1982); G. de Andrés, *El maestro Baltasar de Céspedes y su "Discurso de las letras humanas"* (El Escorial, 1965),

a study and edition of Céspedes's *Discurso de las letras humanas llamado el humanista,* written in 1600. By this time every university graduate wanted to be called a humanist, and Miguel de Cervantes, a keen observer of people and events of his time, in fictionizing the *Querelle* of ancients and moderns, introduced the caricature of a *humanista* into his novel *Don Quijote* (pt 2, chs. 16–22).

20 &🙠 HUMANISM IN FRANCE
Eugene F. Rice, Jr.

A LMOST NOBODY SEES A THING PROPERLY UNTIL HE HAS BEEN
sensitized to see it, a form of blindness—the blindness of the un-
ready—well illustrated by the long interval between the initial
exposure of Frenchmen to Italian humanism (at Avignon during the
"Babylonian Captivity" of the papacy in the fourteenth century and in
Italy itself) and their acceptance and appropriation of the new cultural
and educational program a century and a half later, tentatively during
the lifetimes of Guillaume Fichet (1433–ca. 1490) and Robert Gaguin
(ca. 1430–1501), and fully in the next generation, that of Jacques Lefèvre
d'Etaples and Guillaume Budé. Before the end of the fifteenth century,
the taste of the court was exquisite but backward, that of the aristocracy
luxurious and illiterate, trained to war rather than letters; while French
intellectuals were typically clerics, graduates of the University of Paris,
the repository of French philosophical and scientific culture but in those
years stagnant, mimicking in miniature the grander achievements of the
scholastics of the thirteenth and early fourteenth centuries. Clerics and
nobles remained content with the traditional methods and content of
chivalric and theological education; no other social group of consequence
had yet emerged with the confidence and self-awareness to adapt cultural
forms invented in Italy to meet its own distinctive needs.

By 1500, the cultural and social climates were more receptive. During the last decade of the fifteenth century and the early decades of the
sixteenth, a small group of scholars, men of letters, printers, and patrons—most of them resident in Paris—successfully transplanted to the
alien environment of France an approximation of the *studia humanitatis*
and the moral values associated with their cultivation.

French humanists taught their pupils how to write correct Latin
verse, a Latin letter, a persuasive oration. They reformed the curriculum
of the university's arts faculty by "purifying" instruction in logic and by
putting greater emphasis on literature and mathematics. They restored
Aristotle's philosophy to its original eloquence and meaning, or so they
believed. Like their Italian contemporaries, they stressed the importance
of Plato, reprinted Marsilio Ficino's translation of the *Dialogues,* and
shared his enthusiasm for late antique Neoplatonism and Neopythagoreanism, the writings attributed to Hermes Trismegistus, and the Jewish

kabbalah. They encouraged the study of Greek and a historically more sophisticated reading of the Latin classics. They popularized historical studies by writing patriotic histories of the French monarchy, editing and translating the classical historians, and investigating Roman antiquities and the development of the civil law. The urged a reform of medical instruction and practice by attacking the medieval reliance on Arabic medicine and by recommending a return to the pure Greek sources of the art. They wrote moral essays on a variety of by now traditional topics: true nobility, wisdom, fortune, education, happiness, the true good. They worked for religious reform and recommended a purer, simpler piety recovered from the works of the ancient Christian authors of the first five centuries and from the Bible, corrected by critical philology and read, ideally, in its original languages.

We can better define the program of French humanism in the years between 1490 and 1540 by looking in more specific detail at the intellectual interests of the two humanists who enjoyed European reputations as leaders of the movement, Jacques Lefèvre d'Etaples (ca. 1460–1536) and Guillaume Budé (1468–1540).

*   *   *

Lefèvre was born about 1460 at Etaples, a small port in Picardy, into a family of moderate substance. He matriculated at the University of Paris about 1474 and received the B.A. in 1479 and the M.A. a year later. Until he retired from active teaching in 1508, he lived and worked in the Collège du Cardinal Lemoine, one of the residential colleges of the university, and lectured on philosophy in the faculty of arts. After 1508 he devoted himself increasingly to biblical scholarship. Housed and supported by the abbot of Saint-Germain-des-Prés, Guillaume Briçonnet, later bishop of Meaux, he worked on the text of the Psalms and prepared a new translation of Paul's Epistles with commentary. In the spring of 1521, Briçonnet called him to Meaux to help him put into effect a comprehensive program of diocesan reform. Lefèvre's main contribution was a French translation of the Bible. The fortuitous coincidence of this experiment in reform with the first penetration of Lutheranism into France focused the attention of the faculty of theology on his exegetical works. In 1523 a committee of theologians detected eleven errors in his commentary on the Gospels. When the Parlement of Paris summoned him to appear before it on suspicion of heresy, he fled to Strasbourg in the late summer of 1525. Recalled by King François I in 1526 and appointed librarian of the royal collection (then at Blois) and tutor of the king's children, Lefèvre finished translating the Bible under royal protection and published it in a single volume at Antwerp in 1530. He passed his last years in tranquil seclusion at the court of Marguerite d'Angoulême, queen of Navarre.

Over 350 editions or printings of works written or edited by Lefèvre appeared between the publication of his first book in 1492 and the eclipse of his fame in the 1540s. Contemporaries—Sir Thomas More, for example—usually praised him for restoring true philosophy, especially that of Aristotle. But after the appearance of the *Quincuplex Psalterium* in 1509 and his commentary on the Pauline Epistles in 1512, they often called him "theologian" also, although he had no theological degree and had apparently never studied in a faculty of theology. The notice of Lefèvre in a popular early sixteenth-century biographical dictionary lists his other titles to contemporary admiration: he restored the liberal arts to their antique splendor, freed every part of philosophy from the fog of barbarous sophistry, was the first of the Gauls (like Cicero among the Romans) to join a previously rude and unpolished philosophy with eloquence, and gave himself heart and soul to the study of divine things, helping the professional theologians by restoring, emending, explaining, and publishing scriptural and theological texts.

Lefèvre's principal intellectual interests were Aristotelian philosophy, mathematics, biblical and more particularly New Testament scholarship, patristic literature, and the visionary and speculative theology of medieval Christian mysticism. By means of translations, commentaries, introductions, and paraphrases he tried to recover the precise meaning of Aristotle's works and the original elegance of their style. He edited patristic texts and undertook a major program of biblical research and commentary: in addition to those on the Psalms and Pauline Epistles, he wrote commentaries on the Gospels (1522) and the Catholic Epistles (1524). He searched for mystical manuscripts as indefatigably as Italian humanists had hunted the classics, and published for the first time an important series of medieval mystical texts. Late in life he read the Protestant reformers with sympathetic interest. A common devotion to the Epistle to the Romans gives his doctrine of justification a superficial resemblance to Luther's, while the direct influence of Ulrich Zwingli, Johannes Oecolampadius, and Martin Bucer can be detected in his last works.

Lefèvre built these interests into a consistent scholarly and educational program. "For knowledge of natural philosophy," he wrote in 1506, in his commentary on Aristotle's *Politics,* "for knowledge of ethics, politics, and economics, drink from the fountain of a purified Aristotle. . . . Those who wish to set themselves a higher end and a happier leisure will prepare themselves by studying Aristotle's *Metaphysics,* which deals with first and supramundane philosophy. Turn from this to

a reverent reading of Scripture, guided by Cyprian, Hilary, Origen, Jerome, Augustine, Chrysostom, Athanasius, Nazianzus, John of Damas-
cus, and other fathers. Once these studies have purified the mind and
disciplined the senses (and provided one has extirpated vice and leads a
becoming and upright life), then the generous mind may aspire to scale
gradually the heights of contemplation, instructed by Nicholas of Cusa
and the divine Dionysius and others like them." [1]

This program may not, at first glance, seem a particularly humanistic one; and, indeed, Lefèvre was only approximately a humanist in the
strict professional sense that the words *humanista* and *grammaticus* had
come to have in Italy, namely, a professional teacher of the humanities
(*studia humanitatis*). His only stab at versification was a bit of doggerel
entitled "What is Virtue?"; his few surviving familiar letters are grace-
less; editions of pagan literary works are conspicuously absent from his
oeuvre; he was much more interested in Christian than in classical antiquity. At the same time, he and his pupils worked hard to diffuse Italian
humanist works in France. They expressed their educational ambitions
in a vocabulary shaped by humanistic values, repeatedly advocating and
defining "good letters" (*bonae litterae*), the "humanities" (*litterae
humaniores*), and "liberal studies" (*studia liberales, cultiora, nitidiora*).
Properly understood, indeed, the kinds of education, scholarship, and
piety he advocated were a creative adaptation of the cultural program of
Italian humanism to the educational tradition of the University of Paris
and, more broadly, to the needs and aspirations of his French patrons.

Instruction in the faculty of arts was almost entirely based on Aristotelian texts. Lefèvre did not contest this tradition; in his opinion, Aristotle's philosophy was pure, lucid, and certain, his works "useful,
beautiful, and holy," offering a straight, easy path to knowledge and virtue. His Aristotelianism belonged nevertheless to a tradition distinct both
from the scholastic Aristotelianism of the medieval Latin West and from
the secular Aristotelianism current in the Italian universities of his own
day. An appropriate name for this tradition is humanist Aristotelianism.
Its greatest representative in the first half of the fifteenth century was
Leonardo Bruni; in the second half of the same century the Venetian
patrician Ermolao Barbaro the Younger. Lefèvre was its most important
representative in the first half of the sixteenth century. Humanist Aristotelianism has well-defined characteristics: disenchantment with the
medieval translations and increasing reliance on the Greek text; rejection
of the scholastic commentaries; greater concern with Aristotle's moral
philosophy than with his natural philosophy, logic, or metaphysics; the
implausible conviction, finally, that Aristotle's philosophy harmonizes
admirably with Christianity. Typically, Lefèvre wrote commentaries

on only three Aristotelian works: the *Ethics*, *Politics*, and [pseudo-Aristotelian] *Economics*, the three divisions of moral philosophy; and he supported his belief in free will by citing *Ethics* 3.7, where Aristotle had said that it is in our power to do good or evil acts and that man is the "originator or generator of his actions as he is the generator of his children."

But since study of Aristotle was, in Lèfevre's view, a transitory stage in a program built on the graduated ascent from knowledge of sensible particulars to the contemplation of divine things, from the realm of discursive reason to that of intuition and vision, his larger purpose was to join philosophy to piety, that is, to rise from the human to the divine, from vestiges to exemplars, from shadows to light, from the philosophy of Aristotle to Holy Scripture, the Fathers, and the mystics; or, as his pupil Beatus Rhenanus put it, "to join wisdom and piety with eloquence."

The piety he recommended was humanistic in a number of specific ways. It was eloquent. For how else would men be persuaded to accept the truth, love God and their neighbors, do good and avoid evil? It was warm and simple, which sharply distinguished it, in Lefèvre's mind, from scholastic piety, which he condemned as cold, barren, unnecessarily complicated and subtle, disputatious, intellectually arrogant, and wanting in charity. Like Petrarch, he thought that it was more important to love God than to know him, more important to live virtuously than to split theological hairs. On this humanists and mystics agreed: it is better, Thomas à Kempis had emphasized in the *Imitation of Christ*, to love the Trinity than to argue subtly about the relation of the Persons to one another (such shared assumptions explain Lefèvre's admiration for many of the spiritual writers of the Middle Ages). This eloquent, simple piety had another advantage: it was old, the piety of the ancients, of Jesus himself, of the disciples, apostles, and fathers of the primitive church, in which all things were pure and uncorrupted by time. It followed that the purest source of piety was the Bible, that true piety was an evangelical piety. And indeed from an early date Lefèvre organized his mental life around a scriptural core. What we learn from Aristotle's *Physics* and *Metaphysics* analogically, he taught in his textbooks, we can learn from Scripture directly. We study Greek and Hebrew in order to read Scripture in its original languages. He prized mathematics above all because it opened a path to understanding scriptural mysteries. The usual reason he gave for admiring the Fathers was the perceptiveness of their biblical commentaries. Philology was useful because it helped preserve the purity of the Bible's text. Translation was desirable so that Scripture might be accessible to as many people as possible. "Extra Evangelium nihil scire, id est omnia scire," he wrote in 1522: to know nothing but the Gospel is to know all things.[2]

This emphasis on the centrality of Scripture put a special responsibility on the humanist scholar. His task was to replace the scholastic method of *sic et non,* question and disputation, by philological and historical criticism. The text of Scripture must be correct, the scribal errors of centuries recognized and rooted out. Latin and vernacular translations must accurately reproduce the corrected originals. The commentaries and treatises attributed to the Fathers must be tested for authenticity. The result would be a learned piety (*docta pietas,* the phrase is Petrarch's) based on the foundation of the *studia humanitatis* and shaped by historical and critical insight, yet wholly in the service of that eloquent, loving, uncomplicated evangelical piety which was accessible to the simplest of the faithful.

Lefèvre was not a great textual critic. He does not compare with Lorenzo Valla or Desiderius Erasmus in penetration and flair, though his critical sense grew stronger as he aged. And he had some successes. He was able to show, for example, by using a method and evidence that still carry conviction, that the Vulgate Latin translation of the Pauline and Catholic Epistles was not, contrary to common opinion, the work of St. Jerome, but of some other, anonymous translator. What is more interesting about his textual work is the vivid picture it gives us of the formidable difficulties faced by all the Renaissance pioneers. Lefèvre believed passionately and erroneously in the authenticity of the group of works known as the Dionysian corpus, and he accepted the Dionysian myth in the extreme form given it in the ninth century by Hilduin, abbot of Saint-Denis: that is, that Dionysius the Areopagite, the disciple of St. Paul mentioned in the Book of Acts; the Dionysius described by Gregory of Tours as sent to evangelize the Gauls about 250; and the author of the *Corpus Dionysiacum* (which modern scholars believe to have been written in Syria early in the sixth century) were all the same person; and he set out to prove it. His method was sound enough: find *testimonia* and preferably direct quotations from the text in early authors. He found a reference in a sermon of John Chrysostom (ca. 347–407); the sermon is spurious. He found a quotation in a work by Eusebius of Caesarea (ca. 260–ca. 340), entitled *De theologicis ambiguitatibus;* it is a medieval Byzantine forgery. Best of all, he found a citation in Athanasius (ca. 296–373); but the passage had already been shown to be a later interpolation. Wherever he put his foot, the quicksands of apocrypha and forgery threatened to pull him under. What he could have done and failed to do was to consider the negative evidence and ask himself why Ambrose, Augustine, and Jerome, along with a host of other learned and well-read

Fathers who lived after Eusebius and Athanasius, had never heard of the Dionysian writings.

Lefèvre was once cleverly described by one of his enemies from the faculty of theology as a *humanista theologizans,* a humanist who dabbled in theology. The phrase catches rather well the transitional character of his thought, the uneasy jostling of barbarism and classicism in his Latin style, the complex play of tradition and innovation in his work. Guillaume Budé, Lefèvre's younger contemporary, was a humanist of more mature vintage; yet the principal problem for him too was to reconcile his admiration for classical antiquity with his devotion to the Christian tradition.

*   *   *

Budé was born in 1468 in Paris, the son of a long line of rich and aristocratic royal officers. His great-grandfather, grandfather, and father had all been lawyers, notaries, and royal secretaries, an office that brought with it noble status. The family owned estates and seigneuries all over the Île-de-France. On completing his legal studies at the University of Orléans, Guillaume became in his turn a *secrétaire du roi.* In his early twenties, his passions were riding and hunting. Then he experienced a kind of conversion, and from chasing hares and wild pigs he became a hunter of the wisdom locked up in the *studia humanitatis,* especially in Greek literature and Roman law. He traveled in Italy. He studied Greek with such abstracted application and delight that he is said to have forgotten his own wedding day. The first fruits of his studies were translations from the Greek of several treatises by Plutarch. Two major works of great importance followed: the *Annotationes in Pandectas* (1508) and *De asse* (1515).

The *Pandects* or *Digest* is the bulkiest part of the *Corpus iuris civilis,* the great codification of Roman law undertaken at Constantinople in the sixth century by order of Emperor Justinian. An epitome of many earlier treatises on the law of Rome, containing excerpts from all the great Roman jurists, it is a mosaic of over nine thousand fragments, full of repetition, contradiction, and interpolation of new matter by Justinian's jurists. Nor did the compilers limit themselves narrowly to law: they copied passages of historical reminiscences, etymological observations, quotations from Homer, and philosophical texts. The *Digest* is a legal encyclopedia and a commentator's paradise.

Budé was not the first, of course, to annotate it. From the twelfth century on Roman law had been systematically studied in Europe, and commentaries were numerous. What Budé rightly emphasized was that his method was new and better. He attacked the medieval commentators for their barbarous style, their ignorance of Latin and of the correct meaning of many classical words and legal terms, their lack of historical sense, their innumerable errors of fact and interpretation. In contrast, his own aim was to continue the work begun by humanist scholars in Italy, notably Valla and Angelo Poliziano, to strip away the mountain of accumulated commentary and get back to the original text and its original meanings. He discerned in the Roman law a "picture of antiquity" (*effigies antiquitatis*), which philological expertise and historical imagination could flesh out and bring back to life. The result would be no less than a restoration (*restitutio*) of ancient civilization and a model for the reform of many contemporary institutions.

Budé accomplished his aim remarkably well. The book is fat with a prodigiously miscellaneous learning. It provides material for a Latin lexicon and for a dictionary of Roman antiquities. The digressions include a treatise on the Roman senate, an essay on Homer, a description of Greek and Roman public games, a discussion of the low level of morality in antiquity. Most important was Budé's emphasis on the mutability of law, on the fact that it changes over time, based to be sure on universal principles, but always reflecting the structures of particular societies, the needs and aspirations of particular peoples at specific periods in their history. No one, certainly in northern Europe, had yet studied the Roman world with a comparable historical detachment or so comprehensively, and no one had yet brought to legal history and antiquarian research the same sensitivity to anachronism and historical sophistication. Budé did for the study of law what Valla and Poliziano had done for the study of language and literature and what Lefèvre d'Etaples, but above all Erasmus, were doing for biblical studies.

Budé continued his investigation of Roman history and institutions in *De asse*. The treatise is ostensibly a study of Greek and Roman coinage and weights and measures, its title being taken from the *as*, a copper coin of the earlier Roman Republic. In fact, there is almost no aspect of antique life on which Budé does not shed some light. Here too he was alert not only to what was distinctive and unique in the past but also to what seemed relevant to the present, moving from the coinage to the empire's economy, comparing its wealth with that of modern societies, led on then to a discussion of usury and the incomes of the different professions. In a long excursus, he castigated contemporary abuses in the church: the wealth, worldliness, and nonresidency of bishops; the immorality of monks; the ignorance of the parish clergy. As in the *Annotations on the Pandects*, he attacked the study, teaching, and practice of law. He defended the Italian policy of the French crown and justified the royal claims to Naples and Milan. An early cultural nationalist, he vindicated

French cultural independence of Italy and assured his readers that the French will accomplish anything the moment they decide to do so. The massive and discursive erudition of *De asse* delighted Budé's contemporaries and made his European reputation.

De asse also had a moral purpose to point out the error of those who gave too much importance to the *as*, to money; glory begins only with the study of literature and philosophy. It raised even larger questions: is there danger as well as utility in the restoration of Hellenism (by which Budé meant classical pagan culture as distinct from Judaism and Christianity)? Has philology, the historical and critical interpretation of texts using the tools of the *studia humanitatis*, made faith and reason, reason and revelation, more or less difficult to reconcile? What is the proper relation of the *studia humanitatis* to the Christian tradition? Budé addressed these questions in the two most important books of his later life: *De transitu Hellenismi ad Christianismum* (*The Passage from Hellenism to Christianity*, 1529) and *De philologia* (1532).

The *humanae artes* or humanities consist of *ratio* and *oratio*. *Ratio* denotes all knowledge of human and divine things accessible to human reason operating on its own powers, a classical definition of wisdom. *Oratio* or eloquence is the power to communicate knowledge effectively and persuasively. Together they form an "encyclopedia," a favorite humanist word, made up of the Greek prefix *en*, "in" and the nouns *kyklos*, "circle" and *paideia*, "education, knowledge, culture" (the word and idea Cicero had translated as *humanitas* and which the second-century grammarian Aulus Gellius defined as "knowledge of the good arts"— *eruditio institutioque in bonas artes*). The good arts or good literature (*bonae litterae*) are characteristically human arts because they educate and civilize, because without them men and women can never realize their potentialities for virtue and wisdom. Since good literature, finally, is Greek, Latin, and Hebrew literature, the key to the humanist encyclopedia is knowledge of those languages. Budé worked tirelessly to encourage their study. His *Commentaries on the Greek Language* (1529) remained the foundation of Greek lexicography until the twentieth century. In 1530 he successfully persuaded King François I to establish the *lecteurs royaux*, regius professorships in Greek, Hebrew, Latin, and mathematics, institutional expression of his philological ideals and the nucleus of what was to become the Collège de France.

Clearly, the humanities were of fundamental importance for Budé. Nor can one miss when reading his work the warmth of his regard for pagan literature and philosophy (*philosophia ethnica, saecularis, gentilicia*). At the same time, he was far more sensitive to the potential dangers of a classical education than was Lefèvre d'Etaples. It is only an apparent paradox that it was scholars with a well-developed historical sense, like Valla and Budé, who perceived most clearly the inability of Christianity and classical culture to harmonize; while it was thinkers like Lefèvre and Marsilio Ficino, equally intelligent but less historically minded, whose uncritical admiration for Aristotle or Plato mistakenly convinced them that their idols posed no serious threat to Christian orthodoxy. Lefèvre could discover only two important doctrinal errors in all of Aristotle. Budé was undeceived. To be sure, he found traces of true wisdom in ancient philosophy, especially that of the Platonists. But he discovered much that was false and bad as well: mistaken ideas about divinity, unsatisfactory morals, and ignorance of the true and highest good. The ancient philosophers sowed some healthy seeds (Aristotle was good on human things, the Platonists spoke well about the One), but the plants that grew from them were incomplete and deformed.

Knowledge of the humanities must therefore be completed by sacred studies, secular philosophy corrected by Christian and true philosophy. The liberal arts must not be cultivated as ends in themselves, as they were in antiquity, but only as preparation for learning the philosophy of Christ. A proper model for Christians is Odysseus, who, unseduced by the songs of the Sirens and the pagan ease of the lotus eaters, forced his companions on toward their true fatherland, Ithaca, symbol of the heavenly city. Only there is to be had true peace, pleasure, happiness, and tranquility. So we must not linger overlong among the charms of the *studia humanitatis* (compared to the Word of God all human language is partial and fleeting), but, imitating now the Christian Fathers, move from the *pseudophilosophia* embodied in the classics to the sublime beauty of Scripture. As a young man, Jerome studied Cicero and Plato; in his maturity he meditated on the prophets. Gregory Nazianzus at first delighted only in good letters and the splendors of ancient Athens; but, once he had mastered the humanist encyclopedia, he laid his eloquence and erudition at the feet of Christ. Budé goes further: Hellenism is diametrically opposed to Christian truth ("per diametrum opposita doctrinae sacrosanctae"). To try to harmonize them is equivalent to forsaking the cross of Christ. Greek philosophy is impious and arrogant. It does not know the true God. It proudly rests on human reason alone. It thinks that human beings know the truth and do the good by their own powers alone. But this assumption is false. True knowledge and virtue come to us only from God, "non lege naturae, sed privilegio gratiae." The Greek philosophers located happiness and the highest good in this world. Christians know that this life is a pilgrimage, make God its end, and expect final happiness in an eternal contemplation of the face of God. The proper solution to this conflict is to reject Hellenism and accept

Christ; the Christian knight will flee the camp of Hellenism and cleave to the camp of the Christians.[3]

*　　*　　*

The reception in France of the *studia humanitatis* is closely related to the emergence in the sixteenth century of the social group of which Budé was himself a representative member, that elite corps of royal office-holders known to contemporaries as the *noblesse politique* or *noblesse civile*. The group included the king's secretaries, members of the *parlements* or sovereign courts, the *avocats du roi,* tax farmers, treasurers, and army paymasters, men of bourgeois origin, often trained in law, devoted to royal service and rewarded by the king with wealth, power, and patents of nobility. Their relatives occupied equivalent offices in the church, often possessing, in an age of pluralism, several important benefices at once. Although by the seventeenth century there was to be no counting the number of respectable noble families descended from collectors of the salt tax or presidents of the Parlement of Paris, in the early sixteenth century the social position of these able parvenus was ambiguous and insecure. The old nobility, the *noblesse d'armes et de race,* asserted that true nobility is inherited, not acquired, its origins unknown, lost in the mist of time; that it is biological, inherent in the father's blood, transmitted to the next generation in his "seminal fluid." The true noble is a gentleman, whose particular virtues have been shaped by martial exploits, by brave and honorable actions on the field of battle. The king, they said, can make a noble, he cannot make a gentleman: "The recently ennobled acquire the name and title, but not the race."[4] They naturally disdained the *noblesse politique et civile.*

　　Members of the *noblesse civile* required an alternative idea of nobility, an alternative vision of what living nobly could mean, one distinct from the chivalric aspirations and mentality of the nobility of the sword and adaptable to their conception of themselves and their own style of life, a coherent body of cultural ideals distinct from those of the older nobility with whom they shared and competed for power. They found it in the cultural and educational program of humanism and in the ideal of human dignity implicit in it. A humanist education not only taught them to speak and write persuasively, it also inculcated a self-confident dignity independent of both office and birth and helped to bridge the gap between legal nobility, the reward of service, and acceptance as a gentleman. Preeminence in, or service to, the republic of letters helped legitimize an earned preeminence in the wider republic of men.

　　Humanists had long argued that true nobility was grounded on virtue and merit rather than on birth. The dignity and quality of nobility that the *noblesse de race* located in the blood and defined as honor, bravery, strength, and military brio, the *noblesse politique et civile* redefined as the virtues of peace, eloquence, scholarship, and reason and located in an intelligence and will shaped by the moral teachings of the Greco-Roman classics and the writings of the church fathers. The true noble is the upright and cultivated man. Thus while the old nobles despised the new men as "paper knights" (a reference both to their bureaucratic paperwork and to their patents of nobility), the officer families affected to despise the military nobles as uncultured, ignorant, and bloodthirsty. "What is a *gentilhomme?*" asked a humanistically educated lawyer. "We hear bragging about the nobility and antiquity of his house and race; he knows nothing of the liberal arts and gives himself up instead to the beastly exercise of the hunt; his body's prowess is dedicated to the service of Bacchus and Venus; like a monkey, he copies the ways of princes; gambling, thievery, and murder are his habitual pastimes."[5] Another flattered his readers with the same comparison: "What a world of difference there is between those who wet their pens in ink and those who cover their spears in the blood of their fellow men: the first are surrounded by books, the others are covered with murderous weapons; the first study how men should live, the others are concerned with looting and robbery."[6] The true noble is eloquent in Latin and French; he has some knowledge of Greek; he is well read in histories; he models his behavior on the virtues of the great men of antiquity, Christian and pagan; he supports and rewards scholars and men of letters; he entrusts his children to humanist tutors; he collects coins and medals, antique statuary, finely bound books, and pictures. A humanist education and enlightened taste and patronage gratifyingly distinguish him both from the merely rich and from nobles whose claims rest only on the merits of their ancestors.

Needless to say, the *noblesse de race* was not as rustic, nor the *noblesse civile* as cultivated, as the propagandists would have us believe. By 1540, the circle of humanist patronage in France was visibly widening to include the king, important courtiers, and a certain number of aristocrats of ancient lineage. The old nobility was not stupid. It too was flexibly adapting to changing circumstance. Aristocrats had lost their former military and political independence. The future lay in royal service in a sovereign territorial state. "I would have the courtier devote all his thought and strength of spirit," wrote Count Baldassare Castiglione in *The Book of the Courtier*, "to loving and almost adoring the prince he serves above all else, devoting his every desire and habit and manner to pleasing him."[7] Such service presupposed new standards of manners and more realistic values than the ideals of a decaying chivalry. Above all, it required adequate formal training. Education was becoming an avenue to power and influence for laymen as it had long been for clerics. In order to fit themselves for alternative careers and to compete successfully for royal offices and favors, nobles of the sword began to add a humanist tutor to their households, send their sons to a university, and emulate the patronage of the *noblesse civile*. For the *noblesse civile*, social climbers who had elbowed their way into the aristocracy from below by efficient merit, a humanist education became a substitute for gentility of birth; for the *noblesse de race*, untroubled in their self-esteem, it opened the way to civil and ecclesiastical preferment.

In France, as in Italy, humanism remained the educational and cultural program of a small minority of soldiers, courtiers, and aristocrats of blood or office—plus, of course, of humanist scholars and men of letters themselves. Outside the magic circle were laborers and peasants, shopkeepers and artisans; the *peuple gras* or merely rich, merchants and bankers unambitious of social ascent; and a majority, no doubt, even of the *noblesse civile* and *noblesse de race* (for although interest and position predisposed these elites in favor of humanism, in the end it was individual inclination and personal taste that activated latent affinities). In one important respect humanism did become less elitist as the century went on. The generation of Lefèvre d'Etaples and Budé was the last in which humanists wrote consistently in Latin. By the end of the century most intellectuals used the vernacular. The greatest French humanist of them all, Michel de Montaigne, was a lawyer, royal officer, and member of the Parlement of Bordeaux. His background was the same as Budé's; unlike Budé, he wrote in French.

On the relation of humanists to the development of legal theory in the generation after Budé, consult in these volumes Chapter 34, "Humanism and Jurisprudence." And on the relation between French legal theory and the writing of history see in these volumes Chapter 32, "Humanism and History."

NOTES

The standard work for the earlier period remains A. Renaudet, *Préréforme et humanisme à Paris pendant les premières guerres d'Italie, 1494–1517* (Paris, 2d ed., 1953). For more recent perspectives on this and later periods, see F. Simone, *The French Renaissance: Medieval Tradition and Italian Influence in Shaping the Renaissance in France* (London, 1969; first Italian ed., Turin, 1961); W. L. Gundersheimer, ed., *French Humanism, 1470–1600* (New York, 1969); and A. H. T. Levi, ed., *Humanism in France at the End of the Middle Ages and in the Early Renaissance* (Manchester and New York, 1970).

On Lefèvre d'Etaples, see *The Prefatory Epistles of Jacques Lefèvre d'Etaples and Related Texts*, ed. E. F. Rice (New York and London, 1972); G.

Bedouelle, *Lefèvre d'Etaples et l'intelligence des Ecritures* (Geneva, 1976); and M. Mann, *Erasme et les débuts de la Réforme française* (Paris, 1934). On Budé's life, see D. O. McNeil, *Guillaume Budé and Humanism in the Reign of Francis I* (Geneva, 1975). On his thought and works, see J. Bohatec, *Budé und Calvin: Studien zur Bedankenwelt des französische Frühhumanismus* (Graz, 1950); D. R. Kelley, *Foundations of Modern Historical Scholarship: Language, Law, and History in the French Renaissance* (New York, 1970); and M.-M. de la Garanderie, *Christianisme et lettres profanes (1515–1535)* (Paris, 1976).

1. *Politicorum libri octo,* ed. Lefèvre d'Etaples (Paris, 1506), ff. 123v–124.

2. *The Prefatory Epistles of Jacques Lefèvre d'Etaples and Related Texts,* ed. E. F. Rice (New York and London, 1972), Epistle 134, p. 435.

3. Guillaume Budé, *De transitu Hellenismi ad Christianismum* (Paris, 1535; photographic reprint with trans. by M. Lebel, Sherbrooke, 1973), 152, 239–64.

4. R. Mousnier, *Les Institutions de la France sous la monarchie absolue, 1598–1789,* 2 vols. (Paris, 1974–80), 1:103.

5. Quoted by G. Huppert, *Les bourgeois gentilshommes* (Chicago and London, 1977), 87–88.

6. Ibid., 84.

7. Baldassare Castiglione, *The Book of the Courtier,* trans. C. S. Singleton (New York, 1959), 110.

21 ❧ HUMANISM IN GERMANY
Noel L. Brann

A PARAPHRASE OF SOME FAMOUS HORATIAN LINES ORIGINALLY AP-
plying to the Roman inheritance of Greek culture—"Captive Italy
captured her rude conqueror and introduced the arts into rustic
Germany"—which originally applied to the Roman inheritance of Greek
culture, summarizes the parallel transmission of Italian culture to Germany during the Renaissance.[1] But although the Italian Renaissance must
be viewed as preconditioning the German Renaissance to the north, it
does not explain all facets of the German movement. When the cultural
strains of Italian humanism spread northward into Teutonic lands, they
combined with certain indigenous developments to give German humanism a peculiarly transalpine character.

The inwardly pious nature of German humanism has often been
noted by scholars of the period, with two of their foremost American
representatives, A. Hyma and L. W. Spitz, choosing the phrases "Christian Renaissance" and "Religious Renaissance," respectively, to signify
what they have considered to be the primary interest behind the humanist
revival on German soil.[2] This approach, of course, emphasizes the role
of the Renaissance in helping to prepare the ground for the Protestant
Reformation. Hyma has stressed the part of the so-called "Modern Devotion" (*devotio moderna*) in the making of the German Renaissance—
even to the extent of greatly playing down the Italian influences. In taking
this position, Hyma consciously confronted the dominant scholarly tradition, most notably illustrated by Ludwig Geiger's *Renaissance and Humanism in Italy and Germany*, which accented the reception of Italian
motifs and forms by the German humanists.[3] Professor Spitz has dis-
creetly attempted to navigate a course somewhere between these extreme
positions, as I shall also attempt to do in this essay. However, though
allowing for certain autochthonous elements in the formation of the German Renaissance, I shall bring out at virtually every turn the indispensable role of the "Italian connection" in furnishing German humanism
with that conspicuous character which clearly distinguishes it from the
mystical and scholastic traditions preceding it. In this regard I stand
closer to the "receptivity" theory of Geiger than to the indigenous theory
of Hyma.

The concept of humanism guiding the present essay will be wider in
scope than the narrow literary definition advocated in the many writings

of Paul O. Kristeller, who has declared, for example, that "Renaissance humanism must be understood as a characteristic phase of what may be called the rhetorical tradition in western culture."[4] This essay will be closer to Joachimsen's broader definition of humanism as "an intellectual movement, primarily literary and philological, which was rooted in the love and desire for the rebirth of classical antiquity."[5] German humanism, though initially instigated by what were principally grammatical and rhetorical interests on the part of its proponents, came to embrace mathematical as well as literary studies; it was spurred by a desire for reform, not only within the literary trivium of the traditional liberal arts curriculum, but also within the mathematical quadrivium. This reform of the seven liberal arts in turn helped to set the stage for reform in the professional studies of medicine, law, and theology, for which the liberal arts traditionally had been viewed as foundation stones.

The bond uniting these two basic branches of the German humanist program, literary and mathematical, lies in the principle of classical form or style. By virtue of this bond of form the literary images of the rhetoricians and poets are easily translatable into the visual and tactile images of the painters, sculptors, and architects. In accordance with this principle, in Germany as in other European lands touched by the Italian cultural explosion, the art of rhetoric is shaped in such a way as to conjure, in the minds of its auditors and readers, ideal classical representations of clarity, balance, and proportion. Conversely, the graphic arts are fashioned to evince rhetorical clarity, balance, and proportion in keeping with the rules laid down by the ancient orators. A variation of Horace's famous dictum linking poetry to painting, "Ut pictura poesis,"[6] can be invoked to epitomize this essential unity of the literary and mathematical disciplines: "Ut rhetorica mathematica." At the crux of this outlook, whether expressed orally or visually, lay the Ciceronian precept that true wisdom is not only knowable, but also eloquently expressible. As Cicero had put this point in succinct form: "Eloquence is nothing else but wisdom speaking copiously."[7]

*   *   *

German humanists typically received their higher education in Italy, then returned to the monasteries, courts, and towns of Germany where they served as leaders, secretaries, or teachers. These monasteries, courts, and towns thus served as principal conduits for the spread of Italian humanism into Germany.

The first of these conduits was the monastery. Contrary to a popular impression, the Renaissance cloister was not generally hostile to the new learning. On the contrary, monasteries often proved to be more receptive to the humanistic disciplines than the scholastic-dominated universities, where the literary and mathematical disciplines tended to be subjugated to philosophical logic. The degree of receptivity in a particular monastery, of course, depended greatly on the character of the abbot or prior in charge.

One such cloister, which came to serve as a favored meeting place for Italian and German intellectual currents up to the time of the death (in 1485) of its reigning abbot, Henry of Rees, was the Cistercian monastery of Adwert, near Groningen. Among those who stopped there for a visit were the future great teacher of Deventer, Alexander Hegius; the itinerant humanist, first-rate Greek scholar as well as Latinist, Rudolf Agricola, who was later praised by Erasmus as "one of the first to bring a breath of the new learning from Italy"; and Johann Wessel who, after traveling in Greece and Italy, taught the three ancient languages of Latin, Greek, and Hebrew in various cities of Germany, anticipating Johann Reuchlin's more famous trilingual efforts.[8] The leader among the monastic humanists, however, was Abbot Trithemius (d. 1516), whose Benedictine cloister at Sponheim (until he was drummed out of it in 1505 by his monks, who resented his taskmaster attitude) was praised far and wide as a virtual beehive of vibrant humanist activity.[9]

To promote the cause of learning Trithemius had gathered on his library shelves more than two thousand hand-copied and printed volumes, and he so vigorously applied himself to the humanist program that one grateful guest was provoked to exult: "If there exists in our Germany any Hebraic or Greek academy it is here in this Sponheim cloister, from the walls of which you may absorb more erudition than from the dusty libraries of many other places filled with their inane books."[10] Since his student days at Heidelberg Trithemius had become closely associated with a circle of humanists whom he had met there, the nucleus of the future Rhenish sodality: Rudolf Agricola, Johann von Dalberg, Jacob Wimpheling, and Conrad Celtis. The erudite abbot was no less enthusiastic than his humanist colleagues of this Heidelberg circle in pushing for a revival of the ancient classical authors. One of his heroes, as also that of his Heidelberg friends (Agricola had composed a biography of the same figure while visiting Italy) was Petrarch, lionized by Trithemius in a catalog of ecclesiastic luminaries as one who "recalled the humanistic letters, after they had lain as though dead for a long period of silence, from the lower regions to our higher ones."[11]

This same Petrarch can be credited with being an early intermediary in helping to open up the second major conduit of Italian humanism into Germany, the princely court. Petrarch was in direct communication with the imperial court of the Luxemburg emperor Charles IV (ruled 1346–

78) at Prague, whose chancellor, Johann von Neumarkt (Jan ze Středy, d. 1380) he congratulated in a letter with this effusive compliment:

> Though you were born far from the city of Rome, you nevertheless have been thoroughly imbued with Roman eloquence. . . . By your actions it can now be said for Germany what has previously been said of Italy: in both virtue and might there is nothing more powerful for our future than language, the labor of whose study is highly beneficial to our minds. I find your pen to be a great witness to transalpine fluency.[12]

Neumarkt, who apparently had met Petrarch at Mantua while accompanying the emperor on an Italian journey, represents one important way in which Italian humanism made its entrance into northern courtly circles. Another way was for an Italian humanist to find service in the North. The outstanding exemplar of the latter was the Siena humanist Aeneas Silvius Piccolomini (d. 1464), the future Pope Pius II (1458–64), who, after attending the Council of Basel as a secretary to one of the attending bishops, became subsequently attached to the Habsburg court of Frederick III (ruled 1440–93) in Vienna. Piccolomini's well-deserved reputation as the "apostle of humanism" in the Germanic North is attested by such declarations as the following, written to the Nuremberg jurist and translator Nicholas von Wyle in 1452:

> I rejoice to see the art of oratory finding its way back to Germany, and am confident that the rhetorical art will soon again be revived in this region. For in an earlier time there were many Germans who not only were well educated, but who composed very ornate writings.[13]

The imperial patronage of humanism reached its apogee in Frederick III's successor, Maximilian I (ruled 1493–1519). As the emperor's own personal contributions to literature show, two epic narratives under the titles *Teuerdank* and *Weiskünig*, Maximilian's mind still lay largely within a medieval framework of chivalry, for which reason he has been dubbed by one modern scholar "the last of the knights."[14] But his lavish patronage of many literary erudites who had clearly broken out of that framework, of whom Celtis was the most illustrious example, earns him a place at the center of the humanist revival. "He it was," another scholar has proclaimed, "who drew German humanism out of the schoolroom into the world arena and breathed into it something of the active joy of his own nature."[15] For a number of the humanists Maximilian was an "alter-Hercules," a comparison pointing up not only the heroic character of the imperial patron of the arts, but also the ancient heritage of Greece and Rome that he was actively fostering in the imperial court.[16]

But the imperial Habsburg court was far from monopolizing the role of humanist patronage in Germany during the last decades of the fifteenth century. Among Maximilian's competitors were Joachim of Brandenburg, Philip of the Palatinate, Eberhard of Württemburg, and Frederick the Wise of Saxony. Like the emperors, such princes were sometimes seen in Italy, where they could make contact with its scattered intellectual circles. A case in point was Count Eberhard, whose visit with Lorenzo de' Medici at Florence in 1482, on his way to Rome, also brought him into association with the Florentine Platonic Academy under Lorenzo's sponsorship. In Eberhard's entourage was Johann Reuchlin, who was sufficiently impressed to pay a second visit to Florence in 1490; the result of these two trips was Reuchlin's transmission to Germany of the multilingual and philosophical ideals of the Florentine academy's two leading members, Marsilio Ficino and Giovanni Pico della Mirandola. It was not unusual to see German princes, as they made their way from place to place in Italy, recruiting Italian humanists for employment in their courts, or else German humanists who were currently studying in Italian universities. The law school of Bologna was an especially favorable meeting ground in this regard. The German peregrinations of the jurist Peter of Ravenna, for example, were started in this way, as he was first acquired in 1497 by a German prince, Duke Bogislaw of Pomerania, on his way back to Germany from the Holy Land.

A measure of the widespread appeal of humanism to German courtly culture can be found in the writings of Conrad Celtis, who was mostly associated with the imperial court of Vienna. Crowned poet laureate by Frederick III in 1487, Celtis was recrowned by Frederick's son and successor Maximilian after taking the chair of rhetoric and poetry at Vienna University a decade later. But Celtis petitioned many more princes than Maximilian for patronage of the humanist program. To Magnus of Anhalt, for instance, he wrote in the same year of 1487 in which he was first crowned poet laureate:

Nothing can more gloriously or blessedly enhance the reputation of a prince than, in the midst of his very grave responsibilities attending to the running of his state, to have jealously guarded over the disciplines of the good arts, which alone prepare him eternal profit, fame, and adornment, and render his mind embellished and replete with great things. When these things beautify the prince, it can be truly said that his example is a standard for the lives and customs of his subjects.[17]

In the same spirit Celtis lauded Frederick of Saxony, in the dedicatory preface to his edition of the plays of the tenth-century Gandersheim nun Hrotswitha, as a prince who was attracting not only poets, orators, historians, and jurists of the Roman law into his court, but also the theorists and practitioners in the mathematical and visual arts: astronomers, musicians, and painters. "It is a very fine thing, and to the credit both of the individual German and of the entire German race," Celtis declared to Frederick, "if someone, out of his love of letters, imitates the ancient Greek and Latin models and extends them to the foreign nations." [18]

The third major conduit for humanism in Germany was the town. Of the towns leading the way in the propagation of humanism, three kinds are discernible. The first, exemplified by Schlettstadt and Strasbourg, offered secondary schools that were expressly established to promote the new learning. The second, exemplified by Augsburg and Nuremberg, found the mainstay of support for the humanist program in its patriciate, possibly aided by the establishment of a literary sodality but unsustained by a supporting educational institution. The third was the town that could claim a university.

Among the German schools that helped to establish the humanist educational ideal in Germany were those at Schlettstadt, founded in 1441 by Ludwig Dringenberg (d. 1490), who had been trained by the Brethren of the Common Life at Deventer; and Münster, founded by Rudolf von Langen (d. 1519), trained in Italy. An important product of Dringenberg's school was Jacob Wimpheling (d. 1528), who established humanist pedagogy in Strasbourg, where he also authored some of the most influential educational tracts of his day. Johann Sturm, subsequently a great Protestant educator, studied at Wimpheling's school.

Visiting educators were not the only means through which towns deprived of universities fostered the new learning. Ready recipients could also be found among the patricians, with or without the benefit of a supportive school. At Strasbourg, for example, Wimpheling's educational efforts were complemented by the classical interests of the patrician Peter Schott (d. 1490). It was Schott who drew the great preacher Geiler von Kaiserberg (d. 1510) to Strasbourg, who in turn drew Sebastian Brant (d. 1521), later chancellor of the city and author of the satirical *Ship of Fools*, which became the subject of some of Geiler's most celebrated sermons. At Augsburg an early circle of humanists gathered around the patrician Sigismund Gossembrot (d. 1488), whose literary activities helped prepare the way for those of the patrician Conrad

Peutinger (d. 1547) in the next generation. Celtis, in cooperation with Peutinger, helped found a literary sodality in Augsburg (Sodalitas Augustana) expressly dedicated to the revival of ancient standards of eloquence. The Nuremberg patriciate also acted as a vital intermediary of the new learning in that city, Willibald Pirckheimer (d. 1530) being the chief luminary. The Pirckheimer patrician family could claim links with Italy going back at least to the mid-fourteenth century. Both merchants and students from that family traveled and studied in Italy before Willibald himself entered the University of Padua in 1488 for what was to be a seven-year period of Italian studies.[19]

If any German city can be said to approximate the Italian republican models of Venice or Florence, it was Nuremberg, dubbed by one of its citizens, Christoph Scheurl, the "German Venice."[20] Gerald Strauss has remarked in criticism of what he perceives to have been a vulgar philistine motive operating in the Nuremberg patriciate: "In Nuremberg culture was valued only if it was demonstrably useful and practical and if it added material value or enjoyment of life."[21] But much the same criticism could be leveled against the Italian paradigms with which Nuremberg invites comparison. A central figure was the Italian-trained jurist Gregor Heimberg, whose mediating role his close friend Aeneas Silvius had compared to the role of Cicero in Italy: just as Cicero had carried the eloquence of Greece to Rome, so had Gregor carried the eloquence of Italy to Germany.[22] Further contributors to this intellectual climate before Willibald Pirckheimer came upon the scene were the author of the *Pearl of Poetry*, Albrecht von Eyb; the translator Nicholas von Wyle, who greatly popularized the Italian Renaissance by rendering in the vulgar tongue writings by Petrarch, Boccaccio, Poggio Bracciolini, and Aeneas Silvius; the historian brothers Hermann and Hartmann Schedel, who collaborated on a world chronicle; and the astronomer Johann Muller (Regiomontanus), whose aspiration to return to the pure Greek texts of Ptolemy illustrates the principle that the humanist reform movement could as readily be applied to the mathematical sciences as to the literary arts. The favorable environment created at Nuremberg made it a fitting starting point for Celtis's projected *Germany Illustrated*, the first part of which, the *Nuremberg*, was conceived by its author during a stay in the city in 1487. Nuremberg could also boast the native artist Albrecht Dürer (d. 1528), who chose to remain within his city walls rather than to seek his fortune in foreign places.

Although the towns just mentioned demonstrated their ability to mediate the spread of humanism without the benefit of resident universities, other towns, such as Vienna, Heidelberg, Erfurt, Basel, Ingolstadt, Tübingen, Leipzig, and (after 1502) Wittenberg, revealed that the

German university was far more a positive force than a negative one in the promotion of humanist ideals. One important reason is that the majority of them were founded relatively late in the Middle Ages, thus making them less subject to scholastic entrenchment than older universities such as Paris and Oxford. The University of Vienna was founded in 1365, Cologne in 1389, Erfurt in 1392, Leipzig in 1409, Ingolstadt in 1472, Basel in 1457, Tübingen in 1477, and Wittenberg in 1502. A second important reason for their lesser resistance to the reception of humanism than elsewhere lay in the supporting network of secondary schools already mentioned, which helped feed a steady group of humanist-minded persons—quite often after a period of upper-level education in Italy—into the ranks of the German university faculties. It did not take long for this process to become reflected in the university curricula, which in turn attracted more humanists into the German universities. The long-term effect of this process was to reduce the indispensability of an Italian upper-level education by making the same kind of education available in Germany.

Of the university towns demonstrating their receptivity to humanism, clearly Vienna, the home of the Habsburg emperors, was one of the most important for the success of the movement. The residence of Aeneas Silvius was strongly felt in Vienna long after his departure for Italy to assume the papal tiara. Among those who were early attracted to Vienna were the astronomer-mathematicians Georg von Peuerbach (d. 1461), a disciple of Nicholas of Cusa, and Peuerbach's student Regiomontanus, who made his mark on Vienna before migrating to Nuremberg. In 1470 the wandering humanist Peter Luder (d. 1474) arrived to help influence the course of events in the city, a forerunner of the itinerant humanist Celtis, who took up a newly established chair of rhetoric and poetry at the university. Taking advantage of the mathematical traditions already introduced into the city by Peuerbach and Regiomontanus, Celtis helped institute, a few years after his arrival, the College of Poets and Mathematicians, with the express aim of furthering "the revival of the eloquence of earlier times."[23]

Of the other German university towns, Cologne and Ingolstadt were relatively less open to humanist studies than Heidelberg, Erfurt, Leipzig, Tübingen, and Wittenberg. Erfurt became a strong center of pro-Reuchlin support when the validity of Hebrew studies was challenged. Tübingen was established after the model of the University of Basel, the charter of which, confirmed by the humanist pope, Pius II, in 1459, assured the inclusion of the *studia humanitatis* in its curriculum. Wittenberg obtained many of its faculty from Leipzig. A pamphlet and a lecture written there in the years immediately preceding the Protestant Reformation give a good idea of how strongly the winds of humanism were blowing through many of Germany's universities prior to Luther's theological revolution. In an unabashedly propagandistic pamphlet to help draw students with a humanist bent to the new university, Andreas Meinhardt had one of his protagonists, a student on his way to Wittenberg in conversation with another student on his way to Cologne, characterize the Wittenberg castle of Frederick the Wise as Jupiter's home, the surrounding hills as Apollo's mountains, and the city itself as the "new Rome," adding that good Latin was so much in evidence at the university "that even the peasants in the surrounding region were speaking it." And in an oration delivered in 1510 Otto Beckman, later honored to be Melanchthon's dedicatee in the published edition of the reformer's inaugural lecture in 1518, perorated "in praise of philosophy and the humanities," in the course of which he maintained that the rhetorical arts had achieved such authority at Wittenberg that even the dialecticians were reflecting its powers in the formation of their arguments.[24]

*   *   *

The primary urge of Renaissance humanism, in Germany as elsewhere, was a grammatical and rhetorical one, though it eventually moved beyond this point. By a prior reform of grammar and rhetoric the humanists hoped to produce a radical reform in their sister discipline of logic. A reform of the trivium was to lead to a reform in all higher studies. The humanists thus envisaged a thoroughgoing overhaul of the educational system, both in the secondary schools and in the universities.

The typical attitude of these educational reformers toward the subject of grammar is revealed in a complaint of the Deventer teacher Alexander Hegius that grammar had traditionally been all too subservient to logic. He argued:

> No one is denied the title of grammarian because he does not know which *modi significandi* are essential and which accidental, which material and which formal, which absolute and which representative of the parts of a sentence, but he is unworthy of the name grammarian who does not know how to speak and write correctly, no matter how many words he may write about the *modi significandi*.[25]

The grammatical convention to which Hegius is reacting in this asseveration was based principally on two texts, one by Donatus (fourth century) at the lower levels and one by Alexander of Villedieu (ca. 1199) at the more advanced levels. Frequently associated with Alexander's

Doctrinale was Hugutio's contemporaneously authored etymological dictionary, which was so fallacious in many of its derivations that it sometimes explained a Greek word out of Latin roots.[26]

The view of grammar that Hegius and like-minded educators were taking to task maintained that grammar is essentially subject to the same laws of philosophical logic as any other discipline, and thus is rightfully relegated to logic in the elementary curriculum. Hegius sought to reverse this relationship, making logic, together with its affiliated subject rhetoric, dependent on grammar. The conventional conception of grammar encouraged a heavy preponderance of logical glosses, with one of the most popular in German schools being that of Gerhard von Zutphen's 1488 *Glossa notabilis*. "Who was the inventor of grammar?" Gerhard had asked in the prologue to his second part. "The first inventor of positive grammar," he answered, "was a metaphysician and a natural philosopher, because he, considering the various qualities, the nature, and modes of being of things, imposed various names on things."[27] Hegius was determined to free grammar from the tyranny of logicians and metaphysicians. An identical attitude was reflected in various other secondary schools, most of them with links to Deventer.

To help meet the needs of this educational revolution a number of new grammars appeared. Although most of them were by Italian grammarians (Giovanni Sulpizio [Sulpicius Verulanus], Antonio Mancinelli [Mancinellus], Aldo Manuzio, Niccolò Perotti), the Germans, in Heinrich Bebel and Johann Turmair (Johannes Aventinus), also produced grammars of their own. Aventinus, warning his young readers against the old grammar with its excessive dependence on logic, pointed out to them that "the rudiments of grammar do not drop from the sky or come from nature, but should be formulated by the agreement and contract of men, insofar as that is observation and imitation of the best authors and writers."[28]

Closely bound up with the reformation of grammar was the reformation of logic. Here the principal obstacle was Peter of Spain's *Sumulae logicales* (composed before 1246). The major thrust of this reform movement was the demonstration that logic is, in essence, language; thus the ideal logician is not a metaphysician but a linguistic specialist. The great advantage of this position to the cause of humanism was that it did not necessitate the sacrifice of logic to rhetoric, that is, of substantial content to eloquent form; on the contrary, it preserved the status of logic while reformulating its principles to make them more harmonious with its sister, rhetoric. A cutting edge for this development in German education was furnished by certain Italian writers, most notably Lorenzo Valla and Angelo Poliziano, who sought to restructure logical thought in terms of grammar and rhetoric.[29] Whereas Peter of Spain had argued that "dialectic is the art of arts, the science of sciences, holding the way to the principles of all the disciplines," the exponents of the new humanist version of logic rather argued that "a logician presupposes the signification of terms and how to speak suitably which is obtained through grammar."[30]

Rudolf Agricola was in the vanguard of those in Germany who propagated this revisionist logic. He opened his ground-breaking *Concerning Dialectic Invention* with the kind of appeal that was to be repeated many times among his successors:

Oratory, for whatever reason it was instituted, and every act of discourse with which we reveal the thoughts of our minds, is observed to perform and hold this principal and appropriate office: to teach something to him who is listening to it. Is it not obvious to whomever takes stock of this fact that God, the parent and author of all things, endowed man alone of all the animals, who is capable of rational instruction, with the gift of speaking and of oration?[31]

Agricola's treatise sought to put into practice a plan of logical renovation that he had often advocated in his letters and orations. "I entertain the highest hope," he exclaimed on his return from Italy, "that someday we shall wrest from proud Italy the reputation for classical expression which Italy has nearly monopolized . . . and free ourselves from the reproach of ignorance and being called unlearned and inarticulate barbarians."[32]

One overriding incentive behind the Agricolan appeal was aesthetic, that is, the desire to dress truth in the garb of beauty. Another incentive was moral or ethical. As Agricola aptly put this ethical motive in a letter to a young follower: "If this sort of activity is not absolutely necessary for the development of a moral man, at least it contributes not a little thereto; for when a true interest in scientific investigation has seized upon a man, there is no more room in his soul for low and commonplace effort."[33] Herman von dem Busche argued in a similar vein in his inaugural lecture at Leipzig that "the study of the good arts and sciences, especially poetry and the oratorical art, is not in the least injurious for the morals of youth, but on the contrary exerts a beneficial effect both upon the understanding and upon the will."[34]

Celtis became an eloquent spokesman for Agricola's point of view. In a letter to the University of Ingolstadt in 1492 he complained that "there is no institution for the youth among the Germans dedicated to obliterating our ignorance, nor are we considered to be worthy of knowing anything but what is convenient for our sordid minds." Then he offered this remedy:

> After considering this defect in our young men, I have felt much pain, because in so many of our schools no one has appeared who has straightforwardly and lucidly laid Cicero before its students. Desiring, therefore, out of my love of the republic of letters, to summon a remedy for this disease, I have sought to recover the precepts of speaking and (if I may put it so) all the juice of Ciceronian eloquence in a certain foresightful and clear order. And I have also attended to printing these things . . . so that now Cicero might be thought to have spoken, not the Roman, but the German tongue. This will be the highest ornament and embellishment to you, a perpetual monument, for the stirring up of human actions, for the writing of letters, for preaching or for speaking with whatever man you may wish.[35]

While Celtis was trying to put this program into practice at Vienna, where he went after leaving Ingolstadt, Bebel was making a similar pitch at Tübingen. In an oration "On the Necessity of the Latin Language" delivered in 1508, Bebel lamented that, as he had often heard both at home and abroad, "the majority of scholastics care little for Latin, much less its elegance, so that when they go to foreign lands they are scarcely able to express three words of Latin with confident dignity."[36] A cure for this infirmity entailed a reformation of the science of grammar as a condition for the reformation of rhetoric and logic, liberating it from the encumbrances of natural philosophy and metaphysics. With treatises like his handbook of epistolary style, his *Commentary Concerning the Abuse of the Latin Language*, and his *Facetiae* (modeled on the Italian Poggio's work of the same name), Bebel tried to cleanse Germanic Latin of its "scholastic" corruptions so that his countrymen would no longer need to experience embarrassment in the face of their foreign critics. Indeed, so carried away did Bebel become in this direction that in a treatise *Concerning the Education of Children* he warned youth against becoming exposed at too early an age to Jerome's Vulgate because of its "dry and jejune style."[37]

*   *   *

Italy's critical impact on German learning derived from Greek as well as from Latin study. Venice served as the main gateway from the East for the flow of Greek teachers into Italy; and Florence, ever since its employment of Manuel Chrysoloras in 1397 to lecture on Greek language and literature, proved to be one of the most vigorous promoters of Greek letters. Two noteworthy products of these developments were the Aldine Academy at Venice and the Platonic Academy at Florence. At Ferrara, Guarino of Verona, who had studied in Constantinople, incorporated the requirement of Greek into the curriculum of his humanist secondary school, and Vittorino da Feltre did the same in his school at Mantua. At Rome one might learn Greek from Cardinal Bessarion, and at Padua from Demetrius Chalcondyles and his successor Marcus Musurus. As the German humanists traveled about Italy, they came into contact with this Greek culture as well as with the broader Latin culture in which it was set. Although some southern Greeks also found their way to the North (Bessarion visited Vienna, and Andronicus Contoblachas, a teacher of Reuchlin, Basel), the usual pattern was for a German humanist to travel to Italy to learn his Greek, at least in the beginning stages. Thus Agricola learned the rudiments of Greek from Theodore Gaza in Ferrara and Reuchlin from John Argyropoulos in Florence. Reuchlin is reputed to have been told by his master Argyropoulos at the conclusion of his Florentine lessons: "Now Greek has flown across the Alps."[38]

A reverence for Greek can also be detected in some who did not know the language. Wimpheling, in his *Isidoneus*, notwithstanding an earlier pronouncement that "I regard the Latin language as the noblest of tongues,"[39] went on to express nearly equal admiration for Greek. Though confessing that he had not succeeded in gaining control over the language, he stressed that if he wished to do so in his old age he could easily accomplish the task, just as Cato had done in his old age. Should he apply himself to this project,

> there would be no lack of excellent teachers in Germany. Thus, Rudolf Agricola has learned and taught Greek. Johannes Camerarius Dalberg, Bishop of Worms, devotes himself with ardor to the study of Greek. . . . With no slight ardor does Johannes Trithemius, Sponheim's pious abbot, devote himself to the study of Greek. Among those who at the present time are competent to teach Greek is also Johannes Capnion, or as he is commonly called, Reuchlin of Pforzheim, and the poet laureate, Conrad Celtis. It is, moreover, well known that Augustine in his second book of *On Christian Doctrine* advances the opinion that for those who speak Latin a knowledge of Greek is necessary for the understanding of Holy Writ.[40]

Not named in this list, but an important link between Greek studies in Italy and those in Germany, was Johann Conon, whom the modern scholar in this field Deno Geanakoplos has termed "the true founder of Greek studies in Germany." Conon was charged by the Venetian Aldo Manuzio with helping to gain the protection of Emperor Maximilian for his Greek academy; conversely, through the mediation of Conon, Aldo encouraged the foundation of a Greek academy at Vienna on his Venetian model, thereby hoping to render that city a "second Athens."[41]

It would be a mistake, however, to assume that this campaign to introduce Greek studies into the German curricula experienced entirely smooth sailing, any more than did the parallel campaign to introduce Hebraic studies. Reuchlin, who boldly declared in a letter to Cardinal Adrian in 1518 that "no one who lacks the study of Greek letters can be judged a polished man," conceded in the same letter that the teaching of the language was being discouraged in many quarters on the pretext that, inasmuch as it was the tongue of the Greek schismatics, it could not help but have the same divisive effect in the West if permitted widespread currency.[42] It was of course a similar intellectual posture that was resisting the introduction of Hebraic studies, for which Reuchlin was likewise the foremost spokesman, into the German curricula. Reuchlin's great ally in helping to overcome this resistance was Erasmus, who, though failing to add Hebrew to his first-rate achievements in the Latin and Greek languages, actively campaigned with Reuchlin for the establishment of trilingual studies in the North. It was owing to Reuchlin above all others, however, that the epithet which came to be prized with special jealousy by those who claimed the name of *humanista* in its fullest sense was "one skilled in three languages" (*trium linguarum peritus*).

*   *   *

It might be comforting for some of us to think that the religious argument put forward by the humanists for the acceptance of their program, namely, a "return to the sources" in the field of biblical studies, was alone of sufficient force to justify the learning of the ancient languages. But the idealistic plea for "learned piety" which is so strongly characteristic of the Christian humanists tells only part of the story. If we are fully to comprehend the great success of the humanist movement in Germany, as in other parts of Europe, we also need to look at certain more mundane motives. One such motive, bluntly put, was a narrow patriotic one, with the majority of German humanists happily adopting a role as propagandizers of German cultural nationalism. But other secular interests also helped to further the cause of humanism. Some of these, in spite of the initial antimetaphysical impulses of humanism, continued to be metaphysical in orientation—a tendency abetted by the philosophical influences of the Florentine Platonic Academy. Often uniting with these philosophical currents—also, more often than not, reflecting the impact upon the North of Florentine Neoplatonism—were scientific and even magical ones. As many humanists recognized, along with their patrons, knowledge is power; the force of this truism became ever more poignant as the mathematical disciplines came to take their full place alongside the verbal arts of grammar, rhetoric, and a refurbished logic in the humanist educational scheme. A further interest catered to by humanism, likewise greatly enhanced by its extension to mathematical studies, was that of visual expression in the graphic arts analogous to literary expression in poetry and rhetoric. Such worldly motives as these gave the humanist program a much wider appeal than narrow biblical humanism, converting the *studia humanitatis* into a primary cultural vehicle for secular as well as for religious transformation.

A foremost beneficiary of this cultural transformation was German patriotism. In German lands Erasmus's cosmopolitan brand of humanism, which made him at home on virtually any soil, was clearly the exception rather than the rule. Indeed, Erasmus's German friends were not generally well disposed to his internationalist ways, and some among them pressured him to declare more openly his Teutonic birthright. But to all such efforts Erasmus replied: "I wish to be a citizen of the world, a friend of all men—or rather, a stranger to all men."[43] When the ultranationalist Ulrich von Hutten, in a letter to Erasmus in 1515, praised his correspondent as "the German Socrates," inasmuch as "you have helped us as much in scholarship as he in his Greek," all Erasmus needed to retort to this not very subtly disguised attempt to turn his scholarship to patriotic advantage was that Socrates's main importance for the future lay in his essential citizenship of the world rather than in his accidental Athenian citizenship.[44]

In contrast to the celebrated case of Erasmus, the typical effect of an Italian migration on a German humanist was to bring out in him what was peculiarly Germanic rather than to dissolve his Teutonic peculiarities in a doctrine of internationalism. Ironically, the foremost purveyor of this nationalistic brand of humanism in Germany was the "internationalist" Holy Roman Emperor Maximilian. The Hercules motif, which he actively fostered (Celtis called Maximilian an "alter-Hercules," and the Fribourg jurist Ulrich Zasius seriously argued that he was a direct descendant of Hercules), was closely linked in imperial circles with another myth the emperor was also zealous to promote, that of the Trojan origins of the German nobility. The emperor asked Abbot Trithemius to help uncover these origins. Never mind that Trithemius was forced to invent an entire body of historical material (which he attributed to an ancient historiographer Hunibald) to meet his difficult assignment. Franciscus

Irenicus, relying heavily on Trithemius—since he mentions Hunibald as a source—was so chauvinistic as to claim that the Germans taught philosophy to the Greeks.[45]

A myth sometimes found in close proximity to the Trojan one is that the druids were the priestly class of the Celts. According to this myth, after the druids were outlawed in Gaul by Emperor Tiberius in the first century of the Christian era, they escaped across the Rhine to Germany. The principal promulgators of this myth were Celtis and his disciple Aventinus. Trithemius also accepted this myth. In a letter to Celtis in 1495 he spoke of a recent visit of Reuchlin to "my Sponheim home of the druids." Not inappropriately, then, did Celtis exalt Trithemius in one of his odes as "the druidic abbot in Sponheim."[46] The patriotic motive behind this druidic myth parallels that behind the Trojan one. By putting these two myths together the German patriots could conceive of their ancient heritage, both spiritual and secular, as radically independent of Italy.

The exponents of this highly nationalistic brand of humanism were obviously treading a narrow path between potentially contradictory positions, since they were simultaneously attempting to assert the heroic dignity of their native Germany and their enthusiasm for the customs and languages of ancient Greece and Rome. The ambivalence that necessarily ensued is dramatically illustrated in Celtis's Ingolstadt oration of 1492:

> Emulate, noble men, the ancient nobility of Rome, which, after taking over the empire of the Greeks, assimilated all their wisdom and eloquence, so much so that it is hard to decide whether it has equalled all the Greek discoveries and equipment of learning or surpassed them. In the same way, you who have taken over the empire of the Italians should cast off repulsive barbarism and seek to acquire Roman culture. . . . Consider it a great disgrace to be ignorant of the histories of the Greeks and Latins, and the height of shame to know nothing about the topography, the climate, the rivers, the mountains, the antiquities and the peoples of our region and our own country, in short, all those facts which foreigners have cleverly collected against us.[47]

It is clear from this statement that Celtis's resolution of the ambivalence is a translation of the Roman Empire to the Germanic North through which the Germans became the legitimate preservers of the imperial ideal.

For Celtis, then, Greek culture arrived in Germany principally through the mediation of Rome. Helping to lend valuable archaeological support to this point of view was the Augsburg humanist-antiquarian Conrad Peutinger who, in his book *Concerning the Marvelous Antiquities of the Germans* (1506), assembled a number of ancient Roman inscriptions he had discovered in the area of his home city. Having picked up his passion for antiquarianism while on a visit to Rome, where he was introduced to this kind of study by Pomponio Leto, Peutinger represents one of several German attempts (there were others by Johann von Dalberg, the Schedel brothers, and Jacob Questenburg) to turn the hobby of inscription gathering to the use of German patriotic nationalism. Together with its sister arts of numismatics and epigraphy, the art of inscriptions was employed both to affiliate the Germanic North with the ancient Greco-Roman cultures and to highlight the indigenous antiquity of Germany itself.[48]

Some humanists, however, especially those pushing for a Trojan provenance, were dissatisfied with efforts to emphasize Latin mediation of Greek culture, underscoring instead direct links with the Greek world independent of Roman mediation. Johann von Dalberg, for example, in order to establish philological proof of the Greek foundations of German culture, assembled in a tract "a few thousand Greek and German words which mean the same thing in both languages."[49] Heinrich Bebel rejected out of hand both the Trojan myth and the premise of Roman mediation. In an anecdote in his *Facetiae* one of his characters declares, under the heading "Concerning True Nobility": "The flattery of those Germans who refer their nobility to the Romans is vain and false, since in the entire world there is no purer or more illustrious nobility than among the Germans, nor has there ever been so from ancient times to the present day."[50] Elsewhere Bebel makes it clear that the same principle applies to the Greeks as to the Romans, declaring that the ancient Franks spoke German, not Greek, a position strongly seconded by Beatus Rhenanus in his historical writings.[51] In France Robert Gaguin and Paolo Emilio Veronese were similarly stripping French history of its alleged Trojan beginnings.

To Alsatian patriots like Jacob Wimpheling and Beatus Rhenanus the search for an indigenous Germanic antiquity could also be turned to another advantage, more directly pertinent to their peculiar geographical situation between France and Germany. For Alsatian humanism, which displayed a distinctively anti-Gallic as well as as anti-Italian flavor, could just as easily be exerted against the West as against the South. Wimpheling is a good example of one who simultaneously assumed both of these patriotic postures. To avoid placing too much reliance on the Roman legacy Wimpheling asserted in an *Epitome of German Events* (1505) that

German antiquity antedated Italian antiquity, for although Rome was founded in the mid-eighth century B.C., the city of Trier could trace its origin back two thousand years before Christ.[52] And against the thesis of a corresponding Gallic legacy, which hinged on the presumption that the Aachen-based Charlemagne was French, Wimpheling responded, with such authorities to back him up as the Italian historians Aeneas Silvius and Marcantonio Sabellico, that Charlemagne was an eastern Frank, that is, a German. Calling on an even longer list of authorities—Tacitus, Ammianus Marcellinus, the *Corpus iuris civilis* of Justinian, Pope Innocent III, and Petrarch—to prove that his own beloved Alsace belonged to the same area of eastern Frankland from which Charlemagne came and which formed the modern German nation, Wimpheling vehemently objected to the fallacious Gallic claim to Alsace:

> We [Alsatians] are Germans, not French; hence our land, since Germans inhabit it, must be called Germany, not France. The Romans realized this fact. For after they had subjected us Germans on the Rhine, they moved across the Rhine and then saw that the inhabitants on the other side of its banks resembled us in their bold courage, in the sizes of their bodies and blond hair, as also in their customs and ways of life. Then they named us Germans, that is, brothers.[53]

Although there were some critics of this view, notably Thomas Murner, Wimpheling found a multitude of supporters who agreed that the Rhine River constituted a fully German river rather than a German boundary with France.

German patriotic feeling found support in an appeal, not only to antiquity, but also to certain modern events. The most notable of these was printing from movable type, invented by Johann Gutenberg at Mainz around 1450. Invariably German humanists, when pointing out the great value of the new invention in the revival of classical learning, could not resist bringing out the Teutonic origins of the printing revolution. Celtis, for example, says in his *Amores:*

> All that the Greeks and Latins have composed and all that arose on the banks of the Nile and the Euphrates is now coming to light. Heaven is unlocked, and the earth investigated, and whatever takes place in the four parts of the world is now publicly disclosed through the German art. Printed letters have been taught to serve us.[54]

With a similar burst of enthusiasm Wimpheling exclaimed:

We Germans can be no prouder of a discovery or artistic production than of the art of printing, which has raised us to the role of
new spiritual bearers of the teachings of Christendom and of all
divine and worldly knowledge, making us benefactors of the entire
world.[55]

In making this case, the German humanists were generally not slow to
remind the Italians that they, not the Italians, were the first to enter this
field. Conrad Peutinger at Augsburg, for one, was indignant at the attempt of his Roman teacher, Pomponio Leto, to deprive the Germans of
their invention by claiming it for his own nation.

But if certain of the humanists were more prone to pursue peculiarly
Teutonic forms around which to gather their scholarly investigations,
others persisted in the pursuit of universal forms that could be applied
equally to all places and times. The theological implications of this universalist trend in northern humanism are often illustrated by Renaissance
scholars with Erasmus's famous application: "St. Socrates, pray for us!"
A humanist displaying much the same universalist inclination with more
unmistakably Germanic credentials was Conrad Mutian, who boldly asserted, "Christianity began, not with the Incarnation of Christ, but many
centuries earlier; for the genuine Christ, the true Son of God, is the divine
wisdom, which the Jews as well as the Greeks and the Germans partook
of." In his essential nature, according to Mutian, Christ was not the historical creature of the flesh whose life is narrated in the New Testament,
but a spiritual form that existed before the coming of Jesus, continued to
exist after Jesus' crucifixion, and still exists today for those who have the
eyes to perceive him. "When I say Jupiter," Mutian insisted so as to bring
this divine form to bear on the question of the value of the pagan Greek
and Roman authors, "I mean Christ and the true God; the true Christ is
soul and spirit, not to be grasped with the hands."[56]

Among those who most effectively transferred the Neoplatonic philosophical doctrines lying behind this outlook to poetic theory was the
"German Horace," Celtis, whose invocation to Apollo in an ode "to
visit / Our abode, as once those Italian reaches,"[57] resembles Mutian's
invocation to Jupiter. A salient feature of this development was the combination of conventional mimetic theory—reinforced by poetry's traditional association with rhetoric—with Platonic inspiration theory. An
oration delivered at Leipzig in 1500 by the Grossenhain schoolmaster
Matthäus Lupin (Matthaeus Lupinus), a supporter of Pollich von Mellerstadt in his campaign to legitimize poetry as an adjunct to theology,
reveals the kind of dilemma faced by these poets as they set about
to justify their art. Addressing himself to the potentially embarrassing

question of why Plato outlawed poets from his ideal republic, Lupinus replied that Plato's intention was not to proscribe poetry per se but only its abuse. To lend backing to this conclusion Lupinus cited the Platonic doctrine of the poet as priest and prophet, directly inspired from above by the "divine frenzies," and the ancient role of the poets as theologians.[58] This "inspiration" theory of poetry was also endorsed by Ortwin Gratius of Cologne, who has received such a bad press through the *Letters of Obscure Men*. Gratius invited poetry into the humanistic curriculum through the agency of rhetoric. "Inasmuch as we are striving to praise rhetoric," he proclaimed in an oration, "we should also praise poetry, for the poet is conjoined to the orator, and these arts are tightly bound together by a certain necessity." But he did not stop there. With Boccaccio as his ostensible source but also revealing affinities with ideas radiating from the Florentine Platonic Academy, Gratius went on to add that "poetry is a certain exquisite fervor of invention, speaking, and writing that issues from the very bosom of God, and from this all wisdom and science proceeds, the gift of which is conceded to only a few minds in the act of creation."[59]

*   *   *

If, as Gratius said, "the poet is conjoined to the orator, and these arts are tightly bound together by a certain necessity," the same can be said of the mathematician and the visual artist. A principle shared by diverse humanist disciplines is eloquent form or style, alternatively expressed in verbal, mathematical, and visual language. The possible conversion of poetic into visual imagery (and vice-versa) was most famously pointed up in the Horatian dictum *Ut pictura poesis*. In the Renaissance a new dimension was given to this maxim by the revolutionary alliance of painting with mathematics. Henceforth the nexus between poetry and visual art could be expressed in mathematical as well as in rhetorical idiom. A variation of Horace's dictum, *Ut rhetorica mathematica*, can be taken to sum up this transference of rhetorical form into the mathematical and visual arts.

In a letter written in 1452, Aeneas Silvius raised the question why "the arts, painting and oratory mutually love each other."

> It is a strange thing that as oratory flourishes, so does painting. This is seen from the period of Demosthenes and of Cicero. After eloquence was cut down, painting fell. When oratory revived, painting also raised its head. Painting was an almost wholly unpolished art for two hundred years. The writings of that time are rude, inept, inelegant. After Petrarch letters emerged; after Giotto, the

hand of the painter arose; and we already see that both arts have arrived at a very high point.[60]

Aeneas reveals here an intuitive grasp of the kinship between literary and pictorial renascences that was concurrently being grasped by his friend and fellow ecclesiastic, Nicholas of Cusa. Nicholas is not generally listed in the textbooks as a humanist. Nonetheless, he displayed many of the features we have thus far identified with the humanist personality, including considerable time spent in Italy. His humanist inclinations are nicely illustrated on the first page of one of his more famous books, *On Catholic Harmony* (1433), composed to support the conciliarists during the Council of Basel. With the broader view of the arts that was also to characterize the outlook of Aeneas (also present at Basel, though not yet ordained), Nicholas declared, in a striking echo of a favorite humanist theme:

We see that all the great spirits and those who preeminently exert themselves on behalf of the liberal and mechanical arts, refer with the greatest enthusiasm to the works of the ancients. On all sides men are openly seen to delight in the speech, style, and character of antiquity.[61]

For Nicholas, as for his contemporary Leon Battista Alberti in Italy, the crucial principle allowing the mechanical arts (including painting and sculpture) to be elevated to the dignity of the liberal arts was their convergence in the science of mathematics.[62]

If one sentence can be lifted from the writings of Nicholas that epitomizes the conjunction of the rhetorical and mathematical arts, it is this one from *On Learned Ignorance:* "Every investigation is comparative, using the means of proportion."[63] In elucidating this idea, Nicholas observed that God's appearance in the world, serving as a prototype for all creative endeavor in the human sphere, is always "in an apt proportion, and that is in number. For the eternal mind doth act as a musician which would make His conception sensible; for he takes many voices and brings them into a proportion agreeing to that harmony."[64]

Should we seek one German artist who can be said to bring to fruition Aeneas's declaration that "painting and rhetoric mutually love each other," we can point to Albrecht Dürer of Nuremberg. In the usual manner of humanists, Dürer traveled widely in Italy, first for a short period in 1494 and subsequently for a much longer stay a decade later. Sometime in the course of the latter visit he discovered the influential treatise *On Painting* by Alberti in which, according to the art historian

John Spencer, "essentially, the aims and means of the new painting envisaged by Alberti . . . are similar to the aims and means of the rhetoric advanced by Cicero in his numerous works on the subject."[65] This Albertian legacy of "rhetorical art" is aptly summed up by Dürer in his assertion: "Good judgment comes from good understanding, and good understanding comes from a principle derived from good rules, and good rules are the daughters of good experience, the common mother of all sciences and arts."[66] During a second visit to Venice, Dürer was apprised of an instructor in the technique of mathematical perspective (the art of painting depth on a flat surface) who was living in Bologna. Dürer went to Bologna, learned this "secret art," and carried it back to his hometown of Nuremberg, where he succeeded in translating it into some of the most celebrated artistic output of the entire Renaissance.

*   *   *

The same body of learning that could influence the graphic arts could also influence the scientific disciplines affiliated with mathematics. Astronomy is a notable example. The plea of Georg von Peuerbach and Regiomontanus for a *reversio ad fontes* in the astronomical sciences, that is, a return to the original Greek texts of Ptolemy cleansed of Arabic corruptions (Regiomontanus went to Italy to learn Greek from Bessarion for this purpose), parallels the plea of the rhetorical humanists for a return to the Greek and Roman orators, of the juristic humanists for a return to the pure texts of Justinian's *Corpus iuris civilis,* and of the metaphysical humanists for a return to the original texts of Plato and Aristotle.

Although the principal figures in this development of astronomy, Peuerbach and Regiomontanus, still held stubbornly to the Ptolemaic geocentric conception of the world, they nevertheless can be viewed as helping to prepare the ground for the future Copernican heliocentric conception by clearing away much of the tangled underbrush and clutter of Arabic science that was impeding a change of world views. One possible consequence of this process was the freeing of astronomy from astrology, that is, the science of the stars from the pseudo-science that claims to ascertain the influence of the stars on human behavior. This liberation of astronomy from astrology could in turn have helped to free medicine from its traditional subservience to astrology, as was the issue, for example, in the controversy at Leipzig between Pollich von Mellerstadt and Simon Pistoris over the causes of the "gallic disease" (syphilis).[67]

On the whole, however, the desire to free the sciences from arcane and magical assumptions was the exception rather than the rule among humanists, whether northern or southern. The effect of the Italian migration could just as readily be one of confirming as of undermining the magical predispositions of the traveler. Just as Dürer found his "secret art of perspective" in Italy, so might a magician like Agrippa of Nettesheim (d. ca. 1534) discover in Italy secrets of Hermetic and kabbalistic magic.

Just before taking his first Italian journey in 1511 Agrippa completed the first two books of *On Occult Philosophy,* which he gratefully dedicated to Abbot Trithemius (a magician in his own right who had authored a work on cryptography purporting to send messages telepathically through the medium of angels).[68] In its final three-book version (published in 1531), this work treated the arts, in order, of natural magic, located in the elemental world; celestial or mathematical magic, revealing how to attract and use the influence of the planets; and ceremonial magic, showing how to draw upon the powers of angelic spirits. In the third book, composed after his first Italian journey, Agrippa mediated a key doctrine of the Florentine Platonist Marsilio Ficino, that the melancholy humor, under the sway of the planet Saturn, is the mark of inspired poets, prophets, philosophers, and other extraordinary types. The effect of this doctrine, attributed by Ficino to Aristotle, was to countermand the usual warnings against the mischief-making of Saturn—a view reflected, for example, by Celtis in his *Amores* when he entreats Saturn, who "so often inflicts injury upon me," to keep his "noxious arrows" in their quiver.[69] Moreover, Agrippa extended the Aristotelian doctrine of "noble melancholy" to an area not indicated by Ficino, that of the visual arts. He wrote:

For when set free by the *humor melancholicus,* the soul is fully concentrated in the imagination, and it immediately becomes an habitation for the lower spirits, from whom it often receives wonderful instruction in the magical arts; thus, we see a quite unskilled man suddenly become a painter or an architect or a quite outstanding master in another art of the same kind.[70]

A direct artistic consequence of this passage was Dürer's famed engraving *Melancolia I* (1514). As a modern student of this engraving has correctly observed: "There is no work of art which corresponds more nearly to Agrippa's notion of melancholy than Dürer's engraving, and there is no text with which Dürer's engraving accords more nearly than Agrippa's chapters on melancholy."[71]

In all these explorations, as he well knew, Agrippa was treading on dangerous ground. For it was but three decades earlier (in 1484) that the witch craze can be said to have had its real origin in the promulgation of a papal bull by Innocent VIII declaring illicit magic to be a heresy and in the composition of a notorious inquisitorial handbook by two German scholastics entitled *Malleus maleficarum* (*The Witches' Hammer*).

This kind of climate should help us to understand some of the more vehement opposition to Reuchlin's kabbalism. The very title of his first kabbalistic work, *Concerning the Wonder-Working Word* (1494), betrays this magical motive. As he noted in it, he had recently met a very learned man in Rome "who proposed that no names in magical and lawful enterprises possess a virtue equal to that residing in the Hebrew tongue or in languages most nearly derived from it."[72] In his later work *Concerning the Cabalistic Art* (1517), Reuchlin revealed how he had earned the epithet "Pythagoras reborn." He adopted the view (supported also by Pico) that "by number a way may be had for the investigation and understanding of everything known."[73] According to this theory, the names of God (the tetragrammaton JHVH) and of Jesus, of the angels, and of all other things in the universe can be expressed numerically as well as verbally. The relation between Pythagoreanism and kabbalism, Reuchlin believed, was historical as well as conceptual; Pythagoras, according to this arcane tradition, learned his magical secrets from the Hebrews. Thus in the preface to his treatise on the kabbalah, addressed to the Medici Pope Leo X, Reuchlin proudly announced:

> In Italy Marsilio edited Plato; in France, Jacques Lefèvre d'Etaples restored Aristotle; I, Reuchlin, shall swell the number and exhibit to your brothers and sisters Pythagoras, reborn through me, and dedicated to your name. Now in order to accomplish this, it is necessary to have reference to the Cabala of the Hebrews, because Pythagorean philosophy took its rise from the teachings of the Cabala.[74]

According to L. Geiger, the goal of Reuchlin's two famous books on the kabbalah "was in no way that of magic and astrology, no marvelous secret art, but only the raising of the human spirit to God, the transfiguration of the earthly life and the preparation for heavenly bliss."[75] Spitz accepts this view.[76] At the opposite pole Charles Zika has persuasively argued that Reuchlin's kabbalistic speculations were infused with operational intentions.[77] My own inclination is to accept Zika's revisionist view, but with the understanding that it is not truly an either-or situation, that is, *either* magic *or* religion. For the Renaissance theorist of the arcana in the mold of a Reuchlin or of an Agrippa, magic shared fundamental ground with religion. This fact at least partially explains why the church was so greatly disturbed by the magical renascence in the fifteenth and sixteenth centuries: it saw in magic a competitor threatening its own monopoly of supernatural theory and operations. If magic were to be saved as a legitimate "Christian" discipline, it needed to be theologically justified. That is precisely what the leading speculative magicians of the Renaissance—including the Germans Trithemius, Agrippa, Reuchlin, and Paracelsus—attempted to do. As Paracelsus was later to put this noble aim of magic:

> Magic has the power to experience and fathom things which are inaccessible to human reason. . . . Therefore, it would be desirable and good for the doctors of theology to know something about it and to understand what it actually is, and cease unjustly and unfoundedly to call it witchcraft.[78]

*   *   *

In 1517, the year of Luther's Ninety-Five Theses, a brilliant young humanist named Philipp Melanchthon (d. 1560), a grandnephew of Reuchlin, helped firm up the humanist program at the University of Tübingen. Being, like his relative, a first-rate Greek scholar, Melanchthon came to the attention of Frederick the Wise when a vacancy in Greek occurred in the Wittenberg arts faculty, and he was asked to take the chair. In his inaugural lecture, subsequently published under the title *On Improving the Studies of Youth*, Melanchthon struck what is now a familiar note to us:

> My entire address has the single purpose of raising your hope for elegant literature (I am speaking of Greek and Latin). The studies for youth that are called preparatory exercises—grammar, dialectic, rhetoric—must be learned. . . . Greek letters should be added to Latin, so that reading the philosophers, theologians, orators, poets, wherever you turn, you may gain the very substance, not the shadow of things. . . . For I am fully of the opinion that whoever desires to undertake anything distinguished, either in the sacred cults or in the affairs of state, will achieve but very little unless he has previously exercised his mind prudently and sufficiently with humane discipline.[79]

A fundamental feature of the humanistic reform envisioned in this lecture was the consciousness of a sharp break between the Gothic "dark ages" and the renascence of classical culture with which Melanchthon identified his reform efforts. He wanted to reconcile the improperly divided disciplines of rhetoric and logic. To achieve this goal it was not sufficient to furnish content in a particular proposition; it was also necessary to present that content in an eloquent form. And the purpose of this reform was spiritual and moral excellence. "For where barbarity vitiates the more serious disciplines, the morals of the people are usually endangered."[80]

Significantly, Melanchthon's humanist vision included the visual arts, nicely complementing Luther's corresponding sanctification of the musical arts. It was Dürer above all in whom Melanchthon saw an artistic paragon for the harmonization of Protestant revelation with classical form. He once wrote of Dürer:

> First there is the heroic type of Scipio, Augustus, Pomponius Atticus—or Dürer. It is the noblest type and outstanding in excellence of every kind, since what controls it is a moderated mixture [of humors], and it arises out of an auspicious astral configuration.[81]

Melanchthon believed Dürer was attempting to express visual images analogous to those of the Ciceronian orator, declaring in this regard:

> It is . . . very useful, in forming a judgment, to distinguish the various styles of speaking. . . . There is the simple style, and its opposite the grand. The third is the middle, which is fuller than the first, but yet lacks something of the grand style. These differences may be readily discerned in paintings. For example, Dürer painted everything in the grand manner, variegated with innumerable lines. The paintings of Lucas [Cranach] are simple; . . . Matthias [Grünewald] remained more or less in the middle style. These styles, moreover, intermingle with one another, just as musicians mix their notes; even those which are rather thin occasionally give rise to something which is quite full.[82]

It was fitting that Melanchthon was chosen to inaugurate, in 1526, a new school with a humanist curriculum in Dürer's home town of Nuremberg. If Nuremberg was earlier christened by Dürer's friend Christoph Scheurl the "German Venice," it was now rechristened by Melanchthon the "German Florence." Just as "honorable arts began to revive through the benefaction of the Florentines," exhorted the visiting Wittenberg reformer, "so should the Nurembergers strive to emulate Florence in the transmission of the arts and sciences."[83]

In this way Melanchthon sought to make a smooth transition from Renaissance to Reformation. In his endeavor he found a number of talented allies. Peter Mosellanus, Luther's first choice for the chair of Greek at Wittenberg, counseled along with Melanchthon that the principles of humanism should be instilled in youth at an early age to lead them "as if by a kind of stairway to the style of Terence and the ease of Cicero."[84] Joachim Camerarius, after teaching for some years in the Nuremberg gymnasium opened by Melanchthon, migrated to such well-established humanist schools as those of Tübingen and Leipzig, where he earned a reputation as one of the most erudite classical scholars of his day. These figures and many others in the Lutheran camp give unassailable backing to Professor Spitz's revision of the conventional view which separates Renaissance from Reformation:

> The commonplace notion of a sharp break between Renaissance and Reformation . . . has proved to be a *fable convenue* which must be relegated to the historians' shelves of outmoded curiosities along with the idea of the Middle Ages as the dark ages or the Enlightenment as an anti-historical period.[85]

But there were also many humanists who refused to support Luther's cause, among the most illustrious of whom was Erasmus. Another who, like Erasmus, was initially sympathetic to Luther but pulled away as the Reformation took an increasingly radical turn, was the Nuremberg patrician Willibald Pirckheimer. The essential religious meaning of humanism, as Pirckheimer grasped it in his treatise *In Praise of the Gout* (1530), cut both ways in the Reformation debate. The liberal arts, he said, inasmuch as they help us overcome corporeal sufferings by leading us to nobler incorporeal concerns "should not be condemned . . . but should be learned far into the future. . . . For the knowledge of letters and of the good arts is far superior to external honors and great wealth."[86] This viewpoint also continued to be expressed in the monasteries. Speaking ably for this approach was Trithemius's monastic disciple Johann Butzbach, who proclaimed from his cloister at Maria-Laach: "Without the study of letters I grow lazy in idleness, which is described by Seneca as the burial of a live man."[87]

Thus the torch of humanism helped light the way not only for the Protestant reformers, but also for those Catholic reformers who were searching for an evolutionary rather than a revolutionary solution to the plight of the Christian church.

NOTES

1. For the Horatian line see *Epistles*, 2.1.156. The most concise exposition of this subject so far in English is by L. W. Spitz, "The Course of German

Humanism," in *Itinerarium Italicum: The Profile of the Italian Renaissance in the Mirror of Its European Transformations*, ed. H. A. Oberman and T. A. Brady, Jr. (Leiden, 1975), 371–436. Major trends in the scholarly interpretation of the northern Renaissance are recounted in W. K. Ferguson, *The Renaissance in Historical Thought* (Cambridge, MA, 1948), 253–89, with focus on the German Renaissance, 276–89. Some more recent English-language writings addressed to the spread of Italian humanism to the North, in addition to the Oberman and Brady volume cited above, are: F. B. Artz, *Renaissance Humanism, 1300–1550* (Kent, OH, 1966); M. E. Aston, "The Northern Renaissance," in *The Meaning of the Renaissance and Reformation*, ed. R. L. DeMolen (Boston, 1974), 71–129; *The Late Middle Ages and the Dawn of Humanism Outside Italy*, ed. J. IJsewijn and G. Verbeke (Louvain, 1972); P. O. Kristeller, "The European Diffusion of Italian Humanism," in his *Renaissance Thought II: Papers on Humanism and the Arts* (New York, 1965); *The Northern Renaissance*, ed. L. W. Spitz (Englewood Cliffs, NJ, 1972), 1–12; L. W. Spitz, *The Renaissance and Reformation Movements*, 2 vols. (Chicago, 1971), 274ff.; R. Weiss, *The Spread of Italian Humanism* (London, 1964); and idem, "Italian Humanism in Western Europe," in E. F. Jacob, ed., *Italian Renaissance Studies* (London, 1960), 69–93. For Italian influences in the visual arts see especially O. Benesch, *The Art of the Renaissance in Northern Europe* (London, rev. ed. 1965).

2. A. Hyma, *The Christian Renaissance: A History of the "Devotio Moderna"* (Hamden, CT, 2d ed. 1965); L. W. Spitz, *The Religious Renaissance of the German Humanists* (Cambridge, MA, 1963).

3. L. Geiger, *Renaissance und Humanismus in Italien und Deutschland* (Berlin, 1882). Playing down the humanistic educational role of the Modern Devotion (and thus complementing the "receptivity" theory of Geiger and his followers) is R. R. Post, *The Modern Devotion: Confrontation with Reformation and Humanism* (Leiden, 1968).

4. P. O. Kristeller, *Renaissance Thought: The Classic, Scholastic, and Humanist Strains* (New York, 1961), 11.

5. Cited in Spitz, "Humanism and the Reformation," in R. M. Kingdon, ed., *Transition and Revolution: Problems and Issues of European Renaissance and Reformation History* (Minneapolis, MN, 1974), 154.

6. *De arte poetica*, l. 361.

7. *De partitione oratoria*, § 79: "Nihil enim est aliud eloquentia nisi copiose loquens sapientia." See H. H. Gray, "Renaissance Humanism: The Pursuit of Eloquence," *Journal of the History of Ideas* 24 (1963): 497–514 (with this Cicero quotation cited, 508); and G. M. Logan, "Substance and Form in Renaissance Humanism," *Journal of Medieval and Renaissance Studies* 7 (1977): 1–34.

8. P. S. Allen, *The Age of Erasmus* (Oxford, 1914), 8ff. Allen terms the cloister of Henry of Rees "the Adwert Academy."

9. See K. Arnold, *Johannes Trithemius (1462–1516)* (Würzburg, 1971); and

N. L. Brann, *The Abbot Trithemius (1462–1516): The Renaissance of Monastic Humanism* (Leiden, 1981).

10. Matthäus Herbenus, letter of 1495, cited ibid., 23–24.

11. Cited ibid., 213.

12. Petrarch to Johann von Neumarkt, Avignon(?), 1352–53, in H. Rupprich, *Die Frühzeit des Humanismus und der Renaissance in Deutschland* (Leipzig, 1938), 83. Unless otherwise indicated, translations are my own.

13. Aeneas Silvius Piccolomini to Nicholas von Wyle, Vienna, 1452, in *Enea Silvio Piccolomini Papst Pius II: Ausgewählte Texte aus seinen Schriften*, ed. B. Widmer (Basel, 1960), 298–99 (Latin text and German translation).

14. P. Joachimsen, *Geschichtsauffassung und Geschichtsschreibung in Deutschland unter dem Einfluss des Humanismus* (Leipzig, 1910), 218.

15. H. Holborn, *Ulrich von Hutten and the German Reformation*, trans. R. H. Bainton (New Haven, 1937), 41.

16. See W. C. McDonald, "Maximilian I of Habsburg and the Veneration of Hercules: On the Revival of Myth and the German Renaissance," *Journal of Medieval and Renaissance Studies* 6 (1976): 139–54. Cf. F. L. Borchardt, *German Antiquity in Renaissance Myth* (Baltimore, 1971), 143.

17. Conrad Celtis to Prince Magnus von Anhalt, Leipzig, 13 February 1487, in *Briefwechsel*, ed. H. Rupprich (Munich, 1934), no. 5, p. 11. It is the dedicatory epistle to Celtis's edition of the tragedies of Seneca. On Celtis see L. W. Spitz, *Conrad Celtis: The German Arch-Humanist* (Cambridge, MA, 1957), and idem, *Religious Renaissance*, 81ff.

18. Celtis, *Opera Hrosvita . . . à Conr. Celte inventa* (Nuremberg, 1501), sig. a ii recto.

19. Spitz, *Religious Renaissance*, 156–57.

20. Geiger, *Renaissance und Humanismus*, 384.

21. G. Strauss, *Nuremberg in the Sixteenth Century* (New York and London, 1966), 249.

22. M. Watanabe, "Gregor Heimburg and Early Humanism in Germany," in *Philosophy and Humanism: Renaissance Essays in Honor of Paul Oskar Kristeller*, ed. E. P. Mahoney (New York, 1976), 406–22, at 416. See also Watanabe, "Humanism in the Tyrol: Aeneas Sylvius, Duke Sigismund, Gregor Heimberg," *Journal of Medieval and Renaissance Studies* 4 (1974): 177–202. But on a falling out between Aeneas and Gregor, owing to Gregor's subjection of rhetoric to juristic studies, see H. O. Taylor, *Thought and Expression in the Sixteenth Century* (New York, 1920), 147. Cf. M. P. Gilmore, *Humanists and Jurists: Six Studies in the Renaissance* (Cambridge, MA, 1963), 30–32.

23. Spitz, *Religious Renaissance*, 86. On Celtis's interest in Nicholas of Cusa, see 96–98. See also Spitz, *Conrad Celtis*, 63–71, esp. 68–69.

24. M. Grossman, *Humanism in Wittenberg, 1485–1517* (Nieuwkoop, 1975), 55ff., 72ff.

25. Alexander Hegius, *Dialogi* (1503), cited in T. Heath, "Logical Grammar, Grammatical Logic, and Humanism in Three German Universities [viz.,

Freiburg-im-Breisgau, Ingolstadt, Tübingen]," *Studies in the Renaissance* 18 (1971): 9–64, at 18. Still an important background work for this subject is W. H. Woodward, *Studies in Education During the Age of the Renaissance, 1400–1600* (Cambridge, 1906, reprinted New York, 1967).

26. Geiger, *Renaissance und Humanismus*, 399. See also Heath, "Logical Grammar," 9ff.

27. Heath, "Logical Grammar," 13.

28. Cited ibid., 38–39.

29. See, e.g., E. Garin, *Italian Humanism: Philosophy and Civic Life in the Renaissance*, trans. P. Munz (New York, 1965), 8, 69ff. Valla's crucial writing in this regard is *On the Elegances of the Latin Language (De elegantiis latinae linguae)*.

30. Heath, "Logical Grammar," 48. The humanist objector to Peter is Johann Versor.

31. Rudolf Agricola, *De inventione dialectica/Lucubrationes* (Cologne, 1539; facsimile, Nieuwkoop, 1967), 1. On Agricola as a forerunner of Peter Ramus, see W. J. Ong, S. J., *Ramus, Method, and the Decay of Dialogue* (New York, 1979), 92ff.; and G. A. Kennedy, *Classical Rhetoric and Its Christian and Secular Tradition from Ancient to Modern Times* (Chapel Hill, 1980), 195ff., esp. 208–10. On Agricola's life see Spitz, *Religious Renaissance*, 20ff.

32. Cited in Spitz, *Religious Renaissance*, 25.

33. Agricola to Jacob Barbirianus, in *Sourcebook of the Renaissance*, ed. M. Whitcomb (New York, rev. ed. 1903), 132.

34. Cited in *Humanismus und Renaissance in den deutschen Städten und an den deutschen Universitäten*, ed. H. Rupprich (Leipzig, 1935, repr. Darmstadt, 1964 and 1965), Introduction, 27–28.

35. Celtis, *Briefwechsel*, no. 32, 56–57.

36. Heinrich Bebel, *De necessitate linguae latinae*, appendix to *Heinrich Bebel nach seinem Leben und Schriften*, ed. G. Zapf (Augsburg, 1802; facsimile, Leipzig, 1973), 295. See also Heath, "Logical Grammar," 24ff.

37. Cited in Heath, "Logical Grammar," 25.

38. On the Greek revival in Italy see especially D. J. Geanakoplos, *Greek Scholars in Venice: Studies in the Dissemination of Greek Learning from Byzantium to the West* (Cambridge, MA, 1962), republished as *Byzantium and the Renaissance* (New Haven, 1978), and idem, *Interaction of the "Sibling" Byzantine and Western Cultures in the Middle Ages and Italian Renaissance (330–1600)* (New Haven, 1976). On Reuchlin's role as mediator with Germany see *Greek Scholars*, 275; *Interaction*, 237; and Spitz, *Religious Renaissance*, 61ff., esp. 62.

39. Wimpheling, *Isidoneus*, in Whitcomb, *Sourcebook*, 144.

40. Ibid., 142–43.

41. Geanakoplos, *Greek Scholars*, 136.

42. Johann Reuchlin to Cardinal Adrian, Stuttgart, February 1518, in *Johannes Reuchlins Briefwechsel*, ed. L. Geiger (Stuttgart, 1875; facsimile, Hildes-

heim, 1962), no. 250, p. 283. See also Geanakoplos, *Greek Scholars*, 136ff.
43. Erasmus to Ulrich Zwingli, September 1522, in *Opus Epistolarum Des. Erasmi Roterodami*, ed. P. S. Allen, H. M. Allen, and H. W. Garrod, 12 vols. (Oxford, 1906–58), no. 1314, 5:129. See also Spitz, *Religious Renaissance*, 197.
44. Ulrich von Hutten to Erasmus, Worms, 24 October 1515, cited in Holborn, *Ulrich von Hutten*, 67.
45. Borchardt, *German Antiquity*, 143ff., 196–97. On the Trojan myth see also Brann, *Abbot Trithemius*, 236–41.
46. Borchardt, *German Antiquity*, 170–71. Cf. Brann, *Abbot Trithemius*, 241ff., and "Conrad Celtis and the 'Druid' Abbot Trithemius: An Inquiry into Patriotic Humanism," *Renaissance and Reformation/Renaissance et réforme* n.s. 3, o.s. 15 (1979): 16–28.
47. *Selections from Conrad Celtis, 1459–1508*, ed. L. Forster (Cambridge, 1948), 43.
48. See, e.g., R. Weiss, *The Renaissance Discovery of Classical Antiquity* (Oxford, 1969), 155, 176–77. Cf. Borchardt, *German Antiquity*, passim.
49. Geiger, *Renaissance und Humanismus*, 446. Cf. Brann, *Abbot Trithemius*, 325–26.
50. Heinrich Bebel, *Facetiae*, in *Humanismus und Renaissance*, ed. Rupprich, 192.
51. Bebel, *De laudibus atque philosophia germanorum in opuscula nova* (Strasbourg, 1508), sig. A ii recto ff; Beatus Rhenanus, *Rerum germanicarum libri III* (Basel, 1531), 27. For the role of Beatus in initiating a "new criticism" in historical writing, see Borchardt, *German Antiquity*, 10. But for the stubborn persistence of both the Trojan and the druidic myths in German historical writing, see G. Strauss, *Historian in an Age of Crisis: The Life and Work of Johannes Aventinus, 1477–1534* (Cambridge, MA, 1963).
52. Borchardt, *German Antiquity*, 98ff.
53. Cited in Geiger, *Renaissance und Humanismus*, 364.
54. Cited in W. Andreas, *Deutschland vor der Reformation: Eine Zeitenwende* (Stuttgart, 1932), 494. On the relation of the printing revolution to the Renaissance of letters, see E. Eisenstein, *The Printing Press as an Agent of Change*, 2 vols. (Cambridge, 1979), 1:181ff.
55. Cited in Geiger, *Renaissance und Humanismus*, 326. Cf. Brann, *Abbot Trithemius*, 258–59.
56. Cited in Geiger, *Renaissance und Humanismus*, 435. Cf. Spitz, *Religious Renaissance*, 130ff., esp. 140ff.
57. Celtis, *Ode to Apollo*, in *Northern Renaissance*, ed. Spitz, 14–15. For an alternative translation, see *Selections*, ed. Forster, 20–21.
58. Matthaeus Lupinus, "Quaestio de poetis a republica minime pellendis," in *Humanismus und Renaissance*, ed. Rupprich, 268ff.
59. Ortwin Gratius, "Oratio . . . in commendationem poeticae," in *Humanismus und Renaissance*, ed. Rupprich, 149–50.
60. See *Enea Silvio Piccolomini*, ed. B. Widmer, 298–99. The translation used

is by J. R. Spencer, "Ut Rhetorica Pictura: A Study in Quattrocento Theory of Painting," *Journal of the Warburg and Courtauld Institutes* 20 (1957): 26–44, at 27.

61. Nicholas of Cusa, *De concordantia catholica*, in *Opera*, 3 vols. (Paris, 1514; facsimile, Frankfurt am Main, 1962), preface, sig. AA ii recto.

62. See, e.g., A. Blunt, *Artistic Theory in Italy, 1450–1600* (Oxford, 1940, reprinted 1966), 1ff. Cf. R. W. Lee, "Ut Pictura Poesis: The Humanistic Theory of Painting," *Art Bulletin* 22 (1940): 197–269; and Spencer, "Ut Rhetorica Pictura." On Nicholas of Cusa see E. Cassirer, *The Individual and the Cosmos in Renaissance Philosophy*, trans. M. Domandi (New York, 1963), 1ff.

63. Nicholas of Cusa, *De docta ignorantia* 1.1, cited in Cassirer, *Individual and the Cosmos*, 51.

64. Cited in D. Koenigsberger, *Renaissance Man and Creative Thinking: A History of Concepts of Harmony, 1400–1700* (Atlantic Highlands, NJ, 1979), 116. See also 118.

65. Spencer, "Ut Rhetorica Pictura," 26. On Dürer, see especially E. Panofsky, *Albrecht Dürer*, 2 vols. (Princeton, 1943). On Dürer's association with the Nuremberg humanists, especially Pirckheimer, see Strauss, *Nuremberg*, 272ff., and Benesch, *Art of the Renaissance*, 12ff. An anthology of sources in English translation is furnished by *Northern Renaissance Art, 1400–1600*, ed. W. Stechow (Englewood Cliffs, NJ, 1966), with Dürer writings represented, 85ff.

66. Cited in Panofsky, *Albrecht Dürer*, 1:274.

67. Grossman, *Humanism in Wittenberg*, 42. Pollich later migrated to Wittenberg University, where he became its first rector.

68. Brann, *Abbot Trithemius*, 117. On the magic of both Trithemius and Agrippa, see D. P. Walker, *Spiritual and Demonic Magic from Ficino to Campanella* (London, 1958), 84ff.; and on Agrippa's occultism in particular, C. G. Nauert, Jr., *Agrippa and the Crisis of Renaissance Thought* (Urbana, IL, 1965); and F. A. Yates, *The Occult Philosophy in the Elizabethan Age* (London, 1979), 37ff.

69. Cited in R. Klibansky, E. Panofsky, and F. Saxl, *Saturn and Melancholy* (New York, 1964), 278.

70. Cited in Klibansky et al., *Saturn and Melancholy*, 357. For the relation of Dürer to Agrippa, see Yates, *Occult Philosophy*, 49ff.

71. Klibansky et al., *Saturn and Melancholy*, 360.

72. Johann Reuchlin, *De verbo mirifico*, 1494; *De arte cabalistica*, 1517 (facsimile, Stuttgart, 1964), book 2, sig. c 8 verso. See J. L. Blau, *The Christian Interpretation of the Cabala in the Renaissance* (Port Washington, NY, 1944, reprinted 1965), 41ff.

73. This "mathematical conclusion" of Pico is cited in Yates, *Giordano Bruno and the Hermetic Tradition* (London, 1964), 148, and is applied by Yates to Reuchlin in *Occult Philosophy*, 25. Cf. Spitz, *Religious Renaissance*, 67–68.

74. Reuchlin, *On the Cabalistic Art,* dedication to Pope Leo X, in *Renaissance Philosophy, II: The Transalpine Thinkers,* ed. H. Shapiro and A. B. Fallico (New York, 1969), 28. Also cited in Spitz, *Religious Renaissance,* 67.

75. Geiger, *Renaissance und Humanismus,* 505.

76. Spitz, *Religious Renaissance,* 70–76.

77. C. Zika, "Reuchlin's *De verbo mirifico* and the Magic Debate of the Late Fifteenth Century," *Journal of the Warburg and Courtauld Institutes* 39 (1976): 104–38. Cf. Yates, *Occult Philosophy,* 24.

78. Paracelsus, *Selected Writings,* ed., J. Jacobi, trans. N. Guterman (London, 1951), 211. See Walker, *Spiritual and Demonic Magic,* 96ff.; and N. L. Brann, "Was Paracelsus a Disciple of Trithemius?" *Sixteenth Century Journal* 10 (1979): 71–82.

79. Philipp Melanchthon, "On Improving the Studies of Youth (*De corrigendis adolescentiae studiis*)," in *Transition and Revolution,* ed. Kingdon, 169. The original text is found in *Declamationes,* ed. K. Hartfelder (Berlin, 1891), 1:13–27.

80. Cited in L. W. Spitz, "Humanism and the Reformation," in *Renaissance Studies in Honor of Hans Baron,* ed. A. Molho and J. A. Tedeschi (Dekalb, IL, 1971), 662. Latin text is in *Declamationes,* 1:27ff.

81. Cited in D. B. Kuspit, "Melanchthon and Dürer: The Search for the Simple Style," *Journal of Medieval and Renaissance Studies* 3 (1973): 177–202, at 200, note.

82. Cited in Kuspit, "Melanchthon and Dürer," 185, note.

83. Melanchthon, *In laudem novae scholae,* in Spitz, "Humanism and the Reformation," *Transition and Revolution,* ed. Kingdon, 173.

84. Peter Mosellanus, *Paedologia* (Leipzig, 1521), trans. R. F. Seybold (Urbana, IL, 1927), 4.

85. L. W. Spitz, "Course of German Humanism," 435. Cf. B. Moeller, "The German Humanists and the Reformation," in *Imperial Cities and the Reformation,* ed. H. C. E. Midelfort and M. U. Edwards, Jr. (Philadelphia, 1972), 36: "One can state this pointedly: no humanism, no reformation." See also L. W. Spitz, "Headwaters of the Reformation: Studia Humanitatis, Luther Senior, et Initia Reformationis," in *Luther and the Dawn of the Modern Era,* ed. H. A. Oberman (Leiden, 1974), 89–116.

86. Willibald Pirckheimer, "Apologia seu podagrae laus," in *Humanismus und Renaissance,* ed. Rupprich, 125. See Spitz, *Religious Renaissance,* 155ff.

87. Cited in Brann, *Abbot Trithemius,* 371. Cf. Allen, *Age of Erasmus,* 66ff.

22 ❧ HUMANISM IN THE LOW COUNTRIES
Jozef IJsewijn

THE LOW COUNTRIES OR NETHERLANDS[1] OF THE MIDDLE AGES and Renaissance period do not correspond to any modern country.[2] The Burgundian and later Habsburg or Spanish or independent territories called "Germania Inferior," "Belgium" (or "Belgia" by the poets), "XVII Provinciae (belgicae)," comprise the modern kingdoms of the Netherlands (or Holland) and Belgium, the Grand Duchy of Luxembourg, some border areas in western Germany belonging to Niedersachsen and Rhineland as well as a substantial part of northern France including such towns as Lille (Rijsel/Insulae), Cassel, St. Omer (Sint-Omaars/Audomaropolis), Thérouanne (Terwaan, Teruana or Civitas Morinorum), Arras (Atrecht/Atrebates), Valenciennes, Douai (Dowaai/Duacum) and Cambrai (Kamerijk/Cameracum). There were more or less twenty principalities (Holland, Flanders, Brabant, and so on). Most of them passed under Burgundian rule in the course of the fifteenth century, the signal exception being the prince-bishopric of Liège (Luik/Lüttich/Leodium or Legia), which depended on the Holy Roman Empire. Scholars must be strongly warned against a most common error of anachronism, namely the translation of "Belgium/belgicus" in humanist texts by the English "Belgium/Belgian." Only the translation "(of) the Low Countries" is appropriate, in order to avoid confusion with the kingdom founded in 1830; such confusion renders old texts unintelligible.

Culturally Germania Inferior offered a wide variety of languages and dialects: Frisian was spoken in the North (the Leeuwarden–Groningen–Emden area), various Netherlandic (Dutch) dialects in the major part of the country from Holland to Flanders and Brabant; Low German in the eastern border areas and "Moselfränkisch" in much of Luxembourg; French dialects (Walloon, Picard) dominated in the southern areas of Artois (Artesia), the south of Flanders and Brabant, Hainaut (Henegouwen, Hainault, Hannonia), Namur (Namen, Namurcum), parts of Luxembourg, and Liège. The Burgundian court in Brussels (Brussel/Bruxelles/Bruxellae) and much of the Flemish nobility spoke French, but Spanish became important in the sixteenth century. Finally, in port towns like Brugge (Bruges/Brugae) and Antwerpen (Anvers/Antwerp/Amberes/

Antverpia) there were important Italian and Spanish communities. Latin was the universal language of the church and of higher education, often also of international communication such as diplomacy. Its strongholds were the universities, the abbeys with their libraries (such as Adwerth/Aduard near Groningen, Korsendonk near Turnhout, Park near Louvain, or St. Bertin near St. Omer) and the Latin schools, which existed in nearly every center of some importance or were founded under the influence of humanism. It has often been said that in those schools the so-called Brethren of the Common Life fostered the development of humanism. Even if this claim be true for some places and persons—the most notable being the playwright Georgius Macropedius (1487–ca. 1558) in the early sixteenth century—the Brethren in general did not themselves teach but ran student houses (dormitories), and their concern was mainly religious, not scholarly. And often enough after an initial interest in humanism, they eventually turned hostile to it. The case of the house of Sint-Maartensdal (Vallis Sancti Martini) at Louvain may serve here as an example.

Through Latin, humanism was able to pass from Italy into the Low Countries from the fifteenth century onward and dominate their literature until the early seventeenth century. At the end of the Middle Ages there were no universities in the Low Countries. Students went to Paris (especially from Flanders and Artois) or Cologne (mainly from the other areas). Then and later they even went to more distant places in France (Bourges, Orléans, Dôle, Montpellier), Germany (Heidelberg, Erfurt, Rostock), and Italy (Pavia, Ferrara, Padua, Bologna, Pisa, Rome).

In 1425 a university was founded by Pope Martin V in the Duchy of Brabant at Leuven (called Loven at that time, hence Latin Lovanium, French and English Louvain). It opened in 1426 with the Faculties of Arts, both Laws (civil and canon), and Medicine. In 1432 the Faculty of Theology was added to stop the penetration of Hussitism (*Bohemica haeresis*). Its members for a very long time remained hostile to the humanist movement, which found its patrons mainly in the Arts faculty, sometimes also in Civil Law. Its first stronghold was the Arts College De Lelie (*Paedagogium Lilii*). In 1517 the famous Collegium Trilingue, notwithstanding much opposition, was founded with money left by Erasmus's friend, the Luxemburger and imperial counsellor Jerome (Hieronymus) Busleiden. In this college Latin, Greek, and Hebrew were taught according to humanist principles for all interested students.

For about a century and a half Louvain was the only university in the country, but there were important Latin schools in places such as Deventer (Daventria)—where Erasmus was educated—Zwolle, Alkmaar, Haarlem, 's Hertogenbosch (Bois-le-Duc/Buscum or Silva Ducis),

Brecht, Antwerp, Mechelen (Malines, Mechlin, Machlinia), Gent (Gand/ Ghent/Gandavum), and elsewhere. Their number increased considerably in the sixteenth century.

In the late sixteenth century, when the Low Countries were devastated by unrelenting religious wars, two more universities were founded. A Catholic bulwark was built at Douai in Artois as a sort of extension of Louvain in the French-speaking areas (first approved by Paul IV in 1559; final foundation by King Philip II in 1562). The Reformation camp founded its own university at Leiden (Lugdunum Batavorum or Leida) in 1575. It soon developed into one of the most brilliant centers of humanist learning, attracting such men as Justus Lipsius, Joseph Justus Scaliger, and Daniel Heinsius. Only at a later stage did it become a Calvinist stronghold.

About this time the Netherlands, as a consequence of religious divisions and hatreds, were breaking apart into two separate entities. The North, with the help of England, won its independence and joined the Reformation, though at the beginning the majority of the population was still Catholic. The southern provinces could be kept under Spanish-Catholic sovereignty by commanders such as Alessandro Farnese, and there the existing reformed communities were in one way or another annihilated. This destruction resulted in a heavy brain-drain toward the North, and many of Holland's late humanists were in fact men from Flanders and Brabant: Lipsius from Overijse between Louvain and Brussels, Kaspar van Baerle (Caspar Barlaeus) from Antwerp, Daniel Heinsius from Ghent, Bonaventura Vulcanius from Bruges, Dominicus Baudius from Lille, Philips van Marnix van Sint-Aldegonde (a former burgomaster of Antwerp), and many more.

From that time on North and South in matters of humanism and education followed different paths. In the South no new universities were founded until its temporary reunification with the North, from 1815 to 1830. Latin, however, was taught there in a very thorough way in the Jesuit colleges, six of which (including Brussels and Antwerp) were founded in the years 1556–74 and another nine 1575–1600. A particular mention should be made of the English College founded in 1568 by William Allen at Douai, the first seminary "ad mentem Concilii Tridentini institutum" to train priests for the English mission. There was also an English Jesuit College at St. Omer, and both institutions provided humanist education by means of a sound Latin rhetorical training, including the performance of Latin dramas. Apart from the Jesuits other religious orders too worked along the same humanist lines in their schools—the Augustinians, the Benedictines, and the Oratorians.

In the Protestant North several *scholae illustres* were founded by the municipal authorities, and nearly all of them after a few years developed into a university (*hogeschool* or *academia*). Often the names of famous scholars are linked with their beginnings. In chronological order they were Franeker in Friesland (Frisia), 1595; the Gelderse Hogeschool at Harderwijk (1599 and university in 1648); Groningen (1614 under Ubbo Van Embden [Emmius] after first attempts in 1595 and 1612); the Athenaeum Illustre of Amsterdam (1632) with its first professors Gerardus Vossius and Caspar Barlaeus; finally, Utrecht, 1634 and university in 1636.

As a result, in both the South and the North the humanist teaching of Latin was maintained at a very high level throughout the seventeenth century, but scholarship throve better in the North after 1600. Too often the South became a battlefield for war-waging neighbors; at the same time the anxious conservatism of the dominating theological faculty paralyzed much of Louvain's potential development. Even the Collegium Trilingue ceased to be a center of learning after the middle of the seventeenth century. The *Fasti academici Studii Generalis Lovaniensis* of Valerius Andreas (d. 1655), the last great professor of the college, closed as it were with a historical survey of the glory that had been.

The Low Countries, being a small nook of Europe without natural boundaries except the sea in the west and the north (though the sea more often served as a highway than as a barrier), are open in all respects to foreign influences and exchanges. Humanism came to it from Italy through the Rhine valley, or by way of Paris, or in the luggage of Italians establishing themselves at Louvain, Brussels, Bruges or elsewhere in the country. At the same time, native students and scholars went abroad for education or for a whole career. One cannot study the humanism of the Low Countries without carefully taking into account that continuous exchange of learning and learned men. In the course of the (late) fifteenth century several Italians were at work at Louvain (Raimundus Marlianus, Antonius Gratiadei, Cornelius Vitellius, Stephanus Surigonius, Lodovicus Brunus), but at the same time Rudolf Agricola, the first northern humanist, was in Italy (Pavia and Ferrara), Jacob Canter from Groningen in Augsburg and Bohemia, Matthaeus Herbenus from Maastricht (not a Walloon as was believed until recently) at Rome in the households of Niccolò Perotti and Cardinal Bessarion and later in Venice. This exchange of learning and learned men, facilitated by the universal use of Latin, intensified during the sixteenth and seventeenth centuries, and not rarely the most brilliant scholars in the Low Countries were foreigners, whereas our outstanding humanists often went abroad. The cause of these expatriations could be scholarly (as when courts, printing houses, or universities invited the best authors or teachers available), but very often the reason was a search for spiritual liberty or even a flight from death or imprisonment. Tolerance was hardly known in those days.

In order to assess correctly the overriding importance of these intellectual exchanges, it will be useful to list a few names, the most famous among a host of minor figures. The Spanish (Valencian) Jew Juan Luis Vives found shelter at Bruges in Flanders, and from there he worked in Brabant (Louvain and Breda) and England (London and Oxford). His friend Erasmus from Rotterdam in Holland passed most of his adult years in France, England, Italy, Switzerland, and Germany. One of Erasmus's publishers, Josse Bade (Jodocus Badius) from Asse near Brussels (Brabant), a prolific scholarly writer himself, established his printing press in Lyons and afterward in Paris as the famous Prelum Ascensianum. Later in the sixteenth century a Frenchman from the region of Tours, Christophe Plantin, came to Antwerp (1543) and founded there in 1555 one of the most important centers of late humanist editorial activity on an international scale, printing not only Lipsius and his colleagues, but also many Roman and other humanists (Fulvio Orsini etc.). The German occultist scholar Henricus Cornelius Agrippa of Nettesheim passed the last years of his agitated life in Brabant, where he was appointed court historian by Margaret of Austria (a post held earlier by Erasmus). He had known this noble lady about 1509 in the Franche Comté and written for her his defense of the fair sex (*De nobilitate et praecellentia feminei sexus*). This work was now printed at Antwerp in 1529, followed a year later by his famous *De incertitudine et vanitate scientiarum et artium atque excellentia verbi Dei declamatio*.

This list can be made very long on both sides. Let us mention the Dane Jacobus Jespersön (Gaspari) from Aarhus (ca. 1500–1550); the courtier Miklós Oláh (Nicolaus Olahus, 1493–1568) of Wallachian extraction; the Frenchman Joseph Justus Scaliger (1540–1609), thought to be the most learned man of his time; the English Jesuit playwright Joseph Simons (1593/94–1671); and on the other side, among many others, the Antwerp scholars and poets Joachim Sterck van Ringelbergh (Fortius a Ringelberg, 1499–1536) in France; Janus Gruterus (1560–1627), librarian at Heidelberg; Hendrik Kieffel (Henricus Chifellius, 1583–after 1651), professor at the Sapienza (Rome) under Urban VIII; Petrus Burrus (1427–1505) and Petrus Pontanus (d. ca. 1540), both born at Bruges, teachers and poets in Paris; Johannes Strazelius (d. 1558), professor of Greek; Bartholomaeus Latomus (1485–1570), professor of Latin at the Collège de France; Nicasius Ellebodius (d. 1577) from Cassel in Hungary; Niklaes Cleynaerts (Nicolaus Clenardus, 1495–1542) from Diest, the illustrious Greek scholar, in Spain, Portugal and Morocco; Erycius

Puteanus (1574–1642) from Venlo in Milan before he became Lipsius's successor at Louvain; the Dutchmen Johannes Meursius (1579–1639) at Sorø, Denmark, and Johannes Narssius (1580–1637) at Stockholm; finally, Johannes Heckius (b. 1579) from Deventer, who became one of the founders of the Accademia dei Lincei in Rome, now Italy's national academy. If I add that Thomas More's *Utopia* was conceived, partially written, and first published in the Low Countries (Antwerp and Louvain) but that Erasmus's equally famous *Praise of Folly* was written and published outside his native country, it will be perfectly clear that the international dimension is a fundamental characteristic of the humanism of the Low Countries, perhaps to a much greater extent than that of many other countries, and that it is in any case imperative to keep this aspect in mind for a correct assessment of its historical role and meaning.

*   *   *

The history of humanism and humanist learning in the Low Countries extends over about two centuries, from the middle of the fifteenth to the middle of the seventeenth century. In 1450 culture in the Low Countries was still by and large scholastic and late medieval, but a few individuals were aware of the new humanist currents in Italy. The first specimen of humanist script was produced as early as 1439, when the Flemish scribe George of Oedelem (Houdelem) wrote two quires of a Sallust manuscript in humanistica (the remainder still in Gothic characters) for Antonius Haneron, former professor of Latin at Louvain (1430–37) and at that time in the service of the Burgundian court in Brussels (where he may have met Italians using the new script). But humanists at that time were rare exceptions indeed, and it is quite normal therefore that Poggio Bracciolini, a man widely traveled in Europe from Switzerland to England, in his famous letter of December 1451 to Willem van Heze, dean of Utrecht Cathedral, expressed astonishment that so far north a man could be found with humanist interests: "I marvel that a man can be found so diligent in striving for eloquence and the best arts so far from Italy, to which these studies seem to be native."[3] Even the closer relations of Charles the Bold with Italian states and his occasional contacts with humanists such as Francesco Filelfo do not seem to have fostered very strongly the progress of humanism in his northern provinces. The court remained culturally medieval and French. Classical authors were read in translations (made, for example, by the Portuguese Vasco de Luceña, who translated Poggio's Latin version of Xenophon's *Cyropaedia* into the duke's mother tongue).

The rather late development or acceptance of humanistic learning and literature in the Low Countries and elsewhere in transalpine Europe is certainly not due to ignorance of it. Cultural relations between Italy and the Netherlands are as old as the Roman Empire, and northern scholars always had gone south: Bishop Ratherius of Verona (tenth century), a native of Hainaut and the only known reader of Catullus in the Middle Ages; the Fleming William of Moerbeke, the most famous translator of Aristotle; and his compatriot Dominicus of Flanders (ca. 1425–1479), a scholastic professor at Bologna, Pisa, and Florence, are only a few outstanding names. And conversely Petrarch himself had visited Liège and the Ardennes, discovering there Cicero's speech *Pro Archia*. His most intimate friend at Avignon was Ludovicus Heiligen (Sanctus), his "Socrates," a native from the village of Beringen in the prince-bishopric of Liège (now in Belgian Limburg). His works were widely read and known throughout the fifteenth century, but most of his readers had no inkling whatsoever of his epoch-making humanistic work and regarded him as another moral authority in the line of the old church fathers and St. Bernard.

All this, of course, has to do with the strong and dominating position scholastic philosophy and theology occupied in fifteenth-century life and culture, for which men like Dionysius the Carthusian from Rijkel, Thomas à Kempis, or Wessel Gansfort are far more representative than even Alexander Hegius or Rudolf Agricola, who were rare exceptions. This majority was not prepared at all to leave its powerful and profitable position to a few grammarians and poets who were dreaming of the glory of ancient Rome's bygone language. Moreover, the recovery of that old language could be seen and was seen in Italy by men such as Petrarch and Lorenzo Valla as the only possible means of restoring the lost supremacy of their country. Outside Italy it was only a matter of education and literature, but for people who were satisfied with their scholastic Latin and did not care for the formal beauty of classical Latin and even less for a knowledge of Greek—the language of the abhorred Orthodox schismatics—there was no reason to change or to allow a poet to tell a professor of divinity how to write and how to read the Bible. The whole situation was soon to be complicated in the early sixteenth century, before humanism was as widely accepted as it was in Italy, by the beginning of the Reformation. Although Luther was no humanist at all, theologians at Louvain and elsewhere were eager enough to charge humanism with all their problems and accuse them of being the source of the ecclesiastical disruption. The humanists on their side would often complain that the book market was inundated by theological polemics and quarrels, the ἐριστικὰ θεολόγων, as an irritated Lipsius once put it (*Epistolae* 2 no. 509.9–10), and that no room was left for the "humaniores litterae," a fact clearly confirmed by analyses of the book production in the sixteenth and seventeenth centuries in centers like Basel.

Humanism outside Italy possibly never would have gone as far as it did but for the invention of the printing press and its rapid expansion in Italy. As a result the classics and the new humanist textbooks of Gasparino Barzizza, Valla, Giovanni Tortelli, Filelfo, and others now became available in ever larger quantities. One wonders how many of these texts men such as Erasmus never would have seen at school if only manuscripts had been there and how different a course their intellectual development might have taken! In any case, Erasmus himself never would have been as universally read as in fact he was: Who would ever have written the 2.5 million copies of his works that we know were printed from 1500 to 1925? Therefore the date of the establishment of the first printing presses in the Netherlands—1473—has an outstanding importance in the history of humanism, even if its first publications were mainly patristic and medieval works. The first printers were Nicolaas Ketelaer and Gerrit van Leempt at Utrecht in the North, Dirk Martens and Johann of Westphalia at Aalst (Alost, Alostum) in Flanders. One of the very first books printed at Aalst was the famous *Historia de duobus amantibus* of Aeneas Silvius Piccolomini (Pope Pius II), an excellent specimen of Italian humanist prose. Later on Martens became rightly famous as a printer to the University of Louvain, where he published works by Agricola, Erasmus, Vives, Martinus Dorpius, and last but not least the first edition of *Utopia*. Moreover he was the first in the Low Countries to print Greek (already at Aalst) and Hebrew (1518). He published the Greek grammars of Constantine Lascaris and Theodore Gaza (about ten times!) and a score of classical authors: Homer, Aristophanes, Euripides, Xenophon, Aristotle, Theocritus, and others.[4]

Another incentive and a landmark in the history of humanism was the foundation in 1517 of the Louvain Collegium Trilingue, one of the very first of such institutions in Europe. It followed less than ten years after the Collegio de San Ildefonso (1508), the heart of the newly founded Spanish University of Alcalà de Henares (Complutum), but it preceded by almost fifteen years the Collège des Lecteurs Royaux (Paris 1530) of François I. It is of course sheer coincidence, but nevertheless a kind of symbol of a changing generation, that about the same time two major teachers and grammarians of the previous generation died: Johannes Murmellius of Roermond (d. 1517 at Deventer) and Johannes Despauterius of Ninove (d. 1520 at Komen/Comines in southern Flanders). The

first Trilingue generation, to which belong Erasmus, Vives, Hadrianus
Barlandus, Rutgerus Rescius, Conrad Goclenius, Nicolaus Clenardus,
and its printer Martens, dominated the humanist scene until about 1540.

By that time the religious conflicts had developed to such an extent
that they threatened to suffocate any other intellectual concern. The
number of *Apologiae* the older Erasmus had to write, much as he disliked it, illustrates this nasty evolution, and his complaint apropos of
Zuñiga (Stunica) can be taken as typical for the harm caused to a free
and full deployment of the Bonae Litterae: "I pity you, Stunica, that you
trivialize your mind, pen, paper, and leisure with such nonsense; I pity
the reader who spends some of his good time on such childish stuff; and
I pity myself, because I am forced to read and refute these absurdities."[5]

Humanism did not escape the storm of religious fanaticism and the
unhappy wars it unchained. In the end even the Trilingue was closed
down for many years (1590–1606), and Lipsius in his well-known description of the town and the University of Louvain (*Lovanium*, Antwerp
1605) sighed his melancholy in the words: "At nunc iacent ibi omnia et
silent" (and now all things there lie silent; book 3.4, p. 99). Other fine
and important humanist undertakings collapsed in those years, such as
the Officina Goltziana in Bruges (1562–76), the printing office that the
famous engraver Hubert Goltz (Goltzius)(1526–1583) set up with the
financial help of the humanist-minded Lord Marcus Lauweryns (Marcus
Laurinus, 1530–1581).[6]

More and more writers in both camps had to produce works acceptable to their intolerant theological supervisors. Censorship began its
devastating work, Erasmus being one of their privileged victims, especially so because he had dared to apply the new philological criticism to
the text of the New Testament.[7] Here again one notices the multiplying
and intensifying effect of the printing press. Giannozzo Manetti and Valla
had done much the same before this invention, but their work remained
hidden in a few manuscripts until the moment Erasmus discovered a version of Valla's *Adnotationes in Novum Testamentum* in the abbey library
of Park just outside the walls of Louvain and brought it to Bade in Paris,
or even until modern scholars unearthed Manetti's translation of the
Psalms directly from the Hebrew.

The consequences of these changes for the development of humanist
activities are clearly discernible. Many scholars withdrew into the neutral and safer work of the purely classical philological kind. Yet even
there the censor's eye could find objectionable pages, as the case of Lipsius abundantly testifies. Poetry and drama, except for the pious and
moralizing kinds, withered almost completely in the South, to a lesser
degree (at least for some time) in the North. It is also true, however, that

from the very beginnings of humanism all branches of literature in the Low Countries were deeply impregnated by Christian piety and morals. In this respect the overwhelming success of the Italian Carmelite poet Baptista of Mantua—the Christian Vergil—north of the Alps, almost generally ignored in Italian humanist circles, is quite typical.

The founding of Leiden University in 1575 was another important landmark. It meant that from then on both the old Roman Catholic camp and the new Protestant one had their own academic center. Its first curator was the best possible choice: Jan van der Does (Janus Dousa), a politician, historian, poet, and philologist of the highest quality. Thanks to him and his staff, excellent scholars were called to the new foundation from the very start, in the first place Justus Lipsius and Joseph Justus Scaliger. In order to obtain the latter's services he was hired as a research professor without any teaching obligation.

After many years of teaching and writing, Lipsius eventually went back to his native Brabant and Louvain, to the great joy of the Catholics. His year-long wavering between the two hostile factions characterizes the difficult situation of many scholars and artists in the late sixteenth century. There can be no doubt that most of them were sincere Christians, but their personal interest was primarily the philological, historical, or artistic study and imitation of the classical world, not the endless and often pointless theological squabbles. But as their ill-luck would have it, it was impossible to stay outside when one had a leading position in some field, and sooner or later they were obliged to make a choice in order to survive. So Lipsius had to declare himself a Catholic if he wanted to see his homeland again; but Daniel Heinsius's nephew Jacob van Zevecote (Jacobus Zevecotius), no mean Latin poet and playwright, had to fly from Brussels to Holland because he wanted to leave the Augustinian order and marry.

The early seventeenth century witnessed the last stage of humanist learning and literature. In the South Lipsius (d. 1606) was succeeded by his pupil Erycius Puteanus from Venlo, who began his career as a professor in Milan. He was not a great scholar but a prolific rhetorical author on minor if not trifling arguments, whose style roused an immense and almost universal applause among his contemporaries. Much more important, however, is the fact that he revived the Trilingue and in addition organized in it—with the personal support of Archdukes Albert and Isabella—a "Palaestra Bonae Mentis" or training center of the right mind.[8] To this Palaestra selected students were admitted to receive an additional humanist education in Latin and good morals. On the first Thursday of every month the members met in the Trilingue for a fourfold exercise: a *dissertatio* or extemporaneous oration, a *recitatio* or reading of a composition prepared by a pupil, a *lectio* or explanation of a classical text, and a *disputatio* or study of an ethical or political author. The great models were to be Cicero and Quintilian, Demosthenes and Aristotle. At the end of the year the best student received the golden medal of the sovereigns and a book by his professor with his personal handwritten dedication and his portrait especially engraved for that copy. This program was quite clearly imbued with the old humanist spirit, but it came too late in history to have a lasting influence. Puteanus, having much more of an artistic than a scholarly mind, achieved hardly anything in the tradition of his master Lipsius. In this respect his colleague in Greek at the Trilingue, Petrus Castellanus (ca. 1585–1632), a Fleming from Geraardsbergen (Grammont/Gerardimontium), deserves a more honorable mention for his historical studies on Greek institutions.

Between the southern Netherlands and Baroque Rome there were close humanist relations: from 1619 until after 1650 the professor of eloquence at the Sapienza was Henricus Chifellius from Antwerp, whereas the classical Latin history of the "bellum belgicum" was written in those years by the Roman Jesuit Famiano Strada. In the fine arts we only have to mention a famous visitor to Rome, Peter Paul Rubens, also from Antwerp. His brother Philip was a humanist Greek scholar, he himself one of the greatest painters of western Europe, whose works celebrate in an exuberant style the classical as well as the Christian world. The contemporary painters of the northern Netherlands were much less influenced by those "humanist" themes and turned their attention rather to Dutch daily life and landscape, a striking difference between the two now separated parts of the Low Countries, as pointed out by Frans Baudouin, honorary keeper of the Antwerp Rubens House. Yet literature and scholarship in the North continued to be completely impregnated by classical and humanist learning. Leiden was growing more and more into one of the major centers of classical studies in Europe,[9] and it had close relations with England, Scandinavia, and northern Germany. From Leiden and Holland many branches of literature and scholarship got new impulses: neoclassical drama from Daniel Heinsius's tragedies and theoretical treatise, international law from Hugo Grotius (*Mare liberum*), and more. Philological studies were thoroughly renovated by the younger Scaliger. Up to his time humanist scholars collected notes and explanations on a great number of authors without much rationale (something similar is found in Valla's famous *Elegantiae* or even in Erasmus's *Adages*). Many such notes can be found in their correspondence or were published in books called *Miscellanea* (cf. Angelo Poliziano), *Adversaria critica* (cf. Adrien Turnèbe [Adrianus Turnebus]), *Variae* or *Antiquae lectiones* (cf. Marcus Antonius Muretus, Lipsius, etc.). Scaliger opted for complete critical editions of a single author, based on a systematic study of the manuscripts, and for the first time he tried to get back to the archetype copy. In this conception of philological work Scaliger was far ahead of his time, but perhaps no longer a humanist. So much specialization is a modern approach to the classical heritage; a humanist wanted to wander through all his dear old authors and to enjoy their style and messages. To collate manuscripts is quite another and very dry business. No wonder, therefore, that almost all of Scaliger's colleagues and immediate successors, whose minds were still permeated by the humanist spirit, continued along the old lines of editions based on conjectural corrections and a haphazard use of manuscripts, or of the learned commentaries that accumulated a tremendous mass of various information (from them many modern commentators derive the bulk of their notes, but without acknowledgment).

By about 1650 humanism was nearly exhausted. With the death of Puteanus (d. 1646), his successor Nicolaus Vernulaeus (d. 1649), and his colleague Valerius Andreas (d. 1655) in the South, of Hugo Grotius (d. 1645), Gerardus Vossius (d. 1649), and Daniel Heinsius (d. 1655) in the North, its last great protagonists were gone. There remained a generation of philologists (e.g., Johannes Fredericus Gronovius), who in general had no influence whatsoever on the development of contemporary culture and more and more withdrew into their study and books. By that time Latin was very rapidly losing its prominent place in western society; the great peace treaties of Münster in Westphalia (1648) were among the last written in Latin. Soon its role was to be limited to the education of children and the writing of learned books or documents of the Catholic church. The visible trace of humanism in these remnants remained the pure classical style, to which ever after modern Latinists adhered.

✻   ✻   ✻

I shall now proceed to examine briefly the principal contributions of the humanists of the Low Countries in the fields essential to Renaissance humanism, namely, grammar, rhetoric, poetry, history, and moral philosophy. These areas I shall consider in as broad a perspective as possible so as to include most of the humanists' achievements or aspects of intellectual life influenced by humanism. The impact of humanism on scholarship and sciences in general will be the subject of a further and last section.

The teaching and knowledge of pure (classical) Latin was the cornerstone on which every humanist activity was built. It divided the "barbari" and "obscuri viri" from the "docti" and the "eloquentes," who alone could be real "oratores et poetae," as the humanists presented themselves. This point is stressed over and again by Erasmus (see his *Antibarbari* and other works), his predecessors, his friends and followers: "Grammar especially," says Dorpius in his *Praise of Every Art,* "by its own law, can take pride that it is the parent and nurse of all learning."[10] This formula is central to humanist thinking, and turns up in many similar expressions: sound scholarship (be it theology, or law, or philology for that matter) is impossible without the use of a pure and clear language, which in its turn directly depends on a good grammatical foundation. Otherwise one becomes one of those "pseudodialectici" or teachers of the "Scoticae tenebrae," which the humanists held responsible for the decay of schools and culture in their time.

Many humanists of the old Netherlands contributed significantly to renovating grammatical instruction in their time, and some of them wrote books used far beyond their small country and as late as the nineteenth century or, in derived versions, even to the present day. The history of humanist Latin grammar in the Seventeen Provinces can be formulated as a gradual transition from the old Alexander of Villedieu and his *Doctrinale* to Despauterius and, ultimately, to Gerardus Vossius. If Alexander was the quintessential symbol of late medieval Latin (versified) grammar, so the Fleming Despauterius is for humanist grammar (in a later stage together with the Portuguese Emmanuel Alvares, 1526–1582): more than four hundred editions and adaptations are the manifest proof of its wide and lasting success, which even the Jesuit Alvares could not obliterate.

In the fifteenth century Alexander was still universally used either in his original version or in adapted editions and comments written by schoolmasters such as Godefridus de Traiecto at Tienen, Johan Sinthen in Deventer, or Willem Zenders from Weert in northern Brabant. Next to Alexander and the more philosophical *Modi significandi,* of which Erasmus complained so bitterly and not without reason, several new schoolbooks began to be written in prose. The oldest one is the *Dyasinthetica (Syntax)* of Anthonius Haneron,[11] probably written when he was a professor of Latin at Louvain in the 1430s and surviving in four printed editions of the years 1475–87. Here as elsewhere Haneron appears as a transitional figure, a representative of the medieval grammar and the *ars dictandi* who knows that some change is in the air. The rather awkward Latin of his prologue expresses ideas that a good humanist could approve wholeheartedly: "Certainly it is necessary that one who wishes to obtain the remaining arts be first a grammarian. For how can one who is ignorant of the Latin language know theology or civil law or any of the other arts? How can one understand a Latin text who does not understand the

Latin language, hidden meanings of its words, its grammatical turns, and, finally, the fitting connection of words? Furthermore, how can you believe that whoever is ignorant of grammar can become an expert in rhetoric, especially since latinity and purity of speech has everything to do with rhetorical speech?"[12] Yet his sources are mainly Alexander and the Vulgate, sometimes also Vergil, Lucan, or Terence, but hardly ever the great Roman prose writers.

In the second half of the century the conflict between the traditional and the new methods flared up. Italian books and their principles became known: Perotti's grammar, Valla's *Elegantiae*, Tortelli's *Orthographia*, and a host of minor works. In the wake of Valla, Alexander Hegius at Deventer publicly condemned the *Modi significandi* as a torture for children who deserve better. Matthaeus Herbenus, once an assistant of Perotti in Rome, on his return to the school of his native Maastricht, adapted his master's grammar for local use. Many other distinguished grammarians, such as Johannes Custos from Brecht near Antwerp (ca. 1475?–1525) and his pupil and colleague Johannes Despauterius, began systematically to rework and replace the versified Alexander.[13] Finally, Despauterius produced the most complete set of grammatical treatises, which in the best-known Paris edition of 1637–38 (*Commentarii*) cover the whole range of grammatical questions from the bare essentials (*Rudimenta*, comparable to the *Ianua Donati*) through morphology and syntax to metrics, stylistics, and problems of accents, punctuation, and orthography. Despauterius's method was to formulate a rule in a few mnemotechnical verses and to add an extensive explanation in prose, leaving it to the individual teacher to select from this wealth of information what he deemed sufficient and necessary for his pupils. He also left it to the teacher to add the translations into the vernacular in order to keep his grammar universally usable throughout Europe. The combination of verses and prose would remain for a very long time the typical characteristic of the Latin grammars by northern humanists, most of them simply adaptations or derivations of Despauterius. The most noticeable exception to this rule is the equally successful (thirty-seven editions) *Grammaticarum institutionum libri IIII* (originally Paris 1549) of Lipsius's professor at Louvain, Cornelius Valerius, which is entirely in prose. A strange but typical feature of Despauterius's *Rudimenta* is the addition of a final religious and moralizing chapter: "I have added questions, perhaps not altogether to be despised, about penitence, confession, sin, articles of faith, and other things of this kind, so that from an early age children may be imbued with sacred ideas, without which all things are vain."[14] Here again the ever-present impact of religion on these humanists (these, shall we say, humanist Christians?) breaks through. It is a constant factor in all of them—Erasmus, Vives, Dorpius, Clenardus. The last one even went so far as to abandon his Greek and Hebrew studies in favor of Arabic in order to be able to convert the Mohammedans.

Despauterius's success did not remain unchallenged. In the editions of his works one finds several times an "epistola apologetica," a "recriminatio," or the like. Obviously not only Valla clashed with rivals over grammatical issues! The "Threnodia in temeraria criticorum quorundam iudicia" (1548), a remarkable poem by Despauterius's friend and posthumous editor Laevinus Crucius, ultimately seems to be an apology of his work within the framework of a picture of what Crucius considers to be acceptable in humanism to true Christians.

Despauterius's *Commentarii* have proved to be stronger than their critics, who are now completely forgotten. They became a firm basis for humanist instruction in Latin, and at regular intervals they were "modernized," for example by Simon Verepaeus (1522–1598), a famous teacher at Mechlin and 's Hertogenbosch, whose grammar was printed by Christophe Plantin in 1571–72 and was still reedited for school use as late as 1864. About the same time a similar work by the Düsseldorf teacher Ludovicus Lithocomus was successful in many schools in Holland and the South until it was reworked by Vossius (Leiden 1626), whose version went through an uninterrupted series of editions up to 1837. If we add that many grammars for local use[15] were derived mainly from Despauterius, the paramount importance of this humanist and his renovated grammar books for the teaching of Latin will be self-evident.

At this point it is important to mention a very remarkable book by a Flemish gentleman, George Lord of Halewijn/Halluin and Komen/Comines (Georgius Haloinus Cominius, ca. 1470–1536/37), a friend and protector of Erasmus, Vives, and Despauterius, who for a long time was a teacher at Komen. In 1537 he published at Antwerp his *Restauratio linguae Latinae*, on which he had been working already before 1508. This interesting book remained largely unknown to scholars until a critical edition was published in 1978 by C. Matheeussen.[16] As a polyglot courtier he vigorously defends the thesis that one must learn Latin not from the misleading and faulty grammars, but only by "usus et consuetudo," in other words, by a natural method that consists of listening to speakers of that language (exactly as he had learned his Spanish). Once a sufficient basic knowledge of the language is thus acquired, one should turn to the texts, reading historians in the first place. Haloinus's ideas at least partially coincide with what Erasmus tells us in a letter about his London friend, the famous educator John Colet: "He did not permit striving for the means of speaking rightly by the precepts of the grammarians; he asserted confidently that these impeded speaking well, and that speaking well happens only through reading the best authors."[17] This principle, however, leaves open the question of how to acquire the basic knowledge, and here Haloinus gives an original even if not very practicable answer.

In order to learn Latin more aids are needed than just a grammar book, especially good dictionaries and readers. In this field also many authors from Germania Inferior made important contributions. Several of them published lists of classical words and expressions, some sort of "Elegantiae" so to speak, from the early efforts of Johannes Murmellius to the final *De vitiis sermonis et glossematis latino-barbaris libri IV* (1645) of Vossius. In between there were such books as the *Latini sermonis observationes* (1534) of Johannes Godescalcus from Antwerp (ca. 1507–1571) or the *Phrases linguae Latinae* (Basel 1550 and twenty-six times more) of Antonius Schorus (ca. 1500–1551/52) from Hoogstraten, who had to flee his native country and, later on, Heidelberg to seek shelter from religious and political intolerance at Lausanne in Switzerland. Among the lexicographers the most famous certainly are Plantin's corrector Cornelis Kiliaan (Cornelius Kilianus) from Duffel (ca. 1530–1607) and Hadrianus Junius (1512–1575) from Hoorn in Holland.[18] The Dutch–Latin dictionaries of the first are even nowadays precious sources for our knowledge of both Dutch and Latin as they were used in the sixteenth century (and readers of Erasmus sometimes do well to consult them); the learned Dutchman for his part is the author of a completely new version of Conrad Gessner's *Lexicon Graecolatinum* (Basel 1548) and of a *Nomenclator omnium rerum* (1567) in seven languages. Perhaps it is not improper to remember here that the famous Bohemian pedagogue and language teacher Jan Amos Komenský (Johannes Amos Comenius) in the last and waning days of humanism found a new home in Holland.

A special kind of reference book was compiled to explain the many proper names in ancient texts. To this class belong the *Elucidarius carminum et historiarum seu vocabularius poeticus* (Deventer 1498 and many reeditions), a small but extremely popular historical, geographical, and mythological repertory due to Hermannus Torrentinus from Zwolle (d. ca. 1520). Among the various other dictionaries, special mention must still be made of the forerunner of the later "Gradus ad Parnassum" or prosodical aids: in 1599 the Fleming Henricus Smetius (1537–1612) published his *Prosodia sive exactissima cynosura metrica*, which remained in use by Neolatin poets until the early nineteenth century.

Students also needed special textbooks in order to learn to write and to speak Latin, because nearly all classical authors are too difficult for beginners or do not treat the various aspects of daily life. Two types of such readers were extremely popular, obviously because they filled a need: the letterbooks and the colloquies or dialogues. From the late fifteenth century onward dramatic performances, first of Terence and Plautus, later also of plays written by the teachers, became part of the humanist training in Latin.

The use of letters for instruction based on eminently practical purposes in fact continued the medieval tradition of the *ars dictandi,* which found its last representatives in the Netherlands in Anthonius Haneron, author of a successful *De epistolis brevibus edendis* (which was even used by Georg von Peuerbach in Vienna about 1450) and by his Dutch pupil Engelbert Schut from Leiden, who wrote a metrical *De arte dictandi* in 1454. As a young man, Erasmus, who may have used his books in the Deventer school, wrote a flattering poem addressed to him, but in later years he wrote of him with undisguised contempt. The transition to the really humanist letterbooks, of which Erasmus's *De conscribendis epistolis* (1522) is the most notable example, is Erasmus's black sheep, Karel Maneken/Menneken/Meniken (Carolus Virulus) and his *Epistolarum formulae* (Louvain 1476 and more than fifty editions in France, Germany, and Italy until after 1500). This collection of 337 letters is still largely medieval in style, but not wholly unaffected by humanist influences. After all, one must not forget that Virulus for about half a century was the director of Lily College, which was the main harbor and stronghold of the very first humanists in the strongly scholastic University of Louvain. If it is true that Virulus's style is rather unclassical (though not really bad and even aptly varying according to the addressees), it has for us one excellent merit and quality: it offers a perfect mirror of daily life in and around a late medieval university with real students, professors, and parents.[19]

Virulus's book ultimately had to surrender to the growing competition of Italian humanist letter collections (Filelfo, Poliziano), which were frequently printed in the North, and to the uncompromising condemnation of Erasmus. Several other handbooks *De conscribendis epistolis* followed the latter's example, and often enough their authors are famous: Vives, Macropedius, Verepaeus, down to the *Epistolica institutio* of Lipsius (Leiden 1591), which went through eighteen editions and thus helped to diffuse Lipsius's particular ideas on (non-Ciceronian) style.

If letters served the written use of Latin, colloquies and dialogues had to provide spoken fluency. Among many others, including Hadrianus Barlandus, two authors rise high above all others (even from other countries) as writers of colloquia. They are Erasmus once again and his friend Vives with his *Exercitatio linguae Latinae*. Their school dialogues achieve the status of real literary works both for their splendid form and their rich, varying, and fascinating content. No wonder therefore that they find many readers even today, and that their influence has been enormous. Suffice it here to say that Vives's dialogues were even adapted for use in the first Latin school of Mexico as early as 1554, barely fourteen years after Vives's death, by Franceso Cervantes de Salazar.[20]

Like Latin, Greek was a primary concern of the humanists, and the revival of Greek studies in western Europe was their work and merit. Until the early sixteenth century it was impossible to study Greek in the Low Countries, but individuals learned it in Italy, for example, Rudolf van der Beek (Rolandus de Rivo) from Breda, who studied at Rome in 1380 with the Greek archbishop Simon Atumanos; or the far better-known Rudolf Agricola, who translated from Isocrates, Lucian, and Aphthonius, and on his return to his native country inspired his former Deventer master Hegius to write a Latin poem in praise of Greek. Around the middle of the fifteenth century Johannes de Meerhout (d. 1476) wrote even a *Tractatus de Greca grammatica* in the priory of Korsendonk at Oud-Turnhout (Brabant), but it remains to be seen whether these few pages (unedited so far) are to be connected with humanistic rather than with biblical studies. And according to a recent hypothesis, the Spartan Georgius Hermonymus about 1473 may have come from Paris to Bruges and been busy there as a copyist in the service of Jan Crabbe, the humanist-minded abbot of Ter Duinen at Koksijde on the Flemish coast.[21]

But apart from a few little-known and very short-lived, more or less private efforts to teach Greek at Louvain,[22] the first lecturers deserving that name were Adrien Amerot from Soissons and Johannes Varennius from Mechlin. The first taught Greek to his fellow students of Lily College from about 1515, the second perhaps about the same time or a few years later. Both are authors of grammar books: Amerot of a *Compendium Graecae grammatices ... complectens quicquid est octo partium orationis* (1520), which is praiseworthy for its order and clarity and superior to the treatises of Theodore Gaza and Constantine Lascaris; the second of a *Syntaxis linguae Graecae* printed in 1532 by Rutgerus Rescius from Maaseik, the first Trilingue professor of Greek. Varennius's *Syntax* draws heavily (without acknowledgment) on the *Commentarii* of Guillaume Budé and was often republished in France, Germany, and Switzerland.[23] It followed shortly after the most famous work of Greek grammar from the Low Countries, the *Institutiones in linguam Graecam* (Louvain 1530) and the accompanying *Meditationes Graecanicae* (1531) of Nicolaus Clenardus from Diest.[24] His name became a synonym for "Greek grammar" exactly the way Despauterius did for Latin, so much so that in France the famous verses were written about

>Un écolier qui ne s'amusait guère
>A feuilleter Clénard et Despautère.

The first of the two works treats almost exclusively of Greek morphology and only slightly of case syntax as far as it differs from Latin. Varennius's *Syntax* clearly was intended as a supplement to the *Institutiones*. The *Meditationes* is a handbook for self-study. It contains a letter of St. Basil to St. Gregory of Nazianzus on solitary life (a word-for-word Latin rendering) and the Latin translation of Budé, together with copious notes and references to the grammar. As was to be expected for an extremely successful work, Clenardus's grammar underwent several later "modernizations," the most famous being also the work of Vossius (1626). In its original and Vossian versions it was printed about five hundred times until 1700, and Vossius's adaptation was published in Leiden as late as 1827.

Although it no longer belongs to the period under consideration, it deserves mention here that a fundamental reform of Greek morphology was undertaken by one of the very last professors of the Louvain Trilingue, Jan H. L. Leemput of Rotterdam (d. 1802). In his *Institutiones linguae Graecae* (Louvain 1782 and 1797) he drastically reduced the number of Greek declensions from the Byzantine ten to (the modern) three, and the verbs to two classes, those on -ω and the other on -μι.[25]

Greek was studied not only at Louvain in the time of Clenardus. In Ghent also, to give one other example, Arnold Bergeyck (Arnoldus Orydrius), member of the local humanist circle to which also belonged the Carthusian Laevinus Ammonius, a translator of Chrysostom, and Karel Utenhove (Carolus Utenhovius), wrote a *Summa linguae Graecae* (1531) dedicated to the lawyer Geraard Rijm. Bergeyck was secretary to the abbot of the Blandijnberg in Ghent, which is still known to specialists of the Roman poet Horace.[26] Later, Greek studies were directed more to editions and translations of Greek authors, less to grammar, such as the works of such scholars as the Flemings Bonaventura Vulcanius—first professor of Greek at Leiden—Franciscus Nannius (1525–95) at Leiden and Dordrecht, and the Frisian Willem Canter (1542–1575) at Louvain.

For both Latin and Greek pronunciation important works were published in the Low Countries. Erasmus's lengthy dialogue "De recta

Latini Graecique sermonis pronuntiatione" (1528) rejected for Greek the itacistic pronunciation of the Byzantine scholars and Johann Reuchlin. He was followed by Adolph Meetkerke (Mekerchus) from Bruges, "De veteri et recta pronuntiatione linguae Graecae commentarius" (1565) and finally by Vossius, whose authority established for a long time the Erasmian pronunciation in the Netherlands. Erasmus's views were put into public use for the first time at Cambridge, December 1536, on the occasion of a performance of Aristophanes's comedy *Plutus*. Erasmus's dialogue is historically significant because of its lasting influence, not as a pioneer of new ideas. This honor probably goes to the great Spanish grammarian Antonio de Nebrija, whom Erasmus appears to have followed for his own argumentation.

An offspring of humanist interest in ancient languages is the study of Hebrew, the third sacred language. A first course in the Netherlands was organized in 1518 in the recently founded Trilingue, which hired an itinerant Jew named Matthaeus Adrianus.[27] More famous, however, became professor Jan van Campen (Johannes Campensis, 1521–31), author of a short grammar. His work was very rapidly outshone by the *Tabula in grammaticam Hebraeam* (1529) of Clenardus, who was teaching the language privately. A *Dictionarium Hebraicum* was prepared by the printer Dirk Martens as early as 1520 for use in the Trilingue. Later the study of Hebrew languished at Louvain, but it throve in the North, especially at Leiden.

One student of the Trilingue, however, deserves particular mention, Andreas Masius (1514–1573) from Sint-Kwintens-Lennik near Brussels, a collaborator of the magnificent polyglot *Biblia regia* published by the Plantin press. For this undertaking he wrote the first Syriac grammar ever composed in Europe: *Grammatica linguae Syriacae* (1571), which remained standard for more than two centuries.

In conclusion one can say that next to the brilliant achievements of the Quattrocento Italian humanists, their colleagues and successors in the Low Countries made fundamental contributions in the field of the study and teaching of the classical languages on a scale that surpasses most of the other European countries. Erasmus and Vives, Despauterius and Clenardus, Lipsius and Vossius have indeed a European importance and impact, not just a local one. They are in many respects on the same level with Valla and Perotti, Budé and Philipp Melanchthon, Antonio de Nebrija or Alvares in the history of humanist language studies.

*   *   *

Humanists never felt themselves satisfied with a purely grammatical knowledge. They knew from Quintilian: "aliud est grammatice, aliud est

Latine scribere" (it is one thing to write grammatically correct Latin, another to write good Latin). Their ideal was eloquence, and grammar only laid the foundations for it. The building itself is the work of the *ars rhetorica* and, in poetry, of the *ars poetica*. Rhetorical theory and the practice of eloquence in elegant orations are essential features of the humanist world. How important it was to be an eloquent orator even at the end of the humanist age is proved by Puteanus's initiative in organizing a "Palaestra bonae mentis" within the Louvain Collegium Trilingue and by its counterpart in Leiden: in 1620, at the request of students who wanted a more thorough training in eloquence, the university charged professor Petrus Cunaeus to organize a "Collegium oratorium privatopublicum." It was inaugurated on 10 November with a solemn speech by Cunaeus himself.[28]

Many professors and theoreticians such as Hadrianus Barlandus and Joachim Sterck van Ringelbergh wrote *Rhetoricae institutiones, Libri de ratione dicendi*, and the like, based on Cicero and Quintilian, if not on Greek rhetors. They were handbooks for their students or parts of larger works on the *artes liberales*. They are no more or no less important than scores of other such schoolbooks written all over the humanist world. There are, however, two or three works that have a preponderant importance on a European scale: the three books *De inventione dialectica* of Rudolf Agricola (1479, but printed at Louvain, Martens 1515, and many times more until 1657) and, from the end of Erasmus's life, his massive treatise *Ecclesiastes sive de ratione concionandi libri IV* (Basel 1535). The first enlists, so to speak, the medieval logic of the Trivium, which Agricola knew perfectly well from Peter of Spain's *Summulae logicales*, into the service of the rhetorical humanist invention; the second enrolls the profane art for the service of God. Between them Vives's mature and fundamental work, *De tradendis disciplinis* (1531), built further on Agricola's foundations, and together with the German Melanchthon, they were the most important authorities on the matter in Europe until the appearance of Petrus Ramus's *Dialecticae partitiones* (Paris 1543 and many reissues).[29]

Agricola's work discusses in a personal way[30] mainly the first part of the *ars rhetorica*, namely the *inventio* of the so-called *topoi dialektikoi* or *loci communes*. His starting point is the fact that every *oratio* wants to teach something: "Oratio quaecumque . . . id agere . . . videtur . . . ut *doceat* aliquid eum qui audit" as he puts it at the beginning of his prologue, adding that *movere* (to move) and *delectare* (to please) are secondary tasks and less fundamental than the ancient theories would have it. But in order to teach convincingly we need a method of presenting the arguments of the subject, and this method is the procedure by means of the *loci communes;* therefore "utilissimum videntur fecisse qui sedes quasdam argumentorum (quos locos dixerunt) excogitavere" ("those seem to have performed the most useful service who devised, so to speak, foundations of arguments [which they called commonplaces]"). The *topoi* or *loci* are the theoretically possible points of view, both internal and external, which allow the author to treat an argument in an orderly and persuasive way. To find these *loci* is the task of logic, to put them in the right order and to embellish them with words belongs to rhetoric. In so doing, we shall know what to say and how to formulate it. Logic, however, must be a theory of verbal communication in a correct and understandable language, not one of metaphysical categories expressed in a barbarous idiom or obscure jargon. This last point was stressed even more strongly by Vives, who drew the final humanist conclusions of their approach to language and philosophy. Agricola thoroughly systematized the lore of the *loci* and ultimately distinguished twenty-four of them, which is more than ancient sources had (Cicero knew seventeen *loci,* some Greeks more). In his second book Agricola discusses the correct use of the *loci* and criticizes the modern terministic corruption of dialectics. At the end he gives an example that illustrates his theory: the arguments in favor of and against a most typical humanist *quaestio:* "Philosopho habenda est uxor" (Should a philosopher be married?). The third and shortest book treats various additional problems: "de affectibus, de delectatione" (how to raise the emotions and to captivate the audience), *copia verborum* and *brevitas,* and, most important, the rhetorical *dispositio.* He finds that Aristotle did not touch upon this part of the oratorial art at all in his *Rhetorica* and hardly elsewhere, also that Cicero and Quintilian are very brief on this point. He himself proposes a threefold possible disposition or structure of a work: an "ordo naturalis" for "res, quae statutum quendam et certum ex se habent ordinem" ("things that have a kind of fixed and certain order in themselves"); an "arbitrarius," when there is no natural order or when we do not want to follow it but "utcumque alia alii aptissime ex dicendi occasione subtexi potest" ("when some things in this way, some in that, can most suitably be connected at the moment of speaking"); and finally an "artificialis" when the author disturbs on purpose the natural order (the story of Aeneas as told by Vergil serves here as an example).

Agricola's and Vives's works fit into the overall humanist effort to liberate the trivium and the teaching in the *artes* from the late scholastic metaphysical subtleties and to train children no longer with abstract and often unreal categories of thought, which did not at all appeal to them or to their age, but with pure and understandable rules of a natural and attractive language. In a Christian world, however, this could not be the sole or last aim of schooling. In the end, as Despauterius said in his *Rudimenta*, all is vain that does not bring us to God. As a consequence, the art of speech and persuasion must also be directed that way. And here Erasmus came in with his handbook for preachers, who should care for their words as well as or even better than their worldly counterparts. In the first book Erasmus treats the moral and spiritual virtues required of the preacher: it is the Christian adaptation of the old ideal once formulated by the heathen Cato as "vir *bonus* dicendi peritus" (a good man skilled in speaking). Erasmus points out the eminent dignity of the preacher (exactly as Cicero had stressed that of the Roman orator) and criticizes the decay of preaching and of the church in general. Books 2 and 3 are the technical core of the work and instruct the preacher on how to use the traditional rhetorical schemes and devices (*inventio, dispositio*, the *loci*, and so on) for his Christian task. The application of these rules inevitably would change profoundly the medieval sermon, which is precisely what happened in the Renaissance, as J. W. O'Malley has brilliantly shown in his case study of the Roman sermons held "coram papa."[31] In places Erasmus's suggestions recall famous older texts of the Rotterdam humanist. So when he argues against a long and scrupulous division (LB 874A–877E), one is forcefully reminded of his praise of the sermons of Jean Vitrier in his famous letter to Justus Jonas. Vitrier hardly divided his sermons, as most orators do, in a bookish way: "unde fit ut frequenter sit frigidissima distinctio" ("whence it happens that often the division is very feeble"). The monk of St. Omer spoke with his whole heart—*Amabat quod loquebatur*—and so had a profound impact on his audience, who went home "eruditior et inflammatior ad studium pietatis" (more learned and more inflamed with zeal for piety). Precepts are, indeed, a means, not an end in themselves. In his last book Erasmus gives a sort of repertory of the main themes that usually occur in sermons.

Oratorical theory in the Renaissance was not only important within the walls of the school. Latin still had an undeniable importance in public life and, on certain occasions, it was vital to be able to deliver an elegant speech in the old Romans' tongue. First of all, academic life in the universities was entirely latinized. At the opening of every academic year a solemn Latin oration was delivered by one of the professors (or another member of the Universitas Magistrorum et Studiosorum), usually on the theme of a praise of the arts. We still have, for example, such a "Laus Philosophiae" given at Ferrara in 1476 by Rudolf Agricola, and two "Laudes disciplinarum" from Louvain. The first is by an anonymous professor of canon law about 1450, who inserted a eulogy of Petrarch and quoted from the *Africa*, a recollection of his studies in

Padua.[32] The second is by Martinus Dorpius (1513), who added a long praise of the town of Louvain in the classical and humanist tradition. Many other occasions allowed eloquent professors to demonstrate their abilities: a new appointment, a princely visit, the death of a colleague. Many such orations have been preserved from Louvain, Leiden, and elsewhere, some as individual scattered documents, others published in the collected works of a famous orator such as Puteanus at Louvain or Cunaeus at Leiden. To a large extent Latin also was the language of the Roman church and of international diplomacy. As a consequence, stately visits of princes, bishops, and ambassadors were given added luster by means of official welcome orations, often prepared and even pronounced by professional humanists. In the fifteenth century the University of Louvain sometimes hired an Italian orator for that job, undoubtedly because the local latinists were not yet enough master of the new style. When the new Duke Philip the Handsome made his state entry into Louvain on 9 September 1494 the public *gratulatio* was offered by the north Italian Francesco of Crema (Franciscus Cremensis), who had been appointed "rhetorice artis professor" on 11 January 1493.[33] It is a curious coincidence that Erasmus, who saluted the same duke in Brussels on his return from his voyage to Spain (Epiphany 1504), had been Cremensis's guest on his very first visit to Louvain in June 1498 and had found him a "vir egregie litteratus."[34] Erasmus's *panegyricus,* however, is a splendid example of the kind of speeches Folly would rightly explode a few years later: tediously long and exasperatingly flattering. Certainly, Erasmus was not entirely free to say what he wanted in the way he might have preferred. Those orations were attentively listened to and, if published, carefully read. A wrong word could have far-reaching consequences, as Christophe de Longueil (Longolius)(1488–1522) painfully experienced. This wandering humanist from Mechlin had in his youth in France extolled the Franks against the ancient Romans. When later on his friends in Rome presented him for honorary citizenship in the Eternal City (1519), other Romans remembered that youthful oration, stirred a row on the basis of lèse majesté, and, in the end, the famous worshiper of Cicero had to flee from Rome to save his life.[35]

The custom of diplomatic and public orations lived on far into the seventeenth century, and it is not difficult to find specimens of them even among the works of the most belated humanists. So we possess several public panegyrics of cardinals in Rome by Henricus Chifellius of Antwerp, professor of eloquence at the Sapienza under Pope Urban VIII; and in the Vatican lies the manuscript of a commemoration speech by the same author in honor of Leo X, the great humanist pope who had died a century before. Among the *Orationes* of Dominicus Baudius of Lille

(1561–1613), who taught eloquence at Leiden, there is one of 1603 addressed to James I of England and held on behalf of the "Belgii Ordines" (the Estates of the Netherlands) to discourage an alliance with Spain. It is a fine example of the international use and utility of Latin in its last heyday: a man whose native tongue was French addresses an English king as the representative of a Dutch authority.

Apart from the real orations there are also the fictional speeches or *Declamationes*, which play an important role in school and in literature. Already before the *editio princeps* of 1481 the *Declamationes maiores* of pseudo-Quintilian were used for the training of law students at Louvain, which suggests that these texts then were held in much higher esteem than nowadays, when even classical philologists scorn them. Anyhow, such fictional speeches were written by famous men like Erasmus and Vives. Among the latter's early works there are five *Declamationes Syllanae* as well as a *Pompeius fugiens*, in which he quite aptly introduces the defeated Pompeius speaking after the battle of Pharsalus and so paved the way for later dramatists, who brought Pompeius (and Caesar for that matter) on the humanist scene. Erasmus wrote a *Declamatio*—again too long—that is a refutation of Lucian's similar work *Tyrannicida*, which he had previously selected for translation. If this fictive speech is something very dull indeed, one must not forget that precisely in this declamatory genre Erasmus a few years later displayed the height of his literary art, his humor, and his seriousness. As a matter of fact, *The Praise of Folly* is a speech belonging to the class of the *laudationes* and, since it is fictional, it is a *declamatio*. It is, therefore, a supreme paradox (and not the only one of this work) to see the way that a genre, which already in antiquity was decried as too artificial and the cause of the decline of true eloquence, has given us one of the masterpieces of world literature and an extremely provocative text in many respects.[36] And if rhetoric and theology have caused much harm to humanism in general, we owe them many thanks for the occasion they gave Mrs. Folly to speak out and to do it in such a masterful way.

How typical *The Praise of Folly* is as a rhetorical writing can be seen from certain reactions and from other similar works. Dorpius begged Erasmus to write also a Praise of Wisdom. Now, whatever theological pressures and considerations may have been involved and certainly were acting, the fact remains that this request is perfectly consistent with ancient and humanist usage, that is, the request for parallel declamations in favor of and against a certain subject. Had not Erasmus himself done exactly the same in his Lucianic pair of declamations? Equally usual and widely diffused was the custom of writing a satirical praise of the craziest subjects. The Greek sophists had been good at that, and even Erasmus knew the medieval Hucbald's *Praise of Baldness.* So Folly has a very old pedigree and many children too. At the very end of the period under consideration and in Erasmus's homeland we still find a certain Conradus Goddaeus from Vaassen (1612–1658), who in 1642 published a humorous *Laus ululae ad conscriptos ululantium patres et patronos* at Deventer (in several reeditions). It seems as if something of Erasmus's spirit had remained in the town in which he first learned the Latin that would allow him later to write *Folly.*

Before I take leave of the oratorial art, I want to draw attention to two related points. It was an Antwerp Jesuit, Andreas Schottus, former pupil of the Louvain Trilingue and a friend of Lipsius, who published one of the most important old editions of Seneca Rhetor in 1603. Second, it is in the field of eloquence that the burning question of style was most acutely felt: Shall we be Ciceronians or not? The history of this question and the hot debates it created from the fifteenth century through the seventeenth belong to a history of humanism in general. But it is significant that two of the major protagonists in the debate are men of the Netherlands: Erasmus, who in his *Ciceronianus* wrote the most deadly satire against extremist Ciceronianism and was cursed for that by many an adorer of the Roman orator; and Lipsius, who propagated a quite different style, an amalgam of Plautus, Seneca, and Tacitus, but was rejected by the moderate Ciceronians in the Jesuit colleges, who were finally to win the battle in their ubiquitous classrooms.

* * *

Next to eloquence, poetry in its classical forms was the most genuine expression of the humanist mind. Every major and minor event in private, public, or social life—birth and death, marriage and appointments, the publication of a book or a memorable visit—was "immortalized" in Latin poems, sometimes also in Greek or even Hebrew verses. In the course of the sixteenth century multilingualism, including both the ancient and the modern vernacular languages, began to develop and soon became widely popular. After 1550 most humanists were writing verses in several languages, often including Italian.

For a humanist any conceivable subject could be treated in verse, even mathematics or a chapter of Roman civil law, as the poems of Hugo Grotius eloquently demonstrate. This point is less surprising than it may seem to be to a modern or Romantic reader. In fact, if an intellectual movement attaches paramount importance to a refined linguistic expression of its thoughts in every situation and if, in addition, it considers the *oratio ligata* or verse as the summit of linguistic elegance, it necessarily follows that nothing can be more attractive and beautiful than a versified elaboration, whatever the subject. Well-turned verses are always a joy for a true humanist, even if their contents are as dry as dust.

Even if a Latin adage says that "poeta nascitur," most humanists sincerely believed that writing poetry as well as writing prose could be learned. As a matter of fact it is not very difficult to learn to write correct, fluent, and even elegant verses in classical Latin. Moreover, most of the rules formulated in the *artes rhetoricae* could be applied as well in prose as in poetry, which explains in part why specific *artes poeticae* were written more rarely, especially in the Low Countries. No fundamental contribution in this field seems to have been made in the old Netherlands before the very end of the sixteenth century, that is, many years after Scaliger's influential *Poetica* (1561) or the even earlier and equally widely read *Ars poetica* of Marco Girolamo Vida, not to mention several early Jesuit *Institutiones poeticae*.

The first chair of poetics at Louvain was established in the Faculty of Law in 1477. Its first occupant—after Agricola had declined a call—was the Italian Lodovico Bruni (Ludovicus Brunus) of Acqui, and until the end of the century his successors were all Italian humanists. The results of their teaching, however, were far from brilliant, but that is probably due mainly to the more or less hostile surroundings. In the remarkable *Declamatio de tutelae severitate* (1481), the representative of the (law) students insists on the abolition of the poetics course,[37] which is "ficticiis et fabulis plena," vain and useless. Moreover, poetry offends truth. (A generation later Vives was to say the same at Louvain.) At this point the student quotes a verse of the old Roman Publilius Syrus,[38] which he probably had learned in the class of Bruni. Although the representative of the academic authority pronounces a warm defense and a praise of eloquence and poetry, it is clear from such a text and from others[39] that enthusiasm for Latin poetry cannot have been very fervid. And it certainly cannot be compared with the sparkling zeal with which young Erasmus and his friends such as Willem Hermansz (Gulielmus Goudanus) began to cultivate poetry in the Deventer school.

In the early sixteenth century Despauterius and Vives were most notable for their writings on poetry. The first included a detailed *Ars versificatoria* (1510) and a *De carminum generibus* (1511) in the complete set of his grammatical works; the second is important for his at times wholly unhumanist views on poetry. Vives's attitude toward poetry could be described with the famous words of Catullus on Lesbia: "Odi et amo." In fact, he clearly loved reading and quoting the imitators of classical poets, Baptista of Mantua, Poliziano, and the like. Moreover, he discusses poetry over and again in many of his works, from his youthful *Opuscula*, which include his first *Veritas fucata*, to his mature works on the "Disciplinae" and *De ratione dicendi*. But at the same time he was careful to underline in the presence of the Louvain theologians that he is a philosopher and not a poet. Also, he wrote very scornful lines on poets (who are called the devil's relatives in his *Sapientiae inquisitio*, printed January 1523), and he repeatedly declared that as far as he was concerned erotic and mythological poetry may be destroyed. In the course of the years his attitude shows certain waverings, but fundamentally one finds that the Christian more and more dominates the humanist. Poetry will be accepted and legitimized only insofar as it sings the Christian truth. How much in this thesis is sincere conviction and how much the result of theological pressure is hard to say. Probably Vives underwent the evolution that is evident in so many humanists. They begin as youthful worshipers of the heathen Muses and then slowly turn more and more into a rather narrow Christian moralizing. It is the evolution that Budé so openly formulated in his last great work, with the programmatical title *De transitu Hellenismi ad Christianismum*, from Homer to Christ. And this individual evolution characterizes also to a very large extent the evolution of transalpine humanism in general.

One year before Vives died, Pieter Nanninck (Petrus Nannius) of Alkmaar (1500–1557) succeeded Goclenius as the third professor of Latin in the Louvain Trilingue. In February 1539 he inaugurated his course with an oration on Horace's *Ars poetica*. Unfortunately this text is lost, but we still possess a long verse-by-verse commentary by him on the same work. Here he shows a profound learning in ancient and Italian humanist literature. Its influence on humanism, however, remained limited, since it was not printed until 1608. It is a pity, because the work is not wanting in real scholarly value, as is shown by the fact that the greater part of it was still included in an edition of Horace published in London in 1825, together with similar work by much more famous scholars such as Adrien Turnèbe and Joseph Scaliger.

Nannius's commentary continues a long tradition of hermeneutical work on classical poets in the Netherlands from the late Middle Ages onward. In 1381 Reinerus of Sint-Truiden, rector of the Latin school at Mechlin, finished a vast commentary on Boethius's *Consolatio philosophiae*, using an enormous number of classical and medieval authorities.[40] Arnold Greven made a shorter version of it between 1444 and 1465, and also in 1444 Jan van Meerhout, who was mentioned before, wrote *Commentaria in Vergilii Aeneida*. The series was continued by no less men than Erasmus and Vives, the first with his comments on the Ovidian *Nux* poem, the second with extensive notes on the *Eclogues* and the *Georgics* (the latter lost) of Vergil. Most of these commentaries are less known than many of their Italian counterparts, but they show that between the

late Middle Ages and the great hermeneutical activity of the late sixteenth and the seventeenth centuries there is no interruption but a steady
scholarly development and tradition.

After Nannius nothing important seems to have been written on
poetical theory until the worst days of religious conflicts were over. But
in the meantime foreign works came out of the Antwerp presses; in 1579
the first edition of Giovanni Antonio Viperano (Viperanus, 1535–1610)
De poetica libri IV was published here.

The book by the Jesuit Martinus Antonius Delrio from Antwerp
(1551–1608) on tragedy, written toward the end of the century, deserves
some attention. It is at the same time a witness to the increasing late-
humanistic interest in Seneca, and one of the numerous poetical treatises
by members of the Society of Jesus connected with the lively theatrical
activity in their colleges. Delrio's biographer, his Antwerp confrère Carolus Scribanius, tells us in his *Vita* (Antwerp 1609) that already as a
student—Delrio attended the courses of the Louvain Trilingue—he
wrote a juvenile work on Seneca, which he later redrafted as his *Syntagma tragoediae Latinae* (1593). The first part of it (*De tragoedia*) proposes his ideas on tragedy: its difference from comedy; its subject, which
must be taken (against the ancients' custom) from real history to assure
its moral efficiency; the necessity of a unity of action and time, the question of place remaining open.

Delrio was not the only one to study Seneca: Lipsius, Pieter Schrijver
(Petrus Scriverius) from Haarlem (1576–1660) and in between Daniel
Heinsius are other famous names. Their appreciations could, though,
differ widely. Lipsius greatly admired the *Medea* and the *Phoenissae* or,
as it was called at the time, *Thebais*. Heinsius thought the latter piece to
be a failure because it was too turgid. This difference seems to be a consequence of the opposing stylistic evolution of both critics. Lipsius abandoned classicism in favor of a mannerist style, Heinsius returned from
mannerism to classicism and turned from Seneca to Aristotle.

If Delrio discussed only tragedy, Heinsius and after him Vossius
treated poets and poetry on a much broader scale. Heinsius wrote several
times on this subject, showing, as I said, a remarkable evolution in his
thought. His important theoretical writings all belong to the first decade
of his long professorship in Leiden. Later in his life he sometimes came
back to them, but his attention was drawn more and more to biblical
and (Greek) patristic studies, a not uncommon evolution in the career of
many humanists. The essential texts are his inaugural *Oratio de poetis et
eorum interpretibus* of 1603 and his famous *De tragica constitutione
liber*, first published in 1611 as an addition to his annotated edition of
Aristotle's *De poetica* and republished many years later (1643) in a re-

worked version as *De tragoediae constitutione*. Heinsius's literary theory and its evolution has been studied thoroughly by J. H. Meter, and since I cannot go into it at length here, I refer the reader to his book.[41] In his youth Heinsius was clearly a mannerist poet, strongly influenced by Platonic ideas on inborn talent and divine inspiration, and exalting poetry above all other human activities. As a dramatist (*Auriacus*) he cultivated a predilection for Senecan style with its baroque pathos and rather loose plot structure. The study of Vossius's *Oratoriae institutiones* (1606), Horace's *Ars poetica*, and Aristotle (including *In librum Aristotelis De arte poetica* by the Italian critic Francesco Robortello, Florence 1548) brought about a conversion to a more classical and rhetorical approach to poetry and a new conception of drama as involving a carefully built plot and unity of action. Julius Caesar Scaliger's *Poetica* appears to have been of little or no consequence for Heinsius, himself a pupil of the younger Joseph Justus Scaliger.

The evolution of humanist poetic theory toward a close adherence to Aristotelian-rhetorical principles found its ultimate codification in the work of Gerardus Vossius, who had studied carefully both Scaliger and Heinsius as well as other theoreticians. The result of all this work he published at Amsterdam in 1647 in his *Poeticarum institutionum libri III*, completed by a kind of introductory essay *De artis poeticae natura ac constitutione* and an explicit supplementary treatment of the fundamental problem of imitation: *De imitatione cum oratoria tum praecipue poetica*. In it he carefully distinguishes between the "imitatio puerilis" of the beginner at school and the "imitatio virilis" of the accomplished writer; also between the "imitatio servilis," which slavishly follows its model, and the "imitatio ingenua," which creates the new out of the old.

Both Vossius and Heinsius exercised a profound influence on the authors of Europe's classical seventeenth century, especially in Holland (Vondel), France, and Sweden. They were probably the very last offspring of Latin humanism to convey decisive and seminal ideas to leading writers of their time and to influence the vernacular literature, which by now had reached full maturity. After them literary theory was written in the national languages, even by belated Latin poets such as the Frenchman René Rapin (*Réflexions sur la Poétique d'Aristote et sur les ouvrages des poètes anciens et modernes*, 1674/75) or, if still in Latin, it was simply in schoolbooks, written especially for the Jesuit colleges, such as Martin du Cygne's *De arte poetica libri II* (Liège 1664).

As I said at the beginning of this section, poetry was an integral part of cultural and social life of the Renaissance and the Baroque ages. Instead of sending a telegram of congratulations or filling in application forms, the men of those ages wrote a nice poem in Latin. Until far into

the seventeenth century the educated classes in the Netherlands were perfectly bilingual, the other language being Latin. Even the so-called "Mui-
derkring," those writers and artists who met in the Amsterdam home and
in the castle at Muiden of their common friend, the historian and poet
Pieter C. Hooft, counted many expert latinists among its members. It is
impossible to mention here even the barest outlines of the immense output of Latin poetry written by authors from the Low Countries. Some of
these poets have been treated extensively by G. Ellinger in the third volume of his history of Neolatin poetry,[42] whereas a systematic inventory
of Neolatin verse from the Netherlands is being compiled by Marcus de
Schepper. The history of humanist Latin poetry began in the late fifteenth
century with the verses of men such as Rudolf Agricola (trained in Italy)
and the young Deventer students around Erasmus;[43] its full flowering
extended over more than a century, from the second quarter of the sixteenth century to far into the seventeenth. In fact, Latin poetry in the
humanist tradition did not die completely until the nineteenth century in
the southern and the early twentieth century in the northern Netherlands. It is not by chance that at Amsterdam an international contest for
Latin poetry was first sponsored in the early nineteenth century and survived until 1979, when it ran out of funds. In all those years between
Agricola and men such as Nicolaus Heinsius, Sidronius Hosschius, and
others, several hundreds of educated men and, exceptionally, a single
woman, were zealous worshipers of Apollo and the Muses, some of them
with real artistic skill and poetic talent, with a technical ability increasing
in sophistication through the generations. As was to be expected in the
context of the northern Christian world, pious and moralizing verse pre-
dominates in quantity, from Agricola's early poem to St. Ann or Murmellius's *Elegiae morales* to the elegiac cycle on the "Cursus vitae
humanae" of the Jesuit Sidronius Hosschius, the eclogues of his confrère
Gulielmus Becanus, or the innumerable poems in honor of the Holy Virgin. Even if they are written in perfect Ovidian or Vergilian style, which
is often the case, most of these poems will not be easily palatable to a
modern and lay taste; but one cannot deny their immense success in their
own time and, in cases such as Hosschius and Becanus, until the early
nineteenth century. Fundamentally, these northern humanist poems very
often are only humanist in their Latin words and style. Underneath lies
a purely Christian and often medieval content.

    There is, of course, also a profane strand, which originated for the
most part in the South, but finally survived almost exclusively in the
northern provinces, from which it had been chased at the outset. Young
Erasmus and some of his fellow students at Deventer and at Gouda had
been strongly enticed by classical poetry: Erasmus's first attempt in Latin

verse was an eclogue on loving shepherds. But very soon his friend and poet Cornelius Aurelius had convinced him to prefer the Christian lyre. Not many years later another young man, the Walloon Remacle d'Ardenne (Remaclus Arduenna), who was not locked into a monastery, decided to imitate the amorous poetry of the Italian Fausto Andrelini, royal professor in Paris and a great man in those days of the budding northern humanism.[44] By his decision and his own *Amores* Remacle paved the way for the next generation and especially for the unequaled Everaerts brothers, Janus Secundus, Nicolaus Grudius, and Hadrianus Marius. "The Kisses for Neaera" and the "Elegies for Julia" of the first are among the most famous and influential works in Neolatin poetry. They were read and imitated for many decades all over Europe (e.g., by Ronsard) and they still appeal to modern readers. Jan Leernout (Janus Lernutius) in Flanders, Pieter van der Straten (Petrus Stratenus) in Zealand, Jan van der Does (Janus Dousa), Daniel Heinsius and Jacob van den Eynde (Jacobus Eyndius) in Holland are a few of the Latin poets who were drawing on Janus Secundus when singing to their own mistresses.

It goes without saying that all genres of classical poetry were practiced by authors of the Low Countries: long-winded epics (for example the *Borbonias* of Louis Des Masures [Masurius] from Tournai), didactic and philosophical poems ("De contemptu mortis" of Daniel Heinsius or "De ventis" of the Jesuit Charles Malapert [Carolus Malapertius] from Mons/Bergen), elegies, eclogues, satires (from the early ones by Petrus Montanus from 's Heerenberg or Kempo Thessaliensis from Texel to the Antwerp Juvenal of the seventeenth century, Pieter Scholier [Petrus Scholirius]) and epigrams (such as Grotius's *Instrumentum domesticum*, a congenial imitation and adaptation to Holland of Martial's *Apophoreta*). There is no point in extending this list much longer, but I want to mention a last genre, because it is particularly typical for later humanism: I mean the *emblemata*, a special kind of epigrammatic illustration of moralistic or erotic images, which were cherished by the reading public from the time of Andrea Alciati's epoch-making *Emblematum libellus* of 1531. From the Netherlands came a few of the big successes, which, moreover, mark decisive turns in the development of the genre. The *Amorum emblemata* (Antwerp 1608) of Otto van Veen (Vaenius, 1556–1629) initiated the metaphorical emblem; the *Emblemata partim moralia, partim etiam civilia* (Gouda 1618) of Florens Schoonhoven (Florentius Schoonhovius, ca. 1594–1648) added a long and learned commentary, fraught with classical quotations, to the epigrams; finally the *Pia desideria* (Antwerp 1624) of the Jesuit Herman Hugo (1558–1629), which also carried a prose commentary, introduced the mystic emblem. The many editions and translations of these books are proof of their success as long as this strange genre remained alive in western literature.

Before taking leave of the humanist poets, I must not forget to present another outstanding accomplishment due to scholars from the Netherlands, namely, the collection of some huge anthologies, which preserve large quantities of texts otherwise lost or hard to find.[45] First of all there was Janus Gruterus from Antwerp, a poet himself, who as a librarian at Heidelberg published under the anagram of Ranutius Gherus his famous collections of *Delitiae poetarum*, divided into *Gallorum, Germanorum, Italorum*, and *Belgicorum* (1608–14), which were imitated for other countries by other collectors. A few years earlier his Dutch contemporary Damasus Blijenburgius from Dordrecht had planned five volumes of poetry dealing with ethics, love, household affairs, politics, and wisdom. Only two of them ever appeared, the *Cento ethicus ex variis poetis hinc inde contextus . . . iuventutis maxime institutioni accommodatus* (1599), a perfectly humanistic topic, and the better-known *Veneres Blijenburgicae sive Amorum hortus* (1600), divided into five "flowerbeds" (*areolae*) planted with poems on all kinds of themes concerning love. Not only is the argument typically humanistic, but its almost pedantic completeness is also characteristic of the development of later humanism, which excelled in cataloguing rather than in creative power. To give just a few other examples: in 1597 one of Dousa's sons, Franciscus Dousa, published for the first time the collected fragments of Lucilius; about a century later the extravagant Zealander Adriaan Beverland (Hadrianus Beverlandus, 1650–1716) thought it worth his while to collect a complete corpus of erotic texts from the Bible and from Greek and Latin literature in his unedited *De prostibulis veterum*.[46]

Not less important than poetry are the humanist dramas of the Netherlands, which in this field of humanist activity occupy a foremost position. Latin theater was an excellent means of language training and moral education in the humanist schools. The school therefore was its natural milieu, its authors the professors of the old Roman tongue, its performers the young students. This background must be kept in mind when proffering a judgment on their literary value. In the Low Countries the main center of humanist theater were the Colleges of the Arts Faculty at Louvain; the Latin schools in such towns as Bruges, Ghent, Liège, Gouda, Haarlem, Amsterdam, Utrecht, 's Hertogenbosch, and the like; and at a later stage also the University of Leiden and the colleges of religious orders such as Jesuits, Benedictines, Augustinians, and Oratorians. Apart from an isolated Dutch forerunner in Bologna at the end of the fifteenth century (H. Knuit van Slyterhoven), humanist theater appears to have been nascent in the first years of the sixteenth century and to have come into full growth in the following decades, maintaining itself on a high level until the mid-seventeenth century, in the time of Vondel and Hooft. Texts were written for the purpose or borrowed from Italian, French, and German colleagues, a good example being the Latin school of the Zandberg at Ghent under master Eligius Eucharius in the second decade of the sixteenth century.[47]

The Latin plays offer a wide variety of types. The early decades generally produced *comoediae*, *fabulae comicae*, and *fabulae sacrae*, which present a rather loose structure and, in style, follow Plautus and Terence. The earliest ones were still in prose (Dorpius), but soon we find a mixture of prose and verse (Arduenna's *Palamedes*), dactylic hexameters or iambic verse. Rarely if ever do we find close imitation of Roman comedy in the choice of the argument (the exception is Nannius's *Vinctus*), and the classical use of contamination seems only to be applied in the isolated case of Petrus Papaeus's *Samarites* (1537), which successfully merged the Good Samaritan and the Prodigal Son stories in a new plot, the Son being the victim of the robbers and cared for by the Samaritan.

Although Seneca was read in Flanders in the late fifteenth century, as copies of his tragedies made at that time demonstrate, tragedy did not develop before the middle of the sixteenth century and at first only as *tragoedia sacra* or *christiana*. It is, however, extremely important to remember that as early as 1503 and 1506 Erasmus had translated two plays of Euripides, the *Hecuba* and the *Iphigenia at Aulis* into Latin, and that these plays were performed by students at Louvain and elsewhere in the Netherlands. Only much later were similar translations attempted, such as Aristophanes's *Plutus* by the Fleming Hadrianus Chilius (1533), Euripides's *Medea* by the Frisian Petrus Tiara (1542, more or less contemporary with the translation of the same tragedy by the Scotsman Buchanan), or the works of Sophocles by another Frisian, Georgius Rataller (1570). Until Heinsius's and Grotius's riper years Seneca remained the dominating model for modern tragedians, which means that Aristotle entered only at the final stage of Latin drama: the evolution is noticeable from Heinsius's *Auriacus* to his *Herodes infanticida* or from Grotius's *Adamus exul* to his *Sophompaneas*.

Apart from comedy and tragedy there were several other kinds of plays: *dialogismi* (Nannius's *Dialogismi heroinarum*), *dialogi ioculares* (Arnoldus Madirius's *Pisander Bombylicus*, 1540), tragicomedies, which appear in the Low Countries only fifty years after the first experiments by the Verardis in Rome at the end of the fifteenth century; and even an *amphitragoedia* (Franciscus Eutrachelus's *Edessa sive Hester*, 1559 in

Ghent), the precise meaning of which remains unclear because the author does not explain himself and the piece has not been studied so far. It may be a pedantic variant of tragicomedy, perhaps with some inept reminiscence of amphitheater.

The theme of all those plays is predominantly Christian. The heroes are figures borrowed from the Bible or church history (saints, martyrs, persecutors), a few from classical history (Pompeius) or mythology (Hercules). The latter sometimes will be christianized, as in the allegorical play *Andromeda belgica dicta* by Jan Baptist Gramaye (Gramaius), with which the students of Louvain in 1600 bade welcome to Archdukes Albert and Isabella as the liberators of the Netherlands from the heretic (Protestant) Beggars. Popular life was sometimes the source of comical plays such as Macropedius's village farces (*Aluta, Andrisca, Bassarus*), Gabriel Jansenius's *Fabellae* (1600), Madirius, or the *Vitulus* of Cornelius Schonaeus, but they are on the whole exceptional, as are the students' life plays. Equally rare are translations or adaptations from the vernacular. The most typical case is Eucharius's *Grisellis*, taken from Boccaccio (but through Petrarch's Latin version) and the adaptation of the Elckerlyc (Everyman) theme by Macropedius, Christianus Ischyrius, and a few more.

The high quality of humanist drama from the Low Countries is demonstrated by its international success. Compared to other countries, such as Italy or Germany, so much larger than the Low Countries, the number of plays and authors who found their way far outside their own school or country is strikingly high. I mention, without pretending to completeness, Macropedius, Gulielmus Gnaphaeus (*Acolastus*), Petrus Papaeus, and Jacobus Zovitius in the first half of the sixteenth century, and Cornelius Crocus (*Iosephus*) and Livinus Brechtus, whose *Euripus* (1549), another variant of the Everyman theme, acquired a seminal importance in the development of Jesuit theater from Germany to Spain. In the second half of the century a schoolmaster from Haarlem, Cornelius Schonaeus, the "Terentius Christianus," who achieved a worldwide fame for about two centuries in scores of editions, enjoyed unrivaled success. Finally Daniel Heinsius, Hugo Grotius, Nicolaus Vernulaeus (at Louvain), or even Jacob Cornelius Lummenaeus a Marca (in Italy and in Ghent) close the rich harvest of Neolatin tragedy with works of considerable or even great quality.

＊　　＊　　＊

Two more areas remain that are within the inner core of humanist concern: history and moral philosophy. In both fields the Low Countries have a fair share in the general output of humanist writings. Let us first have a look at history and let us begin with a warning. The Latin word *historia* can have such different meanings as "history," "historiography," and "story." If one is not aware of this very simple fact, the interpretation of humanist Latin texts will suffer heavily and modern students will be led (and already have been led) into very serious errors.[48] Let me also point out here that (auto)biography, according to most classical and humanist authors, is not a part of historiographical literature, but a kind of portrait painting with words, which can be practiced in widely different literary genres (letter, oration, elegy, and so on), in prose as well as in verse.[49] Lastly, it is highly regrettable that, except for Frisia, almost no research has been done on humanist historiographical literature from the Low Countries (by contrast, for example, to the Italian Quattrocento or Germany).[50] Modern historians prefer to study archives and hardly look at their humanist predecessors; literary historians and philologists most of the time limit themselves to Pieter Cornelisz Hooft's *Historiën*, which are a late offspring of humanist historiography but have the advantage of being written in the vernacular. (Let me add that the situation is not much better or even worse for late medieval Latin chronicles, which often are still waiting for the first printed edition.)

Many humanists wrote historical works. Some of them also devoted attention to the question how to be a good historian, a theme already discussed by the ancient Greek Lucian, a favorite author of the humanist world. Vives included history in his search into the causes of the decay of the arts, the first part of his major work *De disciplinis*. One of Nannius's inaugural lectures at the Louvain Trilingue deserves particular mention, his *In T. Livium de laudibus historiae* (printed in his *Orationes tres*, Louvain 1541). The praise of history was a theme that attracted many humanists before and after. Thus at the opening of the Amsterdam Athenaeum Illustre on 8 January 1632, Vossius still chose for his inaugural lecture "De historiae utilitate" and bestowed lavish praise on history as the "magistra vitae," picking up again an expression of Cicero.[51] Nannius in his oration treated (not without some personal views) a wide range of problems: the conditions required to be a good historian (such as personal experience in politics and warfare), the basic need of impartiality, the topics to be included, the order of the narrative, and of course the style of the work. Most of his principles are borrowed, at least in their outlines, from ancient sources, as could be expected from a humanist; and he recommends Thucydides, Sallust, and Livy. As to the style, always a primary concern of humanists, the rule formulated is: "grandiorem esse dictionem historiographi quam sit oratoris, humiliorem quam sit poetae" (the language of the historian is grander than that of the orator, more humble than that of the poet). The comparison with poetry, which may surprise the modern reader, is quite along the lines of classical thinking, in which poetry and historiography have many affinities. Daniel Heinsius similarly compares both genres as to their contents: "The historian sets forth deeds, the poet for the most part qualities; one sets forth the more universal, the other the more particular." [52]

A systematic treatise on the writing of history was published at Antwerp in 1569: *De scribenda historia liber*. Its author, however, was not a native of the Low Countries, but the Sicilian Viperano, whom I mentioned earlier among the theoreticians of poetry.

Historical works are among the first writings of the early humanists worthy to be remembered. A real pioneer is a modest schoolmaster from Maastricht, Matthaeus Herbenus, who had been in Rome for several years in the service of Niccolò Perotti.[53] At that time he had gone to kneel at the tomb of one of the greatest humanist historians, Flavio Biondo. From Italy he sent home three small monographs on the occupation of Euboea by the Turks, on a conspiracy in Ferrara, and on a Turkish attack against Scutari (Shkodër). The first, especially, is a well-written dramatic narrative in Sallustian style. Back home Herben followed in the steps of Biondo's archaeological description of Rome and composed a *Traiectum illustratum*. This work is the humble beginning in the Netherlands of a genre that would culminate in the seventeenth century in the splendid volumes of Antonius Sanderus's *Flandria illustrata* and similar works. Another early historian is the southern Fleming Robert Gaguin, diplomat in the service of the French king. His *De origine et gestis Francorum compendium* (1495), the style of which was still too medieval to be attractive to men such as the great Guillaume Budé, nevertheless has some merits of its own and will at least always be remembered as the book that contains the first printed lines (the final letter) written by Erasmus.

Again it is not possible to write here the history of humanist historiography in the Netherlands. To begin with, there are hardly any preparatory works; moreover, the authors are too numerous to be discussed in a few lines. Among them one finds highly famous names such as Hugo Grotius, Ubbo Emmius, or Erycius Puteanus, and there is a wide variety of types, contents, and style.

There are perhaps fewer works on classical history from humanist authors than one might be led to expect. One may guess that they preferred to read the ancient historians themselves, who were published and commented upon scores of times by leading scholars such as Erasmus, Franciscus Modius, Justus Lipsius and many others. Otherwise, humanists usually chose to write on contemporary or national history, and therefore authors such as Biondo remained exceptions rather than the rule. In the Netherlands one could find some minor works such as Vives's *Descriptio temporum et rerum populi Romani* (1534) or *De veterum ac sui saeculi Belgio libri duo* (Antwerp 1616) by Pontus Heuterus (1535–1602) of Delft, which is, moreover, a historical geography rather than a history in the classical sense, in other words, closer to the elder Pliny than to Livy or Tacitus.

By contrast, works on national, regional, or local history (Res Burgundicae, Res Austriacae, Chronica Flandriae, Hollandiae, and the like) abound, as well as monographs on certain wars or other important events. Church history was less attractive, because it could be dangerous, as Vossius complained in his inaugural lecture at Amsterdam.

The great religious conflict of the sixteenth century and the breaking away of the northern provinces from Spain very strongly stimulated later humanist historiography, in which the so-called "Bellum Belgicum" occupies a central position. This "Bellum" has given us some of the finest works in the field, such as the monumental *Historiae* and *Annales* of Grotius, who in the titles alone pays his respect to Tacitus, or the precious *Historia Belgica ab anno MDLVIII* (1633) in three books by Nicolaus Burgundius,[54] written in a simple straightforward style (its author was a former pupil of Puteanus's Palaestra Bonae Mentis). The two *Decades*—a tribute to Livy—of the Roman Famiano Strada, one of the stylistically most accomplished descriptions of the Farnese campaigns, should also be mentioned. Among the many local historians, let it suffice to mention Jacobus Meyerus and Franciscus Haraeus in Flanders, Hadrianus Barlandus and Petrus Divaeus in Brabant, Jacobus Eyndius in Zealand, Janus Dousa in Holland, Ubbo Emmius and Petrus Winsemius in Frisia.

From what I have said about Herben and Gaguin, one can see that humanists from the Low Countries wrote also about many other parts of the world. When established abroad they often wrote about their new homeland or celebrated the deeds of their new patrons. Again I will limit myself to a few but interesting examples. Johannes Vasaeus from Bruges (1511/12–1561) became a professor at Salamanca and there wrote a valuable *Chronici rerum memorabilium Hispaniae tomus prior* (1552), which in its conception is perhaps still a bit medieval, but nevertheless reveals a new spirit by the inclusion of inscriptions. Even men such as Erasmus were not always aware of the importance of inscriptions as historical or linguistic sources, but about the middle of the sixteenth century and long after Italians (Ciriaco d'Ancona, Pomponio Leto) had set the trend, humanists of the Low Countries also began to collect and study ancient inscriptions (Martinus Smetius and others). Other very interesting cases are Hubert Thomas (Hubertus Thomas Leodius) from Liège (ca. 1495–1556)[55] and the more famous Erycius Puteanus. The latter, when he still was a professor at Milan, wrote a small work in honor of a local war captain. For this *Historiae Cisalpinae libri duo, res potissimum circa Lacum Larium a Ioanne Iacobo Medicaeo gestae* Sallust provided the stylistic model. As that old Roman had done, Puteanus devoted a few introductory pages to moralizing about his time before coming to his subject: "Gradually human affairs grow weak and totter, this complaint is an ancient but unjust one; nevertheless in the present age it has become especially strong." On this theme he goes on for two and a half pages more, then passes immediately to his hero: "When I was going to write history, it seemed proper to me to take Lord de' Medici as the first attempt [sample] of my activity, which will be continued."[56]

The case of Thomas is less known, but at least as interesting as that of Puteanus. This man for more than thirty years was at the service of the Count Palatine Frederick II the Wise at Heidelberg. He wrote several minor works in the field of history, but his masterpiece is the *Annalium de vita et rebus gestis illustrissimi principis Friderici II electoris Palatini libri XIV* (printed Frankfurt am Main 1624), to which he added *De aedificiis illustrissimi principis Friderici*. This work is extremely interesting from the humanistic point of view, since the additional book is a close imitation of a classical model, Procopius, the early Byzantine historian of Emperor Justinian. Procopius not only wrote the history of his emperor, but also an additional *De domini Iustiniani aedificiis libri VI*, which work was printed for the first time in 1531 by Thomas's friend, the Alsatian humanist Beatus Rhenanus.

Before I leave this section on humanist historical literature, a last point must be illustrated. Humanism coincides with the great age of discoveries, and this expansion of the Western world has left numerous traces in humanist works: poems on Columbus or other seafaring heroes and their great exploits, an outburst of utopian fiction beginning with *Utopia* itself, and many historical works such as the *Decades de orbe novo* of Petrus Martyr Anglerius. The humanists of the Netherlands do not seem to have paid much attention to the New World in the early sixteenth century. Erasmus and Vives, for example, barely mention a couple of times the "Insulae novi orbis." The first historical work concerning the Indies written in the Low Countries seems to have been the *Commentarii rerum gestarum in India citra Gangem a Lusitanis anno 1538*, also called *Diensis nobilissimae . . . urbis oppugnatio* (Louvain 1539) written by a Portuguese humanist, Damianus a Goes, who for many years was established in Antwerp and Louvain and had a keen interest in African and Asian affairs. The situation changed later in the century, no doubt because of the growing importance of the Spanish empire—the Spanish king was at the same time sovereign of the Netherlands—and, after the independence of the North, the Dutch expeditions to Brazil or the East Indies. This change explains works, not always equally reliable, such as *De Peruvianae regionis inter novi orbis provincias celeberrimae inventione et rebus in eadem gestis libri V* (Antwerp, 1567) by the Fleming Apollonius Laevinus, *De origine gentium Americanarum* (1642/43) by Hugo Grotius, or Caspar Barlaeus's *Rerum per octennium in Brasilia et alibi nuper gestarum historia* (Amsterdam 1647) on the deeds of John-Maurice, count of Nassau-Siegen, and based on the count's personal notes.

As I said at the beginning, biography generally was not considered to be a historical genre. Nevertheless, a few words here may not be entirely out of place. The number of *vitae* written by humanists of the Low Countries is again very high. Agricola had set the example with his *Life of Petrarch*, soon to be imitated by Servatius Aedicollius (1483–1516).[57] Erasmus is the author of one of the extremely rare modern imitations of Plutarch's *Parallel Lives:* his famous letter to Justus Jonas on the two perfect Christians, Jean Vitrier from St. Omer and John Colet from London.[58] Nor do we lack autobiographies, in prose (Lipsius) as well as in verse, such as the remarkable poem of Gislenus Bultelius (1555–1611) from Ieper (Ipra, Ypres), one of the better Latin poets from Flanders.

*   *   *

Philosophy never was a direct concern of the humanists in general, at least not its speculative branches, and certainly not the late scholastic terministic subtleties of the dialecticians against whom Vives launched his *In pseudodialecticos.* This statement is true in principle, yet historical facts sometimes can be different. The famous Deventer schoolman Alexander Hegius,[59] considered one of the greatest humanist pedagogues, is also the author of epistemological and other speculative opuscules such as *De scientia et eo quod scitur contra Academicos, De tribus animae generibus,* and *De sensu et sensili.*

More generally speaking, philosophy was an integral part of the arts curriculum at the universities; therefore, most humanists had attended these courses in their youth, and many had taught them as senior students (or *legentes* in the late medieval academic jargon). Martinus Dorpius at Louvain offers us a typical case. There can be no doubt as to his profound humanist inclinations. As a *legens* he taught Latin, even taking the initiative—quite new at Louvain at that time—of performing Plautus with his junior students; but at the same time he was a teacher of philosophy, and as such he wrote a handbook *Introductio facilis . . . ad Aristotelis libros logice intelligendos,* which was published at Paris in 1512. And the same Dorpius at a certain moment went so far as to scold Lorenzo Valla in a public speech, because he had read the latter's criticism of Aristotle in his *Dialectics.* In fact, logic or dialectic often became a meeting place or a battlefield between scholastics and early humanists. Valla's work is a perfect example of the point, along with Vives's attack on the Sorbonne dialecticians. But Gerardus Listrius not only wrote a commentary on Erasmus's *Praise of Folly,* but also on Peter of Spain's *Summulae logicales,*⁶⁰ the universal textbook of the time.

Yet it is true and certainly not a happenstance that during the two centuries of humanism in the Low Countries no important name in philosophy can be found, except perhaps the Spaniard Vives, who became a forerunner of modern psychology in one of his major works, *De anima,* and who used to introduce himself as a "philosophus," not as a "poeta et orator." But apart from him, all forces either were drawn to the humanist-literary field or became involved in the endless theological conflicts. The last important name of late medieval scholasticism had been Dionysius (or Denys) the Carthusian from Rijkel in southern Limburg (d. 1472). After him the first names that cannot be passed over in silence in a history of Western philosophy are those of Arnold Geulinx from Antwerp (1624–1669) and his contemporary Baruch de Spinoza (1632–1677), a Portuguese Jew born in Amsterdam. Between these men one finds only unimportant teachers in the Arts faculties such as Vives's Paris master, Jan Dullaert (Johannes Dullardus) of Ghent (ca. 1480–1513), who, according to Vives, at the end of his life regretted having spent so much time on philosophical trifles.⁶¹

Practical philosophy had a stronger appeal to the humanist mind. Ethics, educational theory, and political thought always attracted many pens. This state of affairs is quite normal for men who revered Cicero and Quintilian as their great masters, to say nothing of Seneca and Plutarch. And no work of Petrarch was more popular among our early humanists than his *De remediis utriusque fortunae,* which was copied, read, or abbreviated over and over again. Its theme still returns in Lipsius's most successful *De constantia.* To a modern reader this dialogue may seem downright naïve and hardly fitted to offer consolation in hard times, but that feeling was not shared by Lipsius's contemporaries, who definitely liked very much this rather strange mixture of Christian and Stoic reflections on the troubles of human life.

Equally popular were discourses on the respective values of the *vita activa* and the *vita contemplativa* and the possibility of their combination, questions that one finds in both early and late humanists. Such is Jacob Canter's dialogue *De solitudine* (ca. 1491), in which the contrast is represented by life in town versus life on the land, perhaps a reflection on Horace's famous fable of the town and country mice.[62] Such is still the inaugural lecture of Caspar Barlaeus held at Amsterdam (9 January 1632) and published under the telling title "Mercator sapiens" or, as he explained in a letter to C. Huygens, "de coniungendis mercaturae et philosophiae studiis" (on the way to connect trade and the study of philosophy).[63] In fact, it is a theme that had already occupied the early Florentine humanists of the Quattrocento, and it may even be thought about today by political or academic authorities.

The humanists' traditional concern with moral problems could find a fertile soil in the North, where the medieval Christian way of life easily could be amalgamated with the precepts of the classical thinkers, or at least could be adorned by classical flowers of speech or various mythological images. A good example of such a mixture is the supplement to Sebastian Brant's *Narrenschiff: Stultiferae navis additamentum de quinque virginibus* by Josse Bade (Jodocus Badius). The image of the five unwise virgins is biblical; the theme is a traditional Christian warning against the sins of the human senses, but large parts of the text and its *ornatus* are purely classical-humanistic. Let us read some lines of the song of the foolish girls in the ship of the sense of hearing:

> How far do you men unskilled in music and a little
>   deaf flee the Aonian rhythms?
> Behold, the Zephyrs invite us from afar to the
>   pleasant glades of the sisters and muses.
> . . .
> And the colored birds renew in the
>   grass their familiar and natural songs,
> Which the lyre of Thamyras and Methymnian
>   Arion are unable to equal . . .
> Here harmonious joys continue immortal life
>   with songs.[64]

If it were not for its context, the poem could be taken as a lofty humanist praise of blessed life in company of the Muses.

As can be expected from students and teachers of the *humaniores litterae*, the humanists very frequently concentrated their efforts on questions concerning the education of children and young people. In the Netherlands several interesting pamphlets were written. They begin very early with Alexander Hegius's *Contra modos significandi invectiva* (first draft, ca. 1480), which already stresses the necessity of adapting teaching methods to the children, and Rudolf Agricola's letter *De formando studio* (1484). Next come the important contributions of Erasmus and Vives, and finally, at the end of the sixteenth century, two more remarkable treatises: the Catholic teacher and grammarian Simon Verepaeus (1522–1598) wrote the most complete treatise of humanist Christian paedagogy "ad mentem Concilii Tridentini" ever written in the Netherlands, namely, his *Institutionum scholasticarum libri tres* (Antwerp 1573),[65] whereas the Calvinist Lord Philips van Marnix van Sint-Aldegonde is the author of an extremely interesting *Ratio instituendae iuventutis* (1583), about which I shall say more presently.

All those treatises have one basic concern in common: the religious, moral, and intellectual education of youth, or, to say it with the words of Verepaeus in his dedication letter (par. 3): "In scholis . . . una cum litterarum institutione etiam pietatis et virtutum praecepta proponuntur" (in schools the precepts of piety and virtue are put forth together with the teaching of letters). One should remember what I have said before on this point in the section on the teaching of grammar.

Until the early decades of the sixteenth century the northern humanist educators had to fight against the use of medieval methods and texts, the most famous of them being, apart from the *Modi significandi*, pseudo-Boethius's *De scholarium disciplina*,[66] which—strangely enough—was printed by Josse Bade. How commercial interests here seem to prevail over educational principles, even among humanists! Agricola's letter *De formando studio*, directed to Jacobus Barbirianus from Antwerp, who had tried to hire Agricola for the Latin school of Antwerp, discusses two questions: the relation of one's study to one's aims in life, and the best method of pursuing it. In the first part great weight is given to *eloquentia* against the still omnipresent late medieval barbarism; in the second, three stages are distinguished: first one must understand the matter, next one has to memorize it (an old rhetorical precept), and finally one proceeds to produce one's personal work.

Erasmus's contribution is much greater and more important. He is the author of several treatises such as *De ratione studii*, a protreptic letter, *De pueris statim ac liberaliter instituendis*, *Institutio principis christiani*, *Institutio christiani matrimonii*, not to speak of many of his *Colloquies*, language books (*De copia* and so on), and editions of schoolbooks such as the *Disticha Catonis* and Publilius Syrus.[67] However, since Erasmus is the subject of a special chapter in this series, I shall not analyze here his thought and limit myself to singling out his profoundly humanistic concern for good and pure language as a mirror of correct and orderly thinking, his Christian concern for true religion and piety against all superstition, and his deeply human concern for treating children with due respect and sincere love.

Vives must be mentioned here because of his close bonds with Flanders (his second home) and Brabant, though his most interesting writings on educational problems owe their direct origin to his relations with the English court: in 1523 he wrote his *Epistolae de ratione studii* at the request of Catherine of Aragon as a study program for her young daughter Mary. A year later he dedicated to the same queen his three books *De institutione feminae christianae*, a treatise on the education of girls and women, very much needed, he thought, because nonexistent in the then available literature: "argumento ut maxime necessario, ita nulli hactenus tractato in tanta ingeniorum scribentiumque varietate ac copia" (the subject is extremely useful, but up to now it has not been treated, although there is so great a variety and number of thinkers and writers).[68] It is not entirely true that there were not older works on the subject, since Leonardo Bruni, for one, had written his well-known *De studiis et litteris ad illustrem dominam Baptistam de Malatesta* (ca. 1405) more than a century earlier; but one can agree with Vives that no one had devoted such a complete treatment to the education and life of humanist and Christian women. Of the three books only the first one can be called pedagogical, since in it the girl's education is described from the beginning until her marriage. The other books are more ethical, as they give counsel to the woman as a wife and mother (2) and as a widow (3). In this last book Vives closely adheres to Pauline doctrine on the matter.

Vives's pedagogy is strictly moralistic: the supreme goal is always to bring the girl to a pure and morally noble life, since history teaches us that "nullam fere inveniemus doctam impudicam" (we shall find that almost no one who is learned is unchaste) and most feminine vices find their origin in *inscitia* (ignorance). From his program I shall pick up only the part that is the most relevant from the humanistic point of view, namely, his reading list. Apart from the Bible, which inevitably comes first, the girl will read from the classics the works of Plato, Cicero, Seneca, and Plutarch as well as some "historians" such as Justinus and Valerius Maximus (the latter of course more for the moral value of his exempla than for the historical information he could offer). To these the Fathers Jerome, Augustine, and Ambrose will be added as well as some "modern" authors, such as his friends Erasmus and Thomas More (the latter's *Utopia*). Among the poets Vives in his *De ratione* and *De institutione* recommends Horace and Lucan and, furthermore, the Christians Juvencus, Prudentius, Paulinus, Sidonius, Prosper, and Arator. This list proves that again religious and moral concerns prevail over classical purity of style and language. Finally, if the girl marries, she should read also the pedagogical writings of the Italian humanists Pier Paolo Vergerio and Francesco Filelfo.

Vives's treatises are written for a young princess, but most of his rules can be applied to any young girl. The work of Lord Marnix, on the contrary, is specifically written for noble youth, who must be prepared to become statesmen and war captains. It is a highly remarkable treatise written in a straightforward, elegant Latin prose. Lord Marnix knew the rules of classical style perfectly well (not so common among the nobility), and it is surely not by chance that his *Institutio* ends on a final ditrocheus clausula ("comparabit"), which is a striking parallel even in sound to Cicero's example of this clausula ("comprobavit," *Orator* 214), which—the Roman says—if appropriately used, raises your audience to ecstatic enthusiasm. Marnix wanted to educate the boy's *animus* (religious and moral education), *ingenium* (or intellectual formation), and *corpus,* which not only includes physical training but also rules for elegant behavior and attitudes in all circumstances.[69] He prefers a school with small classes, a strong director, and qualified teachers above private tuition. Permissiveness has no place in education, not even among very young children; intelligent authority is indispensable; the teachers, who will dispose of much freedom in their task, must not be tyrants, but in extreme cases bodily punishment is unavoidable. The training of memory and the formation of personal critical judgment are essential. The study program is very comprehensive, stresses the necessity of a sound knowledge of the native language, Latin, Greek, history, and geography (both ancient and modern) and mathematics. Poetry is considered less important (as is music), and the list of poets to be read is very limited: Vergil, Horace, the Scot Buchanan (obviously because of his Psalm paraphrases), Homer, Hesiod, Pindar, and Euripides. On this point one notices that the overall importance of poetry is on the wane.

Marnix in general follows Quintilian, but not slavishly. From the Roman he no doubt borrowed the principle of a bilingual education for children and adapted it to modern circumstances: Quintilian spoke of Latin and Greek, Marnix expressly proposes the native and another modern language. Marnix also recommends humanist educators such as Erasmus, Melanchthon, Johann Sturm, and Vives. As Vives had done, he urges mothers to nurse their children themselves.

A last point is rather surprising in a humanist context, but explains itself in a religious one. Marnix stresses the importance of journeys to foreign countries, but expressly warns against visiting Italy, at least before the age of twenty-five: "Certe putarim Italiam non secus ac pestis ingenuis adulescentibus esse fugiendam" (I certainly think that Italy should be avoided like the plague by noble youth). Quite clearly the Calvinist here had eliminated the humanist altogether.

Since many humanists were engaged as preceptors, counselors, or secretaries of princes, it follows that the old Isocratean genre of the *speculum principis*, the mirror of princes, would be practiced intensely. Here again we find Erasmus in the forefront with his *Enchiridion militis christiani* and even his long and tedious "Panegyric for Philip the Handsome." Among other authors let me mention Libert Houthem, better known as a playwright, of whom a *De politici magistratus officiis libellus* (1585) written at the imperial court of Rudolf II in Prague, survives in a single copy in that town; also Houthem's contemporary, the poet and philologist Franciscus Modius from Oudenburg near Bruges, who early in 1591 during a visit to Heidelberg wrote a long elegiac poem for the son of the count palatine with which he wanted to lead him into the "sapientum templa serena" (the serene temple of wisdom; verse 9).[70]

Not only young princes, but also actual rulers need the help of wise counselors. One type of advice is very characteristic of humanism in Flanders, care for the poor. Vives's treatise *De subventione pauperum* (1526), directed to the town magistrate of Bruges, is widely known. Less known, however, is the fact that the little book is by no means an isolated case and that it was followed by several texts on the same problem. Christianus Cellarius from Izenberge near Veurne (Furnes, Furnae), in western Flanders, published an *Oratio contra mendicitatem publicam pro nova pauperum subventione* at Antwerp in 1531. Another west Fleming, Jacobus Papa from Poperinge, published also at Antwerp in 1534 two books of elegies, "quorum prior mendicabulum publicum tuetur" ("of which the first has to do with the public beggar's care"). From the same circle as Papa came the well-known Marburg professor of divinity Andreas Gerhard (Hyperius, born at Ieper, 1511, died Marburg 1564), who, a few years before his death, wrote a *De publica in pauperes beneficentia* on behalf of some authorities in Bremen, Germany (published with his works, Basel, 1570). A study of their relation or dependence on Vives would be a rewarding investigation. In any case, from the titles alone one can notice the humanist pleasure at treating the same theme in different literary forms: treatise, oration, poem. Moreover, Papa speaks of the care of the poor at Ieper, not Bruges. An ecclesiastical reaction against the attempts of the Bruges magistrate to organize a welfare service was launched by another Spaniard established in Bruges, Brother Lorenzo de Villavicencio (1518–1583), chaplain of the Spanish merchants in the town. Again a comparison of his *De oeconomia sacra circa pauperum cura a Christo instituta* (Antwerp and Paris, 1564) with Vives's earlier treatise could be interesting. If nothing else, it proves that human-

ists in the Low Countries could not write on many themes without in-
curring the wrath of some theologian.

Another topic, which is omnipresent in humanistic literature, is
peace, or rather complaints for the loss of peace. Erasmus not only made
Folly speak out, but with an equally loud voice he made Peace lament
publicly in the *Querela Pacis* "undique gentium eiectae profligataeque"
(which is cast out and overthrown everywhere). In vain she appealed to
the European princes: "I call upon you, princes. . . . Acknowledge the
voice of your King [Christ] calling you to peace!"[71] Many indeed were
the causes of war and conflict, political as well as religious, and with
Erasmus many others, such as Vives, wrote pamphlets on behalf of peace
and concord in the Christian world, addressing themselves to the pope,
the emperor, kings, or other authorities. Their voices were joined by
those of scores of poets who also lamented the loss of peace or, occasion-
ally, exulted with joy when it seemed to be restored. The Luxemburger
Nicolaus Mameranus and Cornelis de Schrijver (Cornelius Grapheus) at
Antwerp are only two examples out of many during the reign of Charles
V (1519–55).

Political thought was also the subject of more systematic works
(Plato, Aristotle, and Cicero were the bright examples to imitate). They
could be of a more speculative and general kind, or they could search its
practical application in old or modern state systems. Most influential
were Lipsius's *Politicorum sive civilis doctrinae libri sex* (1589), in which
his own ideas were hidden under the cover of a massive collection of
excerpts from ancient authorities. This caution not only was a measure
of prudence in an intolerant age; it also was a well-tried humanistic
scholarly method, the efficaciousness of which had been amply demonstrated by such works as Erasmus's *Parabolae*. Basically, it was a public
application of a most common method of humanist education: every pupil in his school time had to collect well-turned sentences, adages, and
the like on specific themes, as an aide-mémoire for life.

A good example of the descriptive type of political study is Grotius's
partly lost *Parallelon rerumpublicarum* (1600–1604). Grotius, lawyer,
historian, and humanist literator alike, initiated the comparative study
of Greek, Roman, and national (Dutch) institutions. He also laid down
fundamental rules of international law in his *Mare liberum* (1609) and
De iure belli ac pacis (1625). With Lipsius and Grotius, humanists of the
Low Countries for the last time wrote works in the political field, which
were also attentively read outside the classroom and exercised a noticeable influence on the public life of their own and even of the following age.

※   ※   ※

As we have seen, the humanists' efforts first and foremost focused on the improvement of the study of Latin, the care for an elegant Latin style as a means to better learning, and a renewed contact with an exemplary ancient civilization through a better knowledge of its authors, now directly read in improved editions. Latin being the universal language of instruction in grammar schools and universities, sooner or later repercussions of the humanistic ideas must be felt in all fields of scholarship and science. As a matter of fact scholars and scientists in the course of the sixteenth century more and more adapted their language to the new principles and began to write a more classical and stylistically more polished idiom. This does not mean that all became Ciceronians. Ciceronianism was always a trend of the strictly literary prose, and it influenced technical languages much less in their vocabulary than in their style. There it did no harm; on the contrary, the humanists were quite right in positing that a clear and pure style reveals orderly thinking and that an obscure jargon by no means contributes to a better quality of learning.

Also, humanist studies had unearthed scores of forgotten ancient sources, which now helped to advance modern scholarship in many fields: philosophy, history, the natural sciences, medicine, and more. This enrichment of knowledge, together with many new discoveries, laid the foundation for the development of modern science from the seventeenth century onward. During the period of humanism the progress was still modest, albeit real, and the Netherlands can boast a long series of first-class philologists, scientists, and doctors. I do not feel competent to analyze the merits of each of them, but will only recall the most famous names and discuss one or two characteristic cases. Moreover, most of the scholarly and scientific research did not specifically belong to the humanist sphere of activity. Naturally, in some cases humanism and modern science met each other to the profit of both. Such was the case in law, when a famous but not profoundly humanist scholar such as the Frisian Viglius van Aytta published the first edition of the Greek translation of Justinian's Institutes: *Institutiones iuris civilis in Graecam linguam per Theophilum traductae* (Basel, 1533); or when the Antwerp geographer Abraham Ortelius added maps of the ancient world to his modern atlas *Theatrum orbis terrarum parergon sive Veteris geographiae tabulae* (1624), which thus became the humanists' contribution to the genre of historical atlases hardly known before.[72]

Famous names in philology are Erasmus, Willem Canter, Justus Lipsius, Andreas Schottus, Joseph Justus Scaliger, and many others; in law Gabriel van der Muyden (Mudaeus), professor at Louvain 1547–60, who urged a return to the classical sources; in botany Charles de l'Ecluse (Clusius), Dodoens (Rembertus Dodonaeus), and Mathias de L'Obel

(Matthaeus Lobelius); in geography and astronomy Paulus of Middel-
burg, who was in the service of the duke of Urbino and the pope, Gemma
Frisius, Gerrit Cremers (Gerardus Mercator), Godfried Wendelen (Godefridus Wendelinus), and even the Jesuit Ferdinand Verbiest, famous for
his work at Peking; in medicine Andreas Vesalius, Jan Baptist van Hel-
mont from Vilvoorde (1579–1644), the "medicus per ignem" who
coined the word "gas," and Nicolaas Tulp from Amsterdam (1593–
1674), whose valuable *Observationum medicarum libri tres* (first edition
1641) offers the first reliable description of the orangutan and in this way
joins the humanist literature on the Indies, which I mentioned before.

To assess correctly the merits of each scholar is often a very delicate
task. I will give an example from the philological field, which I know
best. When one looks today into a critical edition of Tibullus at book
3.12 (= 4.6), verse 3, one finds in the critical apparatus to the first word
"Tota" a proposal of correction to "Lota," the origin of which is uncertain. The edition of F. W. Lenz (Leiden 1971), which is the most explicit
on the point, offers this rather vague information: "lota: *nescioquis;*
Canterus secundum Müllerum; Guyet secundum Postgate; recentiores secundum Hiller; vetus coniectura secundum Calonghi; probant Müller,
Némethy, Schuster." Nobody really seems to know who first proposed
"Lota," a reading accepted by at least three modern critics of Tibullus.
The name Canterus is too vague to be helpful, since there were several
Frisian philologists of that name in humanist times. Probably Willem
(1542–1575) is meant, perhaps the most famous of them, but I did not
find the emendation in his *Novarum lectionum libri septem, editio se-
cunda tribus libris aucta* (Basel, 1566), in which he discusses several passages of Tibullus. Be that as it may, the real "emendator" could well be
the young and brilliant Lucas Fruytier (Fruterius) from Bruges (1541/42–
1566), who in any case proposed the reading "Lota" in a letter to Marcus Antonius Muretus (see the latter's *Letters,* 1.25). I deem it also highly
probable that the learned French philologist François Guyet (1575–
1655) picked it up later from Muretus's *Epistolae,* published several
times in Paris and elsewhere, without perhaps acknowledging his debt.
Fruytier's fall into complete oblivion may be compared—si parvis licet
componere magna—with Erasmus as a translator of Euripides. In a brilliant essay J. Waszink of Leiden has shown, when he was preparing the
translations for the *Opera omnia* of Erasmus, that on several occasions
Erasmus made implicit corrections to the Greek text of Euripides, the
honor of which is now attributed to modern philologists in our critical
editions.

Also in the field of philology and history I must single out the merits of the Flemish imperial diplomat Ogier Ghislain de Busbecq (Augerius Gislenus Busbequius, 1522–1592). He not only gave us the tulip and other unknown plants, the seeds of which he sent to his friend Charles de l'Ecluse in Vienna, but also a Crimean Gothic vocabulary and the first transcript of the long inscription that preserves, near Ankara, Turkey, the text of the testament of the first Roman emperor Augustus, the so-called *Monumentum Ancyranum*, for humanists, of course, a most thrilling discovery. Busbecq's *Legationis Turcicae epistolae quattuor* (1589) are among the most fascinating documents of humanist literature from the Netherlands.

I do not feel competent to discuss the innovations that humanism may have caused in the field of natural sciences and medicine, except the obvious fact that the scientists, as I have said, also adapted their language to the new style. If one is sensitive to the charm of elegant Latin, the reading of late medieval "scientific" texts most of the time is a torture, Copernicus or Vesalius on the contrary a real pleasure. Although this difference may not be essential for specialists of a scientific discipline, from the cultural point of view in general I think it is not entirely without importance.

Concerning Vesalius and his *De humani corporis fabrica libri septem* (1543), one of the great books in the history of sciences and typography, let me refer the reader to an interesting article of R. Toellner, read at a Wolfenbüttel conference on the reception of antiquity during the Renaissance.[73] Vesalius's work is based on two sources: personal observation during anatomical dissections and the works of the ancient physician Galen. The latter's information is corrected in more than two hundred cases, and proof is given that he worked not on human corpses, but on apes; yet his authority remains fundamentally unshaken and is not contested in matters of interpretation. Toellner gives the typical case of the problem of how the blood is carried from the right to the left part of the heart. Vesalius could not detect any direct communication pores, which should be there according to Galen. Did he jump to the conclusion that Galen's explanation was wrong (and perhaps, in so doing, discover blood circulation)? Not at all. Respectful of Galen's authority, and as a good Christian at the same time, he took it as a proof of God's wonderful power, which could even provide the heart with invisible pores! Vesalius's "renata dissectionis ars," even when it went a step further than medieval bookish learning and tried to free Galen from corruptions introduced into his work throughout the ages, did not liberate itself from the weight of (classical) authority and become a truly new art. To be sure, the humanists had rejected much medieval thinking and often fought hard battles with more conservative colleagues, but the authority of the ancient world remained largely unshaken with many of them. Not many could follow Valla or Vives and doubt if Aristotle was always right.

Not only scholarship and sciences ultimately felt the impact of humanism. Something similar happened to the fine arts, when humanism in the course of the sixteenth century caused a break with the Gothic Middle Ages and fostered a return to classical norms and models. In this process the princely courts, such as those in Mechlin, Brussels, and Liège, often played a decisive role. Princes, bishops, and courtiers underwent a double influence: contact with Italy and its new art through the reciprocal visits of diplomats, bankers, artists, or the rulers themselves; then, local humanism at work through secretaries, counselors, preceptors, and the like, who often were at the same time poets (Remaclus Arduenna) or scholars (Erasmus, Vives) in the first ranks of humanism. The father of Janus Secundus (Everaerts) and his brothers was a prominent officer of the high court in Mechlin, of which he was the chairman during the last years of his life. Another member was Frans Craneveldt (Franciscus Craneveldius), who even in his later years passed his time in Mechlin translating the Greek poet Theognis.[74] These princes and courtiers began to order works of art in the new style, began to build or adorn palaces and churches according to classical principles, and at times even sent their artists to Italy. The porch of St. Jacques at Liège (1552–58) was created by Lambert Lombard, who had been sent to Rome in 1538 by his bishop and had seen there the Septizonium near the Palatine. Nevertheless, the renewal of architecture and the visual arts went much slower than the renewal of language and literature. Only in 1606 did *Den eerste boeck van architecture* appear, being a translation of Sebastiano Serlio's *Regole generali di architettura* (1549), made by Pieter Coecke of Aalst, an important mediator between Italy and the Low Countries in matters of art. But slow as it was, the change was real. It makes the difference between two such important monuments as the town hall of Louvain, a most splendid example of Gothic art, finished by Matthias de Layens about the time Erasmus came into this world, and the town hall of Antwerp, one of the first Renaissance buildings in the old Netherlands. It was erected in 1560–65 by Cornelis Floris de Vriendt, a man who had seen Italy. At that time Lipsius was a student, and literary humanism was already moving to its last and learned stage. One could also compare from the humanist point of view the great artists of the Low Countries in painting or sculpture. Compare, for example, Erasmus's elder contemporary Jeroen Bosch (ca. 1450–1516) and his late medieval allegories, with Pieter Bruegel the Elder (ca. 1528–1569), who had visited Rome and married Coeck's daughter, yet remained largely attached to local popular traditions, and finally with Peter Paul Rubens (1577–1640), who lived in Rome for many years, whose brother Philip was a minor humanist philologist and whose works after his return to Antwerp in 1608 perfectly reflect many of the ideals of humanism in its last stage. At that moment the broad gap between literary and visual arts had been covered, and one understands that many humanist publications of the early seventeenth century were illustrated by Rubens and his workshop: they spoke the same language and met harmoniously in the engravings and the texts of the same books.

٭   ٭   ٭

The age of Renaissance and Baroque humanism was a great one in the cultural history of the Low Countries, the old "Belgium." Situated at the crossroads of important political, cultural, and economic highways of early modern times, literary and artistic life flourished in its many prospering towns, in its schools and universities, its courts and abbeys, not rarely among the cruelties of brutal war or of ideological persecution. But in that respect the Low Countries' humanism did not really differ from that in Tuscany or other Italian states, where often enough war and bloodshed were daily experiences. The generalized use of Latin allowed writers, whose native Frisian, Dutch, or even French would have been of little or no use outside their own region, to speak to the entire Western world from Sicily to Iceland. Without this Latin Erasmus, Lipsius, Heinsius, and Grotius never would have had the worldwide audience they had then and still have now. And because of them and many of their less important colleagues the Low Countries are next to Italy a vital part of the European scene of humanism, a part that largely exceeds the narrow boundaries of that little corner of Europe.[75]

NOTES

1. General bibliographical information is provided by A. Gerlo and H. D. L. Vervliet, *Bibliographie de l'humanisme des anciens Pays-Bas, avec un répertoire bibliographique des humanistes et poètes néolatins* (Brussels, 1972); ten-year supplement for 1972–82 (Brussels, 1981). See also J. IJsewijn, *Companion to Neo-Latin Studies* (Amsterdam, 1977; 2d ed. 1988). Information on recent publications can be found in the annual "Instrumentum bibliographicum" of the journal *Humanistica Lovaniensia*, in the appropriate bibliographical sections of the *Archiv für Reformationsgeschichte*, and in the *Revue d'histoire ecclésiastique*. For the earlier period, the "Kroniek der Handschriftenkunde" in the journal *Archief- en Bibliotheekwezen in België* is particularly important. For the historical background, see the *Algemene Geschiedenis der Nederlanden*, published at Haarlem, especially volumes 4–9 (1980–). Information on single authors is given in the

Biographisch Woordenboek der Nederlanden, 27 vols. (Haarlem, 1852–78); the *Nieuw Nederlandsch Biographisch Woordenboek*, 10 vols. (1911–37); the *Biographie nationale* (de Belgique), 28 vols. (Brussels, 1866–1944), and several supplements since 1956; the *Nationaal Biografisch Woordenboek*, 11 vols. (Brussels, 1964–85), and more in preparation. The latter is not a translation of the French counterpart but an entirely new work. In many cases articles on humanists must be read in this new dictionary and not in the outdated older French volumes.

2. Most place-names have several different forms: the original Dutch or French one and their translations into other languages—Latin, German, English, or even Spanish. They often create great confusion among foreign scholars. Therefore, every time such a name is mentioned first in my essay, I shall give its various forms. As a rule, I shall put first the official native name, even when it differs from the current English one, and add the translations in parentheses; in subsequent references, I use the English spelling. A further source of confusion is the fictional "ancient" names one often finds in Latin humanist texts, especially because some of them are applied to widely different places. Typical examples in the Netherlands are the following: Athenae Grudiae for Louvain (authors calling themselves Grudius were born in Louvain); Civitas Nervia for Tournai/Doornijk; Traiectum Baetasiorum for Maastricht (which is also Traiectum Inferius, as opposed to Traiectum Superius or Vetus or Ultraiectum/Utrecht); the Cimbri are the Flemings (called also Pleumosii) but also the Danes, especially those from Schleswig-Holstein; the Mattiaci are the Zealanders, but Aquae Mattiacae is Wiesbaden in Germany; the Sicambri are the inhabitants of Guelders, but Aquincum Sicambriae is Buda(-pest); Hermopolis can be Antwerp and Glaucopolis Amsterdam, etc.

3. "Miratus sum tam studiosum eloquentiae et optimarum artium virum tam longe ab Italia, cuius haec studia vernacula esse videntur, reperiri." Poggio's letters, book 10, epistle 23. See J. IJsewijn, "The Coming of Humanism to the Low Countries," in *Itinerarium Italicum: The Profile of the Italian Renaissance in the Mirror of Its European Transformations*, ed. H. O. Oberman and T. A. Brady, Jr. (Leiden, 1975), 191–301 at 212.

4. The best list of Martens's printings is that by K. Heireman in the exhibition catalog *Tentoonstelling Dirk Martens 1473–1973* (Aalst, 1973), 264–88. Add now, D. Coq, "Une édition ignorée de Thierry Martens: Les 'Constitutiones synodales episcopatus Atrebatensis' (Louvain, c. 1500–1501)," in *Hellinga Festschrift* (Amsterdam, 1980), 85–88. On the history of printing and editorial activity at 's Hertogenbosch, see now C. J. A. Van den Oord, *Twee Eeuwen Bosch' Boekbedrijf 1450–1650* (Tilburg, 1984).

5. "Miseret me Stunicae, qui nugis huiusmodi et suum ingenium et calamum et chartas et ocium triverit; miseret me lectoris, qui talibus naeniis aliquid bonarum horarum impartit; miseret me mei, qui cogar has ineptias vel legere vel refellere" (Erasmus, *Erasmi . . . Opera omnia*, 9.2: Apologia respondens ad ea quae Iacobus Lopis Stunica taxaverat . . . , ed. H. J. de Jonge (Amsterdam and Oxford, 1982), 82.448–52.

6. See now, the exhibition catalog *Hubertus Goltzius en Brugge 1583–1983* (Brugge, 1983).

7. Fundamental now is J. H. Bentley, *Humanists and Holy Writ: New Testament Scholarship in the Renaissance* (Princeton, 1983).

8. See Puteanus's *Palaestra bonae mentis, eloquentiae et sapientiae officina* added on pp. 479–612 to his volume *Suada Attica sive Orationum selectarum syntagma* (Leiden, 1623); see also Philippus Wannemaker, *Triumphus litteratorum, in quo Borromeianae virtutis imago* (Milan, 1611), 63–64.

9. See the indispensable volume *Leiden University in the Seventeenth Century: An Exchange of Learning* (Leiden, 1975). In the course of the seventeenth century the economic center of Holland, Amsterdam, tried also to gain cultural importance but could not outdo Leiden. See now C. L. Heesakkers, "Foundation and Early Development of the Athenaeum Illustre at Amsterdam," *Lias* 9 (1982): 3–18.

10. "Grammatica hoc uno peculiariter suoque iure gloriari potest, quod parens sit et altrix omnium doctrinarum," fol. A iiii recto of the original edition (Louvain, 1513). See now *Martini Dorpii Naldiceni Orationes IV cum Apologia et litteris adnexis*, ed. J. IJsewijn (Leipzig, 1986). The quotation is from chap. 2.2, p. 28.

11. See J. IJsewijn-Jacobs, "Magistri Anthonii Haneron (c. 1400–1490) Opera Grammatica et Rhetorica," *Humanistica Lovaniensia* 24 (1975): 29–68; 25 (1976): 1–83 (edition of the *Syntax*), 284 (a correction by M. Haverals); 27 (1978): 10–17. To be continued with an edition of *De epistolis brevibus* (see J. IJsewijn in J. M. Van Eijl, ed., "Facultas S. Theologiae Lovaniensis, 1432–1797. Bijdragen tot haar Geschiedenis" [Louvain, 1977], 37–38). J. IJsewijn, "Haneron," *Die deutsche Literatur des Mittelalters: Verfasserlexikon*, 5 vols. (Berlin, 1933–55), 3:431–35.

12. Haneron, *Prologus*, 1.2–3: "Nempe grammaticam prescisse necesse est eum qui velit artes reliquas adipisci. Quo enim pacto quis vel theologie vel civilis iuris vel cuiuslibet artium aliarum habuerit noticiam qui latinam linguam non norit? Quomodo latinum intellegeret qui latinum non intelligat ydeoma, significantias verborum modosque, congruam denique nexionem? Qua deinceps ratione quempiam expertem grammatice expertum rhetorice fore credideris, presertim cum ad rhetoricam orationem latinitas nonnichil attineat et puritas sermonis?"

13. On Herben, see now J. IJsewijn, "Lo storico e grammatico Matthaeus Herbenus di Maastricht, allievo del Perotti," *Res publica literarum* 4 (1981): 93–122. On Custos, Despauterius, and other grammarians such as Simon Verepaeus, of whom I speak further on, see in general the first volume of H. de Vocht's indispensable *History of the Foundation and the Rise of the Collegium Trilingue Lovaniense, 1517–1550*, 4 vols. (Louvain, 1951–55); and the works of M. A. Nauwelaerts, especially his book *Latijnse School en Onderwijs te 's Hertogenbosch tot 1629* (Tilburg, 1974). There is no modern edition or fundamental study of Despauterius. See C. Matheeussen, "À propos d'une lettre inconnue de Despautère," *Lias* 4

(1977): 1–11, on a text in favor of Alexander of Villedieu, written 1509 at Sint-Winoksbergen, now Bergues in northern France (Berga apud Divum Guinnocúm); L. Franzheim, "Das Gymnasium Tricoronatum und sein Lateinunterricht um die Mitte des 16. Jahrhunderts," *Jahrbuch Kölnischen Geschichtsvereins* 48 (1977): 139–50; L. Desgraves, "Contribution à la bibliographie des éditions de J. Despauterius (d. Comines, 1520) aux XVIᵉ et XVIIᵉ siècles," *Mémoires Société d'Histoire de Comines Warneton et de la Région* 7 (1977): 385–402, who gives additions to the article in the *Bibliotheca Belgica.*

14. "Adieci quaestiunculas fortassis non omnino aspernandas de poenitentia, confessione, peccatis, articulis fidei et id genus reliquis, ut ab ineunte aetate sacris pueri imbuantur, citra quae vana sunt omnia."

15. See note 12 and R. Hoven and J. Hoyoux, *Exposition: Le livre scolaire au temps d'Erasme et des humanistes* (Liège, 1969). On Verepaeus, see also M. A. Nauwelaerts, "La correspondance de Simon Verepaeus (1522–1598)," *Humanistica Lovaniensia* 23 (1974): 271–340; on Vossius, see C. S. M. Rademaker, *Life and Work of Gerardus Johannes Vossius (1577–1649)* (Assen, 1981); on Lithocomus there seems to be no recent work.

16. At Leipzig in the Bibliotheca Teubneriana.

17. "Recte loquendi copiam non ferebat peti e praeceptionibus grammaticorum; quas asseverabat officere ad bene dicendum, nec id contingere nisi evolvendis optimis auctoribus": *Opus Epistolarum Des. Erasmi Roterodami*, ed. P. S. Allen, H. M. Allen, and H. W. Garrod, 12 vols. (Oxford, 1906–58), vol. 4, epistle 1211, lines 519–22.

18. L. van den Branden, E. Cockx-Indestege, F. Sillis, *Biobibliografie van Cornelis Kiliaan* (Nieuwkoop, 1978). There is no such work on Junius, but for the study of early modern lexicography in the Netherlands I refer the reader to the works of F. Claes, especially his *Lijst van Nederlandse woordenlijsten en woordenboeken gedrukt to 1600* (Nieuwkoop, 1974). There is also an unpublished doctoral dissertation of the University of Ghent: S. De Baere, "Hadrianus Junius' Nomenclator omnium rerum als deutsches Wörterbuch. Sprache und Quellen" (1981).

19. See A. Gerlo, "The *Opus de conscribendis epistolis* of Erasmus and the Tradition of the *Ars epistolica,*" in *Classical Influences on European Culture, A.D. 500–1500,* ed. R. R. Bolgar (Cambridge, 1971), 103–14. There is no modern edition of Maneken (J. IJsewijn-Jacobs has undertaken work toward a critical edition and Dutch translation). A specimen letter is published in J. IJsewijn, "The 'Declamatio Lovaniensis de Tutelae severitate': Students Against Academic Authority at Louvain in 1481," *Lias* 3 (1976): 5–31, at 9.

20. I. O. Romero, *Floresta de gramática, poética y retórica en Nueva España (1521–1767)* (Mexico, 1980).

21. This suggestion has been made by N. Geirnaert in the exhibition catalog *Vlaamse Kunst op Perkament* (Brugge, 1981), 182–88, nos. 83–86. On Ter Duinen Abbey and its library, see now M.-T. Isaac, *Les livres manuscrits de l'abbaye des Dunes* (Aubel, 1984).

22. See in general the first volume of de Vocht's *History of the . . . Collegium Trilingue Lovaniense.*

23. D. Donnet, "La *Syntaxis* de Jean Varennius et les *Commentarii* de Guillaume Budé," *Humanistica Lovaniensia* 22 (1973): 103–35; idem, "L'humaniste malinois Varennius et la tradition grammaticale byzantine," *Belgisch Tijdschrift voor Filologie en Geschiedenis* 55 (1977): 93–105; R. Hoven, *Bibliographie de trois auteurs de grammaires grecques . . . Adrien Amerot, Arnold Oridryus, Jean Varennius* (Aubel, 1985).

24. L. Baekelants and R. Hoven, *Bibliographie des oeuvres de Nicolas Clénard 1529–1700,* 2 vols. (Verviers, 1981).

25. F. Nève, *Mémoire historique et littéraire sur le Collège des Trois-Langues à l'Université de Louvain* (Brussels, 1856), 223–25.

26. The scholar J. Cruquius from Bruges (d. 1628) collected from old manuscripts of this abbey information on Horace, the so-called Commentator Cruquianus, not traceable from other sources. The Blandijnberg (Mons Blandinius) is situated in the town of Ghent and has nothing to do with the village of Blanden south of Louvain or with a nonexistent Blandigny, as one often reads in works of authors not familiar with the Low Countries.

27. His inaugural *Oratio de linguarum laude,* which he later published at Wittenberg in 1520, was edited from a unique copy in Berlin by H. de Vocht in the first volume of his *History of the . . . Collegium Trilingue Lovaniense,* 533–44. A few years ago the university library of Louvain was fortunate enough to be able to buy a second copy of the original edition.

28. It was his Oratio 5. See P. C. Molhuysen, *Bronnen tot de geschiedenis der Leidsche Universiteit,* 7 vols. (The Hague, 1913–24), 2:95.

29. W. J. Ong, S. J., *Ramus and Talon Inventory* (Cambridge, MA, 1958); C. G. Noreña, *Juan Luis Vives* (The Hague, 1970); *Juan Luis Vives: Arbeitsgespräch . . . Wolfenbüttel . . . 1980,* ed. A. Buck (Hamburg, 1981); J. M. Weiss, "*Ecclesiastes* and Erasmus: The Mirror and the Image," *Archiv für Reformationsgeschichte* 65 (1974): 83–108; J. Chomarat, *Grammaire et rhétorique chez Erasme,* 2 vols. (Paris, 1981); Proceedings of the Groningen 1985 conference on Agricola (forthcoming).

30. In the preliminary letter to T. Plinius/Dietrich von Plieningen, he writes: "Contra veterem vulgatamque persuasionem ausus sum nonnunquam libere proferre quid mihi videretur." Such an attitude was not yet self-evident in Agricola's age, especially when authorities such as Aristotle were involved. Years later Dorp attacked Valla in a speech at Louvain because the latter had dared to criticize the Greek philosopher. Vives, on the contrary, sided with Agricola in this respect.

31. J. W. O'Malley, S.J., *Praise and Blame in Renaissance Rome: Rhetoric, Doctrine, and Reform in the Sacred Orators of the Papal Court, ca. 1450–1521* (Durham, NC, 1979). This book shows that the rules laid down by Erasmus in his last work had already been applied in Rome. It also proves, incidentally, that the negative picture of sacred oratory in Renaissance Rome, which is commonly accepted in humanist studies on the basis of Erasmus's assertions, is both false and profoundly biased. This case shows how a well-

trained rhetor was able to influence public opinion for centuries. A more conservative view is defended by L. Gualdo Rosa, "Ciceroniano o Cristiano? A proposito dell'orazione *De morte Christi* di Tommaso Fedra Inghirami," in *Roma Humanistica: Studia in honorem . . . J. Ruysschaert,* ed. J. IJsewijn (Louvain, 1985), 52–64.

32. J. IJsewijn and P. Lefèvre, "Collatio de laudibus Facultatum Lovanii saeculo XV (1435?) habita, nunc primum typis edita," in *Zetesis. Bijdragen . . . Professor Dr. E. De Strijcker* (Antwerp, 1973), 416–35.

33. Text edited by G. Tournoy, "Franciscus Cremensis and Antonius Gratia Dei: Two Italian Humanists, Professors at Louvain in the Fifteenth Century," *Lias* 3 (1976): 33–73.

34. *Opus Epistolarum Des. Erasmi,* epistle 76, lines 31–32 (1:204).

35. J. F. D'Amico, *Renaissance Humanism in Papal Rome: Humanists and Churchmen on the Eve of the Reformation* (Baltimore, 1983), 110. I think D'Amico's conclusions from Longolius's case as to the later "chauvinistic" development of Roman humanism are not entirely borne out by the facts. The appointments of Marcus Antonius Muretus and Henricus Chifellius prove that there remained room for foreigners.

36. The literature on *Folly* is endless. See now Z. Pavlovskis, *The Praise of Folly: Structure and Irony* (Leiden, 1983).

37. See IJsewijn, "The 'Declamatio Lovaniensis,'" 16, lines 235–36.

38. "Nimium altercando veritas amittitur" is Publilius Syrus, *Sententiae,* 461. This classical source escaped my attention when I edited the text. It must be added, therefore, to my note 10, on p. 16.

39. See, e.g., the verses of the Milanese poet Stefano Surigone on Brabant quoted in IJsewijn, "Coming of Humanism," 234, note 53. In a broader context one could refer also to the *Epistolae obscurorum virorum,* much of the criticism in which is applicable to the late medieval Low Countries (though Master Ortuinus Gratius from Deventer in fact deserves better than to be decried as the typical *vir obscurus!*).

40. See A. Pattin, "Reinerus van Sint-Truiden, rector van de Latijnse school te Mechelen (c. 1370) en commentator van Boethius' *De consolatione philosophiae,*" *Tijdschrift voor Filosofie* 44 (1982): 298–319.

41. J. H. Meter, *The Literary Theories of Daniel Heinsius* (Assen, 1984).

42. G. Ellinger, *Geschichte der neulateinischen Literatur Deutschlands im sechzehnten Jahrhundert,* vol. 3, pt. 1, *Geschichte der neulateinischen Lyrik in den Niederlanden vom Ausgang des fünfzehnten bis zum Beginn des siebzehnten Jahrhunderts* (Berlin, 1933).

43. See J. IJsewijn, "Erasmus ex poeta theologus sive de litterarum instauratarum apud Hollandos incunabulis," in *Scrinium Erasmianum,* ed. J. Coppens, 2 vols. (Leiden, 1969), 1:375–89.

44. See now *Publi Fausti Andrelini Amores sive Livia,* ed. G. Tournoy-Thoen (Brussels, 1982).

45. See L. Forster, "On Petrarchism in Latin and the Role of Anthologies," in *Acta Conventus Neo-Latini Lovaniensis,* ed. J. IJsewijn and E. Kessler (Louvain and Munich, 1973), 235–44.

46. MS Leiden, BPL, 1994. There is a provisional edition in R. de Smet, "Hadriani Barlandi (Hadriaan Beverland) De prostibulis veterum. Een kritische uitgave met inleiding en commentaar van het handschrift, BPL 1994" (Ph.D. diss., Vrije Universiteit Brussel, 1984).

47. On humanistic theater in the Low Countries, see J. IJsewijn, "Annales theatri Belgo-Latini: Inventaris van het Latijns toneel uit de Nederlanden," Album Gilbert Degroote (Brussels, 1980), 41–55; and idem, "Theatrum Belgo-Latinum: Het Neolatijns toneel in de Nederlanden," in Academiae Analecta. Mededelingen van de Koninklijke Academie voor Wetenschappen, Letteren en Schone Kunsten van België. Klasse der Letteren 43 (1981): 1:69–114.

48. See J. IJsewijn and C. Matheeussen, "Erasme et l'historiographie," in The Late Middle Ages and the Dawn of Humanism Outside Italy, ed. J. IJsewijn and G. Verbeke (The Hague, 1972), 31–43.

49. J. IJsewijn, "Die humanistische Biographie," in Biographie und Autobiographie in der Renaissance, ed. A. Buck (Wiesbaden, 1983), 1–19.

50. E. H. Waterbolk, Twee eeuwen Friese geschiedschrijving. Opkomst, bloei en verval van de Friese historiografie in de 16e en 17e eeuw (Groningen, 1952). See also B. A. Vermaseren, De katholieke Nederlandsche Geschiedschrijving in de XVIᵉ en XVIIᵉ eeuw over den opstand (Maastricht, 1941) on Catholic historians of the "Bellum Belgicum," the great war against Spain under William of Orange.

51. Vossius en Barlaeus . . . Het Athenaeum Illustre en zijn eerste hoogleraren, described by C. L. Heesakkers, C. S. M. Rademaker, and F. F. Block (Amsterdam, 1982).

52. Daniel Heinsius, De tragica constitutione, p. 55: "Alter [historicus] enim quae sunt facta, alter [poeta] qualia plerumque fiunt exhibere solet . . . alter enim magis universa, alter magis singula exponit."

53. His historical writings have been republished in IJsewijn, "Storico e grammatico."

54. A full-scale study on Burgundius, historian and poet, is needed. See F. Steyaert, "Puteanus Criticized by a Former Student, Nicolaus Burgundius," Lias 3 (1976): 131–38.

55. Biobibliographical information now in Nationaal Biografisch Woordenboek, 10:629–31 (by G. Tournoy).

56. "Rerum humanarum sensim labi fata et languescere, vetus sed iniqua querela est; nostra autem hac tempestate praecipue invaluit." And: "sed mihi historiam scripturo [cf. Sallust's Iugurtha: Bellum scripturus sum] Medicaeus velut libamentum duraturae industriae placuit."

57. Aedicollius's text has been republished by G. Mezzanotte, "Una nuova testimonianza della fortuna petrarchesca nei Paesi Bassi," Humanistica Lovaniensia 29 (1980): 166–75.

58. Erasme, Vies de Jean Vitrier et de John Colet, ed. and trans. A. Godin (Angers, 1982). See also J. IJsewijn, "Cauletum: Les choux d'Erasme et d'Horace," Moreana 20 (1983): 17–19.

59. J. IJsewijn, "Alexander Hegius (d. 1498), Invectiva in modos significandi,"

Forum for Modern Language Studies 7 (1971): 229–318, and corrections
in *Humanistica Lovaniensia* 22 (1973): 334–35; F. J. Worstbrock, "Zur
Biographie des Alexander Hegius," *Humanistica Lovaniensia* 29 (1980):
161–65.

60. P. Mack, "Valla's Dialectic in the North: A Commentary on Peter of Spain
by Gerardus Listrius," *Vivarium* 21 (1983): 58–72.

61. J. Machiels, "Johannes Dullaert. Gent, c. 1480–Parijs, 10 september 1513,"
in *Professor R. L. Plancke 70. Getuigenissen en Bijdragen* (Ghent, 1981),
69–96.

62. Jacobus Canter, *Dialogus de solitudine (c. 1491)*, ed. B. Ebels-Hoving (Munich, 1981). Corrections by J. IJsewijn in *Wolfenbütteler Renaissance Mitteilungen* 8 (1984): 30–32.

63. I quote from the text in Caspar Barlaeus, *Caspar Barlaeus. From the Correspondence of a Melancholic*, ed. and trans. F. F. Blok (Assen, 1976), 16.

64. Quatenus Aonios modulos fugietis amusi
   Surdidulique viri?
Ecce vocant Zephyri sub amoena vireta Sororum
   Pieriumque latus.
. . .
Et volucres pictae repetunt per gramina notos
   Ingenuosque modos,
Quos nequeant Thamyras et Methymnaeus Arion
   Aequiperare chely . . .
His immortalem perducunt gaudia vitam
   Consona carminibus.
Bade's text is now easily accessible in the facsimile edition of C. Béné and
O. Sauvage, *La nef des folles: Stultiferae naves de Josse Bade* (Grenoble,
1979), 45–46.

65. See Nauwelaerts, "Correspondance de Simon Verepaeus," dedicatory letter
edited on pp. 278–80.

66. Pseudo–Boethius, *De disciplina scolarium*, ed. O. Weyers (Leiden, 1976).

67. Several of these works already have been published in the new edition of
Erasmus, *Opera omnia Des. Erasmi Roterodami*, 13 vols. to date (Amsterdam, 1969–). I must warn the users of this edition that the quality of the
single contributions varies from very bad to very good. I have published
lists of corrections and additions in *Humanistica Lovaniensia* 26 (1977)
through 36 (1987).

68. I quote from the old Mayansius edition, but warn the reader that this edition is not always reliable. See my article, "Zu einer kritischen Edition der
Werke des J. L. Vives," in *Juan Luis Vives*, ed. Buck, 23–34. In the meantime work toward a critical edition of Vives has begun: see *Humanistica
Lovaniensia* 31 (1982): 247. The first volume was published at Leiden,
Brill, in July 1987.

69. The *Ratio* is readily available in *Oeuvres de Ph. de Marnix de Sainte Aldegonde*, vol. 2, *Correspondance et mélanges*, ed. A. Lacroix, 6 vols. (Paris,
1857–60), 17–107.

70. A microfilm copy of Houthem's treatise is in the library (LHUM) of the Seminarium Philologiae Humanisticae of Louvain (Faculty of Letters and Philosophy); on Houthem, see the article of J. IJsewijn in *Nationaal Biografisch Woordenboek*, 10:263–67. Modius's text has been published by J. IJsewijn, "Un poème inédit de François Modius sur l'éducation du prince humaniste," *Latomus* 25 (1966): 570–83.

71. "Vos appello principes. . . . Agnoscite regis vestri [i.e., Christi] vocem ad pacem vocantis!" Erasmus, *Opera omnia Des. Erasmi*, 4.2:98, lines 872–74.

72. It is worth mentioning that Ortelius's *Album amicorum* survives in Pembroke College, Cambridge, and has been published in facsimile by J. Puraye (Amsterdam, 1969). It can serve as a fascinating introduction to the world of northern humanism in the late sixteenth century.

73. R. Toellner, "Renata dissectionis ars. Vesals Stellung zu Galen in ihren wissenschaftsgeschichtlichen Voraussetzungen und Folgen," in *Die Rezeption der Antike*, ed. A. Buck (Hamburg, 1981), 85–95.

74. The autograph manuscript was acquired a few years ago by the university library of Louvain (KUL). It has been studied by one of my students, L. Dalemans, who has found that from a certain point onward Craneveldt used translations of verses he could find in Erasmus's *Adages*—another proof of the universal success of the *Adagia!*

75. One final remark I want to make: serious scholarship on humanism in the Low Countries demands a good reading knowledge of at least Dutch, French, and German, as well as a thorough knowledge of Latin, including rules of style and metrics. The number of stupid errors in recent publications is increasing speedily, due to lack of this basic knowledge. Soon a new Erasmus will have to write about the new barbarians of the twentieth century, who in pompous language write about things they do not understand. *Caveant consules ne quid detrimenti respublica litterarum capiat!*

23 ❧ DESIDERIUS ERASMUS
Albert Rabil, Jr.

IN JUNE 1514 DESIDERIUS ERASMUS (1467–1536) LEFT ENGLAND and made his way to Basel. All along his route through the Low Countries and Germany he was greeted by humanists as the brightest star of the learned world, "prince of the humanists." In terms of actual output, most of Erasmus's work lay ahead of him in that year. He had written a theological handbook (*Enchiridion*), a satire (*The Praise of Folly*), and two educational treatises, one addressed to teachers (*On the Method of Study*) and one to students (*Copia: Foundations of an Abundant Style*). He had edited two books (*Adages* and Lorenzo Valla's *Annotations on the New Testament*). And he had published several translations from Greek authors (Libanius, Euripides, and Lucian). But these works were enough to suggest to his contemporaries the peculiar character of Erasmus's genius. Stated simply, it was that Erasmus succeeded beyond all others in combining the classical ideal of *humanitas* and the Christian ideal of *pietas*. The classical was the ideal of eloquence combined with deep learning; the Christian was the ideal of devotion born of understanding. Erasmus instilled eloquence and learning into Christianity and piety into paganism.

Not only did his contemporaries see Erasmus so in 1514, but by a wonderful (wonderful because so rare) coincidence, Erasmus saw himself in the same way and at that very moment came to believe that it was his peculiar mission to bring about in all Christendom this fusion which his contemporaries saw in him. Erasmus was forty-seven. It seemed that all he had worked so hard for was to be achieved at the very pinnacle of his own life and career.

What was it that brought Erasmus and his contemporaries to this point? How did he arrive at this consciousness of himself and his mission? How did it come to be recognized? And what was the outcome of this dramatic realization? That story requires a close look at Erasmus's life and age. So significant is his life that in some important sense his age is also "the age of Erasmus."

*   *   *

Erasmus was born Herasmus (he changed it to Erasmus as an adult and added Desiderius) in Rotterdam on 27 or 28 October 1467, the second illegitimate son of Gerhard, a priest, and Margaret, the daughter of a physician.[1] He was educated in schools of the Brethren of the Common Life at Gouda (1475–78) and Deventer (1479–85). The headmaster of the latter school was Alexander Hegius, a friend of Rudolf Agricola, the father of German humanism. Agricola spoke at Deventer in 1479 and Erasmus heard him. He also heard Hegius speak on special occasions through his years there. In both of these men, preeminently in Agricola, the winds of humanism were making themselves felt in the North. Inspired by their example, as slight as his exposure to them was, Erasmus developed an abiding passion for classical literature. He himself described it in these words many years later:

> There is a strange power and active force, as it were, in nature . . . which I infer from this fact among others that, though in my boyhood the humanities were banished from our schools and there was no supply of books and teachers, and they had no prestige to spur on a gifted student—quite the reverse: discouragement of them was universal, and drove one into other subjects—in spite of this, a sort of inspiration fired me with devotion to the Muses, sprung not from judgment (for I was then too young to judge) but from a kind of natural feeling. I developed a hatred for anyone I knew to be an enemy of humane studies and a love for those who delighted in them; and those who had acquired any reputation in that field I looked up to and admired as more than human. For this spirit even now, as an old man [he is fifty-three], I have no regrets.[2]

The school itself inculcated a deep inward piety, similar to that found in Thomas à Kempis's *Imitation of Christ*, the most important single expression of the Brethren's attitude. The *Imitation* emphasized the direct spiritual contact between the believer and God, and the removal of all ceremonialism that would interfere with this contact. Erasmus all his life stressed the direct illumination of the heart by God and was a strenuous and consistent critic of ceremonialism of all kinds (so characteristic also of Calvin and Calvinists). The *Imitation* also emphasized the dangers of learning, the distance between learning and piety. Such an attitude could degenerate into anti-intellectualism, which undoubtedly it did among some of the Brethren. But Erasmus took this problem up also in his own way. For, as we shall see, he never countenanced learning for its own sake. His learning, whether eloquence or scholarship, served larger ends than itself. In this way too he was in part indebted to the Brethren.

In 1485 both of Erasmus's parents died from the plague. His appointed guardians applied pressure on him and his brother to enter a monastery. They agreed between themselves that they would resist, but Peter soon gave in, leaving his younger brother stranded. His choices limited, Erasmus finally decided to enter the Augustinian Canons' monastery at Steyn, largely because of the glowing picture painted of it by a friend from Deventer, Willem Hermans, who described the freedom to study and the marvelous library. Erasmus entered in 1487 and remained six years, until 1493 when he left in the employ of the bishop of Cambrai, never to return as a permanent resident. In 1492 he was ordained a priest.

Erasmus's love of learning, in particular the Latin classics, began to find expression in the monastery. He wrote letters to friends urging them to the study of the classics; he wrote poetry; he wrote a tract *On the Contempt of the World* and another *Against the Barbarians*.[3] In one of his letters written to a friend in 1489, we get a sense of his classicism:

> My authorities in poetry are Virgil, Horace, Ovid, Juvenal, Statius, Martial, Claudian, Persius, Lucan, Tibullus, and Propertius; in prose, Cicero, Quintilian, Sallust, Terence. Again, in the niceties of style I rely on Lorenzo Valla above all. He has no equal for intelligence and good memory. I must admit it: I should not dare to make use of any phrases not employed by these authors, while, if you would include any others, I shall by no means hold it against you.[4]

There are three interesting things about this statement. First, all his "authorities" are Latin. There is no trace of the Greek writers to whom he was to turn later. Moreover, only pagan classical writers are mentioned. There is no conception here, as he will develop later, of a Christian classical tradition. Second, his attitude toward these writers is slavish or imitative. What they have not said, he concludes, I will not say either. This attitude is precisely the one he so strongly criticized many years later in his *Ciceronianus*, in which he satirizes those who would not use a word because it had not appeared in the writings of Cicero. Perhaps, however, at this stage of his development, his imitative attitude was a strength, for it enabled him to rid himself of the barbarism he so deplored and develop an elegant classical Latin style in both prose and poetry. The degree of his enthusiasm can be seen in the fact that he memorized all of Horace and Terence. Third, there is his veneration of Lorenzo Valla. Valla's *Elegances of the Latin Language* had been available in published editions since 1471. Erasmus made an epitome or abridgment of this treatise in 1488, arranging the words in alphabetical order as in a dictionary. It was the first of his many efforts to assist his fellow students in acquiring the tools necessary to master the classical tradition.

Not only did Erasmus make an epitome of Valla, he also defended him against his colleagues. Cornelius Gerard half-jokingly wrote to him that Valla was reviled by many, especially Poggio Bracciolini, so that to study Valla was to get oneself disliked. In a spirited rejoinder, Erasmus reminds his friend that a multitude of enemies is evidence of nothing if not the fact that excellence is always disliked and in the minority. As for Poggio's enmity, Poggio was the only one who disliked Valla, and in any case censured him because he himself was an unpleasant man and a personal enemy of Valla's.[5] Even if Valla is harsh against others—and remember that we are not without examples of this from the past: Aristotle objected to everything before him, Cicero's style was despised by Brutus, Seneca by Quintilian, Augustine and Rufinus by Jerome—even if, to repeat, Valla is harsh, he says no more than is deserved. Erasmus concludes:

is anyone so small-minded . . . as not to accord generous praise and the warmest possible affection to Valla, who bestowed such intense industry, application, and exertion in combating the follies of the barbarians and rescuing literature from extinction when it was all but buried, in restoring Italy to her ancient literary glory and even in conferring a benefit on scholars by obliging them to express themselves more carefully in future?[6]

The influence of Valla is evident not only in matters of style and accuracy, but also in Erasmus's thought. Erasmus composed two significant treatises while in the monastery, each of which in a different way reflects (among other things) the persistent presence of Lorenzo Valla. The second of these in point of time, *On the Contempt of the World*, was composed in 1489. The first seven chapters describe the miseries of the flesh and the world, reminiscent of a treatise on the same subject by Innocent III. Chapters 8–11 describe the happiness and pleasure of the solitary life. In chapter 11, the culmination of the latter discussion, Erasmus characterizes that life as Epicurean. He argues that pleasures of the body are vain and fleeting; only pleasures of the mind are perpetual and hence good. One cannot enjoy both kinds of pleasure at once. Given a choice, even Epicurus would expel the pleasures of the body and choose the superior pleasures of the soul. What are the pleasures of the soul? The contemplation of eternal life, which lifts us beyond the depression of our present existence; and the foretaste of eternal life, which is experienced by many here and now. One of the sources for this point of view was Valla's *On Pleasure*.[7]

The second work Erasmus composed in the monastery, *Against the Barbarians*, is also directly indebted to Valla, this time not to *On Pleasure* but to the *Elegances of the Latin Language*. Like *On the Contempt of the World*, *Against the Barbarians* was originally a treatise. Erasmus wrote it when he was about twenty, or just after he entered the monastery. When he left the monastery in 1492 he recast it into dialogue form (1494–95). The work as he originally projected it was to be in four parts. The first (which is the only one extant) was a critique of the enemies of humanism. The second was to provide an answer to the first, in which a fictitious character was to use all the powers of eloquence to pour scorn on eloquence. The third was to be a refutation of the second, and the fourth a defense of poetry. When Erasmus went to Paris in 1495 he showed part 1 to Robert Gaguin, the leader of French humanism, for criticism. Gaguin agreed with the project in principle but counseled him to curtail Batt's long speech—keep a dialogue a dialogue. When Erasmus went to England in 1499 he showed books 1 and 2 to John Colet, who professed himself completely persuaded by the arguments of book 2 pouring scorn on eloquence. Erasmus urged him to hold his judgment until he saw book 3, which would refute book 2, but Colet responded that the arguments of the second book were too persuasive to be refuted. Erasmus revised these two books in Italy and wrote drafts also of books 3 and 4. All of this material was subsequently lost, but during his residence at Louvain (1517–21), book 1 came into his hands and, in order to prevent others from publishing it, Erasmus revised it once again and sent it to Johann Froben, who published it in May 1520.

It is unfortunate that we do not possess the entire work Erasmus projected, *The Four Books Against the Barbarians*, for they would certainly have shown his relation to the humanist tradition stemming from Petrarch, Boccaccio, and Coluccio Salutati. We are, however, fortunate in one respect. The manuscript as Erasmus revised it in 1494–95 survives; it was discovered early in this century by P. S. Allen, that indefatigable editor of the critical edition of Erasmus's letters. A comparison of the earlier with the published version reveals that, while the form remains essentially the same in both, the later edition adds a number of strictures against monasticism and the role of monks in damaging the cause of learning. These complaints are related to the circumstances in which Erasmus made the revisions rather than to those of its original composition.[8]

An analysis of the 1494–95 version of the text suggests that the original work of 1487–88 was the one long speech that in the 1494–95 version, is placed in the mouth of a friend Erasmus met outside the monastery, Jacob Batt. The later dialogue is built around this speech. In the original version, Erasmus was most indebted to Valla's *Elegances*. It was an attack on idleness and ignorance and a lively defense of humanism. The additions of 1494–95 extend the attack to the protagonists of scholastic theology (it was composed before Erasmus actually went to Paris in 1495 and studied scholastic theology) and a wider recognition of the positive values of classical studies. In the 1494 version the world is no longer regarded by Erasmus as a source of temptation. He is moving toward a piety that lives in the world, that is, toward a union of *humanitas* and *pietas*.

The dialogue itself begins with friendly bantering and a description of a bucolic setting in which Plato's *Phaedrus* is explicitly mentioned. But Cicero's *De officiis* (which Erasmus edited in 1501) also stands in the background. The question is then raised: Why has literature fallen on hard days? The doctor in the dialogue suggests that it is the result of fate (he is addicted to astrology). The consul says that it is Christianity that discourages literature. There is an interesting difference at this point between the 1494 and the 1520 versions. In 1494 Erasmus wrote: "Unlettered religion has something of stupidity, which is violently distasteful to those who know letters," a sentence reflecting, perhaps, some uneasiness with his situation in the monastery—or with his colleagues. This sentence was suppressed in 1520 and in its place Erasmus wrote: "Possibly they [Christians] had some perception that there is an incompatibility between pure religion and consummate learning. Piety rests on faith, erudition uses arguments for investigation, and calls the facts in question."[9] In the later statement there is a much deeper awareness of what is at stake for both sides, greater sympathy and less defensiveness. The third interlocutor in the dialogue, Willem, says that the decline of literature is characteristic of all things, for nothing lasts. But Batt, who speaks for Erasmus in the dialogue, rejects all these arguments and contends that the fault is in ourselves; we entrust our children to fools to be educated, thus suffusing the world with ignorance, which religion supports. There are, Batt says, three kinds of enemies of literature: those who want literature destroyed (the uncultured), those who want it controlled within narrow limits (the unskillfully learned), and those who approve literature but want to be considered its best practitioners. The remainder of the treatise appears to be an attack largely on the first group, the uncultured who would destroy literature.

No one attacks literature, Batt argues, who understands it. Those who do not know it are either lazy, or prefer their own craft, or are hiding behind a false piety. The argument that false piety serves as a shield of ignorance is an interesting and important one. Erasmus never ceased to believe that those who later attacked his religion were in reality attacking learning. That is one reason he did not condemn Luther—he believed that the enemies of Luther were also the enemies of good literature. The argument also implies that learning and piety complement one another, that learning will make one a better person. (This concept, as we shall see time and again, is the key to Erasmus's program of scholarship and reform.) Batt cites many examples of pagans who were both learned and good men, whose learning made them humble (it is ignorance, he counters, that makes men arrogant). To be sure, not all men are good, and both the ignorant and the learned are sometimes bad. But ignorant evil is worse because it is less curable (not being open to reason) and never brings any advantage to anyone (which even literate viciousness can do). And of two upright men, one learned and the other ignorant, the learned has more virtue if learning is added to his integrity.

Pagan literature should not be rejected because it is pagan. If we followed this practice, most of the things we use in the world we would have to reject, because they are not of Christian origin. Why do we not rather emulate the attitude of Jerome and Augustine, who criticized the pagans but took what was useful and good from them?

There are some who say that the early Christian apostles were rustic, therefore we should be. But the apostles were not rustic, they were taught by Christ. And even if some of them were, Paul certainly was not. Indeed, there have been many learned Christians: Moses, Solomon, Jerome, Augustine, Justin, Clement, Origen, Basil, Chrysostom (the Greeks were added to this list in 1520). Moreover, these early Christians were educated by their parents in pagan literature, and others throughout Christian history have continued to use it.

Such was the treatise *Against the Barbarians.* Armed with it Erasmus entered the world outside the monastery. In a sense, it was his credo.

*   *   *

Perhaps Erasmus's restiveness in the monastery was observed. Certainly his learning was. And when the bishop of Cambrai needed a secretary in 1493, Erasmus was released from the monastery into his service. He had hopes of an immediate trip to Italy where the bishop looked to gain a cardinal's hat; but this journey did not materialize. It was during this period, between 1493 and 1495, that Erasmus recast *Against the Barbarians.* Instead of returning to Steyn Erasmus went, at his own request and with the bishop's blessing and partial support, to Paris to study for a doctorate in theology. He entered the Collège de Montaigu, headed by Jean Standonck, in September 1495.[10] Standonck had been trained by the Brethren of the Common Life at Gouda, where Erasmus first attended their school. He became the principal of Montaigu in 1485 and at once adopted it as his aim to improve the quality of the clergy by training young men in moral qualities that would make them worthy leaders. The piety of the Brethren was evident in his program. Erasmus studied John Duns Scotus there and heard Standonck lecture on the *Sentences* of Peter Lombard. But the rigid discipline imposed by Standonck during Lent so adversely affected Erasmus's health that he returned to Steyn at Easter 1496 and considered remaining there.

But even while he was studying scholastic theology, Erasmus was introduced to the leader of the humanist circle in Paris, Robert Gaguin. Erasmus, as already noted, showed him his dialogue *Against the Barbarians*, along with some of his poetry. Gaguin had just completed a history of France, and the final quire was not quite filled. He invited Erasmus to fill the space with a letter. Erasmus did so, sidestepping Gaguin's chauvinism by praising his literary style. This letter was actually Erasmus's first published writing. The book appeared on 30 September 1495.

When Erasmus returned for the second time to Paris he did not enroll in the Collège de Montaigu but instead took a course of action momentous for the future. In order to sustain himself he became a private tutor and in this capacity initiated, between 1496 and 1500, most of the educational treatises he was later to publish. He did so in order to provide aid to his students and to other teachers like himself. It was, in fact, as a teacher that Erasmus first defined his role and mission as a humanist. In the absence of proper materials and methods, the teaching of good literature was likely to languish still longer. Erasmus set out to remedy that situation and become, more than any other person, the educator of Europe. It was an important link in his union of *humanitas* and *pietas*.

Between 1496 and 1498 in Paris he wrote three works on education, which were published much later. He wrote first a treatise *On Letter Writing*, providing numerous examples of good literary form. A pirated edition was published in Cambridge in 1521; Erasmus issued an authorized edition in Basel in 1522.[11] He also wrote at least parts of *The Method of Study* and *Copia: Foundations of the Abundant Style*, both of which were revised and published for use in John Colet's school in 1512, after an unauthorized earlier version of the *Method* had appeared in 1511.[12] The *Method* is addressed to teachers, the *Copia* to students. Erasmus regarded the *Copia* as an original contribution to education. In it he enumerates a great variety of ways to express oneself in Latin (copia of words) and to develop persuasive arguments to support one's position (copia of ideas). In the *Method* he argues that the best means of achieving these ends is to develop a sound knowledge of the rudiments of Latin and Greek and to have the student write themes based on his own interests. A good teacher, he argues, could by this method enable a student to be writing independent compositions of good quality within a short time. By way of illustration, Erasmus began to provide as early as 1498 examples of the kinds of independent compositions students might write. When some of this material was also surreptitiously published in 1518 he undertook an authorized version, which appeared in 1522 as the first edition of his *Colloquies*. The *Colloquies* (to be discussed later in this essay) are dialogues on a variety of subjects, some light, some serious, in which good form and proper content can be taught in an entertaining manner. Erasmus believed in exciting a student's interests and eliciting his natural talents. In a treatise he wrote in Paris in 1500 (published in 1529), *On the Instruction of Boys,* he describes a flogging he received at the hands of a teacher who falsely accused him of an offense and then punished him for it. This experience led Erasmus to counsel kindness and persuasion as the proper methods for exciting a love of learning. "Masters who are conscious of their own incompetence," he wrote, "are generally the worst floggers. What else, indeed, can they do? They cannot teach, so they beat."[13] These treatises, and especially the first three— *Method, Copia,* and *Colloquies*—were the important educational treatises of the sixteenth century and stand behind much of that period's educational development.

*   *   *

In the summer of 1499 Erasmus accompanied his English pupil, William Mountjoy, to England, remaining there until January 1500. It was a momentous six months. Near Mountjoy's country estate in Greenwich he met Thomas More, so much like him in interest and temperament.[14] The friendship established on this brief visit lasted the lifetime of both men. In October Erasmus settled in Oxford, where he immediately introduced himself to John Colet (1466–1519), later dean of St. Paul's (1504) and founder of St. Paul's School (1510), for which institution Erasmus revised and published two of the educational treatises just discussed. Colet was at the time lecturing on Paul's epistles at the university.[15] In December, Erasmus left Oxford for London, where he met Thomas Linacre (1460–1524) and William Grocyn (ca. 1446–1519), both of whom had learned Greek in Italy; Grocyn in turn had taught Greek to Thomas More at Oxford.

Erasmus gained much from this English visit. There was first his friendship with Thomas More, to which we shall return. There was also the discovery of a learned circle of *Greek* scholars, something he had so far missed in his pursuit of *humanitas*. Related to this discovery was his encounter with Colet at Oxford. Colet was lecturing on Paul in a new way. Contrary to the medieval scholastic tradition, Colet followed the text of Paul and sought to make clear Paul's meaning in his historical context. In Colet's hands, Paul came alive in a way he had not lived for many centuries. This method was what marked off Renaissance from scholastic theology.[16] Erasmus gleaned this method from Colet, and their employment of it on a point of disagreement between them is instructive. The two engaged in a long discussion one day on the passage in Matthew 26:39: "Let this cup pass from me." Colet maintained that Christ's agony was over the Jews and the guilt he knew they would incur as a result of murdering him. Erasmus, in rebuttal, argued that Christ's agony was his own suffering as a man facing what he knew lay ahead. The discussion deadlocked at this point and was broken off. But Erasmus continued to reflect on it and wrote Colet a letter defending his own interpretation.[17] Why does Christ try to avoid death? What is the will that he submits to the will of his father? If he does not want to die he loved us less; if he never refused to die, why try to avoid what he wanted? A man can have a horror of death who nevertheless does not refuse it. Indeed, he dies in spite of the horror because it will be efficacious for others; he makes the will of his father his own will. Let us grant that at the moment of his death the heart of no martyr ever burned more ardently or joyously. But in the garden there was agony, which is as it should be. Christ was not there in order to give us an example of courage, but rather of patience and obedience. Indeed, his life was throughout exemplary of these virtues. In a response to Erasmus, Colet falls back on the authority of Jerome, who agrees with his interpretation.[18] Erasmus wrote another lengthy reply, making two points that become characteristic of his approach to biblical studies. He argues first that in the text itself there is not a shred of evidence to support Colet's interpretation. Nothing in the passage allows us to refer it to the Jews rather than to Christ himself. And in order to get at the meaning as clearly as possible Erasmus paraphrased the verse, at the same time restating what the verse would have had to say if it had had reference to the Jews. He argues secondly that Jerome is the only Father who holds Colet's opinion; others agree with Erasmus. Why maintain the authority of one Father in one passage so tenaciously? What we should do when the Fathers disagree is not fall back on their authority but attempt to overcome their limitations and interpret for ourselves.[19]

This episode reveals for the first time an interest awakened in the interpretation of Scripture based upon humanist philology. Colet was evidently impressed by his opponent, for he invited Erasmus to lecture on Moses or Isaiah just as he was lecturing on Paul's Epistles. Erasmus declined on the ground that he could not teach what he himself had not learned. What he had not learned was the biblical languages. Colet had not been deterred by the fact that he did not know Greek. He used the Vulgate as an authoritative version in his lectures on Paul. Nor did he, until the appearance of Erasmus's Greek New Testament in 1516, understand the need for such knowledge. But Erasmus understood.

Colet suspected that Erasmus was interested only in secular learning. But Erasmus professed that he never intended to devote his life to secular learning. Colet forced Erasmus, as no one before him had done, to reflect upon his sense of vocation. And while it may be true that Erasmus had never considered becoming a professor of secular learning, it is also true that he had never thought of becoming a biblical scholar. Colet pushed Erasmus's *humanitas* in the direction of a specific *pietas* suited to his training and inclinations.

❖   ❖   ❖

A sure sign that something decisive had happened to Erasmus in England is the fact that he began to study Greek immediately on his return to the continent. In March he wrote to his friend Jacob Batt: "My readings in Greek all but crush my spirit; but I have no spare time and no means to purchase books or employ the services of a tutor. And with all this commotion to endure I have hardly enough to live on: and this is what I owe to my studies!"[20]

Progress came rapidly and was immediately applied in the interests of both *humanitas* and *pietas*. The first edition of Erasmus's *Adages* was published in July 1500 in Paris. He had intended to include only two or three hundred proverbs, but he ended with 818, of which 664 are from Latin authors, 154 from Greek authors.[21] The *Adages* were addressed to the general reader to show him what light the classics could throw on his own life and society. Although his method changed in later editions, in this first edition he began with a classical reference (e.g., a proverb from Cicero), then explained the proverb and sometimes added additional references. His annotations are brief and lack the scope and urbanity of the later editions. Erasmus advertises it as the first collection of Latin proverbs (indicating that he regarded it as primarily a work of Latin scholarship, as indeed it was), although in reality it was contemporary with another collection made independently by Polydore Vergil. The book (as all subsequent editions) was dedicated to Lord Mountjoy, his English pupil. Obviously, Erasmus regarded it as another educational tool by which the barbarians would be vanquished. Finally, it should be added that this first edition is wholly a work of classical pagan origin. Not until the 1515 edition did Erasmus begin to include proverbs from the Christian tradition as well. The fusion of *humanitas* and *pietas* was not yet complete.

Nonetheless, the process of fusion was further advanced than it had been. Erasmus was learning Greek not only in order to appreciate the Greek classical writers but also in order to interpret Scripture. In 1504 he wrote a letter to John Colet in which he said that three years previously he had tried his hand at the exegesis of Paul's Epistle to the Romans and had completed four volumes. He was hindered, however, by his want of Greek and had abandoned the project. Nevertheless, he made it clear that his primary purpose in studying Greek was for the sake of sacred literature.[22] In December 1500 he wrote to Jacob Batt: "My mind is burning with indescribable eagerness to bring all my small literary works to their conclusion, and at the same moment to acquire a certain limited competence in the use of Greek, and thereby go on to devote myself entirely to sacred literature, the discussion of which has long been an ardently sought goal in my mind."[23]

          *   *   *

In July 1501, while still engaged in his Greek studies, Erasmus moved to St. Omer, where he met Jean Vitrier, a Franciscan monk for whom he developed a great admiration and whose life he was later to portray as exemplary for Christians. Vitrier introduced him for the first time to Origen. Of Vitrier's love for Origen Erasmus later wrote: "There was no writer on theology whose genius he admired more than Origen's. And on my objecting that I was surprised to see him take pleasure in the writings of a heretic, I was struck with the animation with which he replied that a mind from which there had issued so many works fraught with such learning and fervor could not but have been a dwelling place of the Holy Spirit."[24] Under the impact of Vitrier and Origen, as well as of Augustine and Jerome whom he had been studying previously,[25] Erasmus wrote his first actually published treatise (written in 1501 and published in 1503), the *Enchridion militis Christiani* (*Handbook/Dagger of a Christian Soldier*). In it we find the first attempted expression of that fusion between *humanitas* and *pietas* which had become Erasmus's aim. The Christian soldier, he says, needs to be on guard. And for this purpose he needs weapons. What weapons are appropriate? There are two: prayer and knowledge. On prayer he spends one page, on knowledge ten. The knowledge the Christian soldier needs is the principles of theological science, that is, the science that interprets Scripture, not the science that constructs a scholastic summa. The first principle that enables us to read Scripture purely is allegorical exegesis. "If you break through the husk and find the kernel, pondering one little line will have more savor and food value than the whole psalter when it is chanted through with reference only to the literal content."[26] How does one go about this kind of reflection? First, one may gain help from Christian writers who have interpreted Scripture in this manner. "From the interpretations of divine scripture choose those which go as far as possible beyond literal meaning. After Paul, the best of the explicators of this sort are Origen, Ambrose, Jerome, and Augustine."[27] But one may also find help in pagan authors, though one should not take up the moral habits of the pagans. In order to be profitable, however, pagan writers, like Scripture itself, must be read allegorically. For "just as divine scripture bears no great fruit if you persist in clinging only to the literal sense, so the poetry of Homer and Virgil is of no small benefit if you remember that this is all allegorical, a fact which no one who has but touched his lips to the wisdom of the ancients will deny. I should prefer, too, that you follow the Platonists among the philosophers, because in most of their ideas and in their very manner of speaking they come nearest to the beauty of the prophets and the gospels."[28] But finally, nothing avails unless the reader comes to Scripture with a pure mind, ready to relate everything to Christ, indeed knowing "that any truth you come upon at any place is Christ's."[29]

Such then are the weapons of a Christian soldier. But no one can properly use instruments given to him for his good if he does not know who he is (and what his good is). Who is man? He is a creature both bodily and spiritual. "Plato puts two souls in one man; Paul, two men in the same man, so conjoined that neither may be divided from the other either in heaven or hell, but also so disparate that the death of one is the life of another."[30] If this is the nature of man, then the task of the Christian is perfectly clear: "You should always try to advance from things visible, which are for the most part imperfect or of a neutral status, to things invisible," to "begin to reject the visible world in favor of the world unseen."[31] For although the body cannot live without the spirit, the spirit needs nothing from the body.

The Christian who becomes spiritual internalizes the Christian message. "I am not impressed by the fact that you never omit a watch, a fast, a period of silence, a prayer. . . . I will not believe that you are spiritual unless I see the fruits of the spirit."[32] The purpose of learning is to make us better.

Erasmus had learned from Colet that scriptural exegesis was one way in which learning could serve piety. In searching through the library of a Premonstratensian monastery near Louvain in the summer of 1504 he discovered another. Quite unexpectedly he came upon Lorenzo Valla's *Annotations on the New Testament*. He carried this manuscript to Paris with him and published the annotations in March 1505. In his preface to these notes he speaks for the first time not about the recovery of the old theology but rather about the recovery of the text of the Bible. Erasmus is aware that this shift will raise the hackles of the theologians. "I am inclined to believe," he wrote, "that the most unpleasantly hostile demonstrations of all will be made by those who stand most to profit, that is, the theologians. They will say it is intolerable presumption in a grammarian, who has upset every department of learning, to let his impertinent pen loose on Holy Scripture itself." But, he asks,

> what is so shocking about Valla's action in making a few annotations on the New Testament after comparing several old and good Greek manuscripts? After all it is from Greek sources that our text undoubtedly comes; and Valla's notes had to do with internal disagreements, or a nodding translator's plainly inadequate renderings of the meaning, or things that are more intelligibly expressed in Greek, or, finally, anything that is clearly corrupt in our texts.[33]

To the charge that it is nonetheless an intolerable insolence for a grammarian to usurp the place of the theologian, Erasmus replies that theologians should not have the exclusive privilege of speaking ungrammatically.

But is there not a very great audacity in the grammarian's assertion that he will employ his erudition to alter Scripture? For does not every jot and tittle of Scripture hold a mystery? Erasmus responds unequivocally: "The sin of corruption is greater, and the need for careful revision by scholars greater also, where the source of corruption was ignorance." Moreover, as Augustine says, just as the reliability of the Old Testament books must be tested by the Hebrew texts, so the accuracy of the New Testament must be checked by rules of Greek usage.

What of the contention that the ancient exegetes, who knew the languages, have provided an explanation for every passage already? In the first place, says Erasmus,

> I should prefer to see with my own eyes rather than another man's; second, much as they did explain, they certainly also left many things for later generations to add. There is also the fact that in order to understand the commentators one has to be reasonably proficient in the languages. Lastly, where is one to turn when one finds the ancient texts in all the languages corrupt, as in fact they are?[34]

Erasmus's attitude toward the authority of the Fathers always remained as stated here: they are to be taken seriously, but they are no substitute for the original text. He had come a long way from the youth in the monastery who would not use anything not found in the authors he then regarded as the best.

The impression of this letter is unmistakable: Erasmus had decided to become a *translator and editor* of the source of theology itself, using his classical and Christian erudition in its service. He did not at this time envision publication of a Greek text of the New Testament. His sense of vocation had not yet arrived at that point.

It would be a mistake, however, to see Erasmus moving univocally toward Christian scholarship. He certainly pursued that course, for shortly after he had published Valla's *Annotations* he made his second visit to England. And while there he worked on his own annotation of the New Testament.[35] But it was also during this same visit that Erasmus engaged in a contest with Thomas More, translating the satires of Lucian (A.D. 120–180), the most eminent satirist of the Hellenistic world. Erasmus translated ten of Lucian's longer dialogues, More another four. One of them, *The Tyrannicide,* was translated by both, and each wrote a declamation in reply to Lucian. They were published by Josse Bade (Jodocus Badius) in 1506, with whom Erasmus left them on his way from England to Italy. Erasmus returned to Lucian more than once after this occasion. While in Italy he translated eighteen additional short dialogues, and upon his return to England in 1509 another eight. Of these thirty-six, only nine had been previously translated.[36] Hence Erasmus did a great deal to make Lucian known. As we shall see, however, even this Erasmus did not do for its own sake. Lucian became the basis for one of the most enduring products of the fusion of *pietas* and *humanitas* to emerge from the Renaissance.

*   *   *

In 1506 Erasmus finally had the opportunity to go to Italy that he had coveted in 1492 when he became secretary to the bishop of Cambrai. Why did he want to go? He himself offers two reasons. One was the acquisition of a doctorate in theology from the University of Bologna. The other was "mainly in order to learn Greek," that is, to perfect his Greek studies.[37] On his way he stopped in Paris, as noted above, and left not only his and More's translation of Lucian but also an enlarged edition of the *Adages.* Instead of 818 there were now 841 proverbs, the additions being largely from Greek authors. Moreover, he gave the Greek equivalents for 143 additional proverbs. This edition, however, was not significantly different from that of 1500.

Erasmus arrived in September 1506 at Turin, Italy, where he received his doctorate in theology (dated 4 September 1506). He regarded it as important in conferring upon him an authority to speak about theological matters (not very different from Luther's later attitude toward his doctorate in theology, received in October 1512). His intended destination was Bologna, but he was almost immediately driven from that city by the approach of a papal army, led by Pope Julius II himself. Erasmus took refuge in Florence for several weeks, where he occupied his time translating Lucian from Greek. He seems not to have been at all mindful that at the time Leonardo da Vinci, Michelangelo, Raphael, Fra Bartolomeo, and Andrea del Sarto were at work in the city or that the secretary of the republic was Machiavelli. His attention was wholly focused on the classical literary tradition. Erasmus returned to Bologna just in time to see Julius II ride triumphantly into the city at the head of his conquering army (11 November 1506), an event that inspired his satire a few years later, *Julius Excluded from Heaven* (1513).[38]

Erasmus remained in Bologna for thirteen months, from November 1506 until December 1507. While there he developed a close friendship with Paolo Bombasio, a professor of Greek in the university, in whose home he lived. How much Erasmus participated in the life of the university is not known, though he certainly must have profited much from his friend's knowledge of Greek to further his own studies in that language. Much of his own work in Bologna was later lost, notably *Against the Barbarians*, discussed earlier. His attention seemed to be focused most on a revision of his *Adages*. For in October 1507 he wrote to Aldo Manuzio, the great printer of Greek texts in Venice, requesting that he reprint Erasmus's translations of Euripides (which had been published by Bade in 1506) in the typography for which Aldo had become famous. The Aldine Press had published nothing in 1506 or 1507 because of the turmoil created by the wars in Italy. One might wonder whether Aldo would choose Erasmus as the first author for his restored press. He did, and the slender volume was published in December 1507. It was the only publication of the Aldine Press during that year.

Erasmus left Bologna and hastened to Venice, where he was gladly received into Aldo's household and invited to join his "New Academy," a group of scholars both Italian and Greek who pledged themselves to speak only Greek at meals and in regular gatherings called for the purpose. Erasmus's contacts with members of the academy were regular and intense. He had come to Venice primarily to work on a new edition of the *Adages*. The composition of that volume as it finally issued from the

Aldine Press in September 1508 was heavily indebted to the Greek scholars of the New Academy, as Erasmus himself testifies in a passage added
in 1526 to one of his commentaries in the *Adages* of 1508:

> At a time when I, a Dutchman, was supervising the publication of
> my book of proverbs in Italy, every one of the scholars who were
> there offered me, without being asked, copies of authors which had
> never been printed, and which they thought I might be able to use.
> Aldus himself kept nothing back among his treasures. It was the
> same with John Lascaris, Baptista Egnatius, Marcus Musurus, Fra-
> ter Urbanus. I experienced the kindness of some whom I did not
> know either by sight or by name. I brought nothing with me to
> Venice but the raw material of a future work, as yet confused and
> undigested, and culled only from well-known authors. It was great
> audacity on my part that set us both on, myself to write and Aldus
> to print. We broke the back of the work in nine months, more or
> less, and meanwhile I had had an encounter with a trouble I had
> not met before, the stone. [Erasmus was later to blame this prob-
> lem on his diet and the poor wine in Italy.] Imagine how much of
> value I should have missed if the scholars had not furnished me
> with manuscripts. Among these were the works of Plato in Greek,
> Plutarch's *Lives* and his *Moralia*, which began publication just as
> my work was ending; the *Deipnosophistai* of Atheneus, Aphtho-
> nius, Hermogenes with the commentary, the *Rhetoric* of Aristotle
> with the notes of Gregory Nazianzen; Aristides together with the
> notes, the little commentaries on Hesiod and Theocritus, the col-
> lection of proverbs which goes under the name of Plutarch, and the
> other called after Apostolius, which was lent me by Jerome Alean-
> der. There were other less important things, which have either es-
> caped my memory or need not be mentioned here. None of these
> had hitherto been printed.[39]

The Aldine edition of the *Adages* was no longer called *Adagia collectanea* but rather *Adagia chiliades*. A glance at its composition reveals that
it was in fact as well as in name a new book and that Greek scholarship
was largely responsible for the difference. Instead of 818 adages (or 841
in the 1506 edition) there were 3,260. Of these, about four-fifths were
either new or substantially altered in form. And 2,734 contained Greek
passages of two to six lines or more in length. This edition was the one
in which the *Adages* was given the structure it was to retain, even though
Erasmus continued to expand subsequent editions until the final one,
which contained more than 4,000 adages. The transformation from the

Paris editions of the *Collectanea* to the Aldine edition of the *Chiliades* indicates the intensity and depth of Erasmus's work with Greek scholars and manuscripts in Italy.

It is important to notice, as Erasmus points out in the passage quoted above, that the Greek sources with which he worked were largely manuscript sources. Although he had worked with Latin manuscripts in England and had published Valla's *Annotations on the New Testament* from a manuscript copy, he had not previously edited manuscripts with a view to the publication of a more accurate text. He first engaged in this process in Venice. He gives expression to its difficulty in his commentary on the adage, "The Labors of Hercules," in which he cites the corruption of the text, the difficulty of collating manuscripts of the same text, the suppression of individual creativity that such work requires, and the toll it takes on one's health as particular problems.[40] Venice was his apprenticeship for his later work in Basel.

The list of manuscript sources cited by Erasmus as having been made available to him at the Aldine Press was almost exclusively manuscripts of Greek classical literature as opposed to patristic theological texts. In his letter of dedication to Lord Mountjoy, Erasmus says of the 1508 edition of the *Adages:*

> I shall discuss theological allegories, since it belongs to my profession to do so, as soon as I have an adequate supply of Greek books on the subject—and will do so the more willingly because I observe that for some centuries now theologians have neglected this department, which is really of the utmost importance, and bestowed all their efforts on subtle questions—a practice which would be less reprehensible if it were not their one and only concern.[41]

In principle, if not in practice, Erasmus had now effected the fusion between *pietas* and *humanitas*, Christianity and classical culture, which was the hallmark of all he subsequently wrote.

The Aldine edition of the *Adagia chiliades* did more than place the crown on Erasmus's Greek studies. It also made him a famous man. Previously known to limited circles among humanists in places he had personally visited, he now became a well-known figure to all men of learning and power in Europe. And this recognition conferred upon him a greater authority than did the doctorate in theology, which he obtained for the purpose.

Even so, Erasmus had not received everything he was to take with him from Italy. Shortly after the *Adagia chiliades* came off the press in

Venice, Erasmus departed and made his way to Rome. He was in and out of the eternal city three times between February and July 1509, when he left Italy never to return. His reputation preceded him, and he was received as a royal guest wherever he went. Among the friends he made may be numbered Giovanni de' Medici, later Pope Leo X (to whom he dedicated his edition of the New Testament), Cardinal Domenico Grimani (to whom he dedicated his first paraphrase, that on Romans), Cardinal Raffaelle Riario, and Tommaso Fedra Inghirami, librarian of the Vatican. Inghirami offered him the use of the Vatican archives, and Grimani, whose personal library numbered eight thousand volumes, suggested that Erasmus might live and work in his home. In a letter written to Grimani six years after he left Italy, Erasmus describes their last meeting, in which he was almost persuaded to remain in Rome, and says that he failed to return to the cardinal's house before departing because he was afraid he might never leave had he done so. He even suggests that he may have made the wrong choice; he often longs for Italy.[42]

So much for what might have been. Erasmus was drawn away from Italy by promises that were as unbelievable as they seemed real. Henry VII died on 21 April 1509. Upon the accession of Henry VIII, Erasmus received a letter from his patron, Lord Mountjoy, urging him to come to England and receive the bounty of a king who appreciated and loved men of letters. He left almost at once to spend the next five years in England.

Erasmus left Italy much enriched. He had obtained the authority of a doctorate in theology and the fame that accompanied the expanded edition of the *Adages*. He had acquired a much deeper knowledge of Greek and of the art of editing manuscripts. And he had acquired friends who in later years would use their power to protect him and to make his controversial biblical work possible.

*   *   *

Shortly after he arrived in England Erasmus wrote *The Praise of Folly*. At the time he was residing in the home of Thomas More, to whom the work is dedicated. *Folly* is to this day the book for which Erasmus is best known. There is justice in this judgment of history, for *Folly* is a new mode of literature but based on a classical model (and so a marvelous illustration of the purpose of *imitatio*) as well as the first complete expression of Erasmus's fusion of *humanitas* and *pietas*.

The Praise of Folly is cast in the form of an oration in which Folly (a goddess) speaks throughout. Since Folly is speaking and in praise of herself, we have here a mock encomium, folly praising folly, a mock praise in which folly is being censured. There is no precedent in the literary tradition for an encomium by folly herself and so no use of irony in the sense in which Erasmus uses it. Making Lucian and Socrates (in the *Apology*) his models, Erasmus reintroduces satiric irony for the first time since classical antiquity, but does so in a way unique to him.[43]

The irony appears even in the dedicatory epistle to Thomas More. "I decided to compose a trifling thing, *Moriae encomium*. . . . inspired by your surname of More, which is as close in form to *Moria* (Folly) as you are in fact remote from folly itself—to which, as all agree, you are a complete stranger."[44] At the beginning of her oration, the goddess Folly launches immediately into the benefits she confers on mankind. All life, she says, is based on pleasure. Take that away and life loses its savor. But in what does pleasure lie? In ignorance. "Never to think, that is the good life."[45] It is ignorance, indeed, which keeps the human race alive, so that the human race owes its very existence to me. What man would want to get married if he first weighed the inconveniences of married life? Or what woman would ever admit her husband to her bed if she had heard or thought about the dangerous pains of childbirth and the irksomeness of bringing up a child? When people grow old only I make life tolerable, for I purge their cares of mind away so that they become young (ignorant) again. Happiness depends upon ignorance, which is in reality delusion. "Everyone is all the happier," says Folly, "the more ways he is deluded." Folly recounts Horace's story about the Greek whose madness took the form of sitting alone in the theater all day long, laughing, applauding, cheering, because he thought fine tragedies were being acted before him (though nothing at all was on the stage). Yet he conducted himself acceptably in other relations of life, "cheerful with his friends, agreeable with his wife." Then he was medically treated and cured of his madness, following which he protested: "Damn it all! You have killed me, my friends, not cured me, by thus wresting my enjoyment from me and forcibly depriving me of a most pleasant delusion."[46]

Erasmus does not omit himself from the catalog of those who are deceived and so made happy by Folly. Let me compare, says Folly, the lot of the wise man with that of the fool.

> Imagine, if you please, a model of wisdom to set over against the fool: a man who has wasted his whole childhood and youth in mastering the branches of learning and has lost the sweetest part of life in sleepless nights and endless painstaking labors, a man who even in the rest of his life has not tasted the tiniest crumb of pleasure, always frugal, poor, gloomy, surly, unfair and harsh to himself, severe and hateful to others, wasted away into a pale, thin, sickly, blear-eyed figure, old and gray long before his time, hastening to a premature grave—though what does it matter when such a

person dies, since he never really lived at all? And there you have a fine picture of your wiseman.[47]

Thus it is that Folly can say, in a passage Shakespeare read, transformed, and immortalized: "Now the whole life of mortal men, what is it but a sort of play in which various persons make their entrances in various costumes, and each one plays his own part until the director gives him his clue to leave the stage."[48]

Actually, *The Praise of Folly* is divided into three sections, of which I have drawn from only the first (this one, however, encompasses slightly more than half the entire oration). In the middle section, the irony is dropped and the satire is direct. Folly makes the transition by remarking: "Let's examine the actual lives of men for a bit, to make it clear just how much they owe me—throughout all society from top to bottom—and how highly they value me. But we will not survey the lives of any and all people, for that would take far too long, but only the lives of outstanding personages—from them it will be easy enough to judge the rest."[49] The "most outstanding personages" whom Folly satirizes are the merchants ("the most foolish and the meanest profession of all"), learned men who instruct or write for others (grammarians or teachers of youth, rhetoricians, poets), lawyers, scientists, theologians, monks, kings and nobles, popes, cardinals, and bishops.[50] Satire against those in power within the church bulks largest. Erasmus had been criticizing scholastic theologians ever since his Paris years, when he had studied under them. But the social satire against those in high places cannot be found in his work prior to this section of *Folly* and, indeed, would have been inconceivable before this time. *The Praise of Folly* represents a new stage in Erasmus's intellectual development. In Italy he had seen at first hand the corruption in high places in the church (most notably in the person of Julius II), and he had gained the confidence and authority necessary to call attention to it. From this time on, much of what Erasmus wrote had as its intention the reform of some aspect of society. His fusion of *pietas* and *humanitas* had now reached the point that he envisioned the restoration of good literature in the broadest sense (Christian and pagan) as the basis for a general social reform. Christian humanism was to become the instrument for social transformation.

What Erasmus says through Folly in this second section of his mock encomium he says directly several years later in "The Sileni of Alcibiades," a commentary on an adage written for the 1515 edition of the *Adages*.[51] The sileni "were small images divided in half, and so constructed that they could be opened out and displayed; when closed they represented some ridiculous, ugly flute-player, but when opened they suddenly revealed the figure of a god, so that the amusing deception would show off the art of the carver." Thus, in a more generalized sense, the word is used "either with reference to a thing which in appearance seems ridiculous and contemptible, but on closer and deeper examination proves to be admirable, or else with reference to a person whose looks and dress do not correspond at all to what he conceals in his soul."[52] Socrates was a silenus. Externally, he was ugly, unfit for public affairs, and (so he said) knew nothing. But viewed from within, he rose above the pettiness of most men. There were other sileni, of whom the greatest was Christ. What power in weakness, what riches in poverty, what grandeur in humility did he not manifest? Within Christianity, many sileni have followed Christ, such as John the Baptist, the apostles, and the great bishops of old. But the situation is reversed today:

> There are those who in name and appearance impose themselves as magistrates and guardians of the common weal, when in reality they are wolves and prey upon the state. There are those whom you would venerate as priests if you only looked at their tonsure, but if you look into the Silenus, you will find them more than laymen. Perhaps you will find some bishops too in the same case—if you watch that solemn consecration of theirs, if you contemplate them in their new robes, the mitre gleaming with jewels and gold, the crozier likewise encrusted with gems, the whole mystic panoply which clothes them from head to foot, you would take them to be divine beings, something more than human. But open the Silenus, and you find nothing but a soldier, a trader, or finally a despot, and you will decide that all those splendid insignia were pure comedy.[53]

It is with this image in mind (though it is not invoked in this section of *The Praise of Folly*) that Erasmus levels his criticisms. Grammarians are exalted people, yet most of their schools are knowledge factories or mills. Writers become famous not by the profundity but by the triviality of what they write. Theologians teach about the formal, efficient, material, and final causes of baptism rather than the true nature of the Christian life. The pope lives in splendor rather than in the poverty of the early church. Monks are regarded as the most religious people, though they are usually the farthest away from religion.

It is clear that in his program of social reform, Erasmus's prescriptions are moralistic rather than political, that is, he believes that the reform of society comes through the reform of those in high places. He does not, therefore, as Machiavelli does, deal with the question of power.

Erasmus's image of society was that of a series of concentric circles around Christ as center or mark at which to aim (*scopos*).[54] Nearest the mark are the pope and high church officials. Next come the magistrates and those in power at all levels, including the learned. Finally come the common people. Change in the larger concentric circles (the common people) radiates from the center. The more those above them aim at the mark (Christ) the more will the common people do the same. Society changes by example from the top.

Folly does not close her speech with satire but with the notion of the Christian fool, the fool in Christ. "The Christian religion taken all together," says Folly, "has a certain affinity to some sort of folly, and has little or nothing to do with wisdom."[55] Indeed, the happiness Christians pursue is nothing if not a kind of madness and folly. Like the Platonists, Christians hold that the soul is shackled by the body, so that it cannot see things as they really are. Those are ridiculed who, like the wise man in Plato's cave, escape the illusory world for the world of reality and then try to communicate this reality to those suffering under the delusions of the body. The religious pay little attention to things of the body, which concern most men most of the time. Thus, from the point of view of worldly wisdom, they are fools. "In absolutely every activity of life, the pious man flees from whatever is related to the body and is carried away in the pursuit of the eternal and invisible things of the spirit. Hence, since these two groups are in such utter disagreement on all matters, the result is that each thinks the other is insane—though that word applies more properly to the pious than to ordinary men, if you want my opinion."[56]

Thus Folly begins by extolling prudence as her special gift to mankind and ends by pointing out the lack of this very prudence among (true) Christians. Christians have a special kind of prudence different from that of the world—it is unworldly. Thus Christians are foolish, but they owe nothing to the goddess Folly since it is not their kind of foolishness that Folly purveys. Christians owe their foolishness to the silenus, Christ.

All of Erasmus is in this little book. We find there his classicism with allusions to virtually all the major classical writers, his special affinity with (and transformation of) the work of Lucian, his sympathy with the attitude of Socrates, whom he likens to Christ in some respects, his agreement with Plato's separation of body and soul. There is also his pietism, traceable to the Brethren, untrammeled by formalism of any kind, whether of learning or of church practice. And there is his learning, which is not for its own sake but at the service of his fellows (*Folly* is an educational treatise in the most profound sense: it seeks to change behavior). The form in which the entire work is cast also reflects Erasmus's personality, for Folly laughs at and satirizes everyone but sides with no one. So Erasmus always prized his freedom above all else. He joined no parties, though (when the Reformation began) he was reviled by all.

Erasmus wrote another satire while in England, but one he never acknowledged: *Julius Excluded from Heaven.*[57] Pope Julius II, the "warrior pope," died in 1513. Later during that year the manuscript of this satire was in circulation. His contemporaries attributed it to Erasmus. He never denied that he wrote it, but he never acknowledged it either. We know, however, that he wrote an epigram satirizing Pope Julius, because we possess it in an autograph; it was sent to Thomas More. We also know that Erasmus did not wish to offend the pope openly. For one thing, Julius had given him a dispensation from wearing the habit of his order while in Italy, since he was once taken for a doctor ministering to plague victims and was almost attacked in the streets. Moreover, he needed papal assistance still in remaining free from the monastery to which his former friend, Servatius Roger, now prior at Steyn, was trying to have him return. The satire is unlike *Folly* and unlike any other satire Erasmus wrote in that it is directed toward an individual. The irony in it is much less subtle than in *Folly,* consisting in pointing out the disparity between what a pope should be and what this one was.

* * *

The wealth promised Erasmus on his return to England never materialized as he had hoped it would. As he said diplomatically on several occasions in his correspondence, he received more than he deserved but not as much as he needed. It was largely for this reason that in 1511 he accepted an offer from Bishop John Fisher to teach at Cambridge University. After a brief visit to Paris in April, the purpose of which was to deposit the manuscript of *The Praise of Folly* with the printer Giles Gourmont (the work was published in June), he settled his affairs in London and made his way to Cambridge in August. There he remained until early in 1514, with side visits to London when he could manage them. In 1511 he worked largely on the *Method* and the *Copia,* polishing and augmenting them for publication as John Colet had requested. In 1512 he spent most of his time revising his *Adages* (published in 1515) in which social commentary was to figure largely and in which, for the first time, proverbs from the Christian classical tradition were included. He also made translations from Plutarch's *Moralia* as a means of getting financial support from patrons. During the first part of 1513 he worked on collating various texts of the New Testament, then turned to emending the texts of Jerome and writing a philological commentary on them.

Sometime during the same period he began, once again, a theological commentary on Paul's letters.

I began this essay with Erasmus's departure from England in 1514 and his triumphal journey through the Low Countries and Germany to Basel in Switzerland. It should be clear now why his contemporaries regarded him as "Prince of the Humanists." It should also be clear why Erasmus believed that he lived perhaps at the dawn of another golden age, in the best of times. He had arrived at full self-consciousness of his vocation as a scholar. The fruits he now regarded as the most important results of his work he carried with him from Cambridge to Basel: the revised adages, the works of Jerome, and the Greek text of the New Testament. It is little wonder that Erasmus believed a flowering of letters was imminent, that it had the power to transform Europe, and that he stood in the vanguard of the movement that would bring it all to pass.

✳   ✳   ✳

The first work Erasmus published after arriving in Basel was the revised edition of his *Adages*. The new edition had 3,400 adages (140 more than the Aldine edition). The additions included nine long essays (only three more long essays were added in all the subsequent editions). What is striking about these additions is the amount of social criticism in them. The edition is thus markedly different in tone from that of 1508, reflecting the kind of commentary we have found in *Folly* and *Julius*. Margaret Mann Phillips calls this the "utopian edition." And well it might be, for it embodies Erasmus's hopes for the reform of society. But Phillips also had in mind the relation between these new essays and More's *Utopia*.[58] Both More and Erasmus attribute disorder in human affairs to abuse of power and to the profit motive. Both believe in elective rule, though Erasmus is more strongly antimonarchical than More. Both depict life in royal courts in uncomplimentary terms. Both believe in a community of wealth. Both disbelieve in war, though More makes room for the notion of a just war, while Erasmus does not (though he does affirm, at the end of his long essay on war, that defense of oneself in case of attack is justified). The wholesale denunciation of war is the most important element of the new *Adages*. Erasmus and More also hold similar views of religion and priesthood, believing in a simplified Christianity and a reform of the priesthood. The idea of a simplified Christianity we find as early as the *Enchiridion*. The idea of a reform of the priesthood appears here for the first time in a positive way; it had, of course, appeared in the earlier satires by way of ridicule. Finally, More advocates the equality of the sexes in *Utopia*, whereas all of Erasmus's remarks about women in this edition of the *Adages* are derogatory. (In the *Colloquies* a few years later he expresses a high view of women.)[59]

There are three essays that deal with the conduct of kings. In one, from the adage "Kings and fools are born, not made," he says that a king, unlike a coachman, does not need to learn his trade, he only needs to be born! Since this situation cannot be changed, the next best thing is to educate him. A teacher will implant the following ideas: that one who wields power for himself is a robber; that there is no difference between pirates and pirate-minded princes; that a king can be of great use to many by behaving like a wise man; that supreme rule in Christian terms means administration, not dominion; that a king should not judge himself by the flatterers around him and should appoint only good men to high office; that he must show mercy and avoid war. Most kings, however, are brought up by women and surrounded by sycophants. They are given whatever they want. With such indulgence, it is no wonder that there are so many bad kings.[60]

Early in 1516 Erasmus was appointed a councillor to the court of Prince Charles, the future Charles V, then fifteen. He wrote—or completed—a treatise to Charles, *The Education of a Christian Prince*, published by Froben in June 1516, which contains all the points made in the essay in the adages as well as a number of others.[61] Both treatises show themselves to be part of the tradition of the "mirror of princes" literature going back to the fourth century B.C. when Isocrates, Plato, Aristotle, and others began to write on kingship in the wake of the rise of Philip of Macedon and his son Alexander the Great. Erasmus, in fact, cites Isocrates as his model, though he is thoroughly familiar with both the classical and the Christian medieval traditions of the "mirror of princes" literature. In all of these it is emphasized that a king should be wary of flatterers and appoint good men to office, that he must look to the good of his subjects first rather than to his own good, that he should strive for justice and virtue, always be watchful, exercise self-control, keep in touch with what his people think. He should be educated by good tutors who instill in him the qualities above described. Both the essay in the *Adages* and the *Education* reveal the emphasis Erasmus placed on the moral education of those in power for the creation of a good and just society.

In a second group of three adages Erasmus levels two kinds of criticism against the clergy: their obscurantism and their moral laxity. The adage "with unwashed hands" may refer to those who attempt to interpret Scripture without knowledge of Hebrew, Greek, and Latin and instead learn the rules of Aristotle.[62] In a second adage, "for the lazy it is always a holiday," Erasmus suggests the reduction of the number of holidays by the pope on the grounds that Christians are never as good at imitating pagans as by their drunken revelry on holidays. Festivals need not be eliminated, but they should be returned to their earlier purposes. (Here is the reformer and the classicist in a nutshell.)[63] But the most important essay in this group is the silenus of Alcibiades. A silenus, as already mentioned, is one who appears different externally from what he is inside. Thus Socrates and Christ were lowly and inconspicuous, but what power within. It is by their fruits that men are known, not by their social class. But today we honor men in reverse order: those who are nobly born are most esteemed. Even the church has given itself over to wealth. In a passage reminiscent of *Julius Excluded from Heaven* Erasmus says: I want to see a pope ride in apostolic triumph, not in bloodthirsty triumph. I wish them to be fierce warriors, but against the true enemies of the church: lust, pride, ambition, anger, irreligion, simony.[64]

Erasmus's comments on war are scattered throughout the *Adages*, but in the 1515 edition he added two long essays on the subject which are the best-known parts of the *Adages*. In the first, a comment on the adage "you have obtained Sparta, adorn it," he makes the point that princes are more concerned about obtaining new lands to govern than in governing well those they already have. He tells the poignant story of Alexander, son of James, King of Scotland, as an example of the folly wrought by such a policy. Erasmus had been a tutor of Alexander in Italy and regarded him as a young man who combined literary brilliance with a fine moral character. At the age of twenty he went into battle with his father and was killed. Had his father not overstepped his bounds, this tragedy would not have happened.[65]

The second essay, a commentary on "war is sweet to those who have not tried it," is perhaps the best known of all the adages, largely because it has been published separately a number of times.[66] As in the case of the "mirror of princes" essays, so this essay closely resembles a treatise Erasmus published in 1517, *The Complaint of Peace,* an oration in which Peace, a goddess, delivers a brief in behalf of concord. Both the adage and the *Complaint* are related to but also contrast with an *Oration on Peace and Discord,* which Erasmus had written for a friend at Steyn in 1488. In the 1488 oration, Erasmus argued that men differ from beasts in that seeds of peace have been planted in human nature, visible in the closeness of human relationships and the ways in which reason supports this closeness (e.g., through mutual protection, friendship, family ties). But ambition, greed, and bad habits have made men worse than savage beasts in their behavior toward one another (Erasmus cites Juvenal, satire 15, to illustrate the point). If we look at the mutual harmony of the parts of the body, at the movement of the heavenly orbs, at the gift of friendship, we will see how contrary to nature this conflict is. It is also contrary to our experience, for discord makes life miserable in so many ways, while peace brings happiness. So necessary is peace for human happiness that all the virtues are as nothing without this virtue. In a final appeal Erasmus says that those who would realize the nature of man, those concerned about faith and duty, those who wish to live safely and peacefully, and those interested in salvation should pursue peace.

How like and yet how different is this early oration from the essay in the *Adages* and the *Complaint*. The unfitness of men for war, the fact that in fighting they are worse than beasts, and the evil motives that bring on war are in all three. But in 1488 there is no word about Christ the King of Peace or reflections on the foolishness of Christians fighting Christians, which permeate the essays of 1515 and 1517. In the latter Erasmus emphasizes that Christ's teachings breathe peace, as do those of his early followers. Christ came to reconcile. Christian princes should look to the image of their Prince and ask whether they are following him. Since all Christians have the same Lord it is ludicrous for them to be fighting one another. What brought about such a state of affairs? The struggle against heretics, in which learning was used as a pretext for combating heresy. Learning should be used to build up faith, not as a basis for war. Christian theologians today give many absurd justifications for war, which only shows that they are not truly Christian theologians. There is no just war. "An unjust peace is far preferable to a just war." Even in the case of the Turk (and if we must fight we should fight him before we fight fellow Christians) we should win them by the example of blameless lives. If we would convert them to Christianity, let us first be Christians.

The 1515 edition of the *Adages* is certainly the "social" if not the "utopian" edition of the work. Erasmus has taken on kings, the church, and the institution of war. What better example could we find than in these essays and those written just following them that Erasmus had become the confident reformer or teacher of western Christendom, that he was using his learning, both classical and Christian, in the interest of creating true Christians, people in whom *pietas* and *humanitas* would be so combined that the promise of "the best of times" would be realized?

*   *   *

But Erasmus brought with him to Basel not only his revised adages; he brought a Greek New Testament, together with notes he had made in England. He had intended to carry this work with him on to Venice and the Aldine Press. But Aldo Manuzio died in February 1515 and Froben pledged to match any offer Erasmus might receive for his manuscript. By

August Erasmus and Froben had reached an agreement. Work began in September and the first Greek New Testament ever published appeared in February 1516, together with his own Latin translation; annotations or critical notes on the text were published on 1 March.[67] This first edition was entitled *Novum instrumentum*. In addition to the Greek text, Latin translation, and annotations, it included a dedication to Pope Leo X, a preface to the annotations, the *Paraclesis* or exhortation to the reader, an *Apologia* for his Greek text and Latin translation, and an introduction to his methodology, *Methodus*. The entire work was about one thousand pages, and all of it was printed in six months, with Erasmus working at the press while the book was being printed.

Dissatisfied in some respects with this effort, Erasmus began immediately to work on a second edition. For the second edition of 1519 the title was changed to *Novum Testamentum*, which it retained thereafter. Much new introductory material was added, including an "Argument" for each book and a much expanded discussion of method entitled *Ratio verae theologiae*, published first in 1518 and included in the 1519 edition. Many additions were made to the annotations. The Latin translation he had made rather hastily in Basel for the 1516 edition was considerably revised. This edition came to more than three thousand pages. In subsequent editions (1522, 1527, 1535) there were expansions of the annotations and a few changes in the text, but the form (and title) of the 1519 edition remained intact.[68]

How does Erasmus interpret Scripture in his annotations? The basic distinction between flesh and spirit he had made in the *Enchiridion* in 1501 remained characteristic of him throughout his life. But the emphasis changes. In the *Enchiridion* he had emphasized the necessity of allegorical interpretation (following Origen to a large degree). His discovery of Valla's *Annotations on the New Testament* (1504) turned him more decidedly to grammatical and literary criticism. Thereafter, the grammatical interpretation became steadily more important to him and the flights of allegory he was willing to countenance increasingly limited.

But within these changes one thing remained constant: the primacy of the moral meaning of Scripture. Here, as elsewhere, Erasmus focuses on redirecting the life of the believer through action rather than through knowledge. In the *Methodus* he wrote: "Let this be the first and most important goal for you, this your prayer, this one thing do, that you may be changed, seized, hasten toward, transformed into the things you have learned."[69] And he adds in the *Ratio:* "God speaks to us truly and efficaciously in the sacred books to the extent that he spoke to Moses from the burning bush only if we come to the conversation with pure minds."[70]

Erasmus made copious use of the Christian Fathers' commentaries on the scriptural text in his annotations. His own growth in his ability to use them is striking. Taking his notes on Paul's Epistle to the Romans as an example, we find that in the 1516 edition he largely depends on Latin writers, among whom his favorite was Jerome (whose writings he was working on at the time). In the 1519 edition Jerome is replaced by Origen, though the Latin Fathers still generally dominate. In the 1527 edition (there were few changes in 1522) there is a striking change. Many additional notes appear, and virtually all the additions come from Greek authors, notably Chrysostom. In the final, 1535, edition, Greek and Latin Fathers are cited (in the additions) with about equal frequency, and virtually all who wrote commentaries on Paul are included. Erasmus gradually became a master of the patristic tradition, as he had become earlier of the pagan classical tradition.[71]

It should be added that Erasmus also cited authors closer to his own time. Among medieval thinkers he cites Thomas Aquinas (generally not favorably) and Nicholas of Lyra, and among his contemporaries or those who belong to the humanist movement, Valla and Jacques Lefèvre d'Etaples. He makes it clear, however, that he prefers the ancients over the moderns.

Erasmus uses the Fathers in four ways in his annotations.[72] First, he reports their opinions when they agree with his own analyses; second, he cites them in defense of his own interpretations; third, he points out differences among them in order to justify his departures from commonly held views (one of the reasons he liked the Fathers more than the scholastics was their heterodoxy, which allowed him to justify differences in the interpretation of a passage); and fourth, he criticizes errors he discovers in their works.

Erasmus criticizes the Fathers almost as often as he finds support for his views in them. The ancient commentators, he says, were amazingly gullible, especially in their willingness to accept books as authentic that were obviously spurious. The Greek interpreters often erred in emending too freely passages of Scripture that have little relevance to apostolic doctrine. The Latin interpreters were equally given to quibbles; many of them have often labored mightily over a passage that is perfectly clear. There was no one among his favorite Fathers who was not singled out at one point or another for explicit criticism. It is the sources themselves that must decide, and final appeal is to them, not to the authority of tradition.

One can more easily take this attitude toward the Fathers than toward the received biblical text itself (the Vulgate). How did Erasmus handle the question of the authority of the Vulgate? There is no doubt that he questioned it. In one interesting annotation, which he augmented with every edition except that of 1522, this fact becomes evident. In the 1516 edition he writes: "Some people think that this Translator [of the Vulgate] never made a mistake and that he wrote under the inspiration of the Holy Spirit. I challenge them then to make some sense out of [his translation of] this passage, if they can." Then, in 1519, he adds an even more radically critical note: "In fact, the flatness of his translation is here so great, and its incompleteness so evident, as to be a sufficient indication of how far we should trust him in other passages." By 1527 he has begun to modify his earlier boldness: "I refer to the awkwardness of his language, not to the content. We do not have to believe that the Holy Spirit inspired him throughout the whole translation." And in 1535 he adds: "In my opinion, the best excuse that we can make for the Translator is that in his day the common people were accustomed to imitate the Greeks in their way of speaking; and his translation was aimed at them, not at the educated."[73]

Shortly after Erasmus completed the first edition of his Greek New Testament with annotations, he began writing paraphrases, a kind of commentary, on the New Testament. The evidence suggests that when he began this project with a paraphrase of Paul's Epistle to the Romans, he did not intend to compose paraphrases for all the books of the New Testament; but eventually he did just that, except for the Book of Revelation. His paraphrase of Romans (1517) was followed by paraphrases of Corinthians and Galatians (1519), then Ephesians, Philippians, Colossians, Thessalonians, Timothy, Titus, and Philemon, as well as Peter, Jude, James, and the Gospel of Matthew (1520). The paraphrase of Hebrews was published in 1521; Mark, Luke, John, and Acts in 1523. The paraphrases were thereafter published in collected editions in 1524, 1532, and 1534. Erasmus made changes in each of the new editions, but in most cases they were not significant. The paraphrases, unlike the annotations, remained pretty much as they had appeared in the first edition throughout subsequent editions.[74]

The paraphrases, unlike the annotations, were not intended solely for scholars but also for laymen. Of course, not many laymen could read the Latin in which they were composed, but they were subsequently translated into the vernaculars. A complete English translation was made between 1548 and 1551, and copies of Erasmus's paraphrases of the Gospels were ordered placed in every parish church in England. This command was fully in accord with Erasmus's wish that (as he expressed it in the *Paraclesis*) the Gospels be translated into every vernacular and the farmer sing verses of it while farming and the weaver while weaving.[75]

*   *   *

In addition to the enlarged adages and the Greek New Testament, Erasmus also brought with him to Basel an edition of the works of Jerome on which he had been laboring. Froben published it in June 1516. It was the beginning of another large project that was to engage Erasmus for the remainder of his life: making available complete editions of the works of the church fathers. He was responsible for editions of Cyprian (1520), Arnobius and Athanasius (1522), Hilary (1523), Irenaeus (1526, editio princeps), Ambrose (1527), Augustine (1528–29), Chrysostom (1530, Latin translation), Basil (1532, editio princeps of Greek edition), and Origen (1536, published posthumously). It was through the publication of these editions of the Fathers that Erasmus gained the familiarity with the patristic tradition of which he made progressively greater use in the editions of his annotations.

*   *   *

Erasmus's work in the theological tradition—New Testament with annotations and paraphrases, editions of the Fathers, criticism of religious practices—involved him in a great deal of controversy, related as much to the time in which he lived as to the work itself. There is no better illustration than in the "Reuchlin affair." In 1511 John Pfefferkorn, a Jewish convert to Christianity, suggested to the emperor that all the books of the Jews should be taken away from them and burned, inasmuch as they contained pernicious lies. Johann Reuchlin (1455–1522), the first northern humanist to learn Hebrew as well as Latin and Greek and the first Christian ever to publish a Hebrew grammar (*De rudimentis hebraicis*, 1506),[76] responded that the Jews possessed many books that were good, and that while any pernicious books they might have should be taken from them, the confiscation should not be indiscriminate. A series of pamphlets was exchanged between the two men. Reuchlin's chief defense was a book of letters from various authorities expressing support, which he entitled *Letters of Distinguished Men*. Finally, both sides appealed to the pope for a judgment. In 1514 the pope turned the matter over to the emperor who conducted a hearing in which Reuchlin was vindicated and his enemies commanded to be silent. By this time, however, the Reuchlin affair had become a *cause célèbre* throughout the learned circles of Europe. To a man humanists believed that Reuchlin's enemies were out to undo the cause of good learning altogether. Among them was Erasmus, who had been silent during the earlier years of the controversy (when it first broke out Erasmus remarked that "it is none of my business"). But in 1515 he wrote to one of his Roman friends, Cardinal Riario, on behalf of Reuchlin, saying that he was accomplished in languages, well known for his published works, and respected both by the emperor and by his own people.[77] He refused to endorse Reuchlin's kabbalistic philosophy (the real reason Reuchlin had learned Hebrew) and upbraided Pfefferkorn for having raised the issue in the first place. The affair reached something of a climax in 1516 when Crotus Rubeanus (1480–1540) wrote a series of letters in which simple-minded monks in monstrous Latin so defended Reuchlin's antagonists as to make fools of themselves. Taking his cue from Reuchlin's earlier *Letters of Distinguished Men*, he entitled this book *Letters of Obscure Men*. He sent a copy of it to his friend Ulrich von Hutten (1488–1526), a German knight, who added a second and much more biting series of letters.[78] Erasmus had helped Hutten in Italy by supplying him with letters of introduction to humanist circles there and had mentioned him favorably in his New Testament. Hutten became an ardent admirer. But in his letters he criticized Erasmus, having become disillusioned because Erasmus had not supported Reuchlin earlier and more fervently.

Erasmus had cause to support Reuchlin in 1515. He had persuaded Jerome Busleiden, a businessman who had the inclinations of a scholar, to make provisions in his will for the establishment of a Trilingual College at Louvain. When Busleiden died on a journey to Spain in 1517, Erasmus, who was using Louvain as his principal residence, became deeply involved in helping the new college get established. Busleiden had wanted the college to be housed in an existing college, but none would have it, so the Trilingual College had to be established separately and supplied with its own buildings. Erasmus sought diligently to hire competent professors of Latin, Greek, and Hebrew to fill the initial three positions provided for by Busleiden. Already suspect in Louvain for his liberal scholarship, he was heartily opposed by theologians who did not believe Greek and Hebrew necessary for a theologian.[79]

The first controversy over theological matters actually involving Erasmus's work came also from Louvain, in the person of Martin Dorp, a theologian who, in 1515, hearing that Erasmus's New Testament project was underway, wrote urging him not to publish a Greek text, both because the Greeks were suspect—since the Greek church was alienated from the church of Rome—and because the Vulgate could not possibly be wrong, having been approved by general councils of the church. Dorp also took the occasion to criticize *Folly* which, he claimed, alienated many learned people; he urged Erasmus to write a Praise of Wisdom to counter its effects. Erasmus wrote a long and patient reply to Dorp.[80] About *Folly* he responded that it contained the teachings of the *Enchiridion* in playful disguise, that people digest things more readily through laughter, and that he had satirized no particular person. About the New

Testament Erasmus replied that the Vulgate was not Jerome's, that Jerome, as well as Augustine and Ambrose, quoted texts of Scripture that differed from the Vulgate, and that no council ever forbade emending the text. The correction of textual errors should alienate no one from following the footsteps of Christ. Dorp had cited the work of Valla and Lefèvre d'Etaples as sufficient; Erasmus commended their efforts but added that much more needed to be done. Erasmus's irenicism, as well as a similar effort by Thomas More, won Dorp over.[81]

But the criticisms that preceded publication of the New Testament were slight compared to those that followed it. Above all, the doubt thrown on the adequacy of the Vulgate text stirred up a storm. Edward Lee, an Englishman, a close friend of Thomas More and later archbishop of York, supplied Erasmus with some corrections of his first edition (which Erasmus had said that he would welcome). When Erasmus treated these disdainfully, Lee let it be known that he had others and that he would publish them without consulting Erasmus (which he eventually did). He was particularly incensed that Erasmus had omitted the Trinitarian verse, 1 John 5:7: "For there are three that bear witness in heaven, the Father, the Word, and the Holy Spirit: and these three are one." Erasmus found it in none of the manuscripts he used and so omitted it. Lee took it as evidence that Erasmus was an Arian, denying that the Son was of one essence with the Father. When challenged in this way, Erasmus promised to restore the passage in subsequent editions if one manuscript could be produced that had it. One was found in England—Erasmus rightly suspected that it had been manufactured for the purpose. But he kept his promise and restored the passage in the third edition of 1522. Eventually this quarrel also was patched up, again with the assistance of Thomas More.[82]

One of the most distressing controversies to Erasmus personally involved Jacques Lefèvre d'Etaples of France. The dispute was over a word in Hebrews 2:7. Should it read: "Thou hast made him a little lower than the angels," or "a little lower than God"? The reference is to Christ. Lefèvre noted that the text was a quotation from the Psalms and read in Hebrew "a little lower than God." But the author of Hebrews had not used the Hebrew text but the Septuagint or Greek translation of the Hebrew Bible, which read "a little lower than the angels." Erasmus retained the reading "angels" because the author of Hebrews used it, even though it was an error (for Christ could not be said to be a little lower than the angels without impiety). Lefèvre made his point before Erasmus's New Testament appeared. In the 1516 edition Erasmus took issue with Lefèvre and when Lefèvre responded, Erasmus expanded his position in fifty-six paragraphs in the 1519 edition. Guillaume Budé, the eminent French humanist, now intervened to patch up the quarrel, writing to Erasmus that his reputation would not suffer if he were silent, while if he continued to speak he would make an enemy. Erasmus took his advice and wrote a conciliatory letter to Lefèvre who, after a year, responded in equally gracious terms.[83]

* * *

These quarrels indicate that the liberal reformation being attempted by the humanists, now that it had become a self-conscious movement, was beginning to meet strong opposition from conservative theological forces. How it might have fared if events had continued in an evolutionary fashion is an unanswerable question. But a revolution occurred that changed the course of events and brought Erasmus within a few years to the point of believing that he lived not in the best of times but in the worst. The revolution, of course, was the Lutheran Reformation.

Erasmus first heard of Luther (though not by name) in December 1516 when Georg Spalatin, the chaplain of Frederick the Wise of Saxony, Luther's prince, wrote to Erasmus that an unnamed Augustinian monk took issue with Erasmus's interpretation of Romans. The monk contended that Paul rejected the entire law, not just the ceremonial law. The first actual contact between the two came in March 1519 when Luther sent a letter to Erasmus, deferential in tone and full of admiration.[84] By that time, Luther's views were known everywhere. In April, Erasmus wrote to Philipp Melanchthon—the young humanist prodigy, teacher of Greek at twenty-one, grandnephew of Johann Reuchlin (but disowned by Reuchlin because Melanchthon would not disavow Luther)—that the quarrels among the learned were the result of a conspiracy against good literature. And so Erasmus saw it for a number of years. His enemies and the enemies of Luther were the same, those who would destroy learning. Erasmus was therefore very sympathetic to Luther, not only for this reason but also because Luther called attention to the abuses to which Erasmus in many of his writings had also pointed. Luther seemed blameless in life, his writings were intelligent exegeses of Scripture in the manner of the Fathers. Those who cried out against Luther did so indiscriminately. They were not interested in the truth but in crushing opposition. Erasmus was convinced of this view by the fact that Luther and Reuchlin were mentioned in the same breath, though they were very different. It was really learning that was endangered.

Thus it was that throughout 1519 and 1520 Erasmus wrote favorably of Luther. In April 1519 he wrote to Luther's prince, Frederick the Wise, deploring the way in which Luther had been handled by Cardinal Cajetan (who would not listen to Luther but demanded only that he recant). No one admonishes Luther, Erasmus wrote to Frederick the Wise, no one instructs him. They simply cry heresy. No author is free from error, ancient or modern. The schools do not agree among themselves, why should they demand that others agree with them? The best part of Christianity is the Christian life. He concludes that Frederick should protect Luther and not suffer an innocent man under the pretext of piety to be subject to impiety.[85]

In November the University of Louvain sent to Cologne for a judgment on Luther. Louvain replied that he was in error regarding confession, indulgences, and the treasury of merits, in addition to which he had attacked the Holy See, for all of which errors his books should be burned. In June 1520 the pope finally wrote the bull excommunicating Luther. It took effect sixty days after it was delivered: because Luther received it in October, it became effective in December. Erasmus regarded the bull as a victory for the obscurantists and expressed concern for the wretched Luther. If the obscurantists pulled this off, he believed, the cause of language and letters would be ruined. On 13 September 1520 Erasmus wrote to Pope Leo X who had requested that Erasmus write against Luther, repeating his contention that opposition to Luther was based largely on hatred of learning and that Luther should not be condemned without a fair hearing. To Nicholas Egmont, rector of the University of Louvain, on whom Erasmus depended for support against those attacking him in the university, he said the same thing. But the response at Louvain was to burn Luther's books on 8 October. And the rector himself denounced Erasmus from the pulpit at the same time.[86] In this matter, as in all things, Erasmus was steering a middle course, maintaining his own independence of mind. But he could not shake the charge that he had laid the egg which Luther hatched and that he was on Luther's side. A similar book-burning took place shortly afterward in England, though Erasmus wrote his friends there in an attempt to prevent it. At the same time, Erasmus tried to persuade Froben not to publish any more of Luther's books.

It was in the midst of all this fracas that Erasmus provided his greatest service for Luther. On 5 November 1520 he had an interview with Frederick the Wise, Luther's prince. Frederick asked Erasmus whether he thought Luther had erred. Yes, replied Erasmus, in two ways: he has attacked the pope's crown and the monks' bellies.[87] In a series of twenty-two axioms on how to deal with the Lutheran question, Erasmus asserted that the bull offended right-minded people and was unworthy of the gentle vicar of Christ; that the universities had condemned Luther but not convicted him; and that his case should be referred to impartial judges.[88] A much fuller recommendation was issued under the name of the liberal Dominican John Faber, most probably with Erasmus's collaboration (Faber presented it later at the Diet of Worms, where Luther was heard). It recommended that the impartial judges should be the emperor and the kings of England and Hungary. Partly on the basis of Erasmus's judgment, Frederick secured from Charles the promise that Luther would not be condemned unheard.

Luther did not make the path of a conciliator easy. In the summer and autumn of 1520 he wrote his *Letter to the German Nobility*, in which he attacked the authority of the pope and the sole power of the church to interpret Scripture; and his *Babylonian Captivity of the Church*, in which he rejected four of the seven sacraments on the ground that they lacked scriptural warrant. And on 10 December 1520, when the papal bull against him was to have become effective, he burned it openly.

After this event, Erasmus began to express more critical reservations about Luther, which appear in his letters from 1521. Finally in 1524 he decided, for reasons not entirely clear, to take up his pen against Luther.

While Erasmus was working on his *On the Freedom of the Will* he published an enlarged edition of his *Colloquies* in March 1524, in which the first new addition is "an examination concerning faith." Barbatius, a Lutheran, is questioned by Aulus (Erasmus) concerning the Apostle's Creed, to discover whether he is a heretic or orthodox. The Lutheran passes the test, going through the Creed with respect to the doctrines of God, Christ, Holy Spirit, church, and resurrection. The point of the colloquy is that on *essential* matters Christians agree. With the exception of the doctrine of the church, the Reformation did not challenge the classical doctrines. On the question of the church, Erasmus skirts the issue of the papacy's authority. He makes the church those who believe throughout the world, in other words, those who are actually holy.[89]

It is instructive to take note of this dialogue before confronting Erasmus's *On the Freedom of the Will*, published in September 1524;[90] for in that treatise Erasmus makes it clear that doctrinal unity cannot be the basis for Christian peace.

> Holy Scripture contains secrets into which God does not want us to penetrate too deeply, because if we attempt to do so, increasing darkness envelops us, so that we might come to recognize in this manner both the unfathomable majesty of divine wisdom and the feebleness of the human mind.[91]

Erasmus then continues:

God wishes that we investigate by venerating him in mystic silence. Therefore Holy Scripture contains numerous passages which have puzzled many, without ever anyone succeeding in completely clarifying them. . . . Other things he wanted us to know with the utmost clarity, as for example, the precepts for a morally good life.[92]

In view of this uncertainty of doctrine, Erasmus is greatly disturbed by the Lutheran claim that the Spirit is an infallible guide in the interpretation of Scripture. To this claim Erasmus puts the question: "What can I do when several persons claim different interpretations, but each one swears to have the Spirit?"[93] The truth is, Erasmus asserts, that there are passages in Scripture that affirm free will and those that deny it. The only reasonable approach in the light of this fact is to find an interpretation that reconciles this seeming contradiction. This reconciliation Erasmus finds in the view that attributes a priority to God's grace but something at the same time to the human will. This view he calls the way of moderation. At the very beginning of his discussion Erasmus confesses:

I have always had a deep-seated aversion to fighting. Consequently I have always preferred playing in the freer field of the muses, than fighting ironclad in close combat. In addition, so great is my dislike of assertions that I prefer the views of the skeptics wherever the inviolable authority of Scripture and the decision of the Church permit.[94]

Luther responded to Erasmus one year later in his *Bondage of the Will* (December 1525). He pondered it longer than was usual with him, because he wanted a response worthy of his opponent. Late in his life he judged it one of the two or three things he had written worth preserving. His viewpoint is precisely the opposite of Erasmus's: it is the doctrine that is clear and the ethical commands that, without clarity of doctrine, are unclear or, rather, undoable. It was the law—ethical law, not ceremonial law—that had cast doubt for Luther on his relationship to God. He had tried to be good but could not do so; the law never made his conscience free and clear. But when he came to believe in the doctrine of the forgiveness of sins he found peace. "The Holy Spirit is no skeptic," says Luther. The Bible is a book about the forgiveness of sins by Christ from cover to cover, and it is in the light of this doctrine that every ethical command must be understood.

The standpoints of Erasmus and Luther were indeed fundamentally different, even as Luther had recognized in 1516. For Luther the most

important thing was that God be God, for Erasmus that God be good.
Erasmus believed in education, Luther in revelation.

         *   *   *

In 1518 someone who had a copy of exercises Erasmus had written in
Paris in the 1490s published them in an unauthorized version. Erasmus
corrected the text (he had retained no copy of this material) and published an authorized version in 1519. In 1522, shortly after arriving in
Basel, he transformed these exercises into dialogues and published the
first edition of his *Colloquies,* to which he was to add material in editions
of 1523, 1524, 1526, 1527, 1529, 1531, and 1533.[95] They were intended
to help students with conversational Latin and so belong, broadly speaking, to Erasmus's educational work. But the fusion of *pietas* and *humanitas,* which emerged by degrees up to 1517, is fully displayed in them.
He pours scorn on religious pilgrimages more than once, blames the immorality of the clergy for the troubles of his age, places Johann Reuchlin
in heaven, describes a "godly feast" in which Socrates, Vergil, and Horace are treated with the reverence given the apostles and fathers of the
church (one guest exclaims: "Saint Socrates, pray for us!"), and agrees
with Luther's idea that love abrogates the law without sanctioning the
sedition that underlies it. These serious themes are mixed together with
others that are entirely playful, and all are written in a dialogue form
that engages the reader. Erasmus is more at home in this genre, because
it allows him to display the many sides of his personality and, above all,
to be himself in the sense of belonging to no party. It should come as no
surprise that the book was condemned by the theological faculty of the
Sorbonne in 1526. The age was no longer playful; it had become deadly
serious, with opposite versions of "the truth" ready to sacrifice lives. The
laughter that prevents us from taking ourselves too seriously was still
possible but no longer worked its magic.

         *   *   *

Once the attacks on him began, not even Erasmus's classicism escaped
censure. Baldassare Castiglione, famous as the author of *The Book of
the Courtier,* slurred Erasmus for writing a barbarous Latin. Erasmus's
reply was his *Ciceronianus,* a critique of those who would be slavish
followers of Cicero.[96] The work is cast in the form of a dialogue among
Bulephorus, Hypologus, and Nosoponus. Nosoponus is represented as
having a serious illness: Ciceronianism. All eloquence except that of Cicero is distasteful to him. For seven years he has read no other writer,
lest some foreign expression slip into his vocabulary. He has made a
lexicon of all the words in Cicero, a second of phrases peculiar to him,

and a third of the metrical feet with which Cicero begins or ends his periods. If a word is found in Terence that is not in Cicero, it is banned. In order not to be distracted he works at night, and labors sometimes over one sentence an entire evening. He refuses to converse in Latin, since he could not do so in Ciceronian Latin.

At this point the other two interlocuters take over. They point out that Cicero did not do all things equally well. Caesar, for example, told jokes better than Cicero. His poetry was also deficient and his translations from the Greek sometimes very poor. Even in oratory his style was not always the best. But there is a deeper problem: it would be impossible to imitate Cicero even if one wanted to, for historical changes cause variations. A Christian prayer could not be expressed only in the words Cicero used; should we try to do so we would only make fools of ourselves.[97] Instead of such nonsense, we should seek to express ourselves clearly, forcefully, and appropriately.

Erasmus goes through many writers, past and present, and assesses their Ciceronianism. The range of his knowledge of humanists from Italy and other countries is astounding. He distinguishes them all from Cicero and points out the nature of their styles. His most interesting comment is on himself. Bulephorus asks Nosoponus what he thinks of Erasmus, to which Nosoponus replies:

He degrades and hurries everything; he does not give natural birth to his creations; sometimes he writes a whole volume at one sitting; nor can he ever have patience to read over even once what he has written; and he does nothing but write, notwithstanding the fact that not till after long reading should one come to writing and then but seldom. What of the fact too that he not even tries for Ciceronian style but uses theological words and sometimes even vulgarisms?[98]

It is a good self-analysis. Erasmus showed in much that he wrote that he did so hurriedly, hated the file, and did not revise carefully what he had written.

At the same time that Erasmus was criticizing Ciceronianism he was growing personally more fond of Cicero himself as a writer. When he edited Cicero's *De officiis* in 1501 what he said of Cicero was slight and artificial. But when he reissued it in 1519 his tone is highly personal. He describes rereading it after these many years and finding in it more uprightness, holiness, sincerity, and truth than he could find in the monks and theologians of his own day. Cicero did not have the Gospels, yet he sounds like a Christian. When he edited the *Tusculan Disputations* for Froben in 1523 he wrote the following in his introduction:

> How it strikes others I cannot tell; for my part, as I read Cicero, especially when he is speaking of the good life, he makes such an impression on me that I cannot doubt that the heart from which all this came was divinely inspired. And this judgment of mine attracts me all the more when I reflect on the immensity, the measurelessness of the goodness of God; which, it seems to me, some people are trying to force into too narrow a conception, simply according to their own ideas. Where the soul of Cicero walks now, it is perhaps not for human insight to decide. But I for one would not be against the views of those who hope that he is at peace in heaven. . . . Never did I more agree with the judgment of Quintilian: the man who really has begun to appreciate Cicero may be sure he has made progress. When I was a boy I liked Cicero less than Seneca, and I was twenty before I could bear to read him for long, though I liked almost everything else. Whether I have gotten wiser as I have gotten older, I don't know; but certainly Cicero never pleased me more, even when I was passionately taken up with those studies, than he has pleased me now that I am an old man; not only because of the wonderful felicity of his style, but because of the uprightness of his scholar's heart.[99]

Erasmus returned to Cicero once again in the last colloquy he wrote in 1533. Fittingly, it recalls his very earliest preoccupations. Hedonius explains to Spudaeus, who has just been reading Cicero's *De finibus*, how Epicureanism is the most Christian philosophy. Epicurus said that happiness was pleasure but, contrary to popular opinion, he defined pleasure in terms of mind and spirit rather than in terms of the body. What most men seek is not true pleasure, for the latter comes from God. Where God is the fount of joy, there immeasurable happiness exists. Even the pains that are outside human control are borne better by those who love godly pleasures. "If people who live agreeably are Epicureans, none are more truly Epicureans than the righteous and godly."[100] And no philosophy better deserves the name of Christian. Christ called us to joy, not to gloominess.

It is in this spirit that we must imagine Erasmus composed the last major work he saw through the press, his *Ecclesiastes or On the Method of Preaching*, which appeared in August 1535.[101] The *Ecclesiastes* is a handbook for preachers, or, as we might say, the rhetorical principles and polish of Cicero applied to the creation of Christian orators. It is, as has been suggested, the counterpart of his handbooks for Christian laymen (*Enchiridion*), Christian princes (*Education of a Christian Prince*), and Christian educators (his numerous works on educational theory and method); here he is prescribing the character of the Christian preacher, the tools he needs to carry out his task, and, finally, sermon topics and how they might be developed. From the time of his intellectual maturity until his death *pietas* and *humanitas* were united in Erasmus; where one is to be found we need not look far for its counterpart.

*   *   *

Erasmus died on 11 or 12 July 1536. In him humanism reached its climax. He was, without any doubt or ambiguity, the greatest of the humanists. He brought humanism to its point of highest self-consciousness and then lived to see its program turned in new directions by a revolution he understood but would not join. He lived in the best of times and the worst of times, and he remained himself throughout both.

NOTES

The standard edition of the works of Erasmus has been, until recently, the *Opera omnia*, ed. Jean LeClerc, 10 vols. (Leiden, 1703–6). One of the great achievements of twentieth-century scholarship has been the critical editing of Erasmus's correspondence: *Opus Epistolarum Des. Erasmi Roterodami*, ed. P. S. Allen, H. M. Allen, and H. W. Garrod, 12 vols. (Oxford, 1906–58); this edition will be referred to hereafter as EE, followed by volume and page number(s). A critical edition has also been published of works omitted from LeClerc: *Erasmi opuscula*, ed. W. K. Ferguson (The Hague, 1933); and of Erasmus's poetry: *The Poems of Desiderius Erasmus*, ed. C. Reedijk (Leiden, 1956). Critical editions of a number of works have been published together with a German translation in *Erasmus von Rotterdam Ausgewählte Schriften*, ed. W. Welzig, 8 vols. to date (Darmstadt, 1967–), referred to hereafter as AS, followed by volume and page numbers where relevant. The works are now being published in a complete critical edition: *Opera omnia Des. Erasmi Roterodami*, 13 vols. to date (Amsterdam, 1969–), referred to hereafter as ASD, followed by volume, year in parentheses, editor, and page numbers where relevant.

Many works by Erasmus have been translated into English, some of which will be mentioned in the following notes. A project currently underway is a complete translation of his letters and works in critical editions: *Collected Works of Erasmus* (Toronto, 1974–), 6 volumes of correspondence and 8 of the works published to date; these translations will be referred to hereafter as CWE, followed by volume and page number(s).

The study of Erasmus has become an industry in itself. For bibliographies of works on him, see *Bibliographie internationale de l'humanisme et de la*

Renaissance (Geneva, 1966–), which appears annually and includes entries on Erasmus (see index); and J.-C. Margolin, *Douze années de bibliographie erasmienne (1950–1961)* (Toronto, 1977); idem, *Neuf années de bibliographie erasmienne (1962–1970)* (Toronto, 1977); idem, *Quatorze années de bibliographie erasmienne (1936–1949)* (Toronto, 1977).

Recently a reference work of Erasmus's contemporaries has appeared: *Contemporaries of Erasmus*, ed. P. G. Bietenholz and T. B. Deutscher, 3 vols. (Toronto, 1984–86). On the interpretation of Erasmus since his own time, see A. Flitner, *Erasmus im Urteil seiner Nachwelt: Das literarische Erasmus-Bild von Beatus Rhenanus bis zu Jean LeClerc (Tübingen, 1952);* and B. Mansfield, *Phoenix of His Age: Interpretations of Erasmus, 1550–1750* (Toronto, 1979); Mansfield is preparing a second volume to cover the period since 1750.

The best brief biography of Erasmus is M. M. Phillips, *Erasmus and the Northern Renaissance* (London, 1949, rev. ed. 1981); see also J. Huizinga, *Erasmus and the Age of Reformation* (New York, 1957). The recent biography of R. H. Bainton, *Erasmus of Christendom* (New York, 1969), takes account of recent scholarship and is an excellent place to begin; he also appends an extensive bibliography. On Erasmus's intellectual development, see E.-W. Kohls, *Die Theologie des Erasmus*, 2 vols. (Basel, 1966); A. Rabil, Jr., *Erasmus and the New Testament: The Mind of a Christian Humanist* (San Antonio, TX, 1972); and J. D. Tracy, *Erasmus: The Growth of a Mind* (Geneva, 1972).

The *Erasmus of Rotterdam Society Yearbook*, published continuously since 1981, is devoted entirely to the life and thought of Erasmus, including as well a birthday lecture delivered each year by a prominent Erasmian scholar and reviews of recent works on Erasmus.

1. I am persuaded by the arguments of A. C. F. Koch, *The Year of Erasmus' Birth and Other Contributions to the Chronology of His Life* (Utrecht, 1969), that Erasmus was born in 1467 and not 1466 or 1469 as most scholars still maintain; see Rabil, *Erasmus and the New Testament*, 2, note 3.

2. CWE, 23:16.

3. For a critical edition of *De contemptu mundi*, see ASD, 5.1 (1977), ed. S. Dresden, 1–86; and of the *Antibarbari*, ASD, 1.1 (1969), ed. K. Kumaniecki, 1–138. For a critical translation of the *Antibarbari*, see CWE, 23, ed. M. M. Phillips, 16–122, preceded by an excellent introduction by the translator, 2–15.

4. CWE, 1:31.

5. CWE, 1:42, 46. A few years later, Erasmus, repeating his defense of Valla, calls Poggio "a petty clerk so uneducated that even if he were not indecent he would still not be worth reading": CWE, 2:92.

6. CWE, 2:48.

7. For an interpretation of the meaning of this treatise, see Chapter 13 in these volumes, "Lorenzo Valla."

8. See Phillips, CWE, 23:11–15.

9. CWE, 32:25.

10. On Standonck and his work of reform, see A. Renaudet, *Préréforme et hu-*

manisme à Paris pendant les premières guerres d'Italie, 1494–1517 (Paris, 2d ed. 1953), esp. 115–54.

11. For a critical edition, see ASD, 1.2 (1971), ed. J.-C. Margolin, 153–580; trans. in CWE, 25.

12. Both are translated in CWE, 24.

13. For a critical text of *On the Education of Boys*, see ASD, 1.2 (1971), ed. J.-C. Margolin, 1–78; and *On the Method of Study*, ASD, 1.2 (1979), ed. J.-C. Margolin, 79–152. The English translation is from *Desiderius Erasmus: Concerning the Aim and Method of Education*, ed. W. H. Woodward (New York, 1904, reprinted 1964), 205–6. *On the Education of Boys* is translated in full, 180–222. A new translation has appeared in CWE, 26, trans. B. C. Verstraete, 295–346.

14. For an account of a prank More played on Erasmus during this first encounter involving the future King Henry VIII, see CWE, 1:230. More was full of pranks. Erasmus recounts a later one in *The Colloquies of Erasmus*, trans. C. R. Thompson (Chicago, 1965), 230–37.

15. In addition to the comments below on these lectures, see Chapter 17 in these volumes, "Humanism in England."

16. On this difference, see R. McKeon, "Renaissance and Method in Philosophy," in *Studies in the History of Ideas*, 3 vols. (New York, 1918–35), 3:37–114. Pages 71–95 are devoted to Erasmus; see especially 92–93.

17. CWE, 1:206–11.

18. CWE, 1:211–12.

19. CWE, 1:212–19. In fact, Colet was more in line with the Fathers than Erasmus, whose views—ironically—resembled those of medieval theologians. See J. D. Tracy, "Humanists Among the Scholastics: Erasmus, More and Lefèvre d'Etaples on the Humanity of Christ," *Erasmus of Rotterdam Society Yearbook* 5 (1985): 30–51.

20. CWE, 1:249–50.

21. See *The Adages of Erasmus*, ed. and trans. M. M. Phillips (Cambridge, 1964). The details on which I draw are taken from this volume, which contains an excellent introduction and a translation of all the adages on which Erasmus made an extended commentary. The adages will soon be published in full in CWE, 31–33. A critical edition of some of them has appeared, ASD, 2.5 and 2.6 (1981), ed. F. Heinimann and E. Kienzle.

22. CWE, 2:25.

23. CWE, 1:295–96.

24. EE, 4:508, lines 24–29; trans. in *Desiderius Erasmus: Christian Humanism and the Reformation*, ed. J. C. Olin (New York, 1965), 164–92, at 166.

25. On the relation of Erasmus to all three of these Fathers (Origen, Augustine, Jerome), see D. Gorce, "La patristique dans la réforme d'Erasme," in *Festgabe Joseph Lortz*, ed. E. Iserloh and P. Manns, 2 vols. (Baden-Baden, 1958), 1:233–76. On his relation to Jerome, see E. H. Harbison, *The Christian Scholar in the Age of the Reformation* (New York, 1956), chap. 3; W. Schwarz, *Principles and Problems of Biblical Translation* (Cambridge,

1955), chap. 5; and now E. F. Rice, Jr., *Saint Jerome in the Renaissance* (Baltimore, 1985), chap. 5. On the influence of Augustine on Erasmus, see C. Béné, *Erasme et Saint Augustin* (Geneva, 1969). On the influence of Origen, see A. Godin, *Erasme et Origène* (Paris, 1983).

26. A critical Latin text of the *Enchiridion* has been published in *Desiderius Erasmus Roterodamus Ausgewählte Werke*, ed. A. Holborn and H. Holborn (Munich, 1933), 1–136, reprinted in AS, 1. There have been several translations. The one I use is *The Enchiridion of Erasmus*, trans. R. Himelick (Bloomington, IN, 1963); the passage is cited on p. 54. For studies of this treatise, see A. Auer, *Die vollkommene Frömmigkeit des Christen* (Düsseldorf, 1954); Kohls, *Theologie des Erasmus*, chap. 3; and idem, "The Principal Theological Thoughts in the 'Enchiridion,' " in *Essays on the Works of Erasmus*, ed. R. L. DeMolen (New Haven, 1978), 61–82.

27. *Enchiridion*, trans. Himelick, 53.

28. Ibid., 51.

29. Ibid., 56.

30. Ibid., 73.

31. Ibid., 101, 104.

32. Ibid., 119.

33. CWE, 2:93.

34. CWE, 2:96.

35. A translation universally thought to have been made by Erasmus in England prior to 1506 (recently published: *Un inédit d'Erasme: La première version du nouveau testament copiée par Pierre Meghen 1506–1509*, ed. H. Gibaud [Angers, 1982]) has now been shown to have been made in Basel, ca. 1514, published in the 1516 edition of the New Testament and subsequently revised for the 1519 and later editions. See A. J. Brown, "The Date of Erasmus' Latin Translation of the New Testament," *Transactions of the Cambridge Bibliographical Society* 8:4 (1984): 351–80.

36. See C. R. Thompson, *Translations of Lucian by Erasmus and St. Thomas More* (Ithaca, NY, 1940).

37. CWE, 2:125. On Erasmus's Italian journey, see R. Marcel, "Les dettes d'Erasme envers l'Italie," in *Actes du congrès Erasme, 1969* (Amsterdam and London, 1971), 159–73; P. de Nolhac, *Erasme en Italie* (Paris, 1898); and A. Renaudet, *Erasme et l'Italie* (Geneva, 1954).

38. The work has been translated: *Julius Excluded from Heaven*, trans. P. Pascal, ed. J. K. Sowards (Bloomington, IN, 1968). Sowards's introduction, 7–32, is a good orientation to this text.

39. *Adages*, ed. and trans. Phillips, 185–186. On Erasmus and the Aldine academy, see D. J. Geanakoplos, "Erasmus and the Aldine Academy of Venice," *Greek, Roman and Byzantine Studies* 3 (1960): 107–34; idem, *Greek Scholars in Venice: Studies in the Dissemination of Greek Learning from Byzantium to the West* (Cambridge, MA, 1962), 256–78.

40. *Adages*, ed. and trans. Phillips, 197–98.

41. CWE, 2:141.

42. CWE, 3:93–99.

43. For a critical text, see ASD, 4.3 (1979), ed. C. H. Miller. There are many modern translations of *The Praise of Folly*. The recent edition by the editor of the critical text in ASD supersedes all previous editions: *The Praise of Folly*, ed. and trans. C. H. Miller (New Haven, 1979).

The literature on *Folly* is immense. Beginners may consult *Twentieth Century Interpretations of The Praise of Folly*, ed. K. Williams (Englewood Cliffs, NJ, 1966). Those who wish to pursue folly further may consult A. E. Douglas, "Erasmus as a Satirist," in *Erasmus*, ed. T. A. Dorey (London, 1970), 31–54; W. Kaiser, *Praisers of Folly: Erasmus, Rabelais, Shakespeare* (Cambridge, MA, 1963), 19–100; B. Könneker, *Wesen und Wandlung der Narrenidee im Zeitalter des Humanismus: Brant, Murner, Erasmus* (Wiesbaden, 1966), chap. 5; and, most recently, M. A. Screech, *Ecstasy and the Praise of Folly* (London, 1980).

44. CWE, 2:161.

45. *Folly*, ed. and trans. Miller, 20 (a paraphrase from Sophocles's *Ajax*, 554).

46. Ibid., 60, 59.

47. Ibid., 57.

48. Ibid., 44–45.

49. Ibid., 76.

50. Ibid., 77–117.

51. *Adages*, ed. and trans. Phillips, 269–300.

52. Ibid., 269.

53. Ibid., 277.

54. This image is mentioned twice by Erasmus in writings dating from this period; EE, 3:368–71, trans. Olin, *Christian Humanism*, 118–23; and *Ratio verae theologiae*, in *Ausgewählte Werke*, ed. Holborn, 202–4.

55. *Folly*, ed. and trans. Miller, 132.

56. Ibid., 136.

57. See above, note 39. See also Sister M. G. Thompson, C.S.J., "The Range of Irony in Three Visions of Judgment: Erasmus' *Julius Exclusus*, Donne's *Ignatius His Conclave*, and Lucian's *Dialogues of the Dead*," *Erasmus of Rotterdam Society Yearbook* 3 (1983): 1–22.

58. *Adages*, ed. and trans. Phillips, 106–19.

59. On Erasmus's view of women, see E. Schneider, *Das Bild der Frau im Werk des Erasmus* (Basel, 1955).

60. *Adages*, ed. and trans. Phillips, 213–25.

61. For a critical text, see ASD, 4.1 (1974), ed. O. Herding, 95–220; see ibid., 1–94 for Erasmus's panegyric to Prince Philip of Austria (1504). The *Education of a Christian Prince* has been translated by L. K. Born (New York, 1936; repr. hardcover, 1964; paper, 1968). Born's introduction to the translation, 1–130, is very helpful. On Erasmus's political "opinions," see J. D. Tracy, *The Politics of Erasmus* (Toronto, 1978); and on Renaissance political thought generally, Q. Skinner, *The Foundations of Modern Political Thought*, vol. 1, *The Renaissance* (Cambridge, 1978).

62. *Adages*, ed. and trans. Phillips, 265–67.

63. Ibid., 267–69.

64. Ibid., 269–96, especially 285, 286.

65. Ibid., 300–308.

66. Ibid., 308–53. For a critical edition of *The Complaint of Peace*, see ASD, 4.2 (1977), ed. O. Herding, 1–100; and AS, 5:359–451. On Erasmus's views of war, see R. P. Adams, *The Better Part of Valor: More, Erasmus, Colet and Vives on Humanism, War and Pece, 1496–1535* (Seattle, 1962).

67. Erasmus's Greek New Testament established him as the most famous man of letters in Europe, and it was the work on which he believed his fame would ultimately rest. Yet his was actually not the first Greek text compiled. That task had been completed in 1514 by scholars working under the direction of Cardinal Ximenes in Alcalá, Spain. But the pages of that text were printed without being bound and distributed. When the cardinal died late in 1517 the project was momentarily halted. It was not until 1520 that the pope ordered the volumes to be bound and circulated. By that time Erasmus's second edition of 1519 had been published. The Spanish edition was superior to that of Erasmus in critical scholarship. Erasmus did not have the best Greek manuscripts with which to work, and in one case, when the verses were missing in the Greek text, he supplied them himself, translating back into Greek from the Latin!

68. See A. Bludau, *Die beiden ersten Erasmus-Ausgaben des Neuen Testaments und ihre Gegner* (Freiburg, 1902). See also Rabil, *Erasmus and the New Testament*, 83–95 and sources cited there.

69. *Ausgewählte Werke*, ed. Holborn and Holborn, 251.

70. Ibid., 179. On the *Ratio*, see G. G. Chantraine, S.J., "The 'Ratio verae theologiae' (1518)," in *Essays on the Works of Erasmus*, ed. DeMolen, 179–85.

71. See Rabil, *Erasmus and the New Testament*, chap. 3.

72. Ibid., 115–27.

73. Ibid., 122 for citations to Latin sources quoted in this passage.

74. Erasmus's paraphrases of Romans and Galatians have now appeared in CWE, 42. See the various introductions, especially Payne, Rabil, and Smith, "The 'Paraphrases' of Erasmus," xi–xix. See also J. Chomarat, "Grammar and Rhetoric in the Paraphrases of the Gospels by Erasmus," *Erasmus of Rotterdam Society Yearbook* 1 (1981): 30–68; A. Rabil, Jr., "Erasmus' 'Paraphrases of the New Testament,' " in *Essays on the Works of Erasmus*, ed. DeMolen, 145–61.

75. A critical text has been published in *Ausgewählte Werke*, ed. Holborn and Holborn, 139–49. There is a translation in *Christian Humanism*, ed. Olin, 92–106. The passage paraphrased here is on p. 97.

76. On Reuchlin, see L. W. Spitz, *The Religious Renaissance of the German Humanists* (Cambridge, MA, 1963), chap. 4.

77. CWE, 3:91.

78. The letters of Rubeanus and Hutten have been published in English, *On the Eve of the Reformation*, trans. F. G. Stokes, new introduction by H. Holborn (New York, 1964).

79. In the 1522 edition of his *Colloquies* Erasmus wrote "The Apotheosis of Johann Reuchlin," in which Jerome is represented as escorting Reuchlin to

heaven and presenting him with a robe of three colors to signify his knowledge of the three languages (*Colloquies*, trans. Thompson, 79–86). On the establishment of the trilingual college see the monumental work of H. de Vocht, *History of the Foundation and the Rise of the Collegium Trilingue Lovaniense, 1517–1550*, 4 vols. (Louvain, 1951–55).

80. Translated in *Christian Humanism*, ed. Olin, 55–91. On Erasmus's responses to criticisms of *Folly*, see M. P. Gilmore, " 'Apologiae': Erasmus' Defenses of Folly," in *Essays on the Works of Erasmus*, ed. DeMolen, 111–23.

81. For More's Letter, see *St. Thomas More: Selected Letters*, ed. E. F. Rogers (New Haven, 2d ed. 1967), 6–64.

82. See Bainton, *Erasmus of Christendom*, 136–37, and sources cited there.

83. CWE, 5:367–83 (no. 810); 6:226–30 (no. 914), 61–65 (no. 155), 66–69 (no. 856), 196–214 (no. 906). For a recent discussion, see G. Bedouelle, *Le Quincuplex Psalterium de Lefèvre d'Etaples: Un guide de lecture* (Geneva, 1979), 127–34.

84. CWE, 6:281–83.

85. CWE, 6:295–99.

86. EE, 4:1153, 362, lines 15–18.

87. EE, 4:1155, note.

88. *Erasmi opuscula*, ed. Ferguson, 338–61.

89. *Colloquies*, trans. Thompson, 177–89.

90. There have been two critical editions, one in *Quellenschriften zur Geschichte des Protestantismus*, 8 vols. (Leipzig, 1904–10): vol. 8 ed. J. Walter (Leipzig, 1910, reprinted 1935); and AS, 4:1–195, with a German translation. The literature on this debate is voluminous from the mid-nineteenth century to the present, most of it highly partisan. Two essays by contemporary scholars that provide a good starting point for understanding the positions of each of the protagonists are B. A. Gerrish, " 'De Libero Arbitrio' (1524): Erasmus on Piety, Theology, and the Lutheran Dogma," in *Essays on the Works of Erasmus*, ed. DeMolen, 187–209; and W. Schwarz, "Studies in Luther's Attitude Towards Humanism," *Journal of Theological Studies 6* (1955): 66–76. See also the introduction to *Luther and Erasmus: Free Will and Salvation*, ed. and trans. E. G. Rupp et al. (London, 1969).

91. Ibid., 8.

92. Ibid., 9–10.

93. Ibid., 18–19.

94. Ibid., 6.

95. A critical edition of the Latin text has been published in ASD, 1.3 (1972), ed. L.-E. Halkin, F. Bierlaire, and R. Hoven; *Colloquies*, trans. Thompson, is a complete translation into contemporary English. Thompson's introductions are an excellent guide into the colloquies. See also Sister M. G. Thompson, C.S.J., "As Bones to the Body: The Scope of 'Inventio' in the 'Colloquies' of Erasmus," in *Essays on the Works of Erasmus*, ed. DeMolen, 163–78.

96. A critical edition of the *Ciceronianus* has been published in ASD, 1.2

(1971), ed. P. Mesnard, 581–710. Critical editions have also appeared together with an Italian translation: *Il Ciceroniano o dello stile migliore*, ed. and trans. A. Gambaro (Brescia, 1965); and with a French translation: "Essai sur le 'Ciceronianus' d'Erasme, avec une édition critique," ed. and trans. J.-G. Michel (Ph.D. diss., Univ. of Paris, 1951). There is an English translation, *The Imitation of Cicero*, trans. I. Scott (New York, 1910), which also discusses some of the major figures mentioned in the work.

97. Erasmus gives an example of what the outcome of such an attempt would be: see *Imitation of Cicero*, trans. Scott, 67–68.

98. Ibid., 105.

99. See M. M. Phillips, "Erasmus and the Classics," in *Erasmus*, ed. Dorey, 1–30, at 14.

100. *Colloquies*, trans. Thompson, 549.

101. There are indications that this work is at last receiving its due among interpreters of Erasmus. See R. G. Kleinhans, " 'Ecclesiastes sive de Ratione Concionandi,' " in *Essays on the Works of Erasmus*, ed. DeMolen, 253–66; and J. W. O'Malley, S.J., "Erasmus and the History of Sacred Rhetoric: The 'Ecclesiastes' of 1535," *Erasmus of Rotterdam Society Yearbook* 5 (1985), 1–29.

24 ❧ HUMANISM IN CROATIA
Dražen Budiša

DURING THE FIFTEENTH AND SIXTEENTH CENTURIES CROATIA WAS the setting of numerous disturbances, conflicts, and wars. "Blood and diaspora," the words that the historian of Croatian literature Mihovil Kombol applied to sixteenth-century developments in northern Croatia, were largely true for the whole Croatian area, and not only in the sixteenth century. The conflicts between magnates and cities, nobility and king, and the Venetian Republic and the Hungaro-Croat kings, as well as problems posed by dynastic struggles and, above all, by the Turkish danger, are the essential features of the social, cultural, and political circumstances of that age.

In the first half of the fifteenth century Venice took Dalmatian cities and islands and extended its possessions into the interior of Istria. Henceforth Croat political life and the appellation "Croatian" was increasingly extended north into the western portion of medieval Slavonia, the area between the Drava River and Mount Gvozd, which was regularly called Croatia from the sixteenth century on. The Turks started penetrating Croatia from the beginning of the fifteenth century, and with the fall of Bosnia (1463) and the defeat of the Croat army on the field of Krbava (1493) there commenced, in the words of the sixteenth-century chronicler Ivan Tomašić, "the first ruin of the Kingdom of Croatia." The Turkish danger cast a shadow over all the Croatian lands. The main direction of Turkish attacks went across the Lika and Krbava into the Modruš region, then all the way to Istria and the Slovenian provinces. Although the Turks made forays into the environs of Dalmatian cities in the possession of Venice, these cities nevertheless were favored by a relative peace and far more advantageous conditions for economic, social, and cultural development. This condition applied especially to Dubrovnik (Ragusa), the city that recognized the supreme authority of the Hungaro-Croat kings from the fourteenth century and later paid tribute to the Turks, but for all that was an independent republic and the most powerful economic and cultural center on the eastern coast of the Adriatic. Other important economic and cultural centers in Dalmatia were Split, Trogir, Šibenik,

This essay has been translated from Croatian by Professor Ivo Banac, Yale University.

Zadar, and the cities on the Dalmatian islands. Northern Croatia, on the contrary, became the European defensive belt against Turkish onslaughts, a veritable *antemurale christianitatis,* the site of centuries-long wars with the Ottoman Empire and a land in which there were no favorable conditions for social development.

Small wonder that the individual portions of quartered Croatia, variously under Turks, Venetians, and Hungaro-Croat kings of various dynasties—and after 1527 the Habsburgs—in the territory administered by the Croatian ban (*prorex*), and in the independent Republic of Dubrovnik, were not equally receptive to cultural and spiritual developments in the age of humanism and the Renaissance. This cultural-historical period was to leave a faint trace in northern Croatia, whereas the European fifteenth- and sixteenth-century spiritual movements provoked a strong response in southern Croatia.

The most important characteristic of humanism was its appeal throughout Europe. Even so, the reception of humanist ideas in individual European countries was quite different. Local circumstances and distinctive cultural traditions conditioned the fact that every European community in which humanism exercised influence received this influence in relation to its own local characteristics. It is sufficient to note here that one of the most widespread motifs in the works of Croat humanists was the Turkish menace, this thematic preoccupation resulting from the fact that the Turks occupied a portion of Croatia and continuously threatened the rest. Numerous Croat humanists wrote epistles, poems, and discourses against the Turks. Anti-Turkish orations, as a special type of humanist eloquence, were widespread throughout Europe, but the *orationes contra Turcas* of the Croat humanists have the breadth of authentic experience, because these orations were shaped in effect by the reality of the Turkish threat. They were addressed to popes and emperors and spoken before ecclesiastical and state assemblies with the aim of interesting Europe in an anti-Turkish Christian coalition.[1] It is quite likely that the Turkish menace and the constant psychosis of fear that the destruction of Christian civilization by the Ottoman invaders engendered also determined two essential characteristics in the work of the Croat humanists: the more pronounced utilitarian-practical tendency in literary works and the more explicit dependence on the Christian tradition. It is the unanimous opinion of students of Croat humanism that its ties with Christian tradition were deeper than elsewhere in Europe. This "ideational conservatism" of Croat humanism, as Mihovil Kombol puts it, was a genuine appellation for one of its chief characteristics.[2] It should be stressed, however, that ties with religious tradition were not specific to Croat humanists alone. This tendency was general, whether the discussion centers on humanists who were the heirs of medieval Catholicism or on their younger colleagues who adhered to Lutheranism and Calvinism. It should be added that our view of European humanism in good part derives from the philosophers of the Enlightenment, who saw the humanist cultural movement as a radical break with the medieval faith— a view that is considerably distorted. Modern research into the relationship of the humanists to the Christian tradition demonstrates that the humanist rootedness in that tradition was greater than is usually thought.[3]

Cultural tradition, too, was an important factor in establishing the character of the reception of humanist ideas in various European countries. The fact that a number of Croat humanist authors—and among them Marko Marulić, the greatest of them all—wrote in both Latin and Croatian is undoubtedly based on the old tradition of the written word in popular language, something that among the Croats can be traced to the first known written monuments from the eleventh century. These works were rich in number, polygraphic in form (they were written in Glagolitic, Bosnian Cyrillic, and Roman alphabets), and, in the medieval manner, both sacred and secular in content. Šimun Kožičić-Benja of Zadar (d. 1535) is an excellent example of a writer educated both in the humanist tradition and in the medieval tradition of Croatian literature. This bishop of Modruš founded the press at Rijeka (Fiume) in 1531, where Croat Glagolitic books were printed; but at the same time he was a Latin author and orator.

The extensive tradition of Latin literary activity among the Croats was essential for the receptivity to humanist ideas in the Croatian lands. The links with classical antiquity were not severed everywhere, especially not in those Dalmatian cities in which the Roman population had been more numerous and had survived longer. Soon after their settlement the Croats, too, accepted the Latin language. The continuity of Latin in public and ecclesiastical affairs dates to the national dynasty, something that is evident from numerous documents, ranging from Latin records of the Croat court chancellery to Latin codices produced in native scriptoria. The indirect evidence of Latin continuity is the numerous medieval manuscripts in the Croat recension of Church Slavonic that were based on Latin models. It is a paradoxical cultural-historical fact that Latin "played the role of the indirect protector of national language" among the Croats.[4] The large role of Latin in the history of Croat printing is evident from the impressive number of some five thousand units recorded in the bibliography of Croat Latinity from the fifteenth century to 1848.[5] Vladimir Vratović's pregnant words speak to the embodiment of domestic Latin literature within the framework of Croatian national literature:

Literature in the Croatian idiom shares with Latinism a significant portion of universal motifs, just as Latinism shares with literature in the Croatian idiom a significant portion of national themes. Croat Latinism safeguards—if we may be allowed to express ourselves freely—duality in unity: duality with regard to its national and international form, unity with regard to Croatian literature as a whole.[6]

Several key starting points for this overview of humanism in Croatia ought to be explained further in order to prevent any possible misunderstandings. The humanist movement in southern Croatia, tied as it was to the developed urban centers on the Adriatic coast, commenced pretty much at the same time as Croatian Renaissance literature in the vernacular. The Italian Renaissance succeeded in awakening very quickly the latent cultural potential of the patrician-burgher stratum in the Dalmatian cities. Inspired by Italian Renaissance models and basing themselves on a very old written culture in the vernacular—a culture that already in the Middle Ages expressed itself also in various artistic forms—Croat writers were creating a Croatian Renaissance literature in the vernacular in the course of the fifteenth and sixteenth centuries. This literature was developed parallel to humanist Latinism, which not only failed to stem the growth of Croat vernacular literature, but, in fact, helped advance it by means of its application of classic poetry's aesthetic canons. In addition to the creative activity in Latin and Croatian that flourished in the Dalmatian cities in the period of the Renaissance and later, creativity in the Italian language was also widespread. For the Croat humanists Italian played a role similar to that of Latin. The highly developed philosophical-scientific structure of Italian and its widespread use offered extensive possibilities of intellectual communication to its users. The use of Italian in the Dalmatian cities and in the works of Croat humanists had many causes. Among them were the proximity of Italy—that fountainhead and center of humanism—the political subjugation of parts of Croatia to the Venetian Republic, the remnants of Roman population in the Dalmatian cities, the frequent arrival of Italian teachers (*magistri humanitatis*) to the eastern Adriatic shores, and the frequent departure of many Croats to Italian cities in order to pursue their education.

It is therefore important to stress that the overview of literary creativity among Croat humanists is only a survey of a portion of the literary creativity in the fifteenth- and sixteenth-century Dalmatian cities. The composition of Latin verses modeled on those of ancient writers was thriving within the walls of these cities during the same period that Croatian poetry, too, was acquiring a distinct artistic shape.

In addition to the Croat humanist authors who were active in their homeland, Croat humanists counted within their ranks an even larger group of those who lived abroad, as well as those authors of foreign origin (Jews, Greeks, but mainly Italians) whose work was connected with Croat cities and lands. At the same time we must be conscious that the national perspective in the study and presentation of such cultural manifestations as humanism is nevertheless a methodological construction. Although there exist numerous proofs of the cultural and emotional connections of the humanists to their native lands, their "area" was nevertheless determined more by the frontiers of the "republic of letters" than by any other ethnic or political borders. Internationalized cultural creativity was the hallmark of genuine humanist centers. The most beautiful example was sixteenth-century Buda, in which the representatives of many European nations worked as cultural producers. Though diminutive in comparison, the humanist centers on the Dalmatian coast and islands were similar. A list of scholars of foreign origin who worked in these centers would be long. A few should be mentioned. Italian humanist Giovanni Conversini of Ravenna lived in Dubrovnik at the end of the fourteenth century. He complained about the low cultural level of the Ragusan community. But the cultural circumstances changed very quickly: in the fifteenth and early sixteenth centuries Dalmatian youths were taught by Italian humanists Filippo de Diversis, Tideo Acciarini, Marino Becichemo (Romanized Albanian), Daniele Clario, and Palladio Fosco. The famed Neolatin poet of Greek origin, Michael Marullus, lived for a while in Dubrovnik, as did several noted Jewish humanists. Nevertheless, high humanist education could not be pursued in the Dalmatian cities. Almost all Croat humanists studied in Italian humanist centers, which obtains equally for humanists from the coastal cities and for those from northern Croatia. Only a few Protestants studied in German universities.

The literary and practical activity of the Croat humanists was noted for all the essential features of humanism as a cultural-historical movement, namely, the awakening of interest in Greco-Roman antiquity, a positive attitude toward the values of earthly life, aspiration to versatile education, attempts to synthesize the thought of the ancients with the Christian tradition, opposition to authority and dogmatism, individualism, and the longing for new insights. Needless to say, these features of humanism were manifested differently in various humanistic disciplines, for example in literature and philosophy, historiography and philology, just as each humanist assimilated the new spirit of the age into his work in a distinctive, individual way.

In this survey of Croat humanism—similar to the approach of

Kruno Krstić in the *Encyclopedia of Yugoslavia*—I shall assume the existence of three different circles: the coastal circle with the developed humanist centers from which numerous humanist authors came and in which they worked; the humanist circle of Croat writers at Buda; and the circle of Croat humanists who operated within the framework of Protestantism.[7]

＊　＊　＊

Dubrovnik, which the poet Ivan Vidal called in one of his sixteenth-century epistles the "crown of Croat cities," was the most outstanding center of Croat Renaissance literature in the vernacular and of humanist literature in Latin and, in good part, Italian.

The most important humanist writers of Dubrovnik were Ilija Crijević and Jakov Bunić. They labored in the fifteenth and sixteenth centuries at the same time as many other Ragusan writers who wrote in Croatian (Šiško Menčetić, Djore Držić, Andrija Čubranović, Mavro Vetranović, Nikola Nalješković, Marin Držić, Dinko Ranjina, Dinko Zlatarić, and more).

Ilija Crijević (Aelius Lampridius Cervinus, 1463–1520) was educated first of all in Dubrovnik and then in Ferrara and Rome, where he attended the academy of Pomponio Leto, one of the best-known humanists of his age. In 1484 Crijević was crowned poet laureate for his youthful poetry, as the humanist Domizio Palladio noted in one of his poems.[8] After his return from Italy to Dubrovnik, Crijević continued his literary work in his native city and maintained ties with noted European humanists, though his personal life was for a time marked by failure, unfulfilled ambitions, and scandals. He held many offices in his native republic, serving as a lawyer, castellan, and rector of the city school. Having been widowed he became a priest.

Crijević was a poet, orator, and lexicographer of extensive interests. His extant poetic opus includes some 240 poems. They include love poems with the accent on erotic and naturalistic motifs, elegies, epigrams, epistolary poems, odes, and hymns. Except for three epigrams published in the book *Natura caelestium spirituum* of Juraj Dragišić (Florence, 1499), all of his poems were preserved only in manuscript. They were published in recent times in the original and in a Croatian translation. Although Crijević "was not a poet of strong internal conflicts, contradictions, or spiritual reflections,"[9] his poetry was nevertheless characterized by spontaneous lyricism, extensive erudition, and rich linguistic utterance. Marin Franičević, a historian of Croatian Renaissance literature, stressed that Ilija Crijević was one of the best Croat

Latinists, more productive, diversified, and untamed than Juraj Šižgorić, Ivan Česmički (Janus Pannonius), and Karlo Pucić. He was a poet expressly tied to the traditions of antiquity. Although it is easy enough to detect classical (Catullus, Tibullus, Propertius, Ovid) and humanist models (such as Angelo Poliziano and Giovanni Pontano) in his works, he asserted his own independence as a writer.[10]

In addition to poetry Crijević tried his hand at both declamation and acting, performing in the plays of Plautus and Terence at the Quirinal Academy, and at the writing of discourses and letters. He, too, just as did many other Croat humanists and Renaissance writers, summoned the West to struggle for the liberation of the South Slavs, and with that aim wrote epistles to Pope Leo X and the Hungaro-Croat king Ladislas II. Particularly notable among his prose works was the Latin encyclopedic *Lexicon* (Bibliotheca Marciana, Venice), which contains explanations of various philosophical, astronomical, medical, and grammatical concepts.

Immersed in antiquity and contemporary humanistic literature, Crijević adored the Latin language. Small wonder that he disparaged his mother tongue—which in his time in the works of Šiško Menčetić and Djore Držić acquired an increasingly refined artistic form—denigrating it as *scythica lingua* (Scythian language) and *stribiligo illyrica* (Illyrian solecism).

Ilija Crijević's free-thinking spirit, relieved from the obsessions of medieval authority, stood in sharp contrast to the spirit of the poetry of Jakov Bunić (Jacobus Bonus, 1469–1534), another important Ragusan Latinist at the turn of the fifteenth century. Bunić, too, was first educated in Dubrovnik and then continued his studies in Florence, Padua, and Bologna. He traveled as a merchant through many European countries, Egypt, and Asia Minor. His creative opus consists of two Latin epic poems and several letters. In 1490 he published in Rome the work *De raptu Cerberi,* which he wrote as a young man in Dubrovnik, before his schooling in Italy. This first epic poem among the Croats was mythological in content and deals with the Greek story of how Hercules overwhelmed Cerberus. In his descriptions Bunić's model was the tragedy of Seneca, but his style and language were basically Vergilian. He clad Greek myth in Christian garb, Hercules clearly standing for Christ, as is evident from the title of the poem's second edition (Rome, 1526), which includes the phrase "sub figura Herculis Christi praeludium." Together with this second edition, Bunić's principal work, *De vita et gestis Christi,* was also published. This was an epic poem in which the life of Christ was described in ten thousand hexameters. Written in the spirit of the

Counter-Reformation, it was, according to Branimir Glavičić, the first Counter-Reformation epic poem anywhere. Writing about Bunić's work, Glavičić noted:

> Bunić's epic poems to a certain degree have retained their literary quality to our day. This is to say that Bunić was the author of a great many very beautiful, original, and developed comparisons, as well as sincere religious-lyrical reflections. In his numerous descriptions of the sea he demonstrated that he was one of the best mannerists of older [Croatian] literature. His high artistic qualities were the main reason why a new edition of this [Croat] poet was contemplated during the 1920s in Italy. V. Zabughin, an excellent authority on Renaissance literature, called [Bunić] one of the "greatest Christian poets of the Renaissance."[11]

Another Ragusan humanist writer, Karlo Pucić (Carolus Puteus, 1458–1522), published his Latin verses in the fifteenth century.[12] His *Elegiarum libellus de laudibus Gnesae puellae* was published in Venice, probably in 1495. Josef C. Jireček collected the scanty facts about Pucić's life that were preserved in the Dubrovnik archives,[13] and the description of his book was provided first by Djuro Körbler.[14] The latter author also collected the biographical facts about Damjan Benešić (1477–1539), a Ragusan humanistic poet whose rich inheritance was more significant because of its documentary—as opposed to poetic—value. Ivan Gučetić (1451–1502), somewhat older than Benešić, left behind only a small collection of poems. As for his contemporary Petar Menčetić (1451–1508), the first Ragusan poet laureate, none of his work has been preserved.

Didak Pir (Didacus Pyrrhus or Jacobus Flavius Eboremsis), whose real name was Isaiah Cohen, ought to be mentioned among the sixteenth-century poets from the Republic of Dubrovnik. This exiled Jew from Córdoba, after wandering through Europe, Asia, and Africa, settled in Dubrovnik, where he taught classical languages and literatures until his death. He was not the only newcomer, but only one of many humanists who came to Dubrovnik and the other cities on the eastern coast of the Adriatic, typical of the unending and lively movement of learned men characteristic of the humanist epoch.

The humanist spirit was manifested not only in literary creativity; it was evident, too, in other humanistic, artistic, and scientific disciplines. The contributions of Ragusan humanists hence were also more than literary and embraced works of multifaceted content. They included the ecclesiological treatises of Ivan Stojković (Johannes de Ragusio, ca. 1390–1443), the great adherent of conciliarism;[15] historical commentaries of Ludovik Crijević Tubero (Ludovicus Aloysius de Cerva, 1459–1527); medical works of the other great Ragusan Jew, João Rodriguez (Lusitanus Amatus, 1511–1568); and especially the philosophical treatises of Juraj Dragišić, known in humanistic circles as Georgius Benignus de Salviatis. Dragišić was born in 1490 in Srebrenica (Bosnia). He removed to Dubrovnik in his boyhood, entered the Franciscan order there, and returned to preach and further interest in philosophy through public philosophical disputations. Teacher at the princely courts of Urbino and Florence, member of the Platonic Academy of George Gemistus Pletho, rector of the monastic school in Florence, and professor of philosophy at the University of Pisa, he was one of the most learned men of his time and, in particular, the foremost expert on oriental languages in Europe. Moderate in his Neoplatonism, Dragišić in his works sought to reconcile the Scotist and Thomist schools. A man of liberal inspiration, he defended the progressive thinkers of his time, among them Giovanni Pico della Mirandola, Johann Reuchlin, and Savonarola. Dragišić fiercely opposed the German Dominicans in their aspiration to burn all the copies of the Talmud and other Hebrew books. In philosophy he pursued above all logical questions, having written, mainly in the spirit of John Duns Scotus, several books in that area, notably *Logica nova secundum mentem Scoti* (1480), *Volumen de dialectica nova* (1489), and *Artis dialecticae praecepta vetera ac nova* (1520).[16]

Of the philosophic-theological writers from sixteenth-century Dubrovnik, it is important to mention three members of the Gučetić family: Petar Gučetić (1493–1564), professor at the Sorbonne and Louvain, better known under the nickname of Doctor Illyricus; Ambrozije Gučetić (1563–1632), a philosophy instructor at Dubrovnik; and Nikša (Nikola) Gučetić (1549–1610), author of numerous treatises in natural science, philosophy, metaphysics, politics, and aesthetics. Nikša Gučetić had a fine grasp of classical literature, patristics, and scholastic and contemporary authors, which he used in writing his numerous—but essentially eclectic—works. He assumed the Platonic form for his treatises, regularly writing them as dialogues in which educated Ragusans of his time appeared as his interlocutors, among them his wife Marija née Gundulić, one of the many educated women of sixteenth-century Dubrovnik, who participated (with Cvijeta Zuzorić, Julija Bunić, Paula Gradić, and others) in the cultural life of the republic.

Gučetić depended on Plato not only for his form, but in large part for his teachings, especially in aesthetics, ethics, and the science of social organization. His Platonism, or better Neoplatonism, was diluted by peripatetic philosophy in its various forms. Moreover, in some of his works the influence of Aristotelianism was expressed more than the influence of Plato's philosophy. The most important works of Nikša Gučetić are *Dello stato delle Repubblice* (1591), *Governo della famiglia* (1589), *Dialogo della Bellezza* (1581), and *Dialogo d'Amore* (1581).[17] Philosophical treatises in Italian were also written by Miho Monaldi (ca. 1540–1592), philosophical and mathematical works in Italian and Latin by Antun Medo (1530–1603), and astronomical and philosophical works by Nikola Nalješković (1510–1583), who was far better known as the author of pious, love, and carnival songs, pastoral plays, and comedies in Croatian.[18]

*   *   *

The central figure of the humanist circle of Split was Marko Marulić (Marcus Marullus, 1450–1524), the "father of Croatian literature." He was educated at Split and Padua. He worked as a lawyer in his native city, served as a judge, and was an examiner of notary books. Marulić wrote numerous Latin and Croat works, several of which were published, but a larger number of which were preserved in manuscripts. Some of the latter, discovered only recently, have been published. It is to be hoped that most of the unsolved questions connected with his enormous opus (lost books, contested authorship) will be cleared up in the critical edition of his collected works, the first volume of which was published in his native Split in 1984.[19]

Marulić reaches his ultimate poetic range in his *Judita* or *Istorija svete udovice Judit u versih hrvacki složena* [*A History of the Holy Widow Judith Composed in Croatian Verse*], a work that he wrote in 1501 and published twenty years later. A didactic-moralistic tendency was pronounced in his other Croatian-language works (*Istorija od Suzane* [*A History of Susanna*]; *Dobri nauci* [*Good Counsel*]; *Poklad i korizma* [*Shrovetide and Lent*]; and so on).

The basis of the majority of Marulić's Latin and Croatian works is Christian moral theology. As a result, his work is often characterized as an example of Catholic reaction to humanism, as an opus in which Croat humanism "perished" in its submissiveness to the Catholic church. At the same time, the moral utilitarianism of Marulić's poetry has been explained in terms of his desire to use his work to mobilize his compatriots in the struggle against the Turks, who in his time were devastating the environs of Split, constantly imperiling the city itself. Indeed, there was a tremendous difference between the lascivious-erotic poetry of an Ilija Crijević and the poetic Christian moral theology of Marulić. Nevertheless, Marulić was not just a representative of the medieval Christian spirit; he also represented the humanist spirit. To be sure, the majority of his works are without any trace of pagan classical influence, their

Christian moral orientation being evident. In others, however, the literary stimulus of classical and Renaissance poetry was also conspicuous, though subject to his Christian world view. Among Marulić's Latin works the more important are *Davidias* (the manuscript was discovered in the twentieth century), *De institutione bene vivendi per exempla sanctorum* (1506), *Quinquaginta parabolae* (1510), *Evangelistarium* (1516), and *De humilitate et gloria Christi* (1519). These works, especially *De institutione,* were published in many editions in various languages.

A more pronounced humanistic orientation was manifested in two of Marulić's works, collections of ancient inscriptions, the first ancient inscriptions from Italy and the eastern shore of the Adriatic (*In epigrammata priscorum commentarius*), and the other inscriptions from ancient Salona, the capital of Roman Dalmatia (*Inscriptiones Salonitanae antiquae*). Marulić also wrote an epistle to Pope Hadrian VI in which he, like so many other Croat humanists, called for peace and unity among Christians and joint resistance against the Turks. His humanist orientation is apparent as well in translations into Latin of the works of Petrarch (*Vergine bella*) and Dante (the beginning of the *Inferno*), as well as in his translation from Croatian (old čakavian dialect) into Latin of a manuscript called *The Croat Chronicle,* which his friend Dmine Papalić discovered in Makarska.

It has been noted that many works of Marulić have not been preserved. Among these lost works was *Psychiologia seu de ratione animae humanae,* in which the word "psychology" was for the first time applied to the science of the nature of the human soul or mind.

By means of his enormous opus, which pointed to his exceptional erudition, excellent knowledge of classical, patristic, and contemporary literature, exquisite philological preparation, and pronounced literary talent, Marulić gained a notable reputation in his homeland and in his time was the best-known Croat in Europe.

The names of a number of other humanists from Split are also known. Their preserved inheritance includes only a poem or two, a prose fragment, or the name alone. Kruno Krstić, one of the best scholars of Croat humanism, has put forth a hypothesis that the "enormous portion of humanist manuscripts from Split shared the fate of Marulić's inheritance, which was burned in the course of one of the many epidemics of plague that repeatedly devastated Split."[20] Of the fifteenth- and sixteenth-century humanists from Split the names of Franjo Božićević Natalis, the author of a brief biography of Marulić and of some seventy Latin poems, and Toma Niger (1450–1531) are worth citing. Niger began his education in Split and finished it in Italy. He was a professor of grammar at Hvar and Split, then a diplomat in a mission to Matthias

Corvinus, and later a participant at the Lateran Council. As a diplomat he traveled to the Low Countries, Bohemia, Poland, and Venice. His preserved opus is modest—several epistles, poems, and a historical work about the bishops of Salona and Split (*Pontificum Salonitarum et Spalatensium series*).

Two notable families of Trogir, the Cipico and the Andreis, contributed several prominent humanists. From the Cipicos came paleographer Petar Cipico, his son Kariolan, and Ludovik Cipico, poet and writer of epistles and epigrams. Of the three, Kariolan Cipico (Coriolanus Cepio, 1425–1493) was the most important. He was the author of the description of an anti-Ottoman expedition led by Pietro Mocenigo, the commander of the Venetian fleet and the future doge of Venice, in which Cipico himself participated. This work was published for the first time in Venice in 1477 under the title *Petri Mocenici imperatoris gestarum libri III,* and was later published in several additional editions both in Latin and in Italian. It was recently translated into Croatian.[21] Cipico's work was the first maritime-martial memoir among the Croats and is very important as a historical source. The reason for its frequent reissuing, however, must be sought in Cipico's exceptional command of Latin and in his direct and clear style.

From the Andreis family came Matej Andreis (Matthaeus Andronicus Tragurianus), poet laureate, author of a lascivious poem full of ambiguous metaphors in honor of the wedding of the Polish-Lithuanian king Ladislas II, and Fran Trankvil Andreis (Andronicus Tranquillus Parthenius, 1490–1571), the most prominent humanist of Trogir. Following his studies in Trogir in Dubrovnik, he continued his education in Padua, Siena, Bologna, Perugia, and Rome. Afterward he went to Vienna, Leipzig, and Paris. In these cities and on other journeys he met numerous European humanists. Having failed in obtaining an appointment as a professor at the University of Louvain, he accepted the position of orator, emissary, and diplomat, first at the court of François I and later with King János Zápolyai. Fran Trankvil Andreis on several occasions traveled from London by way of Paris and Vienna to Buda, Cracow, and Istanbul. His itinerary, according to Nikica Kolumbić, was exceptionally involved, even by our contemporary standards. Kolumbić also notes that some fifty works of Andreis are known. They are mainly poetic epistles, letters addressed to acquaintances, rulers, and notables, dialogues on various subjects, and political discourses.[22]

Numerous writers from Šibenik, too, gained renown as humanists. Some were active in Šibenik itself and others, though by origin from Šibenik, worked either in other Croat cities or in other European countries. The senior humanist of Šibenik was Juraj Šižgorić (Georgius Sisgoreus Sibenicensis, ca. 1420–1509). He received his doctoral degree in ecclesiastical and secular law at Padua. After his return to Šibenik, Šižgorić became the general vicar to Luka Tolentić, the bishop of Šibenik, who, because of his various diplomatic missions, was frequently absent from Šibenik. As a result, Šižgorić effectively administered the diocese for over twenty years. Šižgorić's opus was modest. It consists of two collections of poems, the first of which was published in Venice in 1477 under the title *Elegiarum et carminum libri tres* as the first "poetic incunabulum" among the Croats. The second has been preserved only in manuscript, just as, for that matter, has Šižgorić's historico-geographical treatise *De situ Illyriae et civitate Sibenici.*[23]

Ivan Polikarp Severitan (Joannes Barbula Pompilius or Polycarpus Severitanus, 1472–?), another humanist from Šibenik, unlike Šižgorić found no employment in his native city. He complained about his fellow citizens on many occasions in his works, applying to them the most abusive names. Polikarp studied in Rome where he read at the famous academy of Pomponio Leto, whose program included many disciplines, such as history, archaeology, geography, natural science, philosophy, and grammar. Polikarp, too, was crowned with a laurel wreath in Pomponio's academy, either in 1490 or 1491. Before him this honor had been bestowed on two other humanists from Croatian lands, Petar Menčetić and Ilija Crijević. From Rome Polikarp returned to Šibenik and then went on to further studies at Ferrara, Bologna, and again Ferrara. He repeatedly returned home and went off again, lived and taught in various Italian cities, dying "somewhere in Italy." In addition to being a poet, he was polyhistor, philosopher, grammarian, and translator from Greek. The most notable of his works is *Monoregiae ex qua conjicitur totius humanae vitae modus* (Venice, 1522). This short discourse was the first work of a Croat author to deal with political philosophy. It was, in fact, practical advice to a ruler on how to administer and lead a state in peace and war. It was written in the spirit of an Aristotelian-Thomist understanding of society and state.[24]

Antun Vrančić (Antonius Verantius, 1504–1573), poet, diplomat, and scholar, left his native Šibenik for Hungary as a youth of sixteen. Two of his relatives, Petar Berislavić and Ivan Statilić, notable Croats of the age, assumed responsibility for his education. From Hungary Vrančić went to study at Padua, then at Vienna and Cracow. At the age of twenty-six he entered the diplomatic service of János Zápolyai. He remained in his service and in that of Queen Isabella for a full twenty years. During that time he traveled throughout Europe, visiting all of its important centers. On these journeys he became acquainted with many notables, among others with Philipp Melanchthon and Erasmus. In 1549 Vrančić removed to the service of the Habsburgs as the secretary of the Hungaro-Croat King Ferdinand, who named him his counselor and the bishop of Pécs. He spent four years in a diplomatic mission to Istanbul and several months in Asia Minor as an emissary of Ferdinand. It was there that, together with the Dutch humanist Ogier Ghislain de Busbecq, he discovered the tablets with the list of works of the Roman emperor Augustus, the so-called *Monumentum Ancyranum*. In Asia Minor he collected oriental manuscripts, having discovered and translated into Latin the *Tarihi Ali Khan*, an important Turkish chronicle. After his second return from Istanbul, where he was again in the mission of Maximilian II, he became the archbishop of Esztergom and primate of Hungary, and later regent of Hungary.

Vrančić penned most of his scholarly and literary works in Latin, but some variously in Italian, Hungarian, and Croatian. His collected works, which include mainly his correspondence, were published by the Hungarian Academy in the nineteenth century.[25] The large number of his letters (some four hundred have been preserved), their content, and the stature of the addressees, make Vrančić's epistolary opus the richest and most significant among Croat humanists. Among Vrančić's correspondents one encounters the names of Erasmus, Melanchthon, and Ogier-Ghislain de Busbecq, as well as numerous Croats, Ivan Statilić, Stjepan Brodarić, Fran Trankvil Andreis, Nikola Zrinski, and Juraj Drašković. Vladimir Vratović, a student of Croat Latinism, stresses that Vrančić's epistolographical style was based on Pliny. Vratović has also established that in Vrančić's work one can detect the framework of a special epistolographic theory.[26] In addition to Vrančić's letters and poems (*Elegiae* and *Otia*, Cracow, 1537, 1542), one must note his geographical-ethnographic description of Transylvania, Moldavia, and Wallachia (*De situ Transylvaniae, Moldaviae et Transalpinae*), as well as travelogues that were shaped during his voyages across the Ottoman Empire (*Iter Buda Hadrianopolim* and *De itinere et legatione sua Constantinopolitana . . .*).

Faust Vrančić (Faustus Verantius, 1551–1617) was no less notable than his uncle Antun. From Šibenik he went to study at Padua, Venice, Vienna, and Rome. Antun Vrančić then took him to Hungary, where he discharged various administrative and state services. For a time he lived at the court of Rudolf II in Prague. In 1594 he became the bishop of Csanád. He later left the episcopacy and entered the Paulite order. Faust Vrančić was universally educated, and his scholarly interests were extremely versatile, as is evident from his various practical and scholarly works. Among other matters he worked on the regulation of the Tiber, built fountains in Venice, and wrote historical works, along with some on orthography and lexicography, philosophy, and mechanics. His *Dictionarium quinque nobilissimarum Europae linguarum, Latinae, Italicae, Germanicae, Dalmaticae et Ungaricae* (Venice, 1595), was the first extensive Croatian dictionary,[27] and his work *Machinae novae* (Venice, 1595?), in which he brought forth the descriptions and charts of numerous technical inventions, brought him an enviable reputation in the world of science.

*   *   *

It seems that the first manifestations of humanism on the eastern shores of the Adriatic are connected with the city of Zadar. It was there that at the beginning of the fifteenth century Juraj Benja transcribed the works of classical Latin writers and collected ancient epigrams. At the same time a circle of humanists, gathered round the abbey of St. Chrysogonus (Krševan), was also active in Zadar. The central figure of this circle was Abbot Petar Kršava (Crissava), who was known also on account of his restoration of a Roman triumphal arch, which he dated in the humanist manner by reference to Olympic games. In addition to the domestic humanists of Zadar, the abbey attracted many foreign scholars. Zaratine humanists also gathered around Juraj Divinić, the bishop of Nin, who was by origin from Šibenik. At the literary-scientific discussions in his residence there assembled, among others, the poet Jerolim Vidulić, the physician Pamfilo Castaldi, the famous Italian humanist Palladio Fosco, who lived in Zadar for almost twenty years, the philosopher and theologian Kristofor Niger, as well as Donat Civaleli and Jeronim Križan Kršava.

It is characteristic of Zadar, as of the other cultural centers on the eastern coast of the Adriatic, that humanist literary activity in Latin was accompanied by the flowering of Croatian literature. Sixteenth-century Zadar gave several important persons to the history of Croat letters, notably Petar Zoranić, Juraj Baraković, Šimun Budinić, and Brno Karnarutić.

Federik Grisogono (Fredericus Chrysogonus, 1472–1538), philosopher, mathematician, astrologer, and physician, was also from Zadar. He studied mathematics, philosophy, and medicine at Padua, and after earning a doctorate he became a professor of astrology and mathematics at the University of Padua. He published two of his works in Venice. The first, *Speculum astronomicum terminans intellectum humanum in omni scientia*, dealt with geometry, arithmetic, astronomy, and music, the four subjects of the quadrivium. The second, *De modo collegiandi, prognosticandi et curandi febres, necnon de humana felicitate ac denique de fluxu et refluxu maris* (Venice, 1528), was a discourse of heterogeneous content written in the spirit of Plato's philosophy of nature, which in the fifteenth and sixteenth centuries was increasingly displacing Aristotle's, dominant in the Middle Ages.[28]

The philosophical turn away from Aristotelianism to Platonism was at the foundation of the philosophy of the foremost Croat Renaissance philosopher Franjo Petrić (Franciscus Patricius or Francesco Patrizi, 1529–1597), one of the pleiad of humanists who hailed from the islands of the Adriatic. Petrić was born on Cres (Cherso). At first autodidactic, he later studied at Venice, Ingolstadt, and Padua. He roamed Italy, spent seven years on Cyprus, returned to Italy, and taught Plato's philosophy first at Ferrara, later at Rome. Petrić wrote some sixty works in Latin and Italian, mainly on philosophical subjects, but also on literature, history, theory of music, military science, mathematics, and other disciplines. He was one of the greatest representatives of sixteenth-century philosophical thought. Like so many other Renaissance philosophers (Pletho, Bessarion, Ficino, Pico della Mirandola) he was a follower of that strain of Renaissance philosophy that proceeded from Plato in its opposition to the scholastic tradition. Although his philosophy was antithetical to Aristotelianism, its bounds were not marked simply by rejection of the latter, but by his affirmation of Plato's philosophy and his attempt to prove that Platonism was closer to Christianity than Aristotelianism. Petrić was an original philosopher with his own philosophical system. His conceptions were close to those of Girolamo Cardano (1501–1576), Bernardino Telesio (1529–1588), and Giordano Bruno (1548–1600). Moreover, according to the historian of philosophy Friedrich Überweg, Petrić influenced Bruno. The basis of his emanational system of philosophy, according to which the four basic forms of emanation correspond to the four basic philosophical disciplines, Petrić set forth, as he himself noted, "with his own Patrician method" in his principal work *Nova de universis philosophia* (Ferrara, 1591), which has recently been translated into Croatian.[29] In addition to his numerous original works Petrić translated from Greek into Latin and was engaged in the publication of other authors. Thanks to him a volume entitled *Della mercatura et del mercante perfetto* by the Dubrovnik author Benko Kotruljić (Benedetto Cotrugli, 1400–1468) was published in Venice in 1573. It was the first systematic work on trade and accounting in which the author argued that merchants must be perfectly cognizant of grammar and rhetoric and directed them to the study of Cicero's oratory.[30]

There were no significant centers of humanist life on the island of Cres, the home of Franjo Petrić, nor on the other islands of the northern Adriatic (Krk, Lošinj, Pag, Rab), nor indeed on the northern Adriatic coast. In these areas Glagolitic literary activity lasted for centuries, especially on the island of Krk, that "Eldorado of Croatian Glagolitic literature." The prevalence of Glagolitic culture has in the past been used as an explanation of why these supposedly poor and primitive areas were not receptive to humanism. Contemporary research in the Croat Glagolitic Middle Ages, conducted by Eduard Hercigonja, has turned this traditional picture upside down.[31] Hercigonja's findings point to the high cultural and economic level of Glagolitic centers, something that brings into question the thesis that the Glagolitic tradition was unreceptive to humanism. The reasons why humanist culture did not strike a sufficiently responsive chord in this area very likely must be sought in the fact that its urban life was relatively less developed.

On the islands of the southern Adriatic, however, the cultural stirrings of the Renaissance left a visible trace in literary creativity—equally in Croatian, Latin, and Italian. Just as on the neighboring mainland, the most notable creators here, too, went away to and were active in foreign countries, though many stayed to work at home.

Hanibal Lucić (1485–1553) of Hvar, the author of *Robinja* (*The Slave Girl*), the first Croat secular drama, translated Ovid's *Heroids* on Paris and Helen into Croat verses. His contemporary, Petar Hektorović (1487–1572), also of Hvar, like Lucić was given a humanist education. Hektorović, too, translated Ovid, but only the first part of *Remedia amoris*, in which the principal theme is the perniciousness of sexual love, thereby recasting the classical poet of amorous refinement into a Christian moralizer. Classical reminiscences were present also in Hektorović's original Croat verses.

Vinko Pribojević (Vincentius Priboevus) was notable among the sixteenth-century Latinists of Hvar. Pribojević was the author of *De origine successibusque Slavorum*, an oration he delivered to the nobles of Hvar in 1525 and which he printed in Venice in 1532. This work, which was later translated into Italian, was at the source of the prodromal studies in Croatian and general Slavic history by Mavro Orbini and Ivan Lucić.

Notable among the humanists from the island of Korčula were the diplomat and epistolographer Jakov Baničević (Banisius, 1466–1532), who corresponded with Erasmus, Willibald Pirckheimer, and Pietro Bembo; the jurist Frane Nigretić (Franciscus Niconitius, 1501–1549); and three members of the Petrović (Petreo) family—the Greek scholar Nikola Petrović, the jurist Ivan Petrović, and the writer Pavao Petrović.

Humanist activity in two Adriatic cities that currently are not within the confines of Croatia, Koper (Capodistria, now in Slovenia) and Kotor (now in Montenegro), was inseparably connected with humanist currents in other urban centers of the eastern Adriatic littoral. Petar Pavao

Vergerije the Elder (Pier Paolo Vergerio, 1370–1444), one of the most outstanding personalities of the humanist movement, and Petar Pavao Vergerije the Younger (1498–1565), bishop of Koper who later became a Protestant and cooperated with Slovene and Croat Protestants, were both from Koper. Of the humanists from Kotor, Nikola of Majine (Nicholaus Machinensis), better known as Nikola of Modruš or Nikola of Kotor might be singled out. He, too, was one of those Croat cultural creators of the sixteenth century who wrote philosophical-reflexive treatises in Latin, but at the same time wrote in Glagolitic Croatian. In a Glagolitic letter that he sent to the cathedral chapter and the clergy of Modruš in 1476—that is, seven years after the printing of the first Croat book (the Glagolitic Missal of 1483 in the Croat recension of Church Slavonic)—Nikola defended the use of Glagolitic liturgy with determination. His *Oratio in funere Petri cardinalis S. Sixti* was the first incunabulum of any Croat writer. It was printed in Rome in 1474.[32]

The common fate of the other humanists from Kotor who wrote in Latin and Italian was that hardly any of their works were preserved. This is equally the case with Bernard Pima, who was cited as a poet laureate, and the members of the Buća family (Dominik, Vicentije, and Franjo). The works of three Kotor humanists were published in the course of the sixteenth century: *Rime amorose* (1532) by Juraj Bizanti, *Rime volgari* (1549) and *Carmina* (1551) by Ljudevit Pasković, and *Descriptio Ascriviensis urbis* (1595), an epic poem about Kotor by Ivan Bona Bolica.

❖   ❖   ❖

It has already been noted that political and economic conditions precluded the European intellectual stirrings of the fifteenth and sixteenth centuries from being reflected in northern Croatia with the vigor that obtained in the southern Croat lands. The principal reason for this state of affairs was due not just to the fact that northern Croatia was the battlefield of a seemingly unending war with the Turks—the land having been transformed into a fortress against Ottoman incursions—but in the generally lower economic and cultural level of northern Croatia in comparison to the Dalmatian cities and islands. In the eastern portion of northern Croatia, in Slavonia, there were no urban centers, something to which the poet Janus Pannonius himself referred when he wrote that Slavonia had many villages but not a single city. In the northwestern Croatian regions the situation was somewhat better. This area had a few significant urban centers, which, in addition to the monasteries of various Catholic orders (Benedictines, Cistercians, Templars, Paulites, Dominicans, Franciscans), became the centers of cultural life—but not of humanist activity. In fact, it is difficult to discuss humanism at all in the northern Croat regions, especially in the sense that was applied in the discussion of coastal humanist centers. Still, it is undisputed that the principal tone of humanist activity within the circle of Matthias Corvinus was set by humanists from all areas of Croatia, especially from the northern regions. Two of these men, Ivan Vitéz and Ivan Česmički, belong in the class of the most important humanist creators in general, Vitéz's opus being more organizational-practical and Česmički's literary.

Ivan Vitéz (1405–1472) was born in Sredna in the county of Križevci. He studied in Italy and then went to Hungary, where he was appointed the protonotary of the royal chancellery and bishop of Várad. At the same time he was the tutor of Ladislas and Matthias, the sons of János Hunyadi. After the election of his former student Matthias Corvinus to the throne of Hungary, Vitéz became chancellor, archbishop of Esztergom, and primate of Hungary. Thanks to his efforts the court of Matthias Corvinus became one of the most significant European cultural centers—the most important focus of humanism in central Europe. Vitéz founded the university and an academy at Buda and enriched the Corvinian library.

Vitéz's literary activity was exclusively epistolographic. His letters were published for the first time in the collection *Scriptores rerum Hungaricarum* (Vienna, 1746–48), together with the works of several other Croat authors—the historians Ludovik Crijević Tubero and Ivan Lucić, mentioned above, as well as Feliks Petančić of Dubrovnik, a noted Turcologist, painter, and miniaturist, who also for a time worked at the court of Matthias Corvinus, among a large group of diplomats, artists, writers, theologians, librarians, and historians from Croatia. Vitéz's letters were published recently in a critical edition.[33]

The origin of Ivan Česmički, known in Europe as Janus Pannonius (1434–1472), and his national affiliation are subjects of conflicting opinion among Hungarian and Croat scholars. The overview of various theses about his origin can be found in the very detailed monograph on Janus Pannonius by Marianna Birnbaum.[34] Several relevant contemporary sources argue for the Slavic, that is, Croatian, origin of Pannonius. But in my judgment the appraisal of Pannonius by József Turóczi Trostler is appropriate:

He had no native country but the one he chose; he had no native language but the one he chose. His world was the antique world; he was a priest whose work was permeated with antique gods. It had no determining Hungarian or Croatian features; it belonged to the intellectual universality of humanist Europe.[35]

Pannonius went to Italy at the age of thirteen, where he studied in Ferrara under the famous teacher Guarino of Verona. Already at the age of sixteen he was composing elegant Latin epigrams. After six years of study at Ferrara he went to Padua to study law. In 1458 he left Italy and—at the invitation of his uncle Ivan Vitéz—came to Hungary, where he soon became the bishop of Pécs (*episcopus Quinqueecclesiensis*). Matthias Corvinus counted Pannonius among the principals of his humanist court. Pannonius fought with Corvinus against the Turks in Bosnia, then traveled to Rome on a diplomatic mission to Pope Paul II, and still later fought in the military expedition against the Bohemian king George of Poděbrady. Together with his uncle Ivan Vitéz, Pannonius participated in the unsuccessful conspiracy against Matthias Corvinus. After the plot was detected he was obliged to flee to Croatia. He found refuge at the castle of Medvedgrad, near Zagreb, where he died in 1472 at the age of thirty-nine.

Pannonius's opus consists of original Latin poetry and the translations from Greek of Demosthenes, Plotinus, Plutarch, and some thirty epigrams. One fragment of his translation of the *Iliad* has also been preserved. His original poetry consists of satirical epigrams, sometimes obscene, in the spirit of Martial, panegyrics in honor of famous men, and elegies—his most successful poetical works. Marin Franičević, a twentieth-century Croat poet and historian of Croat Renaissance literature, has said of Pannonius:

> One of our greatest Latinists, Pannonius early on had earned glory for himself in the then Renaissance Europe both as a poet and as an erudite. A choice student of classical Latin, as well as of Greek and Latin prosody, a humanist who was acquainted not just with mythology but with the whole of ancient history and literature, as well as an original poet who also bore in himself his own experience of the world, Pannonius, who was at the same time multifaceted and subtle, propelled by a rich fantasy and sensibility, succeeded in realizing verses of such quality that some of them deserve to be classed with the very summits of Renaissance Latinity.[36]

A number of humanists from the Croat lands were also active at the courts of Ladislas II and Louis II, at the literary society Sodalitas litteraria Hungarorum in Buda, and at a similar society in Vienna (Litteraria sodalitas Danubiana). A group of Croat humanists, too, was numerous at the court of János Zápolyai (Trankvil Andreis, Antun Vrančić, Ivan Statilić, Franjo Frankopan, Juraj Utišenić [György Martinuzzi]). Stjepan Brodarić, too, entered Zápolyai's service. He was born in 1480 in Jerošin "in that part of upper Pannonia which is now called Slavonia" and later studied in Italy. He became a canon, provost, bishop at Vácz, diplomat, and chancellor of the kingdom of Hungary before the battle of Mohács. He penned poetry and letters but is best known for his famous account of the battle at Mohács, in which he himself participated (*De conflictu Hungarorum cum Turcis ad Mohach*, Cracow, 1527).

The battle of Mohács also determined the fate of Bartol Djurdjević (Georgius, Georgievicz, Georgevicz of Croatia). By origin he was probably from Mala Mlaka, but he went to Hungary in his youth and was schooled there. The Turks captured him at Mohács, when he was twenty. He spent nine years in Turkish slavery. In 1535 he succeeded in fleeing across Armenia to Syria and Palestine, and thence to Spain and Rome. That was only the beginning of his wanderings across many European countries, in several of which he published his books about the Turks and ceaselessly and fanatically called upon Europe to unite in the struggle against the Turkish empire. The bibliography of Djurdjević's publications from 1544 to 1686 consists of seventy-seven items,[37] published in various languages. He was among the first authors to acquaint Europe with oriental languages (Turkish, Arabic, Persian, Hebrew, Chaldean), having become, as a result, one of the founders of oriental philology. Djurdjević frequently included small conversational dictionaries of the Croatian language in his books. The translations of his books thereby were occasions for the publication of the first comparative dictionaries of Croatian and several other languages.

* * *

In the Protestant movement the humanists found elements that repelled them, but also some that attracted them. Martin Luther himself was an opponent of humanist thought. He detested the "old philosophy" that "educated only pagans" and referred to it in the most deprecatory terms. Nor was his doctrine on predestination compatible with the humanist ideal of a free man. Acceptance of free will was far closer to humanist conceptions. Nevertheless, the words of Erasmus, "ubi Lutheranismus, ibi litteratum est interitus," are only partially true, and not only because Melanchthon, Ulrich Zwingli, John Calvin, and other important Protestants were more conciliatory toward the ancient classical heritage than Luther. In fact, Luther, too, when he attacked scholastic theology and when he stressed the necessity of interpreting the original sense of Scripture without the intercession of medieval scholasticism, was close to humanist thinking and the humanist orientation toward the sources themselves. This contradiction within Protestantism was an element—perhaps not a decisive one, but certainly notable—that helps to explain the frequent spiritual vacillation of important representatives of humanist thought between Catholicism and Protestantism. Erasmus's case was not isolated. There were irresolute Protestants, too, among the Croat humanists (for example, Pavao Skalić and later Markantun Dominis), but then the Croats also spawned the greatest Protestant zealot Matija Vlačić (Matthias Flacius Illyricus).

The Reformation was introduced into northwestern Croat lands from Slovenia and Hungary, and into Istria from Venice, which at the outset supported the Reformation, due to its political conflict with Rome, only to persecute the reformers mercilessly after a change in political relations. As far as Dalmatia is concerned, Luther's ideas found little response there.

Fierce Catholic reaction against Protestantism in Croat lands was the reason why Croat Protestants lived in exile. Some of them directed their efforts above all to the spread of Protestantism among the South Slavs; others left behind works that surpassed their own religious and national framework. The representatives of the first tendency were active mainly in the so-called South Slavic Biblical Institute in Urach near Tübingen. Their work consisted mainly of the translation and printing of religious and liturgical books. Others, like Matija Vlačić (Matthias Flacius Illyricus), were also driven by religious imperatives, but realized work of such scholarly and humanist breadth as surpassed the frontiers of purely religious activity. Hence, they too must be counted among humanist doers.

Matthias Flacius Illyricus (1520–1575) was one of the most important theologians of the Reformation. He was born in Labin in Istria. Under the influence of his cousin, Baldo Lupetina, Flacius developed a tremendous enthusiasm for Protestantism while a student in Venice. From Venice he went to Augsburg, then to Basel and Tübingen, where he lived with his fellow Istrian Matija Grbac, a professor at the University of Tübingen. In 1541 Flacius went to Wittenberg, the cradle of the German Reformation, where he made the acquaintance of Luther and Melanchthon. After the completion of his studies, at the recommendations of these two, Flacius, at the age of twenty-four, was elected professor of Hebrew and Greek at the University of Wittenberg. With the defeat of the Schmalkaldic League and the capture of Wittenberg by the troops of Charles V in 1547, there commenced the period of Flacius's wanderings and conflicts. Uncompromising to the point of fanaticism, fervent and totally devoted to radical Lutheranism, hostile to any concessions to Rome and the emperor, Flacius placed himself at the head of the struggle against the Interim of Augsburg and conducted fierce polemics against the moderate Protestant theologians Melanchthon, Andreas

Osiander, and others. In spite of his ceaseless conflicts and migrations (Magdeburg, Jena, Antwerp, Regensburg), Flacius nevertheless succeeded in publishing some three hundred works, leaving behind a series of unpublished manuscripts as well.

Although there exist a good many studies of Flacius's life, a bibliography of his works has not yet been assembled. Four works should be singled out from his rich opus. They are, first, *Catalogus testium veritatis* (1556), an extensive anthology of texts from the dawn of Christianity to Flacius's day, in which he pointed to the "errors of papism"; second, *Ecclesiastica historia seu Centuriae Magdeburgienses* (1559–74), the enormous historiographic work of which Flacius conceived, organized, and wrote most of the units in the first five volumes, outlining the first 1,300 years of Christian history; third, *Clavis scripturae sacrae* (1567), an encyclopedic dictionary of biblical concepts that included several hermeneutical discourses; and fourth, *Glossa compendiaria* (1570), a commentary on the critical edition of the Greek text of the Bible with Erasmus's Latin translation, which Flacius, as he himself put it, "corrected in an endless number of cases."

Flacius was one of the most fruitful authors of the sixteenth century. He wrote philological, historical, theological, and philosophical works. He used many languages; besides his native Croatian he knew Slovenian, Hebrew, Greek, Latin, Italian, and German. His contribution to the development of a number of scholarly and humanistic disciplines was exceptionally high. Especially important are his contributions to historiography, in which he introduced a critical examination and use of sources; and to hermeneutics, which Flacius in fact founded as a discipline.[38]

Matija Grbac (Matthias Garbitius Illyricus, ca. 1510–1559), previously mentioned, was also probably from Labin, but unlike Flacius was never a militant Protestant. Moreover, his orientation was more expressly humanistic in comparison to Flacius. Grbac studied in German gymnasiums and universities at Nuremberg, Heidelberg, and Wittenberg, having been appointed professor of classical languages and literatures at the latter. He taught the same subjects also at Tübingen. He wrote poetry in Latin and Greek and translated Hesiod and Aeschylus into Latin. His poems, translations, commentaries, orations, and discourses were published throughout Europe.

Andrija Dudić (Andreas Duditus Pannonius, Dudich, 1533–1589) was born in Buda of Croat parents. He acquired an extensive humanist education that opened for him the road to high political and ecclesiastical functions. Already in his youth he traveled throughout Europe. His parting of ways with the Catholic church began at the Council of Trent. Soon thereafter he left Catholicism and embraced first Calvinism, then Socinianism, and finally Lutheranism. Dudić's scholarly interests were very wide. He pursued philosophy, theology, natural sciences, medicine, and history. He wrote discourses, orations, poetry, and translated from Greek. His works were published in some thirty European cities in more than seventy editions.

Protestantism was briefly embraced by Pavao Skalić (1534–1575), a "gifted adventurist from a poor Zagreb family." Using false titles and falsified documents, he made his way to various courts of Europe. He wrote works of sundry content, from philosophical to occultist, historical to theological. Skalić entered into the history of European culture with his *Encyclopediae* (Basel, 1559), the work in which the term "encyclopedia" was used in the current sense for the first time.

Markantun Dominis (1560–1624), a student of natural sciences and an ecclesiologist, is often included among the Croat humanists. His opus, however, in good part belongs to the first half of the seventeenth century, thereby going beyond the usual bounds of the humanist movement, which is usually limited to the end of the sixteenth century.

✷   ✷   ✷

In general, it is difficult to determine the chronological limits of Croat humanism; neither is it easy to sum up its general characteristics. Every appraisal that would pretend to be general most likely would be subject to various exceptions. As a result general appraisals are only conditionally correct. This problem obtains, too, for the frequently repeated thesis about the "contamination" of humanist tendencies among Croat authors with the spiritual heritage of the Middle Ages. This thesis is certainly accurate in the cases of Bunić and Marulić, but its validity is difficult to maintain in the case of Janus Pannonius or Ilija Crijević.

Any analysis of the opus of Croat humanists will confirm the richness of literary genres and scholarly prose. As far as literary genres were concerned, epigrammatic poetry, elegies, epistles in verse, and epic poetry predominated in verse; in prose, epistolographic works, orations, and scholarly prose of a religious-moralistic, historiographic, and philosophical character. "It is not an exaggeration to say," wrote Veljko Gortan and Vladimir Vratović, "that among the Slavic peoples the Croats had the richest and aesthetically most valuable Latinist literature in the age of humanism."[39] A similar appraisal of Croat humanism and of Croatian Renaissance literature in relation to other Slavic peoples was advanced by I. N. Goleniščev-Kutuzov, the best scholar of fifteenth- and sixteenth-century comparative Slavic literatures, in his principal work *Ital'janskoe Vozrozdenie i slavjanskie literatury XV i XVI vekov* [*The Italian*

Renaissance and the Slavic Literatures of the Fifteenth and Sixteenth Centuries].[40] An exhaustive bibliography that includes practically the whole literature on Croat humanism can be found in the second volume of the Italian translation of this work.[41] In this short informative survey of Croat humanism I have tried to draw attention, too, to some of the more recent works in this area that were not included in Goleniščev-Kutuzov.

NOTES

1. The most important anti-Turkish orations of Croat humanists were translated into Croatian and edited by V. Gligo in *Govori protiv Turaka* [*Orations Against the Turks*] (Split, 1983).

2. M. Kombol, *Povijest hrvatske književnosti do narodnog preporoda* [*History of Croatian Literature up to the National Revival*] (Zagreb, 2d ed., 1961), 80.

3. A survey of this research, as well as a review of the most relevant works that deal with the relationship of humanism and the Christian tradition, can be found in J. D. Tracy, "Humanism and the Reformation," in *Reformation Europe: A Guide to Research*, ed. S. E. Ozment (St. Louis, 1982), 33–57.

4. In northern Croatia Latin was an obstacle standing in the path of germanization and magyarization. On this subject, see V. Gortan and V. Vratović, "Temeljne značajke hrvatskog latinizma" ["The Fundamental Signification of Croatian Latinism"], *Forum* 8 (1969): 606–36.

5. Š. Jurić, ed., *Jugoslaviae scriptores Latini recentioris aetatis*, part 1, *Opera scriptorum Latinorum natione Croatorum usque ad annum MDCCCXLVII typis edita*; vol. 1, *Index alphabeticus*; vol. 2, *Index sistematicus*; addenda, *Ad tomos I et II additamentum I* (Zagreb, 1968–82).

6. V. Vratović, "Hrvatski latinizam u kontekstu hrvatske i evropske književnosti" ["Croatian Latinism in the Context of Croatian and European Literature"], in *Hrvatska književnost u evropskom kontekstu* [*Croation Literature in a European Context*], ed. A. Flaker and K. Pranjić (Zagreb, 1978), 137–51.

7. K. Krstić, "Humanizam kod Južnih Slavena" ["Humanism Among the South Slavs"], *Enciklopedija Jugoslavije* (Zagreb, 1960), 4:287–300.

8. P. Kolendić, "Krunisanje Ilije Crijevića u akademiji Pomponija Leta" ["The Crowning of Ilija Crijević in the Academy of Pomponio Leto"], *Zbornik radova Instituta za proučavanje književnosti SANU* [*Collection of the Works of the Institute for the Study of Literature: Serbian Academy of Sciences and Arts*] 10 (1951): 65–95.

9. N. Kolumbić, *Hrvatska književnost od humanizma do manirizma* [*Croatian Literature from Humanism to Mannerism*] (Zagreb, 1980), 87.

10. M. Franičević, *Povijest hrvatske renesansne književnosti* [*A History of Croatian Renaissance Literature*] (Zagreb, 1983), 314. The remaining literature on Crijević and a list of his works can be found in V. Gortan and

V. Vratović, *Hrvatski latinisti* [*Croatian Latinists*], 2 vols. (Zagreb, 1969), 1:383.

11. This opinion is from the foreword to Jakov Bunić, *Otmica Kerbera, Kristov život i djela (Odabrani odlomci)* [*Rape of Cerberus, The Life of Christ, and Works (Selections)*] (Zagreb, 1978), 8. In the same foreword, B. Glavičić surveys the scholarship on Jakov Bunić.

12. The list of all Croat authors whose works were printed as incunabula has been compiled by Š. Jurić in "Aus der Geschichte des kroatischen Wiegendrucks," *Beiträge zur Inkunabelkunde* 6 (1983): 86–90.

13. J. C. Jireček, "Der ragusanische Dichter Šiško Menčetić," *Archiv für slavische Philologie* 19 (1897): 22–89.

14. D. Kőrbler, "Iz mladih dana triju humanista Dubrovčana 15. vijeka" ["The Youth of Three Fifteenth-Century Ragusan Humanists"], *Rad JAZU* [*Works of the Yugoslav Academy of Sciences and Arts*] 206 (1915): 218–52.

15. The first edition of his work *Tractatus de ecclesia* was published in Zagreb in 1983.

16. Among the more significant works of Dragišić, see S. Zimmermann, "Juraj Dragišić kao filozof humanizma" ["Juraj Dragišić as a Philosopher of Humanism"], *Rad JAZU* 227 (1923): 59–79; B. Pandžić, "Vida y obra de Jorge Dragišić," *Studia Croatica* 11 (1970): 114–31; idem, "Zivot i djela Jurja Dragišića" ["Life and Works of Juraj Dragišić"], *Dobar pastir* [*The Good Shepherd*] 26 (1976): 3–27; Z. Šojat, "Dragišićeva teorija volje" ["Dragišić's Theory of Will"], *Prilozi za istraživanje hrvatske filozofske baštine* [*Contributions to Research into the Croatian Philosophical Heritage*] 2 (1976): 29–66. The last work includes a polemic against those who deny to Dragišić the "qualification of a humanist."

17. Gučetić's numerous works—both published and in manuscript—were surveyed by L. Šifler-Premec in his dissertation on Gučetić defended at the University of Zagreb in 1975. In the appendix to this dissertation, in addition to the list of Gučetić's works, there is a thorough secondary bibliography. The dissertation was published in Zagreb in 1977.

18. These humanists have been the subject of recent scholarship. On Monaldi, see L. Šifler-Premec, "Miho Monaldi, dva dijaloga" ["Miho Monaldi, Two Dialogues"], *Prilozi za istraživanje hrvatske filozofske baštine* 7 (1981): 31–51. On Medo, see E. Pajnić, *Antun Medo, dubrovački filozof šesnaestog stoljeća* [*Antun Medo, a Sixteenth-Century Ragusan Philosopher*] (Zagreb, 1980). On Nikola Nalješković's work in the natural sciences, see Ž. Dadić, *Povijest egzaktnih znanosti u Hrvata* [*A History of Exact Sciences Among the Croats*], vol. 1 (Zagreb, 1982), 77–87. On Nalješković's literary work, see the registry of literature in Franičević, *Povijest*, 1:737–38.

19. The bibliography of Marulić's works was published by J. Badalić in *Zbornik Marka Marulića, 1450–1950* [*A Collection on Marko Marulić, 1450–1950*] (Zagreb, 1950), 317–33. The most up-to-date list of literature on Marulić can be found in the appendix to Franičević, *Povijest*, 719–22. Two recent works should be added to Franičević's list: V. Filipović, "Osnovi

etičko-filozofske orijentacije Marka Marulića" ["The Foundations of the Ethical-Philosophical Orientation of Marko Marulić"], *Prilozi za istraživanje hrvatske filozofske baštine* 9 (1983): 3–22; and M. Tomasović, *Zapisi o Maruliću i drugi komparatistički prilozi* [*Notes About Marulić and Other Comparativistic Contributions*] (Split, 1984). Tomasović includes a report on recent research on the previously unknown editions of Marulić's works, which is also the subject of L. Košuta's contribution at the international symposium, "Les Croates et la civilisation du livre," held at the Sorbonne in 1983.

20. Krstić, "Humanizam kod Južnih Slavena."

21. K. Cipico, *O Azijskom ratu* [*About the Asian War*], trans. and with a foreword by V. Gligo (Split, 1977). The book includes a selected bibliography on Cipico.

22. N. Kolumbić, "Hrvatski humanizam i Franjo Trankvil Andreis" ["Croatian Humanism and Franjo Trankvil Andreis"], in *Franjo Trankvil Andreis, Krvava rijeka* [*Franjo Trankvil Andreis, Bloody River*], ed. N. Kolumbić (Zagreb, 1979), 303–32.

23. This work was published for the first time by M. Šrepel in *Gradja za povijest književnosti Hrvatske* [*Sources for the History of Croatian Literature*] 2 (1899): 1–13. For a recent edition, see J. Šižgorić, *O smještaju Ilirije i o gradu Šibeniku* [*On the Location of Illyria and the City of Šibenik*], ed. V. Gortan (Šibenik, 1981). The afterword by A. Šupuk includes the inventory of literature on Šižgorić.

24. The list of Polikarp's preserved and lost works and a secondary bibliography can be found in S. Krasić, "Šibenski humanist Ivan Polikarp Severitan i njegova politička misao" ["Ivan Polikarp Severitan, a Humanist of Šibenik, and His Political Thought"], *Prilozi za istraživanje hrvatske filozofske baštine* 3 (1977): 7–78.

25. *Monumenta Hungariae historica, Scriptores: Verancsics Antal*, vols. 2–6, 9, 10, 19, 20, 25, 26, 32 (Budapest, 1857–75).

26. V. Vratović, "Pisma Antuna Vračića u okviru suvremene epistolografije evropske" ["The Letters of Antun Vrančić Within the Framework of Contemporary European Epistolography"], in D. Novaković and V. Vratović, *S visina sve: Antun Vrančić* [*From the Heights, Everything: Antun Vrančić*] (Zagreb, 1979), 293–317. Vratović brought out a bibliography of Antun Vrančić's works and the secondary literature in *Hrvatski latinski*, ed. Gortan and Vratović, 1:607–8.

27. A reprint of this work was published in Zagreb in 1971.

28. In 1972 the Yugoslav Academy of Sciences and Arts organized a scholarly conference on Federik Grisogono. The scholarly papers from this conference were published in *Zbornik radova o Federiku Grisogonu* [*A Collection of Works About Federik Grisogono*] (Zadar, 1974). Of the works on Grisogono published after 1974 it is worth noting Ž. Dadić's contribution, "Prirodna filozofija i znanstveni doprinos Federika Grisogona" ["The Natural Philosophy and the Scientific Contributions of Federik Grisogono"], in Dadić, *Povijest*, 1:61–73.

29. This work was published in 1979 at Zagreb by the Institute for the History of Philosophy of the University of Zagreb's Center for Historical Sciences. The same institute organized an international conference in 1979 at Cres on the occasion of the 450th anniversary of Petrić's birth. The conference papers, which deal with most aspects of Petrić's philosophy, were published in a special number of *Prilozi za istraživanje hrvatske filozofske baštine* 5 (1979).

30. In 1975 *Della mercatura et del mercante perfetto* was published in a reprint edition at Zagreb. In the afterword of this edition Andjelko Runjić comments on the literature on Kotruljić.

31. E. Hercigonja, *Nad iskonom hrvatske knjige* [*At the Source of Croatian Books*] (Zagreb, 1983), passim.

32. The description of the life of Nikola of Modruš, the list of his works and their survey, and the comment on the literature on Nikola can be found in S. Hrkać, "Nikola Modruški," *Prilozi za istraživanje hrvatske filozofske baštine* 2 (1976): 145–56.

33. Ioannes de Zredna, *Opera quae supersunt,* ed. I. Boronkai (Budapest, 1980).

34. M. D. Birnbaum, *Janus Pannonius: Poet and Politician* (Zagreb, 1981). See also Chapter 25, "Humanism in Hungary," in this volume.

35. Cited in Birnbaum, *Janus Pannonius,* 12.

36. Franičević, *Povijest,* 294.

37. J. Schwarzwald, *Bartol Djurdjević: Bibliografija izdanja 1544–1686* [*Bartol Djurdjević: A Bibliography of Publications, 1544–1686*] (Zagreb, 1980).

38. A series of books, treatises, and articles have been written on Matija Vlačić (Flacius Illyricus). Among the most important are W. Preger, *Matthias Flacius Illyricus und seine Zeit,* 2 vols. (Erlangen, 1859–61, 2d ed. 1964); G. Moldaenke, *Schriftverständnis und Schriftdeutung im Zeitalter der Reformation,* vol. 1, *Matthias Flacius Illyricus* (Stuttgart, 1936); L. Haikola, *Gesetz und Evangelium bei Matthias Flacius Illyricus* (Lund, 1952); M. Mirković, *Matija Vlačić Ilirk* (Zagreb, 1960). Mirković also wrote a biographical foreword to the selections of the *Catalogus testium veritatis* in Croatian translation. See Matija Vlačić Ilirik, *Katalog svjedoka istine* [*Catalog of Witnesses of Truth*] (Zagreb, 1960), xi–lxix. For other works on Flacius, see Franičević, *Povijest,* 753–54; and I. N. Kordić, "Novija literatura o Matiji Vlačiću" ["Most Recent Literature on Matthias Flacius"], *Prilozi za istraživanje hrvatske filozofske baštine* 9 (1983): 219–28.

39. V. Gortan and V. Vratović, "Temeljne značajke hrvatskog latinizma," in *Hrvatski latinisti,* ed. Gorton and Vratović, 1:13.

40. I. N. Goleniščev-Kutuzov, *Ital'janskoe vozroždenie i slavjanskie literatury XV i XVI vekov* (Moscow, 1963).

41. *Il Rinascimento italiano e le letterature slave dei secoli XV e XVI,* trans. S. Graciotti and J. Křesálková, 2 vols. (Milan, 1973).

25 ❧ HUMANISM IN HUNGARY
Marianna D. Birnbaum

Europe has three pearls: Venice on the waters, Buda on the hills,
and Florence on the plains.

Ambrogio Calepino

IN HUNGARY LITERATURE (AND, IN A BROADER MEANING, WRITING)
in the period from the ninth century to the fifteenth was primarily in
Latin, while from the fifteenth century to the seventeenth it was bilingual. In poetry, during the fifteenth and the sixteenth centuries, Latin
frequently surpassed and almost always equaled in quantity and quality
its Hungarian counterpart. Beginning with the seventeenth century, Latin
became a language of national self-assertion against German. The centers
of Latinity were the royal court, the archiepiscopal and episcopal sees,
the monasteries, and to some degree the courts of the aristocracy.

Although the language of the clergy and the administration was
Latin (and so remained for many centuries, well into modern times),
already in the Middle Ages a literature in the vernacular appeared. The
Latin alphabet was found to be entirely suitable for the notation of Hungarian sounds, and there was increasing need for the translation of leg-
ends, hymns, and the like for beginners and for nuns whose education
did not include Latin.

The beginnings of the Latin language renaissance in Hungary go
back to the rule of Sigismund of Luxembourg (1387–1437). It flowered
during the reign of Matthias Corvinus (1458–90). The Jagiello period
(Ladislas II, ruling 1490–1516, and his son Louis II, 1516–26), was already marked by decline.

The battle of Mohács (1526), and the subsequent Turkish and Habsburg dominations that split the country into three parts, changed the
character of Hungarian Renaissance humanism. The spreading of Reformation ideologies simultaneously gave birth to works in the vernacular. Beginning in the 1530s, Hungarian and Latin writing appeared side
by side, frequently in the oeuvre of the same authors.[1]

From the first decades of the sixteenth century a Christian variant
(as advocated by Erasmus and Philipp Melanchthon) gradually replaced
the Greco-Roman orientation of traditional Italian Renaissance humanism

in central Europe. The new direction took a peculiar and fascinating form in Hungary and Croatia. It developed amidst conflicts between townships and the new aristocracy, against the backdrop of a malfunctioning split kingdom, and in a region devastated by the Turkish occupiers.

The century that saw the birth of large-scale vernacular literature in Hungary and Croatia and was the background to the poetry of Bálint Balassi and the plays of Marin Držić, also was the century in which Latin humanists, uprooted by the Turks, made their last significant showing. Many were eager to gain a new insight into the sacred Christian texts and, in turn, an understanding of the changing values around them. Their efforts were spurred by the proximity of a third faith—Islam—which, next to the Reformation, posed an equally manifest danger for Roman Christianity. In addition to their religious concerns, the humanists of Hungary were engaged in searching for the reasons behind the catastrophe that had befallen their country and guarding the intellectual achievements of the previous generation, who had worked under more felicitous conditions.

Compared to our own times, the politics of the sixteenth century was even less predictable in its pursuits and style. The "international" network was looser, the notion and identification of responsibility less stable, communication slow and frequently unreliable. Hence, individual careers were perhaps even more hazardous, their course even more arbitrary.

The Mohács disaster polarized the humanities. The confusing political situation and the permanent armed conflicts notwithstanding, there was great mobility in this area. Humanists moved to the West in order to escape the Turks, or to the courts of the simultaneously elected, competing monarchs (Ferdinand and János Zápolya), often switching their loyalties to serve first one and then the other. Many, engaged by these rulers, or in the service of the church, traveled as envoys to the sultanate.

When on 12 September 1526, the victorious Suleiman entered the deserted capital city of Hungary, he was mesmerized by the beauty of the town and by the splendor of her royal palace. "I wish I could move this castle to the shores of the Golden Horn," he is alleged to have said. He was unable to move the entire palace, but he did what he could. Laden with the priceless volumes of the Bibliotheca Corviniana which, not long before, Naldo Naldi had called the "sanctuary of wisdom," and with the detachable treasures his soldiers hoarded on board, Suleiman's galleys made several trips from Buda to Constantinople. Soon the fabulous capital became but a skeleton of her previous self, and descriptions about her past were increasingly used as comparisons to the sorry state Buda had been relegated to in the ensuing centuries.

The concept of the "Hungarian Quattrocento," which is frequently regarded as the most glorious period in the country's history, is clearly tied to the person of János Vitéz (ca. 1408–1472), "the father of Hungarian Humanism." At his episcopal see at Várad, and later as archbishop of Esztergom and primate of Hungary and Croatia, Vitéz was a fountainhead and disseminator of humanist learning. His famed library was admired and imitated by many aristocrats; as founder of Pozsony University (Academia Istropolitana) and as patron of scholars and artists all over Europe, Vitéz also contributed to the spread of humanist values far beyond the borders of the country and his own immediate political influence.

Born in Zredna (Sredne), Slavonia, Vitéz is the archetype of that Hungarian Renaissance personality who, originally Croatian, Serbian, Romanian, Polish, or German, came to serve at the Buda court. Related to János Hunyadi, the famed anti-Turkish crusader, Vitéz first entered the services of Sigismund of Luxembourg. His career began at the emperor's chancery, where his name as notary first appears in 1433. Records show that soon thereafter he attended Vienna University, but did not complete his studies, moving back to the chancery in 1437, in the service of Albert of Habsburg. His ardent wish to improve his education and call on the famous Italian centers of learning remained unfulfilled—a distant hope throughout his life. In 1445 Hunyadi secured for Vitéz the lucrative bishopric of Várad, making him a wealthy prelate, who then began sending his relatives and protégés to study in Italy at his own expense. Vitéz accompanied Hunyadi (by then regent of Hungary) on all his important trips, served as his envoy at the courts of Frederick III and Djordje Branković, corresponded with Aeneas Silvius Piccolomini and Pope Nicholas V, and mediated between his patron and Alfonso of Aragon. He was most instrumental in the election of Matthias Corvinus (Hunyadi's younger son) to the Hungarian throne, and was soon considered the most influential member of the chancery at the side of the young king.

The Hungarian chancery functioned much like the ones in Italy during the same period. From a relatively modest beginning a large bureaucracy had evolved by the second half of the fifteenth century. Competent and versatile personalities were needed, who had the diplomatic and political expertise and the authority to deal with the newly arisen functions.

In Hungary, just as in Italy, the papal court was the model of administrative efficiency. Vitéz's contacts with such humanists as Poggio Bracciolini (then secretary to the curia) and Aeneas Silvius Piccolomini (1442–45, secretary to Frederic's Vienna Chancery, and previously to the Council of Basel) made him aware of the importance of epistolary art. It is quite likely that their elegant letters guided Vitéz in his first similar efforts. Humanist correspondence was not an end to his aspirations, but a means by which his political and episcopal functions could attain a high level of success. He became famous for his tact and style, for being capable of couching the most devastating message in an artistically formulated phrase, mellowing its sting by his charm and wit, and often by a disarming personal tone. Even if many of his letters witness to remnants of medieval scholasticism, they are to be viewed as compelling evidence of a sophisticated humanist court in Hungary.

Vitéz's *Epistolae* were first collected and edited by Pawel Ivanich (in or about 1451). Recently a new critical edition was published by I. Boronkai, Hungary's foremost Vitéz specialist.[2] Vitéz's dream of visiting Italy was fulfilled by his nephew, Janus Pannonius, who, for an important period of his life, made *Ausonia* his second home.

Janus Pannonius (1424–1472), one of the most important Neolatin poets of the Renaissance, is almost entirely unknown to the modern reader. Yet he was a many-sided, fascinating person whose career epitomizes the trend of his times. As a youngster he was sent by Vitéz to Ferrara, in order to study with the famous Guarino of Verona. The boy from "North of the Alps," a region considered uncouth and void of culture by the Italians, soon became the pride of Guarino's school, emulated even by his seniors. Guarino had students from all over Europe, about whom the world is informed primarily from Janus's panegyric, devoted to his teacher.[3] Among his fellow students, however, he was famous for his biting epigrams, which, written in the style of Martial, delighted and amused them. Yet Janus also used his epigrams as weapons with which he fought for his own place among the "locals."

> You attacked me and claimed that a bear was my mother,
>   I am ferocious therefore and rough.
> A Pannonian bear was indeed my wetnurse,
>   But Gryllus, your mother was not a bear, but a bitch.[4]

His epigrams were copied, recited, and imitated by his comrades and also by such arrivés as Tito Strozzi and Galeotto Marzio, his closest friend. This genre remained Janus's favorite, of which his erotic epigrams caused the greatest delight among the students of the straitlaced Guarino.

> You say, you bear my child, always hounding me,
>   Silvia, this charge is dirty and unfair:
> If you wander among a forest of roses,
>   How can you say, "It was *this* thorn that pricked me?"[5]

He was sent to Guarino in order to learn what an educated humanist was supposed to know, with immediate plans for his future service in the royal chancery of Hungary. The blossoming of his creative talent was an unexpected bonus and later perhaps the cause of much of his unhappiness. The next station in his life was Padua, where he received his doctoral degree in law and theology. Returning to Hungary in 1458 he first served as secretary to Matthias's wife, Katherine of Poděbrady, but soon received the lucrative see of Pécs and was consecrated "Episcopus Quinqueecclesiensis." Deep in his heart he remained forever bound to Italy, suffering in what he regarded as a cultural desert, furiously confessing, "musis et mihi cano" ("I sing to the muses and to myself"). He became increasingly engaged in politics and the business of government. His poetry also underwent a marked change. The joyful epigrams steadily decreased in number, yielding their place to elegies in which loneliness and pessimism permeate the lines. Also his output became minimal, with the exception of a brief period immediately following his ambassadorial trip to Italy. The journey during which he met all the outstanding humanists of his time—among them Marsilio Ficino—briefly revitalized his creative energies.

His consumption flared up in the harsh climate of Hungary. In a century in which the idealized human body was admired and depicted by artists and poets alike, Janus's detailed naturalism by which he describes the symptoms of his illness transports the reader to this century:

Just as sharpened arrows had been stabbed through my ribcage
  Saliva thickens with blood gathering in my mouth.
Added to this I am gasping for air, refused by my lungs,
  While my wretched inside is feverish, burning up.
What does life mean if it is spent in such suffering!
  Life equals health, and he who cannot conquer illness
No longer lives, but perishes slowly, day by day.[6]

He was not afraid of dying, but he was worried about his name and reputation as a poet, forced to leave unfinished works behind—a torso instead of a complete corpus.

Janus wrote in Latin only. He was truly universal and belonged primarily to the international network of humanists who had no real country and no real mother tongue. His world was the antique world. Italy was his *locus amoenus,* and therefore his oeuvre has no detectable Hungarian or Croatian qualities. But while his work was determined by the Latin universalism of Renaissance Europe, his fate was typically Hungarian. In Hungary he—and his uncle—represented a new class, that of the lower nobility which was the actual carrying force of the Renaissance.

Janus's career and that of his fellow humanists prove that although there was a hothouse character to the Buda Renaissance, there was also a definite need for the development of the class to which he belonged. His fall is also typically Hungarian and unique to the period. Matthias's mistake was that he feudalized his humanists, and then expected them to continue fighting for the aims of centralization, in other words, against their own vested interests.

Following in the footsteps of Sigismund of Luxembourg, Matthias reaffirmed the power of the Hungarian throne and strove for a strong centralized monarchy and, ultimately, for the crown of the Holy Roman Emperor. It soon became clear to Janus that for this purpose Matthias was willing to ignore the increasing Turkish danger and possibly even make a pact with the dreaded enemy. For his wars against the West, Matthias needed more and more money, and the privileges of the estates were increasingly curtailed. Discontent led to two armed conspiracies. Janus remained loyal to Matthias until the second plot, of which he became the guiding force. The conspiring magnates and prelates wanted to dispose of Matthias and elect Casimir, grandson of the Polish king, instead. The plot was discovered, and although several of the conspirators were forgiven, there was no mercy for Janus, the one-time favorite. He fled the rage of the king but died, exhausted physically and mentally, in a renewed attack of tuberculosis on his way to Italy, in the fortress of a coconspirator, Oswald Thuz, bishop of Zagreb.

After the plot Matthias lost interest in humanist scholarship. Many aspiring humanists did not return from Italian schools, fearing the wrath of the king. Only after his marriage to Beatrice d'Este of Naples and Aragon (1476) did a new influx of humanists—primarily Italian—reach the court of Buda.

The view that without Vitéz and Janus Pannonius there would have been no humanist court in Matthias's Hungary is, of course, highly romanticized. Very soon after the country became Christian (1001), students were sent to the great universities of France, Italy, and England. Hungarian students made their mark very early at the universities of Paris, Padua, and Bologna. Another interesting but less frequently quoted fact is that Hungary had early contact with Oxford. The earliest recorded undergraduate of Oxford was Nicolaus Clericus de Hungaria, who studied there from 1193 to 1196. The cost of his education was defrayed by Richard I the Lionhearted, who was distantly related to the Hungarian king: his sister-in-law was Queen Margaret of Hungary, the second wife of Béla III. Of the signatories of the Golden Bull (1222), one bishop was of English extraction, another fought with English barons in the crusades. This contact might have affected even the content of the Golden Bull, which was signed merely seven years after Magna Charta and dealt with the same issues.

Later the lesser nobility usually sent their sons to Cracow or to Prague, while the children of the wealthy continued to travel to Italy. The University of Prague, founded in 1348, followed the structure and divisions of the Sorbonne. The University of Cracow, founded in 1364, was recognized in 1400. By 1440 there were 140 Hungarian students enrolled there, and by the end of Matthias's reign their number had increased to 465.

The sons of the aristocracy had an even wider choice of schools in Italy. The first Hungarian student appeared at Vicenza as early as 1208, and even the faculty had Hungarian members. Regarding Hungarian scholars teaching at Italian universities, Nicholas de Ungheria, who in 1307 became rector of the University of Bologna, and Johannes de Ungheria, who in 1367 functioned as rector of the University of Padua, should be remembered.

By the fifteenth century scores of Hungarian students attended universities in Italy, primarily in Padua and Bologna. Simultaneously the University of Vienna drew a large number of budding humanists to its fold. The short-lived Academia Istropolitana (founded in 1467), Matthias's and Vitéz's common creation, could never reach a comparable peak.[7]

In addition to the University of Vienna, it was Cracow University that had a long-standing relationship with scholars and students of Hungary. There was also a traditional contact between the courts of both countries, and also among the humanists active at those courts.

An ever-increasing number of students visited Cracow University as early as the fifteenth century. Three Thurzós, all bishops, studied there. Also, Pawel z Krosno (Paulus Crosnensis), who had a major influence on the development of Janus scholarship, was a Cracow alumnus. But after the battle of Mohács there was a rapid decrease in Hungarian and Croatian enrollments, and by 1558 the Hungarian *bursa* was closed down.

            *   *   *

During the Jagiellonian period a much broader group was brought into contact with humanist learning in Hungary and Croatia than ever before. Later, however, the defeat of the country shook the foundations of the Renaissance-type cultural life of the lesser nobility. Many lost their properties and possessions and turned into soldiers, or traveling scholars. The new Renaissance literature that flourished among the new aristocracy had a changed focus, befitting the changed times. Iványi's thorough bibliography of libraries and presses in Hungary, however, ascertains that hundreds of lower nobles had considerable book collections also during the Middle Ages.[8] By contrast, after Mohács, many powerful administrators of the court and wealthy prelates lost their independence and were thus forced to revert to the life-style of the penniless courtiers, depending on the wishes and whims of their new masters.

In speaking of Hungarian or, for that matter, Polish or Croatian humanism, frequently the broader term "central European humanism" is used, especially by the native scholars of those countries. However, while each component of this phrase has a special and poignant meaning for the above-mentioned lands, the feature that was common to them was that, as opposed to German humanism (Erasmus) or English (Thomas More), the central European humanism of Hungary, Croatia and Poland was always off-center. It was neither Italian, Austrian, French, nor English. It was outside the mainstream, and therefore often also derivative.

The highlights of the Jagiellonian period's cultural achievements were undoubtedly the foundation of the Litteraria sodalitas Danubiana and the concerted and, by and large, successful efforts to publish the poetry of Janus Pannonius. The personalities involved in those activities were partially the same: their work represents Hungarian and Croatian humanism in the eyes of western contemporaries. By the sixteenth century, Vienna University was attracting more and more students also from Hungary.[9] Its famous Collegium Poetarum, and not the least the presence of Conrad Celtis, made the university an important humanist center. Vienna's fascination for "central European" scholars began, however, much earlier. Its academic coat of arms, which first appeared at the Council of Constance (1414–18), contained fourteen crests—one of them was that of Pécs.[10]

Conrad Celtis was the intellectual model for the first decade of the new century. His *Ars versificandi* (1486) and his *Amores* (1502) were widely read by the humanists of central Europe. He lectured on Horace in Ingolstadt, edited Tacitus's *Germania* (1500), and as Pfeiffer put it, "it was therefore a classical scholar, working after the Italian fashion, who initiated German scholarship."[11] He fails to add, however, that he significantly stimulated scholarship also among the Hungarians, the Croats, and the Poles. Celtis visited Hungary for the first time in 1490. Of this visit very little is known. He returned in 1497, that time with the program to found the Litteraria sodalitas Danubiae, which was to work in cooperation with the Viennese humanist circle. The first president of the society was János Vitéz the Younger, bishop of Veszprém, relative of János Vitéz and Janus Pannonius, a confidant of Emperor Maximilian.

The Sodalitas was founded almost contemporaneously in Vienna and in Buda, where it was called the Sodalitas litteraria Hungarorum. Among its members were also German, Czech, and Italian humanists active in Buda. It was a loosely knit organization with symposia forming the basis for the meetings. Celtis's own works were the group's best-preserved records regarding their activities. The name Sodalitas Collimitiana, often used in Hungarian works, is derived from Collimitius (Georg Tanstetter, royal surgeon and archivist) whose Buda home the society frequented for their meetings.

According to J. Ábel, the Sodalitas, as well as the other scholarly societies founded by Celtis, limited themselves to such activities as electing a president who, together with the members, administered the affairs of the organization, accepted anyone into its ranks who could write a Latin poem, sympathized with the more pleasant aspects of social life, and was recommended by a member.[12] In its organized frequent gatherings—modeled on the *symposia*—a variety of scholarly subjects was discussed, ending at the well-stacked tables where, richly supplied with wine, they undertook to chase away the lowly troubles of daily existence. Yet, Celtis's influence was enormous for eastern European humanism. His *Ars versificandi*, a first proof of modern ideas and methods, became a bible of the young humanists in Jagiellonian Hungary. His emphasis on history and science deeply affected the type and style of writing for the entire century. His philosophy, based on Neoplatonism and Neopythagoreanism, influenced the makeup of the Sodalitas and the ideas of its members, who wrote epigrams in which they celebrated their master. Those also appeared in *De mundo*, published by Celtis. By the time the Sodalitas dissolved in 1511, its Viennese section was already defunct. The death of Celtis brought an end to the enterprise, proving that it was he who was important and not the association that he had brought to life.

Philology, epigraphy, and the study of grammar were also stimulated in the first decade of the sixteenth century by the North, due primarily to the work of Erasmus. His *Antibarbari*, a dialogue in which he and some of his friends promulgated a humanistic program against their opponents, the "barbarians" (first published in 1520), touched a sensitive chord in many a Hungarian humanist. His treatise against aggression (also Luther's!), pleading for *tranquilitas*, connected with tolerance and freedom of *humanitas*, was an attractive alternative for Hungarian and Croatian humanists living in the turbulent decades during the

Jagiellonian rule.[13] The Erasmists thus looked for peace and harmony and rejected war, sedition, and unrest. Among Erasmus's followers, Miklós Oláh (Olahus) perhaps decided against returning to Hungary because of such beliefs shared with his idol.

One of the most interesting personalities of Ladislas II's court was Feliks Petančić whom some scholars, based on Oláh's writing, identify with Felix Ragusinus, active in the workshop of the Corvinian library.[14] Feliks Petančić was dispatched to Rhodes, France, Venice, and the Porte in the service of Ladislas. He drew up a fascinating plan by which the Turks could be attacked on land. Dedicated to the king, he provided a detailed road description and information about the countries through which he had traveled. His work, *De itineribus in Turciam libellus,* which soon became a classic, was first published by Cuspinianus in 1520. It is known that Johann Cuspinian (Cuspinianus) also used Petančić's work while writing his own *De Turcarum origine* (Antwerp, 1541).

Since they were surrounded by humanists, one would assume that the Jagiellonian kings of Hungary were true Renaissance rulers, themselves learned men. The fact, however, was that Ladislas had little interest in the arts, with the exception of music, and Louis found more pleasure in sports and hunting than in books. Ladislas knew little or no Latin and did not develop a desire for book collecting. Instead of enlarging the prodigious collection of Matthias, he lent out or gave away many a precious manuscript to his favorites. He spent no money on books or libraries, or on any large-scale building endeavors. We know of two prayer books commissioned by him prior to his election, but the work on one began in Matthias's lifetime. The collection of the Corvinian Library was merely increased by works that had been received as gifts.

Cuspinian and Wolfgang Lazius (Latius) spread the ideas of the Viennese Renaissance farther during their legations to Hungary. It was the kind of humanism that grew best on the soil of a royal court, and which used the royal chancery as its base. In Hungary it was György Szathmári and, before him, Tamás Bakócz who were the focal points and fosterers of Celtis's thoughts. Bakócz still belonged to the old school; his career had started with Matthias, whom he accompanied to Vienna and at whose deathbed he stood. His own humanist activities diminished during the years in which, for all practical purposes, he wielded royal power. He was respected as the mentor of countless members of his own family, and of students he had found worthy of support.

Szathmári, the son of a merchant, followed Bakócz in the archiepiscopal see in Esztergom. He worked from 1493 in the chancery as royal secretary, later as chancellor. Through his offices he was deeply involved in the foreign affairs of the kingdom. While still in the chancery, a circle of humanist scholars formed around him. It included Pietro Balbo, Sigismund Thurzó, Stjepan Brodarić, and Oláh. His controversial qualities notwithstanding, Szathmári was a generous patron of artists and scholars, to which the numerous dedications to him bear testimony.

The Janus "cult" of the early sixteenth century actually had begun already at the end of the fifteenth, when Matthias Corvinus entrusted Péter Váradi (Petrus of Warda) in the mid-1470s to collect the epigrams of his once-favorite poet. Matthias had Janus's epigrams collected not because, as has been claimed, they included praise of him and his family, but because they were the best-known pieces during the poet's lifetime. He, too, was aware of the fact that Janus was the best publicity his kingdom had had. But there was no national cultural concept behind the royal decision. The entire idea of *patria* is a sixteenth-century phenomenon; thus Matthias had no need to find cultural traditions for a national literature, which was to evolve a century later.

The only Janus poem still appearing in print in the fifteenth century was his elegy composed in Narni in 1458. It was devoted to Feronia, patroness of groves and fountains, and was occasioned by an excursion he had made together with his friend Galeotto Marzio to the nearby spring named for Feronia. Giovanni Ercoli, Galeotto's biographer, also translated the poem into Italian, and a part of his translation is engraved at the site.[15] The elegy first appeared in a publication, *Polybius latine; Jani Pannonii ad divam Feroniam naiadum Italicarum principem carmen*, in Venice, 1498.

Moved by the desire to collect and guard for posterity the oeuvre of Janus, Stjepan Brodarić approached Aldo Manuzio in 1506 and negotiated with him for an edition of the poet's work. His was the earliest attempt in the century, followed by Pawel z Krosno six years later. The publishers of Janus's work were also the most educated humanists in the first quarter of the sixteenth century. They represented the transitional period between the Matthias kind of Renaissance splendor and the Jagiellonian years of successive decline.

Between 1512 and 1526 there were eight editions of Janus's poetry. In view of the great interest in the subject of traveling, it is not at all surprising that by the end of the sixteenth century a part of Janus's Marcello panegyric became separated from the corpus and appeared on its own in Nicolaus Reusner's popular collection of famous travels.[16] Beatus Rhenanus wrote in a letter to Jacob Sturm (Sturmius) that his masters were Erasmus and Janus, an indication that Janus was not merely thought of as equal to his own antique models (about which many of his publishers wrote), but was also considered relevant for the period preceding Mohács. The young humanists of the 1510s could take additional pride from the praise that another of their idols, Erasmus, had lavished on Janus. He reminded the world that the brilliance of Janus was already discovered by his hosts and that it was Italy who first offered him the laurel.[17]

Janus was indeed the first Pannonian poet who had achieved fame beyond the borders of his country, and moreover during his lifetime. Considering that his poetry—written in Latin—was available to the entire West, and that his friends and fellow students had built an international network in the courts and humanist centers of Europe, one may rightly claim that he was the first Pannonian to have achieved world fame.

There was a significant break after Mohács, and the correlation between the events and the silence about Janus is obvious. The country went through a demoralizing defeat; its humanists were strewn about and lacked a cultural center as well as a political focus. The world of Janus became an unattainable realm of security, his problems and topics fast sinking away into a past never to be retrieved. He belonged to the period of glory forever gone, and that alone would have been sufficient to have made his work lose its hold on its sixteenth-century readers. But in addition to such obvious considerations, he was temporarily put aside because of new interests in humanist circles, which were oriented in a more "scholarly" direction. The focus moved from the lyric to the narrative, from the description of the soul to the description of foreign lands, from the imagined to the experienced, and from the existential questions to the problems of survival. Janus simply could not be accommodated in the decades following Mohács. The first one after the lull was János Zsámboky (Sambucus), Trnava-born philologist, poet, and imperial historian in Vienna, who strove for a selection of his best output. "Selegi de multis pauca et de bonis meliora" (I selected a few things out of many and the better out of the good)—as he explained his own editorial policy.[18]

A déclassé nobleman turned burgher, the young Sambucus studied in Vienna, Leipzig, and Wittenberg (where he met Melanchthon). He continued his studies in France and became *magister philosophiae* in Paris in 1552. From there he moved to Padua (1553), where he studied medicine, among other subjects, with the famed Andreas Vesalius. He was a protégé of Oláh who helped defray the cost of his studies. An inquisitive scholar, Sambucus traveled all over Europe, visiting Italy, Switzerland, France, and the Netherlands, until he finally settled in Vienna in 1564, where he remained until his death. His life is representative of central European humanism of the period because his relationships were closer with French and German humanists than with Italians. His concentration on the North is also proved by the fact that of his nearly fifty publications only one was printed in Padua, the rest in Basel and Antwerp. Therefore, it was his conviction of Janus's greatness that made him interested in publishing a Neolatin poet in the middle of the sixteenth century.

Though not an outstanding poet on an international scale himself, Sambucus had significant success with his volume of poetry, *Emblemata* (1564), which allegedly even influenced Shakespeare.[19] Latin was still Sambucus's literary vehicle. He was also active as translator, and rendered Sebestyén Tinódi's Hungarian *Cronica* of the 1553 battle of Eger into Latin. This facet of his personality is interesting because at the time that he began translating into Latin, his Hungarian contemporaries already were writing in the vernacular.

While Janus's work remained the model and the ideal for sixteenth-century Hungarian and Croatian humanists, there was a significant difference: Janus was a lyrically oriented poet and only toyed with the idea of writing a history of Hungary. His historical pieces are of little artistic value and contain all the shortcomings of the panegyrical genres.[20] The newer generation, including Sambucus, by contrast, merely played with poetry and concentrated on the more scholarly side of humanist endeavors, such as historiography, geography, and the like.[21]

*   *   *

A major event in the country's history preceding Mohács was the peasant uprising of 1514.[22] On 9 April 1514, mandated by Pope Leo X, Bakócz called for a crusade against the Turks. Soon it became obvious that the peasants and the lesser nobles gathered outside of the capital presented a danger to the system, and the crusade was canceled. It was, however, too late and the crowds who came to take up the cross turned into an army of insurgents led by György Dózsa, a lesser noble. In spite of initial successes, Dózsa's army was defeated. The captured leader and his immediate deputies were executed. Dózsa was set on a red-hot iron throne, crowned with a glowing iron crown, and some of his men who had been starved for several days were compelled to eat his scorched flesh. The brutality of his punishment caused a shock among western humanists, of whom several treated the event in great detail.[23]

In addition to punishing the participants, a new law was introduced that cast the majority of Hungary's people into "eternal servitude." The infamous edict was drawn up by István Werbőczi, whose code, at the same time, must be considered as a milestone in Hungarian legal literature, and a major step toward the "democratization" of the nobility. István Werbőczi's *Tripartitum opus iuris consuetudinarii inclyti regni Hungariae* codified not only the defeat of the peasantry but also the victory gained by the lesser nobles. Werbőczi established equality of the entire nobility before the law: "una et eademque nobilitas."

The source of Werbőczi's humanist background was Vienna. It is possible that, as a protégé of Mihály Szobi, Werbőczi had already participated in the drawing up of Matthias's lawbook in 1486. His first independent work is dated 1498, when he presented the king with the grievances of the nobility. In 1502 he became propertied and was appointed judge soon thereafter. He formulated the text of the Rákos Diet in which the nation demanded that in case Ladislas's son died, the country was to be permitted to elect a Hungarian king only.

The *Tripartitum* testified to Werbőczi's being well versed in the better-known works of law and history. He spoke Hungarian, German, Latin, and Greek, "fluenter ac eleganter," as Franciscus Chrysologus stated who met him in the printing shop of Syngrenius. Werbőczi, who also served as diplomat at the Porte, died as a judge, arbitrating for the sultan in Buda.

The most important literary response to the Dózsa uprising is, undoubtedly, István Taurinus's *Stauromachia* of 1519, because it determined humanist as well as later attitudes in Hungarian historiography regarding this event. Written in hexameter and comprising five cantos, the *Stauromachia* claimed to present the story of Dózsa and his men in an objective manner. Yet the title, an allusion to the *Batrachomyomachia* (*Battle of the Frogs and the Mice*, a Greek work of unknown date), shows the author's prejudice.[24] With the exception of György Szerémi, all contemporary historians and those following them till 1945 viewed the peasant war from the standpoint of the nobility.

The next event to draw response from the humanists was the battle of Mohács (29 August 1526). Several extant eyewitness reports are from humanists close to the Jagiello court, who spent the fateful days in the company of the king—who died in the battle—and the queen—who was forced to leave the country. The most significant of these is the description by Stjepan Brodarić, chancellor of Hungary, who less than six months after his appointment found himself in exile.[25]

Barely a month before the defeat Brodarić wrote to the pope that only God or fortuitous chance—willed by God—could save the country from perishing. In his last desperate letter to the queen, Brodarić explained his own views about the forthcoming confrontation with Suleiman:

I am considered a coward and a weakling because I speak with caution, and recommend the same caution to our Royal Highness and the nobles. I wish I had no reason for panic. I am not afraid for myself, but mostly I fear for the king, because I know how endangered his position is, even on account of his own men. I cannot believe that our own people behave the way they do and expose the king to such dangers, because they are bent on destroying him. They believe, rather, that this way he will command more respect, and can achieve more result with his actions.[26]

His *De conflictu Hungarorum cum Turcis ad Mohats* was first published in Cracow in 1527. It was written in the form of a monograph, in the third person, and it had been requested by Sigismund of Poland, uncle of Louis II. More than a mere recapitulation of events, *De conflictu* is a polemic directed against Cuspinian and others who had spread incorrect information about the battle.

Although meant to provide a sustained argument, Brodarić's work is not aggressive. He writes in a simple, somber style; his self-description is modest, and he does not relate events at which he had not been present. His work is concise, well-structured. Brodarić is candid about the causes of the disaster. Even his deeply felt grief is couched in a controlled style. His aim is to convince his readership of the truth, and he indeed succeeds precisely by his sobriety and straightforwardness. The flowery meanderings, so well known from late fifteenth-century prose, are decidedly missing from Brodarić's report. He is pragmatic, even in a technical sense. The dramatic tension of the work increases with the king's address and the gathering of his meager defense. The last anxious consultations, tensions flying high, are vividly recaptured in his presentation. The total defeat, which took no more than ninety minutes, unfolds in its entire tragic magnitude. The work ends with the desolate picture of the fallen and captured, amid the destruction and executions ordered by the leadership of the withdrawing conquerors.

Brodarić is remembered for his services on behalf of the national kingdom of Zápolya and for his relentless labor for peace in order to avoid fratricidal bloodshed. Since his role was less spectacular than it was time-consuming, his name in humanist literature is less remembered than he deserved. He put much effort into the piecemeal work of daily diplomacy and had little time left for the pleasures of creativity. G. Székely pointed out that Brodarić's work lacked a central theme. Indeed, his production became fragmented, most probably owing to the turbulent times and to the hierarchy of his obligations. His narrative talent and his gift for characterization are apparent from his description of the battle of Mohács and from his letters to friends, to literary colleagues, and above all to his negotiating partners.

Correspondence was his best literary medium. Over sixty of his colorful and informative letters have survived. Even if his correspondence was meant primarily for the addressee, apparently Brodarić chose his words carefully and always structured his facts in a logical and thoughtful manner with an eye to a broader readership. He spoke his native Croatian, excellent Italian, and a highly educated Latin. He must have known Hungarian, but there are not enough known documents to prove the level of his proficiency or the richness of his vocabulary.

He was proud of his Italian and often mixed Italian phrases in his Latin letters. He read Petrarch's poetry in the vernacular, but with his Italian friends he corresponded in Latin.

D. Kerecsényi, in his sensitive study, wrote that Brodarić had carried on the purest traditions of earlier humanism. He was, in the eyes of the younger generation and among the many feuding factions, the representative of *amitia*.[27] Of those who were to succeed him in Hungarian politics and diplomacy, few possessed his broad cultural outlook, and even fewer his tolerance and integrity. His political legacy was obliterated by the events following his death, and his cultural concepts—expressed in his historical writings—found many more epigones than true followers.

Among those who supported the house of Habsburg Oláh should be mentioned. Notwithstanding the tragedy of Mohács, Oláh's is still an old-fashioned humanist career, similar to that of Janus Pannonius.[28] In the spring of 1510 he was made a page at the court of Ladislas II, where György Szathmári was active in the chancery. The latter was an old friend and fellow student of Sigismund Thurzó, who had preceded him in the see of Várad, when Szathmári became bishop of Pécs in 1505.

Szathmári was a member of the new class, the burghers, who sought a voice in the nation's affairs in pre-Mohács Hungary. He was the son of a rich merchant and became a wealthy and powerful prelate of the church.

Szathmári had an interest in humanist learning and was instrumental in the publication of Janus's poetry. He was a supporter of the "second generation" of humanists in Hungary, among whom were Brodarić and Oláh. As a concerned patriot, in his testament he left six thousand gold pieces (of Matthias's mint) for the redeeming of towns and fortresses "pawned" to Ferdinand. Louis, however, used them for his anti-Turkish war effort.

In many ways Szathmári was a second János Vitéz, committed to the ideals of humanism; a Maecenas of the young, but also of the famous, outside the country. He was the mentor of Jakab Piso, Girolamo Balbi, János Gosztonyi—all of them well-known figures of Jagiellonian Erasmism.

Oláh moved to Pécs with Szathmári and studied theology there. By 1517 his title was listed as canon of Pécs. His future career became assured. By 1526 he was royal secretary, and also a trusted man of the queen. As the Turkish army advanced and Louis moved south with his men, Oláh first remained in the chancery. The king left on 20 August and soon moved to Pozsony (Bratislava), and thence to Vienna—under the protection of Ferdinand, Maria's brother. Oláh decided to follow Maria because, under the circumstances, life at Maria's court was the closest to that of prewar Hungary. It is true, though, that as soon as he left Hungary with the queen's party his political stance became determined. Paradoxically, in Vienna he was able to remain true to the principles of his own past and to the type of culture he had experienced and had learned to rely upon in Hungary. This does not mean that his literary tastes were stronger than his commitments to the cause of the country. But at that juncture of his life there was little to make him believe in the potentials of an active intellectual life in Hungary. He explained his choice of leaving for the West in one of his letters:

> I know that many hold it against me, and would have preferred my having stayed behind during the times of great dangers, instead of spending my life in peace, among foreign peoples. But if they could consider my life style, my nature, and my possibilities, they would cease to hold this against me. . . . I would much rather live in my own country, and believe me that I would rather do this than anything else in the world. Because I also believe that nothing gives more happiness and joy than to share the company of family and friends. But when I see that at home everything is in a turmoil, and that there is not one small nook of security, either from the enemy, or from internal thieves and robbers, I would rather spend this time here, with writing and in contemplation, than there, in the general upheaval.[29]

Oláh's dream was to live like a genuine humanist. He would have much preferred to devote himself entirely to literature and scholarship. The intrigues and machinations of the courtiers pained and alienated him.[30]

Oláh hoped to obtain a political post in exile. But since none materialized, he became increasingly disappointed in the intrigues at court. He withdrew and turned to his studies of the New Testament, St. Augustine, and Ambrose. At this time he had his first contact with Erasmus.

The correspondence with him opened new horizons for Oláh. His first letter to the scholar was formal—written in the name of Queen Maria. He thanked Erasmus for his *Vidua Christiana,* dedicated to the queen, and took the opportunity to introduce himself.

It is obvious that in his correspondence with Erasmus he had never considered an exchange of ideas as taking place between two equals. Oláh and Erasmus rarely touched upon major theological or ideological problems, except for Erasmus's reference to the political attacks to which he had been subjected. Oláh, in turn, responded to his complaints and tried to discourage his adversaries.[31] Although he had first approached Erasmus in his function as diplomat in the service of Queen Maria, after a short while their relationship took on a more private character. Their correspondence became an exchange of letters between two friends. Soon Erasmus started treating him as his *intimus,* writing to him with the admonition, "lege solus." Oláh, for his part, proudly informed his paternal friend that he was gaining further followers for him.

The majority of the letters in Oláh's *Codex epistolaris* were written during his years of exile. They are of a great variety, and though collected by the author with an eye to their publication, they are genuine and very personal. Since their recipients were heads of states, princes of the church, scholars, and artists, as well as private friends, the letters shed light on the thoughts and concerns of an important segment of contemporary society.

They are quite modern compared with Vitéz's epistles, which for a century had served as samples for Hungarian and Croatian humanists active at the court. Vitéz's letters still echo medieval scholasticism. Oláh's correspondence displays, by contrast, a thoroughly Renaissance style and spirit, direct and assertive even when the letter is addressed to royalty. Erasmus's effect is obvious on the literary style of Oláh and of Brodarić.

Although his spectacular career started with Ferdinand's 1542 offer to work in the chancery, in terms of his intellectual growth it was the years he spent at Maria's court that prepared Oláh and provided him with a scholarly milieu that led to the writing of his best works. The years 1536 and 1537 were the most productive. On 16 May 1536, his *Hungaria* was published. It was received with ardent praise. Pietro Nanni wrote that the Turks could destroy Hungary but it would live forever in Oláh's work. This claim, indeed, became to some extent true: his idealized picture of Hungary was in part responsible for the long-surviving myth of a uniquely fertile and abundantly rich land.

The next year, 1537, was marked by the appearance of his *Athila,* and the publication of his poetry by Jan Rutgers. *Athila*'s source was the

Gesta Hungarorum and, therefore, it was only proper that when in 1568 Sambucus published it in Frankfurt, he issued it together with its continuation, Antonio Bonfini's *Decades*.

Both *Athila* and *Hungaria* belong to the genre of descriptive, informative literature flourishing in the sixteenth century. In both works Oláh's aims were twofold: Hungary should learn about its own past, and so should the world. *Athila* is a highly ideological piece of political writing. Its hero is a Matthias of the past, but with victories to his name that Matthias could not have achieved, owing to changed circumstances and his untimely death. J. Szemes aptly refers to Oláh's Attila as the "condottiere" type.[32] When addressing his soldiers, Attila delivers a humanist speech, following the rules of humanist rhetoric, including *exordium*, *tractatio*, and *peroratio*. No event can take place without a speech—a device that becomes a *topos* by the time of Marlowe and Shakespeare. In terms of data, Oláh mostly relies on Bonfini; but in his work Attila is portrayed as an ideal Renaissance ruler, a true ancestor of Matthias. In his literary style he also emulates Tacitus, in addition to Livy. Miklós Istvánffy, who was Oláh's secretary and was influenced by his mentor's writing, incorporated much of it into his own *Historiarum de rebus ungaricis libri xxxiv*.

Hungaria provides an idealized picture of a cherished homeland from which the author was separated. According to this work, Matthias left behind a wonderfully wealthy country whose rich yields were shared in a brotherly manner by Hungarians, Germans, Slavs, and Romanians. Szemes points out that already in Oláh's depiction Hungary appears as a humanist paradise.[33]

Especially Oláh's description of Buda became the favorite source of collective memory in the period after Mohács. He was frequently quoted, and his statements were incorporated into the writings of many of his contemporaries and into works published centuries later. When in 1669 the famous English traveler Edward Brown visited Hungary on his way to Istanbul, he was looking for remnants of what he had read in Oláh's *Hungaria*.[34]

Hungaria and *Athila* are connected not only in terms of their message but also by their composition. In turn, both works are related to Brodarić's *Descriptio Hungariae*. While the latter meant to describe for posterity the losses suffered at Mohács, Oláh strove to recapture for the readers of the future the old glory of Hungary. While his *Carmina* is not worse than many similar collections appearing during the decade, Oláh's memory lives on thanks to his valuable work in education rather than because of his contribution to belles lettres. He became a part of European humanism to the extent that when he considered returning, his western friends implored him not to allow the "spiritus Hungarus" to pull him back to Hungary.

He began late, yet as archbishop of Esztergom and primate of Hungary he made an extremely important contribution to the restoration of the Roman church, and also toward the development of Hungarian education. The center of his activities became Nagyszombat (Trnava), where the archiepiscopate was moved after the Turks overran Esztergom in 1543.

As of 1562, in his position as "locum tenens regius," Oláh held the most important political position of Hungary and Croatia. He used his office not to further Hungary's liberation but to "save" the Catholic church. His *Compendium suae aetatis Chronicon,* dealing with the times from Matthias's coronation in 1464 to 1558, contains the essence of his work for the church. He wanted to weed out heresy by teaching: "Doctrina magis extingui posse" (One could extinguish it better by teaching). Soon he turned entirely to the ideology of conservative Catholicism. Tolerance, inspired by Erasmus, no longer characterized his thinking. His moving away from liberal views culminated in 1561 when Oláh invited the Jesuits to Hungary. The decisive difference between the schools of the fifteenth century and the one at Trnava was in the latter's religious instruction. Religion was taught by the "superintendent." In the lower grades the catechism and the Bible, later the presentation of Catholic dogma with the refutation of the Reformers, were on the curriculum.

In his testament Oláh left two thousand florins to the Jesuits and made provisions for the Collegium Christi. Although the Jesuits did not return to Hungary for another seventeen years, Trnava became a veritable cultural center, fulfilling the dreams and hopes of the primate. Even the Dominican nuns from Margitsziget moved there—bringing their precious codices along. Oláh's religious work was continued by István Szánthó (*Arator*), who played an important role in the activities of the Transylvanian Jesuits. A missionary and religious writer, Szánthó studied in the German College of Rome and was instrumental in its name being changed to Collegium Germanicum-Hungaricum. In 1579 Pope Gregory XIII sent him to Transylvania, but even his ardent labor could not prevent the expulsion of the Jesuits from that region. From Transylvania Szánthó moved to Olomouc. His most important intellectual contribution was the writing of the Hungarian section of Ambrogio Calepino's great multilingual dictionary.[35]

As a patron Oláh was not just generous but very aware of whom to support. János Zsámboky (Sambucus), Ferenc Forgách, and Miklós Istvánffy studied at his expense. With his passing, the last echo of Hungary's fifteenth-century grandeur died out, and the church did not have another representative of Oláh's stature until the appearance of Péter Pázmány.

*   *   *

The representatives of both the Reformation and the Counter-Reformation paid much attention to the schools and were sensitive to the importance of proper education and guidance. During the first half of the sixteenth century both Catholic and Protestant factions had a Latinist orientation and devoted most of their efforts to language teaching and theology.

The first textbook written in Buda, the *Doctrinale* of János Pap (1507), was still being printed in Venice. One of the first to write grammatical rules designed for the new study of classical literature was Janus Pannonius's teacher, Guarino of Verona, whose *Regulae grammaticae* (1418) was widely used also outside Italy. *Rudimenta grammatica* by Niccolò Perotti (1468), the Greek grammar of Manuel Chrysoloras (Guarino's teacher), and Battista Guarino's *De ordine docendi et studendi* (1459), were the most frequently used textbooks for the study of the Latin and Greek classics in Hungary. Among the classical authors, Cicero enjoyed a special reputation (from Petrarch), and Vergil became the most emulated poet in the sixteenth century. Juvenal's writings were made popular by Giovanni Tortelli, who used them to explain his *Orthographia* (written in 1449, printed in 1471).

Lorenzo Valla, in his *Elegantiarum latinae linguae libri VI*, a manuscript that was frequently copied before its 1471 publication, claimed that the power of Latin held the old empire together. "Italy is ours, Gaul, Spain, Pannonia, Dalmatia, Illyria and many others . . . because the Roman Empire is where the Roman language rules." Janus Pannonius, though writing in Latin only, but having been an admirer of Petrarch's poetry, was willing to make concessions—but to Italian only. It was the Reformation that had raised national consciousness, though the problem of the native vernacular had been a recurrent issue from the mid-fifteenth century onward.

Among the Italian universities in the middle of the sixteenth century it was in Padua that scientific thinking and religious tolerance were still practiced. Pietro Bembo taught there in the *lingua volgaris*, and his writings included "bella istoria," as well as madrigals. His work further contributed to making Padua a center of the vernacular.[36] Yet those Hungarians who had studied there did not become imbued with the idea of vernacular literature.

Translations into Latin from Greek had already been popular earlier —Janus translated Demosthenes, Homer, and Plutarch. Translations from the vernacular into Latin were fewer, however. It is important to remember that even after Mohács, Latin had a significant role. Dismembered as the country was, Latin was a real linguistic and spiritual *koine*, a living link with the glorious past, but also a functioning vehicle in parts of the country under foreign rule.[37]

As was the case in western Europe, Hungarian literature had almost no prose fiction written in Latin. When prose narratives developed in these regions, they were already written in the vernacular. Also, while in some parts of Hungary Latin humanism was marked by a degree of conservatism, many Hungarian humanists who had received their education in the West adhered to more liberal ideas, which—upon their return—they transplanted to their native soil.

In the second half of the sixteenth century the Counter-Reformation gave a renewed support to Latinity. After the Council of Trent, Oláh's activities in Hungary and Juraj Drašković's in his Zagreb bishopric promoted Latinity by the founding of centers of higher education. *Eloquentia* in Latin was put into special practice by the Jesuits, in whose usage language became an ideology: once more a vehicle for the message from "the other world." In Hungary Latin remained the language of the court and of scholars, practically to the end of the eighteenth century.

A milestone in the development of Hungarian was János Sylvester's *Grammatica Hungaro-latina* (written in 1536 and published in 1539). Turóczi-Trostler stresses the fact that in the case of Hungarian the enduring application of the vernacular did not coincide with the country's Renaissance but postdated it, marking its impressive beginnings in the 1530s.[38] To this process belong the publications of the Hungarian Reformation, which represent an organic part of the linguistic evolution. While the Latin-language Renaissance had the court, the estates of the oligarchy, and the sees of the upper clergy as its backdrop, the majority of the Reformation-period literary output belonged to the market towns (*oppida*) and represented the ideology of the burgeoning middle class.

János Horváth believes that Sylvester (1504–ca. 1551) never left the Roman church, and although he moved toward Protestantism, his oeuvre actually represents a "general humanist" approach. He supported his claim by referring to a letter of Sylvester, written after his translation of the New Testament, in which he referred to Pope Paul III as "our Holy Father."[39]

Sylvester's earliest involvement with Hungarian came about when, at Hieronymus Vietor's suggestion, he augmented Christoph Hegendorf's *Rudimenta grammatices Donati* and Sebald Heyden's *Puerilium colloquium formulae* with Hungarian vocabulary and comments. Thus his *Grammatica Hungaro-latina* is a work built on considerations identified, and problems solved, in those earlier pieces. The latter, however, includes the discussion of specifically Hungarian problems (definite article, possessive case, etc.). Also, its ordering provides us with the first Hungarian grammar. His first Latin works appeared in Cracow in 1527 (*Rosarium*), his New Testament translation in 1541; yet today he is most remembered for his *Grammatica Hungaro-latina*, because in it he codified the basis of the Hungarian language, placed it alongside the "sacred languages," and made the discovery that Hungarian is suitable for the adaptation of quantitative meter.

Sylvester wrote the first Hungarian grammar essentially by accident. He was planning to write a Latin grammar in which Hungarian had a secondary role. His work was founded on the work of Donatus, which is clearly ascertainable by his retaining the grammatical categories of his model. As has been shown, however, by several scholars, among them primarily by Turóczi-Trostler, the Donatus editions also underwent some changes at the hands of his followers.[40] Thus as has been pointed out before, Sylvester's grammar has to be viewed in the light of Donatus's and Melanchthon's influence. And since Sylvester's grammar is designed with a religious purpose in mind, his work is spiritually closer to that of the German reformer. His originality lies in the areas of embellishments, extensions, and explanations. He still remains under Latin tutelage, and so has Hungarian grammar until recently.

Turóczi-Trostler also called attention to another source of influence, the work of the "new grammarians," especially to Johannes Aventinus-Turmayr.[41] By reading the examples of Aventinus, Sylvester discovered that the rules governing Hungarian make it no less suitable for poetry and translation than the "sacred languages," that is, Hebrew, Greek, and Latin.[42]

While Sylvester's work may be described as containing a number of theological ambiguities, Mátyás Dévai Bíró's *Orthographia Ungarica* (1549) is imbued with the ideology of Lutheran Protestantism. An acquaintance of Luther, Dévai Bíró added direct religious information to his work by completing it with the translation of the Ten Commandments, the Lord's Prayer, and a number of additional prayers.[43] A bonus of such glossaries is their cultural historical information, since they all record the concepts in their synchronic semantic stage.

Another step in the development of the native language is represented by Gábor Pesti's Aesop translation. Based on Valla's Latin translation and Heinrich Steinhőwel's German rendition (which also included Aesop's biography), Pesti set out to complete his task, *decoris patriae:* his is therefore one of the first works in Hungarian conceived as a patriotic program. Gábor Pesti published Aesop's fables in Vienna in

1536. In the same year he completed his translation of the New Testament, and in 1538 he published his *Nomenclatura sex linguarum, Latinae, Italicae, Gallicae, Bohemicae, Hungaricae et Germanicae*. Spurred by the ideas of Erasmus, Pesti was eager to provide new insights into foreign cultures and to raise Hungary among the nations with accomplished translators.

Valla's principles regarding style as expressed in his *De elegantia Latinae linguae* (1471) also determined the writings of those who undertook to address their topic in Hungarian. Latin, Greek, and Hebrew were no less important for these authors; they used them in order to explain Hungarian. In this way they present the opposite approach to the three sacred languages from that of the earlier humanists, who used the national vernacular in order to clarify the more obscure points of Latin or Greek. In the beginning Hungarian humanism was not much less elitist than Latin humanism. Also, most of the scholars remained faithful to Erasmus in principle, only his teachings had become spiced with their Wittenberg experience. Péter Bornemissza (1535–1584), who states, "Hungaricum linguam iam a paucis annis scribi coepisse" (I began to write the Hungarian language a few years ago now) also reached out to the western European editions before he began working on his *Elektra* on the urging of his teacher Georg Tanner. His model was Aldo Manuzio's 1502 Sophocles edition. Similarly to his contemporaries, his source of inspiration was Wittenberg, where interest in the classical tragedies was fostered by Melanchthon. Turóczi-Trostler convincingly argues that Bornemissza's *Elektra* is permeated by the Melanchthon-type conciliatory Protestantism.[44]

Péter Bornemissza's *Elektra* (1558) translation was discovered only in 1923. Comparative philological research has established that he worked from the original Greek text, although his own comments to the drama were in Latin. He admits to having "embellished" it. A. Pirnát, who analyzed the structural components of the drama, maintains that in addition to Camerarius's commentary on Sophocles, Bornemissza also knew Veit Winsheim's 1549 Latin translation.[45] *Elektra* was published in Vienna and most probably also influenced by Tannerus, who lectured on Sophocles.[46] It is not merely a translation but a thoroughly contemporary work, Protestant-inspired and of uncompromising morality. As pointed out by several Hungarian scholars, among the new features of the translation is the elimination of the chorus, which is replaced by an old woman who symbolizes the pain and suffering of the people.[47] Parasitus is transformed into a sixteenth-century empty-headed courtier, a demoralized fop. The royal couple, too, embody the characteristics of contemporary court life.

Péter Bornemissza studied in Kassa (Košice) and later also in Padua, Vienna, and Wittenberg. In addition to his capital work, he published *Négy könyvecske* [*Four Booklets*], his five-volume *Postillák* [*Commentaries*], and *Ördögi kisértetek* [*Temptations of the Devil*]. While *Elektra* is a unique piece in the Hungarian literature of the period, *Postillák*, published between 1573 and 1579, has its roots in the religious pamphlet tradition. They are theological minitreatises and didactic sermons characteristic of the genre. Nonetheless, even in them a personal, intimate voice can frequently be heard, atypical for that kind of writing.[48] Bornemissza was a prototypical Renaissance reformer who also shared the vicissitudes of his humanist contemporaries. Of his secular poetry "Siralmas éneköm" ["My Heartfelt Grieving"] is a thriftily composed lament expressing his pain over being forced into exile:

My departure causes me a heartfelt grieving,
Pretty, blessed Magyar country, I am leaving:
Will I ever have a home in ancient Buda?

Cocky Germans govern all the northern highlands,
Turkish devils conquered all our southern tidelands.
Will I ever have a home in ancient Buda?

While the brazen Germans always seek to hound me
All those heathen Turks are eager to surround me.
Will I ever have a home in ancient Buda?

Magyar magnates caused my spirit to be vanquished,
From this Magyar country even God is banished.
Will I ever have a home in ancient Buda?

God shall bless you, my dear Magyar country, ever,
For your grandeur is already lost forever.
Will I ever have a home in ancient Buda?

Péter Bornemissza, in his cheerful notion,
Wrote this poem in Fort-Huszt with deep emotion.
Will I ever have a home in ancient Buda?[49]

Translations remained for a long while the main avenue by which the Hungarian language became more polished. In 1596 János Decsi of Baranya published his Sallust translations (*Az Caius Crispus Sallustiusnak két históriája* [*Two Stories of Caius Crispus Sallustius*]). The young scholar, who studied in Wittenberg and Strasbourg and perhaps also visited France and Italy, returned to Hungary in 1592 and settled in

Transylvania. Sigismund Báthori's patronage helped him in gaining first a teaching position, later the rector's hat at Marosvásárhely (Tîrgu-Mureș). His work was discovered in Eger, in 1813.[50]

Another special genre flourishing in the second half of the sixteenth century was the chronicles of battles and the heroism of those who had fought them. Acting in the manner of today's war correspondents, the historians of this kind provided their readers with genuine eyewitness reports, and instead of illustrating them, they told about the events in songs, accompanied by music.

The most famous representative of this genre was Sebestyén Tinódi (1505/10–1556). That Tinódi conceived of himself as a man of letters, as well as an artist, is testified to by his self-description: Sebastianus Literatus de Tinód, Lutinista. He shared the need for "objectivity" with his humanist contemporaries, and therefore his work is a fascinating amalgam: the product of a lute-playing entertainer and that of a bona fide historian.[51] His method of narration is that of a bard; his material, however, reveals a man informed about historical writings and familiar with the classics. B. Varjas assumes that the "profile" of the Cronica was developed in collaboration with the printer, Georg Hoffgreff.[52] Tinódi unfortunately used unending sets of quatrains made up of a a a a, b b b b, c c c c, and so on as the rhyme scheme, making his Cronica tiresome reading.

The Chronica az magyaroknak dolgairól [Chronicle of Hungarian History] (1575) by Gáspár Heltai (ca. 1510–1574) treats a much larger segment of Hungarian history, namely from the alleged Scythian past to the battle Mohács. As Varjas points out in the introduction to a facsimile edition, the first who were to write about Hungary's history during the Renaissance were foreigners. Completing the work of Simon Kézai, Pietro Ransano, and Bonfini, Sambucus finally presented a continuous Hungarian history by 1568. It is actually the same conception of history that appears in Heltai's chronicle, but it is dressed up in Protestant garb. Furthermore, it is no longer a mere translation. Heltai's work is a compilation with a clear editorial policy in mind. In his rendering information considered unimportant was omitted, while events conceived of as significant were given more attention. Gáspár Heltai's Cancionale, another compilation, includes "Historia az Bánc-Bánról," treating the rule of Andrew (1205–35) and the murder of Queen Gertrudis (1213).[53] The same regicide later formed the plot of Franz Grillparzer's Ein treuer Diener seines Herrn and of József Katona's Bánk bán [Bank, the Palatine], the great national drama of the Hungarian stage.

In Heltai's case, history was conspicuously viewed from below, representing the ideology of the Protestant burghers. Also, his Matthias portraits reflect the ideology of the lower classes, especially of the towns-people who had profited by his centralizing efforts. Heltai also published a volume in Latin in which he collected material about Matthias as it appeared in Bonfini.[54]

Heltai's forte was the *fabula*. In his *Száz fabula* his moral message comes across in the ingeniously drawn animal characters representing a wealth of Renaissance imagery. His Hungarian is elegant, which is all the more remarkable because as a descendant of Transylvanian Saxons, Heltai only learned Hungarian as an adult. His sermons, a more rigid vehicle for the same religious-moral message, deal with human vices.

Heltai's pamphleteering knack and his strong religious convictions find expression in *Háló* (1570), the translation of Raimundo Gonzales de Montes (Reginaldus Gonsalvinus's) work. The latter, a Spanish Protestant, vividly describes the sufferings of Protestants in the hands of the Inquisition. In this work, Heltai openly confesses his antitrinitarian convictions.[55]

Protestant ideologues also chose the drama as a theologically potent literary genre. It is noteworthy that of the twelve Renaissance dramas written in Hungarian, with the exception of one, all are in prose. Yet they closely follow the rules of the genre based, probably, on Aelius Donatus's Terence commentaries (Bornemissza, who studied with Georg Tanner, must have also been familiar with the latter's lectures on Aristotle's *Poetica*).[56]

As A. Pirnát convincingly argues, all Hungarian dramas of the period tend toward realism—or what was then conceived as such. Each drama is either a *comoedia* or a *tragoedia*, which designations appear in the titles. A popular variant is the *Disputation*, almost exclusively represented by Protestant authors. The best known are Mihály Sztárai's *Igazi papság tüköre* [*The Mirror of True Priesthood*] (Cracow, 1559), and the *Debrecen Disputation* (1572), which is attributed to György Választó. Pirnát also pointed out the Erasmian inspiration of the *Comedy About the Treason of Menyhárt Balassi*, a satyrical dialogue from the sixteenth century.[57]

The first masterpiece of the Hungarian *bella historia* preceded all the above works of missionary zeal. It is *Historia regis Volter*, by Pál Istvánffy (d. 1553), better known by its Hungarian title, *Voltér és Grizeldisz*. Written in 1539, the verse-epic treats tale number 100 of Boccaccio's *Decameron*, though Istvánffy used Petrarch's Latin translation as his source. His finely developed rhymes and technical accomplishments have not yet received adequate attention by the Hungarian students of the period.[58]

As a result of the ravages of the Turkish occupation and the insecurity of any one place for establishing a business, there was little chance for continued printing activity in Hungary proper. Thus, most humanists of the period were patrons and authors of Italian, German, and Flemish presses. It is of interest that Hungarian humanists were published by the best-known printers of the sixteenth century.

Already the pre-Mohács humanists were using the printers of the towns in which they attended universities. Johann Syngrenius in Vienna and Aldo Manuzio in Venice were the favorite choices, the latter being especially well known and appreciated for his beautiful publications of the classics. So also was Antonio Blado, the most famous man of his trade in sixteenth-century Rome.

By the end of the 1570s a large number of Protestant presses were active in Hungary. Several of them were permanent, but some, especially those located in western and northwestern Hungary, were temporary.[59] The next permanent press after that of András Hess (1497) was in use at Sárvár (from 1536 on), actually located at Ujsziget near Sárvár, on the property of Tamás Nádasdy, who was a close friend of Brodarić. He himself studied in Graz, Bologna, and Rome. Here at Ugsziget, János Sylvester's *Grammatica Hungaro-latina* was published by Benedek Abádi, a student of Vietor in Cracow. Abádi also published Sylvester's translation of the New Testament. Soon thereafter, this press too had to fold. Of its publications only the above-mentioned two titles have survived. B. Varjas, who has researched the letter-types of the Sárvár press, postulates that while several letters were cut locally (e, ë, az, t), the matrixes were usually made abroad.[60]

The Sárvár press was active for only six years. Abádi left for Wittenberg in 1543, and Sylvester moved to Vienna, where he again wrote in Latin. In addition to its significance as a linguistic monument, his New Testament translation is also interesting for the history of printing and illustrating, because it includes one hundred woodcuts, Hebrew letters, and initials.

In his essay, "Heltai Gáspár a könyvkiadó," B. Varjas has traced Heltai's activities as printer, and his collaboration with Georg Hoffgreff in Kolozsvár (Cluj). Hoffgreff's first known publication is *Ritus explorandae veritatis*, printed in 1550. Prior to this date he had worked for János Honter, until the latter's death in 1549. Hoffgreff was briefly in partnership with Heltai—a less than happy business relationship, as may be established from the surviving correspondence. In the years 1554–58 Hoffgreff was again alone.[61] However, during the less than four years of his lone activities he published twelve titles. In 1559 Heltai regained the press, possibly owing to the death of Hoffgreff. He continued to publish a variety of works until his own death in 1574. Among his customers was Sebestyén Tinódi, who probably chose Heltai's press because it also printed musical notes.

During this time, with the exception of the workshop of Dávid Gutsgell in Bardejov, there were only temporary printing presses in Hungary. Finally, in 1582, Miklós Telegdi established a press in his own home for the purpose of publishing Catholic literature.[62] After his death in 1586, it was taken over by the cathedral chapter of Esztergom. In 1615 the press was turned over to the Jesuits. The influence of the printed work was appreciated by the emperor. On 8 February 1578, Rudolf banned the opening of any printing press without his imperial fiat.[63]

✻   ✻   ✻

As P. Ács has correctly claimed, both the Erasmist and the Balassi-type ideals regarding the polishing of the vernacular language were nationalistic in their goals. The Erasmists wanted to translate the Bible and the classics, while Bálint Balassi (1554–1594) set out to create a literature ready to express the feelings of "courtly love," couched in the vocabulary of the spoken language.[64]

In the sixteenth century Hungarian texts were primarily composed for theological, political, or educational purposes, and frequently for all three. Almost all Latinists also wrote poetry, simply as another proof of their education. And while Janus Pannonius was the first significant poet to be identified with Hungary, his poetry could not be identified with the cultural interests or free-time pleasures of the majority of Hungarians. His poetry was entirely elitist, in content as well as in language. Therefore, it has often been stated that the first Hungarian poet was Bálint Balassi, because his "register" was undifferentiated as of those Hungarians whose lives and tribulations he had shared. His poetry was *eo ipso* identified as the populist expression of the Hungarian Renaissance, creating the point of departure in a literary tradition that would later directly connect him with the poetry of Mihály Csokonai Vitéz and Sándor Petőfi.

A student of Péter Bornemissza, Balassi received an education designed for the young aristocrats of his time. He was not educated in order to become a vagrant poet and occasional mercenary. His turbulent life, beset with so many hardships, provided him with fluency in an unusually large number of languages. He spoke, in addition to his native Hungarian, Latin, Slovak, Croatian, Romanian, Polish, German, Italian, and Turkish.[65] He read the classics, and owing to his many legal troubles, he also studied law, primarily from the *Tripartitum* of Werbőczi.[66]

In his love lyrics, which are a dominant part of his poetry, Balassi's major influences can be found in the Petrarchan tradition, and especially in the poetry of Marko Marulić (Marullus), Hieronymus Angerianus, and Janus Secundus. The work of these figures had been published by the Pleiade group (*Poetae tres elegantissimi*), and it has been established that Balassi indeed knew and used the volume.[67] But even if Janus Secundus composed a "Julia Cycle," as did Balassi, the Hungarian poet's work is by no means a copy. The conflict between illusion and reality, between love and the opposition of the outside world, are genuine concepts of Balassi's poetry, born out of his nation's and his private history.[68]

Modern Balassi research is still based on the pioneering prewar work of Sándor Eckhardt. His efforts were continued—among others—by T. Klaniczay, I. Bán, B. Stoll, R. Gerézdi, F. Julow, and recently, I. Horváth. Regarding the originality of the so-called Balassi stanza (a a b, c c b, d d b, etc.). J. Turóczi-Trostler stressed the importance of analyzing the entire stanza instead of its meter, rhyme, or rhythm separately. He was the first to call attention to this type of stanzaic structure occurring in the poetry of the Minnesinger, especially in the decades following Walther von der Vogelweide.[69] He also introduced examples found throughout the centuries in which the same constructions had been used. He was the first to note the possibility of its having derived from the German *Leich* sequence, also based on trichotomy. After many decades, during which Balassi's poetry was viewed as the epitome of Hungarian Renaissance versification (secretly ushering in the Baroque), I. Horváth, in his recently published monograph, returns to Balassi's medieval sources. His story, one of the best works of postwar Hungarian literary scholarship, is entirely text-oriented, and therefore is not sidetracked by the adventurous life of his subject, a shortcoming that has blemished most previous Balassi research.[70] Having established the chronology of Balassi's poetry in a previous work,[71] he here reiterates his views on the underlying artistic conception. Also, underpinning his arguments with statistical evidence, he establishes the poet's principles of composition.

This task is a tremendous one, because Balassi is the only known Hungarian poet of the period whose oeuvre remained unpublished in the sixteenth century, and in whose work there is a marked difference between the manuscripts and the items that have later appeared in print. Horváth reexamined all earlier advanced views, and in agreement with Turóczi-Trostler, found the origins of the Balassi stanza in works using the medieval *tripartitus caudatus*. They include such pieces as Jacopone da Todi's "Stabat mater dolorosa," the *Leich*, and the German Minnesang. He rejects any immediate Hungarian antecedents in favor of earlier European models, which in the sixteenth century were also revived in western poetry among the Pleiade group. Perhaps this discovery made

Horváth first reconsider the social stratum of Balassi's poetry. The Pleiade group was noted for its devotion to the native vernacular and its use for poetry of the noblest kind (and for the royal court).

Horváth, though admittedly he found no direct contact between Balassi and the Pleiade, reviewed the vocabulary and themes of Balassi's poetry in terms of "reception." He came to the conclusion that, as opposed to Tinódi's populist oral orientation, Balassi uses almost anachronistic, archaizing structures, which place him among the poets of the troubadour tradition. Thus Horváth contends that it is Balassi's biography that is typical of the Renaissance, and not his poetry. The individual character of his poetry, written during a time of major crises of European religious and social values, reflects the thoughts and feelings of a person who had been denied the security of order. He is, at the same time, a Renaissance poet, especially as displayed in his *Szép magyar comoedia* (a pastoral in the sixteenth-century tradition). Therefore, in one person, Balassi embodies the first Hungarian Renaissance poet and the first Hungarian troubadour.[72] Horváth further argues that his poetry is the *grand chant courtois,* addressed to the upper classes and not to a relatively undifferentiated popular audience. Thus, instead of being grouped together with the *latricane* songs, his poetry belongs to the works of *fin'amors.* A thorough analysis of Balassi's vocabulary indeed supports this thesis. Horváth also demonstrates that all three types of popular songs of the period (the "springtime song," the "woman's song," and the *latricane*) do appear in Balassi's oeuvre but are transformed and fitted into the system of the *fin'amors.*

Balassi's short life was filled with difficulties, ugly court cases and accusations of immorality. While his poetry was the yield of this precarious career, he himself tended to separate it from his private life and hoped that he would not be judged by rumors about his behavior but by the works he had left behind. He never became the envied court poet of a powerful monarch, as Janus Pannonius or Jan Kochanowski, but he was a poet of courtly love, the first troubadour in Hungarian letters.

Among the humanists of sixteenth-century Hungary and his native Croatia, it was that fascinating inventor, Faust Vrančić (Faustus Verantius, 1551–1617) who made the most significant contribution to the science of the period.[73] He was born in Šibenik, lived and worked in Hungary, Bohemia, and Italy, and was therefore often considered Hungarian or Italian. There is ample evidence that he had thought of himself as a Slav, who "never forgot Dalmatia," and was a proud speaker of Croatian, his mother tongue. Of his historical writings, *De Slavinis seu Sarmatis in Dalmatia* and *Regulae cancellariae regni Hungariae* remained in manuscript. But his *Vita Antonii Verantii* was published by Márton György Kovachich, who included it in his *Scriptores minores rerum hungaricum*, volume 1.

Although he was a careful and precise historian, it was Vrančić's scientific and philological work that made him one of the most important figures of Renaissance humanism beyond Italy. His capital work, *Machinae novae*, was published in two different editions, but the year of printing was not indicated in either case and is therefore still in dispute. Some believe that it appeared in 1595 and 1605, while others maintain that the dates were 1615 and 1616.

At the time that Vrančić worked, mathematics and physics were in relative infancy, and engineering was based primarily on practical experience. The chief advantage of his technical designs lies in their simplicity of conception and clarity of explanation. The designs are not all his, but his own inventions as well as those used by him focus on the everyday needs of the public.

Of special interest is still his description of the "flying man," his best-known and most frequently reproduced design: the blueprint for a parachute. Some scholars claim that he had actually tested his quadrangular flapping device by jumping off a tower in Venice. That would make him one of the pioneers of flying *and* parachuting.

Machinae novae placed Faust Vrančić in the ranks of the most eminent engineers of the sixteenth and seventeenth centuries, whose talents extended to architecture, construction, bridge building, machinery, and shipbuilding, and to the domain of measuring time.

Only a year after *Machinae novae* appeared, Vrančić published in Venice a work that was to bring him world fame, and special distinction to his fatherland: his *Dictionarium quinque nobilissimarum Europae linguarum, Latinae, Italicae, Germanicae, Dalmaticae et Ungaricae*, printed by Niccolò Moretti. This dictionary, written probably in the mid-1580s, was the first comprehensive Croatian, though not the first Hungarian lexicographic work of that kind. Because of its importance and excellence, it was enlarged, with the author's consent, by the Benedictine Peter Lodecker (adding Czech and Polish to it), and it was printed in 1605 in Prague.[74] The seven-language edition remained basically unchanged, but in the heading the three Slavic languages were placed next to one another.

Since all important dictionaries of the period were printed in Venice, it is not surprising that the question arose whether Vrančić had been influenced by any of those works. The obvious source of influence was considered to be Calepino, who was not only the most popular lexicographer of the time but whose later editions also included Hungarian.

Calepino's Latin–Italian dictionary (1502) was expanded in 1590 into a dictionary of eleven languages and later reedited as a seven-language work by Jacopo Facciolati in 1718.

Vrančić's own admission of spending merely a short time compiling this work, along with the reputation of Calepino's dictionaries, have made philologists scrutinize both dictionaries in order to establish common features and usage. I have checked the Calepino editions that could have been known to Vrančić, and I suggest a compromise: he probably consulted the 1585 and 1590 editions and used them as his model, but not as his source.

Having buried his wife and having left Emperor Rudolf's Prague court, Vrančić retired to a life of priesthood. As a final gesture, he was appointed by the emperor titular bishop of Csanád. Before he occupied his see, he went to Italy. There he visited the famed Biblioteca de Pesaro of the dukes of Urbino, traveled to Rome and Venice, and saw the Tuscan countryside.

He returned to Hungary, but performed his ecclesiastic duties in a fashion that led to some problems between him and the emperor. Faust, as bishop, almost caused a break between Rudolf and Rome by conferring titles on his own. However, he fought against the Hungarian Protestants and continued his opposition to the Reformation even after he resigned his office. Finally, in 1608 he left his see and in 1609 entered the Paulist order in Rome. He moved to Venice, where in 1616 he published *Logica nova* and *Ethica Cristiana*. The latter was a controversial work that, during the turbulent time of religious strife and heresy, provoked strong reactions.

In his *Logica nova* Vrančić introduced no new ideas. It is based on well-known works with which he had obviously been familiar. The ideas of Francesco Suarez, Lorenzo Valla, Juan Luis Vives, and Melanchthon are reflected in it. Also, it is clear that his years spent in Padua had affected the *Logica nova*. Jacopo Zabarella taught in Padua (1564–78), and his own *Opera logica* was published in Venice in 1578.

Faust Vrančić lived the last years of his life in the seclusion of the Paulist monastery, where he died at the age of sixty-six. His friends mourned in him *un uomo universale,* a typical Renaissance polymath.

*   *   *

The last fifteen years of the century brought about a number of small, regional victories for the Christians. In 1587 the siege of Sárkánysziget, in which the Turkish raiders suffered great losses (allegedly two thousand men died and fifteen hundred were captured), prompted a number of literary responses. György Salánki in his *Historia cladis turcicae ad*

Nádudvar, celebrating the 1580 victory of Ferenc Geszti over the renegade Savrar-Begh at Nádudvar, refers to the event as a second Lepanto.[75]

Similarly, the victorious battle fought by Sigismund Rákoczy at Szikszó (1588) was extolled in an epic by György Tardi.[76] This epic, in which historical events are presented interwoven with mythical happenings, adumbrates Miklós Zrinyi's major work about Sziget written eighty years later. The Szikszó victory captured the imagination of another author, Ferenc Salamon, who published his *Victoria pusilli Christianorum exercitus contra legionem Turcicam* in Prague and dedicated it to Rudolf II.[77] In 1593 the victory at Székesfehérvár was also immediately reported and hailed.

While Austria sporadically sent auxiliary troops against the Turks, after 1600 there was increased fighting between them and the Hungarians, from which, as might be expected, the Turks profited. They suffered a setback, however, when Moldavia, Wallachia, and Transylvania backed out of their alliance with the sultanate in 1595. Also, in 1595 Esztergom was recaptured by the Christians, though the Turks retook Eger in the same campaign.

As a result of the conflicts between Rudolf and the Hungarians, Mohammed Sokolić attacked Esztergom (1605), which the Austrians lost without any Hungarian troops present. It was not liberated until 1683. By the end of 1605 Esztergom, Kanizsa, and Eger were in Turkish hands. Nevertheless, the pashas in Hungary, away from the center of their power in Istanbul and close to Vienna, began to realize the increasing weakness of the Ottoman Empire and the rapid military development of the European states.

The compromise peace at Zsitvatorok (Žitava) of 11 November 1606 was signed by militarily and economically exhausted partners. The Latin version of the treaty became known throughout Europe because it was immediately printed for large-scale distribution, though the authorized document was drawn up in Hungarian. The negotiations and the text of the treaty were published in a number of contemporary works. Some of the signatories at Zsitvatorok were also famous humanist scholars such as Miklós Istvánffy and János Rimay.[78]

To quote Klaniczay's concise formulation:

> Between 1450 and 1490 the royal Renaissance flourished, supported by the Hunyadis. From 1490 to 1526 the period is marked by the patronage of episcopal sees and of an aristocratic Latin humanism, while the period between 1526 and 1570 represent the decades of the Reformation in which the burghers of the market towns and especially Kolozsvár (Cluj) play an important role. The

years between 1570 and 1600 are distinguished by the flowering of Renaissance culture in the courts of the nobility.[79]

In Matthias's court, as well as in the courts of the Jagiello kings, the visiting Italian, Dalmatian, and German humanists later spread the type of artistic and intellectual style that had been typical of Buda to the courts of Vienna and Cracow.[80] The country's desperate state and, in turn, the decline of some of the great humanist courts moved the Hungarian humanists of the Italian school further out of the mainstream. While Janus was still bound to Italy, his sixteenth-century colleagues established their intellectual contacts with the humanists of Vienna, Cracow, and most of all Wittenberg.

The sixteenth century witnessed lively theoretical discussions and heated disputes over practical criticism, such as the language and style of Dante's poetry, Aristotelian poetics and its application to poems (old and new), the quarrel of Lodovico Ariosto and Torquato Tasso, arguments about the difference between the poetic properties of the romance and the epic. These discussions prove that the humanists were eager to take a stand on literary and aesthetic issues and considered them crucial to their craft. Hungarian humanists who a century before would have been passionately participating in such discussions were, by and large, absent. The one notable exception is Sambucus but, while he wrote on the problems of imitation versus originality, he probably got his ideas second-hand, from Adrien Turnèbe of Paris. Nicaisius Ellebodius, who followed the debates even from Pozsony (Bratislava), either did not care to or did not succeed in involving his Hungarian friends in them.

Almost a hundred years of battles, raids, armed resistance, sacrifice, and humiliation took their toll in Hungary. Even the last traces of Matthias Corvinus's grand design had disappeared from the war-torn, dismembered body of that once admired kingdom. A full flowering of a western kind of Renaissance could never come about in the hectic, uncertain atmosphere of a land in which each home could turn into an outpost at a moment's notice. Scholars and artists were not only deprived of the peace and tranquility mandatory for their work, but often also of their personal freedom and livelihood. Poverty, servitude, and exile had been the fate of many. They lived by chance and suffered the hardships and vicissitudes of men without a country.

In the fifteenth century the Hungarian kings "feudalized" their humanists, and often suffered disillusionment when the new oligarchs ceased to serve the interests of a centralized power that they had originally been trained to promote. With the country's falling into the hands of the Turks and the Habsburgs, the new, sixteenth-century humanist was frequently separated from his feudatories or, in the case of a prelate, his see. He was forced to serve away from his homeland and, often, such powers as did not represent his own best interests. The hopes and goals of the previous century were replaced by disappointment and disintegration. While scholarship and the arts flourished, the setting had changed, often literally, to Italy or Vienna. And the yield lacked the trust in a glorious future.

NOTES

1. While the earlier cultural centers were the seats of bishoprics, from the fourteenth century on Buda, though it lacked an episcopal see, became the real focus of cultural life in Hungary, owing to the presence of the royal residence. Its prominence was most obvious during the reign of Matthias Corvinus, whose splendid court was a meeting place of Europe's intellectual and artistic elite. During this period the city of Buda, with its newly built Renaissance royal palace, gained international significance. Of the historians Galeotto Marzio (who also excelled in astronomy) and Antonio Bonfini represented Italy; Regiomontanus, the famed astronomer, Germany; and Ivan Duknović and Feliks Petančic (in the company of many lesser-known Dalmatian and Croatian artists and artisans), the southern Slavs. Scores of foreign authors dedicated their work to the Hungarian king, who was considered a generous Maecenas to the representatives of the New Learning. For a while even Marsilio Ficino considered moving to Buda. Matthias's court could also take pride in its native humanists, who had made the chancery comparable to the most respected ones in the West. The subsequent century, though marred by continual war and the loss of independence, also produced a large number of poets and scholars, who contributed to every facet of Renaissance humanism. Owing to spatial limitations only a small number of humanists active in Hungary could be included in this study. My selection was based on the significance of individual contributions and, to a lesser extent, on the intention to present the broadest possible spectrum. The reader may find the following works helpful in learning more about Hungarian achievements during this period: J. Balázs, *Sylvester János és kora* [*János Sylvester and His Time*] (Budapest, 1957); J. Balogh, *A muvészet Mátyás király udvarában* [*Art at the Court of King Matthias*], 2 vols. (Budapest, 1966); M. D. Birnbaum, *Janus Pannonius: Poet and Politician* (Zagreb, 1981); S. Eckhardt, "Balassi Bálint irói szándéka" ["Bálint Balissi's Literary Aims"], *Itk* 62 (1958): 337–49; I. Horváth, *Balassi költészete történeti poétikai megközelitésben* [*The Poetry of Balassi in a Historical Poetical Approach*] (Budapest, 1982); R. Gerézdi, *Janus Pannoniustól Balassi Bálintig* [*From Janus Pannonius to Belint Balassi*] (Budapest, 1968); idem, *A magyar világi lira kezdetei* [*The Beginnings of Vernacular Poetry in Hungary*] (Budapest, 1962); P. Gulyás, *A könvvnyomtatás Magyarorszagon a XV. és XVI. században* [*Printing in Hungary in the 15th and 16th Centuries*] (Budapest, 1931); J. Horváth, *Az irodalmi műveltség*

megoszlása: A *Magyar humanizmus* [*The Distribution of Book Learning: Hungarian Humanism*] (Budapest, 1954); idem, *A reformáció jegyében* [*In the Sign of the Reformation*] (Budapest, 1953); J. Huszti, *Janus Pannonius* (Budapest, 1931); *Janus Pannonius tanulmányok* [*Janus Pannonius Studies*], ed. T. Kardos and S. V. Kovács (Budapest, 1975); T. Kardos, "A régi magyar szinjátszás néhány kérdéséhez" ["On Some Problems of Early Hungarian Theater"], *Magyar Tudományos Akadémia Irodalom-történeti Osztály* 7 (1955): 16–64; E. Kastner, "Cultura italiana alla corte transilvana nel secolo XVI," *Corvina* 2 (1922): 40–56; T. Klaniczay, *A mult nagy korszakai* [*Great Epochs of the Past*] (Budapest, 1973); idem, *A reneszánsz és a barokk* [*Renaissance and Baroque*] (Budapest, 1961); *La Renaissance et la Reformation en Pologne et en Hongrie . . . (1450–1650)* (Budapest, 1962); I. Trencsényi-Waldapfel, *Erasmus és magyar barátai* [*Erasmus and His Hungarian Friends*] (Budapest, 1941); J. Turóczi-Trostler, *A magyar nyelv felfedezése* [*The Discovery of Hungarian*] (Budapest, 1953); idem, *Magyar irodalom—világirodalom* [*Hungarian Literature—World Literature*], 2 vols. (Budapest, 1961). For the most important series of the period, see Bibliotheca Hungarica antiqua, the new Bibliotheca unitariorum, the journal *Reneszánsz füzetek*, and *Régi magyar kőltők tára*. A most informative catalog on fifteenth-century Hungary, *Schallaburg '82, Matthias Corvinus und die Renaissance in Ungarn,* published on the occasion of that exhibit, contains facsimiles and other illustrative material, as well as an excellent topical bibliography.

2. János Vitéz of Zredna, *Opera quae supersunt,* ed. I. Boronkai (Budapest, 1980).

3. "Jani Pannonii Silva Panegyrica ad Guarinum Veronensem praeceptorem suum," in *Poemata quae uspiam reperiri potuerunt omnia 1–11,* ed. Samuel Teleki, 2 vols. (Utrecht, 1774), vol. 1. All further J. P. quotes refer to this edition.

4. *Epigramma* 1:126. All translations, unless otherwise stated, are mine.

5. *Epigramma* 1:174.

6. *Elegia* 1:10.

7. For more on the universities of Hungary, see A. L. Gabriel, *The Medieval Universities of Pécs and Pozsony* (Frankfurt am Main, 1969).

8. B. Iványi, *Kőnyvek, könyvtárak, könyvnyomdák Magyarországon, 1331–1600* [*Books, Libraries and Printing Presses in Hungary, 1331–1600*] (Budapest, 1937).

9. For more on this, see P. Klimes, *Bécs és a magyar humanizmus* [*Vienna and Hungarian Humanism*] (Budapest, 1934).

10. See J. R. von Aschback, *Geschichte der Wiener Universität und ihre Humanisten,* 3 vols. (Vienna, 1865–88, reprinted Vienna, 1965), as well as the series Studien zur Geschichte der Universität Wien, of which vol. 4 by F. Gall, *Die Insignien der Universität Wien* (Vienna, 1965), treats the subject; and V. Fraknói, *Hazai és külföldi iskoláztatás a XVI. században* [*Local and Foreign Education of Hungarian Students in the Sixteenth Century*] (Budapest, 1873).

11. R. Pfeiffer, *History of Classical Scholarship from 1300 to 1850* (Oxford, 1976).

12. For more on the subject, see J. Ábel, *Magyarországi humanisták és a Dunai Tudós Társaság* [*Hungarian Humanists and the Sodalitas Danubiana*] (Budapest, 1880); R. Gerézdi, *Váradi Péter* [*Péter Váradi*] (Budapest, 1942); Horváth, *Az irodalmi műveltség megoszlása;* T. Kardos, *A magyarországi humanizmus kora* [*The Period of Humanism in Hungary*] (Budapest, 1955).

13. Discussion and evaluation of the philosophical and ethical content of Erasmian thought falls outside the scope of this study. See Chapter 23 in this volume, "Desiderius Erasmus."

14. For a discussion and bibliography, see Balogh, *A művészet Mátyás király udvarában* 1:537–39 and passim. Matthias commissioned a large number of manuscripts, which—in addition to the ones he had confiscated from the rebels—made up the bulk of his famed Corvinian Library. Already Sigismund had a valuable collection of books, but Matthias's outshone it by far. Printing was also introduced to Hungary during Matthias's rule. The *Buda Chronicle (Chronica Hungarorum* or *Chronicon Budense)*, printed by Andreas Hess, appeared in 1493.

15. "Naiadum Italicarum principi Divae Feroniae" was first published in 1497. It is *Elegia,* vol. 1 in the Teleki edition. Ábel also published the Italian translation in *Analecta* (1880): 152–55. For more on the poems, see Birnbaum, *Janus Pannonius.*

16. Nicolaus Reusner's *Hocoepicorum sive itinerarium totius fere orbis libri VII* appeared in Basel in 1580, and in a second edition in 1592. The Marcello fragment was included in both editions (lines 643–54 in Teleki).

17. "Novum non est, apud Hungaros esse praeclara ingenia, quando Janus ille Pannonius, tantum laudis meruit in carmine, ut Italia ultro illi herbam porrigat." Quoted by Cvittinger in *Opuscula,* ed. David Cvittinger (Frankfurt an Main, 1711), 124 and also by Huszti in *Janus Pannonius,* 411.

18. Introduction to the 1559 Padua edition: *Régi magyar költők tára,* 3:468:A3.

19. *Magyar Irodalmi Lexikon* [*Hungarian Literary Dictionary*], 3 vols. (Budapest, 1965), 3:607. A beautifully executed facsimile edition of the *Emblemata* (Antwerp, 1564) was published recently in Hungary (Bibliotheca Hungarica Antiqua, 11 [Budapest, 1982]), including a penetrating study of the work by A. Buck.

20. I do not believe that he wrote *Annales.* For more on this see Birnbaum, *Janus Pannonius.*

21. Sambucus's own interest in history is further proved by his *Obsidio Zigethiensis,* recording the story of Sziget, and his publication of Pietro Ransano's (Ransanus's) *Epitome rerum ungaricarum* in 1558. His most important contribution to Hungarian, however, is his edition of Antonio Bonfini's oeuvre, which for a long time served as the standard historical work for the period. His large Bonfini edition included the first thirty books of Brenner, volumes 31–40 of Heltai, the extant manuscripts owned by Franciscus Ré-

vay and Franciscus Forgách, his own work regarding the years 1496–1526 (i.e., the Jagiellonian period), Brodarić's work on Mohács, Miklós Oláh's *Athila*, his own translation of Sebestyén Tinódi's piece on Eger, and his own history of Sziget. The entire publication appeared as *Antonii Bonfinii Rerum Hungaricarum decades quattor* (Basel, 1568 and Frankfurt, 1581). During the following centuries this work saw five Latin and two German editions. In 1572 Sambucus also published István Werbőczi's *Tripartitum*, and in the 1581 edition he enlarged it by adding to it earlier legal material pertaining to Hungary.

22. For material regarding the documentation of the uprising see *Monumenta Rusticorum in Hungaria rebellium anno MDXIV*, ed. A. F. Nagy (Budapest, 1979).

23. The best known of them was Paolo Giovio, bishop of Nocera.

24. For more on Taurinus, see S. V. Kovács, "A Dózsa háboru humanista éposza" ["The Humanist Epic of the Dózsa Uprising"], *Itk* 63 (1959): 451–73.

25. The best biographies of Brodarić to date are S. Székely, "Brodarics István élete és mű ködése" ["The Life and Work of István Brodarics"], *Történelmi Tár* (1888), 1:1–34, 2:225–62; P. Sörös, *Jerosini Brodarics István* [*Stephanus Brodericus*] (Budapest, 1907); and J. Szemes, *Oláh Miklós* (Esztergom, 1936).

26. On 6 August 1526. Published by Georgius Pray, *Annales regum Hungariae* 5 vols. (Vienna, 1763–70), 1:268–71.

27. D. Kerecsényi in "Nicolas Olah," *Nouvelle revue de Hongrie* 2 (1934): 277–87, republished in his *Válogatott irásai* [*Selected Writings*] (Budapest, 1979), 75.

28. For a thoughtful evaluation of Oláh's career, see Szemes, *Oláh Miklós*. For a more populist view, see V. Bucko, *Mikuláš Oláh a jeho doba* [*Miklós Oláh and His Time*] (Bratislava, 1940).

29. *Codex epistolaris*, 216.

30. "Hoc tamen magno mihi est dolori me per aulica negocia . . . ab hoc otio litterari honesto plerumque avocari": quoted by Kerecsényi, "Nicolas Olah," 238.

31. *Codex epistolaris*, 228.

32. Szemes, *Oláh Miklós*, 16–17.

33. Ibid., 35.

34. Edward Brown, *A Brief Account of Some Travels in Hungaria, Servia . . .* (London, 1673).

35. For more on Szántho, see V. Fraknói, "Egy magyar jezsuita a XVI. században" ["A Hungarian Jesuit in the 16th Century"], *Katolikus Szemle* (Budapest, 1888). Ambrogio Calepino's Latin dictionary, *Cornucopia* (Reggio, 1502), was revised by him in 1505 and in 1509. After Calepino's death fellow humanists kept publishing revised editions, adding Neolatin terminology. By 1590 the dictionary contained eleven languages. Almost all Latin dictionaries depended on his (more on this with regard to Faust Vrančić), until Egidio Forcellini published *Lexicon totius Latinitatis* in 1771.

36. For more on this, see Klaniczay, *A mult nagy korszakai.*

37. V. Gortan with V. Vratović, "The Basic Characteristics of Croatian Literature," *Humanistica Lovaniensis* 20 (1971): 47.

38. Turóczi-Trostler, *A magyar nyelv felfedezése,* quoted by Klaniczay in *A mult nagy korszakai,* 144.

39. Horváth, *A reformáció jegyében,* 139.

40. Niccolò Perotti and Battista Guarino, to mention only two.

41. Turóczi-Trostler, *A magyar nyelv felfedezése,* 35.

42. In 1543 Sylvester became professor at Vienna University and lectured on Hebrew, Greek, and history. There he also published poetry in Latin ("De bello Turcis inferendo," etc.). It seems that at this juncture of his life he moved away from Hungarian and returned to the fold of Erasmist Latin universalism. This part of his biography has not been adequately researched. A facsimile edition of the *Grammatica Hungaro-latina* was published by Indiana University Press (Bloomington, IN, 1968) with a foreword by T. A. Sebeok (Uralic Altaic Series, 55), which includes these most frequently quoted lines of Sylvester: "est enim regulatissima, ut vocant non minus quam una ex primariis, illis, hebraea, graeca et latina."

43. This habit was general among the authors of his time. The best examples of it are the numerous works of Bartol Djurdjević (Bartolomaeus Georgius or Georgievits) who, having returned from Turkish captivity, flooded Europe with his memoirs and travelogues, each including such sample translations.

44. J. Turóczi-Trostler, "A magyar nyelv felfedezése," in *Magyar irodalom—világirodalom,* 1:65.

45. A. Pirnát, "A magyar reneszánsz dráma poétikaja" ["The Poetic Properties of Hungarian Renaissance Drama"], *Reneszánsz füzetek [Booklets on the Renaissance]* 1 (1969): 527–55.

46. *A magyar irodalom története [History of Hungarian Literature],* ed. I. Söter, 6 vols. (Budapest, 1964–66): vol. 1: *A magyar irodalom története 1600–ig [History of Hungarian Literature till 1600],* ed. T. Klaniczay (Budapest, 1964), 376.

47. Among others, see J. Koltay-Kastner, "Bornemissza Péter humanizmusa" ["Péter Bornemissza the Humanist"] *Itk* 57 (1953): 91–124.

48. For example, in vol. 3 he mentions the death of his wife. I. Nemeskürty convincingly argues that *Postillák* moved away from the rhetorical type of literature toward the essay genre (see "Bornemissza stilusa" ["The Style of Bornemissza"], *Itk* 59 (1955): 23–35). See also I. Trencsényi-Waldapfel, "Bornemissza Péter nyelvművészete" ["The Poetic Language of Péter Bornemissza"], *Nyugat [Occident]* 24 (1931): 124–26.

49. Published in *Hungarian Anthology: A Collection of Poems,* trans. J. Grosz and W. A. Boggs (Toronto, 2d ed. 1966), 1.

50. More on János Decsi in the introductory essay to the facsimile edition of his work by A. Kurz, Bibliotheca Hungarica antiqua 10 (Budapest, 1979).

51. For more on his career, cf. T. Klaniczay, "Tinódi Sebestyén emlékezete," in *A reneszánsz és a barokk,* 39–53.

52. B. Varjas, introduction to the facsimile edition of Tinódi's *Cronica*, Bibliotheca Hungarica antiqua 2 (Budapest, 1959), 11.
53. Gáspár Heltai, *Cancionale, azaz historias énekes könyv* [*Cancionale, or A Collection of Poems for Singing*] (Kolossvar, 1574; facsimile, 1962). The title refers to the genre ("historias ének" = sung history).
54. Gáspár Heltai, *Historia inclyti Matthiae Hunyadis* (Cluj, 1565).
55. A new edition of *Háló* appeared in Budapest (1979), in which the editor, P. Kőszeghy, included a selection of Heltai's work.
56. Balassi's *Szép magyar comoedia* was an entirely new chapter in the history of Hungarian drama.
57. Pirnát, "A magyar reneszánsz dráma poétikája." It was T. Kardos who first published a collection of early Hungarian drama (*Régi magyar drámai emlékek*, 2 vols. to date [Budapest, 1960–]). It should also be mentioned that the authorship of the drama has been earlier attributed to the father of Bálint Balassi. R. Gerézdi reevaluated the historical evidence and came to the conclusion that it was written by Gáspár Madách, a contemporary of Balassi senior, who also lived in the region and therefore had knowledge of the events, as well as of the local geography and history.
58. It is pertinent to the tenor of the times that his son Miklós Istvánffy, author of *Historia rebus ungaricis XXXIV* (1622), decided on writing in Latin because he was eager to reach the largest possible readership.
59. Sárvár, Bártfa (Bardejov), Debrecen, Kolozsvár (Cluj), Gyulafehérvár (Alba Iulia), Szeben (Sibiu), and Brasso (Brașov) also had presses. *A Magyar irodalom története* contains a map showing printing presses active in Hungary during the sixteenth century, 1:200.
60. B. Varjas, "A Sárvár-Ujsziget nyomda betütipusai" ["The Types of the Sárvár-Ujsziget Press"], *Itk* 62 (1958): 140–51.
61. B. Varjas, "Heltai Gáspár a könyvkiadó" ["Gáspár Heltai, the Publisher"], *Reneszánsz füzetek* 24 (1973): 291–314.
62. It should be mentioned, however, that the Bardejov Protestant press published twice as many books during the same period as Telegdi's Trnava workshop.
63. *Magyarország történeti kronológiaja* [*Hungary's Historical Chronology*], ed. K. Benda, 4 vols. to date (Budapest, 1983–), 2:405.
64. For more on this subject see P. Ács, "A magyar irodalmi nyelv két elmélete: az Erazmista és a Balassi-követö" ["Two Theories on the Hungarian Literary Language: The Erasmists and the Balassi Followers"], *Reneszánsz füzetek* 53 (1983): 391–403.
65. He also translated poetry from Turkish (see G. Németh, "Balassi Bálint és a török költészet" ["Bálint Balassi and Turkish Poetry"] *Magyar Századok* [*Hungarian Centuries*] 3 [1948]: 80–100), Polish, and Croatian.
66. Balassi's tumultuous life has frequently been treated in Hungarian literary histories—often replacing the analysis of his poetry. Therefore, instead of recapitulating it, I refer the reader to R. Gerézdi, "Balassi Bálint (Rövid élet és jellemrajz)" ["Bálint Balassi (A Brief Life and Character Study)"], in *Janus Pannoniustól Balassi Bálintig*, 485–510.

67. For more on this subject see Klaniczay, *A mult nagy korszakai*, 217.
68. For a thoughtful and thought-provoking study, see V. Julow, "A Balassi-strófa ritmikája és eredetének kérdése" ["The Rhythm and Origin of the Balassi Stanza"], *Studia litteraria* 9 (1970): 39–49. He analyzes "Katona-ének," a bimetric poem by Balassi, and contends that it is not the Hungarian type of meter. Cf. also I. Bán, "Adalékok Balassi-versértelmezésekhez" ["Contributions to the Analysis of Balassi Poems"], *Studia litteraria* 17 (1979): 14–24, referring to M. Hardt, *Die Zahl in der Divina Commedia* (Frankfurt am Main, 1973).
69. Turóczi-Trostler, "A magyar nyelv felfedezése" ["The Discovery of the Hungarian Vernacular"], in *Magyar irodalom—világirodalom*, 111.
70. Horváth, *Balassi költészete történeti*.
71. I. Horváth, "Az eszményi Balassi-kiadás koncepciója" ["The Concept of an Ideal Balassi Edition"], *Itk* 74 (1972): 209–306, and *Reneszánsz füzetek* 35 (1977): 613–31.
72. Horváth, *Balassi költészete történeti*, 219.
73. I am grateful to V. Muljević for having shared with me many of his findings regarding the life and work of Faust Vrančić. I am also using his biographical dating (1551 for the year of his birth, instead of ca. 1540, the date accepted by several scholars).
74. It was reprinted in Zagreb in 1976.
75. The battle took place on 19 July 1580. Salanki's work was published by Gáspár Heltai in 1581.
76. György Tardi, *Historia Szikszoniensis* (Bratislava, 1588).
77. For more on this work see C. Gőllner, *Turcica. Die europäischen Türckendrucke des XVI. Jahrhunderts*, 4 vols. (Bucharest, 1961–78), 2:428.
78. The diary of János Rimay in which he recorded the negotiations and the signing of the documents was published by G. Bayerle in "The Compromise at Zsitvatorok," *Archivum Ottomanicum* 6 (1980) [monograph].
79. Klaniczay, *A mult nagy korszakai*, 164.
80. This is especially true for the arts, primarily of illumination. But even the poetry of Jan Kochanowski contains *topoi* and poetic solutions that derive directly from the oeuvre of Janus Pannonius.

26 ❧ HUMANISM IN THE SLAVIC CULTURAL TRADITION WITH SPECIAL REFERENCE TO THE CZECH LANDS
Rado L. Lencek

THIS ESSAY AIMS TO GIVE AN INSIGHT INTO THE PHENOMENON of Renaissance humanism in the cultural traditions of the Slavic peoples in eastern Europe and attempts a comprehensive survey of the humanist concerns and scholarship of the so-called Slavic Renaissance cultures through the end of the sixteenth century.

Since the end of the nineteenth century saw the beginning of Slavic Renaissance scholarship, many a specialized study has focused on individual Slavic cultural traditions that participated in the Renaissance movement of the West.[1] But while these studies have assembled considerable documentation on the range and extent of the Renaissance humanistic movement among the Slavs, no general, comprehensive examination of specifically Slavic humanism has yet been produced. Many scholars have even appeared to avoid this aspect of the Slavic Renaissance by simply limiting their field of inquiry to the written production in vernacular languages, or even to its belles-lettres. One might have inferred from this focus that classical scholarship—philological, historical, theological, philosophical topics—or even stylistic and rhetorical treatises originally written in Latin were not seen as part of the cultural heritage of most Slavic cultural traditions. Furthermore, though this observation obviously goes beyond such Renaissance research, one formed the impression that this portion of the Slavic culture was not thought to hold any clues for the understanding of our own contemporary world. For this reason, the invitation to reexamine the record of the humanist Renaissance tradition among the Slavs—even if confined to the bounds of a brief essay—seemed opportune and timely. My survey will be concerned exclusively with the Latin and Greek texts of the Slavic Renaissance tradition and will not give an account of the literary production of the Slavic Renaissance in general or of individual humanists and their contributions to particular Slavic vernacular literatures.

The concepts and terminology to be used in this survey are those common to recent Renaissance scholarship, while the concept of Renaissance humanism as well as the parameters of its application as developed by Paul O. Kristeller are used. Thus, in this discussion, the terms Renaissance humanism signifies that broad cultural and literary movement of European Renaissance civilization that dealt with the disciplines of the *studia humanitatis:* grammar, rhetoric, history, poetry, and moral philosophy; and which dominated European culture from the middle of the fourteenth century until 1600. While the Renaissance model developed in Italy, it spread to the rest of the Latin West and to non-Latin Europe shortly after the middle of the fifteenth century. The Renaissance humanists' field of interest was, of course, classical Latin and Greek scholarship. Their activity centered on discovering and studying classical authors whose works were either unknown or neglected during the Middle Ages. Their work of reading, copying, translating, and interpreting the classical heritage later expanded into editing and printing and, eventually, into producing their own prose, orations, letters, historical treatises, and poetry. Guided by the common ideal of imitating the ancients, the Renaissance men of letters cultivated the disciplines of grammar, rhetoric, ancient history and mythology, archaeology, epigraphy, and antiquarian subjects. Latin was their language. By profession they were mostly teachers, chancellors, and secretaries attached to princes or to cities. Erudition, eloquence, and elegance of speech and writing constituted their primary skills and excellence. Originally neither philosophical nor exclusively literary in substance, the Renaissance humanism treated in this discussion is conceived as a manner and method of practicing the *studia humanitatis,* and as the form and process of intellectual contribution to any specific discipline of Renaissance civilization as a whole.

*   *   *

By the first half of the fourteenth century—when Charles IV, emperor and king of Bohemia, entertained the first humanist Petrarch in Prague, his imperial capital (1356)—the Slavic peoples in central and eastern Europe occupied an area that roughly extended as far as the Rüggen, Stettin, Oder–Neisse, Trieste, Adriatic Sea line on the west. Except for what are now Upper and Lower Austria, part of Hungary, Transylvania, and Romanian Wallachia, this territory still represented a Slavic linguistic continuum that stretched across the Vistula River, the Dnieper, and the Don River to the east.

Within this continuum, a number of Slavic ethnic-linguistic nuclei had already unfolded: Russian (though less familiar, the term "Rus'" is perhaps more accurately used to describe the East Slavic reality up to the fourteenth century), Polish, Bohemian (Czech), Bulgarian, Serbian, Croatian, and Slovene. At this time, four of them—the independent Poland, Bohemia in the empire, Serbia, and Bulgaria—existed as states. The early principality of Karantania in the eastern Alps, which united most of the Slovene lands, was soon broken up and divided among German dynasties; in 1270 it became the center of a rapid swell of the Habsburg dynasty in the area. In 1102 an independent Croatian state became part of the Hungarian crown. After 1242 most Russian principalities came under the control of the Mongols, and most western Russian lands became part of the Grand Duchy of Lithuania.

The period 1350–1600 is characterized by the following series of developments. In the East, Dmitrij Donskoj won a decisive victory over the Mongols in 1380, and the Moscow princes began to "gather in" the Russian principalities. By the end of the reign of Grand Prince Ivan III (1462–1505), called the "Great," a consolidated "Muscovy" was ready to become Russia. Under Ivan III's rule the political sovereignty of the Tatars was formally ended (1480), and the old independent principalities—notably Novgorod, Tver, and Vjatka—were successively forced to join Moscow. On the external front, the western lands of the old Rus' had already been annexed by the Lithuanians and the Poles: by 1363 the Duchy of Lithuania occupied the lands along the Dnieper River as far as the Black Sea, and the Kingdom of Poland had expanded into Galicia and Volhynia. Internally, during Ivan III's rule, the power of the independent princes was broken, a new class of boyars (landowners) emerged, and a new form of bondage (serfdom) was created. Ivan III's marriage to Sophia Palaeologus (1472), niece of the last Byzantine emperor, could scarcely make an impact on Russian society of the time. Raised and educated in Renaissance Italy, Sophia introduced Italian artists and tried to spread the glory of the Italian Renaissance that she had witnessed in Rome. But in this endeavor she failed, largely for lack of an educated nobility and middle class, which in other countries had proved the chief patrons and audience of artists. Under Ivan III's successors, Basil III (1505–33) and Ivan IV (1533–84), the latter crowned "czar and grand prince of all Russia" in 1547, a number of other principalities were absorbed by Moscow. A strong autocratic system was established and strengthened and formed the basis for the czarist period of Muscovite history.

In the South, the last decades of the fourteenth century marked the end of both major Slavic independent states in the Balkans: the Ottomans destroyed the Serbian state in 1389 and, four years later, the Bulgarian state. For another half-century, a small Serbian principality with Belgrade as its capital was under Ottoman power but still administered by native princes. For a much longer time an even smaller principality,

practically inaccessible in its location high in the mountains of Montenegro, retained a relative independence and freedom. In 1453 the Ottomans conquered Constantinople and brought the Byzantine Empire to
an end. By 1526 they occupied the rest of the Balkan peninsula; they also
practically controlled the Hungarian plain and all the main roads linking
the Balkans with central Europe. The islands of Dalmatia and their narrow hinterland on the Adriatic coast were part of the territory under
the authority of the doge and senate of the Republic of Venice, and the
tiny city of Dubrovnik (Ragusa), a relatively independent republic of its
own, represented the only oasis of freedom and independence in the Balkans.

In central Europe in the West, the Holy Roman Empire remained in
existence, though after having lost the contest with the papacy and after
the promulgation of Charles IV's Golden Bull (1356), more and more as
Sacrum Romanum imperium nationis Germanicae. After the death of
Sigismund of Luxembourg (1437), the imperial crown, in theory elective,
became hereditary in the Habsburg dynasty of Austria, and its capital
moved from Prague to Vienna. Even as early as 1556, under pressure of
the Reformation and in consequence of an increasing struggle for greater
and greater autonomy among the individual members—electorates of
the empire—such a weakened giant formation meant little more than a
loose confederation of the different princes of Germany.

In Bohemia, the rule of the Luxembourg dynasty (1310–1437) integrated the lands of the Bohemian crown (Bohemia, Moravia, Silesia,
the Lusatian lands) into the central European cultural tradition. From
1348 Bohemia had its own university in Prague, the first such institution
in central Europe. At the turn of the century, it also claimed the first
national religious reform program, the Hussite Reformation, which was
grafted, as it were, on the indigenous Church Slavonic linguistic and textual tradition. In 1415 the reform movement gave Bohemia its first martyr, Jan Hus, triggering a long religious-national civil war in its lands.
George of Poděbrady (1457–71), the only Hussite king of Bohemia, once
again raised his country to the cultural level it had attained under Charles
IV; during George's reign, religious strife came to a temporary halt and
a humanistic movement of the Renaissance returned. Upon the death of
Poděbrady, a dynastic struggle for succession erupted among a strong
Hungary (Matthias Corvinus, 1458–90), Austria (Frederick III, 1440–
93; Maximilian I, 1493—1519), and Poland (Casimir IV, 1447–92; his
son Ladislas II ruled Bohemia during 1471–1516), weakening the status
of the lands under the Bohemian crown and preparing the way for their
ultimate incorporation into the realm of the Habsburg dynasty.

In the Austrian lands, this period represented the growth and strengthening of the dynastic position of the archdukes of Habsburg (in 1452 Frederick III was crowned emperor), the consolidation of their position within the empire and in Vienna. Maximilian I, married to Bianca Maria Sforza, sister of the duke of Milan, Giangaleazzo Sforza, still ruled the empire from outside Vienna. He unified the government of his Austrian lands, however, and through his matrimonial arrangements produced the vast commonwealth that was to pass into the hands of his successor Charles V (1519–56), as well as the long-lasting unity of Austria–Bohemia–Hungary. It was a time of intensified Ottoman pressures on the inner Austrian lands (Styria, Carniola, Carinthia); of the stabilization of defense along the military border; of the first organized peasants' revolts against the feudal order; and of the Protestant Reformation. Two events of foremost cultural significance took place within this period. The year 1365 saw the founding of the Domschule bei St. Stephen in Vienna, the precursor of the University of Vienna and the only academic institution in Austrian lands at the time. In 1438 the imperial chancellery migrated from the Prague of the Luxembourg dynasty to the Vienna of the Habsburgs, bringing with it the German literary language, some sense for Latin eloquence, and the humanist disposition and concern for style.

Succeeding Charles Robert of Anjou (1308–42), Louis I the Great (1342–82), and Sigismund of Luxembourg (1387–1437), Matthias Corvinus (1458–90) ruled a Hungary that, from the early eleventh century, included the Slovak lands and, from 1102, most of the Croatian provinces. The only "true" Hungarian national ruler, Corvinus was engaged in formulating and implementing a most ambitious political and cultural plan for his lands. Successful in his campaigns against the Turks—he had regained Bosnia, invaded the Austrian lands, conquered Styria, Carinthia, and Carniola—he occupied Vienna and made it his capital for fifteen years. His third wife, the Neapolitan princess Beatrice d'Este of Naples and Aragon, was instrumental in helping him attract humanists, poets, and artists to his court. In 1467 he founded the University of Pozsony (Bratislava) and a college in Buda. His library, the Corviniana, was acclaimed as the richest humanist collection in central Europe of the time. Under his successors, Ladislas II Jagiello (1490–1516) and Louis II Jagiello (1516–62), and under Ottomon pressure Hungary rapidly disintegrated. The Mohács disaster of 1526 was followed by the tripartite division of Hungary, which remained in effect for another 150 years.

In the wake of the successive divisions and incursions into its boundaries, Poland entered into a new era at the beginning of the fourteenth century. Crowned king of Poland in 1320, Ladislas Lokietek (1314–33), one of the Piast dukes of Kujavia, revived the idea of Polish unity under a national king. His son Casimir III the Great (1333–70) broadened and consolidated the unity of Polish territories, annexed Galicia and Volhynia to the East, and began a policy of conciliation with the Lithuanian princes. Stimulated by the example of Holy Roman Emperor Charles IV, king of Bohemia, he encouraged learning and through Italian influences at the court of Hungary and the French connections of Prague was able to raise the level of learning among the Poles to match western European standards. In 1364 he founded the University of Cracow. Leaving no male heirs of his own, he bequeathed his kingdom to the son of his sister Elizabeth, Louis I of Hungary, who died in 1382. It was at this point that the Poles accepted Louis I's younger daughter Jadwiga as their queen and helped arrange her marriage to Jagiello, grand duke of Lithuania, who consequently became king of Poland as Ladislas II (1386–1424). This marriage supplied the foundation for the Polish–Lithuanian common-wealth, which for more than three hundred years included the west Russian and Ukrainian lands along the Dnieper River and shaped their cultural orientation. During the next two hundred years, 1386–1572, Ladislas II, Ladislas III, Casimir IV, Sigismund I, and Sigismund II Augustus were among the most representative rulers of the Jagiellonian dynasty. With the real union of both countries in 1569, Poland's political center of gravity shifted eastward. The ensuing prolonged wars with Moscow, the extended periods of elective kings, the setbacks to Polish power abroad and at home, and the shortsighted selfishness of the Polish gentry led to a disintegration of the state, which culminated in the partitions of Poland in 1772, 1793, and 1795. After 1596 the capital of Poland was moved from Cracow to Warsaw. Thanks to Sigismund I's marriage to Bona Sforza of Milan in 1518, the royal court at Cracow became the home of the highest attainments of Italian Renaissance art. Under Sigismund II (1548–72), in the wake of humanist scholarship and Renaissance art, the doctrine of the Reformation entered into Poland.

The situation of the Polish–Lithuanian commonwealth to the east of the western Dvina, the western Bug, and east of the upper Vistula River was especially complicated. By 1386, the Grand Duchy of Lithuania controlled an enormous territory of the west Rus'. This area stretched up into the Polotsk and Smolensk lands and eastward beyond the entire Pripet and Berezina river basin, across the Dnieper River, beyond the Novogorod–Seversk, Černigov, and Kiev regions, and south of Kiev into the Wild Prairies. Galicia and Volhynia had been annexed to Poland since 1349. While most of these territories were part of the commonwealth only until 1598, Galicia and Volhynia remained within the domain until 1772. Even at that time the Orthodox, ethnically East Slavic population of this area represented the two ethno-linguistic bases that are now known as Belorussian and Ukrainian. Their vernacular differences, however, remained barely distinguishable for an exceedingly long period of time.

＊　　＊　　＊

If we wish to understand the extent to which the cultural tradition of the Slavic peoples participated and shared in the development and legacy of Renaissance humanism, we must go back to the time the Slavic peoples became integrated into a Christian Europe. Since approximately A.D. 500, when the Slavs were first recorded in the annals of history, they were the recipients of a Christianity that came to them from both the Byzantine and the Roman cultural orbits of medieval Europe. Historians of Slavic cultures have shown that the linguistic policy and practice of the subsequent Roman Catholic and Orthodox churches proved disastrous to Slavic cultural unity and had profound repercussions in the life of all the Slavic nations. It is known that the Iroscottish, Frankish, Saxon, Bavarian, and Latin Italian missionaries who came to the Slavs from the West were part of a rigid, universal-western Latin tradition, while the missionaries from Constantinople practiced a linguistic tolerance toward the use of ethnic vernaculars in religious texts and in rituals for public worship.

During the second half of the ninth century, two Byzantine missionaries, Cyril-Constantine the philosopher and his brother Methodius, both versed in Slavic, created the basis for the development of a Slavic church and of a literature in the Slavic language. They worked in Moravia and Pannonia in central Europe, where they had been invited by local Slavic princes. Since they were from Thessalonica, the capital of Greek Macedonia on the Slavic–Greek borderland, Cyril and Methodius used a Slavic dialect that was at the time still understandable by all Slavic speakers. They created a Slavic liturgical language, Church Slavonic, and its written tradition, which was used first in Moravia and Pannonia, and for varying lengths of time was practiced and preserved among the Czechs, Slovaks, and Croats. After 885 the Church Slavonic tradition was transplanted to Bulgaria and spread to Macedonia and Serbia. By 989, it had reached Kievan Rus'. First written in a Glagolitic script and later in the so-called Cyrillic alphabet, this Church Slavonic language remained—with only slight modifications through time—the *lingua sacra* of the Greek Orthodox church among the Slavs. This same language, only even more significantly influenced by the vernacular, functioned until the end of the eighteenth century as the literary Slavonic language of the Russian, White Russian, Bulgarian, and Serbian Orthodox cultural communities.

When I say that Latin dominated in the religious practice of the western Slavic peoples who were traditionally Roman Catholic, I do not wish to claim, of course, that the early Slavic Christian communities, in particular the ancestors of the present Poles, Czechs, Slovaks, Slovenes, and Croats, at any time made any attempts to put the Slavic vernaculars to a catechetic and homiletic use. Charlemagne's *capitularia* and the oldest Slavic linguistic records, which predate the recording of the oldest Church Slavonic manuscripts (*Freising Fragments,* ca. A.D. 1000), make it quite clear that Slavic vernacular texts must have existed in Slavic communities in the medieval Latin cultural area, including Moravia-Pannonia, before the mission of Cyril and Methodius. Yet the *lingua sacra* of Roman Catholic Slavs was Latin, as was the language of the presbyter and the monk, of the feudal lord and the secular clerk, of jurisprudence, knowledge, learning, teaching, and scholarship. Through the centuries and even into the present, and to varying degrees—depending on the distance from the western cultural centers and the level of education—the western Slavs were part of Latin Europe, of its Latin institutional bodies and their Latin intellectual universalism. It is against this background that we must understand the remarkable coincidence—almost co-occurrence—of western and Slavic Renaissance humanistic currents, suggesting a much narrower causal relationship than one finds in the evolution of their vernacular literatures and some other literary developments of later centuries.

Yet within the broader framework of European civilization, differences and variations of cultural movements do exist in any period, and, as historians have shown, different phases with different physiognomies in any such period may be found even within the same time and the same geographic area. Consequently, it would be appropriate to identify the variables by which the Slavic humanistic movement of the Renaissance differs from its western model—Italian humanism and the humanism of Germany or of the Low Countries—as well as to demarcate its own distinctive characteristics by which any individual, regional, or even ethno-cultural phases and their specific Renaissance humanist features might be identified in Slavic cultural traditions.

Such are my goals in this survey, organized along a spatial axis that stretches—according to one of the most frequent *loci communis* of Slavic humanist writers—"a mari Adriatica in Asiam ad incognita septentrionalis usque littora" ("from the Adriatic sea in Asia to the unknown north up to the littoral"). It is my objective to present Slavic Renaissance humanism in its origin, development, and transformations. However, it is along this axis, when seen in its entire range, that so-called Slavic Renaissance humanism presents a very complex picture. The variables that appear in this picture and the problems they raise, such as the very presence or absence of a classical tradition in a Slavic society claiming its own Renaissance season; the relative intensity of interest in classical antiquity in individual areas; and, above all, the question of the availability or absence of social mechanisms to generate interest in and to promote classical studies in a society, are far too broad and complex to permit any simple answers.

Still, I would like to focus for a moment on two very specific aspects of these problems, which are especially important for understanding the state, circumstances, and conditions of the Slavic Renaissance in general. One concerns the problem and function of the *studia humanitatis* as a cultural and educational program in a Renaissance society and the relation of such a program to societies claiming a Slavic Renaissance. The other concerns the issue of the existence and functioning of a Renaissance humanist movement in societies as widely dissimilar in their historical relation to the antiquity, classical scholarship, and philosophical values that are usually associated with the classical tradition, as are the societies claiming a Slavic Renaissance and humanist tradition. As has been suggested, both aspects lie at the very core of the recent scholarly debate on the question of a Slavic Renaissance.

The definition of Renaissance humanism adopted in this discussion—a broad cultural movement of the European Renaissance civilization that dealt with the disciplines of the *studia humanitatis* dominating European culture and those cultural centers in Slavic lands participating in this movement—introduces an important practical, professional aspect of the *studia humanitatis* in society. It should not be forgotten that the humanist movement, which inherited the professional practice of grammar and rhetoric from medieval *dictatores,* also added a new dimension to this tradition. This dimension was represented by classical studies and encompassed an admiration of the classical Latin and Greek languages, a mania for their texts, and a fashion for patterning compositions on classical models that ultimately affected all other branches of learning in this era. Manifested in the style and methodology of individual disciplines, in the studied elegance of literary expression, in the increasing use of classical source materials, in the greater knowledge of history and of critical methods, this influence is the achievement and contribution of the Renaissance humanists, the professional heirs and successors of the medieval *dictatores.* They were now, by profession, teachers of grammar and rhetoric—of the *studia humanitatis*—at universities or secondary schools, or secretaries to princes or cities.

Obviously, by calling for specific groups of professionals in a society, this definition and understanding of Renaissance humanists and

Renaissance humanism would scarcely seem applicable to societies in which Latin or Greek or both languages, classical or corrupted in form, were not an instrument of communication for at least some of its social classes, let alone to societies that did not have the professional need for humanistically educated talents. Renaissance humanism was the beginning of the very last period of intellectual universalism in Europe that still allowed itinerant scholars to move freely over the entire continent, from university to university, from city to city, from court to court, and—by implication—away from the lands that did not possess such centers of professional opportunity. Thus, it is only understandable why quite a few fourteenth-, fifteenth-, and sixteenth-century Slavic lands were (one might say) culturally centrifugal. At the same time, it becomes clear why it is sometimes very difficult to speak of a Slavic Renaissance humanism as a cultural historical force in lands and areas in which cultural and social conditions indispensable for the existence of Renaissance humanism did not favor or even allow its development.

The dissimilarities of conditions and circumstances favoring or disfavoring, promoting or obstructing the development of Renaissance humanism in Slavic cultural traditions, therefore, run much deeper in the social, religious, and cultural evolutions of individual Slavic societies. In the final analysis, Renaissance humanism is intimately linked with the fashionable prestige of the revival of antiquity. Ancient classical culture became an ideal and a matter for the education of children, and a classical scholar became a most indispensable professional specialist, needed and wanted to serve the new fashion and style of the day, to teach and cultivate the elegance and decorum of ancient models. It was in such societies that their rich rulers and princes, secular and ecclesiastical, their courts, productive free cities, and educated citizens most generously patronized art and literature. Their scholar-professionals were called on to conduct the classical prestigious forms of social communication—correspondence in the chancelleries, public speaking and oratory—and above all to educate and teach new generations in classical studies. It is only against this background that one can understand the failure to cultivate the *studia humanitatis* in societies in which such conditions and circumstances were lacking.

The sociocultural and sociolinguistic fact that Christianity progressed to the Slavs from two centers—from Rome, which insisted on the universality of the Latin language in religious and public life, and from Constantinople, which used Greek in these same functions but allowed peoples the privilege of conducting Christian worship in their vernaculars—is, as already suggested, a further factor responsible for the creation of the split in Slavic societies in relation to Renaissance humanism. It is not to say, however, that the Greek-Byzantine world, which gave the Orthodox Slavs their *lingua sacra*, did not have its own cult of antiquity and its own revival of classical and philological studies, somewhat earlier in time, yet complementary to the evolution of the cult of *studia humanitatis* in the West.

The critical fact here is that the introduction to Slavic peoples of the vernacular as the vehicle of religious culture, representing, as it were, a victory of the principle of language equality in the history of Slavic cultures, practically meant a departure from Byzantine tradition for at least segments of the Slavic Orthodox societies. Thus, in most of the Slavic Orthodox world the religious and linguistic emancipation turned out to bring an evolution toward cultural isolation. The earliest South Slavic Church Slavonic tradition in immediate contact with the Greek Orthodox church shared a part of the Byzantine religious literature and a tiny fraction of the Byzantine nonreligious literature. There was no direct link with classical antiquity, however, and the translation of Byzantine works into Slavic was far from perfect. As the French Slavic philologist Antoinne Meillet put it, the Church Slavonic renderings of the Byzantine texts, at times even translations made before the eleventh century, were very often poorly selected, clumsily translated, in a language far from the natural dialects, and therefore difficult to understand. Among western Slavs under the ecclesiastical jurisdiction of Rome, Latin was, of course, totally incomprehensible to the people. Yet it was in the West—and perhaps for that very reason—that true vernacular written traditions developed relatively early in natural dialects. In eastern Slavic societies, where church language was all the time half understandable to everybody, for centuries nothing similar happened. There, the language of the oldest Church Slavonic texts, preserved in later manuscripts, copied by poorly trained and half-illiterate scribes, following loose orthographic and grammatical standards of several varieties, became dangerously corrupted. During the fourteenth century, again among the South Slavs in immediate contact with the Greek Orthodox church, a movement for revision of Slavic religious texts began in Bulgaria. It was, if one might compare, a Slavic version of the biblical philology of the Byzantine humanist type, aimed at establishing a pure and unified linguistic norm for all the lands of Orthodox Slavdom. Two principles dominated this reform: modeling of the orthography and grammar of religious texts on the exemplary texts of the oldest tradition of Cyril and Methodius, and examining the language of translation of these texts against their Greek originals. Thus, new models of the oldest pattern of the Church Slavonic language emerged and the revised texts assumed an iconic value in Slavic Orthodox communities. As late as the end of the sixteenth century, the first norm of the Church Slavonic written language was set up; the corrected texts and their grammars, however, made Church Slavonic still less comprehensible and farther from the living language.

At the end of the sixteenth century, among the Belorussian and Ukrainian Orthodox, awakened and stimulated by contact with the Polish humanist Latin tradition, this new standardized Church Slavonic now began to be considered as the "Latin" of the Slavs, as their proper ecclesiastical and classical language to serve as a language of scholarship and culture. This movement, self-contradictorily lining up the Church Slavonic with classical Greek and Latin, certainly represented a revival, a philological renaissance, though by no means a Renaissance humanist movement of the western type. This Church Slavonic revival lacked all the ingredients of Renaissance humanism in the West: classical antiquity, the entire program of the *studia humanitatis,* and the ideas of ancient literatures that served as a ferment and inspiration for the intellectual changes transforming western intellectual and cultural history.

At the same time, one has to recognize the importance of Renaissance humanism's contribution and of the humanistic learning of its representatives outside the limits of the *studia humanitatis,* specifically in the evolution of Slavic Renaissance cultures in vernacular languages. Since their entry into the medieval Latin cultural orbit, Slavic communities in the West had possessed their sociolinguistically prestigious usage of vernaculars, no matter how modest it was, and gradually developed their own written traditions. As elsewhere in western European countries, these written traditions were functionally rarely in open competition with the use of Latin; even during the Renaissance of the fifteenth and sixteenth centuries there was no rivalry between Latin and vernacular literatures in Slavic lands. On the contrary, in areas in which the earliest contact with the Italian Renaissance took place, such as Dalmatia, Dubrovnik, or Poland, many humanist scholars of Latin and Greek classical authors, masters of a classical Latin style, are found among the advocates of the vernacular, and a significant number of authors wrote in both languages, Latin and Slavic. Poetry in particular—to mention only a few names by way of example, Hanibal Lucić (1485–1553), Marin Držić (1520–1567), Dinko Ranjina (1536–1607) in Dalmatian and Dubrovnik letters, or Mikolay Rey (1505–1569) and Jan Kochanowski (1530–1584) in Polish literature—was an important domain of interaction between classical models and vernacular innovations in Slavic lands. For the vernacular introduced new genres of poetry, but no poetics or rhetoric, and as for vocabulary, grammar, and style, vernacular languages had to be educated and developed after the model of Latin before they were able to take over the functions of literary languages. The field of translation from classics, Latin and Greek, including a translation of the entire Bible into several Slavic vernaculars, was another such area of humanist–vernacular interaction. In the religious sphere it represented an extension of the humanistic tradition of biblical philology in Slavic vernaculars. Linked with the Bohemian Hussite Reformation (fifteenth century) and with Polish and South Slavic Protestant Reformation movements (sixteenth century), this tradition is in Slavic cultural histories usually linked with the Renaissance periods of individual Slavic literatures. Thus, the humanists' teaching of poetry and eloquence, their translations and philological activities, exposure to classical learning, humanistic education, and training, and the fashionable prestige of the humanities during the same centuries of a Slavic Renaissance humanism in the strict sense impregnated and fertilized Slavic vernacular cultures for their own independent growth. The presentation and history of this phase of the Slavic Renaissance, however, goes beyond the scope of this survey.

*   *   *

Italian humanism reached Bohemia in the second half of the fourteenth century, during the reign of Charles IV.[2] It reached Prague, the capital of the empire, directly from Italy with appeals to the emperor for the protection of democratic government in Rome and restoration of Roman power and glory. Paradoxical as it may seem, these appeals proved to be significant and consequential more for their rhetorical style than for their substance; they were bringing to the famous emperor's chancellery new patterns of epistolography, models and styles of new rhetoric and poetry so quintessential to the New Learning of the age. The correspondents and visitors to the Holy Roman Emperor and his Czech dignitaries in Prague were no less illustrious men than the famous tribune of the Roman people, Cola di Rienzo (1313–1354), and the first humanist and Italian poet, Francesco Petrarca (Petrarch, 1304–1374). Cola di Rienzo visited Prague in 1350, and Petrarch addressed his first letter to Charles in February 1351. The emperor met Petrarch in 1355 in Mantua, and the next year Petrarch was Charles's guest in Prague. Their correspondence—three letters are preserved from Charles to Petrarch and fourteen from Petrarch to Charles—extends through the years 1351–1361/62.[3]

Two men in Charles's chancellery were in particular influenced by this early contact with Italian humanists: Arnošt z Pardubic (d. 1364), the emperor's archbishop of Prague, a man with an exquisite classical education received in Bologna and Prague; and Jan ze Středy (known also as Johann von Neumarkt, Iohannes Noviforensis, d. 1380), bishop of Naumburg, Litomyšl, and Olomouc, since 1343 a notary in the imperial chancery, between 1353 and 1374 its *senior imperialis aule cancellarius.* This man, a German by birth from Silesia, known also for his role in the development of the contemporary High Standard German literary language, was the first Czech humanist of the new Italian school.[4] There are eight letters from Petrarch addressed to him, and eight letters from Jan ze Středy addressed to Petrarch preserved for the decade 1352–1362/63.[5] Five of Jan ze Středy's letters are official, three personal, devoted to books and manuscripts Petrarch sent to his correspondent in Prague. These letters were copied and recopied in the imperial chancery and became an important source of inspiration in the history of Czech humanism.

This first breeze of Petrarchan humanism, so characteristic for the period of Charles IV and his son Wenceslas IV in Bohemia, was followed by waves of humanistic learning from Italy, sufficiently strong to generate a humanist movement in Czech lands. Among the most important channels of diffusion for this current were, of course, the contacts created by the education of young Bohemian intellectuals at Italian universities, their personal contacts with Italian humanists, and the contacts they had with Italian humanist prelates at the Council of Constance (1414–18) and the Council of Basel (1431), convened in part to mend the damage caused by the Czech reform movement. In addition, three protagonists of the international humanist movement, now already in motion, who influenced Czech literati of the period, should also be recalled here: Girolamo Balbi,[6] Conrad Celtis,[7] both for a time teachers at the universities at Vienna and Prague, and, of course, the famous secretary in the imperial chancery of Frederick III, and the archhumanist of transalpine central Europe, Aeneas Silvius Piccolomini.[8]

Aeneas Silvius had already become acquainted with the Bohemians at the Council of Basel, and later influenced profoundly his Czech colleagues in Frederick's chancery; he entertained a lively correspondence with them even after they had returned to their own country. More than any other contemporary observer of the fifteenth-century Bohemian Slavs, Aeneas Silvius must have understood the intellectual substance of their Hussite movement. In his report to Cardinal Juan de Carvajal on his mission of 1451 to George of Poděbrady in Bohemia, he speaks of his discussions with the Taborite priests at the royal city of Tabor with the unambiguous yet fair posture of a Catholic humanist. His discussions with the Taborites—he says—were attended by "many students and citizens who knew Latin; for this perfidious genus of men has the single good quality of loving letters."[9]

It is also known that Aeneas Silvius's writings—his letters, poems, orations, memorials, and historical treatises—pleasing by their elegance, clarity of style, and vivid personal and historical flavor, were avidly read by his Czech contemporaries and generations coming after them; for he was a master of rhetorical art, a most elegant stylist for his time; his texts, in particular his letters to his Czech friends, were later copied, collected, recopied, and printed in Bohemia for the sole purpose of being imitated. His correspondence and writings were on the shelves of almost every Czech humanist.

Among Bohemian colleagues of Aeneas Silvius in the imperial chancery who later remained in contact with the Italian humanist, we find a number of the earliest humanist activists in Bohemian lands. Václav z Bochova, known as Wenceslaus Bohemus, is one of them, known for the fact that it was he who prepared the oldest known collection of form letters by Aeneas Silvius kept as *candela rhetoricae* in Czech chanceries. One of the oldest codices containing this anthology, preserved in the National and University Library in Prague, also contains the only version of Aeneas Silvius's comedy *Chrysis*, written in 1444 in Terence's style.[10]

Another Czech acquaintance and correspondent of Aeneas Silvius in Vienna was Jan Túšek z Pacova, later known as *proto-notarius civitatis Pragensis;* still another was Václav z Krumlova, a *decretorum doctor*, in Bohemia serving as *cancellarius* of the Czech noble house of Rožmberk. Václav z Krumlova was so much respected by Aeneas Silvius that he invited him to Rome for his installation as Pius II in 1458. At parting, he gave Václav a collection of rare manuscripts which Václav brought to Prague; the manuscripts were later deposited in the Prague archbishopric library.

Prokop Pflug z Rabštejna, chancellor of Emperor Sigismund of Luxembourg and after Sigismund's death the first chancellor of George of Poděbrady's royal Bohemian chancellery, was still another correspondent and close friend of Aeneas Silvius. It is known that this "miles litteratus et praestans," as he is referred to by Aeneas in letters to him, practically and professionally furthered Aeneas Silvius's humanist program in Czech lands after they first met in 1451. It was Prokop z Rabštejna who accompanied Aeneas Silvius on his journey to meet George of Poděbrady at the Benešov Diet, and translated Aeneas's Latin address before the diet and a few Czech documents for Aeneas's elegant Latin *Historica Bohemica*, published in 1475.

*   *   *

As elsewhere in western Europe, the classical learning in Czech lands had, of course, its own medieval tradition, which continued during the fourteenth century. The preserved catalogs of the oldest Bohemian libraries, for instance of the Augustinian canonries and Carthusian monasteries, give references to copies of medieval manuscripts of works by classical authors, as elsewhere in the West. More to the point: the first preserved register of holdings of books and manuscripts of the Charles College in Prague, from the end of the fourteenth century, lists Cicero's *De senectute* and *De amicitia*, Valerius Maximus, Macrobius, Sallust, Ovid, *expositio Oracii*,[11] and so forth, with works that most eloquently speak about a tradition of the *artes liberales*, medieval rhetoric, scholastic theology, and an Aristotelian and even a Platonic tradition of its own. It is against this landscape that we must understand the almost unbroken continuity of interest in a wide spectrum of classical learning noticeable in the oldest group of humanists in Czech lands. The world view and its program, educational and cultural ideals, to be sure, are new, but it is on this background that now little by little the *studia humanitatis* emerge: with new classical standards in rhetoric, Ciceronian eloquence, Greek and Roman philology, and study of newly discovered or newly translated classical authors, including Homer and Sophocles, Herodotus, Socrates, Plutarch, Martial and Horace, Plato, Ptolemy and Aristotle, and above all the poetry of Vergil.

As elsewhere in western Europe and in particular in Italy, the classical learning of the *studia humanitatis* beyond the eastern Alps, including the Czech lands, never reached the awareness of a wider public: the New Learning, including the new literature, remained the exclusive property of that segment of the social elite which was educated abroad, in particular in Italy, and maintained contact with foreign centers; at first the upper nobility with the courts and chanceries, only much later the cities, towns, and universities. At the University of Prague, the humanist movement entered very slowly, more slowly than elsewhere in central European academies; during the religious wars the university lost all scholarly influence and became a theater for polemical disputes. The teaching of classical authors at Prague lagged behind institutions of learning in neighboring countries; scholastic Aristotelianism furiously resisted the Platonic current. Jan Šlechta ze Všehrd, one of the prominent Czech humanists, credits Magister Gregorius Pragensis, 1466/67 and 1470/71 *Decanus* of the Faculty of Arts at Prague, with the introduction of Vergil at Prague University in the seventies of the fifteenth century: "M. Gregorius Pragensis . . . first . . . in Prague University dared to read the books of Vergil with the grammatical explanation of Servius, together with some books of other authors from those studies called the *studia humanitatis*."[12] It was some twenty-five years after Vergil had been introduced at the University of Vienna.

At the same time, the number of students from Czech lands seeking instruction for professions and degrees at Italian universities increased as never before. They were primarily students of law and medicine, very rarely students who would go to Italy for the sole purpose of studying the humanities; during their stay in Bologna, Padua, Pavia, or Ferrara they became involved in the *studia humanitatis* and brought their interests (with their books and manuscripts) back home to Bohemia. It is interesting that in the crucial decades that were the formative years of most known Czech humanists (1430–1475), we find the names of almost all leading Czech humanists matriculated in the registers of Italian universities.[13] There were altogether ten Czech humanists at the University of Bologna during this period, among them Jan Pflug z Rabštejna (1454), Hilary z Litoměřic (1458–59), and Jan z Krčina (1458–59); fifteen at the University of Padua, among them Bedřich Smydel z Chebu (1432–38), Mikuláš z Čech (1439), Václav z Prahy (1444), Václav z Krumlova (1444–49), and Šimon ze Slaného (ca. 1455–60); two at the University of Ferrara: Prothas z Boskovic (ca. 1450) and Jan z Hradiště (before 1456); and two at the University of Pavia: Jan Pflug z Rabštejna (1461, 1464–67) and Prothas z Boskovic (ca. 1450). Of the generation after 1475 should be mentioned: Václav z Chrudimě in Bologna (after 1468); Ladislav z Boskovic in Ferrara (1475); Bohuslav z Lobkovic in Bologna and Ferrara (1475–82); Petr z Rožmberka in Bologna and Ferrara (1476); Oldřich z Rožmberka in Bologna (1487); Martin z Krumlova in Bologna (1491); Augustin Olomoucký in Padua (before 1493); Karl z Doubravy in Bologna (before 1495), and Racek z Doubravy in Bologna (1495–1501). Almost simultaneously with these last names, a first generation of home-educated Czech humanists—Viktorin Kornel ze Všehrd, Václav Písecký, and others—entered the history of Czech humanism.

The fifteenth century in the Czech lands also witnessed a significant increase of studies in classical ancient literature, including new translations of already known texts, and of humanist writings, printed and in manuscripts, original and copied. The books and manuscripts were brought from foreign countries, in particular from Italy, by students, scholars, and diplomats who copied or bought them during their stay abroad or were given them as gifts by their teachers, patrons, or friends. In this way private and institutional libraries grew everywhere in central Europe, including Bohemia.

Thus a few outstanding classical and humanist collections in the present-day Czech lands go back to collections of such institutions as the Chapter Library of Olomouc, inventoried at the beginning of the fifteenth century; to the Metropolitan Chapter Library of Prague; to the College Libraries of the Caroline University in Prague, with a catalog of their holdings preserved from 1460; or to the private libraries of leading Czech humanists, for instance, Jan z Rabštejna, Prothas z Boskovic, Bohuslav z Lobkovic, Hilary z Litoměřic, Václav z Krumlova, Řehoř Hrubý z Jelení, or Viktorin Kornel ze Všehrd. If we wish to understand the preoccupations of the Czech humanist movement, we must go back for a moment to the inventories of these collections.[14]

It is obvious that under normal circumstances the earliest ancient manuscripts of classical writers could hardly, if at all, find their way to Bohemian lands. But there are in Czech libraries numerous fifteenth- and sixteenth-century manuscripts of ancient authors copied in Italy. We have seen that already the oldest catalog of the College Libraries in the Caroline University, dated at the end of the fourteenth century, lists four such manuscripts of Cicero and Seneca, though personal libraries of individual Czech humanists of the same time and later are replete with copies of Latin and Greek texts copied in Italian humanist centers. Paul O. Kristeller's "Iter Bohemicum et Moravicum" (1983) lists, for instance, a fourteenth-century manuscript of Ovid's *Metamorphoses*, property of the former Olomouc Chapter Library, now preserved in the Státní Archiv of Olomouc; or a fifteenth-century "Cicero miscellanea" with Cicero's, Vergil's, and Horace's texts, now in Zámecká knihovna at Kynžvart in Bohemia.[15] Jan z Rabštejna is said, during his stay in Italy between 1455 and 1467, to have bought six valuable manuscripts; among those he brought to Ranštejn, at least one-third were classical texts. Among them were excerpts of Plato's *Politeia*, Livy's *Histories*, Ovid, Horace, Catullus, and Publius Statius's *Achilleis*. We know that when Václav z Krumlova left Rome after the inauguration of Pius II, the former Aeneas Silvius gave him a number of manuscripts whose titles and whereabouts unfortunately are not known. It is known, however, that Bohuslav z Lobkovic had a scribe working for him in a monastery on the island of Crete (then under the rule of Venice), copying Greek texts for him, among them Plato's *Dialogues*, a manuscript still preserved in Prague. It is also known that Augustin Olomoucký, one of the builders of the old Chapter Library of Olomouc, collected and brought from Padua a large number of manuscripts that still constitute an important nucleus of its holdings, today incorporated into the system of the State Archives in Olomouc.[16]

It is interesting that the first humanist Latin translations of the same classics that had been translated before appear in Prague already during the first half of the fifteenth century. The catalog of the Library of the College of the Bohemian Nation, dated 1460, lists among Aristotle's writings also three translations designated *translatio nova: Ethicorum, Metheororum,* and *Phisicorum.*[17] It is quite possible that some of these translations were by Leonardo Bruni Aretino, as there are by him new translations of Plato in a manuscript of a fifteenth-century collection of Plato's works, now in the University Library in Prague.[18] It is remarkable that as many as six other copies of Plato manuscripts translated by Bruni are preserved in Czech libraries today.[19]

The rhetorical theory and practice of the Italian humanists was, of course, well known in the Czech lands. If Petrarch's letters were the first models of a humanist epistolography for Jan ze Středy and his associates, Aeneas Silvius's correspondence with his colleagues and friends in the chancery of Frederick III became the manual of the new rhetoric and style in general use by Czech humanists. Thus, for instance, Prokop z Rabštejna, Jan Túšek z Pacova, and Václav z Krumlova excel in their Latin epistles to Aeneas Silvius, Prothas z Boskovic in his correspondence with Janus Pannonius, Jan Nihil with Georg von Peuerbach in Vienna, and Magister Šimon ze Slaného in his letters to Magister Elias ze Slaného.[20] It is remarkable that almost all the rhetorical works of Gasparino Barzizza, the celebrated representative of Renaissance Ciceronianism and one of the best-known authors of rhetorical treatises from the fifteenth century, could be found in contemporary collections of books and manuscripts now preserved in Prague and Brno.[21] Similarly, writings of the famous Latin stylist Guarino of Verona, whose letters are found in several fifteenth-century codices, exist today in various Czech collections of the time. Even more remarkable is how quickly Czech humanists became acquainted with Lorenzo Valla's scientific analysis of the rules of Latin grammar and style, *De elegantiis linguae latinae*. Bishop Prothas z Boskovic and Jan z Rabštejna already referred to it in their correspondence, and there was at least one copy of this work in Prague, owned by Magister Václav z Chrudimě, and now in the University Library in Prague.[22]

Let us now turn to the literature produced by the Renaissance humanists. We have seen that the first and the most popular Italian humanist in Czech lands was Petrarch. The manuscripts of his *Salmi*, of his epic poem *Africa*, twelve eclogues *Bucolicum carmen*, and the famous hymn *Salve, cara deo tellus*, were part of a Czech manuscript "Petrarch Codex," compiled in Bohemia at the time of Jan ze Středy;[23] some of Petrarch's Latin poems have been preserved almost entirely in these codices, copied and saved in Bohemian lands. Among the most popular of Petrarch's prose writings in Bohemia were his letters (one codex contains eighty-one of his letters), his morally educational *De sui ipsius et aliorum ignorantia*, *De remediis utriusque fortunae*, and the polemical *Invectivae in medicum*. As shown by Arturo Cronia, several copies of such "Petrarch Codices" circulated for generations among Bohemian literati.[24] They are preserved in the Metropolitan Chapter Library and in the university libraries in Prague and Brno.[25]

Interestingly, Dante Alighieri's works were much less known and disseminated in Czech lands during their Renaissance humanist era. Jan ze Středy certainly knew and possibly even read Dante, but the number of manuscripts of Dante's works preserved today in Czech libraries is rather limited. For a long time only manuscripts with a few fragments and excerpts were known, one with two fragments from Dante's *Inferno* in the Metropolitan Chapter Library and one with excerpts from *De monarchia* in the University Library of Prague. Not long ago, a complete manuscript text of *De monarchia*, known as *Znojemský rukopis (Manuscript of Znojmo)* was found.[26] It is also of interest that there is not one of Dante's texts among the earliest printed books in Czech lands, though some translated works of Petrarch, Boccaccio, and even Marsilio Ficino are found among Czech incunabula.[27]

Giovanni Boccaccio was known among Czechs more for his historical writings than for his literary prose. Copies of his historical treatises were made in the original Latin, and his stories were early translated into Czech. Thus, fifteenth- and sixteenth-century manuscript excerpts from *De claris mulieribus*, Boccaccio's collection of biographies of famous women, excerpts from his *De casibus virorum illustrium libri IX,* and the text of the treatise *De genealogiis deorum gentilium* are preserved in the University Library of Prague. Boccaccio's literary prose, of course, is represented with novellas from the *Decameron*. Two novellas were translated very early: the first novella of the day 5 in the *Decameron*, about Tancredo; and the very last novella of the day 10, the story of Griselda; the manuscripts of these two translations are found in the University Library in Prague.[28] In print, a first Czech translation of Boccaccio's *Tale of the Unhappy Love of Two Lovers* appeared in 1504, and a translation of his *Tale of Florion and Biancaforte* in 1519. Both stories became very popular and were reprinted several times.

Obviously, a number of Italian humanists were less popular among the reading public in Czech lands, and their works were accessible only to individual scholars who used them in their studies or who cultivated personal contacts with their authors. To this category certainly belong, for instance, Marsilio of Padua (ca. 1275–ca. 1342), the author of the *Defensor pacis*, the most daring treatise of political thought at the very threshold of the humanist movement; two manuscripts of this work are known to have existed in Bohemian lands, one by the hand of Martin z Tišnova (Martinus Tisnovensis), now in the National Library of Vienna; Coluccio Salutati, the famous Florentine chancellor, with whom the Moravian margrave Jošt corresponded; and Leonardo Bruni, Salutati's successor in Florence, whose Latin translations of Aristotle and Plato, available in Bohemia, have been already mentioned. Among Bruni's original works, manuscript copies of his comedies *Polixena* and *Pamphilius,* and several manuscripts of *Comoedia Poliscenae et Gracii* are known to exist in the Státní knihovna České Socialistické Republiky in Prague. Works of Poggio Bracciolini were also not unknown to Czech humanists: Tas z Boskovic, Jan z Rabštejna, and Augustin Olomoucký very often referred to his historical and polemical literature, and there are several samples of Poggio's correspondence in collections of form letters copied, read, and imitated by Czech humanists of the time.[29]

The rhetoric and epistolographic literature of Gasparino Barzizza, Guarino of Verona, and Lorenzo Valla in the humanistic tradition of the Czech lands has already been mentioned. It might be added here that a few of Guarino's letters and two of his works—the *Life of Plato* and his *Elegia di virgine Alda*—were in manuscript copies in the Metropolitan Chapter Library and in the Prague University Library, now in Státní knihovna České Socialistické Republiky in Prague; and in addition to *De elegantiis*, Lorenzo Valla was known in Czech humanist circles also by his famous exposure of the Donation of Constantine, *De falso credita et ementita Constantini donatione declamatio* (1440), which is preserved in Czech libraries in two late fifteenth-century manuscripts.

One more Italian humanist whose name and work must have been known to Czech scholars of the time should be mentioned here: Marsilio Ficino (1433–1499), in Augustin Olomoucký's words, one of the "clarissimi illi philosophiae triumviri: Joannes Picus Comes Mirandulanus, Hermolaus Barbarus et Marsilius Ficinus," whom he commends for the education of the illustrious Olomouc bishops (*Catalogus episcoporum Olomoucensium*, 1511). It has been suggested that Bohuslav z Lobkovic and Jan Šlechta ze Všehrd used Ficino's Latin translations of Plato's work in their writings, and, indeed, a fifteenth-century manuscript copy of excerpts from several works by Marsilio Ficino does exist in the famous Lobkowitz Collection from Roudnice. The manuscript VI.E.f.11, written in Italy, marked as the property of Bohuslav z Lobkovic, contains, for instance, *Excerpta Marsilii Ficini ex Grecis Proculi commentariis in Alcibiadem Platonis primum, inc. Principium dialogorum Platonicorum totiusque philosophie*, and *Excerpta ex Proculo in republicam a Marsilio Ficino, inc. Plato in Legibus per tuas proprietates*, which must have been used by both men in their discussion of Plato. One of the earliest Czech incunabula, probably published in the very year of his death (1499), is a work by Marsilio Ficino, to which I shall return later.

*   *   *

Czech Renaissance humanism of the second half of the fifteenth century is dominated increasingly by literary and scholarly interests and concerns, transplanted from Italy by young Czech humanists educated in its best schools and academies. The poetry these young men wrote probably imitated Latin classical models with no less versatility than the Latin poetry of the time anywhere; their Latin prose, letters, orations, their works of historiography, their moral treatises and dialogues, were very probably no less sophisticated than most of a similar production elsewhere outside Italy. And yet there must have been "local" differences and specificities, characteristics and achievements in Czech Renaissance humanism as there were in Renaissance movements elsewhere.[30] The continuation of this survey will focus in particular on this aspect of the humanist movement in the Czech lands.

There are eight major representatives of Czech Renaissance humanism who typify this movement of cultural history in Bohemian lands. Five of them are men whose language of scholarship and communication was still, in Dante's words, that universal "speech of the learned," Latin, which included them in the community of Renaissance humanists of western and central Europe; three of them are men whose language in belles-lettres and scholarship was already what Dante called *eloquentia vulgaris*, the Czech vernacular, which marks the rise of a "national" humanist tradition in Bohemian lands. To the first group belong royal chancellors Jan Šlechta ze Všehrd, Jan z Rabštejna, and Augustin Olomoucký, Bishop Prothas z Boskovic, and Bohuslav Hasištejnský z Lobkovic; to the second belong three men whose work is intimately linked with Prague University, Viktorin Kornel ze Všehrd, Václav Písecký, and Řehoř Hrubý z Jelení.

Very little is known about Prothas (Tas) z Boskovic (ca. 1430–1482), a native Moravian, a citizen of the Hungarian kingdom, from 1457 bishop of Olomouc. What we know about him is that between 1447 and 1454 he studied together with Janus Pannonius at the universities of Ferrara and Padua, that the young men became lifelong friends, and that they both became bishops, Janus Pannonius in Pécs, Prothas z Boskovic in Olomouc. We know that they shared friends, among them in particular Albrecht von Eyb, a German humanist, the author of *Margarita poetica* (1475), a popular study in humanist stylistics; and Galeotto Marzio, Prothas's and Janus's teacher, who much later came from Italy to sojourn with them in their residences in Pécs and Olomouc. We assume that in Ferrara (we know that Janus was in Ferrara between 1447 and 1459) and Padua both young men shared their curriculum and teachers, and that among Prothas's teachers must also have been the same famous Guarino of Verona who taught Janus Pannonius.

We also know from their correspondence that about 1461 Prothas z Boskovic urgently requested Janus Pannonius to send him the handbook of the elegant Latin style of the age: "Si habes Elegantiolas Laurentii

Vallae cum Invectivis in Poggium, quas mihi Patavii accomodaveras . . . transmitte."[31] The historians of Czech humanism suggest that Prothas might have been working on a Latin grammar at that time, though nothing more is known about such plans nor about their realization.

Prothas's nephew, Ladislav z Boskovic (1458–1520), also a humanist who between 1475 and 1482 studied at the University of Ferrara with Bohuslav z Lobkovic, very probably inherited his uncle's library and incorporated it into his own collection of books and manuscripts, which he set up in Moravská Třebova. Ladislav's library was known for its rich collection of the first humanist editions of classical Greek and Latin authors, annotated by the hands of both their owners.[32]

Jan Pflug z Rabštejna (1437–1472), known and styled as "Johannes dominus de Rabenstein, Wyssegradensis prepositus, regni Bohemie cancellarius supremus, sedis apostolice protonotarius et referendarius, doctor," was a younger brother of Prokop Pflug z Rabštejna, whose work was closely linked with Aeneas Silvius. Jan studied law and humanities in Italy, at first in Bologna, then in Pavia, where the title of doctor of both civil and canon law was conferred on him. At home he continued the humanist tradition in the chanceries of George of Poděbrady and Matthias Corvinus. For George of Poděbrady he served as Czech ambassador in a diplomatic mission to the Curia Romana. In his Italian years and later, he gathered an enormous collection of books and manuscripts of ancient classical writers and modern Italian humanists and lawyers in a library often compared with the famous Corviniana or with that of his famous contemporary, the German humanist Albrecht von Eyb. The preserved catalog of his *auctores* includes Leonardo Bruni's new translations of Aristotle, excerpts from Plato's *Politeia*, Livy's *Histories*, Cicero, Plutarch, Lucian, Ovid, Catullus, Horace, Xenophon, Isocrates, Hesiod's *Theogonia*, Victor Aurelius, and Publius Statius; in the catalog of his Italian authors, among others, are Lorenzo Valla, Guarino of Verona, Giovanni Boccaccio, Coluccio Salutati, Poggio Bracciolini, Gasparino Barzizza, and Pier Paolo Vergerio the Elder. Among the several scores of manuscripts in this collection, most are fifteenth-century texts.

Jan z Rabštejna used his humanistic erudition and his enormous library more for his own intellectual growth and gratification than for dissemination of classical knowledge to others. He was not a prolific writer, yet what he composed is humanistic writing of the best quality. Two such texts are unquestionably his, although they were not printed in his lifetime. The *Oracio Johannis de Rabenstain in erectione achademie Ingelstatensis aliis orantibus tacite composita*, preserved in a Bavarian chronicle, represents a speech Jan z Rabštejna wrote for delivery at the solemn opening of the University of Ingolstadt in 1472.[33] He expected to represent King Matthias at this event and prepared an exquisite address for the occasion, built on Plato's thought from the *Politeia:* happy are city-states that are governed by princes who have the spirit and power of the philosopher or lover of wisdom!

The other preserved treatise of Jan z Rabštejna is his *Disputacio,* known also as *Dialogus baronorum Bohemorum,* a dialogue on the Platonic model popular in Italy during the Renaissance.[34] The *Disputacio* is dated 1469 and is dedicated to Giovanni Grasso, one of Jan's teachers at the University of Pavia. There are four personas participating in the invented conversation: Iohannes Sswambergensis (Jan ze Švamberka), Zdenko Sternbergensis (Zděnko ze Šternberka), Wilhelmus de Rabie (Vilém z Rabí), and Iohannes Rabensteinensis (Jan z Rabštejna), the author himself. The basic theme of the discussion is given in Jan's opening sentence in the dialogue, epitomizing, as it were, the intimate aspiration of the author himself: "I returned home so that I may live my life on my native soil in fruitful literary leisure." By its content, the *Disputacio* is known for its ingenious political discussion directed against the nobility and pleading for a true ethnic and a conscious national spirit in Bohemian lands. Czech literary historians treat the *Disputacio* as the very first humanistic writing of Czech origin. To a historian of the works of the *studia humanitatis* it is primarily a document of classical tradition and scholarship. And in fact, this text again is based on a most extensive classical apparatus. It certainly represents a most fortunate synthesis of the philosophy and experience of classical antiquity with the contemporary humanist search for individual expression.

Jan z Rabštejna's charters and documents (1463, 1469, 1471), preserved in Czech archives, and fourteen letters written to "Johannes Rosenbergensis" (Jan z Rožmberka) between 1468 and 1473 have biographical value. A major part of his books and codices is found today in the library of a monastery in Schlägl in upper Austria.

Very different but no less important were the interests and activities of Jan Šlechta ze Všehrd (of Wyssehrd, east of Prague, 1466–1525), known also as Johannes Sslechta, one of the leading activists of the humanist movement of the Prague–Budapest–Vienna triangle, for a few years the secretary of King Ladislas II in Prague, later the royal secretary at King Ladislas's Czech chancery in Budapest (1490–1504). The controversy about his learned or half-learned attitude toward the *studia humanitatis,* raised by some historians,[35] has no immediate bearing on this discussion. For almost half a century Jan Šlechta was an active participant in a crucial period of the Czech Renaissance humanist movement. Educated at Prague University (B.A. 1483, M.A. 1484), in 1497 he was a member of the Buda group of the Sodalitas litteraria Danubiana in

Vienna, a friend of Conrad Celtis and Girolamo Balbi, a close friend and associate of Bohuslav Hasištejnský z Lobkovic, Augustin Olomoucký, and of Magister Václav Písecký. With a strong desire to help launch humanist studies at the University of Prague, he successfully promoted Balbi's appointment to its Faculty of Arts, though Balbi's lectures in the college halls did not turn out to be successful.

About 1507 he retired from the hustle and bustle of the court and settled at Kostelec on the Elbe, northeast of Prague, where he occupied himself in the education of his son Jan. At that time he was in close contact with Václav Písecký, a young professor of philosophy at Prague University and a private tutor of his son Jan. Their correspondence (1507–11) shows how much Šlechta influenced his young friend, though in a letter to him, he characterizes himself with all modesty: "I am a little man, who can scarcely speak of philosophy, but I have grasped some shadow of ordinary literature, and I do not echo the sentiments of any teacher" (1507).

As a humanist, Jan Šlechta wrote Latin poetry in the genres and style of the time. He exchanged his verse with Bohuslav z Lobkovic, who had always a word of praise for his Muse. In 1499 he published a collection of poems by Janus Pannonius, *Epigrammata Joannis Pannonii*. Then for some reason he abandoned poetry for prose. In 1500 he completed a Platonic moral-philosophical dialogue *Mikrokosmus*, dedicated to Stanislaus Thurzó, bishop of Olomouc, the manuscript of which remained unpublished and has been lost.

Šlechta's *Mikrokosmus* dealt with the relation between body and soul and the soul's ultimate destiny. According to a short synopsis written by the author himself in a letter to Stanislaus Thurzó, his bishop and friend, the discussion—based on a close reading of Plato in Marsilio Ficino's translations—developed the following argument. The human soul (he uses interchangeably *animus, anima, mens*), arising from God (*prima causa et principium*), dwells in the human body, which, as every physical matter, consists of four elements: earth, air, fire, and water. The body is trying to derange the soul and make her as fragile as it is itself (*caducae fragilitati suae annectere*); the soul, however, conscious of her divine origin (*maiestatis suae recordatione firmata*), is to overcome all the obstacles and to return to her origin. It is obvious that the author of the dialogue tried to remain as firmly as he could within the boundaries of Christian dogma. It is interesting, however, that in addition to the positions of Plato—and from Šlechta's correspondence we know that one of his sources was also Cardinal Bessarion's treatise *In calumniatorem Platonis* (1469)—St. Augustine, and St. Thomas Aquinas, the dialogue also touches on the philosophical positions of Averroës and

Alexander of Aphrodisias, which, as we can judge by the short synopsis, makes *Mikrokosmus* a real symposium of up-to-date humanist positions on this moral-philosophical subject.[36]

About forty-five of Šlechta's letters are known to exist in Czech archives. Of particular value is his correspondence with Bohuslav z Lobkovic and with Václav Písecký. Among Šlechta's correspondence is also one letter addressed to Desiderius Erasmus, the greatest humanist figure in the northern Renaissance. Erasmus's correspondence with Šlechta is printed in his *Opus epistolarum.*[37]

A much more refined Renaissance man of the same circle of poets and scholars in Bohemian lands, a devoted admirer of Vergil and Cicero, was Augustin Käsenbrod Olomoucký or Moravský, known as Augustin of Olomouc, also as Augustinus Moravus (1467–1513). Educated in Padua where he studied law, philosophy, and astronomy, along with the entire spectrum of disciplines of the *studia humanitatis*, he was in 1493 appointed chief secretary at the court of King Ladislas II in Budapest. In addition he was provost of the cathedral chapter of Olomouc, later also provost of the Brno chapter, and canon of the Prague metropolitan see. After his appointment to the chancery he was also a member of the Buda Sodalitas litteraria Hungarorum and participated in its "Poetic Symposia" in Vienna. "*Procul hinc, procul este, profani!*" from Vergil, *Aeneid* (6.258), was the motto of his life; he had this phrase engraved on the golden cup he gave as a present to his congenial friends in the Sodalitas: Conrad Celtis, Johann Spiessheymer (Cuspian), Bohuslav Hasištejnski z Lobkovic, Joachim von Watt (Vadianus), and Vitus Aperbach in Vienna.

Most of Augustin Olomoucký's literary and scholarly work is known only indirectly. Only a few of his verses were printed, and most of his scholarly publications we know only from bibliographic references of the time. Augustin's friends, Conrad Celtis and in particular Bohuslav z Lobkovic, who read his poetic "praeludia," praised his poems and encouraged him to continue to write. Bohuslav saw in him a promise that some day his poetry could win out in a contest with the poetic production of "learned Italy." For some unknown reason, however, Augustin's poetry has not been preserved; infatuated with the ideal of the formal perfection of his classical models, he very probably destroyed it himself. This hypertrophic self-criticism is probably also responsible for the fact that no manuscript of his survived him.

What we know about his work and publications is that his first treatises were in astronomy—two pamphlets, written in Padua, printed in Venice in 1491 and 1495. Sill in Padua he composed his *Dialogus in defensionem poetices*, printed in Venice in 1493. The subject of this *Dia-*

logue in Defense of Poetry, in the style of the dialogues of classical writers, is the value of poetry in everyday life. The discussion is conducted by three personas: Laelius pleading the case of medicine and physicians, the author defending poetry, and Vallarius making fun of their debate. Another of Augustin's treatises on a humanistic subject, known to us again only indirectly from a bibliographical note, was *De modo epistolandi cum nonnullis epistolis quam pulcherrimis,* printed in Venice in 1495.

How deeply Augustin Olomoucký lived Renaissance humanism can be nicely seen from his *Catalogus episcoporum Olomoucensis* (Vienna, 1511), a publication meant to be a register of basic data on the bishops of his bishopric, arranged in the sequence of the years of their tenures. The sequence of hierarchs, indeed, is given in the catalog, representing, however, only a skeleton of the text into which Augustin packed, almost sacrilegiously, numerous humanist scholars and writers, as if he were writing a catalog of Italian humanists. When, for instance, Bishop Prothas z Boskovic enters the list, Augustin defines his time: "Per eius tempora floruere viri omni aetate memorandi, Laurentius Valla, Theodorus Gaza, Guarinus Veronensis, Leonardus Aretinus, Poggius, Franciscus Philelphus, linguae latinae egregi vindices et assertores"; or, before he lists Bishop Stanislaus Thurzó, he pays tribute to his own teachers: "Ea tempestate clarissimi illi philosphiae triumviri effulsere: Joannes Picus comes Mirandulanus, Hermolaus Barbarus, Marsilius Ficinus." It is obvious that he was more concerned with the star humanists than with the order of succession and glory of his bishops.[38]

I have already mentioned that Augustin Olomoucký owned a most valuable library of books and manuscripts, largely compiled from Italian humanist sources, which, after his death, passed into the collection of the Chapter Library of Olomouc.

The most central and influential representative of Czech Renaissance humanism was Bohuslav Hasištejnský z Lobkovic (1460/61–1510), known also as Bohuslaus Hassensteinius, a poet and scholar who, like so many Italian poets and scholars of the age, was able to make his humanist interests one of the chief objects of his life. He was the son of a prominent, wealthy aristocratic family and was never forced to work for a living. He studied at Italian universities, 1475–77 in Bologna, 1479–82 in Ferrara, where he devoted much of his time to the *studia humanitatis* and to making friends with whom he later corresponded all his life. In 1486 he returned home, without an academic title but with the reputation of an "eruditus latine et grece, rhetor, philosophus, iurisperitus et in divinis libris sane instructus"; the tradition has it that while still in Ferrara, he already held an honorary title of "archicancellarius regni Bohemici" in Prague. The fact is that after his return home, he became the soul of the humanist atmosphere in the royal chancellery in Prague, and very soon of the entire Czech Renaissance humanist movement. He made two longer journeys abroad—one to his friend Peter Schott in Strasbourg in Alsace and to the University of Leipzig (1482–86), another to the countries of the eastern Mediterranean, including Cyprus and Jerusalem. Twice he was invited to Ladislas's royal court in Budapest to participate in the cultural life of the Renaissance king's court (1499, 1502), twice he left in disappointment over this post of honor and withdrew to his Tusculum, his castle Hasištejn in the picturesque Bohemian mountains. Here he lived with his rich classical humanist library, devoting himself to writing, research, and correspondence with his friends in Bohemia and abroad. By the time he died, his name and reputation as a humanist poet and erudite were established far beyond Bohemian lands.

Bohuslav z Lobkovic was first and foremost a poet; he was a good poet, the best, in fact, that Czech Latin humanism produced. Just like Italian humanists, he wrote odes patterned on Horace, eclogues and idylls modeled on Vergil, elegies, epistles in hexameters and distychs, invectives and panegyrics, eulogies, epitaphs, and in particular epigrams, the genre of the day as it were—epigrams on everything that may enter a poet's diary. Among Bohuslav's most memorable texts are the usually cited *Carmen heroicum ad Imperatorem et Christianos reges de bello Turcis inferendo* (1499), known from history as one of the most emotional appeals to Christian Europe to defend Europe against the Ottomans; the exquisite satire *Ad Sanctum Venceslaum Satyra, in qua mores procerum, nobilium et popularium patriae suae reprehendit* (1492); a versified epistle to an unknown Bohemian, *De miseria Bohemie* (1493); the Vergilian allegorical *Ecloga sive idyllion Budae* (1502); the *Elegia consolatoria ad Vladislaum Pannoniae et Bohemiae regem de morte uxoris Annae* (1506); and a series of spiritual lyrical poems and prayers in verse patterned on classical models: *Ad Beatam Virginem* and *Praeconium Divae Virginis*.

Only a small part of Bohuslav z Lobkovic's scholarly output in prose has been preserved. Thus, his *Annales Bohemiae*, and the *Hodoeporicon*, two works about which we know only from his correspondence, are lost. What we do have are two treatises of his *Scripta moralia: De miseria humana* (1495) and *De avaritia* (1499), neither printed during his lifetime; and two fragments: *De felicitate* and *De philosophorum nugis*, as well as an *Oratio ad Argentinenses in genere demonstrativo pro Petro Schotto Argentinensi* (1485).[39] While modern literary historians accept Bohuslav's *Oration*, dedicated to his friend Peter Schott, as a good panegyrical exercise, they are more critical about his *Scripta moralia*. Though written in the style of Cicero's and Seneca's philosophical essays on practical ethics, they are far from the sophistication and lucidity of the philosophical thought of their models.

Another of Bohuslav's treatises, the political-philosophical dissertation *De re publica administranda*, his longest prose text, is known to us only from its Czech translation, made by Řehoř Hrubý z Jelení. It was originally part of an epistle to Petr z Rožmberka, the governor of the Kingdom of Bohemia, written in 1497. Its translation is included in a manuscript codex of Hrubý's texts, dated 1513, with the title "On the ideal great man and a good ruler." As has been shown, the portrait of the "ideal ruler" drawn by Bohuslav is not much different from the models of the good ruler drawn in Italian literature of the time. However, when applied to the circumstances of Czech lands in King Ladislas's time, it was totally unrealistic.[40]

Yet, if Bohuslav z Lobkovic was an amateur in philosophy, he was a master of humanist rhetoric. His private letters to his friends, written in flawless Ciceronian Latin, display the polished style of a trained epistolographer. Even today, they are read not only for their documentary information, but as models, enjoyed for the distinction, excellence, and originality of their language and style.

*   *   *

The rise of the Czech local humanist tradition was conditioned by a number of factors that had shaped Czech cultural history. For centuries there had been a cultural diglossia in the Czech society—a practice of Latin higher culture, including liturgy, and a practice of vernacular lower culture, including several forms of religious life. There was a tenth-century tradition of the use of Church Slavonic liturgy and literature in the Czech lands, practiced still through the eleventh century and then abolished; its memory contributed to the rise of a Czech vernacular literature in the late thirteenth century. In the fourteenth and fifteenth centuries, even Czech science and philosophy began to turn to the vernacular language and attempted to adapt it to the Latin cultural pattern. The Hussite concern with the use of the vernacular, of course, supported the functional expansion of Czech, but never challenged the role of Latin as the language of science and international communication. The meeting of this Czech vernacular movement with Renaissance humanism in the sixteenth century could not but lead to the creation of a "national" humanist tradition, the main characteristic of which was its use of the Czech vernacular.

The representatives of the Czech "national" humanism whom I

select for this survey, Viktorin Kornel ze Všehrd (1460–1520), Řehoř Hrubý z Jelení (1460–1514), and Václav Písecký (1482–1511), are only three representatives of the new generation of Czech scholars and writers who were at the turn of the sixteenth century engaged in the transmission of the classical heritage into the realm of vernacular literature. In a sense, this new generation was still rooted in Bohuslav z Lobkovic's world of concepts and values. However, educated at home in Prague, not in Italy, they were increasingly oriented toward Bohemia; though still writing Latin in their private correspondence, their literary production was increasingly in the Czech vernacular. A rapidly expanding printing industry in Bohemian lands, which helped to fill the socio-cultural needs for vernacular literature created by the Czech cultural movement of preceding centuries, became an important factor in the dissemination of their writings; hence the significance of works by classical authors and by contemporary humanists translated into the vernacular. One would be inclined to read in this evolution one of the specificities of the adaptation of Renaissance humanism in Czech lands.

It is interesting to note that the first works translated from Latin by Czech humanists belong to the literature of Christian classics, St. John Chrysostom and St. Cyprian. It is known that John Chrysostom was among the Greek classics with some *translatio nova* and that humanist scholars considered St. Cyprian as one of the Latin Fathers writing a language best suited for grammatical and rhetorical training. Both authors must have had a special appeal to the spiritual needs of Czech society at the turn of the fifteenth century. Thus, in the 1490s, four texts by these two authors, both extant in several older Latin manuscripts in Czech libraries,[41] were translated from Latin into Czech: two treatises by St. John Chrysostom (the oldest was Viktorin Kornel's translation of *De reparatione lapsi*, 1495, the other of *Quod nemo leditur nisi a seipso*, by Řehoř Hrubý) and two of St. Cyprian's texts (both Viktorin Kornel's, dated about 1500). All four translations were published for the first time at Pilsen in 1501, and in a second edition in 1507 at Prague.

Magister Viktorin ze Všehrd was a graduate of the University of Prague and for a period a professor at its Faculty of Arts; later he held an independent legal position in Prague.[42] As a lawyer, he wrote *Nine Books Treating the Laws, Law Courts and Deeds of the Czech Lands* (1502–8), dealing with the history of Czech law. On his own he acquired an extensive humanist education and won Bohuslav z Lobkovic's and Augustin Olomoucký's respect. Later he became the first Czech humanist to translate classics into the Czech vernacular, using a clear, dignified rhetorical style patterned on Latin. As the Romans in their time learned from the Greeks and wrote in their native *lingua Latina*, so he was now writing in his own "good, noble, rational, witty, rich and plentiful God-given Czech language." Viktorin Kornel's first translations of St. John Chrysostom's and St. Cyprian's texts mark the beginning of a struggle for a refined literary language in the Czech cultural tradition.

Another graduate of the University of Prague and of great promise for the *studia humanitatis* was Magister Václav Písecký. In 1505 he became a teacher at the university, in 1508 *Decanus* of its Faculty of Arts. He had close ties with Jan Šlechta ze Všehrd and corresponded with him on his *Mikrokosmus*. He had access to Šlechta's library and used Plato's texts and Bessarion's treatise *In calumniatorem Platonis* from Šlechta's collection of books and manuscripts. Šlechta advised him to specialize in Greek and to continue his studies in Italy. Thus Písecký spent one year in Padua and Bologna; he died in Venice when he was only twenty-nine. Václav Písecký's only contribution to classical studies in Bohemia was his translation of Isocrates's speeches *To Demonicus*, a classical work of a rather popular author in humanist circles of the age, made in Italy and published in Prague one year after his death, in 1512.[43]

By contrast, the third representative of the new generation, Řehoř Hrubý z Jelení, as far as we know—and we know little about his life—very probably had no higher education, no academic degrees, no Italian travel, no prestigious social position, yet an enormous knowledge of the *studia humanitatis* and the most impressive record of humanist writings among Czech scholars and translators.[44] We know more about his son, Sigmund Hrubý Gelenius (1497–1554), also a humanist, a disciple of Erasmus, whose life and work in Johann Froben's press in Basel, however, was not part of the Czech cultural tradition.

In the 1490s Řehoř Hrubý z Jelení joined Viktorin Kornel in translating writings by St. John Chrysostom. It is known that he translated Chrysostom's text *Quod nemo leditur nisi a seipso*, which was printed in 1501. In the meantime, he also translated Petrarch's book of dialogues *De remediis utriusque fortune*, a huge work by the humanist poet, well known in Bohemian lands, extant in several Latin manuscript copies in Czech libraries of the time.[45] It was presumably the first translation of *De remediis* in any language; it was printed in two folio volumes at Prague in 1501.

Other translations by Řehoř Hrubý from classical and humanist authors have been preserved in several manuscripts. One of such codices includes among other texts a translation of three of Cicero's pieces: *De amicitia*, *Paradoxa*, and a portion of his oration *Pro lege Manilia;* and a translation of St. Basil the Great's "Sermon on Envy." Another such codex of texts gathered by Hrubý, much larger, more carefully selected by subject and structured with a definite polemical point, dedicated "to the Lords in the Town Hall of the City of Prague," perhaps typifies best the themes and the extent of Řehoř Hrubý's humanistic interests. This *Řehoř Hrubý Codex XVII D.38*, preserved in the University of Prague Library, contains 531 folios and has translations of the following texts: the treatise *De regendo magistratu ad Franciscum Lucium equitem Senensem, praetorem Romanum* by Giannantonio Campano (1495); a selection of proverbs from Erasmus's *Adagia* (1500) and his *Praise of Folly;* St. Agapetus's *Reprimand to Emperor Justinian; De principe liber unus, Charon, De oboedientia libri quinque,* and *De beneficentia liber unus* by Giovanni Pontano, the famous chancellor to the kings of the Aragonese dynasty; Lorenzo Valla's controversial treatise *De falso credita et ementita Constantini donatione declamatio* (1440); sixteen of Petrarch's *Epistole sine nomine* and his epistle *De avaritia,* addressed to Hannibal, bishop of Tusculum; several passages from the works of St. Cyprian; and finally some extracts from Bartolomeo Platina's *Vitae pontificum Romanorum.*

*   *   *

In closing, a few titles of the oldest printed editions of classics and Renaissance humanist authors published in Bohemian lands during the period of this survey should be mentioned.[46] Several such titles have been already cited: Magister Viktorin Kornel's collection of St. John Chrysostom's and St. Cyprian's texts;[47] Řehoř Hrubý's translation of Petrarch's *De remediis;*[48] the translation of Filippo Beroaldo's version of Boccaccio's novella on Guiscardo and Ghismonda, known to us as "The Tale of the Unhappy Love of Two Lovers";[49] a translation of two other stories by Boccaccio from the *Decameron,* one of them "The Tale of Florion and Biancaforte";[50] and Václav Písecký's translation of Isocrates's *To Demonicus* (Prague, 1512).[51]

Another outstanding title, printed twenty years earlier, was a Czech translation of two of Marsilio Ficino's ethical philosophical texts on the subject "what one ought to do and not to do," two texts known to us from at least one Latin manuscript in the libraries of Czech humanists of the time.[52] These two epistles, one on the human responsibilities of common people, addressed to Cherubino Quarqualio, the other on the responsibilities of prelates and princes, addressed to Cardinal Raffaele Riario, were very probably printed in Prague already in 1499.[53]

Still another significant publication was *Nekrikoi dialogoi (Dialogues of the Dead)* by the great classical satirist Lucian, translated from the Latin and introduced by Mikuláš Konáč z Hodištkova. The book appeared with the title *On the Most Miserable Conditions of the Great Lords,* in Mikuláš Konáč's own printing establishment "At Holy Mother by the Pond," in Prague, 1507.[54] In the same establishment, from which during the next twenty years or so there appeared more than thirty Latin and Czech humanist titles, the *Česká kronyka* (1510), a complete translation of the *Historia Bohemica* by Aeneas Silvius, was also published.[55] It was the first Czech edition of a work thematically and historically linked with Czech lands, which—as the inventories of Czech libraries indicate—was earlier known to Czech humanist intellectuals in several manuscripts and printed editions.

One is, of course, not surprised to find among the titles of Czech incunabula dealing with subjects of classical and medieval antiquities subjects that are intellectually part of the medieval classical tradition. *The Trojan Chronicle* (Pilsen, 1468), a thirteenth-century romance by Guido della Colonna, the oldest Czech book printed in Bohemia; or a Czech version of the *Passional* by Jacobus de Voragine (Prague, 1480); or *The Fables of Aesop* (Prague, 1498), a collection of animal stories derived from Latin medieval compilations; or a Czech version of the twelfth-century encyclopedic *Lucidarius* (*Lucidarz*: Pilsen, 1498) speak of a continuity soon to be broken by the interests of a new generation of thinkers, writers, and publishers of the New Learning in Bohemian lands. Indeed, one of the most obvious causes for cultural change, so easily ignored and forgotten by cultural historians, is the fact that human beings are mortal and are inevitably replaced by new generations.[56] And it is these new generations who in the long run decide how much of what they have received from their predecessors will be preserved or changed, abandoned, or destroyed.

NOTES

1. Notwithstanding all the literature on Slavic Renaissance culture devoted to different aspects of Slavic literatures in the vernaculars, there is no comprehensive treatment of Slavic Renaissance humanism as defined in this discussion. Still the closest to my topic is the survey *Ital'janskoe vozroždenie i slavjanskie literatury XV i XVI vekov*, by I. N. Goleniščev-Kutuzov (Moscow, 1963), now available also in an Italian translation: *Il Rinascimento italiano e le letterature slave dei secoli XV e XVI*, trans. S. Graciotti and J. Křesálková, 2 vols. (Milan, 1973). Numerous valuable and stimulating topical contributions to the subject, however, can be found: M. P. Alekseev, *Javlenie gumanizma v literature i publicistike drevnej Rusi (XVI–XVII vv.)* [*The Phenomenon of Humanism and Renaissance in the Literature and Public Statements of Old Rus' XVI–XVII C.*] (Moscow, 1958); A. Cronia, "Relazioni culturali tra Ragusa e l'Italia negli anni 1358–1526," *Atti e memorie della Società Dalmata di Storia Patria* 1 (1926): 1–39; D. Čiževskij, *Comparative History of Slavic Literature*, trans. R. N. Porter and M. P. Rice (Nashville, TN, 1971); F. Dvornik, *The Slavs in European History and*

Civilization (New Brunswick, NJ, 1962); I. N. Goleniščev-Kutuzov, *Gumanizm u vostočnyx slavjan (Ukraina i Belorussija)* [*Humanism Among Eastern Slavs: Ukraine and White Russia*] (Moscow, 1963); *Hrvatski latinisti. Croatici auctores qui Latine scripserunt*, ed. V. Gortan and V. Vratović, 2 vols. (Zagreb, 1969–70); *Humanizmus a renesancia na Slovensku v. 15.– 16. storočí* [*Humanism and Renaissance in Slovak Lands in the 15th and 16th Centuries*], ed. L'. Holotík and A. Vantuch (Bratislava, 1967); *Italia, Venezia e Polonia tra umanesimo e Rinascimento*, ed. M. Brahmer (Wroclaw, 1967); M. Kombol, *Povijest hrvatske književnosti do narodnog preporoda* [*History of Croatian Literature up to the National Revival*] (Zagreb, 2d ed. 1961); *Krakowskie odrodzenie. Referaty z konferencji naukowej Towarzystwa miłośników historii i zabytków Krakowa z września 1953* [*Cracow Renaissance: Papers Presented at the Scholarly Conference at the Society of Friends of the History and Monuments of Cracow, Sept. 1953*], ed. J. Dąbrowski (Cracow, 1954); S. Lempicki, *Renesans i Humanizm w Polsce. Materialy do Studiów* [*Renaissance and Humanism in Poland: Research Materials*] (Cracow, 1952); R. L. Lencek, "At the Roots of Slavic Cultural History," in *Părvi Meždunaroden kongres po bălgaristika, Sofija, 23 maj–3 juni 1981. Dokladi. Plenarni dokladi* (Sofija, 1982), 29–53; idem, "Humanism in the Slovene Lands," *Nationalities Papers* 7 (1979): 155–70; D. S. Lixačev, *Razvitie russkoj literatury X–XVII vekov. Èpoxi i stili* [*Development of Russian Literature 10th–17th Centuries: Periods and Styles*] (Leningrad, 1973); *Odrodzenie w Polsce. Materialy sesji naukowej PAN, 25–30 października 1953 roku* [*Renaissance in Poland: Materials of the Scholarly Session of the Polish Academy of Sciences, 25–30 October 1953*], 5 parts in 7 vols. (Warsaw, 1955–58); *Renaissance und Humanismus in Mittel- und Osteuropa. Eine Sammlung von Materialen*, ed. J. Irmscher, 2 vols. (Berlin, 1962); P. Simoniti, *Humanizem na Slovenskem in slovenski humanisti do srede XVI. stoletja* [*Humanism in Slovenia and Slovene Humanists Until the Mid-16th Century*] (Ljubljana, 1979); F. Šmahel, *Humanismus v době Poděbradské* [*Humanism in the Age of George of Poděbrady*] (Prague, 1963); J. Truhlář, *Počátky humanismu v Čechách* [*The Beginnings of Humanism Among Czechs*] (Prague, 1892); idem, *Humanismus a humanistě v Čechách za Krále Vladislava II* [*Humanism and Humanists Among Czechs at the Time of King Ladislaus II*] (Prague, 1894); D. Tschiževskij, *Die Renaissance und das ukrainische Geistesleben* (Berlin, 1929); B. Vodnik, *Povijest hrvatske književnosti*, vol. 1, *Od humanizma do potkraj XVIII. stoljeća* [*History of Croatian Literature*, vol. 1, *Humanism to the End of the 18th Century*] (Zagreb, 1913); E. Winter, *Frühhumanismus: Seine Entwicklung in Böhmen und deren europäische Bedeutung für die Kirchenreformbestrebungen im 14. Jahrhundert* (Berlin, 1964).

2. For the remaining sections of this essay, see Truhlář, *Počátky humanismu* and *Humanismus a humanistě*, and Šmahel, *Humanismus v době Poděbradské*. See, in addition, F. Tadra, *Kanceláře a písaři v zemích českých za králů z rodu lucemburského Jana, Karla IV, a Václava IV (1310–1420)* [*Chancellors and Scribes in Czech Lands at the Time of the Kings of the*

Luxembourg Dynasty: John, Charles IV, Wenceslas IV (1310–1420)]
(Prague, 1892); *Catalogus codicum manuscriptorum latinorum qui in C. R.
Bibliotheca Publica atque Universitatis Pragensis asservantur*, ed. J. Truhlář,
2 vols. (Prague, 1905–6); M. Flodr, "Olomoucká Kapitulní knihovna a její
inventáře na počátku 15. stoleti" ["The Chapter Library of Olomouc and
Its Inventories at the Beginning of the 15th Century"], *Sborník prací Filo-
sofické fakulty Brněnské university* 7 (1958): 76–97; A. Patera and A. Pod-
laha, *Soupis rukopisů knihovny Metropolitní kapituly pražské [Description
of Manuscripts of the Metropolitan Chapter Library of Prague]*, 2 vols.
(Prague, 1910–22); J. Bečka and E. Urbánková, *Katalogy knihoven kolejí
Karlový university [Catalogs of College Libraries in the Caroline University]*
(Prague, 1948); B. Ryba, *Soupis rukopisů Strahovské knihovny Památníků
národního písemnictví v Praze. Strahovské rukopisy [Description of the
Manuscripts of Strahov's Library, of Monuments of National Literature in
Prague. Manuscripts Held at Strahov's Library]* (Prague, n.d.); Z. V. To-
bolka, *Dějiny československého knihtisku v době nejstarší [History of
Czechoslovak Printing of the Oldest Period]* (Prague, 1930); F. Horák,
"Five Hundred Years of Czech Printing," in *Pět století českého knihtisku
[Five Hundred Years of Czech Printing]* (Prague, 1968), 115–52; P. O. Kris-
teller, *Iter Italicum, a Finding List of Uncatalogued or Incompletely Cata-
logued Humanistic Manuscripts of the Renaissance in Italian and Other
Libraries*, vol. 3, *Australia to Germany* (Leiden and London, 1983); A. No-
vák, "Dějiny české literatury" ["History of Czech Literature"], in *Českos-
lovenská vlastivěda, Díl VII. Písemnictví* (Prague, 1933), 7–208; idem,
Czech Literature, trans. P. Kussi, ed. with a supplement by W. E. Harkins
(Ann Arbor, 1976).

3. See *Petrarch's Correspondence*, ed. E. H. Wilkins (Padua, 1960): for letters
   of Petrarch to Charles, see p. 14; for letters of Charles to Petrarch, see p.
   122.

4. Jan ze Středy was the author of a number of *dictamina* and collections of
   model letters, e.g., *Summa cancellarii* (manuscript in the Library of the University of Prague), of a *Collectarius perpetuarum formarum* (manuscript in
   the Vatican Library), and of a few German educational works. See J. Tříška,
   *Literární činnost předhusitské university [Literary Activity of the Pre-
   Hussite University]* (Prague, 1967), 13–19. See also J. Lulvès, *Die Summa
   cancellariae des Johan von Neumarkt* (Berlin, 1891); and K. Burdach, *Aus
   Petrarcas ältesten deutschen Schülerkreise* (Berlin, 1929), 28–40. For Jan ze
   Středy's role in the evolution of the literary German used in the imperial
   chancery in Prague, see, e.g., K. Burdach, *Vom Mittelalter zur Reformation*,
   3 vols. (Halle, 1893–1926); for a different view, see L. Schmitt, *Die
   deutsche Urkundensprache in der Kanzlei Kaiser Karls IV* (Prague, 1936).

5. See *Petrarch's Correspondence*, ed. Wilkins, pp. 18 (Petrarch to Jan ze
   Středy) and 126 (Jan ze Středy to Petrarch).

6. Girolamo Balbi (Hieronymus Balbus, 1460–1535), an Italian scholar and
   poet originally from Venice, for years was a leading Italian humanist at
   Vienna University. Balbi studied at the University of Rome; in 1485 he was

teaching at the University of Paris, and during 1490–93 in Padua, where he lectured on Roman Catholic canon law and Roman law. In 1493 he was appointed Professor of Roman Law at Vienna University. In addition to Roman law, he lectured there also on Vergil and soon came into conflict with his colleagues at the university. As a member of the Sodalitas Danubiana, he made friends with Bernhard Perger and Conrad Celtis. In 1499 we find him as Professor of Rhetoric, Poetics, and Roman Law in Prague, in 1512 at Ladislas's court in Budapest where he served the king of Bohemia and Hungary as his special ambassador. He died in Vienna in poverty.

Balbi was a good Latin poet. In Paris he was engaged in polemical and satirical writing, in Vienna he wrote philosophical and political treatises; the latter are of no particular interest for humanism. Known are his *Carmina* and *Epigrammata,* dedicated to his contemporaries (Maximilian I, Ivan Vitéz, Bernhard Perger, Conrad Celtis), two collections of poems modeled on the classical Latin poetry of Martial and Petronius, formally perfect and in an elegant Latin language and style. Of less interest is his *De coronatione* (Bologna, 1530), for which he was accused of atheism and which was later entered in the list of authors of prohibited books.

On Balbi, see G. Bauch, *Die Reception des Humanismus in Wien* (Breslau, 1903); A. Horawitz, *Der Humanismus in Wien* (Leipzig, 1883), 17–25.

7. Conrad Celtis (Conradus Celtis, 1459–1508) was a German humanist, an outstanding Latin lyrical poet, a teacher of poetry and rhetoric at Nuremberg, Ingolstadt, and Vienna universities, friend and correspondent of numerous Czech and Polish humanists. He studied at Cologne and Heidelberg, spent two years among Italian humanists, and two years in Cracow (1489–91), where he studied mathematics and astronomy. Tradition has it that in Cracow he founded a Sodalitas litteraria Vistulana. In 1487, during his stay in Nuremberg, Emperor Frederick III crowned him poet laureate. In Heidelberg he organized the first humanist society, Sodalitas litteraria Rhenana, in 1495. In 1497 Emperor Maximilian I appointed him professor of humanist studies at the University of Vienna. There he founded the Sodalitas litteraria Danubiana, with a subsidiary base in Budapest (1497). Bohuslav Hasištejnský z Lobkovic also participated in the Vienna group; among the *sodales* of the Budapest group were also Augustin Olomoucký and Jan Šlechta. In 1501 Celtis organized a *Collegium poetarum et mathematicorum* at the university. An archhumanist and a wandering apostle of the New Learning, Celtis traveled all over central Europe; he visited Prague several times, first in 1491. It is known that among his friends in Bohemia was Bohuslav Hasištejnský z Lobkovic, with whom he maintained a profuse correspondence.

As a humanist historiographer, Celtis is known as the editor and publisher of Tacitus's *Germania* (1500); as a poet he is known as the author of two masques with music: *Ludus Dianae* (Nuremberg, 1501) and *Rhapsodia* (Nuremberg, 1505), and of several collections of poems: the erotic *Amores* (Nuremberg, 1502), *Epigramma,* and *Odes* (Strasbourg, 1513).

On Celtis, see L. W. Spitz, *Conrad Celtis: The German Arch-Humanist* (Cambridge, MA, 1957); and *Der Briefwechsel des Konrad Celtis*, ed. H. Rupprich (Munich, 1934).

8. Enea Silvio Piccolomini, known in literature as Aeneas Silvius (1405–1464), was a man of letters, a humanist, a diplomat in the service of Frederick III, a bishop of Trieste (1447–48), bishop of Siena (1449–58), from 1458 Pope Pius II.

Born near Siena, Aeneas Silvius studied in Florence under Filelfo. From 1431 to 1455 he lived and worked across the Alps; from 1431 he served at the Council of Basel, in 1442 being sent to take part in the diet of Frankfurt am Main. There he met the German king Frederick III (1415–1493), who made him poet laureate and his private secretary. In Wiener Neustadt he was secretary to Frederick's Vienna chancery (1442–45) and useful to Frederick as an envoy in political missions, including his 1451 mission to George of Poděbrady in Bohemia. He engaged in an enormous literary correspondence in a classical Latin style with almost every significant contemporary writer. He participated in many of the significant events of his time and promoted the humanist fashion, ideas, and interests in central and east-central European lands, including Bohemia and Poland.

On Aeneas Silvius, see G. Voigt, *Enea Silvio de' Piccolomini, als Papst Pius II. und sein Zeitalter*, 3 vols. (Berlin, 1856–63); *Der Briefwechsel des Eneas Silvius Piccolomini . . .*, ed. R. Wolkan, 4 vols. (Vienna, 1909–18).

9. "Bischoff Eneas an den Kardinal Juan Carvajal: Wiener-Neustadt, 21 August 1451," in *Briefwechsel*, ed. Wolkan, 3:36–37.

10. "Comedia Enee Silvii poete que intitulatur Chrysis," 191–204 in the fifteenth-century MS 462 of the Lobkowicz collection in Prague; MS 23 F. 112 of the Národní a Universítní knihovna (now Státní knihovna České Socialistické Republiky) in Prague. The scribe was a Czech scholar connected with the chancery of Frederick III (Kristeller, *Iter Italicum*, 3:164).

11. See the oldest catalog of two hundred manuscripts of the College Libraries in the Charles University, preserved in the National Museum in Prague (MS 1.D.a.1.); Bečka and Urbánková, *Katalogy knihoven kolejí*. See also Tříška, *Literární činnost předhusitské university*.

12. From a letter to Magister Petr Písecký, in *Bohuslavi Hasisteinii Farrago poematum*, ed. T. Mitis (Prague, 1570), 372. See also Truhlář, *Počátky humanismu*, 49; and Šmahel, *Humanismus v době poděbradské*, 29.

13. See F. Šmahel, "Počátky humanismu na pražské universitě v době poděbradské" ["The Beginnings of Humanism at Prague University in the Age of George of Poděbrady"], *Historia Universitatis Carolinae Pragensis* 1 (1960): 55–85.

14. Several libraries of Czech humanists have been preserved and are inventoried. For the library of Jan z Rabštejna, see G. Vielhaber and G. Indra, *Catalogus codicum Plagensium manuscriptorum* (Linz, 1918); and F. Šmahel, "Knihovna Jana z Rabštejna" ["The Library of Jan of Rabštejn"], in *Zápisky katedry československých dějin a archivního studia* (Prague, 1958), 93–113. For Bohuslav z Lobkovic, see *Bohuslai Hasisteinii Farrago*

poematum, ed. Mitis. For Hilary z Litoměřic, see J. Volf, "Knihovna Hilaria z Litoměřic" ["The Library of Hilarius of Litoměřice"], *Český časopis historický* 81 (1907): 131–33. For Václav z Krumlova, see J. Tříška, "Středověký literární Krumlov" ["The Medieval Literary Krumlov"], *Listy filologické* 9 (1961): 93–103; and V. Schmidt and A. Picha, "Das wissenschaftliche Leben und der Humanismus in Krummau im 15. Jahrhundert," *Mitteilungen des Vereines für Geschichte der Deutschen in Böhmen* 42 (1904): 67–77.

15. MS 20 G.13. See "Czechoslovakia, Iter Bohemicum et Moravicum," Kristeller, *Iter Italicum,* 3:149–69.

16. Now Státní Archiv in Olomouc. See M. Boháček, "Literatura středověkých právních škol v rukopisech Kapitulní knihovny Olomoucké" ["The Literature of Medieval Legal Schools in the Manuscripts of the Chapter Library of Olomouc"], *Rozpravy Československé Akademie věd* 70, no. 7 (Prague, 1960): 7; see also Kristeller, *Iter Italicum,* 3:149–69.

17. See Šmahel, "Počátky humanismu na pražské universitě," 72; see also Bečka and Urbánková, *Katalogy knihoven kolejí;* and Šmahel, *Humanismus v době poděbradské.*

18. See E. Pražák, "Český překlad Platonovy *Politeie* z 15. stoleti" ["The 15th-Century Czech Translation of Plato's *Statesman*"], *Listy filologické* 9 (1961): 102–8.

19. See Kristeller, *Iter Italicum,* 3:149–69.

20. The correspondence of Czech humanists has been preserved in various archives and libraries in Czechoslovakia and elsewhere; some has been published, for instance, in Aeneas Silvius Piccolomini's correspondence: *Briefwechsel,* ed. Wolkan; in Georg von Peuerbach's correspondence: "Aus dem Briefwechsel des grossen Astronomen Georg von Peuerbach," ed. A. Czerny, *Archiv für österreichische Geschichte,* 72 (1888), 281–332; and Conrad Celtis, *Briefwechsel,* ed. Rupprich; and (for the Prothas z Boskovic–Janus Pannonius correspondence) in collections such as: *Analecta ad historiam renascentium in Hungaria litteratum spectantia,* ed. E. Abel (Budapest and Leipzig, 1880); and separately, for instance, for Bohuslav z Lobkovic, Racek Doubravský, Václav Písecký, Jan Šlechta, in *Listář Bohuslava Hasinštejnského z Lobkovic* [*Correspondence of Bohuslav Hasinštejnsky of Lobkovic*], ed. J. Truhlář (Prague, 1892); in *Dva listáře humanistické: (a) Dra. Racka Doubravského, (b) M. Václava Píseckého z Doplňkem listáře Jana Šlechty ze Všehrd* [*Two Humanist Letter Collections: (a) Dr. Racko Doubrauský, (b) M. Václav Písecký with the addition of the Collected Letters of Jan Šlechta ze Všehrd*], ed. J. Truhlář (Prague, 1897); and for Jan z Rabštejna in B. Ryba, "K biografii humanisty Jana z Rabštejna" ["Toward the Biography of the Humanist Jan z Rabštejna"], *Český časopis historický* 46 (1940): 260–72.

21. E.g., in the old collection of Augustinians in Brno, in the Universitní knihovna, now Státní vědecká knihovna in Brno.

22. See Šmahel, *Humanismus v době poděbradské,* 33.

23. Such a manuscript of a "Petrarch Codex," part of the former Olomouc

Chapter Library, is today in Olomouc Státní Archiv Library; Petrarch codices are also found in the old Collection of Augustinians in Brno Universitní knihovna, in the Old Chapter Library Collection in Olomouc Státní Archiv, and in the old Lobkowicz Collection from Prague in the Prague Národní a Universitní knihovna. See Kristeller, *Iter Italicum*, 3:149–69.

24. See A. Cronia, "Inchiesta Petrarchesca in Czechoslovacchia, Contributi bibliografici," *L'Europa orientale* 3–4 (1935).

25. E.g., two fourteenth- to fifteenth-century manuscripts, CO 418 and CO 509, of the former Olomouc Chapter Library, now in the Státní Archiv in Olomouc.

26. See A. Fialová, "Znojemský rukopis Dantový Monarchie" ["The Manuscripts of Dante's *De monarchia* from Znojem"], *Listy filologické* 3 (1955): 52–56.

27. See Horák, "Five Hundred Years of Czech Printing"; V. Hanka, "České prvotisky" ["Czech Incunabula"], *Časopis českého museum* 26.3 (1852): 109–26; 26.4 (1852): 62–111.

28. See J. Polívka, *Dvě povidky v české literatuře XV. století* [*Two Novellas in Czech Literature of the 15th Century*] (Prague, 1889).

29. See MSS D. 118, G. 19, G. 20, L. 64 in the Metropolitan Chapter Library, and MSS no. I.C.3 and V.G.15 in the University Library in Prague; see also Šmahel, *Humanismus v době poděbradské*, 41.

30. See P. O. Kristeller, "The European Diffusion of Italian Humanism," *Italica* 39 (1962): 1–20; reprinted in *Studies in Renaissance Thought and Letters*, II, 147–65.

31. See Šmahel, *Humanismus v době poděbradské*, 67.

32. See Truhlář, *Humanismus a humanistě v Čechách*, 61–62.

33. See H. Waltzer, "Beziehungen des böhmischen Humanisten Johann von Rabenstein zu Bayern," *Mittheilungen des Instituts für österreichische Geschichtsforschung* 24 (1903): 630–45; text 637–43.

34. Jan z Rabštejna, *Disputacio*, ed. B. Ryba (Budapest, 1942); idem, *Dialogus*, ed. B. Ryba (Prague, 1946).

35. See Truhlář, *Počátky humanismu v Čechách*, 49.

36. See Truhlář, *Humanismus a humanistě v Čechách*, 98–99.

37. See *Opus epistolarum Des. Erasmi Roterodami*, ed. P. S. Allen, H. M. Allen, and H. W. Garrod, 12 vols. (Oxford, 1906–58), vol. 3, letter 950: Erasmus to John Slechta, 23 April 1519; vol. 4, letter 1021: John Slechta to Erasmus, 10 October 1519; vol. 4, letter 1039: Erasmus to John Slechta, 1 November 1519.

38. See Truhlář, *Humanismus a humanistě v Čechách*, 182.

39. See Bohuslav z Lobkovic, *Scripta moralia, Oratio ad Argentinenses, Memoria Alexandri de Imola*, ed. B. Ryba (Leipzig, 1937); idem, *Epistolae. Accedunt epistolae ad Bohuslaum scriptae*, ed. A. Potuček (Budapest, 1946). See also idem, *Spisy Bohuslava Hasištejnského z Lobkovic, Svazek I. Spisy Prosaické* [*Writings of . . . Lobkovic, vol. 1, Prose Writings*], ed. B. Ryba (Prague, 1933).

40. See Truhlář, *Humanismus a humanistě v Čechách*, 166–70.

41. For instance, in the thirteenth- to fourteenth-century MS II.76 in the Universitní knihovna, now Státní vědecká knihovna in Olomouc.
42. For Viktorin Kornel ze Všehrd, see Truhlář, *Humanismus a humanistě v Čechách*, 123–25 and passim.
43. For Václav Písecký, see Truhlář, *Humanismus a humanistě v Čechách*, 169–71 and passim.
44. For Řehoř Hrubý z Jelení, see Truhlář, *Humanismus a humanistě v Čechách*, 163–78 and passim.
45. For example, in the fifteenth-century MS 274 of the famous Lobkowicz Collection of Prague, in the Národní a Universitní knihovna, now Státní knihovna České Socialistické Republiky in Prague.
46. See Hanka, "České prvotisky."
47. The title of incunabulum no. 18 in Hanka, "České prvotisky," reads: *Jana Zlatousteho O naprawenij padleho . . . & . . . Ze žadny nemuož vražen byti od gine než sam od sebe . . . (millesimo cccc xcvij) & Knihy s Cipriana kterež ğt psal k Donatowi o potupenij swieta . . . & Prawy a gruntownij wyklad na modlitbu panie nayswietieyssij (Leta Božieho milesimo cccc i).*
48. No. 45 of Hanka, "České prvotisky": *Franczysska Petrarchy Poety a welmi znamenitého a dospieleho muže w wymluwnosti knijehy dwoge o lékarzstwij proti sstiestij a nesstiestij . . . kterež gest Pan Rzehorz hruby z Gelenie w nowie z Latinského yazyku w Čzesky przeložyl: gsw w Slawném Starém miestie Pražskiem wytisstieny. Léta Božijeho Tisyczieho Pietisteeho Prwnijeho.* See J. J. Hanuš, "Františka Petrarky: Knihy o lékařství proti štěstí a neštěstí—přeložil Řehoř Hrubý z Jelení a vydal r. 1501 v Praze" ["The Books *De redemiis* by Francesco Petrarch—trans. by Rehoř Hrubý of Jeleni and Published in Prague in 1501"], *Časopis Musea Království českého* 36 (1862): 161–74.
49. The title no. 49 in Hanka, "České prvotisky": *Historie o nešťastně lásce dvou zamilovaných* (V Praze, 1507). Hanka explains that this work is in fact the story of Guiscard and Guismunda, which appeared in Prague in 1504 with the title: *O smutném skončení Gwiskarda i Sigismundy.*
50. The title no. 79 in Hanka, "České prvotisky": *Welmi piekna nowa Kronika aneb Historia Wo welike milosti Kniežete a Kraale Floria z Hispanij A geho milee panie Biantzeforze . . . W slawnem Miestie Praze . . . Letha . . . tisytzyho Pietisteho Dewatenatzeho.*
51. The title no. 54 in Hanka, "České prvotisky": *Isokratesa napomenutij k Demonykowi. Od Václava Píseckého z řečtiny přeložen ve Vlaších* (V Praze u Jana Motavusa, 1512).
52. See Kristeller, *Iter Italicum*, 3:149–69.
53. The title no. 44 in Hanka, "České prvotisky": *Listy dva Marsília Ficína, první o povinnostech lidských všelikého stavu, Cherubínu Quarqualiovi; druhý kardinalu Rafaelu Riarovi o povinnostech prelatův a knížat* (octavo, 16 pages, no date, no translator's name).
54. The title no. 50 in Hanka, "České prvotisky": *Luciana dvoje rozmlouvani. Charon a Palinurus. O rozličných lidských stavích a zvláště o nejbídnějším*

stavu velikých panu. Terpsion a Pluto. O těch kteří lidí starých smrtí pro zboží žadají (W Praze, 1507), (quarto, 20 pages).

55. The title no. 52 in Hanka, "České prvotisky": *Czeska kronyka. W starem Miestie pražskem. Leta božyeho patnatctisteho desateho v matky božije na Luži.*
56. See P. O. Kristeller, *Renaissance Thought and Its Sources*, ed. M. Mooney (New York, 1979), 108.

CONTRIBUTORS TO VOLUME 2

MARIANNA D. BIRNBAUM ("Humanism in Hungary") is Professor in Residence of Hungarian Studies at the University of California, Los Angeles. She is the author of *Janus Pannonius: Poet and Politician* (1981) and of *Humanists in a Shattered World: Croatian and Hungarian Latinity in the Sixteenth Century* (1986).

NOEL L. BRANN ("Humanism in Germany") is currently engaged in independent research. He is the author of *The Abbot Trithemius (1462–1516): The Renaissance of Monastic Humanism* (1981).

DRAŽEN BUDIŠA ("Humanism in Croatia") is curator of the rare book and manuscript collection at the National and University Library in Zagreb. His works include *Počeci tiskarstva u evropskih naroda [The Beginning of Printing Among the Nations of Europe]* (1984). IVO BANAC, translator of this essay, is Associate Professor of History at Yale University and author of *The National Question in Yugoslavia: Origins, History, Politics* (1984), among other studies in the cultures of eastern Europe.

OTTAVIO DI CAMILLO ("Humanism in Spain") is Associate Professor of Spanish at Queens College of the City University of New York and at the Graduate Center. He is the author of *El humanismo castellano del siglo XV* (1976).

JOZEF IJSEWIJN ("Humanism in the Low Countries") is Professor at the Katholieke Universiteit Leuven. He is the author of *Companion to Neo-Latin Studies* (1977) and of "The Coming of Humanism to the Low Countries" (1975), among many other studies of humanist culture in the Low Countries and of Neolatin literature.

RADO L. LENCEK ("Humanism in the Slavic Cultural Tradition with Special Reference to the Czech Lands") is Professor of Slavic Languages and Cultures at Columbia University. He has published *A Bibliographical Guide to the Literature on Slavic Civilizations* (1966), and he has written several articles related to Slavic humanism: "Humanism in the Slovene Lands" (1979), "At the Roots of Slavic Cultural History" (1982), and "A Lesson from Bulgarian Cultural History" (1983).

ALBERT RABIL, JR. (Editor; "Desiderius Erasmus") is Distinguished Teaching Professor of Humanities, State University of New York, College at Old Westbury. He is the author of *Erasmus and the New Testament* (1972), one of the translators of *Erasmus' Paraphrases of Romans and Galatians* (1983), and author and editor of *Knowledge, Goodness, and Power: The Debate over "Nobility" Among Quattrocento Italian Humanists*, 2 vols. forthcoming.

EUGENE F. RICE, JR. ("Humanism in France") is William R. Shepherd Professor of History at Columbia University. He is the author of *The Renaissance Idea of Wisdom* (1958) and, most recently, of *Saint Jerome in the Renaissance*

(1985). He is editor of *The Prefatory Epistles of Jacques Lefèvre d'Etaples* (1972).

RICHARD J. SCHOECK ("Humanism in England") is Professor of English and Humanities at the University of Colorado at Boulder. He is editor of *Editing Sixteenth-Century Texts* (1966) and of a number of other volumes; and author of *The Achievement of Thomas More* (1976), *Intertextuality and Renaissance Texts* (1984), and many articles on English and French humanism and jurisprudence during the Renaissance.

RETHA M. WARNICKE ("Women and Humanism in England") is Professor of History at Arizona State University. She is the author of *William Lambarde: Elizabethan Antiquary* (1973), *Women of the English Renaissance and Reformation* (1983), and numerous articles on Tudor women, most recently several on Anne Boleyn.

INDEX TO VOLUMES 1–3

References to volume numbers are set in italic type. Notes are cited only when they contain discussions of issues; otherwise, consult the Bibliography.